The Evolution of the GAA

Ulaidh, Éire agus Eile

Armagh and Kerry contest the All-Ireland Senior Football final at Croke Park in 1953. (*Gerry Murphy*)

First Published 2009
by Stair Uladh
(an imprint of Ulster Historical Foundation)
with the Cardinal Ó Fiaich Library and Archive
and the Ulster Council of the GAA

© The individual contributors and the joint publishers
ISBN: 978-1-903688-83-0

Printed in the European Union
Design by Cheah Design

The Evolution of the GAA

Ulaidh, Éire agus Eile

Editors:

Dónal McAnallen, David Hassan and Roddy Hegarty

Comhairle Uladh CLG
Leabharlann an Chairdinéil Tomás Ó Fiaich, Ard Mhacha
Stair Uladh

CONTENTS

ACKNOWLEDGEMENTS

The co-operation and assistance of many individuals and organisations have made the publication of this volume possible within what has been a very short period of time. The success of the conference from which this volume is in a large part drawn was due in no small measure to the excellent collaborative efforts of the staff of the Cardinal Tomás Ó Fiaich Memorial Library and Archive and that of Comhairle Uladh, Cumann Lúthchleas Gael.

The subsequent publication represents the combined efforts of a range of individuals and the editorial team wish to pay tribute to their contribution and assistance. First, the contributors who, at short notice, provided the raw material for the publication. The quality of their work is a measure of their dedication and efficiency.

The collections and facilities of the Ó Fiaich Library provided the working environment for much of the editorial toil and we would like to thank Monsignor Réamonn Ó Muirí and the management committee of the library for their assistance and patience. In particular we would like to thank Joe Canning, Librarian and Armagh GAA stalwart.

Without the moral and financial support of Comhairle Uladh CLG this project would never have become a reality and we pay tribute to their foresight and generosity in this regard. The provincial body continues to forge a strong leadership role within the GAA and civic society generally. We wish to acknowledge the role of the Ulster Council's 125 committee, including Mark Conway (Cill Dreasa), Tom Cullen (Gaeil na hEirne), Jennifer Cultra (Cumann Camógaíochta na nGael), Gerry Doherty (Cumann Peile Gael na mBan), Micheál Greenan (Drumalee), Michael Hasson (Ros Earcáin), Niall Laird (An Ómaigh), Martin McAviney (Ballybay), Naul McCole (An Clochán Liath), Fergus Magee (Leitir Ceanainn), Aoghán Ó Fearghail (Droim Dhúin), Catherine O'Hara (Cumann Camógaíochta ns nGael) and Dr Eugene Young (Moneymore) as well as council staff Stephen Donnelly (Achadh Lú), Sharon Haughey (Granemore), Damian Kelly (Ballymena) and Bernie McGlinchey (Goirtín). Particular thanks for their vision and unfailing support throughout this process must go to Tom Daly (Uachtarán Chomhairle Uladh), Danny Murphy (Stiúrthóir Chomhairle Uladh) and their colleague Ryan Feeney (Nuachongbhail), who co-ordinated the Ulster GAA's 125 celebrations.

We wish to acknowledge the forbearance of our designer, Jill Morrison of Cheah Design, who delivered several draft versions of this work and dutifully obliged our late alterations and corrections; and Fintan Mullan and the staff of the Ulster Historical Foundation whose combined efforts have worked wonders.

A great many people have contributed images and documents to this collection, whilst still more have offered advice and guidance when sought. These include: Micheál Ahern (Corcaigh & Doire); Michael Anderson (Poyntzpass); Jack Bratten (Armagh Harps); Jarlath Burns (Béal Átha an Airgid agus Cathaoirleach, Coiste 125 Bliain CLG náisiúnta); Joe Canning (Whitecross), Jack Devaney (Killoe & Bredagh); Nora Donnelly (An Eaglais); John Dooher (Leckpatrick); Éamon Fegan (Warrenpoint); Mick Gribbin (Newbridge); Roy Hamilton (Prehen); Anna Harvey (Belfast); Séamus and Niall Hasson (Dungiven); Noel Haughey (Seamróga Iúir Cinn Trá); Joe Lavery (Ardoyne); Joe Lennon (Gormanston); Jim McDonnell (An Cabhán); Gilly McIlhatton (John Mitchel's, Belfast); Gearóid Mac Gabhann (Cill Mochuda); Jim McKeever (Ballymaguigan); Éamonn McMahon (Béal Feirste); Jim McQuaid, Art and Helen McRory (Dún Geanainn); Brídín Uí Mhaolagáin (Dún Lathaí & BÁC); Peter Mossey (Goirtín & Dundee); Fabian Murphy (Muineachán); Danny O'Kane (Gleann Iolar); Dr Geraldine O'Neill (Open University / Queen's University Belfast); Rose O'Rourke and family (Inniskeen); Frankie Quinn (Páirc Mhic Cáismint); Jerome Quinn (Bredagh); Kathleen Bell and the *Irish News*; Ray McManus and Sportsfile; Mary McVeigh and the staff of the Irish and Local Studies Library, Armagh; Belfast Central Library and Newspaper Library; Brendan Scott (Béal Tairbirt) and the staff of Cavan County Museum; Tom Sullivan (Moynalty) and the staff of Cavan County Library; Arlene Crampsie, Ann-Marie Smith and the GAA Oral History Project, Boston College Dublin; the staff of Donegal County Archive, Donegal County Museum and Fermanagh County Museum; the library staff at the University of Ulster. In addition, Marc Mac Conmidhe, Gabhán Ó Dochartaigh (Doire), Alan Rodgers (Bearach) and Paul Rouse (Tulach Mór) rendered exceptional assistance with the preparation of certain chapters.

On a personal level we would like to thank Breandán, Bríd, Cormac RIP and Fearghas for their constant support and encouragement; Pauline and the Conway family for their kindness and tolerance through many woes and broken memory-sticks; the Hassan family of Fincarn and the inspirational Gaels of St Mary's, Banagher; Máire Bn. Uí Éigeartaigh agus na gasúirí, Ruairí, Eoghan, Dónall, Cathal agus Oisín.

Go raibh míle maith agaibh uilig.

DÓNAL McANALLEN, DAVID HASSAN, RODDY HEGARTY
2009

LIST OF CONTRIBUTORS

The following list, in keeping with a principal theme of this collection, includes the names of the clubs and native counties of the contributors. Where a contributor does not have such an affiliation, he or she is allocated to the GAA unit(s) of their native area – all in accordance with the relevant membership byelaws, of course.

Alan Bairner (Dúnedin Connolly, Alba) is Professor of Sport and Social Theory at Loughborough University. He was formerly Professor in Sports Studies at the University of Ulster, having taught on the Jordanstown campus for 25 years. He is the co-author (with John Sugden) of *Sport, Sectarianism and Society in a Divided Ireland* (1993), author of *Sport, Nationalism, and Globalization: European and North American Perspectives* (2001), and editor of *Sport and the Irish: Histories, Identities, Issues* (2005). He has written extensively on the relationship between sport and national identity.

Cardinal Seán Brady (Laragh, An Cabhán) is the Catholic Archbishop of Armagh and Primate of All Ireland. In tandem with his distinguished clerical career, His Eminence had a noteworthy involvement with the GAA at all levels. He played Gaelic football for the Laragh club and on one occasion for the Cavan senior team. As a professor at St Patrick's College, Cavan, he trained numerous school football teams. In the 1970s he was also Cavan's delegate to the Central Council of the GAA.

John Connolly (Naomh Breacán, Lios Dúin Bhearna, An Clár) is a lecturer in research methods at Dublin City University. His current research interests include figurational-sociological approaches to the study of sport and organisations, specifically the development of Gaelic games (with Dr Paddy Dolan). His work has been published in *Journal of Consumer Culture* and *Sport in Society*.

Eoghan Corry (Ard Cloch, Cill Dara) is a journalist and sports historian. He has written fifteen books, including *Catch and Kick, Kingdom Come, Kildare GAA: A Centenary History* and *An Illustrated History of the GAA*. He has written for various national newspapers, and held editorial roles with the *Sunday Tribune*, *Irish Press* and *Evening News*, *Gaelsport* annual and *High Ball* magazine. He also lectured in journalism at Dublin Institute of Technology and wrote the storyline for the GAA museum in Croke Park. He is currently the editor of *Travel Extra* magazine, a travel correspondent for RTÉ 1 radio, and the scriptwriter of the ten-part TG4 series *GAA@125*.

Paul Darby (Naomh Éanna, Aontroim) is a senior lecturer in Sport and Exercise at the University of Ulster at Jordanstown. He is author of *Africa, Football and FIFA: Politics, Colonialism and Resistance* (2002), and *Gaelic Games, Nationalism and the Irish Diaspora in the United States* (2009). He was also joint editor of *Soccer and Disaster: International Perspectives* (2005) and *Emigrant Players: Sport and the Irish Diaspora* (2008). He has represented Antrim in Gaelic football at all levels and still plays for his club, St Enda's, Glengormley.

Paddy Dolan (Baile an tSaoir, Baile Átha Cliath) is a lecturer in consumer research at Dublin Institute of Technology. His PhD in Sociology (Goldsmith College, University of London) examined the development of consumer culture in Ireland using the figurational sociology of Elias. He is co-founder of DIT's consumption and leisure studies group and has published in the *Journal of Macromarketing*, *Journal of Consumer Culture* and *Sport in Society*. He is also joint editor of *Approaches to Qualitative Research* (2009).

Regina Fitzpatrick (Gabhal Mhaigh, Cill Chainnigh) is an oral historian working for the GAA Oral History Project, Boston College-Ireland. She carried out postgraduate work in history and in cultural policy at University College Dublin. Her research interests currently include camogie, the GAA in Kilkenny, Irish language and culture and the GAA. She has also written and presented on oral history, museum studies and offers a course on Irish cultural history at the Institute for the International Education for Students, Dublin.

Simon Gillespie (Aodh Ruadh, Dún na nGall) works as a primary schools coach for the Ulster Council of the GAA in Derry City. Previously he graduated with a BSc in Physical Education and a masters degree in History from the University of Limerick. He is a member of Aodh Ruadh club in Ballyshannon, which celebrates its centenary this year (2009).

Brian Hanley (Mungairit, Luimneach) is a lecturer in modern Irish History at St Patrick's College, Drumcondra. He obtained his PhD from Trinity College Dublin. He is the author of *The IRA, 1926–1936* (2002) and *Lost Revolution: the Story of the Official IRA and the Workers Party* (2009), as well as articles on Irish republicanism in *Saothar*, *History Ireland* and *Irish Political Studies*.

Mickey Harte (Aireagal Chiaráin, Tír Eoghain) is the manager of the Tyrone senior football team, and technical director of a company. He has managed the county to its first three All-Ireland senior football successes (in 2003, 2005 and 2008); National Football League triumph in 2003; All-Ireland under-21 titles in 2000 and 2001; All-Ireland Minor title in 1998; three consecutive under-21 Ulster titles (2000, 2001, 2002), and four-in-a-row McKenna Cup titles, 2004–07. As a player he won county and Ulster championship medals with his club, and he represented Tyrone at minor, under-21 and senior levels. For several years he taught at St Ciaran's High School, Ballygawley. In 2006 he received an honorary doctorate from Queen's University, Belfast.

David Hassan (Beannchar, Doire) is a senior lecturer in Sport and Exercise at the University of Ulster. In 2006 he was awarded a Distinguished Research Fellowship in recognition of outstanding contribution to research. He is the current academic editor of the international, peer-reviewed journal *Sport in Society*, and has had over thirty academic articles published in the last five years. He is the joint editor (with P. Darby) of *Emigrant Players: Sport and the Irish Diaspora* (2008). He has played senior inter-county Gaelic football and hurling for his native Derry.

Maurice Hayes (Cill Chléithe, An Dún) is the Chairman of the National Forum on Europe. He was the county GAA board secretary when Down won the Sam Maguire Cup in 1960 and 1961, and also sat on the Ulster and Central Councils. He obtained a PhD in English from Queen's University, and worked as a teacher before becoming town clerk of Downpatrick. He was chairman of the (Northern Ireland) Community Relations Council, Ombudsman, Permanent Secretary of the Department of Health and a member of the Patten Commission on policing. From 1997 to 2007 he was a member of Seanad Éireann. As well as works on conflict research and community relations, he has written three books of memoirs, *Sweet Killough: Let Go Your Anchor*; *Black Puddings with Slim: A Downpatrick Boyhood*; and *Minority Verdict: Experiences Of A Catholic Civil Servant*.

Roddy Hegarty (Cumann An Phiarsaigh, Aontroim) is a native of Strabane, Co. Tyrone, and Director designate of the Cardinal Ó Fiaich Library in Armagh. He was formerly a development officer for the Federation for Ulster Local Studies. He has taught local history courses across Ulster and has contributed widely to local studies journals on a range of topics. He is currently editor of the local studies journal *Due North* and an active member of the Patrick Pearse's club in north Belfast, where he now lives.

Tom Hunt (Clonea-Power, Port Láirge / An Iar Mhí) is a teacher in Mullingar. He played inter-county Gaelic football for Waterford between 1975 and 1984 and also under-age hurling for the county. He was on the Munster inter-provincial panel from 1982 to 1984 and unusually for a Waterford footballer won a Sigerson Cup medal with UCD in 1973. Tom has also served as player, PRO, chairman and treasurer of Mullingar Shamrocks club. He has written extensively on economic and sports history and is the author of *Portlaw, County Waterford: Portrait of an Industrial Village and its Cotton Industry* (2000) and *Sport and Society in Victorian Ireland: the case of Westmeath* (2007).

Joe Lennon (Achadh Dearg, An Dún) is a retired PE teacher and meteorologist, and has written several books. He obtained a Dip.Phys.Ed. and M.Sc. at Loughborough College / University and a PhD at Dublin City University. His published works include *Coaching Gaelic Football for Champions* (1964), *Fitness for Gaelic Football* (1969); *The Skills of Gaelic Football* (1988) (with an award-winning video), *The Playing Rules Of Football and Hurling 1884–2000*, *A Comparative Analysis of the Playing Rules of Football and Hurling 1884–1999* and *Towards a Philosophy for Legislation in Gaelic Games* (2000). He played football for Down for eighteen seasons, winning five Ulster senior titles, three All-Ireland medals (one as captain in 1968), three National Leagues, and many other honours. He played for Ulster for ten years and won three Railway Cup medals.

President Mary McAleese (Ard Eoin, Aontroim / Ros Treabhair, An Dún) has had many connections with Gaelic games from her youth right up until her election as head of state. She played camogie with the Ardoyne club in Belfast and as a student was an ardent fan of the Queen's University Gaelic football team, for whom her later husband, Dr Martin McAleese, was a star player. Her brother, Phelim Leneghan, also played for the Down county football team. During her presidency GAA achievements have frequently been recognised in Áras an Uachtaráin.

Dónal McAnallen (An Eaglais, Tír Eoghain) is an education officer at the Cardinal Ó Fiaich Library and Archive. He studied History at Queen's University, Belfast, and NUI Galway. He has written articles for academic journals about Michael Cusack, amateurism, Gaelic games on newsreel and in the universities, and has compiled records for *The Complete Handbook of Gaelic Games*. He was formerly secretary of Comhairle Ardoideachais of the GAA, and editor of *High Ball* magazine.

Kieran McConville (Naomh Pádraig, Coilleach Eanach, Ard Mhacha). He is a librarian with the Northern Ireland Library Service and was formerly librarian-in-charge at the Cardinal Tómas Ó Fiaich Memorial Library and Archive in Armagh. He holds a B.A. and M.A. from Queen's University, Belfast. He has been involved with St Patrick's G.F.C., Cullyhanna, for many years and is currently secretary of that club. He has written a history of the Cullyhanna club and also articles for such periodicals as *Seanchas Ard Mhacha* and *Creggan Journal*.

Paddy McFlynn (Cumann Uí Dhonnabháin Rossa, Machaire Fíolta, Doire / Tulach Lios, Doire) is a retired teacher and former *Uachtarán* of Cumann Lúthchleas Gael (1979–82). He played Gaelic football for Derry in the 1930s, before serving as county secretary (1941–45) and delegate to Central Council. At the end of the 1940s he transferred to Down, where he was the county treasurer from 1955 to 1973. He was also *Cisteoir* (1947–54) and *Uachtarán* (1961–64) of Comhairle Uladh, before acceding to the highest office in the association. *Cén contae is fearr leis? Briseann dúchas trí shúile an chait.*

Jim McKeever (Baile Mhic Uiginn, Doire), a graduate of Loughborough College (1953) and the University of Leeds (1974), is a retired Head of Faculty at St Mary's College of Education, Belfast. He played football for Derry for fourteen years and captained the side to the All-Ireland final in 1958, when he was named 'Footballer of the Year'. He played for Ulster for eleven consecutive years and was selected to play for the Ireland team against the Combined Universities on six occasions. In Derry he has acted as chairman of the county board, Central Council representative and manager of the county football team. He served as a member of the Youth and Sports Council for Northern Ireland and its successor the Sports Council for Northern Ireland. He was the first Gaelic football commentator and analyst on BBC NI television.

Stephen Moore (Naomh Bríd, Baile Átha Cliath) is a final-year doctoral student at the University of Ulster, researching the history and development of the GAA in London. He has co-authored several papers on the GAA in Britain, including 'The "Temporary Diaspora" at play: The Development of Gaelic Games in British Universities' (with Peter Mossey and Dónal McAnallen) in 2007. He is a fluent Irish speaker and is an active Irish teacher with the Spleodar youth organisation. He currently plays intermediate Gaelic football and hurling for his native club, St Brigid's, Blanchardstown, in Dublin.

Aogán Ó Fearghail (Droim Dhúin, An Cabhán) is a primary school principal and vice-president of the GAA's Ulster Council. He has been involved at all levels of the association. A keen historian and researcher, he has delivered many historical lectures and is currently studying the War of Independence in Cavan/Monaghan. As an active *Gaeilgeoir* he is also the administrator of Coláiste Uladh in Gort an Choirc, Donegal, the oldest *Gaeltacht* college in Ulster. He is married to Frances and has four children.

Art Ó Maolfabhail (Cumann Fág an Bealach, Baile Átha Cliath) is the former Chief Placenames Officer of the Ordnance Survey of Ireland. His book, *Camán: 2000 Years of Hurling in Ireland* (1973) was a landmark work in the historiography of Gaelic games. He has also written *Ó Lyon go Dún Lúiche: Logainmneacha san Oidhreacht Cheilteach* (2005).

Peter Quinn (Tigh Mór, Fear Manach) is a financial advisor, company director, *Cathaoirleach* of Bord TG4 and *iar-Uachtarán* of Cumann Lúthchleas Gael (1991–94). He was previously a lecturer in accountancy at Queen's University, Belfast, and lectured in corporate finance and corporate banking at Manchester Business School. He is also a former member of the Parades Commission. With the Tigh Mór club he won four Fermanagh senior football club championships. He was formerly *Uachtarán* of Comhairle Uladh, from 1986 to 1989.

Paul Rouse (Tulach Mór, Uibh Fhailí) is a lecturer in History at University College Dublin. He is the author of the agricultural history, *Ireland's Own Soil*, and a range of articles on the history of Irish sport. He is a director of the GAA Oral History Project and a founder member of the Sports History Ireland project. Previously he was a reporter and researcher for the *Prime Time* series on RTÉ, and he produced a documentary for TG4 on the Tailteann Games. As co-founder of InQuest Research Group he has been writing the online pages for the National Archives 1911 census project for some time.

RÉAMHRÁ

Bhí na cluichí Gaelacha i gcónaí i ngar don chroí ag an Chairdinéal Tomás Ó Fiaich. D'imir sé peil Ghaelach go díograiseach ina óige, agus cé nach raibh sé ábalta imirt nuair a bhí sé ina shagart, bhí suim mhór aige i gcónaí i gCumann Lúthchleas Gael agus in imeachtaí éagsúla an chumainn. Ba bhreá leis dul go dtí na cluichí idir-chlubanna agus idir-chontae, bheith ag caint faoi na cluichí agus staidéar a dhéanamh ar stair na gcluichí. Is mór an trua é nach raibh sé beo agus i bPáirc an Chrócaigh le breathnú ar Ard Mhacha ag fáil an lámh in uachtar ar Chiarraí i gCluiche Ceannais Peile na hÉireann 2002, ach tá mé cinnte go raibha lán daoine, cosúil liom féin, a d'iarr air idirghuí neamhaí a dhéanamh dúinn ar an lá sin!

It is fitting and timely to recall the late Cardinal Ó Fiaich in the preface to this comprehensive book on the history of the Gaelic Athletic Association. Fifty years have passed since Tomás himself contributed the preface to the first known published GAA club history book, that of Crossmaglen Rangers (by Con Short) in 1959. For many subsequent GAA history publications as well, particularly during the 1980s when he was Cardinal, he was asked to write the introductory article. On every occasion he provided an apt and enlightening preface. A chapter later on in this collection outlines his work in greater detail. While I could not attempt to emulate his masterful overtures, the duty falls to me to write the foreword on this occasion, and in doing so I must pay tribute to Tomás for the inspiration that he gave to us and the legacy that he left behind.

Part of his legacy was the construction of the Cardinal Ó Fiaich Library and Archive. Since its opening in Armagh in 1999, the library has had five broad subject areas of special interest. Irish sport, and in particular Gaelic games, is one of these. From 2007 to 2009 the library has held exhibitions of the history of Gaelic games in Armagh and Ulster, and numerous related events have taken place, such as lectures and collectors' fairs. The principal event was an historical conference in the library in March 2009, to celebrate one hundred and twenty-five years of the GAA. That conference, organised jointly by the Cardinal Ó Fiaich Library and Comhairle Uladh CLG, brought together many of the leading authorities on Gaelic games history and leading playing and administrative personalities from the last sixty years.

Nár mhór an onóir dúinne Gaeil gur oscail a Soilse Máire Mhic Ghiolla Íosa, Uachtarán na hÉireann, an chomhdháil ar an chéad lá agus an Cairdinéal Seán Mac Brádaigh ar an dara lá, agus nár bhreá a gcuimhní pearsanta ar Chumann Lúthchleas Gael!

The proceedings of that conference, entitled *Pobal, Club, Contae agus Tír / For Community, Club, County and Country*, are collected in this volume and have been augmented with additional contributions to form a lasting legacy of Ulster's celebration of 125th anniversary.

Over the past decade the Cardinal Ó Fiaich Library and Archive has made great efforts to expand its collection on our national games. The library now houses one of the most comprehensive collections of GAA match-programmes in the country. The archive has been similarly expanded and now includes the minutes of Comhairle Uladh from 1917 to 1972, alongside those of the Armagh County Board and a number of clubs. There is also a growing library collection that includes around three hundred club and county histories, newspaper-cuttings, audio and visual recordings, and valuable historic photographs, together with other memorabilia such as trophies, medals and jerseys have been donated or given on loan. Much of this work over the last three years has been made possible due to the generosity of the Heritage Lottery Fund, which continues to support the library's education and outreach project enabling these collections to be made available to an ever wider audience.

Finally, the Cardinal Ó Fiaich Library and Archive would like to acknowledge the generous support and assistance of Comhairle Uladh, Cumann Lúthchleas Gael and to thank the council in general and in particular, Uachtarán, Tom Daly, and Runaí, Danny Murphy. Without that partnership and generosity, the commemorative events of the last year and this publication would never have become a reality.

Molaim na heagarthóirí agus a lucht cúnta a chuir an leabhar álainn stairiúil seo le chéile. Bainfimid uilig taitneamh as agus beidh sé mar chuimhneachán ar laochra na nGael do na glúnta atá le teacht.

RÉAMONN Ó MUIRÍ
Chairman, Cardinal Tomás Ó Fiaich Memorial Library and Archive, Armagh

FOREWORD

Cuireann sé ríméad orm réamhrá a scríobh don leabhar seo a dhéanann taifeadadh d'ócáid a bhí iontach tábhachtach mar chuid dár gclár ceiliúrtha 125 bliain de Chumann Lúthchleas Gael.

This book is a record of the 125th anniversary history conference hosted in the Cardinal Tomás Ó Fiaich Memorial Library and Archive, Armagh, on 13–14 March 2009, in conjunction with Comhairle Uladh CLG. What began as an historical commemorative event became an historic and memorable event in its own right, attended as it was by many distinguished guests and personalities from the last seven decades of the GAA in Ulster. The presence of her Excellency Mary McAleese, *Uachtarán na hÉireann*, and Dr Martin McAleese, added to the prestige of the occasion and was also a reflection of the esteem in which the GAA is held by Irish society.

Comhairle Uladh and the Ó Fiaich Library have developed a solid partnership in recent years. Whilst we have shared a mutual interest in Gaelic games and cultural affairs, it has become clear that working together in a strategic way has great value for both organisations. Comhairle Uladh has spelled out our intentions in that regard in our newly published strategic plan, *Teaghlaigh agus Pobail: An Fabraic de CLG* ('Families and Communities: The Fabric of the GAA') which will direct the work of Ulster GAA up to 2015. The library, in addition to its broader roles, continues to develop as a unique resource for the GAA and the breadth, depth and preciousness of its Gaelic games archive material grows by the day. Comhairle Uladh wants to foster and promote that growth; we would encourage others to do the same.

In August 2008 the Ulster Council established a special committee to plan and oversee a series of events and projects to celebrate the 'GAA 125' theme. The Ulster 125 Years Anniversary Committee was deliberately structured to comprise key members of the Ulster Gaelic games family. This committee worked hard to produce and implement an outstanding '125' programme. It was a great privilege for me to chair this special group of people.

Over the past 125 years the GAA has grown to become Ireland's largest sporting, cultural and community movement with over one million members, spread across 2,500 clubs. In Comhairle Uladh we are responsible for supporting 250,000 of those members and almost six hundred of those clubs across the nine counties in Ulster. Many influences, most of them positive but some of them malign, have come together to make the story of the GAA in Ulster different from elsewhere. Our March conference aimed to present, analyse and discuss some aspects of that story. In Ulster we are proud of our history but equally we do not want to be constrained by it. We should learn from history and that is part of what our conference was about; but it dealt with also what much of Comhairle Uladh's current and planned work is about, as we seek to improve not just what we do, but also people's understanding of it.

Because the two days of our conference were so successful and thought-provoking, we thought it essential that the proceedings should be documented. That is the essence of this book. From the outset of our '125' work we were determined that our programme should leave a legacy for those who come after us. I believe this book will contribute significantly to that legacy. And I also believe it does some justice to the heroic efforts of the many tens of thousands of Ulster GAA men and women who created the GAA we enjoy so much today.

I am thankful to the many people who have contributed to this book, not least the authors of the various articles. I am particularly thankful to the editorial team of Dónal McAnallen, Roddy Hegarty and Dr David Hassan, who were supported by Ryan Feeney and Mark Conway on behalf of the Ulster Council. In Dónal we have a keen historian and someone who has an unrivalled commitment to the GAA. His contribution to the GAA generally over many years has been very significant; I am pleased to acknowledge it here.

These conference proceedings represent an important contribution to the GAA story. We have published them so that people could read and be inspired by them. Above all we would like people to then act on that inspiration and in turn to do their bit for our Association, particularly by contributing their talents on a voluntary basis.

TOMÁS Ó DÁLAIGH
Uachtarán
Comhairle Uladh CLG

INTRODUCTION

This volume of GAA history originates from a conference in March 2009, entitled 'For Community, Club, County and Country: celebrating 125 years of the Gaelic Athletic Association'. The event was held in the Cardinal Tomás Ó Fiaich Memorial Library and Archive, Armagh, and was organised in partnership with Comhairle Uladh CLG (Ulster Council GAA). The conference was very well attended and was so well received that before its conclusion the idea of publishing a collection of the proceedings to commemorate the event had begun to emerge. Hence in April the library and Comhairle Uladh embarked on a further collaborative project to produce a publication that would indeed act as a fitting legacy for both the conference and 125th anniversary celebrations in Ulster.

The book that has resulted combines aspects of the history of Gaelic games at Ulster, national and international levels, through a blend of articles of personal recollections and thematic academic studies. The main part of the title, *The Evolution of the GAA*, acknowledges both the long period of history covered herein – back to 1884 and far beyond – and the great degree to which the association has changed since then. The second part of the title, in the Irish language – *Ulaidh, Éire agus Eile* – reflects the different areas (Ulster, Ireland and other) of the GAA on which the book focuses, and adverts to some of the numerous layers of identity with which its members can simultaneously identify. The story of the GAA, as relayed through the pages of this book, is one of extraordinary passion and significance in the lives of its members and others affected by its enduring role in Irish societies at home and abroad.

The opening section of the book comprises personal reflections on the GAA, by seven prominent figures who have played significant parts in the GAA in Ulster and nationally, and indeed in Irish national life, over the last seventy-five years. They include the President of Ireland, Mary McAleese; the Catholic Cardinal and Primate of All Ireland, Seán Brady; two former GAA presidents (Paddy McFlynn and Peadar Ó Cuinn); a pioneering county official (Maurice Hayes); a renowned player and lecturer (Jim McKeever); and a recent manager of All-Ireland senior title-winning teams (Mickey Harte). These contributors describe some outstanding memories of their experiences and make some general observations about the role of the association in their communities, clubs and counties, in Ulster and Ireland, during their lifetimes. Their stories are recalled in remarkable detail, epitomised by a fascination with otherwise incidental occurrences which sets the folk memory of the association apart from those of other sporting and cultural movements.

The middle sections of the book each contain seven academic chapters on various GAA-related themes. Utilising fresh research, much of which is drawn from newly available sources – newspaper archives, church archives, oral-history interviews, census records and others – this compilation presents a thorough examination of a broad range of subjects. 'The Origins and Development of the GAA' is the first of these academic sections. 'From Cú Chulainn to Cusack' traces the many references to hurling and sister games in Ulster from mythology up to the 1900s, and considers the links between *camán* and *shinny* as played in the north of Ireland with hurling as played in the south and with shinty in Scotland. Paul Rouse's chapter provides a timely reappraisal of the motives of Cusack, Davin and colleagues in Thurles in 1884, and strips away much of the myth about 'why the GAA was founded'. Tom Hunt's analysis of the structures and social activities of clubs continues in his vein of groundbreaking work on the GAA and sport in the late nineteenth and early twentieth centuries. Eoghan Corry's chapter carries out a fascinating survey of the role of the printed press in propagating Gaelic games over two centuries. The chapters on the links between the Catholic Church and the GAA up to 1902, and the history of camogie up to 1950, go some way to addressing two topics which have been surprisingly neglected in GAA historiography to date. *Ina theannta sin tá alt ann faoin chéad seasca bliain de CLG i gCúige Uladh, atá tábhachtach ní amháin toisc go gcuireann sé eolas nua ar fáil ar an ábhar sin, ach mar gheall ar go bhfuil sé scríofa as Gaeilge agus is beag atá foilsithe maidir le CLG sa stair acadúil go dtí seo.*

Section Three, 'The Expansion and Modernisation of Gaelic Games', focuses more specifically on the progress of the games themselves, in Ireland and abroad, in more recent years. The contribution of John Connolly and Paddy Dolan, on the 'civilising' of Gaelic games, confronts the myth (often promoted in the media) that the games have become more violent of late. Joe Lennon's work provides a neat synopsis of his authoritative tomes on the evolution of the playing rules, and reviews developments since their publication. Previous academic historical studies of the Irish republican movement's attempts to wield influence in the GAA and other sports had been largely confined to the pre 1923 period, but Brian Hanley's valuable contribution to this collection tackles this subject for the subsequent period. The chapters on the GAA in the USA, Britain and Europe bring greater attention to the development of Gaelic games abroad, while Aogán Ó Fearghail and Paul Darby reassess the extraordinary All-Ireland football final of 1947 in New York, which remains an evocative episode in GAA history over six decades later. In the closing chapter of this section, Alan Bairner, places the modern GAA in a global sporting context and considers whether its special attributes such as amateurism and community values can withstand the encroachment of commercialisation and urbanisation.

The penultimate section of the book comprises an appendix based not on conference proceedings, but on other parts of the Ó Fiaich Library's project to commemorate 125 years of GAA history in 2009. The first of these outlines the research undertaken by library staff to discover the final resting place and family background of John McKay, the sole Ulsterman present at the inaugural meeting of the association. A chapter chronicling the relationship of Cardinal Tomás Ó Fiaich with the GAA, provides a fitting remembrance of the late primate almost two decades after his death, and demonstrates why the library built in his honour features Gaelic sports prominently. The final section contains lists of Ulster senior football and hurling championship results and final teams from 1888 to 2009 – the most complete set of Ulster records compiled yet. These annals capture the vital details of provincial championships that have earned a special renown of their own. Finally there is an extensive bibliography drawn from the Gaelic games collection housed at the Ó Fiaich Library. This list of holdings, divided according to the various levels and themes of the association at various levels, should make researchers of GAA history aware of the extent of not only the Ó Fiaich Library collection but also of the wide range of GAA-related publications that exist.

The book is illustrated throughout with photographic and documentary images, which are mostly drawn from the Ó Fiaich Library's Ulster GAA history exhibition of 2009. Although almost all are of Ulster origin, these images are intended to represent points that are quite universal to other quarters of the association. Of course, the text does not discuss certain topics, such as handball, rounders, *Scór* and women's football in great depth, but these are valuable aspects of Ireland's sporting culture and deserve detailed and considered appraisal in the time ahead.

A significant amount of the content of this book focuses on Ulster, and in many respects it constitutes the most comprehensive coverage of the history of the association in the province. The Ulster dimension is important in that it provides a unique context for the study of the GAA. From the start and particularly during the last third of the twentieth century the story of the association in the northern province has been quite unique. In view of the difficult and exceptional challenges faced by GAA personnel and ordinary followers of Gaelic games in that part of Ireland, the remarkable achievements of recent years merits special attention. The successes of several Ulster teams in claiming All-Ireland titles in recent decades is the most palpable indicator of the vibrancy of the GAA in Ulster at this time, but the community spirit that is championed by the association inside the province and beyond is equally worthy of appreciation. For many people the simple pleasure of watching their kith and kin play, or helping out their local club, represents the *buille bháire* of the association over the past 125 years. And if you want to know what a *buille bháire* is, read 'From Cú Chulainn to Cusack' in section two of this book.

Finally, in a year which has witnessed a timely upturn in the publication of GAA-related books, just as in the centenary year of 1984, this compendium aspires to be one of enduring quality by serving as an essential source of knowledge and reference in years to come. In publishing this extensive collection of new material, we endeavour to raise the standard of historical scholarship on the association and its games. This book may not win any All-Ireland medals for us, but as our voluntary contribution to this anniversary of the association we are confident that it will stand the test of time.

It is now time to throw in the ball.

Go mbainigí sult as an leabhar seo a léamh.

On a triumphant visit to St Patrick's College, Cavan,
in 1948, winning captain John Joe O'Reilly holds the
Sam Maguire Cup, in which sits a young pupil, Peter Shaffrey.

Section 1: Reflections

Radharc ón Pháirc: A presidential perspective on the GAA
President Mary McAleese

Parallel Pilgrimages: A personal journey through the GAA
Cardinal Seán Brady

75 Years out of 125: A Lifetime in the GAA
Paddy McFlynn

Down through the Years
Maurice Hayes

The Coming of Age of Gaelic Games in Ulster, 1950–1970
Jim McKeever

From Tigh Mór to Croke Park
Peter Quinn

Dua, Bua agus Ré Nua: The Rekindling of the Northern Flame
Mickey Harte

Radharc ón Pháirc: A presidential perspective on the GAA

Uachtarán na hÉireann, Mary McAleese

Tá an-áthas orm an chéad alt a scríobh don leabhar seo ar an ócáid speisialta atá a cheiliúradh, 125 bliain de Chumann Lúthchleas Gael. Ba mhaith liom buíochas a ghabháil le heagarthóirí an leabhair, le Comhairle Uladh CLG; leis a Uachtarán, Tomás Ó Dálaigh; leis a Rúnaí, Dónall Ó Murchú; agus leis an institiúid iontach agus clúiteach sin, Leabharlann agus Cartlann Chuimhneacháin an Chairdinéal Tomás Ó Fiaich, as ucht a gcuireadh an moladh seo a thabhairt. Go maire sibh uilig.

It is a great pleasure to be part of the celebration of 125 years of Cumann Luthchleas Gael, an organisation which has given each of the contributors to this collection and millions more, a personal store of powerful, long-lasting memories, allegiances, friendships and connections which have brought colour, vibrancy, meaning and magic to our lives. The GAA, as an organisation, is extraordinary in terms of its reach into home and parish, into county and province, into our nation, in fact wherever two or more are gathered, at home and abroad.

This book will look at how, over all these many years of its history, through the drama that produced so many variegated chapters in Ireland's turbulent history, the GAA was born, survived and thrived. If two shortens the road, then the company of the GAA has shortened the road from 1884 to 2009. It has been companion and friend, family and community to generations. It has been and is deeply loved, occasionally a little resented, for it has taken tough stances in the face of history's demands and it has been generously courageous in moving beyond them and beyond the vanities of history.

There is a narrative of sheer pride in the story of these 125 years and a fresh narrative up ahead as the GAA strides comfortably and confidently through its second century, a legacy of fabulous facilities all over Ireland, not least in Croke Park, four hundred dynamic clubs outside Ireland, Gaelic games in Asia going from strength to strength, new facilities in San Francisco, the first full-time Gaelic coach in an English school – all this the result of the work of amateurs, volunteers, who are driven by a determination to make the GAA the best it can be. Why do they bother, year in, year out, the punishing training schedules, the fundraising, the jersey-washing, the aggravation, the committees, the conflicts, and the craic? They do it, to borrow a phrase, for community, club, county and country. It is a rallying call to goodness, to decency, to mutual interdependence, to sporting excellence, to skill, to working to win and to graciously accepting defeat. In a world that spins and changes, the GAA adapts and endures because its fundamental values endure. Here is an organisation of pure, national solidarity, where people of all backgrounds meet as equals, share a passion for sport and for showcasing our country at its best.

I grew up in Belfast but I was the child of a Down mother and a Roscommon father. That set my GAA allegiances in stone. I remember the 1960s as a sea of red and black, of soaring, mad rip-roaring pride in the accomplishments of those men whose names I could never forget, who came to Croke Park, took on the princes and kings of Kerry and brought the Sam Maguire Cup north. I still get an anxiety attack thinking about that late penalty from Paddy Doherty that stopped a few Kerry hearts. There is a story told that, just after the penalty, as Paddy was strolling back past the legendary Mick O'Connell, Mick asked Paddy how much time was left and the answer was, '365 days, Mick!'

How could we ever fully evaluate the influence of those giants of the 1960s for those of us growing up in the divided Northern Ireland of that time? Here were men who seemed to lift, carry and disperse those high-banked clouds of resignation that Seamus Heaney writes about so brilliantly in his poem, 'From the Canton of Expectation.' These men changed the mood, infused us with a fierce self-belief, a vision of ourselves as winners and as serious shapers of the GAA.

Years later while I was living in Rostrevor and on the local church pastoral council, I took part in a diocesan workshop in the cathedral in Newry. We gathered delegates from every parish in Dromore. They gave us massive sheets of paper on which to draw our parishes and the important places in them. When the

President Mary McAleese with her husband, Dr Martin McAleese, receiving a specially mounted Ulster championship medal from the Ulster GAA President Tom Daly on the occasion of her address to 125 years history conference at the Cardinal Ó Fiaich Memorial Library and Archive in Armagh. (*Comhairle Uladh*)

eighty charts went up on the wall, there it was for all to see –shouting at us from every single piece of paper – were the words 'GAA'. We stood amazed, confronted by a reality we had always known but overlooked – this for many of us was our heartland, the place that united us as family, friends and neighbours. In that same era George Morrison produced his epic film *Mise Éire* with Ó Riada's thunderingly moving and evocative music. Our story was being told and beautifully; our story was changing driven by a new purpose and a fresh voice.

A well-known unionist sports commentator recently described Croke Park as 'the epicentre of Irish sport' – he got that right between the posts. There is no way I could do justice to my own debt to the GAA, the inimitable days of football, hurling, camogie, handball, from under-sevens to senior level, from the Sigerson Cup that Martin (my husband) won to those that he lost, but when I heard *La Marseillaise* blast out at the first Six Nations rugby match in Croke Park I felt a peace of heart and mind like no other. When the English came, an hour and a half before Ireland beat them, the sheer genuineness of the welcome given to them was one of those memories a person takes to the grave; grateful to have been there, to have felt the shared mood, the infectious mood of goodness and decency. It was proved once again that the GAA holds a people's heart with care and with compassion.

Early this year I was in Croke Park for the launch of the GAA's social initiative, designed to reach out to and embrace older men living alone who do not want their lives to be simply solitary but long for sociability again. To be in that room in the famous stadium with the first two hundred men, to hear their excitement and see their happiness was a privilege. To see the massive growth of ladies' Gaelic football; to live in hope that Antrim hurlers will one day shake my hand on a September Sunday; to hear my husband groan under the relentless weight of bad economic news, 'Dear God, would the Gaelic season ever start!'; to watch my kids who once painted their faces red and black head for Parnell Park dressed in Dublin blue; to argue the footballing and hurling toss with every Seán and Sinéad from Belfast to Beijing – these are the gifts of the

Seán O'Neill of Down rises to contest a ball with Mick O'Connell of Kerry in the 1968 All-Ireland final. For people like Mary McAleese and GAA fans all across Ulster, the Down teams of the 1960s have always held a heroic status.

The Queen's University team that won the Sigerson Cup in 1971. Martin McAleese is picture fourth from left in the second row. The then Mary Lenaghan, also a student at Queen's at that time, was one of the team's most ardent supporters. (*John Devaney*)

GAA. I met a young Newry man in Dubai last month; he was coaching fifty under-tens in Gaelic football in his spare time. I asked him why. He said it all simply – 'the GAA has given me so much, it is only right to give something back'.

It is a debt that a lifetime could not repay in my own case alone from my days as an undistinguished camogie player, to the days of trudging after my husband and children as they played, the family days as spectators following Rostrevor and Down, the summers spent begging and borrowing tickets for All-Ireland finals so our kids would know and love Croke Park as we knew and loved it, and these eleven years as President with the best seats in the house. Camaraderie like no other, craic like no other and community like no other – that is my GAA. And the best is yet to come. Enjoy this collection and this start to the next 125 years. I wish Ulster football, camogie and hurling – especially Antrim – well; I have two more years of good tickets and I dare to hope!

Parallel Pilgrimages: A personal journey through the GAA

Cardinal Séan Brady

I am very pleased and honoured to be asked to contribute to this book. I congratulate the GAA and the Cardinal Ó Fiaich Library and Archive for compiling such an impressive volume from an array of contributors. A collection focusing upon the GAA is very appropriate and timely because in an age where individualism is rampant, and volunteerism is on the decline, it is good to reflect on the benefits and advantages that working for the community brings. It is good to recognise the joys to which such work gives rise. It is important not just to pay lip-service to the value of community work. It is also important to identify the things which threaten those ideals of amateurism and to oppose them.

Cardinal Séan Brady

When I consider the landscape upon which the Cardinal Ó Fiaich Library rests I recall the first occasion I arrived there. It was not in the cause of religion. It was way back in 1954 to the MacRory Cup Final. We travelled, by train, from St Patrick's College in Cavan to play Abbey Christian Brothers School, Newry. Unfortunately the referee died during the match and so it had to be, of course, called off. We were winning at the time but alas we lost the replay.

Ultimately this short piece gives me an opportunity to thank the GAA for the enjoyment I have derived from so many activities offered by it. Not just from playing but from coaching, training, attending meetings, administration and so on. I am very grateful also for the friends I have made in the association, especially those who give, and gave, so generously of their time down through the years.

As a Cavan man myself, and in the context of 125 years of the GAA, you will forgive me if I draw attention to one of the greats of Cavan football and the only surviving member of that famous 1947 team, Mick Higgins. He was admired for his exploits on the field of course, having played in several All-Ireland finals and winning three All-Ireland medals. But he was admired also for what he gave to the association after he retired from playing. He managed teams, at county and provincial levels and he refereed at the very highest level. I remember him speaking with Seán O'Neill about the 'battle of Ballinascreen' in 1968, when he was in charge of the Down versus Derry match in what would have been a day out for the yellow and the red cards now! I was struck by the fact that quite soon after he retired he was already involved in other activities and I admire him for that. For example, I recall, as a minor, being brought by Mick and the late Victor Sherlock to minor trials. I wonder is that happening now? Are young men, immediately after they retire, putting enough back into the association?

As I have outlined I am grateful for the friends I have made and the opponents I met and learned to respect throughout my involvement with the GAA. I am grateful too for the moments of nervousness and anxiety which I endured before matches and which I now realise were preparing me, possibly, for the other challenges and, indeed, for the defeats of life. One of the great things about taking part in games is that you win some and you lose some. You realise that we all have God-given gifts which enable us to win but we are also limited – very limited. We are sometimes weaker than we care to admit whilst we will always meet people who are better than we are, and that is an important lesson.

After spending a lot of time as part of an organisation that places such emphases on the community and on the club, it was a great consolation to me personally to discover that one of the basic principles of our faith is the principle of communion. Our way to God, and God's way to us, is a communal way. What does that mean? Our religion brings about an encounter between ourselves and our God. It is a personal and individual meeting with our God. But this encounter is made possible only with the help of a community of faith. So for that reason I do not regret the many hours spent, especially in the 1970s, attending meetings

The Cavan team of 1933, the first All-Ireland senior football champions from Ulster.
Back: P. Mac Seáin, J. Tiernan, J. Rahill, P. Brady, L. Blessing, V. McGovern, M. Dinneny,
T. McCormack (vice-president, Cavan Co. Board), P. O'Reilly (treasurer).
Middle: S. McCormack, W. Connolly, T. O'Reilly (Mullahoran), W. Young, T. Coyle,
T. O'Reilly (Cornafean), H. O'Reilly, J. Smallhorn, M. O'Reilly (trainer).
Front: S. Gilheaney (president, Cavan Co. Board), P. McNamee, D. Morgan, P. Phair,
J. Smith (captain), P. Lynch, P. Devlin, M. J. Magee, J. J. Clarke. (*Gearóid Mac Gabhann*)

and coaching teams at club and college levels. I know that is exactly why the GAA people are often the backbone of the parish. It is good to be part of a team, one that loses occasionally and in so doing reveals our limitations.

When I was preparing this piece, I had to attend a meeting in Belfast. It was hosted by the leaders of the six main Christian churches here in Ireland: The purpose of that meeting was to provide people with a means of expressing their rejection of violence and of the killings and the murders which took place in March 2009 and that threaten to take us back to a place we do not wish to go. It was a call to pray – a call to pray in the privacy of your own heart or in your families or in your church or in the church of another community, that the peace which we have been enjoying in this part of the world for the last number of years may not be disrupted. There is far too much at stake here at the moment and we cannot just take the peace for granted. We have to play our part in consolidating it and indeed, I want to pay tribute to the association for its part in the building of that peace.

During my own GAA career, growing up as a young lad in Cavan, I played for Laragh and a couple of other clubs as well, and that was due to a thing which is very much in vogue now called 'strategic planning'. It was not 'strategic planning' on my part, but on the part of other people. But it reveals a side of the GAA which is very real and, I think, after the profound examination of the association and of its motivation and ideals (such as that contained in this collection), it is no harm to take a look at another side of it which, I know, you will appreciate.

In 1956 in Cavan there was a rule which allowed a parish – for minor purposes – to pick players from any parish that bordered it. The parish of Killinkere is famous in the history of Cavan football because it was the birthplace of the late, great Jim Smith, who captained the first Cavan All-Ireland-winning team and was a holder of thirteen Ulster championship medals. Killinkere was in turn surrounded by six parishes

Cavan midfielder Phil 'the Gunner' Brady in action
(Cavan County Museum)

and so a strategic planner in 1956 decided that this would be a very good team to enter in the minor championships, and resultantly we could have representatives from seven parishes playing on the one team. Those parishes included Bailieborough, Mullagh, and Virginia – all strongholds of Gaelic football. And so it was that I was lucky enough to get my place on that team and to win a Cavan minor championship medal in 1956. By 1960 I had become a member of the Laragh Sons of O'Connell club. However, by the time I came home from Maynooth that year the Sons of O'Connell were already out of the Junior Championship, as was their wont!

At this stage the strategic planners in the Laragh Sons of O'Connell realised that there was a danger that I might be poached, I suppose you would say, and that I would go to Stradone. You know how we GAA people love one another, especially our nearest neighbours! Some strategic action had to be taken to ensure that that didn't happen! Somebody, who was creative with the truth, came and told me that Father Gargan, who was formerly my dean in the college and a priest in the diocese, wanted me to play for Cavan Gaels. So, out of respect for my former dean, I went in and said I would join and play for Cavan Gaels. The result was that after I left Laragh I ended up being a member of Cavan Gaels, not for very worthy motives, I admit, but that is how it happened and these things do happen in our beloved association.

On that theme I am reminded of a funny story concerning Tomás Ó Fiaich. One night he was introduced to a man called Father Larry Hannan. Tomás thought for a while and he said: 'Larry Hannan. I marked you in a challenge match between St Patrick's Armagh and St Mary's Dundalk in 1937, when you were playing left half-back and I was playing right half-forward'. And Larry Hannan said: 'You are quite right'. This is just the kind of memory that the GAA gives rise to, not least when one considers often how much time has passed after these reminiscences are evoked.

I grew up in Cavan in the 1940s and 1950s. Living in a county that won eight Ulster senior titles in the 1930s and nine in the 1940s it was hard not to be interested in the GAA. I would attribute my knowledge of the GAA principally to the *Anglo-Celt*, the Cavan man's bible. I can remember well when I got my first football. My father and mother went to town in the horse and trap – my brother and I must have known what they intended to buy because I clearly remember going out the lane as far as my neighbour's house to meet them on their return and my father throwing the football out to us as we passed. It was that same neighbour's house where we gathered late one September evening for the broadcast of the 'Polo Grounds' game in 1947. The kitchen was jammed to the door. The radio was on the window sill and the overflow was on the street. I know Aogán Ó Fearghail and Paul Darby cover this game in greater detail later in this collection but I recall that Batt Garvey was playing havoc in the opening stages of that encounter. Obviously the Cavan defence decided some remedial action was called for and some time later it was proclaimed: 'Batt Garvey has gone down injured'. One of my less charitable neighbours was heard to say: 'I hope to blazes he never gets up!'

Many of the places I visited when I was appointed to the Archdiocese of Armagh were also GAA strongholds, which I remember travelling to when I was involved in youth football. I remember visiting

Ardboe, Coalisland, Killeavy, Eglish, and Dungannon, for example. The generosity of those clubs in making their pitches available to college teams was remarkable and for that I am again very grateful.

A memorable, but very sad event in my native parish when I was growing up was the untimely death of P. J. Duke. He was our hero, our icon, a role model when we were young boys. By the age of 25 he had won every honour in the game: two All-Ireland medals, and the Sigerson Cup three times (once as captain), whilst his last appearance in Croke Park was on St Patrick's Day 1950, before he sadly died on 1 May 1950. I can still remember the shock that his passing created. Worse was to come in 1952 with the death, after a short illness, of John Joe O'Reilly. His passing meant that two of that famous half-back line of P. J. Duke, J. J. O'Reilly and Simon Deignan were dead.

By 1960 I was, for a short while, a member of the Cavan senior football panel. Cavan lost the National Football League final that year, having been beaten by Dublin by three points. Later that year, in October, I was asked, by Bishop Austin Quinn, a native of the Armagh archdiocese, if I would like to go to Rome to continue my studies for the priesthood. Upon my return in 1967, I joined the staff of St Patrick's College, Cavan, and began working my way up the GAA ladder from there. Do you know how difficult it is to work your way up the ladder in the GAA? I won a hotly contested election for a place on the GAA Central Council in 1980, only for another Armagh man, Cardinal Ó Fiaich, to intervene and send me back once more to Rome! It is one of my regrets that I only survived long enough to qualify for Ardchomhairle tickets for one All-Ireland final!

The GAA is my family. I feel very much at home in the GAA but because of this I also feel comfortable about saying a few things about the association. The first one surrounds the amateur status. My heroes are, of course, the footballers that play on the field but they are also the people who turn up much earlier in the day to open the gates, who stand in cold and dusty turnstiles, people who still support their club but who might not have a son or daughter near the team. I also applaud the GAA for its initiatives surrounding drugs.

What do I not like about the association? Not a lot. I like the GAA very much, but I am not happy with the win-at-all-costs mentality. It sometimes comes across that winning is all that matters. Winning is not all that matters because half the time you win and half the time you don't. I am also uncomfortable with

The funeral procession of P. J. Duke making its way along O'Connell Street, Dublin, in 1950. Duke had been a student at UCD and died suddenly at the age of 25. *(Cavan County Museum)*

the sponsorship of GAA competitions by alcoholic drinks companies, and I know that many members feel disappointed with the GAA at central level on this point. I would also appeal for your help in keeping Sunday special. Sunday is a day of rest. It is a day of worship. If we do not worship God, we end up worshipping ourselves and that is a very dangerous situation. I commend things like *Scór*. The GAA is not just another games-playing organisation. It is about culture. It is about real life and it is about history. It has a soul and we need to go back to that soul every so often and be nourished.

I want to finish this short piece by quoting a poem about the late great P. J. Duke that was written by Pádraig Purcell and it moves me every time I read it. It still gives me a lump in my throat because it goes right to the heart and that is what the GAA is about.

As I was walking through Dublin city,
One pleasant morning in the month of May,
Near Stephen's Green I met a student,
With tear-dimmed eyes this to me did say.

This morning early as the birds were singing,
And Mass bells ringing in fervent tone,
To His great promise the Lord took from us,
Our fearless champion from sweet Stradone.

The banshee keens by Breifne's border,
Beyond Lough Sheelin in the morning breeze,
By lake and river the rushes quiver,
In silent sorrow for one so young.

No more he'll trod the green soil of Croke Park,
But we see him still; his manly feeling
And manhood pealing
And red hair flying in battle still.

New stars may rise in the years before us,
but none like him will they then bethrone,
The boy from Breifne, the pride of Ulster,
God rest you P J in sweet Stradone.

75 Years out of 125: A Lifetime in the GAA

Paddy McFlynn

Paddy McFlynn

Clubs were low on the ground in Derry back in the early 1930s when I first became involved in the GAA. But in 1934 a group of teenagers, including myself, set about changing this by forming the O'Donovan Rossa's club in Magherafelt. We were the officers, selectors, trainers and players. There was no such thing then as a management structure of the modern type. Everything was done to the best of our ability, like our monthly *céilí*. Money was very scarce. The first man on the list was always Canon John Ward, who would have started the collection with a few pounds. That was how we raised the money for jerseys and a football. We began as a minor club, and replaced an earlier side called St Joseph's which folded, leaving the way clear for us. A minor league began under the auspices of the South Derry Board, of which I was the very young secretary. For us Rossa's was the beginning and end of everything.

Two series of events in 1933 had led to my rapid immersion in the GAA. The first was the revival meeting of the GAA in Derry, held at St Joseph's school in Magherafelt on 9 March 1933, and attended by the Ulster secretary, B. C. Fay from Cavan. Previously, the GAA surfaced in Derry City and north Co. Derry in mere fits and starts, and in the south of the county it had only emerged in the mid 1920s, before falling away again. At the time of that meeting just two clubs existed in south Derry: Lavey, playing in Antrim; and Ballinderry, playing in Tyrone. A match was held as part of the revival between the two clubs; it took place in Ballinascreen and I remember going there with my father.

Going to inter-county matches with my father was the second major influence of 1933 that brought me towards the GAA. He was from the Loup – while my mother was Brigid McNicholl, from a very old Magherafelt family – and I always thought that someone had a wry sense of humour, because he was born on the twelfth of July and named William. He had an interest in football, and we travelled on bus trips to big matches. The first big game he took me to was at Breifne Park in 1933, when Cavan beat Kerry by 1-5 to 0-5 in the All-Ireland semi-final. M. J. Magee scored a great goal; he was part of the famous half-forward line of Smallhorn, Blessing and Magee. Jim Smith was a tremendous footballer, as were the O'Reillys. They then went on to win the All-Ireland final, which was my first visit to Croke Park. I remember it as a tremendous match and occasion.

My own participation in inter-county football began in 1936, when I played at centre-forward on the first county minor side from Derry. We played against Tyrone in the Ulster championship at Omagh in 1936. There were six Rossa's lads on that team, but I recall that a couple of players from St Columb's College in Derry City were introduced, whom we felt were not up the standard of the south Derry lads. We had trained hard for the game: we did early morning training runs around Ballyheifer, led by P. J. Robinson, who, as a well-known boxer, claimed to be an expert in physical fitness. We lost the game by four points. Soon afterwards, I began to play for the Derry senior team – though we were graded as 'junior' at that time. My selection was understandable, as I was secretary to the selection committee! After one National League match against Donegal at Ardara, I lost an almost-new pair of football boots. For a schoolboy like myself, boots were not easily obtained, and I lamented the loss of this pair!

From 1937 to 1939 I attended St Mary's College, Strawberry Hill, London. There was no teacher-training college for men in the six counties, so we had to go there to be trained. A dozen went over every year on a 'king's scholarship' for the two-year course, so there were twenty-two Irishmen in attendance at any one time. I used to be very happy at home in Derry over the holidays, and I did not relish the long journey away again. I would have to get up early, get the bus to Belfast, then the boat to Liverpool and the train to London. The

Programme from the 1933 All-Ireland football final. This final, the first of its kind won by Cavan and Ulster, was also the first occasion on which Paddy McFlynn visited Croke Park. (*Gearóid Mac Gabhann*)

return fare from London to Magherafelt was two pounds and half a crown. It was while at Strawberry Hill that I first began to learn Irish. John Bell from Louth took us for a class two or three times a week. There were no Gaelic games at the college then, but I did play rugby and indeed made the first team. I was wing-half forward and played for the two years that I attended the college. We played the London Irish, London Welsh and London Scotch third-string teams in competitive games. There were also very tough matches against the other teaching colleges in London, St Mark's and St John's. Of course, there was no mention of this in dispatches back home. At that time the in-word was PE, which began to develop, and there would be an annual college sports meeting in which I attempted the distance-running, but otherwise never really took part.

When I returned home to Magherafelt in 1939, my participation in the GAA expanded once more. Rossa's club was flourishing. We won our first senior football championship in that year. With the county board I was involved in setting up the Bellaghy club, at a meeting in a little wooden hut on the Castledawson Road. Among the prime movers in the Derry County Board then were the chairman, Fr Mick Collins; his successors, Seán Mac Diarmada of Ballinascreen and Paddy Larkin of the Loup; Basil Guidera of Moneymore; and Hugh Corey of the Loup. Seán Dolan of the city was county secretary from 1936, but he was interned around the start of World War Two. Fr Collins informed me of his arrest, and I was asked to serve in his stead. Thus I became county secretary in 1941. That same year Dolan died tragically on the prison ship *Al Rawdah*, aged just twenty-eight.

I first became a member of Comhairle Uladh, the Ulster Council, in 1939. After many years of difficulties, it was beginning to make significant progress. Bhí sí ag dul ó neart go neart. The improvement in fortunes owed a lot to the quality of leadership we had then – people like Gerry Arthurs, Pádraig Mac Con Mí, Seán Ó Cinnéide, Séamas McFerran, Willie Harvey and Alf Murray. They were very inspiring personalities and orators. We had a very strong sense of cultural mission back then, and in 1942 we decided to hold all of the meetings *trí Ghaeilge* from then on. The presentation and commencement of the Dr Lagan Cup, for the Ulster section of the National Football League, was an important step too. This competition saw my provincial duties expand further, as I refereed a few games in the Lagan Cup. In particular I remember an Armagh game, in which I whistled for a few free-kicks for over-carrying against Alf Murray. Ní raibh sé sásta liom!

Simultaneous with that in the early 1940s I began to work as a substitute teacher. I was all over the country in those days. I taught in Ballinascreen for a while, and then Coalisland for a few months also. In 1942 I moved on to Crossmaglen. During the war there was double-summertime, but the local people did not accept it. School used to start at 11.30 am and finish at 5.30 pm, though I would always cut it short by an hour. Crossmaglen was a real hive of activity with the cross-border smuggling, and the football was every bit as prominent as it is now. I remember a crowd of lads in the goalmouth and another group further out the field, and if you wanted a kick you had to win the ball first. It was a far cry from the sophisticated training methods of today. While in that area I played illegally for Culloville. I used to go out on my bicycle to line out for them. In the summer of 1942 I was out practising football every night. Culloville team practice sessions could be up to twenty-a-side games, and real rough stuff. 'Mind "the Master",' some of them would shout when I was coming out with the ball. A great character called Joe Watters was involved there. The wife of the Ulster secretary, Gerry Arthurs, was teaching in a school in nearby Anamar. He came there every Friday evening, so I would ride out to meet him and stay the weekend. We went to matches together and I remember cycling into Armagh to get a bus to various locations and venues. In a letter to my brother Charlie, I wrote about going to an Ulster championship game that year: 'I met a lot of people in 'Blayney on Sunday, who asked, "How did you get here". "Cycled," *arsa mise* – Gasps of astonishment.'

While all that was going on I still managed to play for Magherafelt in 1942. On Friday evenings I would get the bus from Crossmaglen to Newry, from there to Belfast, and then on to Magherafelt. We won our second Derry senior title that year. I played centre half-back initially and in the forwards later, but I was

The Ardchomhairle (Central Council) of the GAA pictured in 1942. The photograph contains three of the leading officials from Ulster in the twentieth century. Pádraig Mac Conmidhe (Uachtarán CLG, 1938–43) is in the centre of the front row; a twenty-something Pádraig Mac Floinn (Uachtarán CLG, 1979–82) is third from left in the second row; and Gerry Arthurs (Rúnaí Chomhairle Uladh, 1934–76) is third from left in the third row.

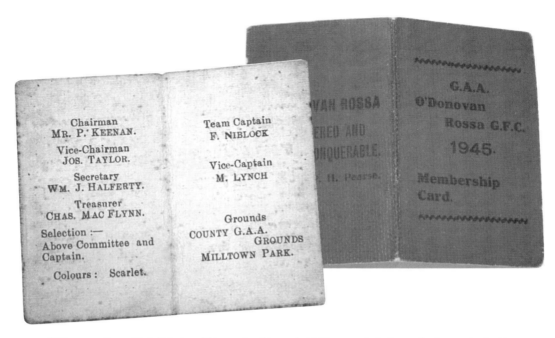

O'Donovan Rossa Club (Magherafelt) membership card, 1945 – a symbol of organisation, and of pride in membership of both the club and the GAA. (*Pádraig Mac Floinn papers, CÓFLA*)

probably more vigorous than skilful. An infamous incident involving me arose in the 1942 county final, against Dungiven. One of our best players, Pat Keenan, had not been well and his marker was giving him a tough time. So our captain, Paddy 'Sticky' Maguire, told me to go up and do something to sort the situation out. Their man went up for the ball and I hit him with all my fierce strength, putting him out over the endline. Now I was county secretary and the referee, Paddy Larkin, also happened to be the county chairman, and he ordered me off. As was our custom, the county board held a meeting on the evening of the county final, because everyone was present, but I had to sit outside, suspended due to my sending off. But when any contentious issue cropped up they had to come out to consult with me for clarification! The club went on to win the championship again in 1946 and 1949. Some other clubs did not like us very much, however. They claimed that we were 'swell headed', that we got too many men on the county teams, that these men let the county teams down, and that we had players dabbling in soccer. Once, in protest at the adoption of a referee's report which listed the wrong score, Rossa's wrote to the county board announcing its withdrawal from the GAA. The threat was not carried out, but the club clearly felt that it was being victimised.

We were a proud club. By the 1940s, when I was back living around home, we produced club membership cards each year, listing the officers and a quote from O'Donovan Rossa. In 1947–48 we also put together a regular club newsletter or magazine, which was named *The Hawk*, because O'Donovan Rossa was known as 'the Hawk o' the Hill'. I proposed the name since my party piece at the time was Patrick Pearse's oration at the grave of O'Donovan Rossa, which had been given to me by Hugh Gribbin, whose sons went on to represent Derry in the 1958 All-Ireland Final. All of our literature carried the line, 'A Rossa Production', at the bottom. It was all done by hand on a very antiquated old machine for duplicating manuscripts. I was the main editor and I tried to include humorous items. So as well as articles about club matches and Irish cultural matters, there were pieces entitled 'Moustaches', 'Going to the Pictures' and 'On Keeping a Date'. But there were also serious editorials, such as one in 1947 which criticised how southern attitudes towards Ulster teams alternated between condescension, demanding playing-rule changes to stop the northerners' alien style, and tolerating violent play as a means of stopping the northern style.

The immediate inspiration for that article was the rough treatment of the Derry team in the National Football League final of 1947, by the opposition, Clare. Derry won in any case, and it was, remarkably, one of three trophies the county won that year – the others being the Dr McKenna Cup and the Dr Lagan Cup

– after having been no-hopers just a few years previously. Goal-scoring was a special knack of that Derry team. Another important landmark for the county in that decade was the purchase of Celtic Park, Derry City, in 1943. I was among those who took part in the purchase, along with the chairman of the Derry City Board at the time, Eddie McAteer (who later became leader of the Nationalist party). We went up to see the ground and it was in terrible shape altogether because it was used as a sort of dump. There was a zinc-tinned shed on the site and a key factor was the acquirement of the land from the gasworks. That was a big achievement.

I joined the ranks of the Central Council for the first time in 1942. The idealism and commitment of many of them I met on this body, and at congresses, made a deep impression on me. I was present for the amazing decision to hold the 1947 All-Ireland final in New York. It was only at the meetings after the congress that it was definitely decided to go. The Connacht secretary and Pádraig Ó Caoimh had gone to America and reported back that it was practically impossible to hold the final there, and advised strongly against the move. The Central Council met in private session at 7 pm, before the public meeting an hour later. President Dan O'Rourke was in the chair, and a vote was taken against going to America. Cavan was due to play Roscommon in the All-Ireland semi-final, and he made some disparaging remark that no son of his would fly on an aeroplane to America. The Ulster people took umbrage at this, because they felt that he was implying that Roscommon would win. So the Ulster delegates changed their minds and this swung the vote to decide to go. Dan couldn't believe this, so he had a second vote taken and counted it very carefully. The main people who opposed making the trip were the four provincial presidents and secretaries, and Pádraig Ó Caoimh. But when the decision was taken to go they were all appointed as officials to attend. Martin O'Neill, the Leinster secretary, refereed the game, and the rest were umpires and linesmen, including Gerry Arthurs.

Idir 1947 agus 1954 toghadh mé mar chisteoir Chomhairle Uladh. Bhog mé go Baile na hInse, Co. an Dúin, i 1948. Theagasc mé ar scoil ansin. I 1949 phós mé Kathleen i mBaile Meánach, Co. Aontroma, áit a raibh a athair lonnaithe ag an am sin. Tionóladh an aifreann phósta trí mheán na Gaeilge ar fad. B'as Tulach Lios, Co. an Dúin ó dhúchais í.

In my new county I became involved first with the Ballynahinch club and also as chairman of the East Down Board. The Ballynahinch club reached its first county junior football championship final in 1949, playing against Laurencetown (Tullylish). Only after I moved to teach in Tullylish in 1953, did I discover that half of the Armagh county team had played against Ballynahinch that day: men like Harry McPartland, Bill McCorry and several others. Soon I became chairman of the South Down Board. It was quite unusual for someone to have held positions on both the south and east boards. There was also once when, having been the Derry representative on the Central Council, I switched to represent Down on the same body a year later.

My tenure as *cisteoir* of Comhairle Uladh came to an abrupt end in unusual circumstances in 1954. Around then the tax officials in the north were pushing very strongly on the GAA to pay income tax on gate-receipts and other income. Gerry Arthurs was always very adamant that we were merely a branch of the association in Dublin and that the association's bank account was based there. Hence he sent all correspondence with regard to this to Pádraig Ó Caoimh. It was felt that our case would be stronger if there was someone from over the border as treasurer of Comhairle Uladh, so I stepped aside to allow Harry Carey of Donegal take up take this role. Also I recall an entertainment tax being introduced in the form of stamps. Every ticket that was sold had to have the stamp, but the GAA did not recognise this. Instead, about a dozen stamps would be purchased and kept aside just in case a stranger came in to check up. There were never any prosecutions.

In 1955 I was elected as treasurer of the Down County Board – a position I held for the next eighteen years. My time in that role coincided with Down's success in the All-Ireland during the sixties and I obviously handled a lot of the financial matters. I followed the county teams to Clones, Cavan and Croke Park as keenly as a native of the county, and also on the team trips to play in Wembley and America. I remember in particular being shocked when the bill for £9,000 came for our trip to the USA in 1962. We chartered a Paskin Airlines flight from Dublin to New York. I remember an amusing scene on the plane when the priest was saying the rosary via megaphone surrounded by the stewardesses in sarongs.

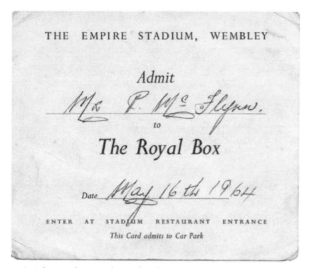

THE EMPIRE STADIUM, WEMBLEY

Admit

Mr P. McFlynn.

to

The Royal Box

Date *May 16th 1964*

ENTER AT STADIUM RESTAURANT ENTRANCE

This Card admits to Car Park

A ticket to the Royal Box for the annual GAA tournament at Wembley stadium. This competition was held at the famous venue from 1958 until the mid 1970s, and attracted large crowds. Down won the football competition on a record four occasions.

When I became Ulster Council President for the 1961–64 period, I succeeded 'big' Frank O'Neill. My travelling companion to meetings was Gerry Arthurs. No matter where we were going the routine was always that I would pick him up. He was great craic. He would start by saying the rosary with all the trimmings, and then tell old yarns and stories about former days of the GAA: all the problems that they had in the 1920s with the pogroms and bans on Gaelic games; how money was such a big problem then and it was often a case of just keeping things going; and how he beat Eoin O'Duffy to the Ulster treasurership. The gates were increased from two shillings to half a crown, he said, because it was easier to count! Gerry loved draws. I remember one particular year when the two semi-finals ended with last-minute points in extra-time. He could not understand why the referees could not have ensured draws, which would have meant another gate! We had an income one year of £15,000, which was like a dream for us.

A lot of the big issues that cropped up during my Ulster presidency were perennial issues, and some of them still arise today. The old problem of teams playing 'ringers' persisted; perhaps it was coming back to haunt me since I had been one in former days! One of the biggest problems we had in the early 1960s was separating Collegeland (Armagh) and the Moy (Tyrone), because the players would always adopt a more flexible approach, shall we say, to parish and county boundaries. Media coverage of GAA games was also a big issue in the 1960s. But during that period we didn't even go to the BBC and we were even struggling with some of the newspapers. The *Irish News* gave us fairly extensive coverage, as did the *Irish Press*. A big debate then surrounded the strength of the signal of the new RTÉ television service. Many northern people were deeply annoyed that they could not get the signal for what was supposed to be a national service. Many of these concerns were relayed through the GAA, and I, as president of the Ulster Council, lodged these concerns in the strongest possible terms. The problem was that RTÉ was not permitted by international guidelines to broadcast into BBC territory, and a suggestion was made to put a booster close to the border. The matter was never officially resolved, but the two organisations began to work more closely together in later years anyhow.

Alf Murray was a great influence on me, always encouraging to run for different positions. He had been president and it was he who sowed the seed in my mind of running for president. I thought about it for a number of years, although there was a period when I thought the chance was gone. Holding the position was a great honour because the office of president is very highly respected, whoever the incumbent may be. But it is also a position which carries great challenges and sometimes there were very serious problems. I was very lucky to have come in during 1979 at more or less the same time as Liam Ó Maolmhichíl, then the new *Ardstiúrthóir*. I had been a member of the committee that selected him. We were both new to our positions and became very friendly as a result. Even then Liam was a very capable man whose legacy to the association is, of course, immense.

A major development during my presidential term was the construction of the Ceannáras, the new GAA administrative headquarters at Croke Park prior to the construction of the present Hogan Stand. Obtaining the money for that was a major undertaking, and Seán Ó Síocháin was probably the main fundraiser. But Con Murphy had probably completed most of the work in relation to this, and I suppose I was only in to see its completion.

The big issue, however, was the hunger strikes, which were terrible altogether. He understood the position in Northern Ireland and I think the association was fortunate to have had a northern president during that time, because things became very fraught. Marcus de Búrca wrote in an article that the three occasions when the GAA might have split were the Parnell controversy, the Civil War of the 1920s and the hunger strikes. There were very high emotions on both sides and there was a terrible struggle for publicity and support. The hunger strike and H-Block people were very keen to use the GAA's strengths and numbers to back up the marches which were being held.

It was very difficult to cope with that, and not just because Rule 7 loomed in the background. Many of these young men came from strong GAA areas and were part of local communities. In Ireland, the local community is very strong and the people supported them. On the other hand, many people felt that it was none of our business. A strong line was taken in some counties, but other counties let things drift and allowed the clubs do what they liked, when they should have taken control of the situation. The fact that I was a native of south Derry and living in Down was definitely a big help for me as president during that time. I was meeting people on the ground and we have to remember that the rank-and-file GAA people, especially those with families that included young teenagers, did not want the GAA taking part in parades and so on, for fear of their children becoming involved in activities. I could feel greatly for parents of teenage children because it was a terrible worry for them.

Much of my job was taken up with preventing the association from splitting and yet it could have split easily. While parents were obviously very concerned, on the other side there was a feeling that we were a nationalist organisation and these were young people who were dying for a nationalist cause. I remember in particular two people whom I trusted very much, who had very strong opinions on this issue, from opposite perspectives. Sometimes they disagreed with decisions that I made as president, but the GAA came first with them and overrode all political considerations and always put what was best for the association first.

There were also some worrying moments on television, including the occasion when the IRA brought a lot of newly obtained weapons into Casement Park. Hugh McPoland was Antrim chairman at the time and a great friend of mine. He phoned me asking what should be done. I told him to open the gates wide and get away for the day, because there was nothing that he could do about it. An interviewer asked me why I

260/79

17th July, 1979

Mr. P. McFlynn,
236 Banbridge Road,
Gilford.

Dear Mr. McFlynn,

   I have been directed by the Magherafelt District Council to inform you that they are unable to offer their congratulations to you on the occasion of you being elected President of the G.A.A.

Yours faithfully,

Clerk to Council

A letter received by Paddy McFlynn from Magherafelt District Council after his election to the position of Uachtarán Chumann Lúthchleas Gael in 1979. A motion to acknowledge the achievement of local native McFlynn was not universally supported, due to the antipathy of some councillors towards the GAA.

had let the guns into Casement Park, a question that perhaps I was not expecting so quickly. The interview was taking place at Croke Park during some work, and before I got the chance to answer the question this man let a hammer drop and the interview was temporarily halted. When it started again I said the GAA could not be expected to keep them out when so many thousands of troops could not do it.

Another difficult occasion was John Joe Sheehy's funeral. As Liam Ó Maolmhichíl and I were going into the chapel that day, I saw a platform up at the grave. There were shots fired over the grave and Dáithí Ó Conaill asked me to speak about Sheehy's activities in the GAA, which I did, relating how John Joe had been President of the Munster Council, Vice-President of the GAA, and that I was duty-bound to attend as President of the GAA. At the 1980 Congress, held in Newcastle, Co Down, a motion was forwarded which was going to cause big problems. I kept it off the agenda and when the proposer came over from London I went to him to explain that the eyes of the northern press were on us and the motion could do immense harm. I said that I had no right to take it off the agenda, but told him that if he wanted to raise it then the motion would be put back on the agenda. He agreed and his decision shows how helpful people were when called upon. The loyalty of many members to the association is a wonderful basic principle and a great strength.

When my presidency ended, I was probably in a different position from a lot of my successors because I was much older. I was ready for a rest, after a very exhausting and tiring time. It was a tough job because of both the social and administrative demands and commitments which were – and indeed still are – placed on the president. One of these was to be the chairman at Congress and I remember someone being amazed that I was in that role throughout the event because at trade union or party political conventions there are two or three people who take it in turns to chair the meeting. Nevertheless, I was lucky because I was the first president-elect, and had a year's apprenticeship under Con Murphy. So it was only a matter of carrying on his example. The other presidents prior to that had a difficult time, as they were elected straight into chairing the meeting.

The best thing about the GAA, for me, is the friends that I have made. Even now I am flattered that, after all these years on the sidelines, clubs still invite me to various events. Of course, I always enjoy returning to my native south Derry and functions in the McFlynn Suite at Rossa's club. Each year after the All-Ireland hurling final, a friend, George Ryan, takes me down to Tipperary. We travel around the county for a week, meeting all the GAA people. Another great man I respect greatly is Pat Fanning, the *uachtarán* of 1970–73; when I am visiting people in Tramore I always spend an evening with him. He is still very involved and interested in the progress of the association.

There are aspects of the GAA at the moment which would cause concern. Barney Carr, who coached the Down teams of the 1960s, said to me that if you read the newspapers nowadays you would think that it was the managers and not the players who won and lost matches. In our day it was down to the players who played, and managers, if any, were very much in the background. This and some other aspects of the GAA which have changed in recent years would cause me annoyance sometimes. All this terrible handpassing is one trend in the game of which I would prefer to see less. One of the greatest skills was the high catching, as I saw demonstrated by big Jim McCullough, Mick O'Connell and Jim McKeever. If the midfielder catches the ball now and comes down he is surrounded and managers seem to have this tactic of immediately surrounding the player perfected to such an extent that a free is given against him for over-carrying. I think the game has been spoiled by these aspects.

Hurling has always been a great love of mine, even though I did not play it to any great extent. In the early years we tried on a number of occasions to get it up and running in Magherafelt, without much success. Alf Murray was a great advocate or the game and was always anxious to 'bring back the hurling'. Galway people certainly acknowledge his influence in revitalising the game under An Coiste Iomána in the 1960s. For many years I was involved in Féile na nGael, which was very enjoyable. Clubs from every county were represented, and it was enlightening because it provided the opportunity to talk to people in the weakest areas, some of which do not even have the population to sustain football, let alone hurling. But the efforts of two or three individuals to keep the game alive have been absolutely vital. It's very hard work. Here in Down we have been trying to build the game up with the Non-Ards team, but so far only with limited success. It is such an unbelievably skilful game, which is why it is so difficult to match the top counties.

A telegram sent to Paddy McFlynn, as GAA president, after the death of republican prisoner Kevin Lynch on hunger strike in August 1981. This message demonstrates the types of pressure that the GAA faced during that period. Lynch had captained the Derry under-16 hurlers to an All-Ireland title success nine years earlier and the hurling club in Dungiven is named after him today.

Cé nár fhoglaim mé Gaeilge ar scoil, bhí grá agam don teanga i gcónaí. Mar a dúirt mé cheana anseo, d'fhoglaim mé an Ghaeilge ar dtús i Strawberry Hill agus ina dhiaidh sin ag coláistí de leithéid Rann na Feirsde i nDún na nGall. Sílim gur theip orainn beagainín i gCLG ó thaobh cothú agus forbairt na Gaeilge de, agus sílim gur chóir dúinn í a spreagadh ní ba mhó ar fud na tíre ná mar a rinneadh. Rud amháin atá iontach maith ná Cúrsa na Gaeilge de chuid Chomhairle Uladh sna Dúnaibh, Dún na nGall. Ailf Ó Muirí agus mé féin a bhunaigh é i 1959. Lean sé ar aghaidh go dtí na 1970idí, ach thit sé as a chéile ansin. Buíochas le Dia, thóg Comhairle Uladh an cúrsa ó mhairbh thart fá fiche bliain ó shin, agus bhí Seamus de Faoite as Dún na nGall lárnach san obair sin. Téim ansin gach bliain, sa tseachtain tar éis chluiche ceannais peile Uladh. Bíonn sé eagraithe go maith ag Tomás Ó Cuilinn agus Nollaig Mac Cumhaill. Sna blianta beaga anuas bhí imeachtaí éagsúla mar chuid den chúrsa – mar shampla ceoilchoirmeacha ina raibh iomaitheoirí *Scór* páirteach, leabhair a sheoladh agus léachtanna, go háirithe Léacht Chuimhneacháin Shéamais de Faoite. Ar a laghad déanann Ulaidh iarracht an 'G' a choinneáil i gCLG, fiú muna bhfuil sé sofheicthe in áiteanna eile.

Since my retirement as GAA president I have served several terms as chairman of Tullylish club, and I am currently an honorary president of both the club and the Down County Board. I still attend both the county and club meetings and take a keen interest.

In the summer of 2009 I was in the Loup for the funeral of my cousin, John McFlynn. I was there early and went to the grounds, and who was playing a game there only the Rossa's and the Loup at under-8 and under-10. I saw some of the grandchildren of the original Rossa's who were involved with me during the early years of the club. It makes me very proud to see that happening and the great work that is being carried out at underage level in Magherafelt and of course throughout the GAA.

I have always been asked whether I am a Derry man or a Down man. It's a difficult question to answer, especially when the two counties meet. At this stage the Down people more or less accept me, but at the same time the Derry people would still claim me. It's very difficult to get away from your roots.

Down through the Years

Maurice Hayes

The title to this chapter seems a sufficiently wide label to enable me to write in general terms about the emergence of Down as a significant force in football in the early 1960s. Having had an insight into the administrative workings of the GAA at all levels as far back as the 1940s, I would also like to include a few more general remarks from that time, and to recount a few amusing memories along the way.

Maurice Hayes

One of the earlier significant GAA events that I happened to attend was the 1947 Annual Congress, which took the decision to export that year's All-Ireland football final to the Polo Grounds in New York. The Cavan story of the 1947 final has already been written about quite extensively and referred to again during the course of this compendium. Without in any way taking away from the glory of that great Cavan team, which I admired greatly, I feel obliged to record that there is a Kerry narrative too of the same event. In this version, Kerry, who had dominated the first half, were so far ahead that the organisers were concerned that the fickle New York audience, which had been built up to expect a titanic struggle, would become totally disillusioned. To avoid this, the umpires disallowed two further Kerry goals, which put them off their stroke and brought Cavan into contention. Maybe it is just how they rationalise defeat in Kerry. The umpires, incidentally, were the four provincial secretaries, any one of whom could have been trusted to take a pragmatic view of proceedings.

But to come back to how the teams got to be in New York in the first place, we must go back to the GAA congress held that year, and what a bizarre occasion that was. It was my first congress, and I got there entirely by accident. I was minding my own business on the street in Downpatrick when a county board member, Alf Oakes, told me that Brian Denvir, a fellow member of Kilclief who had been appointed as a delegate, could not travel and no other substitute could be found. It seemed as good a way to spend a wet weekend as any other and a chance to see the Railway Cup final and so off I went.

The convention, or at least the morning session, was held in Dublin City Hall. The scarcity of Down delegates was explained by the fact that the Down convention had passed a motion proposing the deletion of Rule 27 (the 'foreign games' ban), which could then be raised any year. With none of the great or the good of the county being ready to 'face the music' at congress, it was left for Alf to propose the motion, which he did, after a suitable apology, and for me to second, monosyllabically. They did not even bother to take a show of hands. So much for the will of the people of Down! The congress adjourned at lunchtime to enable members to attend the Railway Cup final at Croke Park. The final had been delayed from its usual St Patrick's Day date by the prolonged freeze of that winter and spring. Congress was due to reconvene at Croke Park after the game to consider the only other item on the *clár*, a motion from Clare to send the football final to New York and thereby mark the centenary of the Great Famine.

So there we were, cooped up in an airless, small room, with a sloping roof, and without windows, under the old Hogan Stand. Numbers were reduced, many having gone home after the morning session or after the game. Others had enjoyed a long and liquid lunch. In the gathering dusk, Canon Hamilton, a very forceful man – in these less reverential times he would be recognised as a clerical bully, too used to getting his own way – made an impassioned address, proposed the motion, and then an emotive 'letter', purportedly from an Irish emigrant, was read out; even then I suspected that the canon had written it on his way to the meeting. He was opposed by several practical men, among them Gerry Arthurs, but it was an amazing occasion, in an amazing atmosphere. It was a bit like the Anglo-Irish Treaty negotiations, delegates cooped up while the canon threatened immediate and terrible consequences for failure to agree his terms. Rationality

THE BRITISH BROADCASTING CORPORATION

Head Office : Broadcasting House, London, W.1

Broadcasting House, Ormeau Avenue, Belfast

TELEPHONE AND TELEGRAMS : BELFAST 27411

31st March, 1948.

M. Hayes, Esq.,
Denvir's Hotel,
DOWNPATRICK.

Dear Mr. Hayes,

Since I last saw you I have received a
directive from the Head of Programmes which
instructs me that I am to leave out all reference
to Sunday Sport. There are many reasons for
this, which are no doubt evident to you, but we
are fully prepared to broadcast news of sport of
all kinds, provided that it is not on a Sunday.

It may have struck you that I was hesitant
about this and I awaited a definite ruling, which
I have now been given.

If there is any way in which we can cover
Gaelic Football, other than advertising it prior
to Sundays, then I am willing to do so. I shall
be grateful for any suggestions.

Yours sincerely,

(Kenneth Best)
Sports Assistant

PL

Maurice Hayes did not pursue a career in the media after this early rebuff. BBC Northern Ireland's refusal to broadcast sports on Sundays obstructed the development of the GAA locally up to the 1950s and beyond. In 1934 the station briefly allowed GAA results to be mentioned as news items, before a sabbatarian storm and the intervention of Prime Minister James Craig put a stop to it. For almost two decades afterwards, the station declined to broadcast any Gaelic games items on Sundays. The station did not have a problem with broadcasting music and other entertainment pieces on Sundays. (*Maurice Hayes*)

went out the window (which wasn't there anyhow) and people made a decision on a flood of emotion. For some it seemed the only way of getting out if trains were not to be missed and another night in Dublin avoided. Anyway a decision was taken, against the wishes of the leadership (not least Paddy O Keeffe) and the game was sent to New York in a grand gesture of magnanimity – hang the consequences!

On another theme, I wonder how many people know of the award of an All-Ireland medal other than on the field of play? The first, I believe was to the coxswain of the Rosslare lifeboat about 1914 for the heroic rescue of the crew of a Norwegian boat. The other, of which I have direct knowledge, arose in the early 1950s when I was on the GAA Central Council. Meetings were held on a Friday evening, and there was a newsflash that an Aer Lingus plane had made a forced landing near Birmingham, having run out of fuel, miraculously without casualties. It turned out that the pilot was a Mayo man, and Paddy Mullaney, an emotional man of great enthusiasm, proposed that his heroism be recognised by the association by the immediate award of an All-Ireland medal. Since it would have seemed churlish and derogatory to refuse to recognise a palpable hero, the proposal was carried without a vote. The next night I was at a reception in Belfast when I ran into Dónal Ó Moráin of Gael Linn, a man who always knew the inside story. He nudged me slyly and said 'I hear you gave a medal to the pilot.' I mumbled that it seemed the decent thing to do, at which he added, even more mysteriously 'He was a bigger hero than you all imagined: he had a full tank of petrol when the plane crashed.' And so it turned out at a subsequent inquiry at which the pilot was held culpable. I do not know if the medal was ever awarded. Another Paddy Mullaney initiative was the naming of the Nally Stand. This had been completed to replace the old Corner Stand in Croke Park, and I don't think anybody had any great idea of calling it anything else until Paddy, in another emotional outburst at a Central Council meeting, proclaimed the necessity of calling it after P. W. Nally, an athlete and a prominent Fenian from Mayo, of whom most of us had never heard.

I was a member of the Ulster Council some time after they had decided to carry out all business in Irish. I got there mainly because I 'had' Irish. It was a laudable project from the point of view of promoting the language, but not necessarily so from the games angle – a victory of idealism over practicality. One effect was to reduce the representation of former prominent players and to produce a disproportionate membership of teachers (of whom I was then one) and priests, simply because they also 'had' the Irish. I was reminded of this position years later when I heard a disgruntled Gerry Fitt bewail his position as a socialist in the largely middle-class SDLP as 'up to my arse in country schoolteachers.'

It is an honour to share these pages with Jim McKeever, whom I have admired for many years, both as a man and as an outstanding athlete. On one occasion in 1953, he, I and Malachy McEvoy crept, as far as we could ensure unseen, into the only house in Downpatrick with a television, to watch the FA Cup final – the famous 'Stanley Matthews' final – hoping that the act of apostasy by three pillars of the GAA would not become a cause of public scandal. I remember too, an occasion about that time when we responded to an advertisement to join a first-aid class organised by the local branch of the Red Cross. Being involved with Gaelic games and the coaching of young players, we thought it would be sensible and useful to learn how to deal with minor injuries. The first night went fine. On the second evening there was a visit from the Dowager Lady Londonderry, who became greatly enthused at the sight, as she put it, of such stalwart and athletic young men who could carry the standards and the Union flag at the next Remembrance Day parade. We did not attend a third class and the cause of sports medicine in east Down was put back by a generation!

Hurling was always my first love, and remains so. In the absence of hurling I can tolerate football, but increasingly only just. Sometimes I think that, as in football, modern coaching has taken much of the gay abandon, the sense of adventure and uncertainty out of the game. In this religion, Thurles is the great temple, and the Munster final the object of pilgrimage. I have not missed many over the years. The great sadness, and one that should concern the GAA, is that in spite of all the efforts, hurling is still confined to the traditionally strong counties, and in some of them is just hanging on. Tom Hunt's very interesting work on the sociology of the first All-Ireland winning hurling teams could be replicated today – with, I suspect, much the same results – confined to parts of parishes in parts of even the strong counties, and handed down through families. In most counties, football has an advantage – it can be enjoyed by more people at a lower level of skill, and it is less expensive, needing less by way of equipment and gear.

Seán Purcell (Galway) and Kevin Mussen (Down) leading their respective teams out at Wembley stadium in London in 1959. Seán O'Neill has claimed that the experience of this match laid the foundations for the county's All-Ireland successes of the following decade. (*Éamon Fegan*)

Hurling in Ulster in the 1940s and 1950s was dominated by Antrim and Down; they contested Ulster final after Ulster final, with Antrim inevitably winning except once in a blue moon. Donegal could field a reasonable junior team, backboned by *gardaí* from the south of the country, and Cavan likewise, depending on agricultural students in Ballyhaise. There was some hurling in Armagh and a little in Monaghan, but hardly any that I remember in Derry, Tyrone or Fermanagh. Indeed the later growth of Derry hurling is effectively the creation of one man, Liam Hinphey. In the late 1940s and early 1950s I was involved in developing Ulster colleges hurling – again only in Down and Antrim. Even there the problem was that games-masters in strong football schools did not want the competition of another (even GAA) game. An Ulster under-sixteen team played a Dublin schools team as a curtain-raiser to one of the legendary Oireachtas tournament finals between Wexford and Clare, and showed that at that age, they were as good as anybody. Sadly, it ended there for most of them.

In Down, at that time, there were strong centres of hurling outside the Ards: Kilclief (the strongest team), Ballela, Newry (Clann Uladh) and Liatroim. Antrim hurling was backboned by the Glens, Ballycastle, Loughgiel, Cushendall and Dunloy, but hurling was also very strong at the time in Belfast, with teams like Mitchel's, O Connell's, Rossa, St John's and St Gall's. Kilclief played in the South Antrim league, for want of serious competition in Down at the time, as the Ards clubs were to do later. There were hurlers like Noel Campbell, as good as I ever saw, who would have had six All-Ireland medals if he had been born in Cork, Dessie Cormican and Séamus 'Stout' McDonald. Kevin Armstrong, Billy Feeney and Brian Denvir were three who could play for Ulster in both hurling and football.

To my mind, the greatest blow to hurling in Antrim and Ulster was the demolition of Antrim by Cork in the 1943 final – the worst hammering of any team until Kilkenny beat Waterford in 2008. Antrim had beaten Kilkenny, admittedly in horrible conditions in Corrigan Park, and hopes were high. Cork too were an exceptional team, winning four out of five All-Ireland titles, but still, had Antrim been left with a bit of pride, they might have come back.

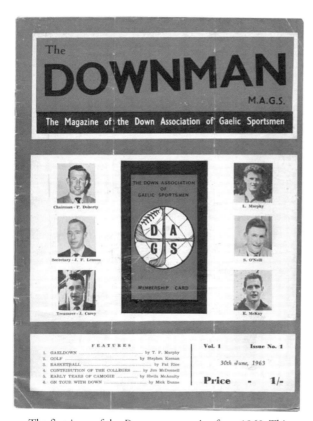

The first issue of the *Downman* magazine from 1963. This short-lived publication, from 'the Down Association of Gaelic Sportsmen' epitomised the precociousness and innovation widely associated with the Down football teams of the 1960s. The articles covered a wide range of topics, far beyond those ordinarily featured in Gaelic games writing. (*Michael Anderson*)

A later bizarre experience of hurling was of a film-actor being allowed to join in the players' parade before an All-Ireland final, in order to assist the making of a feature-film, entitled *Rooney*. This was the story of a Dublin dustman who won an All-Ireland in hurling. The actor, John Gregson, joined the Kilkenny team in the march before the 1957 game between Kilkenny and Waterford. The finished film contained action-shots of the game, with clips of Gregson artfully spliced in, showing him heroically scoring the winning goal. I remember a long day spent in Croke Park after the final, in which Des 'Snitchy' Ferguson patiently tried to teach Gregson how to hold a hurley, and a few Kilkenny and Waterford players mimed support or opposition as he eventually managed to hit the ball.

But back to the main burden of my contribution to this collection, the effort which produced the 1960–61 Down team. This too is surrounded by myth, not the least of which appears on the Down website through a link to a *Wikipedia* entry which attributes credit to an initiative taken by members of the Queen's team that won the 1958 Sigerson Cup. Nothing could be further from the truth. The only connection between Queen's and Down at that time was the young Seán O Neill, who was just then making his way on to the senior team. The real genesis of that team lay much earlier, was entirely home-grown, and involved a wide range of people. There tends to be a lot of talk about a five-year plan, as if it were all magic. There was a five-year programme, but that came fairly late in the process, after a lot of painstaking preparatory work had been done. We were lucky that there was a group of extremely talented players available at the same time that was prepared to make the effort and to stay together until their goals had been achieved. It was my good fortune to be associated with an interesting group of intelligent and talented young men from whom I learned an awful lot by way of man-management, planning and human relations, which I found very helpful in many of the jobs I subsequently undertook. It was a very close group, and remains so to this day – 'We few, we happy few, we band of brothers' we would proclaim, and the mutual respect and trust developed over those years remains to this day. I owe them a lot. There had been good footballers in Down, and a high standard of club football in the 1940s, when inter-county competitions were limited by wartime travel restrictions. That no trophies were won (apart from a Junior All-Ireland in 1946) I put down to failure of ambition, the absence of management and lack of self-confidence.

I tend to date the beginning of the renaissance to the early 1950s, with the establishment of an all-county league in Down. This broke down divisional barriers and gave teams a regular schedule of games in which discipline was strictly maintained. After that an inter-barony league enabled the best players to join with their peers in a higher level of competition. At the same time the Newry colleges were emerging as strong nurseries and the new intermediate schools staffed by trained coaches like my fellow contributor Jim

McKeever were beginning to make their mark. None of this was reflected in senior inter-county success. Teams were picked to fail, and then the county board talked of imposing suspensions on those who did not turn up. My view was that there was little hope of success with a team if players would only play under duress. The answer was to create a team which everybody wanted to play on. After a few dreary seasons in which we scarcely even won the toss, there was one game in which we almost had to give the taxi driver a jersey to make up the numbers.

A few of the younger members of the county board, who had got fed up with losing year after year and fed up with being cannon-fodder for the stronger teams in Ulster, decided to do something about it. They were fed up, too, with the lack of ambition which heaved a sigh of relief when the county team was out of the championship so that they could get ahead with local leagues. It was an odd phenomenon at the time, fed by the success of a very good team which won the All-Ireland junior title in 1946 (which could have been built on, but was not) that Down should aim at success at this level. Good players were sometimes deliberately not selected for the senior team one year so as not to disqualify them from playing junior the next. I was reminded of the composition of these junior teams years later when I was nominated to Seanad Éireann. There I saw the same thing in political terms – last year's good minors on the way up meeting the previous year's ageing seniors on the way down, and both groups wishing they were somewhere else.

The first job was to get team selection out of the hands of the county board. This is not a criticism of the board as such, simply a means of selecting a team. We all know the definition of a camel as a horse designed by a committee. Like most other counties, the county board took seriously its responsibility for county teams by insisting on selecting the teams themselves. The whole board (all twenty-five or thirty of them) picked the teams, voting on each position in turn, fighting for 'their' man, one by one, with no great idea what the finished article would look like. I remember one particularly stubborn clerical gentleman who, if he did not get his man on at right full back, would turn his chair to the wall and read his breviary until the meeting was over. There was another, too, who, having taken full part in the selection, would greet his colleagues after the inevitable defeat with the salutation, 'That was a fine team yeez picked!' There was even one who, having taken a set against a particular player, would sit among the subs loudly demanding that the player be taken off, only to be told he was not playing that day. It was not a great way to develop team spirit and a sense of common purpose.

My preference would have been for a single team manager, but the best the market would bear at the time was a selection committee of three – Barney Carr and Brian Denvir (who had been distinguished county footballers) and me. We soon added, unofficially, T. P. Murphy, and the team doctor, Martin Walsh. After a bit too it was possible to recognise Barney Carr as manager. This could not have been achieved without the support of the younger members of the county board and also the chairman, George Tinnelly, who was consistently supportive. Many of the others were convinced that the whole thing would end in tears and were quite happy to distance themselves from a foolish escapade. It was only later when success had come and the whole thing seemed easy that they began to 'want the ball back'.

It was at this stage that the 'five-year plan' emerged – not a Stalinist work-programme, but a set of achievable, if stretching objectives we set ourselves in order to give players a sense of development, and to prepare them for the steps that had to be taken, and to enable them to see periodic defeats in the context of steady progress towards a goal. We had not read the books at the time, but found out afterwards that we had blundered into a version of management by objectives. Indeed, that is what we were doing, learning by experience, learning to do the simple things consistently well, to pay attention to detail, looking after people, trying not to make the same mistake twice, learning from each other in what was a fairly collegiate style of management in which all were equally involved and in which players too were encouraged to contribute their ideas.

What we did was to make a pact with the players to maintain the group as a unit, to keep faith if they were prepared to stick the course, with the promise of success in the end. Our end of the bargain was to look after the players, to treat them well, providing facilities for travel and training, good hotels, medical care and support when they were injured, help with employers and holiday jobs, and otherwise when difficulties arose. Part of the plan was to get people to commit to a programme of training from early in the year and

'Blanket defence', 1968 style. Four Down players converge on Kerry's Mick O'Connell, one of the most graceful players of his time. Although Kerry was traditionally the supreme county in football, Down never lost to 'the Kingdom' in the championship. (*Éamon Fegan*)

to take every effort to bond as a group. We wanted to build on the natural skills and abilities of what was a talented group of footballers, and to allow them to express themselves in what would be recognised as a distinctive flowing, exciting brand of football. All the time, however, it was almost more about building self-confidence and team spirit than success in football.

We were, unashamedly, creating an elite set, a group that players would be glad to be part of, and others anxious to join: no need to threaten them with suspension, standard-bearers for the game in the county, and role-models for the young. It was all part, too, of giving people the self-confidence needed if they were to win anything and take on the best in the game. People who did not like it called it cockiness, at best, or arrogance; we preferred to call it assurance and self-belief. I am reminded of the story of the Kerryman who had an inferiority complex – he thought he was just as good as the next fellow.

The idea of a five-year cycle, aimed at winning an All-Ireland title in 1961, was based on the maxim of 'one step at a time' gaining experience all the time: two years to get to an Ulster final, only to lose, then a win in Ulster, but lose the All-Ireland semi-final; then get to the All-Ireland final and lose; before finally winning out. If success came earlier, so much the better, and it did through the added experience of a drawn semi-final in year four. In the meantime too a problem arose in that the combined experience of the players soon outran that of the management, none of whom had played in provincial finals or National League Finals, Croke Park or Wembley Stadium. At one stage in 1960 senior players expressed the view that they needed more help than management could give them, and this was resolved by bringing in Peter McDermott to support Barney Carr and to prepare the team mentally for the experience of playing in an All-Ireland final. Looking at the confrontational way in which similar situations have been handled in other counties in recent years, I am rather proud of the way we managed back then.

Another noted declaration of intent at this time was the decision to break with the Down tradition of pursuing success at junior level. A highly successful junior team, which had won Ulster in a canter, would almost certainly have won an All-Ireland in 1959 had the county board not taken the courageous decision to sacrifice it in the interests of the senior team. In the event, six of that team had the compensation of senior medals the next year, and the county had the greater glory of success at the highest level. This, although largely unnoticed, was in my opinion the most significant declaration of intent during this era.

We were just at the beginning of the television age in the north as far as Gaelic games were concerned. I think we saw something of the same effect as Ulster Television (UTV) began to compete with the BBC in the north. Indeed, I believe, that were it not for the games being taken up by the newer channel, the BBC (which gave obsessive coverage to minority interests like motor-sports) would not then have opened its doors to Gaelic games. I think, too, that there were deeper roots to this lack of interest amongst those involved with the BBC. In 1948, in my last year at Queen's, as a hungry student trying to earn some money, I persuaded a producer in BBC radio (there was no other station at the time) to engage me to contribute a commentary each Friday on the weekend GAA fixtures. My first script was submitted, but not broadcast. I still have the letter from a chastened producer telling me that he had received a directive from the Head of Programmes to leave out all reference to Sunday sport, and that was the end of the matter. Later they relented to the extent of giving out results on the Monday, but not affording prior publicity to games on the Sabbath; they could report that sin had been committed, but would not provide prior information about the occasions of sin. They also, at the time, sent a cheque for seven shillings and sixpence (less than 40p) for my trouble, which, in a fit of high-minded moral outrage I refused to cash – and have now sadly lost, but the scar remains. Even on UTV we got fed up explaining during interview after interview that the ball was round, there were fifteen players on a team, that a goal was under the bar and equalled three points, which were over the bar. In 1961 Paddy Doherty was even voted sports-star of the year (partly because Briney McCartan went round handing out pre-addressed postcards with his name on them). The name was received with stunned silence on the night, and Paddy never got his trophy from UTV.

But back to the main business at hand and we took the view that the main barrier to a northern team winning a senior All-Ireland title in football was psychological. Armagh should have won in 1953, and Derry could have done so in 1958. They seemed to be convinced that southern teams were somehow better, that southern footballers were a race of giants whom it was presumptuous to think of beating. One could only do one's best and put up a good show. And then there was Cavan, lying like a dragon in the path of any other Ulster county. They did not meet in the National League or the McKenna Cup, only in the championship, which Cavan had won with monotonous regularity, year after year, almost without working up a sweat. As a result, the highest ambition any Ulster county could have was to beat Cavan once in a blue moon. That was their All-Ireland final. After that they had nothing left to achieve.

We concluded that to have any hope of winning an All-Ireland, a team needed to be able to beat Cavan while still having enough in reserve, both physically and mentally, for the greater tasks ahead. Down's contribution to the other Ulster counties was to slay the Cavan dragon. Our contribution to them and to less successful counties everywhere was that it was possible to dream, even to hope that with effort and preparation, harnessed to skill and ability it was conceivable, every now and then, for David to take on Goliath, and to win. We broke the spell for the men of Ulster which released the other counties to achieve similar success later. I thought at the time it was a bit like the four-minute mile: until Bannister did it, everybody said it could not be done, and then everybody started doing it. They were exciting times too: Everest had been climbed for the first time (it is now commonplace); Paddy Doherty got his nickname, 'Paddy Mo' from an American tennis prodigy who was herself named after a battleship 'Mighty Mo'; and Cassius Clay, not yet Ali, was emerging as a sporting superstar. It was a wonderful time, when anything seemed possible, and we felt part of it.

In winning the All-Ireland title, Down did much to raise the spirits not only of their own community, but right across the north. President McAleese has rightly identified earlier in this book about how it gave new confidence to the minority nationalist community in the north. That said there were, I think, few people in the county interested in any sport who did not give us some measure of support and we took care to appear to represent all areas in the county by making tickets available to every district council. They all took them up in any event – in a note that is now topical, some even claimed travelling expenses for going to Croke Park. We did, oddly enough, contribute to the removal of the playing of *Faith of Our Fathers* from

Maurice Hayes, team-manager Barney Carr, and a squad of fifteen Down players of the 1960s at a reunion held in the Cardinal Ó Fiaich Library, Armagh, in June 2009.

the pre-match ritual, which some people thought unduly pietistic. What we did get was a huge amount of voluntary support right across the board, especially from hospital staff and employers. In any event the whole thing – raising the team to win an All-Ireland title – was done on a shoestring budget.

One piece of back-projection that was imposed on us by the media and a few romantics, and is now part of the folklore, is that Down wanted to be the first team to bring the Sam Maguire Cup across the border. The thought never crossed our minds. We went to Dublin to win a football match and that was all. There was no more significance in doing so than in beating Cavan in Clones and bringing the Anglo-Celt Cup back to Down. In any case, as members of an association whose ideal was a united Ireland it would have been illogical for us to glory in breaching a line we thought should not exist. Some people did think otherwise. On the morning of the National League win over Cavan, the local postman, an Orangeman and a B Special, on seeing the cup displayed in Kevin Mussen's home, could not contain his feelings. 'Begod', he burst out, 'we took it off the friggers!' We took support where we found it, and were glad to do so. Actually I did not see the cup cross the border, and did not go home with the team, although in hindsight I missed much of the joy of the occasion. As far as I was concerned, the job was done – until the next year. I went to Listowel races, along with Paddy O Keeffe, to be joined the next day by the McCartans and Patsy O Hagan, and where we were warmly welcomed by Kerry players and fans, who taught us that to lose gracefully was as much of an accomplishment as to win. That said, it is interesting to chart the change in attitude to Down as a northern team. When we were going down to be beaten by twenty or thirty points, we were great people indeed. 'You don't know how much we admire 'ye', keeping the flag flying up there against all opposition!' Win an All-Ireland or two, however, and it was 'How can we compete with ye – getting free milk from the British government!'

It was amusing too to see the reaction of the ultra-orthodox to some of the things we did for purely practical reasons. I remember being berated by an eminent theologian from Kerry in Croke Park one Sunday for the deviant tendencies displayed by Down in having decided to wear black knicks (shorts). This was creeping 'californication' and 'soccerisation' of the worst type – a threat to the moral fibre of the nation. There was little point in arguing about peripheral vision or the importance of players having a common point of reference when the jerseys changed. Similarly tracksuits were introduced, not to be trendy, but to overcome the problem – caused by the fashionable drainpipe trousers of the time – for subs who were then accustomed to strip out and pull their trousers on over their boots before sitting in the dugout.

Of all the strange places the Sam Maguire Cup has been, and they are many, few know that it spent an evening in the Crumlin Road gaol in Belfast. I was asked by the Catholic chaplain, Fr McAllister, to bring the cup and a few players up to a Christmas concert which he staged for prisoners. I brought Leo Murphy, George Lavery, Kevin Mussen, James McCartan and Jarlath Carey and we carried the cup through locked door after claustrophobic locked door to a stage on which James Johnson was singing and a young Frank Carson was telling jokes and a few scattered and probably smuggled pieces of red-and-black cloth fluttered in the upper galleries. The occasion is not mentioned in Eamon Boyce's prison diary of the period – he told me that convicted prisoners had been excluded and that we had entertained the internees. I hope it cheered them up.

The Down team did a coast-to-coast tour of the USA in 1962, one of the most extensive ever by a GAA team. We played in Boston, Cleveland, Philadelphia, Chicago and San Francisco, but not New York. We were the guests of the North American Board, a sort of rival organisation to New York, which was causing trouble for Croke Park at the time. I think we were sent out to strengthen the cities and to put a shot across John Kerry O Donnell and his group, who responded in kind. The North American Board were nearly all new immigrants, much more naïve and idealistic than the people in New York.

Finally, what I would want you to take from this is the lesson that success does not come easily; there is no magic formula, no substitute for commitment, hard work and careful preparation. All the five-year plans will not work if the ground has not been prepared. That is why I weep at counties who think that throwing money at a moderate team and a mercenary manager will bring instant success. It is why I admire Tyrone and Kilkenny in their different games: they do the work; they look after the grassroots and keep renewing themselves. All of us who were involved with that great Down team gained a great deal from it, not least in nostalgic reflection. To quote the next greatest Derry man after Jim McKeever, Seamus Heaney, we were like youngsters playing in an ill-defined field, and enjoying it so much they continued playing in their minds after dark. It is a poem about transcendence, and in a sense, great players, great games and great teams enable us to transcend the drab, the mundane and the merely dull grind of the daily round. Like Heaney, again, in *The Point*, 'Is it you or the ball that goes sailing higher and higher and ruefully free?' That the proud county of Down managed it in those years indubitably changed the trajectory of Ulster football for years to come.

The Coming of Age of Gaelic Games in Ulster, 1950–1970

Jim McKeever

To reflect on the considerable development of the GAA in Ulster during the middle part of the twentieth century, is the task that I have been handed for this publication. I am not entirely delighted that in celebrating 125 years of activity I should be considered representative of the medieval period. Nevertheless I have taken up the challenge to assess this period, based on my personal involvement, which was often deep and wide-ranging. Among the experiences which inform my perspective are the following: playing competitively from 1947 to 1969; serving in administrative roles as club secretary, county committee delegate, Central Council member (in the mid 1960s), higher education council (chairman), and a member of the special commission on the GAA which reported in 1971; and my professional interest in Physical Education, as one of the earliest batches of its teachers in Ireland and then as a lecturer from the late 1950s, which acquainted me

Jim McKeever

with all forms of sport; sitting as a member of the statutory Youth and Sports Council of Northern Ireland from the early 1960s, and its later equivalents; and plumbing the depths by writing a weekly article for a Sunday newspaper and being a match-commentator and -analyst on television. Though this article cannot aspire to give the definitive account of the period, I can at least recount those groundbreaking developments that I was fortunate enough to witness.

I grew up in a community mainly interested in Gaelic games and my memories of them date back over the 1940s and indeed the late 1930s. I recall that in those years Ulster football – Cavan excepted – was of a poor standard, compared to the giants of the game in the south, Kerry, Cork, Galway, Mayo, Roscommon, Dublin, and, of course, Cavan. They were the aristocrats; we did not figure in their thoughts and we accepted this as a fact of life. We did not fully realise that these counties had been playing the game for the first fifty years of the GAA, whereas for us it was relatively new. The cliché that the GAA spread like wildfire following 1884 is an exaggeration. Some sparks were scattered and landed randomly here and there. The further north the less likely it was to catch fire.

Derry did not have a permanent county board until I was almost three years old, in 1933. (There had been several previous boards in the county, mostly based in Derry City and district, but each one expired after a few years.) Even *Mars* bars were launched a year before the Derry GAA became finally established. 1933 was also the year that Cavan won its first All-Ireland senior football title, whilst Kerry had already won ten. There was clearly a lot of ground to cover and a lot of catching up to do. Leaving Cavan aside, the 1930s and 1940s could be regarded as the formative years of the GAA in Ulster. Over those two decades Cavan won seventeen Ulster championships, losing only to Monaghan twice in the 1930s and to Antrim in the 1940s. They also won four All-Ireland titles and lost three finals, two of them after replays. We all supported and respected Cavan as our champions. They gave Ulster respect but, as a consequence, emphasised the impoverishment of the rest.

In the 1940s some green shoots of recovery began to appear. In 1946 Down won an All-Ireland junior title, St Patrick's College, Armagh won the Hogan Cup, and Antrim beat Cavan to win the Ulster Senior Football Championship. In 1947 Derry won the National League, somewhat shortened by an outbreak of foot-and-mouth disease and the worst winter weather in living memory. Tyrone and Armagh won All-Ireland minor titles in the last three years of the decade.

There were clearly grounds for optimism at the beginning of the 1950s, in spite of the almost total dominance of Cavan, a fact made palatable by recognising that the Cavan team of that era was one of the greatest Gaelic football teams of all. In the first Ulster inter-provincial team I was selected on I was placed

The 1958 Derry team at a meeting in Newbridge prior to the county's first-ever appearance in the All-Ireland senior football final. Team-manager Roddy Gribbin instructs the players, including Jim McKeever (second from right on the front row), and Leo O'Neill (brother of Martin) and Sean O'Connell on either side of him. (*Jim McKeever*)

in the right corner-forward position. The left half-forward was Hughie McKearney of Monaghan but every other spot from midfield, that is six out of eight, was occupied by a Cavan player and each one a household name. And there were Cavan backs as well. In the corner position I was surrounded by Tony Tighe, Mick Higgins, and Peter Donohoe.

Though we did not know it in 1950, Cavan's dominance was at an end. The championship in that decade was shared by six counties: Cavan won three titles, Armagh and Tyrone claimed two each, with Derry, Antrim, and Down winning one each. Though only Cavan actually won an All-Ireland, Armagh and Derry reached their first finals in this decade. Throughout the 1960s successes were not as widely distributed, mainly due to the emergence of a remarkable generation of Down footballers. They won six Ulster titles and three All-Ireland championships, while a still competitive Cavan won four in Ulster; though it is fair to say that both were pushed hard by several other counties.

A look forward to the 1970s illustrates a clear change in the landscape of Ulster football. Again six different counties shared the provincial championship; Derry won the title on three occasions, Down and Donegal won two championships each, whilst Tyrone, Armagh, and Monaghan again claimed one apiece. Though Cavan reached two provincial finals, for the first time in any decade they failed to win a single Ulster championship title. Senior provincial championships wins are not, of course, the only indication of success.

Indeed one of the virtues of sport is that with appropriate goal-setting, virtually everyone can experience periodic levels of achievement.

But I do believe that the quality of the best twenty or thirty players in a county is a reasonably reliable indicator of the strength and effectiveness of the association in that setting, not over one year but over the previous five to ten years. There are, however, some factors with a significant influence on success, which lie outside the control of county committees.

One such factor highly correlated with success and outside of county control is the size and composition of its catchment population. In most Ulster counties a further complication is the fact that Gaelic games have so far been confined to the Catholic population. The only county yet to win a senior championship in Ulster, Fermanagh, is the one that probably suffers most from a combination of these two factors. Clubs on the other hand, unlike counties, can control the size of their catchment population to some extent. The vast differences in club-team successes can often be explained by population comparisons, especially true in rural or semi-rural parishes.

In a similar vein a sports organisation, especially one involving team-games, can only function if teams can travel the distances needed to fulfil competitive fixtures against other sides. For the vast majority of people this only became possible from the mid nineteenth century onwards with the advent of railway systems. The new travel possibilities at the time explain why the five different football games associations in the world were founded in the twenty-five years prior to 1884. In Ireland travel difficulties initially hindered contact with games played in the seminal growth-points throughout Munster and south Leinster and further inhibited GAA developments in Ulster until the post-war years.

Derry's first senior football championship match in my lifetime was played in 1945 at Letterkenny, Co. Donegal. It required an overnight stay. One south Derry player cycled to Magherafelt on Saturday, caught a bus for Derry city, and transferred to a train for Letterkenny. On Sunday there was not even time for a meal between the conclusion of the match and the return journey home. My first experience of playing against southern opposition at that time – essential for my development as a player – was for the Ulster colleges' side against Connacht colleges in 1948, a match staged at Tuam. The journey on the Saturday meant leaving St Malachy's College, Belfast – where I was then a pupil – before nine o'clock in the morning, travelling to Armagh by train and then by bus, collecting players en route. We arrived in Tuam at nine o'clock in the evening following a twelve-hour journey. Such journeys could not be undertaken regularly and consequently Ulster teams rarely benefited from games against better quality teams in the south of the island. Today transport difficulties have all but disappeared. But in the 1950s club competitions were organised on a county divisional basis for ease of travel. Now clubs play, without difficulty, in an all-Ulster league, which has served to refresh interest in club games.

In spite of these and other difficulties during the 1950s and 1960s the pattern of widespread success in senior championships and in the All-Ireland series indicates that standards throughout Ulster had risen to a level comparable with that of other provinces. The GAA here, at least in football, had truly come of age. What brought about the evolution? It seems to me that the important elements were: a change of emphasis in the administration of the game, an acceptance of team coaching / management and a revolution in the provision of facilities.

The administration of the GAA was governed by its *Official Guide*, which identified responsibilities and procedures for managing club competitions and fielding county teams but made no reference to the preparation of a team. Since the county committee consisted of club delegates, the welfare of the clubs was its primary concern and the interests of county teams were but a secondary consideration. Nevertheless the power to select county teams was jealously guarded and, in some cases, was suspected of being heavily politicised. There is a whole folklore connected with the team selection of county and provincial teams, which many of us could no doubt contribute to. In brief, a delegate was regarded as successful if he had 'his' player(s) selected. However no-one had specific responsibility for the team that was ultimately selected and the resulting lack of confidence affected the morale, the performance focus, and the commitment of its chosen players.

The Derry team that played in the 1958 All-Ireland football final. And a fluffy-dog mascot.
Back: P. McLarnon, S. O'Connell, H. F. Gribbin, P. Breen, P. Stuart, B. Murray, P. Smith, R. Gribbin (trainer).
Front: D. McKeever, B. Mullan, O. Gribbin, J. McKeever (captain), C. Higgins, T. Doherty, C. Mulholland, P. Gormley.

For example, Roddy Gribbin is rightfully regarded as the Derry manager in 1958, when the team reached its first All-Ireland final, but he was never appointed or authorised to hold the position. He was a member of the county board, as well as an injured member of the playing panel, and being a natural leader he took over the team willingly. The board still, in theory, selected the team but never questioned his recommendations, which were based on discussions with players and his own judgment.

Having one person as a reference point, as opposed to control by committee, was the norm in college teams and much valued by players, many of whom became county footballers and brought their college experience with them. Such an arrangement quickly caught on and county committees began recruiting what were called 'trainers' to prepare the team but only for the final stages of a competition, when presumably the players had proven they were actually worth training. Initially recruitment of trainers was from other sports such as boxing or soccer where, it was assumed, greater expertise could be found. The hope was to make fitter players rather than better footballers. There was then, as there is to some extent today, an inordinate belief in the value of fitness in bringing about team success.

In 1950 when Derry reached an All-Ireland junior semi-final the county board recruited as trainer Frank McGreevy from Newry, whose expertise derived from having trained Newry Town F. C. He was an endearing man, approaching sixty years of age at that time, who knew very little about Gaelic football, indeed scarcely enough to referee a practice game. His specialism was doing drill exercises. But his presence focused us on preparing for the game, was a source of interactive enjoyment, and much valued by the team. Though short-term appointments continued there emerged quickly a preference for ex-players, sometimes with additional experience, such as John Vallely in Armagh, who had a background in athletics; or Gerry Browne, who was involved in Down and Tyrone and was a Physical Education (PE) teacher. Importantly these ex-footballers added team-play and skill-coaching to the preparation. It was not until the end of the 1950s that year-long managerial appointments became common.

Derry players relaxing in their Dublin hotel and reading the match-reports on the morning after their shock All-Ireland senior football semi-final win over Kerry in 1958. (*Jim McKeever*)

I like to believe that we in the six counties had a head start in coaching and managing as a consequence of the 1947 Education Act, which required the building of secondary schools, including sports facilities, for pupils up to the age of fifteen years (later sixteen years) and the employment of PE teachers to instruct them. For the first time Gaelic games were included on the course syllabus for PE student-teachers, enjoyed equal status with other activities, and featured on Ministry of Education and later Queen's University, Belfast, final examination papers. This was particularly important for those students who had little experience of the games. The planned coaching of football in these new secondary schools formed the expectations of young players and created demand for similar arrangements at club and county level. Since the employment of PE teachers began about two decades earlier in the north than in the south of the country the impetus towards coaching was felt more strongly in the former during the 1950s and 1960s.

Specialist coaching of talented school-aged players was offered at summer coaching schools provided by education boards, notably the Orangefield courses, which included football and hurling as well as other sports. Courses for adult players and potential coaches followed. I can recall courses at Castlewellan and Casement Park financed by the Northern Ireland branch of the (British) Central Council for Physical Recreation in the mid 1960s and, later, week-long courses at Stranmillis College and the University of Ulster at Coleraine, organised by Sports Council for Northern Ireland (now Sport NI). However, the GAA authorities were generally unenthusiastic about coaching and probably delayed its progress somewhat. The reluctance seemed based on a suspicion that it would dilute the Gaelic ethos (though how this was the case was never specified) and might lead to professionalism (the jury is still out on that!). The courses I have referred to were outside the direct control of the GAA. When Joe Lennon, also in the mid 1960s, proposed national coaching courses in Gormanstown College, Co. Meath, he also found officialdom to be unsupportive, though he was not discouraged. The obscurantism shown towards coaching at the time damaged the authority of the association in the minds of many.

From the mid 1940s to the end of the 1960s was a major period for the purchase and development of grounds. In 1944 Clones was opened at the most important railway crossroads in the province. It brought increased gate receipts to an Ulster Council struggling financially and in turn released money for ground investment throughout the province. In 1947 Davitt Park opened in Lurgan, and co-incidentally I played my first county game there – for Antrim minors – in what was surely the first Ulster championship game hosted at the new venue. In the five years prior to 1950 the Ulster Council allocated £10,000 in grant-aid to grounds across the province many of which became county venues, including Dungannon, Magherafelt, Newcastle, Ballybay, Irvinestown, Newry, Castleblayney, Ballybofey and others. The small grant was an important stimulus, but it did not eliminate the importance of clever dealing. My first club, Newbridge (Co. Derry), for more than ten years, had been spoilt for choice with very good pitches on a flat plain and where I saw my first half-dozen county games. Subsequently a war-time airfield was constructed on the flat terrain and the club was dislodged. In 1943 a small, barely adequate ground was purchased for £200. In 1953 a farm alongside was bought for £500 and having enlarged the pitch the remaining land was sold for £550.

Maybe the most iconic statement about the future of GAA in Ulster was the opening of Casement Park in 1953, on a new site, of modern design, alongside the main road to the south and in the middle of a rapidly growing Belfast suburb. I had witnessed its early construction when passing almost daily as a student and, in what must have been its first senior championship game in June 1953, I left the field to have stitches in my face; attributable, I believe, to a lack of match fitness, having arrived home the previous evening from a year in Loughborough College in England.

The purchase of grounds, begun slowly in the post-war era and continued for the next twenty years and transformed the GAA throughout the province until virtually every club had its own ground. In the early 1950s I played against almost every club in south Derry, east Down and some clubs in the English midlands, and I recall permanent pitches only at Newbridge, Magherafelt, Newcastle (Co. Down) and, strangely enough, Birmingham. When I stopped playing in 1969 almost every club had a laid-out, fenced pitch, with good clubrooms. In each case a combination of courage and prudence was needed to see the development through to completion and take on the almost inevitable debt. It required what current American President Barack Obama would call the 'audacity of hope'.

When the Magherafelt ground was purchased in 1941 for £500 the county board thought the club a little too audacious and, fearing the impact of possible financial difficulties to the good name of the GAA in the county, insisted on taking over the ground themselves. They then leased it back to the club for a lengthy period under certain conditions, including the right to play county fixtures there. For two generations it was known as the county grounds but now as Rossa Park, it is fully in possession of the Magherafelt club. Indeed in the past year the club has purchased additional ground and, at the time of writing, is currently developing a second pitch costing over £500,000. When this latest decision was made no one blinked an eyelid.

Grounds development was accelerated by a new source of grant-aid which came on stream in 1962. The Stormont government, following established practice abroad, took on the role of promoting sport. The 1962 Youth Welfare, Physical Training and Recreation Act enabled sports clubs to receive grant aid for expenditure on administration, coaching and sports facilities, and therefore established for the first time the possibility of the Northern Ireland state doing business with the GAA.

A council was appointed to vet applications and establish priorities. I was invited to be a member of this committee. Correspondence emphasised that appointees were not representatives of particular sports but were to assist informed decision-making. It was ground-breaking for both the government and the GAA. I sensed in the civil service wariness of both a GAA voice in committee and equally of possible reactions from some who might well be suspicious of the GAA's motives. The pen-pictures of members of the new body were circulated prior to the first meeting. Mine was carefully worded, perhaps not to attract attention, stating that I was a lecturer in St Mary's College, Belfast, had been awarded half-colours for athletics at Loughborough College, had represented Northern Ireland in basketball, and was formerly associated with a boys' club in Downpatrick, where I had organised basketball and trained football teams. Gaelic football,

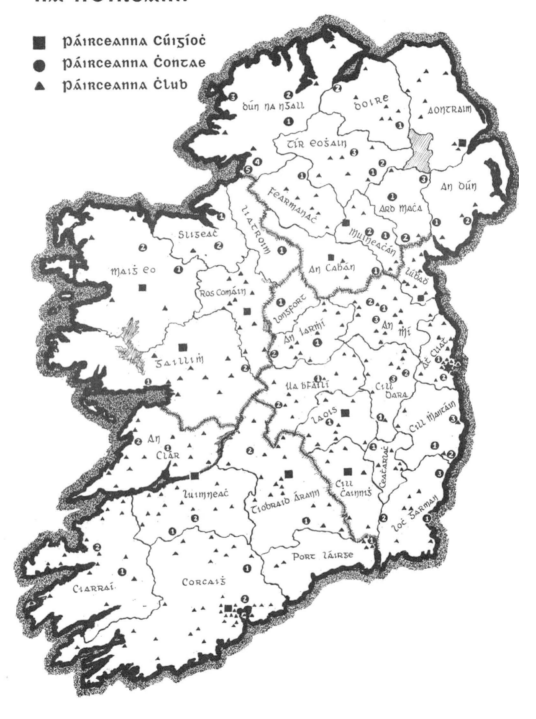

páirceanna imearta na héireann

- ■ páirceanna Cúigíoc
- ● páirceanna Contae
- ▲ páirceanna Club

Dún na nGall

Doire

Aontraim

Tír Eoġain

An Dún

Fearmanaċ

Ard Maċa

Muineaċán

Liatroim

Lúḃaḋ

Sligeaċ

An Caḃán

Maiġ eo

Ros Comáin

Lonġfort

An Mí

An Iarṁí

Áṫ Cliaṫ

Gaillim

Ua bFailí

Cill Dara

Laois

Cill Mantáin

An Clár

Ceatarlaċ

Cill Ċainniġ

Loċ Garman

Luimneaċ

Tiobraid Árann

Port láirge

Ciarraí

Corcaiġ

Club, county and provincial playing facilities for Gaelic games as outlined in the *Our Games* annual of 1963, the year after Jim McKeever joined the Youth and Sports Council. It was only since about 1950 that clubs began to acquire their own grounds.

Playing facilities attracting grants under the Youth Welfare, Physical Training and Recreation Acts (Northern Ireland) 1947, and the Youth Welfare, Physical Training and Recreation Act (Northern Ireland) 1962.

	LOCAL AUTHORITIES			VOLUNTARY ORGANISATIONS		
	Completed in the period		Work in progress	Completed in the period		Work in progress
	1948-65	1962-65		1948-65	1962-65	
Soccer pitches	72	14	15	6	4	-
Gaelic pitches	2	1	-	-	2	1
Rugger pitches	6	-	1	6	12	-
Tennis courts	80	8	20	17	5	-
Netball courts	2	2	4	-	-	-
Hockey pitches	22	1	11	2	4	-
Cricket squares	14	1	5	3	3	-
Cycle tracks	3	-	-	-	-	-
Athletics tracks	2	-	-	-	-	-
Ball alleys	-	-	-	1	2	-
Swimming pools	3	2	1	1	-	-
Sports halls	-	1	-	-	6	1
Changing Accommodation	29	9	4	15	5	3
Playgrounds	54	14	8	2	1	1

Local authorities were notoriously poor at providing adequate facilities for Gaelic games, and the GAA had been largely disinclined to apply for what few capital development grants were available.
(*Minutes of the Youth and Sports Council for Northern Ireland*)

which I thought was the reason for my appointment, was not mentioned – though two others members of the committee were listed as rugby players and a further two as former soccer internationals.

The 1962 Act enabled sports clubs, for the first time, to apply directly for financial support. Until then local authorities (under the1947 Education Act) had been providing playing fields for public use but Gaelic games had been virtually ignored. In Belfast, of 183 playing fields provided for public use only four were Gaelic pitches, all situated in Falls Park (seventy-five were soccer pitches). In the four years prior to 1962, and the establishment of the Youth and Sports Council, sixty-seven pitches throughout Northern Ireland became available for public use or were in the process of construction. None of them were for Gaelic games; but twenty-two were soccer pitches.

Having been overlooked by local authorities, GAA clubs were not slow to avail of the new opportunity offered by central government. At the first meeting of the new council there was an application from Clonduff GAC for the purchase and levelling of a pitch, erection of fencing and building changing accommodation at a cost of £2,100. Within the next year applications followed from the GAA clubs of Rathfriland, Newcastle (fencing pitch), Dunloy (purchase of smaller pitch) and Carnlough (purchase of pitch). All were recommended for grant-aid.

At the end of three years the Youth and Sports Council reported as follows: work in progress – Newry (accommodation upgrade) and Ballycran (pitch); ready to start – Shaws Road, Belfast (three pitches), Roslea (a handball alley), St Enda's, Omagh (pitch and pavilion) and Carnlough (drawings awaited); finally, temporarily deferred – Clonduff (no replies), Dunloy (seeking new site) and Rathfriland (planning refused). Further triennial reports also brought good news. In 1965 to 1968, of eighteen playing field / accommodation schemes approved, twelve were for GAA clubs and of twelve others under consideration, nine were for units aligned with the association. So clearly it can be established from these figures that by this stage Gaelic clubs were very much on the move.

The 1968 to 1972 report listed total grant paid under fifteen headings. Gaelic games came third. An interesting irony is that soccer clubs, which had been favoured by local authorities, were now at a disadvantage because ownership of a ground was a requirement when applying for a development grant, which partly explains the predominance of Gaelic clubs when receiving grant approval. A major disadvantage for Gaelic clubs was the reduction of grant from 50% to 33%, which applied if the club was 'single-activity' or had 'closed membership'. All GAA clubs were categorised as 'closed' because of the exclusion of security forces from their memberships. Former pupils' rugby and hockey clubs were also classified as closed but by taking on a few talented players from outside they qualified for 50% of cost. Reduction to 33% was a significant handicap, which continued for some years after the Youth and Sports Council was replaced by the Sports Council of Northern Ireland in the early 1970s.

The Sports Council had a broader role in sports development than the Youth and Sports Council and was largely independent of the civil servants who, in my experience, see obstacles more clearly than they do opportunities. The GAA continued to be represented by, in turn, Paddy O'Donoghue, Jarlath Carey and Seán O'Neill, and assistance of various forms for Gaelic games continued. I succeeded Seán O'Neill as a member of the Sports Council and remained so for close to twenty years. Sometime in the 1990s a summary of the sports lottery allocations was presented at a particular meeting. It showed that the GAA had been allocated the greatest amount of all, in excess of £11 million. The next highest was swimming, mainly because of the construction of a pool at Bangor, which had received over £5 million. The discussion which followed was the only time in nearly thirty years of such meetings that I remember a degree of acrimony in a Sports Council chamber-room.

I regard the 1960s as an 'ice-breaking' experience, which operated both ways. GAA clubs found the application process and the visits of inspectors helpful and friendly and ministry officials and council members were assured that the GAA business was sporting and managed by well-meaning and pleasant people. The consequent reconciliation of views was important as some fellow committee members, particularly the older ones, would have linked the GAA to earlier antagonisms and in fairness the GAA in the north had made little effort to appear friendly. I would like to put on record that after an initial defrosting period, I found in both the Youth and Sports Council and the Sports Council only continuous goodwill and

Schemes approved in principle for grant under the
Youth Welfare, Physical Training and Recreation Act.

Swimming Pools	Estimated Grant	Date of Approval in Principle
Dungannon	£110,000	27.4.1967
Banbridge	£130,000	8.8.1966
Castlereagh	£260,000	26.3.1964
Newtownabbey	£150,000	7.7.1966
Peter's Hill, Belfast.	£225,000	12.8.1966
	£875,000	

Voluntary Schemes	Grant	Date of Approval in Principle
A. SPORTS ORGANISATIONS		
Old Ballyclarians' Association	£3,500	18.12.1963
Holy Cross G.F.C. Playing Fields	800	7.10.1965
Leitrim G.A.A.	1,000	11. 1.1966
Newbridge G.F.C. Pavilion	1,000	24. 6.1966
Bangor R.F.C. Pavilion	15,000	4. 7.1966
Drumsurn G.A.A.	1,500	7.10.1966
Rathfriland Swifts F.C.	2,000	18.12.1966
Kickham G.A.A. Randalstown	10,000	18. 1.1967
East Antrim Boat Club	1,300	5. 5.1967
Church of Ireland Young Men's Society	4,000	25. 5.1967
Windsor Tennis Club	8,000	5. 7.1967
Aghaderg G.F.C. Playing Field	1,300	6. 7.1967
Ballerin G.A. Club Playing Field	1,400	9. 8.1967
St. Peter's G.F.C. Playing Field	6,000	30. 8.1967
Ards Rugby Football Club Playing Field	600	4. 1.1968
Bellaghy G.F.C. Playing Field	8,400	7. 3.1968
N.W. Football Association	1,000	7. 3.1968
Strabane Cricket Club	600	8. 3.1968
John Mitchell's G.F.C. Playing Field	2,000	8. 3.1968
East Down Yacht Club New Premises	Not known	20. 3.1968
Ballymurphy Tenants' Association Community Centre	Not known	25. 3.1968
St. Patrick's G.F.C. Pavilion	1,800	2. 4.1968
	£71,200	
B. YOUTH ORGANISATIONS		
Charter Youth Club	£4,500	5.12.1963
Limavady Scouts and Guides	4,000	10. 3.1964
Dungannon Youth Club	25,000	20. 4.1964

Grant assistance to sporting organisations from the Northern Ireland Youth and Sports Council 1963–68.
Its consideration of applications for funding was predicated upon sporting need alone, and this approach helped to
accelerate the rate of development of GAA club facilities. (*Minutes of the Youth and Sports Council for Northern Ireland*)

open discussion leading to impartial decision-making. I believe that occasional confrontational approaches by upper levels in GAA not only contrasted with club attitudes but were misjudged.

The GAA I grew up in was almost defiantly an isolated 'no-man's-land', remaining outside not only sport in general but much of society and defined by various rules of exclusion. In fact, one chapter in the *Official Guide* was actually entitled 'Exclusions'. I was troubled by this even before I spent a year in Loughborough University with young men from all sports. I knew in my soul that the game I played was the equal of any other and that people involved in it were overwhelmingly splendid human beings, that it was something to be shared and enjoyed. Yet it chose to stand alone in the world of sport. I took the view, as did most of my contemporaries that the controversial rules and attitudes were non-essentials, which had become encrusted, unquestionable articles of faith but like most of my friends, I simply got on with the game. But the foolishness of isolation would continue to confront me at odd times.

On a visit to a sports summer school I was walking along a path with a young man who introduced himself as a representative of hockey. I told him my name and that I was representing the Sports Council. 'Jim McKeever,' he said, 'Did you play Gaelic for Ulster?' He then described how he had grown up on a farm near Dungannon in a strict Presbyterian family. Sundays were long days. He would go to church, but later reading or radio or recreation was not allowed. He would retire to his room and listen at low volume to Michael O'Hehir, especially when Ulster was playing and he wished us on from that unlikely setting. The scenario that he portrayed horrified me – that young boy could not, and accepted that he could not, openly support his team and his neighbours, including Iggy Jones and Jody O' Neill, who were probably playing. And again we know that the barriers were on both sides. However, the 1960s can claim credit for the first major breach of the isolationist stance by its clear rejection of Rule 27 – the 'excluded games' ban. Though technically the removal was in 1971, the thinking was more borne of the 1960s. Uniquely it had been referred to clubs for a decision and rarely has there been a more decisive result.

The 1950s saw the arrival of television, the supreme medium for enjoying sport, as part of an expansion in the popular media. Many of my generation will recall the interest in watching for the first time the FA Cup final or rugby international on television. We looked forward to having our big games seen by the whole population. Disappointingly, the BBC in Northern Ireland, for years the only television station available, ignored Gaelic games, reinforcing existing prejudices on both sides of the community. The controlling influences in the BBC, I found out later, were of a strongly unionist mindset and not always able to conceal their caricaturist understanding of the GAA. Shamefully they failed to televise the 1960 All-Ireland final won by Down. The widespread celebrations and receptions which followed the win only added to the BBC's embarrassment.

When Down reached the 1961 final, and were defending the championship title, the BBC accepted the responsibility to televise it and asked me to do the commentary. On match-day at Croke Park the main problem and principal concern of the producers was the directive not to broadcast the Irish national anthem but to go live only at the throw-in. So as we stood for the *Soldier's Song* in the stand, where we had been located, surrounded by supporters, the BBC showed a fixed caption throughout and played a very long version of *Greensleeves*. The broadcast had a big audience and Down's win again ensured great interest. The numerous comments from non-Gaelic followers were especially encouraging and I even wondered if my Dungannon friend might have had a television in his room by this time.

The quaintest comment from a new viewer was from a television newsreader. I had been asked to do an interview on Monday's news and during a break he told me that having watched it he was fascinated by the player's names. He recited a long list of very Irish-Catholic names: Leo Murphy, Dan McCartan, Jarlath Carey, Paddy Doherty, P. J. McElroy, Seán O'Neill and then out of the blue, he said, came John Smith – (the left half-back from Ballykinlar). The newsreader was not a sports fan; he had lectured in English and enjoyed deconstructing the language of the names and the intrusion of Smith. But he had watched the game and that was significant. Television coverage of Gaelic games became a regular occurrence in the 1960s and helped to locate all of us more centrally in our own community. As a committed, card-carrying midfielder I am convinced that that is the place to be, as it is from the centre that real influence can be exercised.

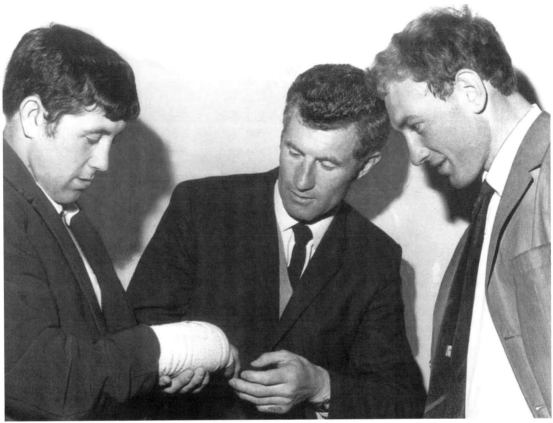

Three men who have served the GAA in Derry in numerous roles: an injured young Éamon Coleman,
Jim McKeever and Tommy Diamond. (*Jim McKeever*)

In conclusion then, the coming of age of the GAA in Ulster in the middle part of the twentieth century was both caused and evidenced by the following factors: widespread development of playing facilities; positive team-coaching and management; raised competitive standards throughout the province; admission of games into statutory educational programmes; engagement with government bodies and mainstream media; a reduction in exclusivism; and a movement towards accommodation with, and acceptance by, wider society.

The GAA has had a wonderful 125 years to date and Ulster is at last the leading province in football, entering this year holding the three major All-Ireland trophies, national league, minor and senior championships. As we have heard repeatedly from our financial advisers and know now with certainty, past success is no guarantee of the future. So too this is true of the GAA. We have a more educated, more cosmopolitan, more critical and more exposed young population than ever before in our history. They will look at us with more searching eyes and we need to win both their minds and hearts, and maybe in that order. And if we do not have committed players then sadly we will have nothing.

From Tigh Mór to Croke Park

Peter Quinn

There's a story attributed to some unknown Irishman, who, when asked directions to some place, replied that if he was going there he wouldn't start from here. In a way, Teemore is like that – for most people, it is not the most obvious place from which to start any journey; but if one lives there, or comes from there, it's a logical enough place to start, because it's the centre of one's world. And Teemore was, and in a very real way still is, the centre of my world, certainly as far as the GAA is concerned, but in other respects too.

Peter Quinn

Not many people know much about Teemore. It's a small enclave, bounded to the east by upper Lough Erne, to the west by Slieve Rushen, to the south by the Fermanagh-Cavan border and to the north by the other club area in the parish. In total, it covers about 4½ square miles. When I was growing up there, it had no village and no school – it was just another town land, which happened to have a Catholic church, with a small temperance hall and a shop, but no settlement as we would now know one. In fact, the GAA club, worried by the declining population and the effects that might have on the club, spearheaded a battle for public housing in Teemore, without success, for almost forty years, until a local business, owned by a former player, decided to build houses privately and sell them to local people 'at cost'.

It had a total population of less than six hundred people and a nationalist population of around four hundred. Like many other areas with their own GAA clubs, it was entirely rural, with an economy which depended on farming, supplemented by a bit of smuggling, and with a football field which was more than two miles from Teemore itself, on what was – and still is – known as the Mountain road. But also like many other rural areas, it suffered massively from emigration, from the 1930s right through to the mid 1970s. After winning their fifteenth Fermanagh senior football championship in 1935, no team could be selected in 1936, until after Sunday Mass, because no one knew who had emigrated during the course of the previous week. The reality is that, in the early 1950s, the club nearly folded, and it struggled throughout that entire decade, with a small number of enthusiasts keeping it alive.

What made Teemore a bit different was that it had a split personality – a sort of communal bipolar complex. Up until the 1860s, most of what is now accepted as Teemore, including where I was reared, where the current GAA pitch is and where the previous pitch was, were all part of the old parish of Tomregan, which is now Kildallan, the parish which includes Ballyconnell, in Co. Cavan.

Then the Diocese of Kilmore decided to realign the parish boundaries to reflect the county boundaries, and the Fermanagh part of Tomeregan parish was transferred into Knockninny, which is essentially Derrylin. Since then, Teemore has formed about forty per cent of the land area of its parish and about thirty per cent of its population. But some things never change, and most of the population of that part of Teemore continued to identify with Ballyconnell as their local centre. For most of the families in my area, their burial place was in Ballyconnell, rather than in Teemore; my grandparents are buried there and so are my father's only sibling, his brother-in-law, and his niece and nephew, all of whom lived in Fermanagh; and my father always expected that he too would be buried there.

Ballyconnell / west Cavan was where we socialised, where we shopped, where people went for a pint; it was where most people met their spouses – there was and still is a massive level of inter-marriage between south Fermanagh and west Cavan. Our diocesan college was St Patrick's in Cavan. The landlord to whom farmers and householders paid their ground rent had been based in the estate house a couple of hundred yards south of the border. We bought our cattle in Arva and Carrickallen, and even in Boyle and Granard, but never in Irvinestown or Derrygonnelly, or Tempo or Rosslea.

The all-conquering Teemore Shamrocks from the early years of the twentieth century. The club won three consecutive Fermanagh football championships between 1904 and 1906, and eight-in-a-row between 1910 and 1917. The club benefited from its proximity to Co. Cavan, the hotbed of Gaelic football in Ulster at that time. The Shamrocks won only two more between then and Peter Quinn's team in 1969. (*Fermanagh County Museum*)

We got to know west Cavan and north Leitrim very well, while we knew virtually nothing about north Fermanagh. We knew Cavan town better than we knew Enniskillen; we knew Belturbet and Ballinamore better than we knew Belleek or Brookeborough. And apart from one member of our own club, who was an outstanding member of the county panel for well over a decade, we knew more about Mick Higgins and John Joe O'Reilly, or Victor Sherlock and 'the Gunner' Brady, than we knew about any Fermanagh player, because we read the local Cavan paper rather than the Fermanagh one. Not only that, but we also identified with Dublin and the 'Free State' (as the Republic was called around Teemore, in my youth) in a way that we never identified with Belfast or Derry, or the north, even though Belfast and Dublin are equidistant from Teemore. The first time I was ever in Belfast was the day I enrolled at Queen's University, though I had been in Dublin several times by then (mostly in Croke Park). Teemore and the majority of its people were in Fermanagh, but not really 'of' Fermanagh; they were in the 'six counties', but not really 'of the six counties' (as the north was then referred to in that area). In almost every nationalist house in Teemore, parents, who had lived through the War of Independence and the Civil War, believed that the failure to implement the recommendations of the Boundary Commission had, in one way or another, deprived them of their proper home in the Republic of Ireland, and they resented that fact. That's how things were fifty years ago. They are significantly different today, largely because of the changes in the education system in the north, and the consequent increased interaction of teenagers on a county-wide basis, but also because of the increased industrialisation of the area, the vastly improved communications and connections, and the 'peace process'.

A GAA parade in Fermanagh in the association's centenary year, 1984. Despite never having won a provincial senior title in football or hurling, there has remained great pride in the county identity. (*Fermanagh County Museum*)

I raise these issues of identity and allegiance because I believe that what I have described in relation to the Teemore of my youth still resonates in many border areas, and still has both relevance and implications for nationalists generally in the north and for members of the GAA in particular. For me, identity has always been central to the GAA's aims and ideals; it is what makes the local GAA club the focal point of so many communities and what allows it to provide leadership and a sense of place and identity within those communities too. I have long argued that the core ideals and values of the GAA are about the creation of a positive sense of identity and the development of greater confidence within our communities and among our membership; and I believe that, by and large, we have succeeded in that role.

In that respect, I see the Teemore of my youth as a microcosm of the wider nationalist community in the north of Ireland. I believe that there is still a large element of a bipolar sense of identity and allegiance, particularly in border areas; and I am convinced it is not restricted to the north – it exists on an island-wide basis too. In my youth, the main thing which gave Teemore its own sense of identity was its football club. Teemore Shamrocks and the Mountain Road Pipe Band represented Teemore in the eyes of all its residents. They were 'ours' and we were proud of them; and the football club in particular had the unequivocal support of every Catholic family in the area and of many Protestant families too.

Long before I was born, the Shamrocks had developed a proud history, going back almost to the founding of the GAA. Having been part of Ballyconnell for centuries, no changes in parochial boundaries could change historic allegiances. As most people know, the first officially registered GAA club in Ulster was Ballyconnell, later known as the 'First Ulsters', and the first game played under GAA rules in the province was also played in Ballyconnell. Not so many may know that at least three, and probably four, of the players in that game were from the Teemore part of Fermanagh, though they attended Sunday Mass in Ballyconnell rather than in Teemore, as some people from the townlands along that border still do. And members of the Church of Ireland in that area still attend their Sunday services in Ballyconnell too.

Pádraig Mac Floinn
President of the G.A.A.

Thursday 25/2/82.

Firstly President I must start of this note by appologising for not being able to write to you in our own language (which I am in the proceeds of learning at the minute) But dispite this treadgy I beg you to have patience with me, and kindly help me with my request if you please.

I am here in the H-Blocks of Long Kesh and I would dearly love to Promote the G.A.A. sport, How to go about this properly I believe I would need to start of firstly by doing a lecture or lectures on the entire history of the sport and then proceed from there, But unfortunaly I do not have this information to lecture or lectures of this kind, so that is the reason why I am writing to you President, and I beg you President Please do not let me down, Please forward a good lecture or lectures on to me as soon as possiable, Below are a few points which might let you know the kind of lecture or lecture's that I am looking for, though I dare say you know exactly what I need for such a lecture.

1. I would like to know the very first existence of Gaelic football, Hurling, Handball, that was ever played on Irish soil, How many took part in a game, what way the scoring was done, How long the game lasted, The type of ball to, Sticks which were used in those days, How the games Gaelic football, Hurling, and Hand-Ball came into being, Were there many people interested in the games at that time, was it promoted in any way, plus everything in general about Gaelic football, Hurling, Handball, and any other sport that was played in Ireland at that time.

2. When the G.A.A. was first Founded and by whome, The rules that were laid down at that time, and how they have changed over the years right up to this present day, When was Gaelic football + Hurling first played on a proper pitch, was club football and Hurling played before they were played at county level, and for how long did clubs represent the county.

3. At what times did the different grades of G.A.A. come into being example senior, Junior, Intermediate, U-21, Minor, and other grades, example school football, this for both football and Hurling as well as Camogie and girls football, and at what time did the National football and Hurling League's come into being, as well as other things in general.

4. What is the present standard size of Gaelic football pitches, and Hurling pitches, and Camogie pitches, as well as the present day rules for these sports.

5. I would like a list of the county which has won the all Ireland most times at all grades in football, and Hurling, and Camogie, and girls football, as well as the National football, and Hurling League's.

6. Also when it was Gaelic

An extract from a smuggled letter or 'comm', written on government-issue toilet paper by a republican prisoner from Co. Tyrone in February 1982, to seek the assistance of the GAA president (Pádraig Mac Floinn) in delivering a series of talks to his fellow inmates on the history of the association. (*Pádraig Mac Floinn papers, CÓFLA*)

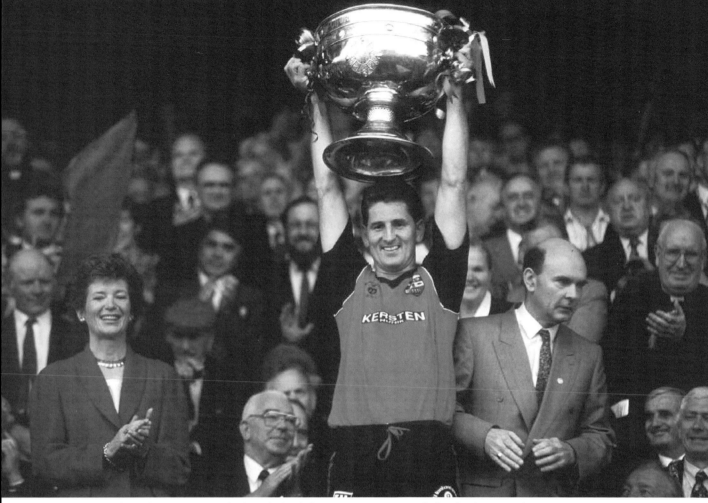

Thosaigh an Tuaisceart. The first of Ulster's four-in-a-row sequence of All-Ireland victories, by Down in 1991.
Peter Quinn had the unique honour of presenting the Sam Maguire Cup to an Ulster captain in each year
of his presidency of the GAA (1991–94).

So the football pedigree was there from the start. Teemore won the first Fermanagh football championship and, in later years, went on to establish a record which it held until the end of the twentieth century, being the only club in Ulster to win eight successive county senior football championships. In the current century, Crossmaglen Rangers has since smashed that record comprehensively and I congratulate them on it; they are a credit to our province of Ulster.

I can never remember a time when I did not aspire to playing for the Shamrocks and to winning championships with them – and even to winning an Ulster title with Fermanagh. Unfortunately, when I was seven years old, I suffered a serious illness, as a result of which I nearly died; as a consequence I lived for over twenty years on penicillin injections and, in my entire life, I never played a game of football that was not played contrary to doctor's orders. I still played senior football for nineteen years, starting when I was fourteen, but possibly not at the level I might have achieved had my health been better in my youth.

For most of those years, I had no interest in the administrative side of the association. I became an officer of the club while still a teenager, but I did it for the club, rather than for any broader association. Without any planning our achievements were modest but that all changed in 1969, when I was lucky enough to captain Teemore to senior championship success, scoring the equaliser three minutes from the end and the winner in the last minute.

It might seem odd that, at twenty-five years of age, having played senior football for over ten years, I had never been present at the awarding of the county championship trophy to a winning captain. My only experience of acceptance speeches was at Clones or Croke Park, and they always started with at least a few sentences in Irish, so I spoke in both Irish and English when accepting the New York Cup – the Fermanagh championship trophy – from the late John McElholm.

Three months later, the nominations for county convention were published and I was one of three people nominated for the two positions of representatives to the Ulster Council, which conducted its entire business through Irish, at that time. I knew Teemore had not nominated me, because I had filled in the club's nomination form. I attended the county convention and just before the election of officers I noticed that a former county chairman, the late Gerry Magee of Irvinestown, then President of Fermanagh county board, was speaking to every delegation in the room, but he never came near us. We wondered why!

On the first count, the late John Vesey, former president of Comhairle Uladh and one of the best GAA administrators I ever met, was elected. In fact I can state that John Vesey and Malachy Mahon, who is also a former president of Comhairle Uladh, were the two best administrators I ever worked with in Fermanagh. Consequently there was a second ballot between Mickey Brewster, who had played for Fermanagh and Ulster for years, and myself, who had played for the county team for a couple of hours. I won by fifty-four votes to fifty-three and it was much later that I learned that I had been nominated by Irvinestown, whom we had played in the county final, and that Gerry Magee had been canvassing for me at the convention.

I was not to know it then, but my 'road to Croke Park' started that day. Just over ten years later, I became treasurer of Comhairle Uladh and, within a year, the association generally, and Comhairle Uladh in particular, found themselves embroiled in the problems of the hunger strikes. As most GAA people are aware, the hunger strikes were a particularly emotive issue within the association, with many of our northern members demanding that we should adopt a strongly supportive stance and many others insisting that we avoid anything that smacked of politics. It was a time for careful judgment and strong, steady nerves. The GAA at a central level clearly did not know what to do and attempted to keep a low profile, apparently unaware of the potential for a major, damaging split within the organisation; and we did lose some members and a small number of clubs at that time, though the majority returned later.

But one man saved the GAA in Ulster and nationally from the sort of major split which could have done irreparable, long-term damage; that was the then president of Comhairle Uladh, Peter Harte from Tyrone, a man of the highest integrity and commitment, who, virtually single-handedly, charted a way through the problem. He subordinated his personal views in favour of the best interests of the GAA nationally, and invested an enormous amount of time and energy in protecting the association from what could have been a disaster. It still disappoints me that, while others have trumpeted their roles over that period, Peter Harte has never been accorded the recognition he deserves for what he did for our association in 1981; without his input and his sound judgment, the association would, in my opinion, be much weaker today.

Twenty years later, I saw, at first hand, another example of another Ulsterman who did not allow his own prejudices or personal views to distract him from doing what he perceived to be in the best interests of the association. Using the mechanism of a special congress, Seán McCague steered the change of the rule banning members of the security forces from membership of the association (Rule 21) through the association's decision-making structures. This was because he foresaw the potential for damage to the association, if its rulebook was to become an impediment to the realisation of a cessation of violence and the creation of a more peaceful society on this island.

I have always believed that it is easy to argue a case which accords with one's personal biases, but it takes real strength, real courage and real leadership to pursue a course, which one's head says is right, but which one's heart rejects. I am exceptionally proud of those two Ulstermen who placed the best interests of the GAA ahead of their own preferences, who demonstrated outstanding leadership and who contributed massively to making our association a stronger, more respected and more potent organisation, by facing down the obstacles which confronted them, with courage, integrity and commitment. Pat Fanning had played a similar role in 1971 and he too deserves great credit for that.

By comparison with what those two men contributed and achieved, my time as president was reasonably straightforward. I first stood for the presidency of the GAA in 1997. Although I knew my name had been mentioned, I had absolutely no intention of standing and I knew that the late John Dowling had been in contact with virtually every county and was getting a positive reaction. Then I got a call from a senior officer of the Donegal county board, who asked me 'What about the presidency?' 'I haven't given it a thought', I answered. 'Well', he said, 'We intend to help you to make up your mind, because we intend to nominate you tomorrow, at our convention.' By the next evening, I was a candidate for the presidency of the GAA!

Of course, the result was predictable – so much so that I wrote out my loser's speech before breakfast on the morning of the vote and did not bother to write a winner's speech. But I was still disappointed; I had not stood to lose, but I lost and John Dowling's track record within the GAA was, by a considerable distance, greater than anything I had achieved. A couple of years later, I decided that I would not run again. Then, towards the end of that year, I got a call from a close relative, who insisted I should run. I discussed it with my wife, Mary, who told me that if I did not run, I might regret it one day. I thought about it and I decided to run again.

I did no canvassing and made no commitments to anyone, but others canvassed for me. There were seven candidates and, in the end, I won easily enough. I was under no illusion about why I was elected. A couple of years earlier, I had been a member of a sub-committee which had reviewed the Croke Park staffing situation. We recommended a reduction in total staff numbers from twenty-three to eighteen and management training for some staff, and, on the casting vote of the Chairman, decided not to recommend more radical change. When the report came before Central Council, it met some opposition and, in supporting it, I knew I had made a few enemies. I also knew that many of those, who later voted for me, did so on the basis that I would sort out the association's staffing problems and its head office structures, and I was very aware of that from the outset. As it turned out, I probably disappointed those supporters. The presidency can be a lonely place – exposed to scrutiny and criticism and antipathy, often with little support, and sometimes with none. I soon discovered that being a northerner was not an advantage in dealing with the Dublin media.

Virtually as soon as I took office, I was faced with a choice; I realised that I could concentrate on sorting out the association's staffing problems and its management structures (as many wanted me to do), or I could put my emphasis on redeveloping our national stadium. I knew that I could not do both in tandem. To this day, I am not sure whether I made the right choice, but I opted for the development of the stadium. The events at Hillsborough in Sheffield, as well as similar incidents in other places, had created a huge awareness of the importance of safety at sports grounds and of the need for them to be 'fit for purpose'. Clearly, Croke Park needed massive investment; unbeknownst to most of the association's members, it was facing the very real prospect of having its permissible capacity – then 67,000 spectators – reduced dramatically, probably to 50,000 or less within five to ten years.

In my year as president-elect (1990), I had accompanied John Dowling to meetings with the then Minister for Sport, Frank Fahy, in relation to the possible construction of a national stadium, to be owned and funded by the Irish government, for use by the three main field-sport organisations. The Minister was very keen on the project. Soccer, rugby and ourselves were asked to contribute £20 million each, with the government providing the balance. We could not get agreement that all three would subscribe that amount and the GAA was not prepared to be the main funder of such a project. Eventually, that proposal was abandoned. Long before my accession to the presidency, we had plans and designs for the redevelopment of our stadium; so we were now faced with the choice of going ahead with the project or waiting for a resolution of the issues with the other bodies. We took the decision to go ahead on our own, knowing there would still be other issues to be resolved.

In the late 1980s, when I was on the GAA's management committee as president of the Ulster Council, I had argued that the GAA should buy the Phoenix park racecourse, which was for sale at that time, and build a completely new state-of-the-art stadium there, with acres of parking space and better infrastructure. For reasons which I fully understood and accepted, the management committee decided that tradition, history, the symbolism of Hill 16, the memory of Bloody Sunday and a myriad of other factors dictated that we should rebuild Croke Park on the existing site. It was probably the right decision, but it meant that we had either to close the stadium for at least two or three years and play our major games elsewhere, or we could continue to use it and undertake the project on a phased basis; we opted for the latter.

When the project was put to the membership, it received a very lukewarm response in many places. At £110 million, to be spent over twelve to fourteen years and paid for over more than twenty years, it was deemed too risky. We were accused of providing boxes and premium seats for those with money, at the

Peter's Palace. The Armagh and Tyrone teams parade before the 2003 All-Ireland final, soon after the redevelopment of Croke Park, instigated by Peter Quinn, was completed.

expense of the ordinary member, even though the proposed increase in capacity was well in excess of twice the number of seats being made available to the business sector, who were going to be funding almost sixty per cent of the cost. We were channelling money into fixed assets – money which was needed for the promotion of the games at 'grassroots' level; we were converting a sporting and cultural organisation into a commercial entity; and we were elitist and just wrong!

We commissioned a model of the stadium and took it round the country to show members what the stadium would look like when it was completed, and it was impressive. Support was strong in the greater Dublin area, in most of Ulster and in Cork; in the rest of the country, it ranged from outright opposition to apathy, or lukewarm acceptance. When we put it to Central Council, it got reasonably strong support, with Ger McKenna (Kerry) and Seán McCague (Monaghan) as well as the members of the Management Committee, being particularly influential in persuading the members to support it. Phase One was budgeted at £37.75 million and we brought it in, almost on time, at just under £37.4 million. I was not involved in the Canal End phase, but returned to become involved in the rebuilding of the Hogan Stand and the northern end; the latter came in well under budget, but both the Canal End and the Hogan Stand exceeded budget. In the end, the stadium, including the land which we had to buy, cost almost €240 million and when it was finally opened, excluding what was owed to Central Council, borrowings were reasonably small.

Ultimately, my three years as President were defined by the successes of Ulster teams, with Paddy O'Rourke being the first Ulster captain to accept the Sam Maguire Cup for twenty-three years; he was followed by Anthony Molloy and Henry Downey, and Ulster's run of success did not end there, with Down returning to win it in 1994 and Tyrone almost winning it in 1995. Of all those events of that period, my outstanding memory (though I was no longer President at the time) is of the game in Celtic Park, in the first round of the Ulster Championship in 1994, between Derry and Down – by a mile, the best game of football I ever watched. In the end, what we enjoyed that day is what the GAA is all about – manly competition between rivals who are not enemies, who have similar aims and aspirations, and whose ethos is determined by their roots in their respective communities and by their sense of identity and their pride in their county and its jersey.

Since then, Ulster has being riding the crest of a wave; eight of the last eighteen All-Ireland senior titles have been won by Ulster teams and it should have been nine and might even have been ten. Five different counties have won those All-Irelands. Ulster teams, led by Crossmaglen, have done very well in the All-Ireland Club championships. Seven different counties have won the Ulster senior championship over the past twenty-five years and no other province comes near that – and it should have been an eighth one (my native Fermanagh) in 2008! I can't take any credit for those achievements, but they make me proud to be an Ulsterman, as well as an Irishman.

It is now fifteen years since my term ended. Before I ever became involved at administrative level, I was hugely enthused and motivated by the radicalism which pervaded the GAA's earliest years, some of which carried through to more recent times, but much of which has been lost – possibly inevitably – as the association has matured into one of the most stable entities in Irish society. But I still hanker after that radicalism, after the willingness, which its founders demonstrated, to be innovative and entrepreneurial, and after the vision-driven momentum, which propelled it to its current status. I continue to be invigorated by the resilience it has shown in prospering through two world wars, two civil wars, a land war and the War of Independence. I am proud of its contribution to healing differences in Irish society, especially in the early 1920s, but more recently too.

However, I worry about what I see as a reduced emphasis on vision and its being replaced by progressively more bureaucratic structures. I am delighted with the increasing success of Ulster teams and the heightened profile of the games in this province as well as with the overall strength of the games nationally and internationally; I welcome the growing emphasis on the promotion of the games at youth level and their increasing capacity to attract and cater for the so-called 'new Irish'; and I am pleased with both the imaginative initiatives recently undertaken by Comhairle Uladh, and the start made by the new regime in Croke Park.

But I am disappointed by the rate of burnout of young players, by our loss of market-share in many areas and by the inadequacy of our response to those losses; I regret the years in which we lost momentum and failed to make the progress we could and should have made; and finally, I believe that, in football (but not necessarily in hurling) we need to have a very serious look at both our playing rules and our refereeing, if we are to continue to be attractive to both potential young players and a significant section of our supporters. Despite those reservations, I have immense confidence in the young people of modern Ireland, in their sense of identity and their pride in their communities and their counties. I am convinced that we can harness their sense of Irishness in building an even better association, that the next generation of GAA leaders will be far better than anything we have had to date and that we have a very bright future. I have absolute faith and confidence in the future of the greatest sporting, cultural and social organisation in Ireland, or anywhere in the world.

Do I regret my three years as GAA president or my overall involvement in the association? Absolutely not, though I know there were some more things, which I didn't do, but which I should have done, and some which I did, but should have done better.

But would I do it again? *Sin ceist eile!*

Dua, Bua agus Ré Nua: The Rekindling of the Northern Flame

Mickey Harte

My involvement in the GAA spans forty-odd years, and it has been a very eventful period. At club level, most clubs have undergone tremendous development, both materially and in terms of their role within communities. The county identity which raises the GAA's public profile has grown and grown. Within Ulster, most counties have enjoyed unprecedented success on and off the field. The province as a whole has done extraordinarily well to come from a less advanced position than other sectors of the GAA, to overcome significant adversity, to catch up and lead the way in some respects. Meanwhile the GAA as a national organisation has increased further in significance. Indeed, the profile of Gaelic games has expanded globally, and new possibilities have arisen for their promotion worldwide.

Mickey Harte

In this chapter I will attempt to describe and analyse not only the triumphs, but also the less prosperous times of the GAA in Ulster over the last four decades. For people such as I who have been involved throughout, the successes of the recent era have been cherished all the more because not so long ago they looked like distant prospects. Everyone's viewpoint of events is unique, and the GAA means many different things to different people, but I will draw on some of my experiences with family, community, club and county, to illustrate certain general aspects of the association and its games in the modern period, with which I hope other members in Ulster and beyond can identify. Further, I will outline what I think have been the key building blocks in the process of development.

Most GAA members of my generation grew up in families that had a definite interest in, and focus on, the association and its games. Not every house or family was that way inclined but for nearly all of us in Tyrone who were, life revolved around football. It was a much more local affair then. It was a man's world, with women confined to being spectators or (in a small minority of clubs) helping on the margins. My father Peter did not play football, but he was a dedicated clubman for Ballygawley, looking after the senior team jerseys. I was the youngest of seven boys in our family, and we practised with a pigskin ball. I got my first pair of football boots when I was about ten years old. They were of the old style, with leather cogs and a hard toecap, small size thirteen. My eldest brother, Paddy, bought them for me when he was working in London. Six of us played for Ballygawley at different stages, but only once all together, in a tournament game. My brother Peter played for the Tyrone senior team from 1962 to 1972, and also for the Combined Universities team against Ireland. It was an unsuccessful decade for the county, but we were very proud of his achievements, and really looked up to him.

Another formative sporting influence came from media publicity. GAA coverage was much more limited than it is now. The *Irish Press* was our main source; we read it from back to front every day. However, the northern broadcasting media effectively ignored Gaelic games, there was no local radio in place, and only a few inter-county championship games were covered on RTÉ radio. RTÉ television showed the All-Ireland semi-finals and finals, and the Railway Cup finals, but few people had sets to watch them. Only two houses in our townland had televisions in the 1960s. Crowds of two dozen or more would turn up at either house to watch the big games. Thus a football game became a social event, even a community event. As more adults came in to watch, we younger ones were relegated in the seating ranks until we had to sit on egg-boxes. Afterwards, a lot of us, perhaps a dozen, would go outside and try to replay the action. Even though we had only impromptu goalposts, with baler-twine as a crossbar, we thought we were playing in Croke Park. Everyone adopted a player's name: the goalkeeper would pretend to be Johnny Geraghty of Galway; full-backs proliferated, such as Lar Foley (Dublin), Noel Tierney (Galway), Jack Quinn (Meath) and Dan

The Tyrone minor team that lost to Cork in the All-Ireland final of 1972. Mickey Harte and Frank McGuigan are seated in the centre of the front row. This was the second of Tyrone's six Ulster minor titles in the 1970s, which raised the county's hopes to new heights.

McCartan (Down); a player taking a '50'-kick was Tom O'Hare of Down; and Seán O'Neill of Down was probably the favourite forward to imitate.

My first game for Ballygawley was a juvenile match in 1965, at just eleven years old. I started at corner-forward, in a pair of jeans, in order to make up the numbers. The club's struggles to field teams in those days demonstrated that the GAA's appeal, even within the nationalist population, was confined to certain families. But because it was a big and scattered parish, we had a minibus to go around and collect all the young players to go to games. In 1969 I made my debut for the senior team in a tournament at Clogher, and by the next year, aged sixteen, I was playing more regularly. From May to August every year local tournaments were still as much a feature of the club scene then as the official leagues, and we thought nothing of playing in a league game and a tournament on the same day. For as long as I can remember Tyrone club games could draw big crowds, probably more so than those in other counties. There was a greater tolerance of fisticuffs back then; if it did not spread from the initial pair sparring, it was unlikely to result in sendings-off. Although the GAA has always had a strong cultural ethos, its activities in Tyrone were almost always focused on football. Handball and hurling were not readily available in most areas, and we did not go looking for them. Apart from a brief revival in the mid 1960s there was no camogie in our parish from the 1930s until 1980. And although Ballygawley took part in *Scór* from 1973, it was more of a sporadic effort than a structured one.

Preparation for games then was rudimentary by today's standards. Training typically consisted of the running of laps, and two groups of players kicking in and out of a goalmouth, vying for possession. This tended to suit the bigger players who could catch the ball high. The availability of only one proper football in the club limited our possibilities. Improvement rapidly became visible though. Even the use of a blackboard to demonstrate tactics seemed innovative for a club in the 1960s. The opening of St Ciaran's High School, Ballygawley, in 1967, enabled the club to train indoors in the early months of the year, where previously it had been impossible. By the early 1970s many clubs were moving towards proper, enclosed pitches. In most years Tyrone played in challenge matches to mark the opening of local pitches inside and outside the county. MacRory Park, Dunmoyle (Ballygawley's ground), got its first, primitive 'floodlight' for evening training by the late 1970s, but it was not fit for games; it just helped you to see where to run! Yet a lot of clubs still relied on unenclosed, flat fields, and few had any sophisticated changing facilities. Several dressing-rooms had no electricity or running water. When Omagh opened its new complex in 1984 it was probably the first Tyrone GAA facility with a telephone.

Within the county the club horizons were widening. Traditionally most counties had organised their internal competitions on a divisional basis, due to the practicalities of travel and so on. Tyrone, like other counties, had embraced an all-county set-up for senior leagues by the late 1960s, though intermediate and junior club competitions were divided on an east and west Tyrone basis for a few years longer. You only ever got to play teams from the 'other half' if you got to the junior final or intermediate semi-finals. For example, across the middle of Tyrone you had a line of clubs – Kildress, the Rock, Galbally, Killeeshil and Aghaloo – that were in the east Tyrone GAA world, whilst right next door to them was another line – Greencastle, Carrickmore, Pomeroy, Ballygawley and Augher – that was in west Tyrone. Those clubs rarely met in competition and almost turned their backs on each other, as though we had two different counties in Tyrone. The east/west structural divide also created unnatural tensions about the selection of county teams. There was always talk of one side or the other having too much influence or say. It was more perception than reality, but such distrust probably hindered Tyrone at inter-county level. I believe that going 'all-county' at all adult levels was central to developing the strong sense of county that we enjoy in Tyrone, and which works to our advantage.

Football then in Tyrone, apart from the limited youth fare and tournament or carnival games (on week evenings), was unequivocally a Sunday afternoon game. Around 1979 Tyrone began to fix championship replays for Friday nights, and people thought that innovation very strange. It marked an important willingness to do things differently and to broaden the scope and structure of Gaelic games. In Tyrone a couple of years later we introduced gradings to youth football. This move did much to improve the appeal of the games to our young people, as up to then our bigger and town-based GAA clubs tended to dominate the single-grade underage competitions.

The area of communication was of course very different, with no teletext, mobiles, texting, emails or internet. Monday's *Irish News* gave the first listing of the previous day's results, and Tuesday's revealed the next Sunday's fixtures. Our local papers in Tyrone – the *Ulster Herald*, the *Dungannon Observer* and the *Democrat* – were very important for coverage of the games. Even then the east/west split was reflected: the *Herald* focused on west Tyrone affairs, and the others on the east. The first Tyrone GAA annual, covering 1973, was seen as very new and innovative. Around then clubs started appointing public relations officers, who submitted regular material to the papers. Before that the coverage was dominated by match-reports of the bigger games, written by the papers' GAA journalists.

When I began playing for Tyrone minors in 1972, we had high hopes. In the previous year the county won the Ulster minor football title. The 1972 team went further, reaching the All-Ireland final, which we lost to Cork. I played at full forward on that team, and enjoyed the distinction of scoring from play in every game of that campaign. Making the

Frank McGuigan lifts the Anglo-Celt Cup after the 1984 Ulster football final at Clones, in which he scored a phenomenal eleven points from play – five with his right foot, five with his left foot, and a fisted point. (*Jerome Quinn*)

county breakthrough carried with it an elevated status. When I arrived back at Omagh Christian Brothers School for my final year, I was named as captain of the MacRory Cup team, despite not having been a regular starter on previous school teams. We lost the 1973 MacRory Cup final to St Michael's, Enniskillen, but a year later, when I was gone, Omagh claimed the famous trophy for the first time. I had more 'near misses' when attending St Joseph's Training College, Belfast from 1973 onwards, though we had some great teams. St Joseph's was a GAA college if ever there was one, owing to the tutelage of Jim McKeever. We trained or played each Monday, Wednesday and Saturday – more often than we would with our clubs at home – and the experience converted many young students into inter-county players.

Back then, Ulster teams saw good prospects for regaining the Sam Maguire Cup. Down had won it in 1968; Derry and Antrim won All-Ireland under-21 titles in 1968 and 1969; St Colman's (Newry) in 1967, and St Mary's CBS (Belfast) in 1971, were Hogan Cup champions; Queen's University won the Sigerson Cup in 1971; and Tyrone had won national vocational schools titles in 1967, 1969 and 1970. From a Tyrone standpoint at least, 1973 seemed to confirm the upsurge in fortunes. In that year the minors completed the mission by winning the Tom Markham Cup; the seniors collected the Anglo-Celt Cup for the first time in sixteen years, and the county achieved the first-ever Ulster treble of senior, minor and under-21 titles in one year. Tyrone went on to win three more Ulster minor titles in the 1970s, three Ulster senior championships in the 1980s, and reached the All-Ireland final of 1986. But on the whole, Tyrone, like other Ulster counties, did not realise the great promise of the early 1970s. As a player I rarely got my hands on silverware either. After our Ulster minor success in 1972, I won little of note in the next two decades, other than two Dr McKenna Cup medals (in 1978 and 1982), a Tyrone division two league medal with Ballygawley in 1974, and a local McElduff Cup medal later.

It may be a bit hackneyed, that is true, but 'the Troubles' had a major impact on the GAA in Ulster, in the 1970s and 1980s. For over a quarter of a century the turmoil gave people other concerns and priorities. During my time at St Joseph's, Belfast, I seldom played in Casement Park – it had been unilaterally occupied by the British army and turned into a fortified military base. With hindsight, it is surprising how quickly the abnormal became normal. One infamous event demonstrates that. In 1973, I was on the Tyrone under-21 team which met Mayo in the All-Ireland semi-final at Dungannon, a week after Cork beat our seniors in their semi-final in Croke Park. A huge crowd turned up, but a car-load of our players were arrested by the British army at Coalisland on the way to the game. In Dungannon, the players, managers, county officials, and, above all, the spectators, insisted that nobody was going anywhere until our players were released and the game was played. The stand-off was not face-to-face, but it lasted a couple of hours. Eventually, sanity prevailed, the players were freed, the game went ahead, and we got a draw. It was a bizarre preparation for one of the most important games of our lives. By the way, after the drawn game Tyrone swapped around the goalkeeper (Patsy Kerlin) and full-forward (Jake Quinn). Few team-changes today are quite as dramatic as that one! We lost the replay in Carrick-on-Shannon, but that day in Dungannon stands out as an occasion when our GAA stood up.

None of us won another Ulster under-21 title. Often I have wondered how many other Ulster teams were similarly affected over the years. Having lived through it all, I have no doubt that the GAA had a huge stabilising effect on the broader nationalist community in those often difficult times. When you could not rely on simple things like being safe, you could still rely on the GAA, on your club and county, and on the games and the camaraderie that went with them. The GAA gave (and still gives) to young people a very positive sense of identity, and a vehicle for them to express their Irishness. Sadly, this meant that others viewed the GAA with suspicion and it was targeted in a variety of ways. Many GAA people lost their lives as a result. When suspicion reigns, distortion is likely. Any game in Clones, for example, invariably involved long queues at military checkpoints on the border. For many years in Tyrone, being stopped by the police or army was officially accepted as a reasonable excuse for teams taking to the field late. My brother Peter served as Ulster Council president from 1980 to 1983, and had to deal with problems at their height. Few major titles came north in the 1970s and 1980s, but the GAA's role in holding together communities that were under intolerable pressure, and developing them, was possibly a greater achievement. The GAA provided true leadership within our communities, so perhaps they were not lost decades for the association here.

A section of the crowd for Tyrone's All-Ireland semi-final victory over Galway in 1986. This was as close as any Ulster team came to winning an All-Ireland senior title in a period of over two decades from 1969. Nonetheless northern fans raised their hopes (and home-made banners) at championship time every year. (*Irish News*)

There was also a sense in Tyrone (and much of Ulster) of being partially isolated from the GAA mainstream. When I studied in Belfast in the early 1970s there was no RTÉ television signal, so we did not see even its limited Sunday night coverage. Imagination remained central to our understanding of southern players and teams. This may have fed a notion that their teams were somehow naturally or genetically superior to ours. Des Fahy, in his book *How the GAA Survived the Troubles*, has depicted how in those years Ulster GAA people felt on the outside looking in, our noses pushed up tight to the glass, desperate to be in the action but essentially out in the cold. It was not a pleasant feeling. But Ulster GAA people did not lose faith.

We had not the same discipline of preparation that we have now. In the mid 1970s a non-GAA Gaelic football tournament in Cookstown severely disrupted Tyrone team-training on the eve of the Ulster championship. Emigration and other factors were also constant drains on us, and on other counties. Today our county teams tend to roll seamlessly from one year to another; back then there would invariably be significant changes in personnel from one year to the next. In 1980 I played on a Tyrone team in the Ulster senior final, but when we played (and lost) our opening game in the 1981 championship, seven of our 1980 team had gone. For years many of our best players were living and working in the USA in particular.

All through these years, even if Ulster seemed to make little progress at inter-county level, the constant core of the GAA remained the club. That is where we all start and finish, and in my time in the GAA, it has been an unchanging constant. In Ballygawley, the story was not simple, as a dispute in a parish league in 1982 led to a split in the club. My area of the parish, Glencull, formed a separate club. For the next eight years Glencull was not allowed to affiliate to the county board, but we carried on as an ordinary club. We played up to twenty games a year, organised our own youth-training sessions, and also ran a playgroup and an Irish class. (*Níl mórán Gaeilge agam go fóill, ach ba mhaith liom bheith ábalta í a labhairt go líofa sa todhchaí.*) We probably excelled in adversity. Gaelic games and culture were still our life, and we felt no less a part of the GAA than anyone who was affiliated. This goes to show that the GAA is much more than an organisation; it is a state of mind.

I think that Ulster's GAA clubs have championed the notion of the club being the engine of it all. Clubs have become increasingly aware of the merits of good coaching from an early age and of its provision for all age-groups. The Ulster Council has rolled out informative courses and seminars for many years. These continuously push up standards, and the numbers of attendees provide proof of the parallel wish for

Brian Dooher loses his head bandage in the race towards goal during Tyrone's All-Ireland semi-final defeat against Meath in 1996. He became one of the leaders of a new generation of players, under Mickey Harte's management, who won the Sam Maguire Cup three times in the new millennium. (*Irish News*)

improvement by coaches and clubs. Other developments, though quite unnoticed at the time, later proved significant. Tyrone made its under-12 football non-competitive, years before 'Go-Games' were heard of. This decision helped our youngest players to focus on skills rather than a win-at-all-costs attitude. In our early years my generation tended to play a disorganised football, which was purely about enjoyment and in which one could learn some key skills. It became accepted, however, that to do proper justice to our game and our players, we need to apply good coaching across all aspects of the game.

In Ulster we have had over the past three decades a phenomenal improvement in facilities, virtually all provided by clubs and only recently with any significant outside financial help. These pitches and buildings represent success in their own right. They act as anchors for our communities. They are open and free to all. They generate intense local pride. And of course they ratchet up the quality of our games. They have contributed enormously to 'the rekindling of the northern flame'. In recent years a great dynamism has driven the massive fundraising needed to provide these facilities. Notionally small GAA clubs have raised up to £100,000 through 'gala dinner' events, and up to £400,000 through organising their own draws. Not just a few clubs have done this. Such effort, in galvanising communities to reach a goal, has brought about development and growth. I think that Ulster also got it right, maybe unlike other provinces, by concentrating on developing club facilities rather than several big inter-county stadia.

Happily, though, the county grounds in Ulster have been enhanced considerably in the last two decades. When I played at Clones, in Ulster finals in 1972 and 1980, the ground had changed little since its opening in the 1940s. Yet Clones still had an aura all of its own. You wanted to play there and tens of thousands were drawn to it. By the early 1990s, when I returned there as a minor manager, new dressing-rooms had been added, but not the Gerry Arthurs or Pat McGrane stands, and 'the Hill' was just that – a grassy hill with more than twenty thousand people standing on it. The quality of the pitch was also poor. Some club grounds we trained on in Tyrone were much better. But Clones was soon totally re-developed, and by the mid 1990s we had a stadium befitting the province. Yet I think it was Ulster's focus on club infrastructure that really laid the ground for future playing success.

Ulster's GAA counties of course have benefited from all that work. But they too have made their own input. Just relying on what the clubs, schools and colleges 'delivered' to them would not have sufficed. I think that Ulster is blessed in having a competitive province in football. We cherish our provincial GAA competitions. Contrary to what some seem to believe, we are not the deadliest of enemies. Collaboration and sharing are valued highly in the GAA in Ulster. I think that has encouraged us to put the right focus on working with young players; on organising development squads; and, above all, on identifying and disseminating best practice at an early age. In Tyrone we are now in our second decade of structured, county-wide GAA summer camps, which attract about forty per cent of all the eligible children in the county. They are organised by the county but largely delivered by the clubs in club facilities. It is a very powerful combination.

Schools have done a great deal to build on the foundations laid by clubs, in terms of coaching and player-development. The huge (and often unmentioned) role of vocational schools in improving Tyrone's status is something that I can attest to from my experience of teaching in St Ciaran's, Ballygawley, from 1982. The individual vocational schools competitions, started in the early 1970s, gave a new degree of recognition and confidence to boys who previously had no playing outlet beyond their clubs. Gaelic football has been the dominant sport in the Tyrone schools. The enthusiasm of teachers and a keen rivalry between the institutions have helped to raise the overall standard. Eight vocational colleges in Tyrone have won Ulster titles, and six have won All-Ireland titles. The vibrancy of vocational schools games in the province in general has owed much also to the dedicated sponsorship of Ulster Bank throughout this period.

The return to glory of the GAA in Ulster in the early 1990s had many facets, and fortunately I experienced it most acutely at club level. Our parish split was resolved in 1990 and the Aireagal Chiaráin club was born. The new club engendered a fresh zeal, and three years later we exceeded our expectations by winning both the Tyrone and Ulster club senior football championships – becoming the first and as yet only Tyrone club to win the Ulster title. I was a substitute on that team, twenty-four years after my senior debut, and it was an occasion of great joy for many reasons. Yet probably its greatest legacy was the fervour it spawned for Gaelic games in the parish. Our GAA population increased tremendously on foot of those victories, and this in turn laid the platform for a club dynasty in the years to come. Numerous senior and youth football honours have come our way since, and the Ulster senior club title was recaptured in 2002. Over time Aireagal has become a more substantial club all round. Our participation in *Scór* has risen in the last two decades, and we have won Ulster titles in the solo singing, ballad group and quiz sections. Camogie has fallen by the wayside, but our women's football team soon emulated the men by winning an Ulster senior championship. We have very impressive facilities now, including a second field at Dunmoyle, and we also have access to a council-owned field in Ballygawley village. Such features are quite common to many clubs now.

Down's success in 1991, in bringing the Sam Maguire back to Ulster after an absence of 23 years, seemed to inspire the rest of Ulster to believe that we could follow where they had led. It was hugely significant in creating for us 'the breakthrough factor'. Three more consecutive All-Irelands came north in the early 1990s, and with a bit of luck Tyrone could have made it five-in-a-row in 1995. Undoubtedly the experiences and building-blocks that I outlined above were crucial to Ulster's run of glory. And just as the civil conflict in the north had hampered the GAA in the north, its abatement in the 1990s enabled our teams to come back to the fore. Meanwhile, I had begun to manage the Tyrone minor team with Fr Gerard McAleer in 1991. We won the Ulster championship in 1993, but felt that we stumbled on bad luck once or twice between then and 1996. My chief ambition in management was to win the Tom Markham Cup, for I had just missed out on winning it as a player. 1997 was our turning-point. In that year our minors had to overcome the tragedy of Paul McGirr's death. We did not win a national trophy, but one game was, in retrospect, hugely significant. Our 0-23 to 0-21 win over Kerry, after extra-time in the All-Ireland semi-final replay, was for many people the epic game of games. I believe that it brought home to a lot of Tyrone people the great

Peter Canavan kicks the winning point from a free-kick in the All-Ireland football semi-final of 2005, as Armagh's Paul McGrane attempts to block. The rivalry between these Ulster neighbours, both at the height of their power helped to raise the profile of Gaelic games across the province. (*David Maher, Sportsfile*)

potential of this group of players, and also in a wider sense just what a game of football could deliver. In 1998 we came back and claimed the All-Ireland minor title. Many of us had sought this sort of outcome for several years: now it looked like we would deliver it consistently.

I think the quality of play by Ulster teams then also broadened out interest in the GAA and got more people to take a look at what we were doing for our communities. Our broadcast media in the north, particularly the BBC and UTV, were at last providing a substantial coverage of GAA games. That ability to turn on your television and see clear pictures of major games was very significant for the promotion of the games. Moreover, over the last years the GAA media in Ulster has developed in a useful way. This media has analysed and dissected carefully, resisting the dual temptations of sensationalism or just telling us what we want to hear – neither of which does anyone any favours.

All the while small things were falling into place which worked together to create a momentum. Among the many notable national football titles won by Ulster sides in the late 1990s were those by St Patrick's Academy, Dungannon, and St Colman's College, Newry, in the Hogan Cup in 1997 and 1998; Tyrone and Down minors in 1998 and 1999; and Crossmaglen club in 1997 and 1999. Unlike the transition from the late 1960s to the early 1970s, fate did not thwart this momentum. Since the year 2000 Ulster teams have won six All-Ireland minor titles (Tyrone, three; and Derry, Down and Armagh one each); three under-21 titles (Tyrone in 2000–01, and Armagh in 2004); four Hogan Cup titles (for Maghera, Abbey CBS, Omagh CBS and Dungannon academy); four Sigerson Cup titles (shared by Queen's and Jordanstown); three All-Ireland club titles (Crossmaglen two, and Ballinderry one); and six National Football League titles (Derry and Tyrone, two each; and Armagh and Donegal, one each); while Ulster stayed at the top of the Railway

Cup roll of honour, with four more victories. Above all, Armagh achieved the ultimate accolade of lifting the Sam Maguire Cup; and Tyrone emulated this historic feat three times, in 2003, 2005 and 2008. After the relative doldrums of the 1970s and 1980s, it is remarkable that in the 2000s Ulster lifted more football honours than any other province. Or, to provide a more graphic long-term statistic: in 106 years of the GAA from 1884 to 1990, Ulster teams won the All-Ireland senior championship on eight occasions; but it took only another eighteen years to win the next eight.

There have been many other notable milestones along the way, such as a first all-Ulster All-Ireland senior final, in 2003; Fermanagh's first All-Ireland semi-final, in 2004; Ulster finals held in Croke Park, before crowds of over fifty thousand people, between 2004 and 2006; an All-Ireland senior-minor double for Tyrone in 2008; and Antrim's voyage in 2009 meant that for the first time ever all nine counties had reached the Ulster football final within a decade. It has not been a narrative of endless glory and progress. The GAA in Ulster has a lot to do still to enhance its position, not least in hurling, for example. And of course, tragedy has visited the GAA, its teams and players often. The shocking loss of Cormac McAnallen in 2004 put sport in perspective, and the reaction by ordinary GAA members reminded us of the special communal spirit of our association.

Team preparation and support are now at unprecedented levels, with nothing but the best in terms of gear, transport, medical back-up, hotels and so on. We now get fit to train rather than train to get fit, and we encourage individual and personal responsibility to do things. Our drills now emphasise the ethos of the whole team or the whole person, and we take what is good from the psychology of sport. It is as much about the 'how' as the 'what'. Maybe most important of all, we now have a definition of team that goes far beyond the players on the field and those close to them. In the GAA the real team is multi-layered and multi-faceted, so that when victories bring 'success' and honour, many thousands of people share in them.

Indeed, a wider spectrum of people in the north are now coming to an appreciation of the GAA. Abraham Lincoln once said: 'I don't like that man. I must get to know him.' This attitude is becoming more prevalent generally. As a result, increasingly more people who have been previously outside the GAA fold now want to unlock the secrets of its huge positive community influence, and to try to apply them in new and different settings. We should welcome that, and take it as an encouragement to appreciate and guard the wonderful community asset that we have in the GAA.

Ulster has not rested on its laurels in recent years and appears unlikely to do so in the near future. I, for one, would subscribe to the view of the great basketball coach, John Wooden, that success is 'an admission ticket to the next challenge', and hopefully the GAA in Ulster will continue to be ambitious and embrace the challenges that lie ahead.

Sown seeds always take time to grow and mature. But history tells us that the wait is always worth it. GAA growth across Ulster over the past four decades has taken time and multi-layered input. No one thing started it all off and no one thing maintains it. Throughout my life the GAA has unfailingly produced a sense of identity and community and a way of life built on their importance. It has provided opportunities for development at a wide range of levels and in a host of places. It has delivered excellent engagement with people, giving them game and non-game skills. It has moved on in new and positive ways. What happened for the GAA in Ulster after 1990 was not due to a sudden sea-change, but rather the benefits of previously unheralded work, both on and off the field, and some key strategic long-term decisions taken by GAA people at all levels here.

At 125 years of age, the GAA has much reason to be proud. Over time it has changed dramatically in appearance and it has become a much-enhanced organisation with a wider appeal than ever before. Some of its core values may have been diluted occasionally, but thankfully they have remained strong on the whole during the time of my involvement in it, and little or nothing has been lost along the way. The basics of people and place are as strong now as they were back in Ballygawley in the 1960s. Those are elements of the northern flame that never needed to be rekindled!

Two young boys with camáin in hand admire the Cooley Mountains. The mythology of Setanta / Cú Chulainn and the Cattle Raid of Cooley have inspired the holding of the modern annual poc fada competition in these mountains, in which hurlers try to hit the sliotar between two points using the fewest strikes.

Section 2: The Origins and Development of the GAA

From Cú Chulainn to Cusack: Ball-playing, Camán, Shinny and Hurling in Ulster before the GAA
Art Ó Maolfabhail, Roddy Hegarty and Dónal McAnallen

Why the GAA was founded
Paul Rouse

Parish Factions, Parading Bands and Sumptuous Repasts: The diverse origins and activities of early GAA clubs
Tom Hunt

The Mass Media and the Popularisation of Gaelic Games, 1884–1934
Eoghan Corry

Camán and Crozier: The Catholic Church and the GAA, 1884–1902
Simon Gillespie and Roddy Hegarty

The Freedom of the Field: Camogie before 1950
Regina Fitzpatrick, Paul Rouse and Dónal McAnallen

Cén fáth a raibh cúige Uladh chomh lag chomh fada sin?: Deacrachtaí CLG ó thuaidh, 1884–1945
Dónal Mac An Ailín

From Cú Chulainn to Cusack: Ball-Playing, Camán, Shinny and Hurling in Ulster before the GAA

Art Ó Maolfabhail, Roddy Hegarty and Dónal McAnallen

In the history of Gaelic games there is no more iconic figure than Cú Chulainn. The name and exploits of this epic warrior have often been invoked to illustrate the antiquity of hurling, to depict it as heroic in nature, and to encourage Irish youths to take up the game. His image has inspired the greatest reverence in Ulster, for, according to retold mythology, it was there that he performed his greatest sporting feats, and he defended ancient Ulaidh single-handedly against invasion. The problem with this story is its very mythological nature: there is little solid evidence that Cú Chulainn ever lived or played hurling, or indeed that hurling was played in prehistoric times. Besides, some recent studies have argued, we cannot prove that hurling or related games in Ireland through the centuries were truly distinguishable from other un-codified stick-and-ball games played in various parts of Europe since ancient times. The point has also been well made that suppositions about a direct lineage of hurling from ancient to modern times may tend to overlook regional variations, change over time and gaps in chronology and knowledge.[1]

Yet for all these caveats, since the medieval period at least, hurling, in one form or other, has been consistently identified as the indigenous stick-and-ball game of the Irish, and the most popular field-sport on the island. Within modern Ulster, the regional variants of hurling – *camán / commons* and *shinny* – featured prominently in more recent times. This chapter will explore the antiquity of hurling in Ireland, with particular reference to its various manifestations in the province of Ulster before the founding of the GAA in 1884. It will analyse various written references to stick-and-ball games drawn from sources such as mythology, statutes, ecclesiastical registers, surveys, song, poetry, fictional literature, oral accounts and historical works. These texts appear in the (old and new) Irish, Latin, Norman French and English languages. This chapter will present excerpts in their original wording, rather than in the problematic translations that emerged in the nineteenth century and early twentieth century; and where appropriate it will endeavour to translate or interpret them in an accurate, value-free way. Some consideration will also be given to the history of football and similar team ball-games, but the long history of handball in Ireland will require separate examination elsewhere. Finally, the chapter will examine to what extent hurling, *camán* or *shinny* survived up to 1884 in Ulster,[2] and whether the arrival of the GAA did much to preserve these traditions of play.

Séadanta (Setanta), also known as Cú Chulainn, is the earliest named exponent of the game, hero of *Táin Bó Chuaille* (or *Chuailnge*) – the Cattle-driving of Cooley – and he is generally acknowledged as an Ulsterman. The name Séadanta is interpreted as meaning 'pathmaker, leader', from *séad* ('path'). His prowess as a hurler was reported around one thousand years ago and long after his supposed lifetime. Séadanta, living in Maigh Muirtheimhne, near Dundalk in modern Co. Louth, heard accounts of the young men of Eamhain Mhacha, which was near the city of Armagh, and wished to join them. After speaking with his mother, he set off for Eamhain Mhacha, where his uncle, Conchúr mac Neasa, was king. In Armagh Séadanta showed his prowess in the games, and later as a fighter defending his people. When setting out for Eamhain Mhacha Séadanta took with him his wooden shield and his javelin, his *liathróit* ('ball') and his *lorg ána*[3] ('driving stick'). The word *áin* (and its derivative form *táin*, as in *Táin Bó Chuaille*)[4] – means 'to drive, to hurry along'. The word *drive* in English is used similarly, and also, in a special sense, means 'to hit a ball with force'. The *Táin*, as presented to the modern reader, is a synthesis of at least three earlier versions. According to Strachan's *Stories from the Táin*, while he resided at Eamhain Mhacha, Séadanta was invited to a feast by his uncle's smith, Culann, but he stayed behind to finish a game of hurling with a group of boys. Arriving late at the feast, the young boy was attacked by Culann's fierce guard-dog. Séadanta flung his *liathróit* and then *loirg*, and then killed the dog with his hands.[5] In compensation for this, he agreed to guard the smith's cattle until another dog was found, thus earning the name Cú Chulainn (the hound of

A depiction of the boy Setanta in a game of hurling. The retelling of the Setanta/Cú Chulainn story has relied ever more heavily upon the hurling motif, and in an effort to depict the central hero within the context of the modern game the original versions of the saga have become lost.

Culann).[6] At some time, probably in the nineteenth century, this story became embellished to the extent that Séadanta struck the *liathróit*, hurling-style, into the dog's mouth,[7] and it was said that this alone killed it; finding an original written source for this account is quite difficult, though.

At Eamhain Mhacha Séadanta took part in the game of *áin phoill* – 'the driving of a hole', as it is called in the oldest version of the story, which is in the manuscript called *Leabhar na hUidhre* (The Book of the Dun Cow), written about the year 1100.[8] In the later version of the story, in *An Leabhar Laighneach* (The Book of Leinster), written *c.* 1180, this game is called *cluiche poill*, meaning literally 'the game of a hole'; and two new words, *báire* and *iomáin* are introduced in the phrase *bheireadh sé bua báire agus iomána*,[9] meaning 'he used to be victorious in activity and in hurling'. Also in this later version, the word *camán* replaces the earlier *lorg ána* 'driving stick'. This game involved competing against an opponent or opponents. Indeed he was said to have taken on and beaten a group of fifty boys by himself.[10] This suggests a game that required physical power, speed and strength as well as the skill of accurate shooting or driving.

As opposed to *áin* / *táin* meaning 'to drive', the word *iomáin* / *tiomáin* means 'to drive about', and seems always to have signified a vigorous physical activity in which injuries could be sustained. The terms *lorg ána*, *áin phoill* and *cluiche poill* have long been obsolete. However *iomáin* has never gone out of use in Ireland or Scotland, and later it developed another form, *iománaíocht*, which is widely used today to signify 'hurling'. Likewise the word *camán*, for the implement, the hurl(ey), is understood universally today in Ireland, and in Scotland (where the general Gaelic word for shinty is *camanachd*). The word *báire* will be discussed later. Thus it is possible that two different types of play may have been confused in the written stories of Séadanta. Whether or not 'the game of the hole' resembled golf, or even cricket with defending of the hole involved,

This fifteenth century grave-slab from Clonca in the north of the Inishowen peninsula, Co. Donegal, clearly depicts a shinty-style *camán*. The grave is that of Magnus Mecorriston, a native of Iona who may have come to Ireland as a gallowglass or mercenary soldier. (*Roy Hamilton*)

is a subject for conjecture, as no further reference to such a game is found in Irish. Although obviously not a simple matter, it is natural that many readers would see 'the driving game' of the sagas as a precursor to modern hurling,[11] especially with the introduction of the term *camán*. Cú Chulainn did not have a monopoly on hurling in mythology. Later the game was also associated with Fionn Mac Cumhaill, and it appears in local folk legends such as that of O'Creamon, King of Mourne, who crossed a great level *faithche* (green), 'upon which the "Aois Og", the youths of the rath are hurling, and practising many other athletic exercises'.[12]

Unlike these mythical accounts, subsequent references to hurling can be placed in a certain period of history, although themselves quite mythical in nature. Perhaps the earliest association of the game with an historical person is that relating to Saint Colmcille, a patron saint of Ireland, who was born at Gartan in Co. Donegal, *c*. 521 A.D. Mánas Ó Dónaill compiled a life of the saint in 1531. His text recounted that during a game the son of the king of Connacht and the son of the chief steward of the King of Ireland got into a dispute, in which the young prince killed his antagonist with a *camán*, and the prince fled immediately to the sanctuary of St Colmcille.[13] The incidental nature of this reference to hurling, in a biography of a saint, enhances its importance. The original author(s) did not set out to explain hurling, or prove its antiquity, nor did they have to; the intended audience was, presumably, already familiar with it as a traditional game.[14]

From the late nineteenth century onwards a large corpus of manuscript material relating to the early Christian era was transcribed and published. These texts provided further documentary evidence of some form of hurling in Ireland in the first millennium A.D. The ancient Brehon Laws are among the richest sources of information on customs and practices of the ancient Irish.[15] A principal manuscript of these laws, *Senchus Mor*, was first set down in the fifth century; but it is generally accepted that they applied much earlier and were passed through the generations by oral tradition.[16] Because the Norman system of government from the twelfth century was largely confined to the Pale, these laws retained a currency within Gaelic Ireland until the early seventeenth century. While the manuscripts were annotated and glosses added in the intervening centuries, the laws remained essentially unchanged. Under the Brehon Laws, someone who injured another party in the course of play was exempted from liability: *'Islan lim don ti buailis in liathroid da luirg o poll na himana co log na grifid'*. In the nineteenth century this was translated as referring to he 'who strikes the ball with his hurlet from the hurling hole to the place of the 'grifid'. Mention of a 'hole', 'grifid', and a subsequent reference to 'the place of division',[17] seem to differentiate the game portrayed from modern open-field hurling, but this does not disqualify it as a primitive form of hurling; no other modern sport bears a close resemblance to it, except perhaps rounders, baseball or golf – none of which involves the same danger of injury with the ball as does close-contact hurling. These laws were probably of more direct relevance to the *rithe* (kings) than to the lower orders of Gaelic society. The Laws also stipulated the habitual fosterage of children between the various Gaelic chieftains and their vassals, and the obligations pertaining to this practice. One such example required the sons of the king of Ireland to have brass rings upon their driving / hurling sticks and those of the 'sons of chieftains of lower rank' to be similarly adorned.[18] Based on his interpretation of these Laws and more recent folklore, P. W. Joyce stated that 'Hurling or goaling has been a favourite game among the Irish from the earliest ages'.[19]

The first known reference to hurling in a contemporary tract appeared among the Statutes of Kilkenny, written in Norman-French, and passed in 1366 under the reign of Edward III. The motive behind the Statutes was to restrict 'native' Irish customs and habits, so as to secure the Anglo-Norman lordship in Ireland. The law in question prohibited *'les Jues qe home appelle horlinge oue graundz bastons a pilot sr la terre'* – 'the games which men call hurlings, with great clubs at ball upon the ground'. This ban sought to avert the perceived physical danger of the game, and to encourage the colonial community to practise drawing bows and throwing lances, and other pastimes which could be useful militarily, to keep 'the Irish enemies in check.[20] It should be noted that royal edicts against popular sports, and encouraging military skills such as archery, were issued periodically in England, France and Scotland during the fourteenth and fifteenth centuries.[21] The Statutes of Galway (1527), which were written in English, specified a ban on 'the horlinge of the litill balle with the hockie sticks or staves'[22] and handball, but not football. It may be deduced from these statutes that *horlinge* and / or *hockie* were native to Ireland, as the same game or different games; it is likely that these terms, especially *hockie*, were used only by the colonisers to describe this popular game(s). No other documentary reference to these terms is available in Ireland from the times of the statutes.[23]

From around this time, however, there is a reference to an illegal game called *galbardy*. In the register of Archbishop John Swayne of Armagh, 1418–39, the newly installed Primate of Ireland sought to reaffirm many of the views expressed by his predecessors. Writing in Latin, he stated, *ad instar Domini Johannis*[24] – in the manner of Lord John; most probably John Colton, Archbishop of Armagh, 1381–1404. He then continued to criticise *'quia per quendam Ludum illicitum vocatum Ludum Galbardy in Crastino Sancta Pascha et Feria tertia sequéti hucusque communiter usitatum peccata Mortalia et verbera etiam et Homicidia pluries committuntur'* – a certain unlawful game called the game of Galbardy, commonly used on the morrow of Easter and the third holiday following, which leads to mortal sins and beatings and often homicides being committed. In a translation of this document, published in the 1930s, D. A. Chart suggests that this game was 'probably hurling', but the term does not feature in any other text and thus this claim cannot be verified. Swayne used the term *ludum reprobandum*, a reprehensible game and described those who would play it during Easter week, having so recently approached the altar, as *recidivam sentinam*[25] – the backsliding rabble or dregs – which was hardly a reference to the upper tiers of society. Excommunication was threatened on those who played the game. Swayne was exercising his authority over the province of Armagh, which covered all of the province of Ulster and parts of Connacht and Leinster, including the Diocese of Meath.

In contrast, the word *iomáin*, signifying a type of ball-playing, occurred in literature down through the ages and with reference to places widely scattered around Ireland and Scotland. The term is usually used respectfully in relation to the participants, whereas later accounts in English of hurling very often depict it as an unruly peasant game. For example, of special interest to Ulster is a poem written about 1425. Dubhthach Mac Eochadha, writing in Leinster, sent a poem of thirty verses to Aodh Buí Ó Néill, wishing that he could be with Aodh in his house in Carrickfergus, as he had been on another occasion.

> *Ní aistear níos sia ná sin*
> *a bhí i mo chionn car an earraigh,*
> *dul ón lios go taobh trá(gha)*
> *le hAodh d'fhios na hiomána.*[26]

> [I had no further journey
> before me throughout the springtime
> than to go from the dwelling to the strandside
> with Aodh to watch the hurling.]

The words *iomáin* and *iománaíocht* are widely used today for the game of hurling. *Báire* is another word used to refer to the game, and it seems to have meant originally 'activity, action'. As shown above, it was used in the twelfth century in the later version of the saga of Séadanta / Cú Chulainn, in which it is said *bheireadh sé bua báire agus iomána* – apparently meaning that he used to be victorious in activity and in hurling. The word is used in modern Irish in phrases such *i dtosach báire* ('in the beginning of the matter') and in *i lár báire* ('in the midst of affairs').

The poet Tadhg Óg Ó hUiginn, who died in 1448, referred to *báire an bheatha* – 'the game of life'. The poet Pilib Bocht Ó hUiginn, whose death is recorded in the *Annals of Ulster* in 1487, made frequent metaphorical use of *báire*, and the term *buille bháire* seems to mean the 'winning / final stroke of a game'. He called the Virgin Mary *buille bháire na mban* ('the winning stroke of women'), and he terms the 'judgment day' the *buille bháire* of God:

> *Buailfidh Dia a bhuille bháire.*
> *buille dá nach bia truaighe*
> *a díoth a-tá in ár dtáille,*
> *críoch a bháire, lá ar Luain-ne.*[27]

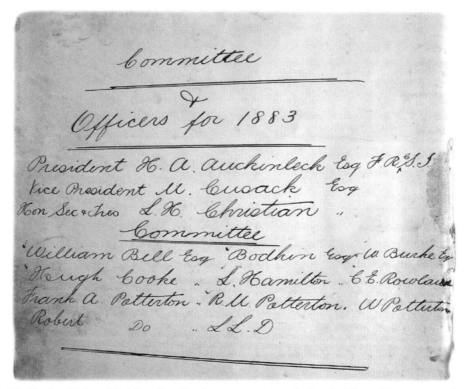

Committee

&

Officers for 1883

President H. A. Auchinleck Esq F.R.C.S.I
Vice President M. Cusack   Esq
Hon Sec & Treas L. H. Christian   „
Committee
William Bell Esq Bodkin Esq W Burke Esq
Hugh Cooke „ L. Hamilton „ C E Rowla...
Frank A. Potterton „ R. M. Potterton. W Potterto...
Robert   Do   „ LL.D

Dublin Hurling Club codified the rules of hurling at a meeting at the Royal College of Surgeons in Ireland, in January 1883. Michael Cusack was the club secretary, and Hugh Alexander Auchinleck (a native of Ardstraw, Co. Tyrone) was the chairman, The Potterton brothers were originally from Newry.
(*Bailiúchán Chíosóig, Ollscoil na hÉireann, Gaillimh*)

Professor George Parks, a Belfast native and president of the Royal College of Surgeons in Ireland, along with the then GAA president, Seán McCague (Monaghan), presided at an event at the RCSI in 2002 to commemorate H. A. Auchinleck's part in formulating the rules of hurling.

[God will strike His winning stroke;
a stroke which will give no mercy.
The expiry of that mercy is our reckoning,
the end of his game is our judgment day.]

From these examples it is obvious that *báire*, as an activity, was referred to with much respect.

The oldest known pictorial representation of a *camán* in Ireland is probably contemporary with those Ó hUiginn poets of the fifteenth century. In the extreme north, in Clonca, near Malin Head in Inishowen, Co. Donegal, is a grave-slab nearly two metres long. On it is carved a two-handed sword, and a ball and a *camán* shaped very like the modern Scottish shinty stick. It also bears an inscription in Irish which states that it was made by Fergus Makallan to the memory of Magnus Mecorriston of Iona. There are some similar stones with similar swords in Iona and on the island of Islay, but none have a *camán* and ball, or an inscription in Irish.

In *An Leabhar Eoghanach*, composed about the year 1580, Muiríoch, son of Eoghan Ó Néill and grandson of Niall Naoighiallach ('Niall of the Nine Hostages') in the fifth century A.D., was depicted as a Cú Chulainn-like hurler in his youth. At the age of thirteen Muiríoch defeated the son of the King of Leinster and his company of three score youths who had come for a hurling contest (*iomarbhá iomána*) on Tráigh Inbhir (probably Portstewart Strand, in modern Co. Derry), and three days later defeated a Scottish team in Scotland.[28]

The Ulster Plantation of the early seventeenth century caused tremendous upheaval, but it appears not to have diminished whatever form(s) of *iomáin / báire* or *camán* were traditional there, as reference(s) to such a game(s) increased in later centuries. It is possible that the influx of Scottish planters reinforced the game in Ulster, or even introduced different varieties of play. Alternatively, Irish *gallóglaigh* or gallowglass soldiers may have introduced *camán* to Scotland. The common names of the game(s) in Ulster and Scotland suggest a shared heritage. *Camanachd* was the Scotch Gaelic term for the stick-and-ball game also known as, and later codified as, Scottish shinty.[29] From the eighteenth century onwards, the main stick-and-ball game(s) in Ulster were identified as *camán / common(s)* and *shinny* – remarkably like *camanachd* and *shinty*; though it is true that *camán* or similar-sounding words were also known in Munster and the midlands.[30] The other significant similarities between *camán* and *shinny* in Ulster, and shinty in Scotland – inasmuch as sources over the next couple of centuries appear to indicate – were that they were played primarily in winter and with striking on the ground.[31] (*Cammag* was also a popular winter sport on the Isle of Man, played with a *cammag* – more similar to shinty than hurling – and a *crick*.)[32]

Meanwhile, in the south, especially in Leinster, a much greater abundance of written material on 'hurling' appeared. These accounts related to games played mainly in the summer season, and with apparently more carrying of the ball and aerial play than in the *camán / common(s)* games of the north and west.[33] In 1700 John Dunton, an Englishman living in Dublin, wrote one of the most graphic accounts of 'their hurling', which he had seen in the Dublin-Kildare area.[34] There were many eighteenth-century newspaper reports of hurling games held with the patronage of the local landed gentry, and handsome sums as prizes, particularly in Munster and Leinster.[35] Arthur Young, who toured Ireland in the 1770s, wrote of witnessing the sport in various places – and of 'a very ancient custom' in Tipperary, of hurling games in which 'a marriageable girl is always the prize'[36] – but not in Ulster. Similarly, Coquebert de Montbret, a French revolutionary government diplomat in Ireland between 1789 and 1791, observed in his travel diaries that hurling was played in Munster and Connacht, and football in Leinster; but 'In Ulster the Presbyterians are scandalised by Sunday play.'[37]

Principally because of attitudes to Sunday play, most extant reports of *camán / common(s)* in Ulster in this period relate to special feast-days. (Henceforth this chapter will use '*camán*' as a generic name for this game, and will cite similar-sounding colloquial variants where appropriate.) In the southern provinces Sunday was the most accessible and accepted day for play among the mainly Catholic populace; but in most of Ulster, the Lord's Day Observance Act was more rigidly enforced and a popular sabbatarian spirit actively discouraged organised games. If games could not be played on Sundays, there was no suitable time for most people during the ordinary week, and so they were limited to feast-days. The infrequency of such games hardly assisted their popularisation and long-term preservation, though (as we will see) *camán* lasted well into the nineteenth century in places.

There was a paucity of reports of hurling or *camán* in Ulster in eighteenth-century newspapers, but the gentry were not entirely detached from local forms of the games. A report from the parish of Donaghcloney, Co. Down, described a tradition in the grounds of Waringstown House, the home of a local clergyman: 'It is an old custom for the young men of the neighbourhood to assemble on Easter Monday in front of the house to play at a game called hurling or, as they term it, "to play common".'[38] Similarly, a poem by John Anketell, published in 1793, described 'a patron, or rural meeting, held annually each Easter Monday in Stramore,' which is near modern Glaslough in north Monaghan. The verse provided a vivid depiction of a game of *commons*:

> Lo! There at commons two form'd parties stand,
> Each grasps the bended weapon in his hand;
> Then near each other in the ground are fix'd
> Two sticks at each end, some score yards betwixt;
> Thro' one of which the ball must run,
> Before the game is either lost or won.[39]

The poem proceeded to portray the game as very competitive, with a lot of tripping in the play, inspiring 'loud laughter' from the crowd. Afterwards, 'two selected bodies' of youths engaged in a robust game of 'foot-ball' – 'They justle, trip, kick, wrestle, fall, and rise / And shout and swear with loud confused cries'. The violence continued after the day's sports, when the crowd retired to tents, drank heavily and began brawling.[40] Such behaviour undoubtedly lent justification to the deliberate curtailment of sporting assemblies in the repression after the United Irishmen's rising of 1798. In addition, the sheer danger of the game itself probably became a deterrent in some cases. A meticulous history of landed families in Co. Fermanagh recorded that Paul D. Dane Esquire married in 1779, died in 1800 (aged 68), and his youngest son, Alexander, 'had his head cut off playing *Commons* on the ice at Killyhevlin'.[41] This form of play may be seen as a precursor of ice-hockey, so it is noteworthy that *shinny* is the popular name for an unregulated type of ice-hockey played (especially by youths) in Canada, up to the time of writing (2009).[42]

The playing of *iomáin* along the Ulster-Leinster border was also captured in verse. *Iomáin Ionnas Caoin* describes a contest in 1806 between Inniskeen, Co. Monaghan, and Channonrock, Co. Louth; *Iomáin Óméith* (or *Iomáin Léana an Bhadhbúin*) comes from the Louth-Armagh border.[43] The poems gave few details of the games. The opinion has been proffered that in this region and in these verses *iomáin* was used to describe football[44] – if so, the composer apparently knew no Irish term for football – but the evidence for this argument seems rather thin.

Unlike hurling and its variants, evidence of football in Ireland before the sixteenth century is scant. In the seventeenth century it was mentioned rarely, mainly around north Leinster, but two references to football in Co. Down in that century can be found, albeit in secondary sources written up in the nineteenth century. The first relates to Newtownards,[45] and the other, collected from oral tradition, relays that the killing of Rev. Carolus Magrorey, a Catholic priest, near Kilkeel, Co. Down, in 1686 – whose gravestone inscription (in Latin) translates as 'cruelly done to death' – occurred after he tried 'to settle a dispute which commenced at a game of foot-ball, [and] was stabbed to death by one of the disputants'.[46] In the Irish language there was no reference to football before the eighteenth century. Football references during this century remained largely confined to north Leinster.[47] As stated previously though, Anketell's poem of 1793 referred to 'football' in north Monaghan.

Two published socio-economic and geographical surveys provide tantalising evidence about styles of hurling in Ulster during the nineteenth century. Between 1814 and 1819 details of seventy-nine recent parochial surveys from around Ireland (as submitted by local Church of Ireland ministers), appeared in three volumes compiled by Rev. William Shaw Mason. More than one-third (twenty-eight) of the surveys related to Ulster parishes.[48]

An early *sliotar* probably made from horse-hair or cow-hair, dating from the sixteenth century. (*Cavan County Museum*). The second picture shows a late nineteenth-century leather ball from the CÓFLA collection beside a modern-sized hurling ball. The former is almost twice the size of a modern ball, but there is little difference in weight.

Shaw Mason's survey of the parish of Holywood, Co. Down, where the vast majority were Presbyterians, mentioned only 'the game of *shinny*, as it is called by some, and *common* by others,' played most generally at Christmas.[49] The survey went on to say that this game 'resembles golf in Edinburgh', and that it 'prevails all through Ireland, and in the Highlands of Scotland'. That was a very confused statement as it equates the non-contact individual game of golf to physical-contact team-games. The custom of hurling around Christmastime may have had a pre-Christian origin, as its timing coincided with festivities pertaining to the winter solstice. Continuing play until the twelfth day of Christmas – the Epiphany, *Nollaig na mBan* or Little Christmas – probably had its origin in the Gregorian corrective calendar, which was introduced in 1582 and adopted by the English government in 1752. The custom of *iomáin* at this season was widely recorded in Scotland in the nineteenth century and may have come to Ireland thence.

In Shaw Mason's surveys it was reported that *common* or *shinny* was played on Christmas Day and New Year's Day on the strand at Whitepark, near Ballintoy in north Antrim. 'This formerly was frequented by old and young, and the amusement generally ended by drinking whiskey and broken heads: but of late years, only young people appear on these occasions.'[50] This practice of playing on the shoreline in north Antrim has also been recorded through the local song tradition. The song known as *Aird Tí Chuain*, which was composed by a native of Cushendall, Co. Antrim, and first put into print by Eoin Mac Néill in the nineteenth century, belongs to this tradition:

> Is iomdha Nodlag a bh' agam péin
> Ar a' bheagan beagan céill'
> A' rith ag iomain ar a' tráigh bháin,
> Mo chamán bán in mo dhorn liom.[51]

> [Many is the Christmas I spent
> when I was of little sense
> running to the white strand to hurl
> with my white *camán* in my grasp.]

The account for Culdaff, in Inishowen, Co. Donegal, stated that 'during the Christmas holydays they amuse themselves with the game of *Kamman*, which consists of impelling a wooden ball with a crooked stick to a given point, while an adversary endeavours to drive it in a contrary direction'.[52] The aforementioned (fifteenth-century) grave-slab at Clonca, located nearby, may indicate the type of *camán*-stick used in

Culdaff. From Tyrone, the account for Ardstraw parish, published in 1814, pointed up the hostility of establishment forces to the game in Ulster.

'There are no patrons nor public sports, except playing at *common*, as it is called: this diversion resembles hurling in the south; but since the institution of the yeomanry, it has been seldom practised.'

By way of further explanation, the report stated:

> The ball they play with is a small wooden one, which they strike with sticks inflected at one end. In the south of Ireland, the curve of the hurl is broad, and the ball large, and of a soft substance, covered with leather. Formerly they spent here eleven days successively at Christmas time in this exercise, now they idle only one; a manifest proof of the increase of industry.[53]

The name and type of ball used in hurling and *camán*-playing varied greatly from place to place. Although *sliotar*, a word of Munster origin, has become the standard name for a hurling ball in the GAA, before 1884 it was more often known as a *cnag* or variants (*nagg, cnaig, crag, creg, nig, nog* or *eag*) in Ulster and parts of Connacht, and in Scotland too; *cnag* meant a (wooden) lump or knob. The two different names may advert to a distinction in substance of ball. As cited in the Ardstraw survey above, the *cnag* used in the north was usually made of wood (often a brier root); likewise the *bool(e)* used in parts of Donegal, such as Ardara, was also wooden. The journalist and author, John Clarke ('Benmore'), who was born in Ballycastle, Co. Antrim, in 1868, wrote (in 1906) of the *nog* as 'a hard little wooden ball, which had been seasoned by boiling and resting for a time in the corner of a chimney'.[54] By contrast, a hair-ball or leather-covered ball was used often in the southern provinces, Munster and Leinster.[55] *Camán* was apparently played mostly as a winter cross-country game in Donegal.[56]

The second significant collection of sources for hurling in the nineteenth century are the Ordnance Survey Memoirs. These memoirs were compiled during the first mapping of Ireland by the Ordnance Survey of Great Britain, in the 1820s and 1830s, and were intended to contain detailed information that could not be included on the printed map. Unfortunately this aspect of the survey was discontinued in 1840, leaving most of the country untouched.[57] However, as the project began in Ulster, the information gathered, particularly for counties Antrim and Derry, provided an unequalled account of life in the far north before the Great Famine. Information was recorded under a series of specified headings. Under the heading 'Amusements' were listed wrestling, putting the shoulder stone, bullet-playing, handball, cockfighting and ball-playing; and the terms *cammon* or *common(s)*, *hurling*, *shinny* seem to have been employed interchangeably. For example, in Loughguile (or Loughgiel), Co. Antrim, it is stated, 'A sort of hurling or cammon playing as it is called in the north is still kept up here chiefly among the Catholics.'[58]

In Co. Antrim, the game(s) of *cammon, common(s)*, hurling or *shinny* was also mentioned in the memoirs of the parishes of Ballymoney,[59] Carrickfergus,[60] Derriaghy,[61] Finvoy,[62] Magheragall[63] and Rathlin.[64] Sometimes this game(s) was described as a 'former' custom. Similarly, *cammon* or *common* was mentioned in Co. Derry, in the parishes of Aghanloo, Dunboe,[65] Ballyrashane,[66] Desertmartin,[67] Desertoghill,[68] Dungiven,[69] Killowen, Magherafelt,[70] Magilligan or Tamlaghtard, Tamlaght O'Crilly[71] (Greenlough) and Termoneeny (Knockloughrim).[72] These reports are supported by verse. A poem, entitled 'The Camán Playing on Cashel Green', depicts a match between Dungiven and Ballinascreen on 17 January 1825. While there are few details of the game itself, the usual reference to a *nag* is found:

> Here's health to Francis Pheadair
> Gave the nag the first hoise
> Which made all the Screen boys
> Look on with surprise.
> We played them so briskly
> Before they did go ...[73]

The Ordnance Survey Memoirs also mentioned football in Dungiven and Magherafelt. In south Co. Monaghan, hurling was listed in the parish of Inniskeen,[74] and football was mentioned in the parishes

The earliest known GAA trophy from Ulster, this 1891 Derry county hurling championship cup was won by St Patrick's GAA Club from the Waterside. In the first twenty-five years of the GAA, hurling was often the leading Gaelic game in Derry City and district (with teams from north-west Tyrone and east Co. Donegal taking part). (*Danny O'Kane*).

of Donaghmoyne, Killanny and Magheracloone.[75] *Common*-playing was also recorded in the small portion of Co. Donegal covered, in Carndonagh and Clonmany parishes.[76] Contemporary with the Memoirs there was a newspaper report of *common*-playing from east Donegal:

> Monday the 6th inst. being Old Christmas-Day, which is observed by the Presbyterians generally, at which time the young people are apt to indulge in field sports, four young men had commenced what is called common-playing, at a place named Craghadoes, on their own land, and about half-way between Lifford and St Johnstown, when about forty of the opposite party came into the field, quarrelled with the young men in question, who narrowly escaped with their lives.[77]

The most significant aspect of this 1834 account is that the players in the game were all Presbyterian. Various sources from the time confirm that *camán* and / or hurling was still played by Protestants and in several predominantly Protestant areas, well into the nineteenth century – a hitherto largely forgotten fact. It is also notable that hurling was apparently played at Trinity College Dublin in the early nineteenth century – according to a reference by W. H. Maxwell, from Newry, Co. Down, who attended the college between 1809 and 1813.[78] Most Trinity undergraduates were Protestants, and many were from Ulster. The subsequent decline in Protestant participation nationwide may have been influenced by the growth of Irish nationalism and its links with the game. In *Rody the Rover* (1845), a novel set in Co. Tyrone, William Carleton depicted a hurling game as a cover for Ribbonism.[79] The increasingly nationalist complexion of Irish rural society generally, coupled with the lack of support for the games among the (largely Protestant and ultimately unionist) landed classes in Ulster, probably did much to distance the Protestant community from hurling. The evangelical religious revivals during the century, and the growing influence of temperance and sabbatarianism that they brought, was a major factor too.

The Great Famine and the consequent depopulation of the countryside had a huge part in the overall decline of hurling and *camán* after the 1840s. The general economic malaise in rural areas was illustrated by a Belfast newspaper in 1882, under the heading, 'Distress in County Antrim'. The writer reported that in Cushendall the game of *shinney* or hurling was in decline, though, owing to the harsh prevailing economic climate; due mainly to rack-rents, the spirit of the people was 'completely broken' and the young men were depicted as being prematurely aged. An older resident reminisced wistfully of playing 'in innumerable hurling matches where the reputation of a whole parish was at stake'.[80] Cardinal Joseph MacRory, who was born in 1861, later wrote: 'when I was growing up in Tyrone, Tyrone of the O'Neills, the real spirit of Irish Nationalism was all but dead even on the hillsides'. This decline he ascribed to the famine and the collapse of the 1840s Young Ireland movement. 'Gloom and apathy hung like a heavy cloud especially over the rural areas; and the National Games, language, music and dances were fast disappearing where they had not already disappeared.'[81] Similarly, P. J. Devlin, who was born in 1877, later wrote of his first decade at Damolly, near Newry, where 'distinctive games and pastimes had long been suppressed'; 'life was drear and aimless during leisure hours, especially for the young,' while older people only had card-playing and cock-fighting. Having 'never seen either football or hurling' or rural team games, he could only read about their likes in the south.[82]

The gradual disappearance of *camán* and hurling of whatever sort from the social scene in many areas of Ulster, as well as other parts of the country, during the nineteenth century also reflected a general discouraging of such activities in the pursuit of what was considered social improvement. The Ordnance Survey Memoirs reported from Killowen, Co. Derry, that *common* had been popular thirty years previously, 'but a general complaint of a want of money and time is stated as reasons for not indulging in it at present'.[83] In Magilligan, an account of the recent decline of various forms of recreation explained that 'the people must apply themselves wholly to industry in order to meet the demands of the landlord'.[84] It is likely that some parents dissuaded their children from playing, due to the physical (and possibly social) danger involved. In England during the same period traditional bandy and hockey came to be looked on as being too rough, and both the play and the stick were refined to suit colleges and public schools. Of course, most of the population had no access to such schools. The Irish Constabulary, formed in 1822 and later with the 'Royal' prefix after the suppression of the Fenian movement in 1867, was instructed to clamp down on games where a breach of the peace might occur and in numerous instances it did so.[85] Landowners throughout Ireland were probably strongly opposed to widespread cutting of young trees or saplings from the hedges to make 'instant' sticks for ball-playing,[86] though in parts of Ulster, as elsewhere, a whin bush, which had a flexible stalk and a broad root, would be split and used as a rudimentary hurling stick instead of a *camán*.[87]

Despite the obvious decline, there is much evidence of the survival of hurling, *camán* and *shinny* in Ulster up to the eve of the GAA's birth and later. A lexicon of local words in counties Antrim and Down, published in 1880, recorded *shinney* as 'hockey, a boys' game, played with *shinneys, i.e.* hooked sticks, and a ball or small block of wood called the "golley" or "nag"'[88] (or '*knur*').[89] Although the aforementioned newspaper report from Cushendall in 1882 referred to the decline of the game, the writer imparted that during his recent visit to the area, some 'neighbours' gathered for 'a game of "shinney", or, to be more correct, shinty'. There were other press references to *shinny* and *camán* around then (of which more anon), but most of our information on such games in the immediate pre-GAA period is garnered from recollections by people of that time, recorded in the early twentieth century, either by their own pen or in oral history interviews. One of the first such accounts came from John Clarke ('Benmore'), who was born in 1868 in Ballycastle, and wrote an account in 1906 of past games in the Glens of Antrim. He recalled his own faint memories of

> past days in the valleys of the North, at festive times, when the manly, generous-hearted boys of the glens turned out to wield the caman'. … Matches were not uncommon on Christmas day in the olden times. Crowds would travel from the distant end of a glen, over miles and miles of rugged ways covered with snow and sparkling frost, to witness a trial of strength – a test between parishes for a prized trophy.[90]

It is important to note that while the GAA had been established in Co. Tipperary in 1884, it had little or no impact on north Antrim until two decades later: there were no affiliated clubs or games under the official aegis of the GAA until *c.* 1903–04.[91] Another account of *shinney* games between teams from Cushendall and Ballyeamon, at Legge Green in the 1880s, was written in a nostalgic article some fifty years later. These games took place every Christmas Day, from after Mass until nightfall, it was recounted, and with little or no regulation:

> It was a game unencumbered with rules. As many as a hundred players formed a team; a hundred on each side and as many fields as they required as a playing pitch! One acre, two, three, even four acres, it didn't matter. If the ball took a notion of wandering, so did the players. … The goal 'posts' were made up of heaps of stones, and the ball, a hard wooden object, had to roll along the ground between the two heaps for a goal. If it went an inch above the ground it was no good.[92]

There are, furthermore, accounts of *shinny* being played in the nineteenth century in Glenariff (where handling the *nig* was not allowed)[93] and Glenarm,[94] Co. Antrim, and of *camán*-playing at Christmas on the beaches of Magilligan in Co. Derry, Portrush and Bush Bay' in the same county.[95]

Similarly, eyewitness accounts from north Donegal, gathered from men born in the late nineteenth century, describe a game played under local rules, like 'one-handed shinty in Scotland', at times across a stretch of land perhaps 'four to five miles in length'; and matches as far back as the 1860s between teams of up to forty men each from Burt and nearby Newtowncunningham.[96] Playing equipment, like the rules or conditions of play, varied from one region to another. Peculiar styles of *camán* sticks in north Donegal (especially in Burt), up to the early days of the GAA, had a narrow *bos* and a ridge; while in the south of the county a wider *bos* with ridge was favoured, and forwards used a broad-*bos* hurley with hollow for carrying.[97]

The prevalence of *camán* in south Co. Donegal in the 1870s–90s is apparently confirmed by the numerous references to it in the works of Séamus McManus (1869–1960), a famous author, from Knockagar, Glen Ainey, near Mountcharles. In *The Bend of the Road* (1898), a 'patriarchal old tailor' reflects on the 'bright days long syne, when he used to shoulder his caman on a Christmas morning, and, followed by many an admiring dark eye, hie him to the frozen lakes for a rare day's sport'.[98] A *camán* match between two townlands, watched by a large crowd, provided a backdrop to *Through the Turf Smoke* (1899).[99] The term 'crooked kippeen'[100] (from the Irish, *cipín*, or 'little stick') seems also to be used to refer to the *camán*-stick. In *Yourself and the Neighbours* (1914), 'the Back-o'-the-Hill was to engage the Mountain-Foot for the caman championship,'[101] and the narrator hid his *camán* in the graveyard during Sunday Mass, before joining the team 'going to Glen Mor "to take the consait out o' the Glen boys" who thought they could play caman'. The local fervour and rivalries of handball also feature, as do other games.[102] The most vivid portrayal of all, in *Bold Blades of Donegal* (1935), details a keenly contested *camán* game between teams from Knockagar and Glen Ainey, trying to score *hails* (goals) with the *niag* (ball). A clear impression is given of local pride, local rivalries, heroic players, hundreds of supporters, and all-in participation.[103] There are obvious drawbacks to using this literature as historical evidence, such as the need to make fiction exciting to the reader. There is also the issue of from which game(s) McManus drew his memories. In 1905 he organised a large 'caman parade' in Mountcharles[104] which led to the founding of the Donegal County Board of the GAA,[105] and he was one of its officials up to 1909. Perhaps his later depictions of 'caman' games were embellished by memories of matches under the GAA's aegis.

Yet there is ample consistency of detail of these games throughout McManus's various works, to indicate that his depictions were reasonably true reflections of *camán* games in pre-GAA days in south Donegal – as corroborated by players of that period. In an article based on interviews with some of them, P. J. McGill outlined the playing of numerous games of cross-country *camán* between teams from Glengesh and Scadaman, near Ardara, in the 1897–1906 period; described the manufacture of *camáin* and *bools*, various methods of play and the scoring of *hails*; and listed the names of the players, as well as their disputes and injuries![106] *Hail*, as a term for 'goal', was apparently 'hails' derived from the Gaelic word, *tadhall* ('to touch'); it was used similarly in Cavan.[107] As with north Antrim, the fact that the GAA was not formally organised in south Donegal until the 1900s seems to have prolonged the survival of the local tradition of *camán*.

There is abundant evidence of these traditions surviving in other counties too. 'Towards the end of the last century it was still a custom in country districts to play a caman match on Christmas Day, in which the

The Red Hand Hurling Club of Belfast won the Antrim Hurling Championship in 1902. (This is not the same club as Lámh Dhearg, Hannahstown, of more recent times.) The revival of hurling in the city around the turn of the century owed a lot to the growth of Conradh na Gaeilge, and the adoption of the red hand as a club name and symbol was the archetypal manifestation of cultural nationalism.

Planter population joined as heartily as the native stock,' recorded an article on the GAA in Co. Derry in 1934.[108] The same publication recalled pre-GAA contests of *camán* or *shinny* between townlands in Co. Down; 'the prowess of many a wielder of the caman was talked of around the firesides of forty years ago'.[109] Many people who were interviewed for the Irish Folklore Commission from the late 1930s, were born before or around the time of the GAA's founding, and recalled witnessing or hearing of traditions of such games. In Fermanagh, such interviews tell us that *camans* or *cooley* – possibly derived from the Irish *cúl* (goal) – was played with crooked sally sticks at Landrock, near Newtownbutler, in the 1870s.[110] Meanwhile, on Upper Lough Erne, teams from two neighbouring islands reputedly played *camans* or *kites*, often using a tin can as a ball.[111] Of Co. Cavan, these interviews reveal that for hurling in the 1860s playing-sticks were made from whin-bushes, blackthorn or branches of apple or crab-trees; that the ball was usually made of wood, but elsewhere hay covered by rabbit skin (Castletara), corks covered by corduroy (Kildallan), and leather packed with sawdust (Mullahoran); that it was played on the road at Gowna; that lifting the ball into the hands was not allowed; and that there were few other rules or regulations, with the result that games were very dangerous.[112] More of this type of information was gathered by GAA clubs compiling their own histories. In Tyrone, for example, there are vivid recollections of *camán* in the mid to late nineteenth century in Clonoe[113] and Carrickmore.[114] *Camán* and hurling traditions in areas such as east Down and south Armagh in the immediate pre-GAA period have also been recorded more recently.[115]

The Burt Hibernians team that won the 1906 Ulster Senior Hurling Championship. Burt's distinctively shaped *camán* remained a controversial feature of their game for many years afterwards.

Fifty-two years later four surviving players (Jamie McLaughlin, Johnny Whoriskey, Josie Campbell and Willie Gallagher) review the same photograph. (*Damian Dowds*)

In the two decades before 1884, a form of play called 'hurley' was played at Trinity College, where there were students from all over the country. Among the players was Edward Carson, the later Unionist political leader.[116] 'Hurley' was played also by masters and pupils in some Protestant schools for boys in the Dublin area.[117] There is no similar record for similar Catholic schools. In the late 1870s a number of 'hurley clubs' arose in Dublin and Michael Cusack sought the co-operation of these in promoting hurling using a broad stick, but without success. When the Hockey Association was established in England in 1886, these colleges, schools and clubs abandoned 'hurley' and adopted the English rules of hockey. Photographs show that the kind of stick used in 'hurley' was of narrow natural timber, cut from the hedge, suitable only for playing the ball on the ground, and quite different from the flat stick eventually adopted by the GAA.

Before the GAA arrived, 'hurley' was turning into a game for a small privileged section of society, while hurling at large was being supplanted by other games. Team-games largely of English origin – such as cricket, hockey and rugby – made sizeable progress during this time. Above all, football of various types was making inroads by the 1880s. Association football – as played by newly organised, urban clubs – was viewed by nationalists as a 'garrison game', due to the fact that the British army introduced it into some Irish towns.[118] On the other hand, the 1850s–1880s period also saw the growth of unregulated folk football among sections of the rural (and largely nationalist) population. Football apparently overtook *camán* in popularity in Cavan; the 'kickers' used balls made of straw, rags, rope or leather.[119] 'Football, as we played it,' wrote Shan Bullock (born near Newtownbutler in 1866) of his schooldays, 'even as I have seen it played in the north – a parish against another, no rules, no bounds, except to kick the ball to blazes. Such sport is apt to rouse mad, wild passions in the players.'[120] Such free-for-all football before 1884 is described in south Armagh and Monaghan.[121] The eclipsing of hurling traditions by football occurred elsewhere too. Whereas in 1841 a tourist from England wrote that 'the great game in Kerry … is that of "Hurley"',[122] *caid*, a local form of football, was reportedly in vogue before the GAA was born,[123] and thereafter Gaelic football was easily the dominant code in the county – notwithstanding a solitary All-Ireland hurling title in 1891.

Partly due to fear of its extinction, Cusack was inspired in the early 1880s to seek – as he said later – 'to bring back the hurling'.[124] Cusack, who had taught in Newry and married an Ulster woman, found himself in 1882–83 in the company of several men from the province at the founding of Dublin Hurling Club. The club president was Dr Hugh Alexander Auchinleck, a native of Mulvin, Victoria Bridge, in the parish of Ardstraw, Co. Tyrone, where *common* was observed in 1814. It is possible that he saw or heard of the game in his youth. At a meeting on 3 January 1883, Auchinleck occupied the chair when the club adopted the first codified set of rules for hurling, based on a draft submitted by the secretary, Frank Potterton – a Newry native whose brothers were also committee members.[125] Within two years the GAA, under Cusack's direction, began to revive hurling, with considerable effect, but in doing so in a standardised fashion it may have accelerated the disappearance of local traditions of *camán* and *shinny* in Ulster.

Initially in Ulster, there was an apparent perception of the GAA as an incoming southern influence, bringing change in ways of play, though contemporary sources paint a confusing picture. In reviewing sporting activities in Beragh, Co. Tyrone, on Christmas Day, 1885, a newspaper reporter stated that while local men engaged in 'shooting matches through the country' – probably target-shooting, with guns – he 'could only see a few youngsters engaged in "cammen" playing, from which the reader may know that the Gaelic Athletic Association has not made way here yet'.[126] The writer seemed to identify 'cammen' as the game of the GAA, and one that had failed to spread to his area; alternatively, but less likely, did he mean that 'cammen' was *still* played locally, *despite* the GAA 'hurling' revival? In north Antrim, north and south Donegal at least, old traditions of *shinny* and *camán* lingered on. A letter to the press in 1888 proposed 'a grand hurling match to be played on Christmas Day', near Belfast, for novelty value; 'besides the game is so well known and popular, and under the name of 'shinney', has been played by every one brought up in the country'.[127] Well into the 1900s and 1910s, children in the Glens of Antrim played *ad hoc* games of *shinny* or *shinty* (with a 'wee wooden neug') in their schooldays – as they recounted later.[128] It appears that Protestant participation lasted longer in north Antrim than elsewhere. William Clarke Robinson, a Presbyterian resident of Glenarm,[129] wrote enthusiastically about *shinny* in a poem about the area in 1907.[130]

In south Donegal, even under the GAA's aegis after 1905, the custom of referring to a 'caman match' (rather than 'hurling') carried on colloquially and for official purposes,[131] but after 1910 it was eclipsed by 'hurling', and football soon became the more popular game locally anyway. In north Donegal, the continued use of a distinctive local *camán* (stick) occasioned much comment. In 1890, local hurling teams were repeatedly advised to 'replace the camans with hurleys',[132] but they carried on wielding them for a long time yet. Indeed, as late as 1932 a columnist remarked of Burt that '[s]ome of the hurlers in that district play with the caman; with a little training these players would make splendid rivals to our Scotch cousins at a game of Shinty'.[133] Significantly, north Antrim and the Burt area of north Donegal remained among the handful of hurling strongholds in Ulster throughout the GAA's history.

The rapid propagation and popularisation of Gaelic football under GAA auspices from the 1880s onwards probably cemented the displacement of surviving *camán* and *shinny* traditions in most of Ulster. It is said that young people of Carnally, near Crossmaglen, Co. Armagh, kept up the *camán*-playing tradition until the importation of football in the 1880s by adult residents effectively spelt the end of it in the area.[134] The greater difficulty and expense of obtaining *camán* sticks, vis-à-vis the ease of playing football, did much to alter the sporting allegiances of young men in areas such as Carrickmore, Co. Tyrone.[135]

From the documentary sources, it appears that hurling, in one form or other, was widely known in Ireland through the last millennium, but not necessarily universally practised at any given time. Accounts of earlier hurling were written long after the reported events, so their true antiquity cannot be verified. Of course, the game(s) attributed to Cú Chulainn and various historical figures through the centuries may have born little resemblance to the hurling codified and promoted by the GAA since the 1880s. Yet under the GAA's control, the game has changed dramatically in just 125 years, and in many aspects of play hurling in 2009 is barely recognisable as the game of the same name played in the 1880s. Hurling as we know it today is, like a wide range of sports, the result of a long (and ongoing) process of evolution. Therefore the diverse references to hurling and variant games throughout Irish history should not be dismissed or de-constructed to the point of insignificance. Long before the GAA existed, hurling was recognised as Ireland's national sport, both inside the country and abroad, and thus – irrespective of how it was played from place to place, or how accurately it was documented – it was an important symbol of a developing Irish national identity. The *camán* occupied a similar position in Scottish culture, albeit not quite as prominent. And even if one were to dispute the homogeneity of *camán* and *shinny* traditions with hurling before 1884, the commonality of these Ulster ways of play with *camanachd* / shinty is obvious, which in turn triggers the question as to whether they together represent one of the more tangible manifestations of Ulster-Scottish heritage. That question may be tackled more firmly on another day.

Why the GAA was founded

Paul Rouse

On Saturday afternoon, 1 November 1884 a small group of men gathered in the billiards' room of Lizzie Hayes' Hotel in Thurles, Co. Tipperary. The attendance was poor. Depending on which newspaper report you read, there were either seven or eight or thirteen or fourteen men in the room. Two men dominated proceedings. Michael Cusack and Maurice Davin had organised the meeting and immediately took centre-stage. Cusack opened by stating that their purpose was the establishment of a new athletics association for Ireland. He quickly deferred to Davin, who made a speech outlining the reasons for establishing such an association, one which would run Irish sports for Irish people using Irish rules. It was not that there was anything wrong with British rules in themselves, he said, merely that they did not suit Irish sports. By the end of the meeting, it was agreed that a Gaelic Athletic Association for the Preservation and Cultivation of National Pastimes would be established.[1] This chapter – aspects of which have also appeared in Paul Rouse, 'Michael Cusack: Sportsman and Journalist' in Mike Cronin, William Murphy and Paul Rouse (eds), *The Gaelic Athletic Association 1884–2009* (Dublin, 2009); and Paul Rouse, 'Gunfire in Hayes' Hotel: the IRB and the Founding of the GAA' in James McConnel and Fearghal McGarry (eds), *The Black Hand of Republicanism: The Fenians and History*, (Dublin, 2009) – will explore the simple question: why were those men in that room on the particular Saturday afternoon?

To answer that question it is crucial to attempt to separate myth from history, to separate possible conspiracies from probable causes, in analysing the founding of the GAA. Every sport has its own invented myths. Such myths imagine, for example, that rugby was founded by William Webb Ellis catching a ball and running with it across a school field in the midlands of England, one afternoon in 1823. Such myths also imagine that Abner Doubleday stopped a game of marbles outside a barbers' shop in Cooperstown, New York, one summer's afternoon in 1839 and used a stick to sketch out in the dirt a plan, which he had just imagined, for a game called baseball. Neither event happened – their very neatness as defining moments in history is enough to suggest their implausibility. The Webb Ellis story was concocted in the 1890s by members of the Rugby Football Union desperate to claim sole ownership of the heritage of a game which was splitting into Rugby Union and Rugby League. The lone source of the story was not even in the school when Ellis is supposed to have performed his act. Against that, by the time the story was paraded, Ellis was dead and could be relied upon to say nothing unhelpful, like 'No, I didn't'. The Doubleday story is even more fanciful. By the time he was credited with the invention of baseball, Doubleday was as conveniently dead as Ellis was. Not that his death was particularly convenient for Doubleday himself. He was able to talk from beyond the grave, however. He had been a hero of the American Civil War and had written a two-volume history of his own life, in which he had somehow managed to forget to mention that he was supposed to have invented baseball. Ultimately, of course, both rugby and baseball were the products of long processes, not the sporting equivalent of the Big Bang.[2]

The GAA's own invented myth is more complex. It sees the story of the foundation of the GAA in political terms and imagines that the GAA was primarily focused on a project of national liberation, one which used sport as a weapon to define Ireland against British rule. There is logic to this. After all, the 1880s was a decade defined by the struggle for land and freedom. Debates on Irish affairs dominated the House of Commons in London. The establishment of a home rule parliament in Dublin, led by Charles Stewart Parnell, emerged as a genuine possibility. The Irish Republican Brotherhood (IRB), a secret society dedicated to the overthrow of British rule in Ireland, was also actively organising in the 1880s; on its extreme fringe, a group called the 'Invincibles' targeted the very heart of British rule in Ireland when the two most important British officials in Ireland were murdered while out walking in the Phoenix Park in the summer of 1882. Wrapped up with such political upheaval was a dramatic battle over land-ownership between

Michael Cusack, the driving force behind
the formation of the GAA.

landlords and their tenants. For month after month, whole swathes of the countryside were in tumult, with newspapers filling their pages with stories of evictions, boycotting and agrarian outrages by secret societies.

The divided politics and contested identities of Ireland in the 1880s inevitably coloured the origins of the GAA. As the first historian of the association, T. F. O'Sullivan, put it, the men of the GAA founded the organisation to 'foster a spirit of earnest nationality' and as a 'means of saving thousands of young Irishmen from becoming mere West Britons.' As if to emphasise the political aspect of the early GAA, various members of the IRB were present at the founding meeting of the association.[3]

It is usually presumed that the involvement of such men in the GAA is rooted in their politics. This is an unwise presumption – one that at least needs qualification. The story of J. K. Bracken is a case in point. Bracken was at the founding meeting of the GAA. He was one of the most important figures in establishing the association across Tipperary and, as an active IRB man, he regularly featured in police files as a committed revolutionary. On the surface, he seems to epitomise the manner in which the GAA was shaped by the IRB. And yet, the lengths to which Bracken went to further the cause of his club, Templemore, are not easily explained by politics. In October 1887 Templemore was playing the semi-final of the first ever All-Ireland Football Championship against the Limerick Commercials. With the game nearly over and the Commercials pushing for a winning goal, a Commercials player found himself alone with the ball in front of the Templemore goals. He was about to shoot the winning score when he was grabbed by Bracken and thrown to the ground. The tackle has always been difficult to define in Gaelic football, but this was a clear foul – one made considerably worse by the fact that Bracken was actually a match umpire, and not a player.[4] Later, in the mid 1890s, when the GAA came extremely close to disappearing altogether following lengthy internal disputes, Bracken remained involved, working to organise hurling and football across Tipperary, refereeing matches and serving his club.[5]

Despite evidence such as this, some historians have lent credence to the notion that the GAA was actually founded by the IRB. To support this idea, they have relied on police reports such as one written in the mid 1880s by Inspector A. W. Waters of the Royal Irish Constabulary's Crime Branch Special department in Dublin Castle. This report claimed that the IRB had founded the GAA in order to get 'the muscular youth of the country into an organisation, drilled and disciplined to form a physical power capable of over-awing [sic] and coercing the home rule government of the future.'

Historians have anointed hysterical police reports in a font of rumour, half-truth and folklore, and made leaps of faith which defy any reason. For example, the belief that the IRB founded the GAA crystallises around an IRB meeting in June 1883, when it is claimed, a sub-committee was established to consider the idea of establishing a nationalist athletics movement. Having decided upon the establishment of a sporting body, this sub-committee is then said to have approached Michael Cusack, winning his support for the plan.[6] It cannot, of course, be proven whether this meeting and subsequent process happened or not, but its provenance seems more than a little suspect.

First of all, the story of the IRB sub-committee seems not to have emerged until it was included in a newspaper supplement, published in 1934 by the *Irish Press* to celebrate the fiftieth anniversary of the founding of the GAA.[7] It is not mentioned in any other pre 1934 GAA publication. Second of all, at least one of the men who were supposed to have been at that IRB meeting was most likely in America at the time. James Boland had fled there having been suspected by the police of involvement in the Phoenix Park murders. Third – and the most important reason of all – is quite simply Michael Cusack.

Michael Cusack held Fenian sympathies – of that there is no doubt – but he was never a member of the

IRB in any meaningful way. His personality could not have permitted it. There was a restlessness, an individuality, an outspokenness to everything he did, which renders impractical the idea that he could ever be part of a secret conspiracy. As much as he was capable of extraordinary generosity and vision, he was often incapable of diplomacy and was devoid of perspective in personal exchanges. There are many examples of outrageous behaviour. In the year after the GAA was founded, the new association got embroiled in a bitter row with the Irish Amateur Athletic Association, which had been formed by existing athletics clubs in response to the arrival of the GAA. Cusack was in his element as he attacked his opponents week-after-week in a series of newspaper columns. At one point, for example, he described the IAAA as a 'ranting, impotent West British abortion'.[8] And when John Dunbar, the secretary of the IAAA wrote a conciliatory letter to Cusack, in the midst of their dispute, Cusack replied to him: 'Dear Sir, I received your letter this morning and burned it.'[9]

The thing about Cusack was that he made enemies within the GAA as easily as he did without. A mere eighteen months after the GAA was founded, he was removed from the association at a special meeting. Any suggestion that this was an IRB-led heave, motivated on the understanding that Cusack had outlived his usefulness as a front for the IRB, is wide of the mark. The GAA was thriving beyond all expectation by the middle of 1886, but Cusack had succeeded in alienating almost every section of the association. He had managed this thanks to what one Cork GAA club noted was 'the unfortunate knack possessed by Mr Cusack in a superlative degree of offending and insulting those with whom he comes in contact.'[10] On top of that, his administrative and organisational shortcomings were of biblical scale. Any suggestion that Cusack was a front for the IRB should be dispelled by the extremity of his attacks on those members of the IRB who replaced him at the head of the GAA. In another series of newspaper columns he condemned them as 'a junta of knaves and fools', 'a miserable mischievous traitorous gang,' and, simply, 'bastards.'[11] In return, he claimed he was physically assaulted at least three times, and also had shots fired over his head in the lobby of Hayes' Hotel in Thurles during the hot summer of 1887.[12]

What ultimately made possible the establishment of the GAA was not Cusack's relationship with the IRB, rather his relationship with Maurice Davin. The alliance of Cusack and Davin was an unlikely one. Davin had been born into middle-class comfort to a Tipperary family of large farmers who also operated a river haulage business along the River Suir. He inherited the running of the family farm and business, before he had turned eighteen. As a student he had been given private tuition in the violin, becoming an accomplished player, and, in general, was considered a diligent and studious boy. He maintained this aspect throughout his life, constantly striving to expand his store of knowledge by buying encyclopaedias and compendiums. He used this knowledge to design and build his own boats, most notably a 35-foot four-oared racing gig (named the *Cruiskeen Lawn*), which he raced at regattas around the south-east of Ireland. It was this meticulous planning which defined every aspect of his life.

What brought Michael Cusack and Maurice Davin together was the dramatic change during their lifetimes in how people played sport. Traditions of play were as old as history itself, but the nineteenth century brought a revolution in sport which had its roots in the profound social and economic change which transformed life in England. The industrial revolution turned England from an agricultural society to an urban one. The informal, traditional recreations of previous generations were recast on an urban stage as modern codified sports. For example, centralised organisations such as the Football Association and the Rugby Football Union now set rules for football, changing a game which had previously been played according to local rules in communities all across the country. Other sports such as athletics and rowing were also now organised by central organisations. Sport became more commercialised as events involving amateur and professional competitors drew enormous crowds to purpose-built stadiums. And all across England many more enthusiasts played games in the parks and pavilions of the growing suburbs. Everywhere the British went they brought their sports with them leaving it inevitable that the sports revolution would spread across Ireland. The spread of this revolution was as critical to the establishment of the GAA as any political context.

It must be remembered that public schools shaped the development of sport in Britain during this period, not least in drawing up the first rules for many of the modern sports we see around us today. And, a key factor in the spread of organised sport across Ireland was also this same education system. Some Irish students were sent to public school in England and brought organised games home with them. The most obvious example of this was the establishment of the Dublin University Football Club at Trinity College in 1854. Over the following decades, sport – in particular rugby and cricket – came to find a central place in the growing number of public schools in Ireland. It was through these public schools that Michael Cusack entered Ireland's Anglocentric world of sport. Having been born into a poor, rural background in Co. Clare, Cusack had trained to be a schoolteacher. Through the 1870s he had moved – year on year – teaching around the elite public schools of Ireland, including St Colman's College in Newry, Kilkenny College, Blackrock College in Dublin and Clongowes Wood in Kildare. In 1877 he established his own grind school – Cusack's Academy. By the time he had founded the GAA, nobody in Dublin was more successful than Michael Cusack in preparing students for the examinations which brought entry into the civil service of the British Empire.

Through his career in the public schools, Cusack became a particular devotee of cricket. As late as the summer of 1882, for example, he wrote: 'You may be certain that the boy, who can play cricket well, will not, in after years, lose his head and get flurried in the face of danger.'[13] He wrote that cricket was Ireland's national game and that every town and village in Ireland should have its own cricket field.[14] And, if he loved cricket in the summer, he was devoted to rugby in the winter. For the 1879–80 season, he founded the Cusack's Academy Football Club and affiliated it to the Irish Rugby Football Union. The team played out of the Phoenix Park. Cusack was club secretary, trainer, as well as playing in the forwards, where he built a reputation as a powerful operator. His interest in these sports apparently dissipated from 1882, however, and after 1884 he did not involve himself in any sports outside the GAA's ambit.

The sporting revolution in England was not merely passed across the Irish Sea and adopted unchanged. Local factors coloured the way in which the new sports were organised. In Dublin and Belfast, acceptance of English ways was most pronounced; beyond the cities old traditions were not easily displaced. Athletics was a case in point. Through the 1860s the notion of holding athletics meetings spread across Ireland. In most areas of the country there was already a long tradition of athletics where men gathered together to compete on Sunday afternoons or during the long nights of summer. Weight-throwing was perceived to be a great form of exercise and was practiced in many variations across the countryside. In Co. Cavan, for instance, men would gather weights at the end of a rope and attempt to lift them with their teeth.[15] Several of these old-style practices – including 'throwing the blacksmith's sledge' and throwing a wheelstock, which had a rope inserted in the axle shaft, were included in the new sports-days.[16] In many places, despite the obvious influence of the English sports revolution, the Irish rural sports day was often considered 'more of a holiday than of a purely athletic gathering.'[17] Mostly, it was only local men who competed and this was the target for occasional sneers from the Dublin press. While attending a sports meeting at Kilmallock, Co. Limerick, one reporter laughed at the attempt to stage a two-mile bicycle race, saying that he had had time to go and eat his dinner during the race and was still back in time for the finish. The reporter also recounted with relish that the meeting had ended up in a free fight.[18]

Michael Cusack had emerged from the rural tradition of weight-throwing and, when he arrived in Dublin, it was a natural progression for him to join in athletic activity in the city. It was through athletics that he first met Maurice Davin, most probably in Lansdowne Road at the Irish athletics championships in 1875.[19] Cusack came to regard Davin as the greatest authority he had ever met on the sport of athletics – both national and international.[20] In the 1870s, Maurice Davin had revolutionised preparation for athletics events. He constructed what might be considered a mini-gymnasium at his home in Deerpark. There, he practiced weightlifting, and used dumbbells and assorted weighted clubs to increase the power in his muscles. He was meticulous in his diet, neither drank nor smoked, believing that anyone who used cigarettes would never be any good at anything.

Davin became the dominant figure at the Irish athletics championships in the 1870s, winning ten gold medals for performances in weight-throwing events. In some years he was reckoned to be so untouchable that he was given a walkover. In common with Cusack, however, Davin disapproved of the manner in which Irish athletics had developed. The early promise of a vibrant, organised athletics scene had fallen away and what had emerged by the early 1880s was a shambles. No one club or federation had managed to elevate

Minutes

Dublin Hurling Club

A general meeting of this club was held on Wednesday 3 Jan 1883 at 35 York St a 6.30 P. Dr Auchinlick in the chair. A draft of rules was submitted by Mr F.A. Patterton & after some discussion was with some slight alterations adopted temporarily. On the Motion of Mr F.A. Patterton seconded by Mr Cusack Dr ~~Auchlor~~ Auchinlick was elected President of the club on the motion of Mr F.A. Patterton & seconded by W. Bell. Mr M Cusack was elected vice President & on the motion of Mr Cook seconded C E Rowland Mr L H Christian was elected Hon Sec & Treasurer. The following gentlemen were elected on the committee Mes.rs W Bell Bodkin, Burke, Cook, & Hamilton, C E Rowland, E P Rowland, F A Patterton R M Patterton & W Patterton. The subs was then fixed at 5/- per annum & it was decided to hold the first match in the Phoenix Park on Saturday 15th inst.

Hugh A. Auchinlick, M.C.S.I.
Chairman

This extract from the Dublin Hurling Club minutes illustrates the extensive Ulster connections within the club and their contribution towards formulating a codified version of the game before the establishment of the GAA.
(*Bailiúchán Chíosóig, Ollscoil na hÉireann, Gaillimh*)

With the passage of time the motives of the GAA founders became the subject of ever-increasing speculation and extrapolation. Later depictions of the founder members' actions were shaped to a large extent by a desire to make them fit with contemporary thinking. In the *Irish Press* GAA golden jubilee supplement in 1934, the seven men identified at the first meeting are depicted as having seven core values in mind, although it is debatable as to whether they were really foremost in their thoughts at that meeting. (*Vincent Halpin*)

itself and establish proper control over Irish athletics. The sport was also dogged by petty internal squabbles and personal disputes. The annual athletics championship was, on several occasions, on the verge of collapse and the entire sport suffered for the want of a proper organisational structure.[21]

In the early 1880s the English Amateur Athletic Association (AAA) began to fill this vacuum, its rules being accepted by increasing numbers of clubs along the east coast of Ireland. The expansion of the English AAA rules offended Cusack for several reasons. On a matter of sporting taste, the English AAA rules were concerned more with running than with the weight-throwing events, which Cusack believed most suited the Irish character. On top of that, athletics was increasingly being confined to those of a certain class. Firstly, officially recognised athletics meetings were held on Saturdays, yet the traditional day for sport in rural Ireland was Sunday. Secondly, the rules of the English AAA narrowed the range of athletes who could compete. Their definition of amateurism excluded all those who had competed for money, or who took their livelihood from sport, but also excluded every 'mechanic, artisan or labourer.' This was sport not for the 'amateur' but for the 'gentleman amateur'.

Crucially, throughout 1883 and 1884 more and more athletics meetings across Ireland were organised under AAA rules. Cusack and Davin resolved to act. An exchange of letters between the two in the summer of 1884 led to a general plan to hold a meeting in Tipperary on 1 November 1884 to establish an Irish athletics association. It should be remembered that at the first meeting of the GAA it was the idea of reforming athletics which dominated the meeting. Davin told those present that they needed to establish a proper code of rules for Irish athletics and to design those rules in such a way that they would provide recreation for the bulk of the people of the country, especially the working man, who he said seemed now to be born to no inheritance other than an everlasting round of labour.[22]

It was as a secondary act that the GAA set about drawing up, what Davin referred to as, proper rules for hurling and football.[23] In the case of football, that essentially meant inventing the game of Gaelic football. Various types of football had existed in Ireland – just as it had in Britain, across Europe and in other regions – for centuries. This folk football had evolved into soccer and rugby in England in the middle of the nineteenth century, and Cusack and Davin now set about constructing their own football game.

Hurling was another matter altogether. The Victorian games revolution with its passion for uniformity and centralised control, did not bring immediate change to the hurlers of Ireland. In those places where hurling survived, it did so in much the same form as it always had. There was no immediate move to establish formal hurling clubs in rural Ireland. As with so much else in modern Ireland sport, Trinity College was involved in changing the way in which hurling was organised in Ireland. A game called 'hurley' had been played by a club at the college at least since the 1860s. The rules included provisions for off-side, hitting off one side of the stick only, and should be considered a forerunner to modern hockey, rather than to modern hurling. Amongst those who played the game was Edward Carson.[24] Through the 1870s the game was spread out of the university and into the city by Trinity graduates. The steady growth in the number of players led to the establishment of the Irish Hurley Union at Trinity College on 24 January 1879. Over the following couple of years, the Hurley Union sought to draw its own rules closer to the game of hockey as played in England. The impact of these changes was to make the game of hurley progressively less physical and this seems to have led to a disaffection amongst certain players, several of whom were instrumental in founding the Dublin Hurling Club.

The first meeting of the Dublin Hurling Club took place in the Royal College of Surgeons on York Street in December 1882 in the lecture-room of Dr Hugh Alexander Auchinleck. One of those who attended the meeting was Michael Cusack, who became vice-president of the club. Four times in early 1883 the Dublin Hurling Club played matches amongst themselves in the Phoenix Park.[25] Around twenty players turned up, many of whom were Protestants and were part of the established hurley clubs of the city.[26] Despite the apparent promise of the club, it disintegrated as suddenly as it had formed. The reason for the sudden demise of the Dublin Hurling Club in the spring of 1883 was clear-cut. Following its establishment, hurley clubs had immediately sensed the threat of a rival organisation, which would poach its players and launched a counter-attack. Initially, several players had taken part in both hurling and hurley matches on the same weekend, hoping to combine the two games.[27] Faced with confrontation between rival bodies, those players drifted away and the Dublin Hurling Club collapsed.

Michael Cusack was undaunted. He began to gather hurling enthusiasts in the Phoenix Park on Saturday afternoons. At first there were just four of them, but their numbers grew until they were in a position to form the Metropolitan Hurling Club. This they did at a meeting in Cusack's Academy at 4 Gardiner Place on 5 December 1883. Michael Cusack was later in no doubt that this was the club out of which the GAA sprang.[28] By the spring of 1884 there were sometimes fifty hurlers on the field on Saturday afternoons. The game they played was physical and free from the rules which so constricted hurley.

What was crucial was that Cusack's interest in hurling was sparked at precisely the same time that he and Maurice Davin were moving to reform athletics. The decision to integrate the revival of hurling and the organisation of football into their proposed athletics association proved a masterstroke. It gave the GAA a breadth of activities which immediately distinguished it from its rivals. It also allowed the GAA to stress the 'Irish' aspect of its endeavour. In the context of social and political upheavals of the 1880s this was to prove a potent weapon.

All of this is by way of arguing that, when you address the founding of the GAA, it is clear that politics mattered and mattered a lot, but so did much else. Indeed, it seems equally clear that Cusack and Davin's first ambitions were sporting ones. On that November Saturday evening in 1884, as they left Hayes' hotel, Michael Cusack and Maurice Davin were not to know it, but they had just turned Irish sport on its head.

Parish Factions, Parading Bands and Sumptuous Repasts: The diverse origins and activities of early GAA clubs

Tom Hunt

In the last decade or so the writing of general GAA history has become much more comprehensive and scientific, as a result of a gradual embrace of sports history in universities in Ireland and abroad. Previously the prevalent model – and one encouraged from Croke Park – was a single-author narrative placing a deliberate emphasis on the association's growth in the context of Irish nationalism, particularly in the pre 1922 era.[1] Recent works of scholarship on the GAA and Gaelic games have tended to comprise a multi-author, thematic approach to wide-ranging aspects of the association's activities. This latter method has expanded the parameters of historical examination of GAA-related subjects, providing valuable new insights and ideas for further study of the association. This more empirical, multi-faceted approach has been slower to percolate down to the writing of GAA history at club-level.

In a notable collection published earlier in 2009[2] this author provided an initial examination of the socio-economic profile of the early GAA athlete and the clubs associated with these players.[3] This chapter will continue in a similar vein. By sampling details from club histories from the four Irish provinces, it will attempt to illustrate common themes that may be emphasised by the club historian, and to provide some direction as to how new and illuminating types of data can be found.

The GAA takes special pride in the primacy of the club as the basic unit of the association. The parish-centred club has provided one of the great organisational and communal strengths of the association. However an examination of early GAA clubs provides a different perspective on its territorial base and its *modus operandi*. Indeed placing the emphasis on people rather than place during the analysis of a club's origins might lead to a better understanding of clubs than has previously been recognised.

The GAA rules of 1895 provided for the formation of hurling, football or athletic clubs in towns and rural districts or parish throughout Ireland. Members were required to reside or be employed in the area concerned in order to be considered eligible to represent that club in competition. The rules specified 'that not more than one club of the same kind can be formed in any town or parochial district without the consent of the County Committee or Central Committee'.[4] This permission was normally forthcoming and examples abound of several clubs emerging from a parish in the early days of the GAA. Three clubs – Ballydine, Boherlahan and Suir View Rangers, from the parish of Boherlahan-Dualla contested the 1897 Tipperary hurling championship, for instance.[5] Even more significantly, three clubs from the parish of Moycarkey-Borris won five All-Ireland senior hurling titles between them in the years 1895 to 1900. Indeed, Tubberadora, Horse and Jockey and Twomileborris clubs won Tipperary senior hurling titles before selecting players from their parish rivals to bolster their ranks when contesting the provincial and national championships.

Things were not as simple elsewhere. In some instances, county boards tried to enforce the rules that allowed only one club per Catholic parish, but found intra-parochial divisions too resistant to unity, or at least that many people identified with their immediate townlands more than with the parish as a single unit. In 1888 the Cavan County Committee tried to implement the rule in the case of the parishes of Mullagh, Lurgan and Bailieborough, which had at least two clubs each. Provisional committees set up in these parishes to amalgamate the clubs 'failed hopelessly to achieve unity'. The group attempting to merge Maghera and Virginia reported that 'it was a moral impossibility to expect an amalgamation of these two clubs'. The initiative was abandoned, and within the year the parishes of Drumlane, Belturbet, and Bailieborough also had at least two affiliated clubs each.[6] Likewise, there is evidence that the GAA's Central Council was prepared to overlook the principle of one club per parish when the occasion demanded it. In January 1900, the Tuam Kruger Football Club was founded in Co. Galway. The club was refused affiliation on a number of occasions and the county committee twice rejected the instructions of the Central Council

This photograph, probably taken about 1888, shows Owen McMahon of John Sheares' team of Cullyhanna, south Co. Armagh. Local research some years ago unearthed the story behind the picture. It is claimed that his sister Mary A. McMahon, knitted the jersey and stockings for Owen in the colours of the local club for which he played. At this time, Mary was running the local pub, but she married in early 1886 and shortly afterwards left Cullyhanna, possibly for America.

to affiliate the new club. Eventually on 1 July 1900 the Central Council instructed the Galway County Committee to affiliate the Tuam Kruger Football Club and thus overruled the only organised county unit of the GAA in Connacht. Twelve months later in July 1901 the Kruger club won its only Galway senior football title and again had to pay a number of visits to Central Council to defend in the boardroom the title they had won on the playing-field.[7] These examples illustrate that the stylised ideal of the 'parish club', and the idea of devout loyalty of parishioners to such a club, were not really familiar to many early GAA members, and in truth they were later constructs.

Early club units formed specifically to play Gaelic games were transient structures whose lifespan was often very short. Many matches in the early days of the GAA took place not between properly constituted clubs but instead were the consequence of *ad hoc* arrangements made by groups of young men living in an area. In such cases they would challenge their peers living in a neighbouring district to a football game often without any prior experience of the game. In Westmeath, for instance, ninety different groups are recorded in the newspapers as having played a Gaelic football match between 1886 and 1900. Of these combinations sixty played a maximum of three (reported) matches only. Inevitably a hierarchy of clubs developed from this improvisation. At the base were the ephemeral non-affiliated teams, whilst at the apex were a small number of semi-permanent, formally constituted clubs.[8] Even those units that were successful tended to have a somewhat brief existence. The revered, three-time All-Ireland hurling title winning Tubberadora team of 1895 to 1898 played only twenty-three matches between 11 August 1895 and the 1898 All-Ireland hurling final of 25 March 1900.[9] The Horse and Jockey combination that won the 1899 All-Ireland hurling title disbanded after the final and it was 1912 before the Jockey reappeared with junior and senior teams.[10] The Dundalk Young Ireland club, wishing to avoid the divisions associated with the Parnell split, discontinued its involvement with Gaelic football in mid 1891, seven years after its formation, opting to concentrate on pastimes of a non-controversial nature.[11]

Several factors contributed to the transience of many early GAA clubs. These included a lack of success or (paradoxically) a fulfilment of ambitions, unfamiliarity with the codes and conventions of football and

Members of the Seaghan an Díomais club from west Belfast on an outing to Feymore, Lough Neagh in 1904. This was one of the more well-off GAA clubs in Belfast, as seen in the fancy regalia being worn by members. Social outings were a very important part of club activities from the early days. (*Gilly McIlhatton*)

hurling, the loss of key members through death or emigration, the Parnell split, clerical opposition, financial difficulties, failure to access a playing field, and internal disputes with controlling county committees. The history of the Kerry hurlers who won the county's first All-Ireland hurling title in 1891 is instructive in this regard and illustrates the tenuous links between the individual and his club and sport. The Kerry team was selected from the Ballyduff and Kilmoyley clubs. Of the twenty-six man panel for the final against Wexford eighteen never again competed in the county hurling championship. Similarly twenty-one Kilmoyley and Ballyduff players who featured in the 1891 county final never again competed in the county championships. The victory in the All-Ireland final left many disillusioned hurlers in north Kerry. The players had to pay their own train fare and accommodation expenses and therefore finished their playing careers in protest. Three players from Lixnaw were particularly aggrieved with this turn of events. They had to walk the twelve miles from Tralee to Ahabeg after arriving from Dublin, with one man suffering from an injury that had forced his retirement during the game.[12]

In rural districts the strongest and most stable clubs were based on neighbourhood networks that were grounded in contiguous townland alliances. These clubs emerged from the informal arrangements that evolved among members of the farming communities. These were based on the practice of farmers pooling their resources in peak times during the farming season to complete essential works.[13] Some of the most successful of the early clubs were based on these strong community networks. The core group of Tipperary's All-Ireland title winning teams of 1895, 1896 and 1898, were neighbours from the Tubberadora townland and its adjoining townland of Nodstown. The powerbase of the Horse and Jockey combination of 1899 was centred on the townland of Curraheen, with eight of the players from the district. In 1900 it was the turn of Twomileborris to capture the All-Ireland hurling title for Tipperary with this team based on the townland of Leigh and Borris.[14]

The importance of a strong neighbourhood network, underpinned by family involvement and supported by inspired leadership from prominent individuals, to the early GAA club is clearly illustrated in the early history of the first club established in Co. Down. The Leitrim Fontenoy's club was founded in 1888, mainly due to the influence of James L. Savage of Backaderry House and the three McAleenan brothers of Ballymaginthy. All four had spent some time in Dublin advancing their professional careers and had some contact with the founding fathers of the GAA. Savage studied in Dublin under Michael Cusack at his Civil Service Academy and participated in his hurling sessions held in the Phoenix Park. The McAleenan brothers were apprentice builders in Dublin when they reputedly met Maurice Davin, who introduced them to the new game of Gaelic football. On their return from Dublin they established the Leitrim club with its core personnel from the townlands of Backaderry and Ballymaginthy. Fourteen of the early players hailed from these areas. However, as the only club in the locality Fontenoy's also attracted players from outside the parish boundaries. Joe McAleenan's love of a ballad entitled 'the Battle of Fontenoy' inspired the club's title. The club was very active and by July 1892 it had played twenty-one matches. The club then disbanded and it was not until 1902 that Fontenoy's became a fully-fledged club again.[15] Ten years later the same principle operated. The reconstituted club in 1902 still drew its core membership from the same townlands. The hurling team of 1902 had ten players from Ballymaginthy and Backaderry. In 1903, the Shane O'Neill club was formed in Glenarm village, Co. Antrim. Teams were also established in outlying parts of the parish including Mullaghsandal, Feystown and Carnagear. Two hurling clubs were founded in Mullaghsandal.[16] However these were, without exception, short-lived entities.

In urban areas the 'parish rule' was often irrelevant, and the most effective clubs originated from pre-existing socio-economic networks formed by employees of the retail trade that included shopkeepers, shop-assistants, clerks and sales personnel.[17] The working environment of these men facilitated their involvement in organised sport. They normally lived in accommodation provided by their employer and the constant contact with their fellow workers, customers and neighbours facilitated effective organisation. They were also guaranteed work-free Sundays. These men were enthusiastic joiners of clubs and organisations that expanded their opportunity for social or cultural activities. These social organisations provided the network from which some very important football clubs emerged. One such organisation was the Young Ireland Society founded at Dundalk Town Hall on 10 March 1884. This organisation embraced all shades of nationalism; its objectives included 'mutual improvement, the study of National literature, the promotion of concord and unity among Irishmen, the cultivation of National ideas and opinions and the Irish language'. Irish classes and talks on topics relating to Irish culture and Irish nationalism were organised. Members' entertainment nights were also held that included piano and poetry recitals, singing and storytelling of an Irish orientation. The society established a members' reading-room where the national newspapers as well as books, periodicals, magazines and articles dealing with aspects of Irish history were available to its members. An annual dance was held and plays with Irish themes performed on St Patrick's Day. In the summer months outings to areas of historical interest were organised.[18] Following the formation of the GAA a Gaelic football club was formed amongst the members of the society and on 8 November 1885 the team had its first public practice session, and 'The Dundalk Young Ireland Society Gaelic Athletic Club' became the first Louth club to affiliate to the GAA. The club then played in the first inter-club football games staged in Louth, against Tullyallen on 11 April 1886, with Michael Cusack travelling from Dublin to referee the game.[19]

The men of the Young Ireland Club played a significant role in the development of the GAA in Louth. Vice-president James Moore became the first president of the Louth GAA County Committee; Thomas Smyth was the second chairman of this committee. Charles McAlester became the first secretary of the Louth GAA committee and Joseph M. Johnson played a leading role in the establishment of both the Young Ireland Club and the Louth county committee. Johnson was known to Michael Cusack and was invited to attend the Thurles meeting that established the GAA. The distance probably prevented Johnson from travelling but instead he sent a letter of support to Cusack extracts from which were later published in *The Nation* newspaper. The history of the Dundalk club provides important insights into the means by which knowledge of the rules of football were diffused. The members of the Young Ireland club spent some time familiarising themselves with the rules of Gaelic football before proffering a public performance. After their inaugural game members of the club such as Michael Carroll, Charles McAlester, John Lennon and Bernard Whately were instrumental in helping to establish football clubs in places such Haggardstown, Dundalk, Dowdallshill and Kilcurry in Co. Louth and Crossmaglen in Co. Armagh. Club members, in their role as referees in counties Louth, Monaghan, Meath and Armagh, also played an important part in ensuring that matches were played according to the rules of the GAA.[20]

If the Young Ireland Society provided the focus of entertainment and informal education for the young commercial men of Dundalk, a (Catholic) reading-room provided a similar function for the youthful, upwardly mobile men of Armagh City. Reading-rooms were used by a variety of organisations during the nineteenth century as a means of disseminating ideas conveyed through print and they also serviced the growing demand for printed material.[21] In 1888, the Armagh reading-rooms were well stocked with newspapers and magazines and its library contained about four hundred books. Membership cost one shilling per quarter with honorary membership available for two shillings and sixpence. The men that formed the Armagh Harps club in 1888 had a strong association with this club. Dundalk Young Ireland's were the first opposition for the new club.[22] An idea of the social standing of the membership of the Harps in the Armagh business community is evident from its Gaelic ball held on 26 December 1890. The entrance fee to the event was set at six shillings. This was the equivalent of at least the weekly wage for an agricultural labourer of the time. When the club was reorganised in 1903 after a brief lull, the reading-rooms had metamorphosed into the Catholic Reading Room, but the Harps club maintained strong links with the organisation. Some members of the GAA club shared membership with the Armagh Harps Cycling Club, which was also associated with the reading-rooms. In the early 1900s Armagh Harps, as an urban club with 'links to local government personnel, enjoyed a level of stability and prestige not witnessed by the association elsewhere in Ulster' at the time. The Harps included two local councillors John Conway and Patrick Hughes and town clerk James Lennon on its committee, as well a number of prominent Armagh citizens and businessmen.[23] The story of the origins of the Dundalk Young Ireland and Armagh Harps clubs provide classic examples of pre-existing social networks providing the focus for GAA club development; in urban areas all over the country a similar pattern was repeated.

The industrial economy of an area was also an important influence on the establishment of GAA clubs and the socio-economic construction of a club. One of the largest industrial complexes outside of Belfast was located in the south-western section of Dublin city where there was a concentration of brewing and distilling industries and their spin-off associates. The Guinness brewery employed over sixteen hundred people in 1900 and the nearby Anchor Brewery employed over three hundred individuals. The John Power distillery and various Jameson distilleries were located in this industrial sector of Dublin as well. The Great Southern and Western Railway (GSWR) terminus at Kingsbridge also formed part of what was Dublin's most significant industrial zone.[24] The Henry Grattan GFC in Inchicore was composed of railway-workers. The quality of their facilities suggests that the Grattan club received some patronage from the railway company, as in 1889 its grounds hosted the All-Ireland senior hurling and football finals.[25] The Guinness workforce was one of the best-paid and best-catered for in the country. It was difficult to gain employment in the firm and as a result of this discipline was well maintained amongst the men by the 'knowledge that no one was indispensable'.[26] Well-paid and disciplined workers were ideal candidates for the formation of a GAA club. Several clubs emerged from this district, the most successful was Young Ireland GAC, founded in January 1888 among Guinness employees. Many of the founding members were not only united by a shared workplace but were also natives of Co. Wexford. The Phoenix GFC was formed from the employees of the Phoenix Brewery, Watling Street, in 1887. In 1889, the Watling Street enterprise was incorporated into the Guinness business empire and several of the members of the Phoenix club transferred to the Young Ireland club. The club disbanded in 1898, but during its brief existence it won four Dublin senior football titles and provided the bulk of the Dublin team that won three All-Ireland titles during the 1890s.[27] The Eblana Hurling Club was founded in the James' Street area in 1886, with a membership comprised mainly of Guinness employees and others who lived in the locality. The club was progressive enough to establish its own gymnasium in 1894, located at 60 St James Street, with two instructors in attendance.[28] Parnell's GAA club was formed in 1888 in connection with Power's distillery but it disbanded a year later and merged with the Sunbursts club.[29] Small-scale industries in smaller urban centres also provided a focal point for club development. In Stradbally, Co. Laois, E. S. Nolan, the manager of the Malt House in the late 1880s, was responsible for the formation of a football team in the town. The club's first set of officers included a local tailor, an hotelier and a publican as well as Nolan, the club's president. The connection with the Malt House continued through the following decades and most of the early Stradbally players worked there.[30]

Armagh Harps club
minute-book from 1904 and
membership card from 1906.
The Harps club was one of the
best-organised clubs in Ulster
in the early years of the GAA.

Ardoyne camogie team aboard a charabanc at Hazelwood, Antrim Road, Belfast. The carriage was owned by Henry McNeill who operated tours along the Antrim coast road but this journey brought the party from Ardoyne to what is today the location of Belfast Zoo, a distance of less than five miles. The young ladies' attire nevertheless suggests that the occasion was of some significance. (*Joe Lavery*)

The Monasterevan Brewing and Distilling Hurling and Football Club, playing *c*. 1887, was another such combination founded from an association of workers.[31]

Dublin's student-population provided another important social group from which early GAA clubs were formed. The Metropolitan Hurling Club was the original of the species, being founded by Michael Cusack in 1883, prior to the formation of the GAA. The membership was made up of the students of his Civil Service Academy and the club was the first to affiliate to the GAA. It won the first Dublin Senior Hurling Championship in 1887.[32] Cusack was later to declare that this was the club 'out of which the GAA sprang'.[33] The students and professors of the Carmelite College, Terenure were one the first groups to form a GAA club in Dublin.[34] The Erin's Hope club in Dublin was composed of national teachers from various parts of Ireland who were undergoing training-courses in Marlborough Street Training College. This club faced the disadvantage that the courses ended around 1 July each year, after which the members of the team became dispersed in all directions.[35] The 'brethren of the birch', as Cusack termed them, were successful in the initial Dublin football championship defeating the Grocers' Assistants in the final. The students had benefited from practising 'three times a week' on a 'five-acre field somewhere in Marlborough Street' whilst the Grocers, with their long hours of work, had 'little practice' for the final.[36] Feagh McHugh GAC in Blackrock, Co. Dublin was a similar type of club. Pupils from Blackrock College provided the main playing members of the club, but the club's playing strength was regularly depleted when the students left Blackrock on completion of their studies.[37]

Pre-existing sports clubs sometimes provided the nucleus from which hurling or football clubs emerged. This study has been focused on what was essentially a ban-free time-zone and as such there was considerable movement between sports and inter-changeability was an important characteristic. Nil Desperandum in Cork began life as a rugby team known as Berwick Rangers. Demoralised by their lack of success, the members disbanded the club, but later reconsidered their decision and re-formed in 1887, taking to the newly designed Gaelic football code with much success.[38] Laune Rangers Gaelic Football Club was initially founded as a rugby club.[39] The commercial assistant-cricket network was also an important nucleus from which early GAA clubs emerged. In Mullingar, Mount Street Cricket Club members formed the Young Ireland Gaelic Football Club in 1902 and it was this club's members who were instrumental in setting up the Westmeath County Committee in 1904.[40] The relationship between the early GAA organisation and cricket is more complex than is generally considered. Historians make brief reference to two aspects of their relationship. The formation of the GAA in 1884 is generally considered to have been a cause of the decline in rural cricket's popularity, and then in 1905 cricket was included amongst the list of banned sports.[41] Recent research has emphasised the popularity of cricket in Westmeath,[42] Tipperary[43] and Kilkenny.[44] In Wexford in the late 1880s and early 1890s cricket was extremely popular and 'a club or two existed in almost every parish'.[45] In Galway, cricket clubs were common in the mid 1880s and later and 'was played by all kinds of people'. Tuam had several flourishing clubs at this time that catered for different social groups.[46] Many early footballers and hurlers gained their first experience of modern organised team-sport from participation in locally organised cricket matches. Cricket provided an apprenticeship in the virtues of codification and the positive dimensions of regularised sport. Many continued to combine cricket with their hurling or football activities. The creation of the hurling district of north Westmeath was essentially due to the activities of a Gaelic League activist, Peter Nea, and the familiarity of the young men of that district with a stick-and-ball game through their participation in cricket. Ringtown Hurling Club was founded in February 1904 and shared a direct lineage with the area's cricket club. It benefited from the patronage of landowner Denis Smyth JP, who had acted as captain and main patron of the cricket club for many years. Smyth always placed the 'back field' at the disposal of the hurling club for practice and games.[47]

Soccer also provided an occasional recruitment source for early GAA clubs. Soccer was popular in the Beragh district of Tyrone where at least two clubs, Sixmilecross Stars and Beragh Scorchers were active in the late 1890s and early 1900s. A soccer tournament on St Patrick's Day 1904 was, according to the *Ulster Herald*, 'certainly as enjoyable a day as has ever been spent about Sixmilecross'. Many of the players who lined out that day were within a year representing the Sixmilecross Wolfe Tone's GAA team.[48] Some of the founding fathers of Cootehill Football Club had returned from Glasgow where they had become acquainted

A football match near Loughinisland in Co. Down in the early twentieth century. The bicycle in the foreground is a reminder that this was the regular mode of transport for many participants in Gaelic games at a local level for many years. (*CLG Loch an Oileáin*)

with the soccer exploits of Glasgow Celtic Football Club. They initially intended to form a soccer club in the town but accepted the majority view and supported the formation of a Gaelic football team.[49] Armagh Harps included in their ranks in the early 1900s many men who had lined out with local soccer teams such as Armagh White Stars and Greenpark Rovers. Barney Corr of the Harps was considered to be one of the great all-round sportsmen of the time, excelling in Gaelic football, hurling and soccer.[50]

Many early GAA clubs and competitions provided much more than the basic opportunity to participate in, or observe a match. Membership of a GAA club introduced young men to lifestyle opportunities that were enhancing and liberating. However, there were serious concerns about the excessive consumption of alcohol associated with GAA occasions. Contemporary newspaper reports are remarkably similar in their reportage of GAA events. We read about the team's journey to the game, often accompanied by a local band. The welcoming party of the opposition is then featured, followed by the parade through the town or village. The game is then briefly described, after which the post-match entertainment is referenced. Often a meal was served and it was invariably sumptuous. The final part of the report describes the departure of the away team, and depending on what club has submitted the report the return of the 'conquering heroes' may conclude the report.

Sociability amongst GAA personnel varied from the rudimentary open-air drinking sessions enjoyed by both spectators and players, which were a feature of many of the early tournaments organised by GAA clubs, to the more sophisticated hotel-based occasions enjoyed by the clerks and shop-assistants of the urban-based clubs. In Cavan in 1889, for instance, there were ten half-barrels of porter at Maghera MacFinn's tournament in 1889.[51] Tournaments were day-long events and featured at least two or three matches as well as athletic events. It was not unusual for spectators and sometimes players to be heavily intoxicated by evening-time. Celebrations continued for days after Colmcille's first county championship victory in 1890 in Longford. On the way home, a half-barrel of porter was obtained at Ballinalee, a full barrel was produced at Bunlahy, and the celebrations continued when the team eventually arrived back to Smear Cross.[52] Apparently the beaten finalists, Rathcline John Martin's, celebrated in a more sophisticated manner. On account of their controversial defeat, the county committee presented the club with a special set of medals, inscribed 'Honest Johns for superior merit'. After the medal presentation in Lanesboro, the team

Geraldines club hurlers, north Belfast, pictured about 1910. The elderly man in the centre of the photograph is probably the local schoolmaster. Two of the young boys in the front row are holding cricket bats. This may suggest that both codes coexisted as late as the early twentieth century with some degree of harmony. The former Cliftonville cricket grounds are less than half a mile from where the Geraldines were based in Ardoyne. (*Joe Lavery*)

– led by Rathcline Fife and Drum Band – marched to the Shannon; from there the party took *Lady Balfour*, a large cruiser, to an island in Lough Ree, where the group celebrated with music and song well into the early morning.[53] It is not reported whether barrels of porter were consumed on the island. No venue was too sacred for the celebratory drink. In June 1894, when Selskar Young Ireland's team arrived home to Wexford after winning the 1893 All-Ireland football final a special thanksgiving Mass was held in the town, and later four barrels of stout were consumed at the club's headquarters in Selskar Street – a temperance hall![54]

If drinking was much practised it was also much criticised. These occasions met with clerical condemnation and county GAA committees tried to discourage them. In 1888 the Cavan convention passed a byelaw that required each club to appoint three or four men to take charge of the travel arrangements of a team and to prevent 'riotous behaviour'.[55] In February 1893, the Westmeath committee, in an attempt to control the post-game drinking culture, prohibited after-match receptions for championship matches.[56] The drinking culture associated with early GAA activities was of particular concern to the Catholic clergy from the level of the patron of the association down to the curate at parish-level. The association's patron, Archbishop Croke of Cashel, specifically condemned drinking in 1888 when he warned of the 'grave matter of drink in connection with our Gaelic games'.[57] Clergy in various parishes in Ulster reported on the drunkenness, quarrelling and fighting at such games, and their likely impact on the moral order (see Gillespie and Hegarty in this section).[58]

Neal Garnham has suggested that Sunday play had an added advantage in that it allowed GAA players and supporters an opportunity to obtain drink legitimately. Since 1878 Sunday closing of public houses was enforced by law outside the five largest urban centres of Dublin, Belfast, Cork, Limerick and Waterford. A '*bona fide*' traveller could legally obtain drink provided he had travelled more than three miles from his place of residence. The journey to a match was 'usually enough to ensure that a legal drink was available on a Sunday'.[59]

More sophisticated, abstemious and status conscious club members used the opportunity associated with playing a game to engage in a type of cultural tourism. In June 1893 the members of the Charles Kickham club travelled to play an away match against Mullingar Football Club. From the railway station they were escorted to the rooms of the Catholic National Young Men's Club 'where refreshments were lavishly provided and the best of good cheer was the order of the day for an hour or more'. Many of the Dubliners then took the opportunity to explore the Mullingar hinterland and travelled out to view a local lough.[60] Similarly, when the Mullingar club travelled to Ballinasloe in September 1891, its members were accompanied by a reception party to Whelehan's Temperance Bar, where they received 'a sumptuous supper'. On the Sunday morning they availed of the opportunity to visit local places of interest. After the match 'hall and club were thrown open to the visitors, and singing and dancing kept up till the departure of the Mullingar men by the morning train'. When Cusack's Metropolitan HC travelled to Monasterevan in December 1887, the time between lunch and the first match was spent touring the brewery and distillery.[61] In 1898 the secretary of Wolfe Tone's club, Bluebell, gave the visiting Charles Kickham second team an account of the history of Drimnagh Castle and surrounding areas on their way to the playing-field.[62] Dublin clubs participated in a remarkable variety of organised tours. They organised trips to Glasgow and London as well as playing in many country tournaments.[63] In September 1893 the Brian Boru club travelled to Glasgow to stage an exhibition hurling match at Glasgow Celtic's ground at Parkhead. Members of Rapparees, Grocers and Faughs-Davitt's were included in the travelling party, and two teams picked from the players provided the spectators with a closely contested sample of the glories of hurling.[64]

An additional layer was added to the extra-curricular programme of clubs associated with Gaelic League branches in the post 1900 era. The Archbishop Croke's club of Dublin was founded on 24 April 1904 from members of the civil service and the members of An Craoibhinn branch of the Gaelic League. This club placed a heavy emphasis on its cultural programme. The Irish language was taught to the members during the winter months and papers dealing with events in Irish history were read to the members on a weekly basis. Sunday night entertainment events in which only Irish dancing was allowed and Irish-Ireland songs and recitations performed, were held regularly.[65] The post-game entertainment was strongly influenced by the ethos of the Gaelic League. Donaghmore Éire Óg team of Co. Tyrone played its first match in 1904 away to Coalisland Fianna and travelled to the game accompanied by the Donaghmore Fife Band. After the match the teams and their supporters were entertained at an Irish concert in St Patrick's Hall, Coalisland. The full concert of song and dance was in Irish and performed by members of the Donaghmore team.[66] The Donaghmore club placed particular emphasis on the promotion of Irish as a spoken language and weekly language classes were held over the winter months. Sunday night meetings were also organised where debates, lectures, readings, and discussions of Irish history and other matters of public interest were held. [67]

Early GAA events were associated with much pomp, ceremony and pageantry. It was standard practice to have a visiting team met at the local railway station or on the outskirts of town and accompanied to the football pitch or reception hall by one or more musical ensembles. Music was an important part of the sporting occasion at the time and no self-respecting race committee or athletics meet organiser would promote an event without having some form of musical entertainment.[68] GAA organisers went a step further and took the band out of the arena and onto the streets and marched participants to and from the event of the day. Again it was not uncommon to have visiting teams arrive with their own musical ensemble. These practices helped to create a sense of occasion and were great publicity-generating devices drawing public attention to the event of the day. Marching in military formation presented the footballers or hurlers of the day with an opportunity to publicly display their orderliness, organisation and sense of mission. However for the individuals involved the experience must have added to the attraction of the experience. For the farmer who worked long hours in the anonymity of his fields, and for the retail-assistant who was equally isolated behind the counter, the personal enhancement associated with participation had added significance.

Contemporary newspapers abound with descriptions of these occasions. The inclusion of these descriptions in the reportage of GAA provides an indication of the importance attached to this aspect of the early GAA. In August 1887 Moycarkey hurlers travelled to Dublin for a challenge match with the Faugh-a-Ballagh club in the Dunleary festival of hurling and football. The Dunleary Brass Band met them at Kingsbridge Station and on their way to the Angel Hotel they were met by the Shamrock of Erin Fife and Drum Band. In the evening the Moycarkey men were entertained to dinner at Brazil's Hotel in Kingstown where 'there were any amount of toasts and oratory'.[69] Armagh Harps travelled to Dublin on 16 November 1890 with 250 supporters accompanied by the William O'Brien Fife and Drum Band for the All-Ireland football semi-final against Cork, but were heavily defeated.[70] In April 1903, Shamrocks Hurling Club, Mullingar travelled to Longford by special train to play the local Leo Casey Club. The special train was organised for the convenience of buyers attending the big Longford cattle-fair. Members of the Longford club escorted Shamrocks from the station to an hotel, where they ate 'a substantial lunch'; both teams then marched 'with camans on shoulders' behind a fife and drum band to the park. After the match the visitors returned to the hotel for dinner. On their return to Mullingar, the Shamrocks players were met at the railway station by a local brass and reed band and played to their clubrooms followed by a large crowd.[71] This was the standard *modus operandi* of the well-organised urban retail-assistant-dominated hurling and football club and placed these clubs on an equal footing with their rugby and soccer counterparts, which at this time were mainly middle-class institutions.

This chapter builds upon the exploration of some of the themes unpacked by the author and examined in recently published academic GAA history, referred to at the outset of this chapter. These articles provide an introduction to the origins of GAA clubs, their socio-economic profile and the multi-layered activities associated with them.[72] Club historians can add to this process and contribute to a fuller understanding of the early GAA. Newspaper reports that include reports of a club's social activities should not be ignored. Microfilm copies of county newspapers can normally be accessed in the local history section of county library headquarters. Quality of GAA reportage varies, but some such as the *Anglo-Celt* and the *Dundalk Democrat* are particularly comprehensive on early GAA matters. Most county and university libraries also have some national newspaper archives. The National Library in Dublin has the widest range of old newspapers, while there are also particularly extensive collections from across Ulster in both the Belfast City Library newspaper department and the Irish and Local Studies Library, Armagh. The increasing digitalisation of old newspapers on online archives of late has made it possible to do more historical research from home.

The gradual introduction of the 1911 census reports to the internet has made it easier for the club historian to construct socio-economic profiles of the early club players and officers. At the time of writing the census forms of nine counties – including Antrim, Down and Donegal – are available on the internet at the National Archives of Ireland website, with all counties due to be available by the end of 2009. When this is completed the 1901 returns will be added. This presents tremendous possibilities for the club historian. Names of club-members can be cross-referenced with the census material and information regarding the age, marital status, family members, occupation, and ability to speak the Irish language compiled. In this way a more complete socio-economic picture of GAA membership is created. Alternatively, one can visit the National Archives in Dublin, where the 1901 and 1911 census forms are available on microfilm as part of a system that is wonderfully user-friendly after a little orientation. It is crucial for the researcher to compile a list in advance of names of players of the 1890s and 1900s, with their townlands of residence; with such a list a few hours spent researching in the National Archives should be productive. Most county libraries include microfilm copies of the 1901 and 1911 census returns for their counties in their local history departments so these can be accessed locally also. The enthusiastic club historian can also identify the extent of the landholding of a player from a farming background, by visiting the Valuation Office in Dublin where the cancellation books contain full details on the amount of land held by a family and its valuation and any changes that occurred from the 1840s to the 1960s.[73] This again is organised on a townland basis so if travelling on a research mission one should make sure to know this basic information (and its correct Ordnance Survey spelling).

There are, furthermore, excellent collections of GAA-related material in county libraries and other archives. For instance, the county libraries in Cork City, Thurles ('The Source') and Cavan Town have comprehensive collections of club histories for their respective counties. Histories of Tipperary clubs are plentiful and it is doubtful if any other county has its clubs' affairs so well documented. The variety of approaches adopted can provide inspiration to the prospective club historian. The Cardinal Ó Fiaich Library and Archive, Armagh, has impressive holdings of club histories from all over Ulster and beyond, as well as

The Clann Uladh club from Newry who won the Down county football championship in 1912.
This was a short-lived club formed in 1910 and disappeared on the outbreak of the First World War.
The captioning of the team in the photograph, with their jobs identified, provides an interesting case study
on the occupational profile early GAA members / players.
Back row: Hugh O'Neill (brewery-cart driver), Jimmy Quinn (emigrated to Australia), James McGauley (painter),
Michael Murray (printer), Paddy Howley (clerk).
Middle row: Johnny Kinney (Urban Council mason), Joe Smith (baker), Johnny Devlin (mason),
Willie Marshall (butcher), Geordie Weller.
Front row: Barney Duffy, John McAteer (baker).
Others pictured include John McArdle (with the cup), Martin Power, Michael Evans, John Daly, 'Poppy' Polin,
Paddy Donnelly, Barney Polin, Christie Miller (Painter), Micksie Lennon, Joe Mason, James O'Hare, Owen Rankin,
Pat Larkin, George McCall, Tommy Mc --, Willie McCaul, Ernie Hillen and Mick McCreesh. (*Noel Haughey*)

programmes and minute-books. The GAA Museum, Croke Park, has possibly the largest collection of archival material about the organisation, but the lack of a catalogue for visitors at the time of writing limits research possibilities. Another valuable resource is the Limerick City Library, which contains many rare GAA newspapers and magazines in its Séamus Ó Ceallaigh collection.

Adopting a more expansive approach to the writing of club and county histories will provide a more comprehensive understanding of the workings of the GAA and its multi-faceted contribution to the quality of life of local communities.

The Mass Media and the Popularisation of Gaelic Games, 1884–1934

Eoghan Corry

The late nineteenth century saw the beginning of a golden era for print journalism that lasted well into the television age. Rapid progress in technology, literacy and the self-confidence of newspaper contributors all converged to produce a body of writing that serves as a window into the social mores, concerns and debates of the times. Out of some of the liveliest of these newspaper debates emerged the Gaelic Athletic Association. In the five decades before the foundation of the GAA, print-journalism was boosted by the evolution of universal education, the rotary press which churned out newspapers at speeds of up to thirty thousand per hour, railways which conveyed these new printed newspapers quickly throughout the land, and supply-side technological developments such as the telegraph and shorthand note-taking systems. Circulations were still small: in the absence of properly audited figures, an estimated seven thousand for the *Weekly Freeman* and three thousand for its nearest rival. But the new journals and their contributors carried great influence.

New technology and the interests of their new audience enabled newspapers to turn their attention to another revolution, one that was happening on the sports-fields. By the turn of the nineteenth century, horseracing tip-sheets had begun to evolve into the new sporting press. The presentation of race results was established by the 1820s in a form that punters today would recognise. At the same time London produced the first powerful sports weekly newspaper in these islands, *Bell's Sporting Life*. The *Freeman's Journal* began to carry racing columns in the 1820s and cricket reports soon afterwards. The development of coherent sports sections was well under way by the 1850s, when the first multi-sports county clubs were founded in provincial towns.[1]

On the advice of Edmund Dwyer Gray, proprietor of the *Freeman's Journal*, Athlone-born Thomas Power O'Connor introduced comprehensive sports coverage into his newspaper in London through *The Star*, with instant success.[2] Dublin did get its first sports weekly in 1869, the *Irish Sportsman and Farmer*, with Margaret Dunbar as proprietor and William J. Dunbar as editor. Twelve years later, in 1881, the *Freeman's Journal* launched a sporting weekly, simply entitled *Sport*, which was edited by Fred Gallaher, *Sporting Life's* Irish correspondent. W. J. Dunbar (whose two sons were to become active in the athletics movement) and Gallaher became great rivals and benefactors of a sporting revival in their own right.

Naturally, an influential media was of more than passing interest to the people behind the foundation of the GAA, a process far more complex and lengthy than the traditional story of seven men in Thurles would suggest. From the beginning the GAA had its friendly media, which it used to propagate the myth that the infant organisation was larger and more powerful than it was, and which then fuelled its phenomenal growth in the first six months. This growth was unmatched by sporting organisations elsewhere. From the outset the GAA had a hostile media too, and it also served the association well. The many GAA-related controversies were reported vividly, colourfully and often in an entertaining way. Whatever the people of 1880s Ireland felt about the nascent GAA, they could not but notice it. This media coverage, from both sides, was arguably the most important catalyst in creating the GAA and sustaining it through its early crisis-ridden years. It also sheds light on the peculiarities of relationship between the GAA and the media that endures to this day.

From our modern perspective the newspaper archives – now more accessible than ever, thanks to the digitalisation process by Gale and Proquest technologies – assist greatly in research of the early years of the GAA. They enable us to track the scale of pre-GAA sporting activities, and the careers of the founders before 1884; to identify some of the writers of the articles that provided the context for founding the GAA; and to assess the early coverage of the GAA, its accuracy and its impact on sporting culture at that time. Accordingly this chapter will outline the crucial role played by newspapers and their staff in increasing the popularity and significance of Gaelic games between the eighteenth and twentieth centuries. Special consideration will be given to some previously underemphasised themes, such as what part the press had in

PARTY SPIRIT—DREADFUL OUTRAGE.—We regret to find that a spirit of organization is beginning to manifest itself among the lower classes of the Roman Catholics, in the parishes of Lifford and Taughboyne, which, if not speedily put an end to, may lead to fatal results. Monday the 6th inst. being Old Christmas-Day, which is observed by the Presbyterians generally, at which time the young people are apt to indulge in field sports, four young men had commenced what is called common-playing, at a place named Craghadoes, on their own land, and about half-way between Lifford and St. Johnstown, when about forty of the opposite party came into the field, quarrelled with the young men in question, who narrowly escaped with their lives. While this scene was acting, James Middleton, a weaver, returning from Strabane, where he had been for yarn, stopped to see what was the matter, when one of the ruffians came behind him, and, without any offence on his part, struck him a blow with a bludgeon, which fractured his skull; he is now under the care of Surgeon Harvey, of St. Johnstown, but in such a dangerous state that his life is despaired of. We have not heard whether the perpetrator of this foul deed is known, but as some of the party are, we trust that he will be identified, and that the disturbers of the public tranquility, in that hitherto peaceable district, will be severely punished.

Londonderry Sentinel, 11 January 1834. Newspaper references to hurling, *camán* and *shinny* in pre-GAA times are being found in greater number, particularly since digitalisation began. It is worth noting that those who had gathered to play the game of commons were from a Presbyterian background and their assailants were Roman Catholic.

propagating new ideas concerning organised sport from mainland Europe to Ireland, and whether these influences had as much to do with the birth and expansion of the GAA as those emanating from Great Britain did.

It is important that we understand the newspaper sources and their shortcomings as we begin a process that will no doubt grow in depth and breadth as more newspaper sources become more readily accessible. Journalists, then as now, were writing for an immediate audience and had different priorities and objectives than some of us viewing the material retrospectively make allowances for.

The dozens of references to hurling and football in the eighteenth-century printed press usually (but not always) emphasised the undesirable consequences of early matches; riots, drunkenness, the desecration of the Sabbath, and the suspicion, echoed in the state papers, that every gathering of *cosmhuintir* was to cloak a political gathering.[3] More of these references are being uncovered every year, as local history groups grapple with the enormous body of printed material available and more archives arrive online.[4] Most of these are brief notices, which give no indication of what form the play took, but they do indicate some characteristics of the games which the GAA inherited. It is clear that inter-county matches were popular even at this early stage as evidenced in the grand hurling match between Waterford and Tipperary played in September 1788 at Churchtown, near Carrick-on-Suir, 'on as bad a piece of ground … as ever was chosen … a miserable match it was … play commenced at nightfall and lasted only ten minutes.'[5]

There are indications that prizes such as barrels of ale were staked, as well as stakes of money laid (as in a *Freeman's Journal* report of August 1777) to enable 'two waiters from a noted coffee house in the city, to hold a match of hurling for five guineas a side in Crumlin.'[6] It is also clear that games were well attended, as in a report of July 1779, when 'upwards of 10,000 spectators' were present at a match in the Phoenix Park, and 'the number expected next Sunday will be at least double.'[7] Above all, hurling then was a match sport, part of the gambling culture that emanated from the King's Plate races, as in the report of 3 November 1792 that 'Colonel Lennox proposes to establish a prize of 100 guineas annually for superiority in hurling, on the fifteen acres, in the Phoenix Park.' We do not know if Colonel Lennox's proposed plate transpired. By the nineteenth century the references were less favourable. The *Freeman's Journal* reported that there were political meetings under the pretence of hurling in Dublin in 1821[8] and Kilkenny in 1831,[9] and pieces harking back to the time when hurling was a common practice. When the same newspaper stated on 23 April 1844 that 'the national and athletic exercise (hurling) is again being revived in some of the parishes north for the Slaney', there appeared to be grounds for optimism, as it reported that thirty thousand spectators were present at the contest.[10]

We can also track the arrival of new sporting ideas into Ireland through the pages of these newspapers. Sadly, they give rise to more questions than answers. To what was *Dublin University Magazine* referring in 1761, when it described hurling as 'a truly national game?' What was the event or the context which inspired the *Dublin Evening Post* of 16 October 1792 to write that 'this is one of the native sports of this country', and 'we would be glad that an English garrison or the family of an English minister should dare to enter into competition with us in this instance, where, and not in an English exercise – cricket – Irishman have a right to excel.'[11] Were these instances (and there are likely to have been more) important in forming the opinions of 1798 insurrectionist James Hope in calling for a hurling revival, something that Pádraig Puirséal, for one, saw as a precursor to the GAA? It has been his comfortable assumption that the United Irishmen were the first to develop a political philosophy around the national games,[12] but our bank of newspapers suggest that the idea preceded them by at least three decades, and that it preceded even their role-models in revolutionary France whose view of sport as desirable, ennobling and egalitarian served as the foundation of the international sports industry that we know today.[13]

Over the coming decades the evolution of pastimes into organised modern sports, including the GAA, was presaged by writers and activists such as Johann Bernhard Basedow, Friedrich Jahn, and Per-Henrick Ling.[14] Jahn's *turnverein* were among those who paraded to welcome Thomas Francis Meagher to America in 1852, four years after Meagher had famously remarked, paraphrasing Lord Byron, 'you have the Irish dance as yet, where is the Irish hurling gone?'[15] This became one of the major symbolic references to the games, cited by nationalist GAA writers such as Séamus Upton, during the period immediately pre- and post-independence.[16]

In 1867 there were signs of a more sinister sporting culture having arrived in the country. Though attributed to Charles Kingsley, the term 'Muscular Christianity' had not been used by him, but was first printed in the *Edinburgh Magazine* in 1857. This was an opposing view to that expressed by Rousseau and Friedrich Jahn; it was one in which sport was understood as a conquest, where the colonial power brought its own rules and invited the natives to watch and sometimes play on their own terms. It was exclusive rather than inclusive, and it caused consternation throughout the Irish sporting community.

During the 1860s, as a result of a fear of military invasion scare, the country's highly ritualised public-school culture became fused with the idea of raising a volunteer corps to support the army. This new sporting movement followed Germany's lead in celebrating athleticism. The movement spread rapidly and generated separate controlling bodies for soccer, rugby, rowing, tennis, croquet, and lacrosse all within a sixteen-year period. The English sporting codes resembled the continental ones in their concerns for measurement and achievement. English sports culture, imbued as it was with the country's medieval class system, impeded equality of opportunity. In turn, continental sports abhorred wagering, prizes or admission charges – all of which were tolerated by the British. On the continental mainland there was a concern with health, moral improvement and ideology, which later transformed into a latent patriotism. Because of its peculiar position, as an occupied country with an ascendancy that regarded Ireland as a poor relation of Britain, Ireland soon became subject to both influences. Many of these new English sporting bodies saw themselves as inherently English in nature, and propagated the first international sporting contests against Scotland and Ireland.[17] Eventually the efforts of some of these bodies to claim jurisdiction over existing Irish sporting clubs would help create both the GAA and its rival, the Irish Amateur Athletic Association.

The *Freeman's Journal* reported in September 1867 that the Civil Service of Ireland Society for the encouragement and practice of athletic sports 'held their first meeting for actual exercise on Saturday evening at the Leinster Cricket Ground, Upper Mountpleasant Avenue.' It said that 'a more successful meeting could not have been desired by even long-established and prosperous associations of the most devoted advocates of the system of muscular Christianity which has obtained so much popularity of late years in these countries.' The patrons of the new sports included the Lord Lieutenant.[18] In that same year, *The Irishman*, founded by Denis Holland, echoed Meagher when it complained 'the nation that has lost its relish for athletics is incapable of winning its independence.' In contrast, the *Irish Times* declared on July 19 1873 that 'Ireland is coming to the fore as a nurse of the fleet of foot and the strong of limb,' with the hope that this country would turn out athletes to compete with the *turnverein*, and the champion English runners. Ireland and England competed against each other in the first athletics international three years later, with Maurice Davin's two brothers Tom and Pat included on the Irish team.[19]

'Benmore' (John Clarke) was a journalist, nationalist and a leading promoter of Gaelic games from the north of Antrim. He had a very distinctive descriptive style of reporting on Gaelic games, and tended to write more about the scenery and the national virtues of Gaelic games than about the players, as he (like some other GAA scribes) thought it invidious and against the team spirit of the games to focus on individuals.

The evolving newspaper industry funded a new group of professional writers who specialised in rapidly evolving news-reportage, comment and what is today referred to as colour-writing. Some were later to distinguish themselves in literature and politics. The market for which they wrote was dominated by four dailies: the *Morning Post*, *Evening Mail*, *Irish Times* and, most significantly, *Freeman's Journal*. There was a growing audience for news of these sporting developments, and more important, a small group of sporting activists who learned how to manage the media coverage of sporting developments. Due to the absence of professional sportswriters in most cases, they supplied their own reports. For instance, the foundation of the Hurley Union in 1879 and the Dublin Hurling Club in 1883 were recorded in short news items that appear to have been supplied by the bodies themselves. Indeed the first item on the agenda of the inaugural meeting of the Dublin Hurling Club in 1883 was to instruct the honorary secretary to request the press to favour the club by inserting reports of the proceedings under the heading of hurling, and not hurley.[20] The said secretary was Lloyd Christian, a prominent banker, a cousin of George Bernard Shaw, and one of the brothers who were at the heart of the early athletics movement in Ireland.[21]

Meanwhile, an equally energetic debate was being conducted in an array of underground and mainstream political journals of the time, which sometimes outsold the national newspapers. For example, the circulation of *The Nation* peaked at 10,730, while its closest rival, the *Weekly Freeman*, sold 7,150 copies at its height. Michael Cusack was among the amateur polemicists and writers (as was his fellow Clare-man David Comyn) who contributed to a cluster of nationalistic journals, including the two journals sold by Richard Pigott in 1881, the *Flag of Ireland* and *The Irishman*, edited at that time by William Lynam. He also contributed to Alexander M. Sullivan's 'paper for boys', *Young Ireland*, and William O'Brien's *United Irishman*. As with many writers who had a prodigious output, Michael Cusack's prolificacy appears to have served as an unexpected barrier to understanding his real feelings and motives at the time. His writings in various journals, under several by-lines, and often no by-line at all, run to hundreds of thousands of words and are often puzzling and contradictory in form. His children's column in *The Shamrock* in 1882 famously advocated that cricket be played as the 'national game.'[22] This is cited often nowadays in discussions about Cusack's endeavours. But was this suggestion tailored to suit the readership of *The Shamrock*? Cusack had fallen out with various editors and owners, notably *Freeman's Journal* proprietor Edmund Dwyer Gray by 1884. However, at the time of his correspondence with Davin about the foundation of the GAA, he still had access to the Parnellite newspaper *United Ireland*, which had been launched under William O'Brien's

THE

Shan Van Vocht:

A NATIONAL MONTHLY MAGAZINE.

Edited by ... ... ALICE L. MILLIGAN.

Offices (pro tem)—

65, GREAT GEORGE'S STREET, BELFAST.

American Agent—

M. J. O'BRIEN, Room 70, 195, Broadway, NEW YORK

Subscriptions—1/3 Half-yearly ; 2/6 Yearly.

Agents' Orders to be addressed to the Secretary, Miss Anna Johnston ; Literary matter to the Editor.

The Revival of the G.A.A.

AN APPEAL TO THE YOUNG MEN OF BELFAST.

AT a time when the Gaelic Athletic Association is being revived all over Ireland, will the young men of Belfast allow the present deplorable condition of apathy and indifference towards purely national movements to continue?

This is a question well worthy of careful consideration, for upon the answer depends, to a great extent, the position to be occupied by the youth of this city in the unceasing struggle between the Celt and the Saxon. It cannot, it must not be, that you are content to remain a mere collection of units without the slightest semblance of cohesion or unity of purpose, and this appeal is addressed to you for the purpose of pointing out one way by which you could be welded into a solid mass. Until you are so, it is impossible for you to be reckoned among the effective forces of Irish Nationalism or regarded as other than belonging to that class which, of all grades of contemptible meanness, is looked upon with the greatest loathing by honest men—the willing slave. Elsewhere in the "Shan Van Vocht" will be found an interesting account of the G.A.A. by "Celt." It is, therefore, unnecessary to refer here to the rise of the Association or to any of that brilliant array of athletes who have placed no fewer than *nineteen* world's records to the credit of the G.A.A., and who have proved that Old Ireland is still able to produce men remarkable for their physique, as well as men mentally capable of governing any nation in the world—except their own. To the chief pastime cultivated by the G.A.A., however, it is necessary to refer and call immediate and earnest attention. Hurling is the oldest and finest physical exercise practised in any part of the world. Compared with it in either respect the popular games of Bel-

fast are poor and insignificant. Besides, they are un-Irish—football is Scotch; cricket, English; and cycling—well, anything you like, but *not* Gaelic. Hurling, on the contrary, is an eminently Irish game. Its history is easily traceable through the last two decades, and right back to that terrible calamity, the Great Famine, the awful effects of which, so largely the result of the demoralising and emasculating policy of "Liberating" and "Head Pacificating" Leaders (!) we are experiencing to this day, and shall experience to the end of time perchance. Before 1847 every parish in the country had its hurling team, and 1798 showed that wielding the "caman" was not mean practice for wielding the pike. During the dark and bitter days of the Penal Ages it was still the national game of Ireland, just as it was

"Ere Norman foot had dared pollute
Her independent shore."

Further back yet, to the days when St. Patrick preached on Tara's Hill, we find it prominent, so much so, indeed, that every able-bodied man in the land played it. Even at that far distant date it was an ancient game, for do we not read that before the first battle of Magh Tuireadh, in the year 1272 B.C., between the Firbolgs and the Tuatha De Dananns there was a hurling match played with three times nine men on each side? For a space of over three thousand years, therefore, hurling has been the national pastime of Ireland. The physical aspect of the game is equally creditable and well attested. Look at the record-breakers of modern days and the Fianna Erion of ancient days — all trained on the hurling field—the latter entirely so, which speaks volumes for the system of training pursued by the most famous body of athletes and warriors of Pagan Ireland.

Many of our most ancient literary productions are merely accounts of the exploits of famous heroes in the hurling field. It is a very noticeable fact that most of the heroes mentioned were Ulstermen. How many famous modern hurlers has Ulster produced? Not one. To Munster belongs the credit of preserving the game.

Men of Belfast, how much longer will you be content to hear it said that you have lost the spirit of your forefathers? Rouse yourselves from your slumbers ; shake off your apathy and the indifference which is clogging your energies ; and set an example to the province of which your city is the proud capital. A hurling club is in course of formation in Belfast. Fall into line immediately, and let it not be asserted, to your discredit, that it was a failure, and that your country has nothing to hope from you, for if you will not keep alive your ancient games you can hardly be expected to keep alive your distinctive nationality. Let no one excuse himself on the plea that he cannot hurl. All can learn, and there will be teachers galore. Now, what answer is to be made to the opening question?

F. P. BURKE.

The *Shan Van Vocht* newspaper played an was an important newspaper in the revival of Gaelic games in Belfast around the turn of the twentieth century. It gave regular space to GAA propagandists in Dublin such as Michael Cusack, P. J. Devlin and F. P. Burke to stir Belfast nationalists to reorganise for hurling.

editorship in August 1881. Thus Cusack's three newspaper articles of October 1884, published simultaneously in *United Ireland* and in *The Irishman*, served as the clarion call for the new association.[23]

Calls for an independent Irish sporting organisation or a revival of hurling did not divide along predetermined national or colonial lines, even allowing for the complexity of politics at a time when all parties anticipated Home Rule within a few years, when there was no suggestion of partition and no indication that the Home Rule political movement would be effectively sabotaged at Westminster. Rather, the GAA was founded at a time of confidence that the constitutional issue between Ireland and England was about to be settled or at least substantially remedied. The foundation of the revivalist Dublin University Hurling Club and subsequently the Irish Hurley Union was almost exclusively a colonial-unionist affair.[24] The breakaway revival of hurling, rather than hurley which later merged with hockey, was activated by Frank Potterton, writing under the name 'Omega' in the *Irish Times*. Subsequently as an IAAA officer, he became one of Cusack's most strident opponents.

Similarly, although the journals of Pigott and O'Brien served as a sounding-board for Cusack, newspapers and journals of all political shades were involved in the run-up to the foundation of the GAA. In January 1884, Dunbar's nominally unionist-inclined *Irish Sportsman*, which interspersed athletics results with articles proclaiming the superiority of the Saxon race and acclaiming imperialism in Africa, called for 'Home Rule in Irish athletics' – fairly unambiguous terminology in the political context of the time.[25] Cusack had contributed three articles on athletics unity to Dunbar's *Irish Sportsman* in 1881, including a warning that the Irish rugby team needed 'a strip of green across their colours and their ground.'[26] Indeed tracking Cusack's output is a task in itself. His two major biographers have puzzled over the contradictory opinions, argued passionately and forcefully, often in two opposing directions within a short period of each other.[27] His dream of an Irish-run athletics movement and the revival of the Tailteann games received a lot of publicity, and the impact of this publicity was maximised by the series of media debates that immediately followed, including a mean-minded attack from the *Daily Telegraph*.[28] Instead it is appropriate to record that, in modern terms, Cusack achieved a public relations coup when founding the GAA, securing its future beyond that which any of the previous seven attempts to set up a sports body in Ireland had proved capable of doing.[29]

He wrote across several journals at the same time, nationalist and unionist, before founding his own title in 1888. He engaged in a series of enthusiastic battles in print with several opponents, many of whom had been close colleagues and allies at some stage in his career; for example, he assailed John 'Bones' Christian in print for seven years before Christian emigrated to the USA in August 1887. Ironically, much of Cusack's most strident criticism took place at a time he was friendly with Christian's two younger brothers. In due course John Houston Stewart from Castlederg, Co. Tyrone, later a vice-president of the GAA, acted as intermediary to bring the two together and establish an uneasy truce. Other adversaries included Henry Dunlop, founder of Lansdowne Road Stadium; Val Dunbar, the *Irish Sportsman* editor, and his brother John (at the time of the foundation of the IAAA in 1885); Fred Gallaher, the editor of *Sport*; Edmund Dwyer Gray, *Freeman's Journal* proprietor; P. T. Hoctor, the editor of *The Gael*, the official GAA journal in 1887,[30] when Cusack simultaneously managed and single-handedly produced the *Celtic Times*.[31]

Cusack's later, more polite, writings suggest that the force with which he engaged these debates may have been inspired by a desire to maximise publicity for his various undertakings. Indications of this are contained in Cusack's correspondence of twenty years hence the foundation of the GAA, when he wrote as follows:

> Christian was a keen thinker, from his point of view. He was an Irishman, brave to the point of recklessness. He was an incisive writer and an ardent supporter of the then encroaching new school of athletics. His warm personal friend, yet formidable public opponent, was a restorer and a conservator of the Tailteann games. Bones must have believed that I wanted to do away with the sports in which he and I took part. I wanted to add to the building. If I appeared to propose to put an end to a small building, and to be destructive in my methods and criticism, it was because I had constructive methods arranged. In committee we reasoned our case. In the Press we thrashed it out. In private and social life we never referred to it. We hit one another hard in business places, but every blow was well short above the belt. Would that my now friends of later days could act as we did of yore.[32]

It helped Cusack's already well-fuelled publicity machine that the attendance of the foundation meeting of the GAA on 1 November 1884 included two professional journalists, as well as Cusack himself, who single-handedly generated an enormous volume of newspaper material. The event was widely reported; it gave rise to more news reports of the event than there were individuals present at the meeting. Cusack probably wrote the reports in *United Ireland*, *The Irishman* and *The Shamrock*;[33] John McKay, who was listed as representing the Cork Athletic Club at the meeting, presumably wrote the report in the *Cork Examiner*, which at about fifteen hundred words represents the longest and most detailed report of the foundation meeting of the GAA.[34] Similarly, John Wyse Power penned the report of this gathering for the *Leinster Leader*.[35] In contrast, whilst Wyse Power may have provided some detail, it is almost certain that Fred Gallaher and John Dunbar provided inaccurate reports of this historic meeting, gathered from second-hand

Souvenir of Dr. Croke Cup Football Final, Jones's Road, Sunday, June 13th, 1897.

DUBLIN YOUNG IRELAND FOOTBALL TEAM.

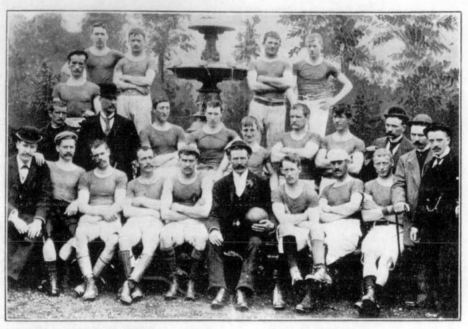

J. Mahony. J. Heslin. — Gannon. J. Teeling. J. Ledwidge.
S. Mooney. E. Hessian. A. Graham. R. Flood. —Brady.
P. Heslin. R. Curtis. M. Byrne. L. O'Kelly. J. Kennedy. M. Hayes. G. Roche. T. Errity.

TIPPERARY (ARRAVALE) ROVERS FOOTBALL TEAM

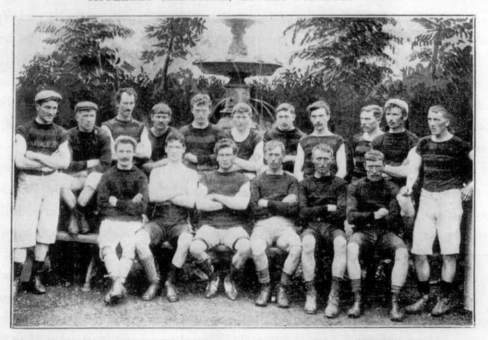

R. Quane. M. McInerney. P. Glasheen. R. Swords. W. Shea. M. Connor. W.J. Ryan. P. Dwyer. J. Carew. M. Walsh. J. O'Brien.
W. P. Quane. M. F. Ryan. W. P. Ryan. M. Harris. J. Heffernan. R. Butler.

CAHILL & CO., PRINTERS,   35, 36 & 37 GT. STRAND ST. DUBLIN.

Photographs of two of Ireland's leading Gaelic football teams, in the *Gaelic News* of 1897. This was the only edition of this official GAA newspaper, but in printing these team photographs together it broke new ground in coverage of Gaelic games. (*Eoghan Corry*)

information, in the *Freeman's Journal*, *Daily News* and *Irish Sportsman*. Interestingly these reports added the names of John Butler, T. K. Dwyer, C. Culhane, M. Cantwell and William Delahunty (all from Thurles), and William Foley (from Carrick-on-Suir) to the attendance. Tellingly, the 116-word report in the *Freeman's Journal* ('From Our Reporter') did not record Bracken's first name, although the initial 'M Cusack' suggests that the report may have come from a note by Cusack himself.[36] It is generally accepted among historians that the two other journalists, John McKay and John Wyse Power, attended not just because of their interest in the new association, but also because there was a story to report. Puirséal suggests that Power's membership of the Irish Republican Brotherhood gave him another reason for making the journey from Naas to Thurles for the meeting.[37] Both became immersed in the donkeywork of establishing the organisation and so it is reasonable to conclude that their motives for attending this gathering were at least partly sincere.

Thus Wyse Power and McKay's contributions to the early spread of the organisation went beyond their professional roles. Wyse Power had come to journalism from another profession, and both were from the new breed of professional writers who moved from newspaper to newspaper in the course of their careers. Significantly, both were to attend another foundation meeting a decade later – of the first professional body established to secure better conditions for journalists, which included access to public events. John McKay had worked in Belfast, before moving to Cork and became involved in the various disputes there over the rules of football that marred the organisation of the game in Munster in 1885 and 1886. He had come to Cork in 1878, returned to Belfast around 1896 to join the *Irish News*, then went to work at the *Freeman's Journal* in Dublin, and back to Cork again, before finally moving to London, where he died in 1923 (see McConville and McAnallen in section 4).[38] Wyse Power was editor of J. L. Carew's *Leinster Leader* at the time of the meeting but was soon to move to the *Freeman's Journal*, only in turn to become editor of the *Evening Herald* by the early 1890s. He was an active and hard-working secretary of the GAA nationally and in Dublin; later he was involved in several trades councils and nationalist organisations, and chaired the first Irish branch of the Institute of Journalists.[39] He stood unsuccessfully in the local elections of 1902. His wife Jenny is better known nowadays, due to her prominence in the suffragette and independence movements; she became a senator in the Free State and a trustee of the disputed Sinn Féin funds.

As the GAA and its rivals fought for the allegiance of the existing sports clubs and sportsmen, a robust and often intemperate debate was conducted in print. The arguments were primarily between Gallaher's journal *Sport* and Dunbar's *Irish Sportsman*, but also unfolded at a local level as many towns had rival nationalist and unionist newspapers or even nationalist newspapers in rivalry with one another. Jacques McCarthy's oft-quoted putdown of Gaelic games (as savage games played by savages) set the tone for a debate that was echoed at local level through the country.[40] The highlight of the several 'newspaper wars' that erupted around the early GAA was undoubtedly the libel action taken by Cusack against the Dunbars and their newspaper, the *Irish Sportsman*, in 1885. The report of the case was headlined 'An Amusing Libel Action' by the *Irish Times*, while the *Freeman's Journal* said the case 'seemed to excite considerable interest and the court was crowded.' Cusack was represented by D. B. Sullivan and Tim Healy, whilst John Monroe and Charles A. O'Connor stood for the Dunbars. Cusack sued for £500, an exorbitant amount which would have bankrupted the newspaper. The Dunbars lodged £2 in court, showing how much they valued Cusack's reputation. The jury awarded Cusack £10 as well as the £2 lodged.[41]

The libel took the form of a poem, entitled 'A Simple Sarcasm', and 'a song suggested for the next concert promoted by the Gaelic Athletic Association,' to be sung to the tune of a current Gilbert and Sullivan song in their light opera *Patience*. It coincided with the exchange of letters between Cusack and John Dunbar, in which Cusack famously told Dunbar 'I received your letter this morning and burned it.'[42] John Dunbar may have written the poem but it is difficult to distinguish precisely what was written by which brother and how much collaboration was involved. Within eight stanzas the poem managed to mock the GAA's definition of a 'pure athlete' and its disdain of 'Saxon games'; its preference for 'weight throwing and leaping' in athletics; violence in hurling (in which 'man assaulted man'); and its promotion of the Irish language. The verse also characterised the association as politically orientated and 'a narrow minded boorish lot'. Cusack ('our sec in Gardiner Place') was depicted as 'the obese academician', but the crux of the libel action was the portrayal of his Civil Service Academy, as one in which it would be 'an awful fluke' for his 'much neglected class' to pass an examination.

Cusack's own account of the foundation of the GAA, in *The Nation* of 12 October 1889, is often quoted because of its use of the phrase, 'for sixteen months the Association spread out with the devastating rapidity of a prairie fire.' The rest of Cusack's article refers to the 'infusion into the Association of those disintegrating agencies that burst up the Young Ireland Society' in Dublin.[43] The prairie fire he referred to was no longer burning and was about to be almost extinguished by the Parnell split and other problems. The tone of the article is of a somewhat more reflective Cusack, his energy no doubt exhausted by his enormous input into the *Celtic Times*, which wasted an unknown amount of Morrison Millar's money before it folded. At the end of 1888 the cumulative financial and intellectual toll had also closed Cusack's academy.[44]

The ongoing controversies maintained a high level of coverage of GAA affairs. Several of the police files in the National Archives consist simply of newspaper reports, faithfully cut and pasted in. This appears to indicate that the policemen who compiled the files were convinced that the shorthand proficient newspaper reporters of the day gave more accurate accounts than the men who were supposed to be monitoring the events for subversive activity. Though coverage declined after the split of 1891, newspaper files give an indication of continuity of games even in unaffiliated counties. Skilled professional writers were beginning to emerge, part-timers at first like Wexford born P. P. Sutton the correspondent of *Sport*; James Furlong, also from Wexford; Frank Dineen, the *Freeman's Journal* correspondent who died at his desk while filing his weekly column, but who is best remembered as the man who acquired Croke Park for the GAA; and eventually in the 1920s the first full-time GAA correspondents, P. J. Devlin ('Celt') and Paddy Mehigan, who left his job in the civil service to write for the *Cork Examiner* and *Irish Times* and to bring out *Carbery's Annual*.[45]

After the GAA revival of 1900, inspired by the establishment of provincial councils, members of a more confident association were anxious to ensure adequate media coverage, as in 1912 when the GAA congress condemned William Martin Murphy's *Irish Independent* for a partial boycott of GAA affairs.[46] The coverage

A cartoon from the *Gaelic Athlete* depicting the 1923 All-Ireland senior hurling semi-final between Limerick and Donegal. Cartoons have rarely been used in newspaper features of Gaelic games, particularly in the late twentieth century.

As Gaelic games became more popular they generated more specific publications. The *Northern Gael* was a Belfast-based periodical in the late 1940s. *An Camán* was an official joint newspaper of the GAA and *Conradh na Gaeilge* in the early 1930s, but it was not a profitable venture and it ceased publication in 1934.

in the *Independent* was to become more extensive, but a suspicion persists that the complaint may have been inspired by Dineen, who had more than a passing interest in the growing rivalry between the *Freeman's Journal* and the *Independent*.

Sport again played its part in the rise of newspaper circulation during the first third of the twentieth century. In the case of the *Independent*, already the best-selling daily in the country in 1906, this helped to boost circulation more than fourfold from 30,000 to 132,000 over a twenty-five year period.[47] That sport would prove a circulation builder was apparent to the founders of the *Irish Press*, who wrote individually to each county board in advance of the launch of the paper seeking co-operation with regard to results and other matters, and launched the paper on the day of the Cork versus Kilkenny All-Ireland hurling final. Sports editor Joe Sherwood, who had been recruited from Workington, England, famously billed the start time for the match as 'kick off 3 pm'. The *Irish Press* ran daily reports from special correspondents billeted in the two training camps as the match fortuitously went to two replays and in turn boosted the new paper's circulation still further. The *Irish Press* approach did raise the standards of reporting on Gaelic games generally, but its impact on other newspapers has been overstated greatly. Gaelic games had enjoyed progressively more extensive coverage in the *Irish Independent* during the 1920s and in the *Freeman's Journal* before that, and the greater coverage of GAA events in the 1930s owed as much to the sharp growth in popularity of the association and its games within a short number of years. The fact that the *Press* had an extensive network of country correspondents, designed to cater for a rural readership, only served to amplify a process that had long been under way, as the GAA's attendances and structures grew considerably. In more recent times Rupert Murdoch, the media mogul behind the rise of the satellite broadcaster station, BSkyB, famously described sport as his 'battering ram' into the living rooms of his potential subscribers. However, the *Irish Press* used the GAA in exactly the same fashion as far back as 1931. Ironically, the *Daily Star* later deployed Gaelic games as one part of its offensive against the *Press* in a circulation war that ensued between the newspapers after 1988.

The Leaving Certificate results of 1932 listed Patrick Purcell of St Kieran's College, Kilkenny, as the joint highest score in English in the state at that time. Purcell (or Puirséal) was to become the foremost of the new breed of GAA writers as an *Irish Press* correspondent, replacing the part-time insurance executive, Donegal-born Seán Bonner. In similar fashion, John D. Hickey became GAA correspondent of the *Irish Independent* in 1951, and Paddy Downey, whose first reports in the *Irish Times* were run in 1962 when he was correspondent of the *Sunday Review*, took over from Paddy Mehigan as *Irish Times* resident GAA writer in 1963. In the same era Paddy O'Hara arrived as the central figure in GAA journalism in Ulster. Among his unsung achievements was convincing the BBC to broadcast GAA reports; even the relaying of results had been banned by its director, George Marshall, in 1934, following a public debate in which Northern Ireland Prime Minister James Craig personally intervened to prevent GAA results being aired.[48] For most of the mid twentieth century GAA followers in the north-east had to rely on the *Irish News* for daily coverage of Gaelic games, for which they owed a considerable debt to Jack McKeever, the sports editor.

The first, short-lived GAA Writers Association was founded in 1961, with Paddy Mehigan as patron, Michael O Hehir of RTÉ as president, John D. Hickey as chairman, Val Dorgan of the *Cork Examiner* as vice-chairman, Paddy Downey of the *Sunday Review* as treasurer, and Mick Dunne of the *Irish Press* as secretary. The primary motive of the association was to present 'player of the year' awards to the leading GAA figures of the day. In fact Dunne, who later moved to RTÉ, was behind the All-Stars awards, which originally stemmed from a *Gaelic Weekly* enterprise of the 1960s, and which is still selected by a panel of journalists today. Indeed the All-Star awards are just the latest manifestation of the marked and serious contribution that journalists have made to the evolution of the games.

At provincial level full-time GAA correspondents were less prominent, although many writers were hired because of their GAA knowledge and assigned to other tasks during the week. Some fascinating literary product was being offered, notably by Edward Ramsbottom ('Thigeen Roe') in the *Leinster Leader*, Phil O'Neill in the *Kilkenny Journal*, Séamus Upton ('Vigilant') in several Munster publications, and Paddy Foley ('P. F.') in the *Kerryman*. Similarly, colour writers were applying themselves to All-Ireland events, and producing some memorable reports, such as those of Jacques McCarthy at the 1903 All-Ireland football final, an unnamed writer who attended the 1921 and 1922 finals for the *Irish Independent*, Gertrude Gaffney's account of the All-Ireland hurling final of 1931 for the same paper, and Brinsley McNamara's accounts of the 1937 finals in the *Irish Times*.[49]

The subsequent history of the GAA and its journalists has been one of enduring relationships. Surprisingly perhaps, the GAA had no full-time press officer until the appointment of Pat Quigley in the mid 1970s, albeit some of its previous general secretaries had been active part-time journalists, including Dineen and Luke O'Toole. Similarly Pádraig Ó Caoimh took an active interest in the prevailing GAA coverage of the day, including the approach adopted by broadcasters towards the sending-off of players or other unseemly incidents during the course of matches and, most famously, during the 1946 All-Ireland semi-final between Kerry and Antrim.[50] President Seán Ryan seems to have been behind the strange decision in 1929 to lock radio engineers out of the All-Ireland hurling final at Croke Park – a decision that was quickly overturned by the Central Council of the GAA. The association was already expressing pride in its hosting of the first field-broadcast of a sports event in Europe, and the first outside of Pittsburgh, when P. D. Mehigan commentated upon the 1926 All-Ireland semi-final for 2RN.[51] Problems continued, however. Central Council was unhappy with the commentaries of Éamonn De Barra, editor of *An Camán*, and prevented a live broadcast of the 1937 Railway Cup finals, and the following September's All-Ireland hurling final from Killarney. Instead de Barra and Seán Ó Ceallacháin, whose results programme had been aired without intermission since 1930, ran to the local post office from the ground with their notes to provide a simulcast of proceedings. A compromise seemed to have been found by the year's end when Fr Michael Hamilton, former chairman of Clare County Board and the man who instigated the 1947 Polo Grounds Final, was chosen to broadcast the All-Ireland football final. Despite his premature announcement of Cavan

SPORTS COVERAGE SURVEY OF THE BELFAST TELEGRAPH
(Issues 14-10-1982 — 30-10-1982 inclusive)   COVERAGE IN COLUMN INCHES

SPORTS	Th. 14/10	F. 15/10	Sa. 16/10	M. 18/10	Tue. 19/10	W. 20/10	Th. 21/10	F. 22/10	Sa. 23/10	M. 25/10	Tue. 26/10	W. 27/10	Th. 28/10	F. 29/10	Sa. 30/10	TOTAL	%
SOCCER	197.3	94.7	17	111.3	119.8	201.8	113.9	86.1	18	97.3	126	104.1	44.2	71	10.1	1472.6	29.4
HOCKEY	105.7	2.1	7.8	17.9	—	24.6	81.4	26.4	6.1	5.9	17.9	20.9	80.1	—	12.8	409.6	8.2
RUGBY	—	57.3	—	2.6	26.5	38.4	3.6	63.9	—	29.0	26.6	40.1	35.6	45.7	15.6	384.3	7.7
MOTORSPORT	22	34.2	8.7	37.2	16.6	45.4	15.5	20.9	—	24.7	52.7	20.1	36.9	29.7	—	364.6	7.3
GOLF	26.2	21.8	47.9	18.9	21.5	10.6	31.1	15.8	—	8.5	13.0	31.3	34.8	5.8	18.2	305.4	6.1
SNOOKER	—	3.3	79.1	12	4.0	5.0	12.9	3.8	57.4	5.0	6.5	5.6	30.4	—	70.5	296.5	5.9
EQUESTRIAN	3	5.1	—	—	170.2	—	40.4	—	—	2.9	2.2	—	8	21.8	6.2	293.8	5.9
CRICKET	—	4.4	31.8	19.8	10.4	—	—	21.8	57.9	35.8	9.8	45.1	18.9	14.1	10.8	280.6	5.6
DOG RACING	—	—	—	—	22.8	18	20.7	31.8	16.2	16.0	15.2	4.5	14.0	27.1	15.8	202.1	4.0
G.A.A.	—	21.6	—	26.8	—	15.6	—	17.7	—	25.1	—	10.8	—	20.9	—	138.5	2.7
BOXING	14.1	—	16	—	—	4.9	1.3	—	—	7.5	—	—	53.3	—	3.5	132.1	2.6
SQUASH	28.4	—	—	5.8	—	—	27.6	—	14.8	6.2	—	4.5	6.3	5.3	11.8	110.7	2.2
BOWLS	—	15.8	2	2.8	23.5	3.7	6.9	3.6	2.8	—	3.5	24.9	2	1.9	2.4	95.8	1.9
ANGLING	11.6	17.9	13.3	—	—	—	—	22.1	—	—	—	—	—	20.5	—	85.4	1.7
TABLE TENNIS	—	11.4	—	7.4	—	—	—	18	—	12.9	—	—	4.9	24.4	—	79.0	1.5
TENNIS	—	1.2	10.4	1.1	—	—	19.1	—	—	9.4	9.7	—				65.2	1.1
BASKETBALL	—	16.8	—	1.1	—	—	9.4	8.3	—	6.9	—						
ATHLETICS	—	16.8	7.7	2.4	—	—	—	—	—	1.6	—						
SWIMMING	—	—	5.5	—	—	—	—	—	—	—	25.2						
KARATE	—	—	—	—	—	—	31.4	—	—	5.1	—						
WATER POLO	5	3.0	—	10.3	—	—	—	—	—	6.1	—						
ROWING	—	—	—	—	—	—	—	—	24.3	—	—						
CYCLING	12.2	—	—	—	—	—	1.4	—	—	—	—						
SAILING	—	4.4	—	1.8	—	—	—	2.3	—	8.5	4.0						
BADMINTON	—	—	—	—	—	—	9.2	—	—	—	—						
NETBALL	—	—	—	—	—	—	—	—	—	—	10.1						
VOLLEYBALL	—	—	—	—	—	—	—	—	—	—	—						
SKI-ING	—	—	—	—	—	—	—	—	—	—	—						
HANDBALL	—	—	—	—	—	—	—	—	—	—	2.7						
DARTS	—	—	—	—	—	—	—	2.2	—	—	—						
BASEBALL	—	—	—	—	—	1.3	—	—	—	—	—						
OTHERS																	

The lack of coverage of Gaelic games generally in the northern Irish print and broadcast media, was long a bone of contention for GAA followers before a subcommittee of the Down County Board produced this meticulous and damning report in 1982. The report had a considerable impact in increasing the amount of coverage of Gaelic games in the region, but until recent times many GAA supporters believed that their favourite games were not given the amount of positive media publicity that they warranted.

A REPORT ON THE COVERAGE OF GAELIC GAMES IN THE NORTHERN MEDIA

by Down G.A.A. Communications Committee

as victors in the game – it ended in a draw – he was retained for the replay, but his career as a broadcaster did not survive the winter break. The search for a new voice of the GAA in 1938 turned up the teenage Micheál O'Hehir. The issue of who would choose the commentator never again arose between the GAA and Raidió Éireann.

The national broadcaster incurred the disfavour of the GAA again in 1954 nonetheless. The new issue was whether the GAA would share the St Patrick's Day broadcast on Radio Brazzaville with an inter-league soccer fixture. The GAA allowed the Railway Cup finals to go ahead without them being covered, but this time Raidió Éireann's position prevailed and relations were sufficiently restored with the director of RTÉ, Maurice Gorham, to deliver the new television body's first live sport at a nominal fee of £10.[52]

The presence of three journalists at the founding meeting of the GAA has helped create an intrigue about its birth. For a body established by just seven acknowledged individuals the GAA enjoyed enormous publicity during its first few months. Of course journalists cannot match schoolteachers in their contribution to the GAA as administrators. Cusack was also a schoolteacher and it is this profession that has dominated the GAA's administration ever since. But journalists have made their contribution in several ways that distinguish it from other sporting bodies. Newspapers created the context in which the GAA could be founded and could spread. In turn the GAA was the most active of several sports bodies established at the time in realising the potential of the print media, broadcasting and television in Ireland. The reward for historians of the GAA is the vast newspaper legacy created in relation to the association. They record the diligence and enthusiasm, the passions and the prejudices of the GAA writers of previous generations, many of their names lost to anonymity forever. That is their failing, yet simultaneously that is their beauty.

Camán and Crozier: The Catholic Church and the GAA 1884–1902

Simon Gillespie and Roddy Hegarty

To many followers of Gaelic games, the image of a member of the Roman Catholic hierarchy throwing in the ball or *sliotar* on All-Ireland final day is a familiar one, albeit no longer current. The throw-in was generally preceded by the bishop meeting and greeting the players when the latter would reverentially kneel to kiss the episcopal ring. Following this, a chorus of *Faith of our Fathers*, played by the Artane Boys Band, would take place followed in turn by the national anthem. This practice continued until 1979, when it was dispensed with for logistical rather than political or religious reasons. So as not to compromise the decorum of the bishop, it was subsequently decided to let the referee begin proceedings on All-Ireland final day. All too often the bishop's hat would fall off in the heavy gales of September, as he hurriedly made his way from the field of play. If one considers that this level of reverence towards the Roman Catholic clergy at key GAA occasions was until relatively recent times commonplace, it may be surprising to learn that the relationship between the church and the association was not always such a cordial one.

This chapter will attempt to provide an insight into the perceptions and attitudes of the Roman Catholic hierarchy in Ireland towards the GAA in the years 1884–1902 – the period of Archbishop Thomas Croke's patronage of the association, and arguably the time in which clerical influence reached its zenith in pre-partition Ireland. The various attitudes displayed by the key clerical figures of the period, how these were shaped and what consequences they had, will all be outlined. Consideration will be given to whether certain aspects of the GAA, such as (in)temperance at games, Sunday play and links to secret societies, caused the differences in clerical reaction from diocese to diocese. The chapter will touch briefly on some aspects of relations between the GAA and the Catholic Church at parochial level, but this subject will merit much greater study on another occasion.

The emergence of the GAA in the last quarter of the nineteenth century was contemporary with one of the most divided eras in Irish politics. The Fenian rising of 1867 was still fresh in the memory of many and the Home Rule campaign and opposition to this, particularly in Ulster, was being played out both on the national stage and at Westminster. From a political perspective, the GAA was conceived of a much more strident view of Irish nationalism than Charles Stewart Parnell's Irish Parliamentary Party, having as it did a sizeable contingent of Fenian activists. Scholars are divided, however, as to the number of physical force advocates that there were amongst its seven founders: Austin Reid claims four,[1] Mark Tierney five,[2] while the official historian of the GAA, Marcus de Búrca, argues that at least two of the seven founders of the association were then active members of the Fenian brotherhood.[3] Indeed the GAA's founding father, Michael Cusack, later claimed to have formerly been a member of the Fenians around the time of the 1867 uprising.[4]

Nationalism and the GAA would appear synonymous to many, particularly in post-partition Ireland. Yet the Catholic Church's response to more militant manifestations of Irish nationalism has at times given rise to a variegated relationship as that manifested itself in support for secretive or violent organisations. In her extensive and wide-ranging survey of Catholicism in Ulster Marianne Elliott makes only the slightest of reference to the relationship between the church and the GAA. Indeed for this period before partition that relationship is portrayed uniformly as one that witnessed the church taking increasing control of the association and employing the indigenous nature of Gaelic games and culture to emphasise the Irishness of Catholicism and the foreignness of Protestantism.[5] This, she argues, was facilitated by the GAA's ban on the playing of foreign games. Such a simplistic analysis of the relationship between the association and the Catholic Church demonstrates the lack of serious scholarship which exists for one of the most pivotal periods in modern Irish history relating to two of the largest influences on Irish society over the last century and a quarter.

To fully comprehend why the attitude of the Irish Catholic clergy should have had any influence upon the growth and development of a sporting organisation, with or without political affiliations, it is critical

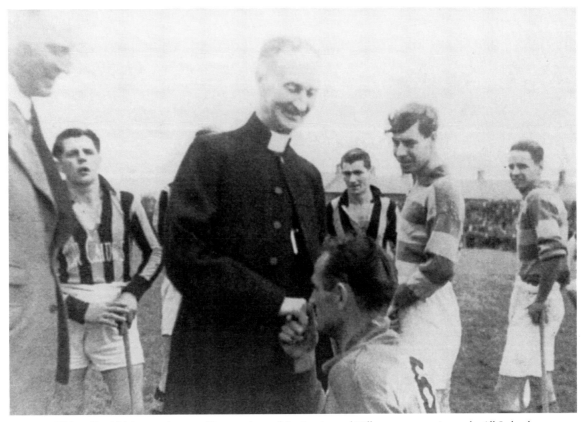

Bishop Daniel Mageean is greeted by members of the Antrim and Kilkenny teams prior to the All-Ireland semi-final at Corrigan Park, Belfast in 1943. (*Anna Harvey*)

to understand the extent to which the church's own position within Irish society had gained prominence in the mid nineteenth century. In the years after the Great Famine, the Catholic Church came to dominate political and religious life in Ireland to a level that would be difficult to overstate. This was the era of 'devotional revolution', as described by Emmet Larkin. As the structures of Irish life, particularly in rural areas, adjusted to the new economic and social realities of the post-famine decades, these changes were mirrored by an unprecedented growth in religious orders and numbers of clergy. The result of this was that Catholicism was much more visible and had the opportunity and personnel to allow it to extend its already considerable influence over the moral and political education of the Irish people. With a presence in virtually every parish in the country and with a sophisticated and structured hierarchy, Catholic Church leaders in Ireland found themselves increasingly drawn into the social and political life of the country during the last quarter of the nineteenth century.

Charles Stewart Parnell had constructed an effective, if informal, alliance between the Irish Parliamentary Party (IPP) and the Catholic Church to increase the popularity of the Home Rule movement. This effectively created a clerical support base for the nationalist cause, serving, indirectly, to a heightening of agrarian outrages during the 1880s. Many of the country's Catholics, who represented the overwhelming majority of the Irish people, may have believed that they had the backing of their church leaders in their defiance of landlordism.[6] To state that there was at least a tacit approval for the Home Rule cause is not to suggest that the Catholic Church in Ireland was supportive of Irish nationalism. On the contrary, some within the church could be described as ambivalent and at times hostile towards any form of separatist politics. It could be argued that some members of the episcopacy, for instance, Archbishop William J. Walsh suffered for their political opinion. Despite being the leading contender to succeed Archbishop McGettigan as Primate of All Ireland, Walsh was passed over in favour of the more politically neutral bishop of Raphoe, Michael Logue.

SUNDAY FOOTBALL PLAYING IN ARMAGH.

We re-print the following notice of an event which took place in our city on Sunday last ; and which appeared not in the slightest degree to have been noticed by the civil authorities :—During last week the dead walls of the city were covered with posters announcing that to-day a grand football match would be played in the Gaelic grounds here, between the Harps of Armagh and the John Dillons of Keady. This is only the second match played here, Gaelic football having but recently been introduced into Armagh. This morning at 8 o'clock Mass in St. Malachy's Chapel, his Grace the Primate preached, and in the course of his observations referred to the Gaelic Association, the working of which he strongly condemned. So far as we could ascertain, he said he did not object to young men engaging in football or hurling for a few hours on a Sunday afternoon, but he was opposed to their going away to play in places where they would have to mix with members of secret societies. Many of them, he had no doubt, were in the pay of the Government, who would do all they could to entrap them. He also said that he had received several complaints as regards the way the association is being worked in other places, and already in Louth the clergy had dis-associated themselves from it. Apart from other evils attendant on it, the system of going from one parish to another was a heavy drain on the slender resources of small farmers and others in the country whose sons are members of the association.

The match between the Harps and the John Dillons came off this afternoon, and was witnessed by nearly one thousand people, but probably this is the last time a distant team will visit Armagh to play Gaelic football.—*Cor. of News-Letter.*

Report of Archbishop Michael Logue's sermon against Gaelic games at St Malachy's chapel in Armagh in January 1888. (*Armagh Guardian*)

The emergence of the GAA during the last quarter of the nineteenth century was indicative of the change in Irish society. Indeed one could interpret the establishment of the association in 1884 as a natural product of an increasing self-confidence resulting from the growing prominence both of the Roman Catholic Church, the contemporary cultural revival and the increasingly nationalistic nature of politics in Ireland at that time. The evidence of this can been seen today in that many clubs and grounds affiliated to the GAA bear the names of religious figures or nationalist personalities who were prominent during the late nineteenth and early twentieth centuries. The symbolism of the GAA further reflects this in that it combines the political, patriotic and Gaelic with the religious. Even in the modern era most medals won by GAA members take the form of a Celtic cross, most clubs and some other branches have a clerical patron, and new grounds are typically blessed by a local priest prior to their official opening.

A close relationship between the church and the GAA was never a certainty, however, and in the period immediately following the foundation of the association clerical leaders seemed indifferent and even hostile towards a body with an expressed support for the pursuit of independence or separatism for Ireland. It is not at all surprising to find that in their attempts to popularise this new and national sporting organisation, the founders of the GAA approached a number of well known and highly respected figures from both walks of life to act as patrons.

Dr Patrick Duggan, Bishop of Clonfert, a central figure during the land agitation of the 1870s, was the initial clerical candidate for patronage of the GAA. By 1884, however, Bishop Duggan was an elderly man and increasingly prone to illness.[7] Instead, Duggan advised Michael Cusack to seek out Thomas W. Croke, Archbishop of Cashel and Emly, who (in Duggan's words) was 'a fine Gael, young, vigorous and energetic' to act in his stead, while Duggan promised to promote the success of such a 'fine, manly national movement'.[8] Two other nominees, Charles Stewart Parnell and Michael Davitt, both of whom were immensely popular figures within Irish society and politics at this time, wrote to Cusack accepting the invitation to become patrons of the GAA. It was Croke's letter of acceptance, however, which had a truly lasting effect on the GAA. His response to the request for his patronage has frequently been described as the founding charter for the association. The letter, written on 18 December 1884, was re-published along with the association's first set of rules in 1885, with the recommendation that it ought to be read as an order of the day at every general meeting of the GAA. In his reply to Cusack he wrote:

> I beg to acknowledge the receipt of your communication inviting me to become a patron of the Gaelic Athletic Association, of which you are, it appears, the Hon. Secretary. I accede to your request with the utmost pleasure.
>
> One of the most painful, let me assure you, and at the same time, one of the most frequently recurring reflections that, as an Irishman, I am compelled to make in connection with the present aspect of things in this country, is derived from the ugly and irritating fact, that we are daily importing from England, not only her manufactured goods, which we cannot help doing, since she has practically strangled our own manufacturing appliances, but, together with her fashions, her accents, her vicious literature, her music, her dances, and her manifold mannerisms, her games also, and her pastimes, to the utter discredit of our own grand national sports, and to the sore humiliation, as I believe, of every genuine son and daughter of the old land.
>
> Indeed if we continue travelling for the next score years in the same direction that we have been going in for some time past, condemning the sports that were practised by our own forefathers, effacing our national features as though we were ashamed of them, and putting on, with England's stuffs and broadcloths, her masher habits and such other effeminate follies as she may recommend, we had better at once, and publicly, abjure our nationality, clap hands for joy at sight of the Union Jack, and place 'England's bloody red' exultantly above the green.[9]

Croke's vision of a Gaelic Ireland was not shared by all of the Irish Catholic hierarchy, however. So why then, when at least some of their senior colleagues could be counted among the most ardent critics of the association in its early years, would two of the country's bishops appear to endorse the association in such glowing terms? The answer lies in the fact that the Catholic Church was itself eager to tackle several issues prevalent in Irish society at the end of the nineteenth century. One such example was the problem of intemperance, which was commonplace in Ireland in the 1880s. Many clergymen loathed the excessive consumption of alcohol that was all too frequent in rural and urban areas especially on the Sabbath. Intemperance was denounced with regularity from the pulpit and leading clerical figures saw the GAA as a vehicle that might be used to drive what Croke himself had described as the 'holy crusade against intemperance'.[10] Later under his advice the GAA banned alcohol from its meetings and this was very well received by the temperance movement who fully endorsed and promoted Gaelic sports and pastimes as an alternative to those events where the excessive consumption of alcohol was a feature.[11]

In establishing how the GAA was of importance to the church it is also necessary to analyse why the GAA needed the endorsement of church leaders. It must be remembered that in its infancy the GAA relied on athletics rather than hurling and football to provide its showcase events. The association may have hoped to benefit from the pre-existing structures of the church in promoting these activities to the public. If an organisation such as the GAA could be seen to draw on support not only from the Home Rule and Land League movements, as it had from its inception, but also from the church to which most of the country's population belonged, it could hope to count on a substantial public interest and involvement. If this had been the theory behind the association's approach to Duggan and subsequently to Croke then that decision may have been predicated more upon an ideal than a reality.

The GAA had, in its early days, been prospering despite the largely indifferent approach taken by members of the clergy towards the association and it could draw attendances of up to ten thousand people at its athletic contests without significant clerical involvement.[12] If, however, the association was simply seeking the public endorsement of the church then it may not have fully appreciated the price at which such approbation would be granted. Similarly for the church that relationship may have proved more complex than had been obvious at the time of Cusack's letter to Croke.

Croke's initial enthusiasm was to be tested by no less a figure than Michael Cusack himself. The Clare man was notoriously hot-headed and prone to bouts of extraordinary rhetoric. It would seem to have been only a matter of time before the cordiality struck by Croke's letter would be challenged. Relations began to sour between the editor of the *Freeman's Journal*, Edmund Dwyer Gray, and Michael Cusack. Cusack had, at the first annual convention of the GAA, condemned the *Freeman's Journal* for not reporting on GAA events. This was a rather strange action as other organisations such as the Irish Amateur Athletic Association had criticised the same newspaper for what it regarded as a bias in favour of the GAA.[13] On 15 March 1886 a statement, which became known as the North Tipperary resolution, and which was in all likelihood the work of Cusack, stated that 'we hereby call upon all Gaelic men to beware of the sporting representatives of the *Freeman*, and of all papers hostile to the national pastimes'.[14]

One of Cusack's accusations was that Gray had deliberately edited a speech by Dr Croke in which he had praised the work of the GAA. Croke subsequently wrote to the *Freeman's Journal*, exonerating it from Cusack's allegations and denouncing the North Tipperary resolution. Cusack was furious with the Archbishop's reaction, responding to Croke, 'as you have faced the Pope so I will with God's help face you and Gray'.[15] By now Cusack had become an embarrassment to the GAA's Central Council, on account of his constant feuding with figures in high office. In due course he was dismissed from the GAA's executive council for 'failing to keep accounts, answer letters and for being violent and offensive to anyone who had disagreed with him'. In so doing the GAA had sacked its own founder less than two years after its inception.[16] This was not to be the last of Cusack, however, and he would remain involved in GAA affairs periodically throughout the next few years and up to his death in 1906, often with controversial effect.

The Catholic episcopacy had for the first few years, with Croke as the exception, generally ignored the GAA. Indeed in a letter to the *Freeman's Journal*, in 1887, Croke hinted that he was planning to resign his own position as patron. He condemned the executive's ongoing row with the *Freeman's Journal*, and wrote, 'my connection with the association is fast drawing to a close. I shall however take the deepest interest in it'.[17] Further controversy loomed for the GAA, as throughout this period the reinvigorated Irish Republican Brotherhood (IRB) was positioning itself for a takeover of the organisation's Central Council, much to the

To be censured

Rettonism, very prevalent in Killean district & Meigh district also in Cloughoge = also football is a feeder to Rettonism, it interferes with Catechism, Rosary and meetings of S. Heart and leads to drink = Dances very frequent especially at Xmas, drink and immorality at same = Also leaders opposed to religion and opposed to religion's support are very numerous. In Killean district Thomas Sloan, Thomas Conyery Laurence Murphy, Owen Kenny In Cloughoge district, John D'Arch Terence Quin, Farrell, McGuirk Joseph Campbell who has been tried

Extract from the parish schedule for Upper Killeavy parish, Co. Armagh, returned by Fr Thomas Hardy who served as parish priest there from the establishment of the GAA in 1884 until 1902. It is most likely that this particular return dates from about 1890. (*CÓFLA parish schedules*)

Bishop Joseph MacRory pictured with the Gaelic football team from St Malachy's College, Belfast, in 1922. At the time MacRory was Bishop of Down and Connor and it is possible that this is one of the first formal photographs of a senior Irish clergyman along with a Gaelic team. (*Gilly McIlhatton*)

delight of the advanced nationalists within the association, and had now decided to make its move for control of the association.

At the annual convention of 1886 the IRB secured multiple positions on the executive and clearly signposted its political intentions by installing John O'Leary, the previously exiled Fenian, to the position of fourth patron of the association. The 1887 convention proved to be a decisive turning point in the political orientation of the GAA and was to be the most controversial in the organisation's history. The event created a 'split' in the GAA between the large IRB element and those factions of the association which had by that stage come under clerical influence. During the convention a priest, Fr Scanlan, had attempted to disrupt the gathering, being chaired by IRB member P. N. Fitzgerald, only to be 'hustled about' and insulted before finally withdrawing his supporters from the meeting. Following this drama the convention returned to its business and dubiously passed a resolution that 'the association shall be non political' to the extent that a motion of sympathy for the imprisoned MP William O'Brien was ruled out of order.[18] These events met with a predictable response from the Catholic clergy with Croke writing to the *Freeman's Journal* on 10 November 1887 stating that he refused to be associated with the new executive. 'I heard with deep regret and afterwards read with pain and humiliation an account of the proceedings of the Gaelic convention, held here on that day. Nothing then remains for me to do but to dissociate myself as I now publicly do from that branch of the Gaelic Athletic Association, which exercised such a sinister influence over yesterday's proceedings'.[19] Further hostile reaction from the clergy became widespread in the *Freeman's Journal* with several letters from the Scanlan faction accusing Fitzgerald and his supporters of being 'advanced men of one particular character … against the National League, against the Archbishop of Cashel, against the priesthood of Ireland'.[20] Croke also wrote to William J. Walsh, Archbishop of Dublin, stating 'I had as you have seen to break with the Gaelics, their meeting here was disgraceful. It was packed to the throat with Fenian leaders and emissaries, the priests made a bold but not a very effective stand'.[21]

The proceedings of the reconvened convention held in January 1888 to find a compromise between the two opposing groups, was to be in marked contrast to that held previously. Under the watchful eye of Croke, Maurice Davin was re-elected president of the GAA and a new constitution approved by Croke himself was accepted. Croke later summed up his feelings on the split in an entry in his diary: 'The Gaelic Athletic Association gave a great deal of trouble during the latter part of 1887. It was, however, grabbled [sic] with and finally settled satisfactorily at the convention in Thurles on 4 January 1888'.[22] It is ironic then that in the same month Archbishop Logue made one of his first pronouncements concerning the GAA. In a pastoral letter Logue condemned the GAA for its links with intemperance and desecration of the Sabbath: 'Laudable as the object may be if it can be gained only by the sacrifice of Sunday duties of the spirits of religion and the habits of temperance among our young men, it is not worth the price'.[23] This was a clear demonstration that the clergy and in particular the senior bishops did not have a consistent or uniform collective view of the association.

Although located in a different part of the country from Croke it is natural to question what circumstances may have influenced Archbishop Logue's decision to condemn by name the GAA. The record of parish priests' reports to Logue available to view in the Cardinal Ó Fiaich Library and Archive in Armagh begin to cast some light upon this. For the year 1888 there are a number of references from priests in the diocese regarding the negative impact of the GAA within the diocese. Canon James McGee of Dunleer parish reported, 'I wish to call attention to the harm to religion football is causing, it is leading the young men to drink … this game is also attended by the young girls, the result is they are brought into the company of young men with no good results … coming home at very late hours'.[24] At the same time, Rev. Patrick McGeeney reported that 'football matches on Sundays cause quarrels, accidents and drunkenness and keep children and others from Mass and catechism'.[25] In the neighbouring Dromore Diocese, Fr Rooney, preaching in Newry Cathedral in April 1889, attributed the decline in Sunday church numbers to 'This football playing on Sundays which is the invention of the devil for the purpose of destroying souls and is the cause of much drunkenness and quarrelling'.[26] Similarly in the Kilmore diocese in south-west Ulster one of the few clerical GAA stalwarts in Cavan, Rev. Francis Teevan, controversially resigned from the GAA following the deterioration in behaviour of several club members at tournaments and claimed that 'on account of the drunkenness, disorder and consequent desecration of the Sabbath begotten by matches … I feel it is my duty as a priest to withdraw altogether from the GAA'.[27]

In the midst of these denunciations Archbishop Walsh of Dublin made one of his first public pronouncements on the GAA. In response to a letter published in the *Times* newspaper in London, which stated that the episcopacy had condemned the GAA, not only did Walsh completely distance himself from these sentiments but stated that 'I am fully aware that efforts have been made in some parts of Ireland to engraft upon the Gaelic Athletic Association a secret society of a political character. Let its members follow the advice of the Archbishop of Cashel that they may laugh at the foolish intrigues and plotting of their enemies.'[28] Walsh and Croke, of course, oversaw dioceses in parts of the country with substantial Catholic majorities. Logue and his Ulster bishops by contrast had to contend with the potential for public criticism by their Protestant neighbours, many of whom had been greatly influenced by the religious revivals of the previous generation and for whom sabbatarianism and temperance were fundamental both to religious practice and public life.

Notwithstanding all the aforementioned causes for clerical complaint, what would almost instantly lead to the GAA's near collapse was its unflinching, relentless support for Parnell and Parnellism over the next few years. Parnell had made only a limited contribution to the GAA as its patron. When, in December 1889 he was named as a co-respondent in the O'Shea divorce case, most people and in particular the clergy hoped that, as in the case of the earlier Pigott forgeries, which had erroneously and maliciously linked Parnell to the Phoenix Park Murders, these charges would be dismissed. Crucially, however, the verdict against Mrs O'Shea and Parnell was delivered on 17 December 1890. It was to have far-reaching and disastrous implications at a number of levels. When the news broke, Dr Croke was returning home to Ireland from the Vatican, and he wrote to Archbishop Walsh stating that 'it is fortunate for me, that I had left Rome before this sad catastrophe had occurred. The Pope would surely 'have at me' about it for he had a personal dislike somehow to Parnell, and was not pleased with me for having constantly defended him.'[29]

At this point the GAA decided overwhelmingly to nail its colours to the Parnell mast. At a GAA meeting in Dublin, chaired by Michael Cusack, sixteen Dublin clubs passed a motion of confidence in Parnell.[30] GAA members throughout the country were also instrumental in the setting up of various Parnell leadership committees.[31] The president of the GAA, and IRB member, Peter Kelly, stated that 'the Gaels and the hillside men would stand or fall by Parnell'.[32] Throughout 1891 the country was politically polarised. Croke, in a letter to Walsh wrote, 'the issue is Parnell or no Parnell. There can be no compromise – there is no medium possible'.[33]

At a parochial level the GAA was to endure a new level of vitriol from the clergy. One of the association's strongest opponents was, somewhat ironically, Dr Patrick Duggan's coadjutor Bishop of Clonfert, Dr John Healy, who appeared to take a particular dislike to the GAA. By February 1891 Healy was to the fore of episcopal opposition towards the GAA, which prompted by Pat Flynn, the prominent IRB and GAA stalwart, to threaten that should Healy come to Sooey in Co. Sligo, 'there would be 200 men lying in wait for him'.[34] The Archbishop of Tuam, John MacEvilly, wrote to Bishop Gilhooly of Elphin in March 1891, lamenting the prevailing political climate, wondering,

> Are we not fallen on awful times? It will take all the united efforts to stop the evil, rely on it if he [Parnell] and his hillsiders succeed religion will suffer … I was always at our meetings against the Gaels … some of our more prominent men made nothing against it [a reference to Croke] … the Gaels or rather Fenians are our greatest cross.[35]

Parnell's untimely death at the age of just forty-five did little to resolve the controversy. Reactions to Parnell's passing in October 1891 varied dramatically. The *Freeman's Journal* reported that 80,000 people had come out to see Parnell lying in state. Twelve pallbearers, representing the GAA carried Parnell's coffin for a period during the procession while two thousand members of the GAA, with 'cámans draped in black', led the cortege with 'splendid military precision'.[36] Leading members of the GAA were in the fourth carriage of the funeral cortege and were joined by members of the IRB. In this carriage were GAA patron and Fenian John O'Leary, IRB and GAA members P. N. Fitzgerald and James Stephens, and two of the GAA's founders, Michael Cusack and John Wyse Power. Parnellism though was not to die with Parnell. The grief-stricken Gaels left a message intended to be read by the clergy on a wreath by the graveside of Parnell, in purported revenge for their fallen patron. It was sure to be understood by those who had, in their opinion, murdered Parnell. Quoting from the Book of Matthew, it simply read, 'an eye for an eye, a tooth for a tooth'.[37]

By 1892, however, the GAA was faced with more urgent concerns than exacting revenge for the treatment afforded Parnell as it had fallen into total disarray at an administrative level. County conventions and championships were not staged, in many cases, until 1893, if at all.[38] At the 1891 annual convention, delayed until January 1892, Patrick Tobin, the secretary of the GAA, noted how 'in 1888 the GAA was in its heyday of its existence with close on 1000 affiliated clubs … [but] in 1891 the total came down to 220'.[39] Nor was there any significant sign of improvement for the GAA in 1893.[40] However by 1894 some level of revival was apparent within the association as several counties began to re-organise. However, according to historian William Mandle, this was merely a result of the IRB's resurgent participation in the GAA.[41]

Instead several GAA historians identify the year 1895 as a turning-point in the fortunes of the association. This was to be the year when the GAA firmly moved away from the political arena and focused more on its *raison d'être*: the promotion of Gaelic games and Irish culture. Some suspicion amongst the clergy persisted, however, as in April 1895 the GAA received fresh criticism from Bishop Coffey of Kerry, who withdrew his permission for a Gaelic football tournament in Killarney, to be held on Easter Sunday in aid of the Sisters of Mercy. The bishop claimed that the GAA was again connected with 'secret societies' and was therefore unworthy of his patronage. Coffey, who had previously been described by Croke as 'a rank Tory', incurred a very public admonishment from Croke for his outburst.[42] Dr Croke issued a statement in support of the GAA and dismissing Coffey's remarks: 'As far as I know … the Association is purely an athletic body and that alone … [A]s regards the statement made by Dr Coffey that the GAA was connected

Cardinal MacRory presenting the MacRory Cup to the captain of St Patrick's College, Armagh, following their victory over St Macartan's College, Monaghan in 1931. The trophy was first presented in 1923 but the Ulster colleges competition had begun in 1917/18. Previously St Patrick's and St Macartan's had played each other in annual soccer games, until around 1917 the Armagh pupils refused to continue these games.

with secret societies, I am totally unaware of it and surprised that Dr Coffey had made such a statement, as far as I know he has no foundation for it'.[43] In July of this same year Croke celebrated his silver jubilee as a Catholic bishop. In celebration, a special Gaelic games competition, the Croke Cup, was established in 1896. This competition continued up to 1915,[44] but there is still a Croke Cup today as the prize for the All-Ireland senior colleges' hurling final each year. Most of all, Croke's name would become forever synonymous with Gaelic sports as a result of the renaming of the Jones' Road stadium as Croke Park in 1913 – a fitting tribute to his contribution to the association.

Croke's death in July 1902 was an occasion of great sadness for the GAA as he had been patron of the GAA for seventeen years. As a mark of respect all matches due to be played the following Sunday were postponed. There was a huge GAA presence at the funeral that included all of the members of the Central Council and several county board delegations.[45] Croke was succeeded as Archbishop of Cashel and Emly, as well as patron of the GAA, by Dr Thomas Fennelly, although Archbishop Walsh of Dublin had been the first choice of the GAA's Central Council.[46] It is a mark of how far the relationship between the GAA and Catholic Church had evolved by this time that, during his installation as Archbishop of Tuam on St Patrick's Day 1903, Dr Healy, formerly of the Diocese of Clonfert and one of the fiercest critics of the association, welcomed a GAA delegation to congratulate him on his appointment. Indeed during the course of his address Archbishop Healy expressed his 'warm sympathy with the GAA movement to develop the rigour, discipline and strength of our race'.[47]

Throughout the period 1884–1902 there was a significant variation in attitudes from the clergy towards the GAA. These ranged from staunch support to complete indifference and even vehement opposition to the association. This range in attitudes from the bishops and priests is not exclusive to the GAA but is rather typified by it. The clergy was split on many issues, the GAA being only one such example of this division. The mollification of the more condemnatory of these can in part be explained by the more settled state of political affairs in Ireland by the turn of the twentieth century. The Home Rule movement was beginning to coalesce once more around the figure of John Redmond and in turn seemed to have won the support of the Liberal Party in Britain. Physical-force nationalism appeared to be, for a time at least, on the wane. Perhaps with control of the GAA having been wrested away from what the church saw as dangerous elements, the tacit support and even public association of the clergy with the GAA at last had time and space to develop without contention.

The period covered in this chapter was one of great change in Ireland. The rural population continued to decline, while urbanisation and to a degree industrialisation began to makes its mark. This was a time of challenge for the church as it was for society at large. The contrasting opinions of the episcopacy on these, as on other matters at this time, are perhaps indicative of a lack of a clear hierarchical structure, which allowed each bishop the freedom to decide his own views on such matters, without directives from their archbishops or consultation with their episcopal peers. In fact, no single, coherent attitude towards the GAA was adopted by the Catholic Church during this period; rather there were disparate responses depending on the attitudes of individual members of the clergy, varying circumstances within different dioceses and the GAA, and, crucially at times, the opinion of the local bishop.

The Freedom of the Field: Camogie before 1950

Regina Fitzpatrick, Paul Rouse and Dónal McAnallen

Much work remains to be done in researching the history of camogie in Ireland. No substantial history of the game exists and such published work as has been produced raises as many questions as it does answers. The relative importance of class, education, geography, politics and personality in the development of camogie through the twentieth century needs to be assessed. These issues are raised in this chapter, which is intended as an overview of the first five decades of camogie in Ireland, with a particular emphasis on Ulster. It is hoped that the issues which are raised here will be taken on and that the game of camogie will receive the attention from historians which it merits.

When the GAA was founded, it was pledged that the new association would be open to men of every class. Speaking at the inaugural meeting, Maurice Davin made particular reference to men from poorer backgrounds, who, he related, seemed to be condemned to a life which was little more than an endless round of labour. That women might also have wished to play the sports organised by the GAA does not seem to have occurred to the founders. There should be no great surprise in this. In the propaganda which attended the sporting revolution of the late nineteenth century, most notably in Victorian Britain, it was the crucible of sport which made boys into men. The playing field was posited as the perfect academy for learning the virtues of courage, vigour, strength and stamina considered vital to a successful life.[1] All the major sporting organisations which emerged in Europe and North America during this period were dominated by men. The GAA was no exception.

That is not to say that women were not involved in the early years of the GAA. Far from it. Women turned up in their droves to football and hurling matches throughout the 1880s and 1890s. The GAA welcomed their attendance, hence they were usually admitted for free or at a discounted price. Both their presence and their finery were commented on frequently in newspaper reports. According to Michael Cusack, Tipperary women turned up at hurling matches, dressed in their 'gala attire to flash looks and smiles of approval on their rustic knights.'[2] Cusack noted that those women were

> amongst the most earnest admirers of the play. Indeed so much taken was one of them with the dexterity and skill of the play, that she expressed her regret they were not eligible for election as members of the GAA, because, she said, if they could not play itself, they could decorate the jerseys for the boys.[3]

This statement was clearly reflective of the wider sentiments of society. Women's involvement in sport was perceived to be decorative in function.[4] Young adult women were expected to be devoted to their families first and foremost, as hard-working housewives and mothers. Wealthy women, who might have been expected to lead a sporting movement for women, usually held other priorities. Fashions came and went, but it was considered vulgar to have a robust fitness. Science fuelled a belief that men and women were complementary opposites. It was widely held that excessive sporting activity could diminish a woman's capacity to procreate.[5] Such attempts as were made by women to organise sport for themselves were routinely sneered at, or were simply ignored.

Undaunted nonetheless, some women in Britain, America and certain other countries began to organise their own competitive sports. The emergence of modern codified and formally organised sports for men in the late nineteenth century, stirred the interest of some women to emulate them – a 'me-too' feminism, as described by Richard Holt.[6] Developments in technology and communications in the late nineteenth century enabled these intrepid young women to engage in sporting pursuits. The invention of the 'safety' bicycle afforded some women with a new degree of physical mobility and freedom. From the 1880s onwards two sports in particular came to be popular among women in Britain and America: lawn tennis, which had women's competitions at Wimbledon and the U.S. Open from 1884 and 1887 respectively; and hockey, in

A youthful camogie team, possibly from north Antrim. (*Éamonn McMahon*)

which a proliferation of schools' teams and clubs led to the founding of the All-England Women's Hockey Association in 1895. Among the other sports participated in by women in the late nineteenth century were croquet, badminton, yachting, rowing, archery, golf, ballooning, cricket and baseball. Several female competitors, most of them from the host country, took part in the 1900 Olympic Games in Paris – despite the disapproval of the father of the modern Olympics, Baron Pierre de Coubertin. The critical criterion for the social acceptance of a sport for women was whether it was perceived as too strenuous or dangerous. Most of those listed above gained general acceptance over time, overcoming various reservations that were held about them. Sports like athletics and football, however, would take many more years to convince the public that they were suitable for women.

In Ireland, change came slowly, but by the end of the nineteenth century the boundaries had begun to shift. Wider changes in Irish society brought change to the playing of sport. Women were appearing in far greater numbers than previously in secondary schools, in teacher training colleges, in universities and in the civil service by 1900. As these emancipated women sought their own place in the world, sport played a significant part in shifting the perceptions of what a woman was capable of doing. This shift involved a leap over the sideline and onto the playing field. Due to their popularity elsewhere and particularly in Britain, it was natural that tennis, golf and hockey numbered among the first competitive field-sports to be taken up in earnest by Irishwomen.[7] With their class and imperial connotations, however, these sports were held in disregard by a large section of Irish nationalists. The reintroduction of the GAA's ban on certain sports of English origin from January 1903 increased the stigma around these games. So it became expected that to be a patriotic Irishman or woman was to eschew sports like soccer and hockey. If Irish nationalist women were to take part in sport and gain approval for it, they would have to follow the GAA's example and innovate.

The birth of camogie was an initiative which was framed by the involvement of women in the Gaelic

League. The League was founded in 1893 with the promotion of the Irish language as its principal objective, but branches were also committed to the promotion of all aspects of Irish culture. Many male League members were involved with the GAA. Female members of the League in turn resolved to play ladies' hurling. One account traces the game back to an exhibition match among League members from Navan, Co. Meath, as part of a local commemoration of the 1798 rebellion, at a field near the Hill of Tara.[8] We must look to 1903 for the recognised birth-date of the game, however. The Keating Branch of the Gaelic League in Dublin already had prominent male hurling and football teams. In 1903 a group of women members, including many who had travelled from various parts of Ireland to work in Dublin, determined to play the game of hurling. Led by university graduate Máire Ní Chinnéide, a code of rules that was based on hurling was devised. The rules of hurling were amended in ways that were considered to make the game more suitable to women – and this game was renamed *camóguidheacht* (or *camógaíocht*), roughly translated as 'junior hurling',[9] but more commonly abbreviated to 'camogie' in common English-language usage. The *camóg* (or stick) and *sliotar* were to be smaller and lighter than the equivalent equipment used by the men. The pitch was shortened so that its dimensions were to stand between 60 and 100 yards in length and between 40 and 60 yards in width. The number of players per team was set at twelve, in recognition of the possible difficulties in getting sufficient numbers of women to play. Unique amongst the rules was one which cited as a foul the deliberate stopping of the ball with the long flowing skirts then fashionable amongst early players.

The women of the Keating Branch began their practices in the summer of 1903, first in Drumcondra Park, and later in the Phoenix Park. The founding of another club, Cúchulainns, in Dublin in early 1904, allowed for the staging of the first recorded camogie match in July of that year. The game was played at the Meath Agricultural Society Grounds (later Páirc Tailteann), and Keating's claimed victory by a single goal to no score.[10] Camogie was spreading quickly. The first club in Ulster (Fág-an-Bealach) – and reputedly the second in Ireland – was formed in Newry,[11] and the game was even played in Glasgow in 1904.[12] By the end of 1904 there were five teams playing in an organised league in Dublin. The progress was sufficient to allow for the formal establishment of An Cumann Camógaíochta (the Camogie Association), with Máire Ní Chinnéide as president, at 8 North Frederick Street in Dublin on 25 February 1905. The impetus created led to more clubs being established around Dublin. 1905 also saw the first camogie clubs emerge in Cork[13] and Dundalk,[14] and the sport began to make inroads into Belfast, after the West End *craobh* of the Gaelic

Ardoyne's first camogie team in 1909. (*Joe Lavery*)

League organised a team to go to play Newcastle (Co. Down) at Feis an Dúin. The thinking behind this initiative, as with so many early camogie endeavours, was that 'if women can play hockey and golf there is no earthly reason why their more patriotic sisters should not gain healthy exercise by participating in this ancient Irish game'.[15] By the summer of 1906 there were regular practices on Tuesday evenings at Seaghan's Park, Belfast.[16] Parallel to this there was a flurry of play in Derry. A 'ladies' camoguidheacht match' took place at an *aeridheacht* in Derry City on St John's Eve (23 June) 1905,[17] and a couple of Gaelic League-based teams were organised in the following months. In March 1906 it was also claimed that Omagh (Co. Tyrone) and Moville (Co. Donegal) 'already have their Camoguidheacht clubs'.[18] Meanwhile, the game also reached Co. Monaghan[19] and Co. Galway, where the hope was expressed that the new club at Uachtar Ard 'will keep our fair sex from trying to imitate the accent and manners of the local gentry'.[20] By 1908 Ballymoyer and Lissummon had teams in Co. Armagh,[21] and the game was played in Co. Cavan.[22] It appears that camogie had spread more widely in Ulster than in any other province.

The influence of the Gaelic League was underlined by the appearance of the game in areas where hurling was not well established, and also by the fact that, more so than their GAA menfolk, camogie teams were prone to adopt names from Irish mythology and literature, as well as female saints. Like the League, camogie prospered most in urban centres. There was, moreover, a healthy social life associated with the game. For example, in 1909 the camogie players of Crokes club in Dublin joined the club's hurlers on a trip to the Devil's Glen in the Wicklow mountains, and organised to play a camogie game there; and in 1910 the Ardoyne camogie team had an outing on charabanc to Hazelwood, outside Belfast.[23]

If the rapid spread of camogie in the 1900s was like the GAA's 'prairie fire' of the 1880s, it burnt out even quicker than the first phase of the men's association. Within a short space of time it perished in most of the above mentioned counties. There were the practical difficulties in spreading a stick-and-ball game. After all, the GAA had much more success in diffusing Gaelic football among men than it had in promoting hurling. There were also hostile attitudes to women playing the game. Early camogie players were pioneers who flew in the face of public opinion; many of them hid their hurls under their coats as they travelled to play, in order to deflect ridicule from the wider populace. One of the men who did much to assist the development of camogie in Dublin, Seán O'Duffy, a Mayo native who was a leading hurler and official with Crokes club, wrote to the press that the growth of the game was largely 'unaided and unorganised', and hindered by 'adverse circumstances'.[24] The challenges faced by those trying to promote camogie were legion, and were not always overcome. Even when progress was made, it was sometimes lost at a later date. For example, the league which was started in Dublin in 1904 fell into abeyance and the cup which had been presented initially went missing. The sporting aesthetics of camogie were found wanting as well. In these early years, skills were scarcely developed, the ball stayed close to the ground most of the time, few goals were scored and even fewer points. Games often appeared little more than random scrambles between well-intentioned women in ill-suited outfits, huddled over the ball, swinging to hit it as far as possible, without aiming to pass to anyone in particular.[25] By 1910, the sport had drifted into stagnation in Dublin. By contrast, six Belfast clubs formed a camogie board in that year, with an all-female administration.[26]

In April 1911 letters to the Dublin newspapers signalled a new attempt to put camogie on a sound footing. A letter from one player, Cáit Ní Dhonnchadha, outlined the motivation for their endeavour: 'We want something to supplement the ballroom and the skating rink. We want to organise the womanhood of Ireland into one grand body, whose sole object, under that of national emancipation, would be the raising of the sex from the slough of a false and foreign civilisation.'[27] The letter announced a meeting to reorganise the association and revise its rules, at the Calaroga Hall, Rutland Square, Dublin. On 21 April 1911 An Cumann Camógaíochta was relaunched at a meeting attended by thirteen Dublin clubs. Eleanor, Dowager Countess of Fingal, was appointed president, and declared: 'I will be delighted to do anything I can to help what I consider a splendid work, for I believe if we could make the boys' and girls' lives in Ireland more happy and cheerful we would keep many more of them at home.'[28] The association's new chairman, Mrs Hamilton, stated that ladies should have their own form of recreation which would give healthy exercise, counteract the evils of living in a city and make them better and nobler living. The potential of the game

Cumann na mBan Hurling Cub, Newry, 1918. The naming of this club, apparently after a republican female auxiliary body, was one of several radical associations of camogie. (*Noel Haughey*)

to improve women's health was stressed in the newspapers too. One journal argued that with a little organisation, camogie could provide 'a means of recreation for many hundreds of indoor workers in Dublin'.[29]

This time a determined effort was made to establish the game on a nationwide basis and by the middle of 1912 camogie matches were being played regularly in each of the four provinces. The game was dominated by single women, who were students, graduates or out at work. The first official inter-county game was played in that summer of 1912, when Dublin defeated Louth by 2-1 to 0-0 at Jones's Road. The Louth team was based on a Dundalk club that had written to the reorganisation meeting of 1911, pledging a willingness to help in any way possible. It says much for the profile of the game in Dublin that when newspapers published photographs of the two teams, the caption referred to 'Irish ladies' new Gaelic game'. The match was played as a part of a wider *aeridheacht* involving music and song and dance. Dublin was considered much the stronger team, playing more scientifically, although all the players were hampered by constant slipping caused by having no studs on their boots.[30] An estimated four thousand people were present. Other early camogie games also attracted large crowds, even if no prize or previous rivalry existed. The novelty of seeing girls playing hurling was a big 'pull' factor.[31] Alas for promoters of the game, by 1914 the organisation of camogie itself slipped away again in most counties where it had recently appeared.[32]

Then, in 1915, the first national camogie competition, an inter-varsity championship, was initiated, with the Ashbourne Cup as the prize. The trophy was donated by Lord Ashbourne (Edwin Gibson), a rather eccentric nationalist who often wore a kilt. He was reputedly prompted to do so by Agnes O'Farrelly, a lecturer in Modern Irish Poetry at University College Dublin, a prominent Gaelic Leaguer, and a native of Mullagh, Co. Cavan.[33] She would serve as president of the UCD Camogie Club from 1914 to 1951. The Ashbourne Cup remained the leading camogie competition, albeit small and confined, up to the early 1930s. By comparison with other women, female students had more leisure time and access to suitable facilities to play the game. In those first two decades, University College Cork won the title more often than not, but the other participants, UCD and University College Galway, both recorded several successes.

The adoption of camogie by convent schools from the late 1920s was a crucial development to the long-term sustainability of the sport. These images were taken at the Dominican Convent in Portstewart, Co. Derry.

The cup was reputedly destroyed during the disturbances of Easter 1916, but quickly replaced.[34] Every year thereafter without fail, the names of all winning players were inscribed in Irish on the plinth of the cup, thus reinforcing the ties between camogie and the language revival.[35] The presentation of the Dr Merriman Cup for Cork schools, by a UCC professor in 1917, gave an important boost to the burgeoning schools' camogie scene in that county,[36] and emphasised the centrality of the universities to the propagation of the game. The Ashbourne Cup encapsulated much of the social side of camogie: exciting trips, hearty receptions and dances, and a couple of games as well. College journals of the time are littered with hints of romances initiated at finals weekends.[37] Yet teams were usually chaperoned, and impeccably behaved.[38]

The Camogie Association had a firm nationalist outlook. A letter from Cáit Ní Donnchadha and Seán O'Duffy to the *Evening Telegraph* newspaper outlined the broader vision which underpinned the game:

> Notwithstanding the excellence of certain foreign games, it is obvious that the country at large, and the city of Dublin in particular, would be strengthened and purified by our women cherishing and practising games of native origin and growth. The energy displayed by so many Irish ladies in advocating women's rights proves that active forces are still to be won over to national objects. I would respectfully suggest to those ladies to devote portion of their organising energy and resources towards ameliorating the lot of their less fortunate sisterhood, who toil in vitiated shops, stores, warerooms, etc. and whose social life needs brightening. … The realisation of such an ideal would naturally give rise to a more independent and more self-respecting race. When we have secured national freedom – which is the goal of all true Irish women, no matter how they may differ in trivial matters – let us have our own national pastime as an essential element of our existence as a nation.[39]

Later, Seán O'Duffy fought in North King Street during the 1916 Rising, and was detained in Stafford Gaol.[40] Participation in camogie could also bring young women into defiance of the authorities. Joining a camogie club brought a few young women closer to the female republican auxiliary body, Cumann na mBan.[41] Like the GAA, camogie officials refused to apply for police permits when public meetings were prohibited. When Crown forces barred entry to Croke Park on 'Gaelic Sunday', 1918, a game of camogie was played on the road outside. The name of the 'Cumann na mBan Camogie Club' of Newry in 1919 at least suggested a republican allegiance on its part.

With the GAA concentrating on organising games for men, An Cumann Camógaíochta and its players were quite reliant on the Gaelic League for support. The GAA could have done more to help, but leading camogie officials preferred to retain their autonomy – though never independent in the true sense. Occasionally, GAA branches or officials rendered assistance, and in some cases their offers were spurned. In 1917 the Dublin GAA board offered to run the city's camogie league and its financial affairs, but the league officials declined, on the basis that as a subcommittee of one association it could not affiliate to another body. The GAA board aided camogie in various ways over the years anyhow.[42]

Despite much turmoil on the streets, camogie still made steady progress in Dublin in the early 1920s. A record number of teams were competing in the Dublin colleges' leagues. In 1922 the first officially designated camogie grounds became available at Phoenix Park. In the city the game was played mostly over a winter-spring season, because it was regarded as too much an 'ordeal' to play in the summer 'under the broiling sun', and better to allow players off on their holidays.[43] More regular practices enabled players to become more adept at skills such as volleying the *sliotar* in the air, as demonstrated in a cinema newsreel of 1922.[44] Camogie matches were also played at the Tailteann Games in 1924 and 1928. The game proved to be remarkably popular among the Irish in British cities in the 1920s. The sheer symbolism of the *camóg* seems to have reassured girls of their Irishness in an unfamiliar or alien urban environment. Some started to play the game in Britain, despite not having played (or had the opportunity to play) it in their rural parishes in Ireland; for example, one woman recalled that she got introduced to the game through meeting a girl carrying a *camóg* on the London 'tube' in the 1930s.[45]

Yet elsewhere any progress being made by the association was negligible. In Belfast the game was scarcely played at all between 1914 and 1927, and in rural areas (and hence most counties) it barely existed, making little progress in the 1920s.[46] In fact, in 1923/24 Wicklow was the only county that had an active camogie scene outside of Dublin.[47] There were many reasons for these difficulties: a chronic lack of funding for the game; gate-receipts were virtually unobtainable; a lack of transport in rural areas; a lack of suitable playing facilities; and a shortage of leisure time for young women to attend practices or meetings, due to their long working hours as domestic servants, mill-workers and so on. There were also concerns that the sport was unladylike. A strong body of global opinion endured against female participation in sport that was vigorous or immodest of dress; it was only in 1928 that the Olympic Games began to include contests for women in the more strenuous pursuits, chiefly track-and-field athletics, which Pope Pius XI said were 'irreconcilable with woman's reserve'.[48] The contemporary camogie uniform was uncontroversial though: it consisted of a gymfrock that covered the knee, a white blouse, long black stockings and even a beret for some,[49] so only the face and forearms were bare. Some girls simply thought the game would be 'too rough' for them, and shied away from it.[50] For similar reasons many Irish Catholic convent schools opted for less forceful games like hockey instead; this disappointed Gaelic games enthusiasts, who had got used to most clerical-run boys' schools promoting Gaelic games. In many areas girls joined in with boys playing hurling informally,[51] and it was no coincidence that many successful camogie players were the brothers or daughters of successful hurlers. Generally, any mixed play was informal and uncontentious. In UCG, however, a 'men's camogie team', formed in 1923/24, incurred the chagrin of both the college hurling club and the lady players – who, after the initial novelty value, found it detrimental to have 'an enormous swain or a possible Apollo in pursuit of the leather' alongside them – and the experiment ended swiftly.[52]

For most of the second half of the 1920s, the Irish countryside saw no camogie other than one-off challenge games and tournaments, most often on the programme of a cultural festival or sports-day.[53] Around 1928 the game began to turn the corner. The founding of a county camogie board in Galway was a considerable development. The 1929 annual congress of the Camogie Association launched a new rulebook. Amendments to the existing rules were made, and it was recommended that an additional crossbar be introduced at the top of the point posts, to put a height limit on point-scoring. Antrim and Dublin were noted among the few champions of the top crossbar, but it did not prove popular.[54] Despite the production of this new rulebook and the attempt to regularise the sport on a national level, it remained that some camogie clubs played by the camogie rules and others by the GAA rules of hurling.[55]

That nuns and convent schools were gradually warming to the sport did a lot to improve its fortunes,[56] not least in Ulster. An Ulster colleges' camogie competition, inaugurated in 1929, comprised convent schools such as St Louis', Kilkeel; St Louis', Ballymena; Cross and Passion, Ballycastle; and Poor Clare's, Newry. St Mary's Training College fielded its first camogie team in 1929, and in 1931 it ran a seven-a-side house league, comprising seven teams.[57] Due to the strict rules of St Mary's and the apathy of its authorities towards sport, however, the college dropped out of competitive camogie for the next three decades.[58] In Leinster the Brigidine convents' camogie league also did much to elevate the game.

The 1930s was a defining decade for camogie. It saw an explosion of participation in camogie nationwide. New clubs and teams were formed in almost every county, and the sport developed a proper local administrative structure for the first time, through the establishment of county boards and provincial councils. There was also an increase in the number of women organising and officiating at their own games, and the development of the game outside of Ireland. Two initiatives early in the decade were critical to the development of the game: the standardisations of the rules of the game and the establishment of an All-Ireland championship.

One of the main underlying reasons for the 1930s camogie boom was the rising tide of cultural nationalism. The upsurge in Gaelic cultural revivalism at the start of this decade had resonances of that of three decades earlier which had originally given birth to camogie. A rapid growth in participation in Gaelic games generally, and in Gaelic League activity, in the early 1930s, created more favourable circumstances for camogie to take root. Individual GAA officials, and the GAA as an organisation, gave more active support to camogie, as they saw the necessity of getting more women involved in the project of re-Gaelicising the nation. In their view it would be futile to demand the full commitment of the menfolk to restoring a Gaelic Ireland if their wives and daughters were not similarly committed.[59] Such thinking certainly informed the

Camogie Association members from Antrim standing in formation at a ceremony. Camogie quickly came to mean a lot to its players in terms of their personal, local and national identities. (*Éamonn McMahon / Catherine O'Hara*)

sudden expansion of camogie in Ulster. A southern visitor wrote of how he 'knew Belfast was part of Ireland still' when he saw girls playing the game there, and he realised 'what a perfect medium camogie is, as a step-together movement for the rising generation of Irish womanhood'; camogie 'could be the centre and shield around which the women of Ireland could give expression to their latent genius'.[60] In view of this emotional impact on some ideologues, the prominence of male nationalist figures in Belfast especially was understandable; all ten of the Antrim County Camogie Board chairmen between 1928 and 1948 were indeed men, and several had connections with nationalist and republican politics.[61] Former IRA leader Dan Breen was equally to the fore in the extraordinary growth of camogie in New York from the turn of the 1930s. The seven teams in New York in 1931 included those adopting the names of Cavan, Leitrim, Roscommon and Longford. The irony was that the original counties of these names in Ireland were still barren of camogie.[62]

The need to standardise the codes of play was a central reason why a special convention was held at 41 Parnell Square, Dublin, on 24 April 1932. The convention, which marked a watershed for the development of camogie, was attended by sixty delegates from all over Ireland; Liverpool and Manchester were also represented. Motions were passed on the playing rules, and these motions eventually led to general acceptance of a standard set of rules.[63]

The convention revolutionised the organisation and administration of camogie. Most significantly, plans were laid for an All-Ireland championship. The idea of such a championship, which Seán O'Duffy had written about as far back as 1910,[64] and which had been attempted (unsuccessfully) in previous years, was not realised until 1932. Dublin beat Galway in the first final, played in Galway. Remarkably, Máire Gill, then in her tenth year as president of the association, became the first captain to receive the Seán O'Duffy Cup.[65] From then on the All-Ireland finals were played in Dublin. Dublin and Cork shared out the titles between them over the next decade.

The Tailteann Games of 1932 enhanced the profile of camogie. Such was the organisational vigour of camogie beforehand that one newspaper commented that the sport was promoting the Games single-handedly: 'Camogie alone advertises Tailteann activities: What of the others?'[66] The camogie matches captured the public imagination and were well covered in the press. One reporter, 'Caman', remarked:

'Camoguidheacht is catching among our cailíní … The big crowd who waited over for the closing event

Up to the 1950s many players of camogie and the GAA learned of their selection (or non-selection) by post. The author of this letter of notification, Jean McHugh, was the national secretary of Cumann Camógaíochta na nGael for several years. (*Éamonn McMahon*)

of yesterday's opening was agreeably surprised and highly thrilled at the skills shown by representatives of the Leinster and Connaught in the initial tie. These sturdy girls wielded a camán in a manner that many hurlers might envy. It is a strenuous pastime this camogie but our girls seem perfectly fitted for it – their stamina is wonderful.'[67]

Seán O'Duffy, who was a representative on the Tailteann Games Council, cherished this success, which confounded those who had doubted whether camogie merited a place on the programme; 'since the opening day the prestige of the game, as well as that of the association, had grown high, and it was now looked upon by many as being equal to, if not superior to, any other of the competing sections.'[68] Buoyed by the momentum of 1932, camogie enjoyed great boom years in 1933 and 1934. The national and local press – which within a short space of time had begun to display a greater interest in Gaelic sport, culture and nationalistic causes generally – gave generous publicity to the burgeoning sport. The appearance of weekly columns in print about camogie in areas where it was not played at all perhaps only three years earlier,[69] hastened the process of its acceptance. Lay concerns about the propriety of camogie subsided when some Catholic priests became leading advocates and officials of the game.[70] Such clerics took the view that it was better recreation than 'lounging around the roads and engaging in things which are not very creditable'.[71] The fact that Louth, a weak county in hurling, reached two All-Ireland camogie finals in the mid 1930s, led by two early star players of the game, Nan and Kathleen Hanratty, was widely attributed to the dynamic work for the sport over the previous decade by Fr Tom Soraghan in Darver parish.[72] When posted to An Port Mór, Co. Armagh, in 1939, Fr Soraghan turned it into another camogie cradle.[73]

But parish and county structures were not as strong in camogie as they were in the GAA. The university colleges continued to occupy a relatively more prominent position in camogie. Even into the 1940s, several Cork players wore frocks emblazoned with the distinctive UCC skull-and-crossbones symbol when playing for the county.[74] Queen's University Camogie Club debuted in 1932, joined the Ashbourne Cup competition in 1934 and hosted the prestigious finals weekend a year later – the first major national camogie matches to take place in Ulster.[75] Workplaces were also central to the advance of camogie in Dublin and Cork. Various manufacturing companies in Dublin, including three tobacco factories, had their own teams in the 1920s; insurance firms had teams too; a transport employees' club was formed and later renamed as

Córas Iompar Éireann (C.I.É.); and the civil service had an inter-departmental league by the 1930s.[76] In Cork, a scientific company donated the county championship cup, and Lee Hosiery club, set up by employees of a clothing firm, became one of the sport's leading clubs.[77] This club soon adopted the ceremony of camogie players standing in uniform in two lines with their *camóig* aloft to form an archway before a newly married team-colleague;[78] this custom, albeit copied from other sports, spread and became a popular symbol of camogie's place in the community. The holding of regular camogie club *céilithe* – and Dublin camogie supporters held an annual 'all-sports *ceilidhe*' in the Mansion House as well – re-emphasised the part that camogie, like the GAA, was playing in the Gaelic revival movement.

The provincial councils of the Camogie Association were formed in quick succession in 1934. After the Leinster and Munster councils were founded on 6 May, the Ulster Council followed suit on 26 May. Dr Cassidy (Fermanagh) chaired the Ulster meeting at Armagh, which was addressed by Seán O'Duffy, and which elected Agnes O'Farrelly as the Ulster president and Vera Campbell (Tyrone) as secretary / treasurer. Twelve delegates, all but one female, from eight of the nine counties – all but Monaghan – attended. Notwithstanding their close ties with the GAA, many camogie county boards registered different colours from their male counterparts: Antrim, saffron and blue; Armagh, green and navy; Cavan, deep blue and black; Derry, purple and black; Down, red and black; Fermanagh, black and white; and Tyrone, gold and green.[79] From the off Antrim dominated the Ulster Camogie Championship, prevailing in the years 1934–39 and 1942–47 consecutively; only Cavan, in 1940 and 1941, broke the chain.

The Camogie Association had made terrific progress in all the four provinces. By 1935, 423 teams were affiliated, representing 10,000 players; and twenty-eight counties were affiliated. From a standing start in 1927, by 1934 Belfast had three adult camogie leagues, comprising twenty-four teams in all. In the rest of Ulster, there were no clubs in 1930, but over eighty in 1934.[80] Whereas in Dublin it remained primarily a winter game, summer was the preferred season of play around the country.

Between 1945 and 1947 Antrim won three All-Ireland titles in a row – a record which the county is unlikely to equal in the foreseeable future. (*Éamonn McMahon*)

Throughout its history, the Camogie Association had used the rhetoric of national struggle to recruit women to the game, but in the 1930s ideological differences emerged in the expression of this. Its close relationship with the GAA meant that the Camogie Association would have to consider bringing in its own ban on foreign sports, either out of ideological symmetry or sheer pragmatism. At a meeting (in the GAA rooms in Cork City) early in 1933 a motion proposed a ban on foreign games for camogie members in Cork. A Cobh delegate argued that the spirit of camogie should be at one with the spirit of the GAA; failure to impose the ban could prove damaging to their relationship and, in turn, to the organisation of camogie in general. In theory, it was also believed that the ban would make schools and individuals choose to play camogie rather than hockey. The motion was lost,[81] but the decision caused controversy. In reaction, the Cork County GAA Board chairman (and national president of the GAA), Seán McCarthy, said that camogie officials had 'cut themselves off' from the GAA. 'While they maintained that attitude they could not remain members of the association, having flouted one of the fundamental rules.'[82] A split ensued in Cork camogie, with the creation of a pro-ban county board. A representative of the official (anti-ban) branch subsequently claimed that it was the one which was thriving. In Galway, a motion to enact a ban was passed, and so the proposal went before the camogie congress for the first time in 1933, but it was shelved for one year, on the suggestion of Seán O'Duffy, to see how it would affect the association.[83]

A motion to impose the ban rules on camogie players returned to the national congress in 1934, again forwarded by the Galway delegation, and on this occasion greater support was forthcoming. Ulster was particularly to the fore. Brendan Kielty, a Belfast delegate, supported the motion 'not only because foreign games were detrimental to the progress of the national games, but also the soul of the Gael. Girls who attended functions under the auspices of non-Irish games, he proceeded, would be expected to stand up while an anthem to a foreign King was being played.' Miss Kleeshaw (Dublin) opposed the motion: 'Girls should be Irish enough to support Irish games without coercion'. Miss Sinéad Crotty warned delegates that the ban would 'train children to be cheats and given to subterfuge in their attitude to games'.[84] Fifteen of the twenty counties represented voted for the motion; Cork and Meath were split; and only Dublin, Laois and Westmeath voted against. By 26 votes to 17 it was decided to ban 'foreign' games. A camogie columnist in Belfast's *Irish News* declared the result 'a decided victory for the true Gael' and the north, and 'an eye-opener to the people from Dublin and Cork'; the writer ascribed Dublin members' acceptance of hockey to the city being 'the heart of the Sassenach garrison'.[85] These emerging urban-rural and north-south fault-lines, and perhaps personality clashes too, would later prove harmful.

The 1935 congress extended the ban to the attendance of members at 'foreign' (non-*céilí*) dances. Yet the meeting was most notable for the decision to exclude male delegates from future congresses.[86] The opposition to male involvement, suggests Mary Moran, owed to a belief 'that men wanted to lay down the law, argue the point but not do the work'.[87] In 1936, congress went further, by deciding that in future all games would be refereed by female officials only.[88] Yet in many areas there were still few women who were sufficiently conversant with the rules or confident to referee.[89] Most Ulster delegates, fearful of the potentially adverse effect on the game in the north, opposed the decision. A Tyrone official reported back to her county board that 'it seemed that the Ulster delegates would not be given a hearing at the congress'.[90] This was apparently an allusion to the fact that certain counties, Dublin in particular, had a dominant voting strength – more so than in the GAA. (Counties were entitled to a delegate for their first three clubs, and one for each five thereafter; on occasion, Dublin, with seventy-plus clubs, had more delegates than two provinces together.) The decision was not universally enforced anyhow. One male official in Belfast explained that he got involved in refereeing camogie out of concern that too many serious injuries were occurring, and he proceeded to instruct players on 'tackling methods, caman control, and the known arts of the game'.[91]

In tandem with rising tensions at administrative level, various other problems beset camogie, so that by the late 1930s the progress of the game had stalled, and in many areas there was even decline. Between 1935 and 1938, it was on the wane in most of Munster,[92] in spite of the mass popularity of hurling in the province. Although not quite so bad, Ulster and Leinster too endured significant dips in participation in most counties.[93] Players often had to pay their own way to play,[94] and doing so regularly, especially to distant inter-county games, proved beyond some of them. Parental disapproval and domestic duties remained

A major factor in Antrim's All-Ireland-winning run of the 1940s was the playing of many of the semi-finals and finals at Corrigan Park, Belfast. There the sizeable and partisan crowd, as well as the dubious state of the pitch, were possibly worth several points advantage to Antrim in each game. (*Éamonn McMahon*)

obstacles. 'Since my daughter began playing camogie she neglects to milk the cows,' complained one mother.[95] Above all, the game's faltering fortunes reflected recurring difficulties of player turnover in this and other female sports: groups of players tended to be dispersed within a few years, moving away from home for education or employment, or being sidelined by marriage and children.[96] In some places married women were debarred by rule from playing.[97] With the departure of the former stalwarts often went the interest and wherewithal to organise a team, especially as they did not have proper club administrative or youth development structures, and so over the decades it became habitual for teams / clubs to form and fold cyclically in many parishes.

Some members, particularly in Dublin, also believed that the ban on 'foreign' games was weakening the association, by persuading some women to choose hockey over camogie. Dublin's attempts to remove this rule caused only more discord, however. In 1939 a motion to rescind it was forwarded to the national congress. The Ulster Council called a meeting with the Central Council, warning that unless a 'one county, one vote' system were implemented, its delegates would not attend the special congress to be held to debate the resolution. This demand was refused. Only Leinster counties attended the congress, and Dublin and Kildare swung the vote to remove the ban.[98] The majority of counties, led by Ulster, severed their links with the Camogie Association and joined a new camogie body which would retain the ban. This new pro-ban association, led by Mrs M. Dunne (Wexford) as president and Jean McHugh (Antrim) as secretary / treasurer,[99] and known as the 'National Camóguidheacht Association', sought the support of the pro-ban GAA in its endeavours. It requested the use of Croke Park for its own all-Ireland championship – 'Knowing that the GAA has the full national faith and that it is the vanguard of the national resurgence, it is the desire of the cailíní of Ireland to be in full communion with this premier national association. We therefore call upon the Central Council of the GAA, the provincial councils and the 32 county boards to help us form a

Some Antrim camogie players stretching in training. City-based teams traditionally had an advantage over rural county teams, insofar as they could gather players together for practice and training sessions with relative ease, while their country cousins had to deal with greater complications in terms of transport and working hours. (*Éamonn McMahon*)

truly national association.'[100] The original *Ardchomhairle* of the Camogie Association, led by Máire Gill of Dublin (president, 1923–40), ignored the new council despite its increasing strength and support from several counties. The decade ended with a divided camogie organisation.

Both associations worked in isolation of each other until 1941, when Pádraig Mac Con Mí and Pádraig Ó Caoimh intervened to mediate the dispute. A special congress was summoned in December,[101] and the reunified body elected the following officers: Prof. Agnes O'Farrelly (UCD) as life-president, Lil Kirby (Cork) as chairman, Jean McHugh (Antrim) as secretary / treasurer, and Paddy Higgins (Galway) as national organiser. There were other signs of a brighter future. The All-Ireland final replay of 1942, between Cork and Dublin, was the first camogie match broadcast on Raidió Éireann. In 1943 games were extended from forty to fifty minutes in length, producing a more substantial viewing spectacle. Despite wartime hardship and travel restrictions, the All-Ireland final replay of that year drew a record crowd of 9,136.[102] Up to then the organisation of schools' camogie was haphazard outside the cities, but the launch of an Ulster colleges' championship in 1943, and then the Ulster Colleges Camogie Council in 1945, began to change that; some years later, colleges councils were set up in the other provinces.

Yet from 1944 another dispute over men holding office hampered the sport. Cork was torn asunder again. Its county board refused to affiliate to the association due to the ongoing participation of men in administration and allegations of misspending of local funds; a few clubs did affiliate to the centre separately, but the county's championship prospects were ruined for the rest of the decade.[103] Then, after heated debate at the 1945 congress, the official Leinster Council disbanded, and Dublin withdrew. In April 1947, Louth, Laois, Meath, Wicklow and Cork decided to set up a new association, and issued a statement calling on all male officials to withdraw.[104] In September, however, a new Leinster Council, adhering to the organisation as before, was formed.[105]

Southern woes provided Ulster's opportunity. Antrim took it. Having not even appeared in the final before, the northern county recorded a remarkable three-in-a-row of All-Ireland senior titles, 1945–47. The first victory was inconspicuous, even surreal: the Antrim players packed into a few cars to travel to play away to Waterford in the final, at Cappoquin, with hardly any supporters. Antrim's joy was slightly dampened by the non-presentation of the O'Duffy Cup; Dublin had refused to hand it over. The Antrim captain, Marie O'Gorman, did, however, receive a box of chocolates, and a pound of tea was presented to her Waterford counterpart, Biddy McGrath, in return – these gifts were in high demand in the respective jurisdictions, due to wartime rationing.[106] The Antrim team arrived home to be met with almost complete indifference. A major factor in the county's three triumphs was the arrival in Belfast of an expert team coach, Charlie McMahon, from Dublin in 1944. There was also a generous set of fixtures: all but one of the county's five All-Ireland camogie semi-finals between 1942 and 1947 were home games, and both the 1946 and 1947 finals were played at Corrigan Park, Belfast.[107] The park's long grass was as issue for visiting teams, and in the first ten minutes of the 1946 final Galway reportedly put four 'goals' into a second (bogus) set of goalposts left at one end.[108] Antrim's good fortune continued in the 1947 national final, as Dublin had a goal disallowed and perhaps a second when the ball allegedly crept over the goal-line.[109] The large and fervent home crowds at the Belfast ground provided a further advantage to Antrim; there, wrote a Tipperary journalist after that county's defeat in the 1947 national semi-final, camogie was 'a religion'.[110]

Ulster's successful run ended in 1948, when Co. Down – despite a modest record in hurling – reached the All-Ireland final, but suffered a heavy defeat to Dublin. The successful Dublin team was drawn entirely from C.I.É., the only capital club that stuck with the association throughout the recent administrative tumult. Inspired by the sport's most successful player ever, Kathleen Mills, Dublin embarked on an unparalleled winning streak of eighteen titles in nineteen years, 1948–67; only Antrim in 1956 broke the sequence.

The administration also reflected the increasing prominence of Ulster in camogie in the 1940s. Jean McHugh continued as national *Ard-rúnaí* from 1939 to 1953, while two Ulster officials were elected as national presidents: A. Hennessy (Cavan) in 1945; and Síghle Nic An Ultaigh, 1949–53. The 1947 team also contained two future national camogie presidents, Lily Spence and Nancy Mulligan (Murray).[111] In the more immediate term, Nic An Ultaigh came to the rescue of the sport: as *uachtarán* of the Ulster Council, she presided over a series of meetings towards reunifying the association; by the next spring all the counties, except Cork, and Nic An Ultaigh was elected as president. In 1951 the rebel county finally relented and affiliated to the Munster Council, and in 1952 the Co. Down official's presidential term was extended by an extra year, on account of her special service to the association.[112]

Few sports were confronted with as many obstacles as camogie before 1950. The women's Gaelic sport endured a much more precarious existence than hurling or football, but managed to survive through all the challenges. Although separate in constitution, camogie achieved unity of spirit with the GAA, and was an integral member of the family of Gaelic games. Hence it had become established in the four provinces for many years to come as Irish ladies' national game.

Cén fáth a raibh cúige Uladh chomh lag chomh fada sin?: Deacrachtaí CLG ó thuaidh, 1884–1945

Dónal Mac An Ailín

Anuas go dtí na 1950idí, ba é cúige Uladh an cúige is laige ó thaobh Chumann Lúthchleas Gael de in Éirinn. Ba mhinic go raibh contaetha éagsúla sa chúige neamheagraithe chomh déanach leis na 1920idí; bhuaigh contaetha ó na trí chúige eile craobhacha peile sinsearacha Uile-Éireann sula ndearna contae Ultach a leithéid; agus ó thaobh na hiomána de, ba é cúige Uladh amháin nach raibh ábalta dushlán maith a dhéanamh do chraobh na hÉireann. Is iad sin na fíricí bunúsacha, ach go dtí seo is beag atá scríofa sa stair acadúil chun laigí Uladh a mhíniú. Déanfaidh an t-alt seo iarracht anailís a dhéanamh ar stair an chumainn sa tuaisceart ó 1884 go 1945, agus díriú ar na tosca ba mhó a chuir moill ar fhorbairt CLG sa chúige.[1]

Scaip CLG timpeall sa chéad chúpla bliain ó 1884 mar a bheadh 'fallscaoth' nó 'tine phortaigh' ann, a scríobh a bhunaitheoir Micheál Cíosóg. Is fíor sin ar an iomlán, ach is amhlaidh nár spréigh tine an chumainn úir i dtuaisceart na hÉireann chomh gasta agus a spréigh sa deisceart. Maireann tagartí go dtí an lá atá inniu a chruthaíonn gur tionóladh cruinnithe ó mhíonna tosaigh 1885 amach d'fhonn clubanna CLG a chur ar bun (i gContae Dhoire go háirithe),[2] ach is dócha nach raibh club amháin eagraithe agus cleamhnaithe mar ba cheart le hArdchomhairle an chumainn go dtí 1886 – mar a bhí Club J. G. Biggar, Béal Átha Conaill, Co. an Chabháin, an chéad chlub oifigiúil sa chúige. Idir 1887 agus 1889 d'fhorbairt CLG go forleathan go gasta. B'amhlaidh sin in Ultaibh: rugadh na dosaenacha de chlubanna agus d'imir siad (peil Ghaelach den chuid is mó) in aghaidh a chéile i gcomórtais go rialta. Bunaíodh cúig bhord contae (An Cabhán, Muineachán, Ard Mhacha, Fear Manach agus Doire) agus chleamhnaigh breis agus céad club sna naoi gcontae ar fad.[3] Reáchtáladh craobhchomórtais idirchlub sna contaetha sin agus eagraíodh Craobh Peile Uladh d'fhoirne idirchontae ó 1888 ar aghaidh. Do chuid mhór fear náisiúnach faoin tuath sa chúige, ba é seo a gcéad eispéaras de spórt a bheith eagraithe go foirmiúil, agus thaitin sé go mór leo.[4]

Laistigh d'Ultaibh bhí difríocht mhór ann sna rátaí fáis idir tuaisceart agus deisceart an chúige. Má thairringimid líne samhailte ar an léarscáil a scoilteann an chúige ina dhá leath (idir thoir agus thiar), chímid go raibh níos mó ná céad club faoi stiúradh CLG sa leath theas den chúige (taobh ó dheas de Loch nEachach) sna 1880idí agus nach raibh níos mó ná fiche sa leath thuaidh an chúige ag aon am amháin sa tréimhse chéanna. Bhí na constaicí céanna ann do na cluichí Gaelacha sa dá leathchuid den chúige, ach is réasúnta a rá gur mó dochar a rinne na constaicí seo d'fhás CLG san oirthuaisceart. Ar feadh blianta fada bhí deacrachtaí timpeall an chúige agus sa réigiún sin ar leith maidir le cluichí a eagrú agus a imirt ar an Domhnach de dheasca láidreacht an tsabóideachais – dian-dheasghnáth na Sabóide ó thaobh na hoibre agus an spóirt de – sa phobal.

Níos mó ná aon rud, bhí sabóideachas taobh thiar de chuid mhór fadhbanna ag CLG i gCúige Uladh sna blianta tosaigh. Ó aimsir na plandála sa seachtú haois déag bhí tionchar Preispitéireach láidir sa chúige agus rinne an Lord's Day Observance Act (1695) cluichí Domhnaigh mídhleathach. Cé nár cuireadh an tAcht i bhfeidhm go minic sa deisceart agus gur imríodh cluichí iománaíochta go fóill, bhí sé éifeachtach go leor sa tuaisceart agus ba bheag cluiche a imríodh ar an Domhnach ansin – agus bhí sabóideachas i measc na réasún gur tháinig meath ar chluichí na cosmhuintire go ginearálta sa naoú haois déag. Nuair a bunaíodh CLG ba é cúige Uladh an t-aon chúige amháin ina ndearnadh iarracht an tAcht a úsáid in éadán na gcluichí Gaelacha. Ar Dhomhnach amháin go luath i 1886 chuaigh imreoirí ó chlub Bhéal Átha Conaill (Co. an Chabháin) amach chun an chéad chluiche oifigiúil faoi rialacha an chumainn a imirt. Tháinig drong de phóilinigh ó Chonstáblacht Ríoga na hÉireann (R.I.C.) ar an láthair agus thaifead siad ainmneacha na n-imreoirí, ach ní raibh siad ábalta síniú a fháil ó ghiústís áitiúil chun na himreoirí a chúiseamh os comhair na cúirte.[5] Ní dhearna na péas aon iarracht stop a chur le cluichí Domhnaigh sa chúige ina dhiaidh sin.

Ach níorbh é sin deireadh le fadhbanna CLG in Ultaibh maidir leis an sabóideachas. Ar ndóigh, b'iad eaglaisí Protastúnacha ba mhó a chothaigh sabóideachas, agus is nadúrtha gur chuir a ministrí i gcoinne na

Ballyconnell J. G. Biggar's club: the first affiliated club in Ulster, in late 1885 / early 1886.

gcluichí Domhnaigh.[6] Sna míonna tosaigh den bhliain 1889 rinne roinnt easpag agus sagart Caitliceach sa tuaisceart cáineadh láidir ar chluichí an Domhnaigh ón phuilpid.[7] Is fíor gur thug baill éagsúla den chléir sa deisceart dúshlán do CLG chomh maith thart fán am céanna, ach dhírigh siad sin a ngearáin ar na nascanna idir CLG agus cumainn rúnda, leithéidí na bhFiníní. Ba i gCúige Uladh amháin a rinne easpaig agus cléir (ach chan iad uilig) cáineadh faoi imirt Dhomhnaigh. Ba é An tArdeaspag Micheál Ó Laodhóg an fear eaglasta ba thábhachtaí a labhair ina n-éadán, mar a rinne sé in eaglais Naomh Maolmhaodhóg, Ard Mhacha, i mí Eanáir 1889;[8] ach bhí daoine eile ann freisin.[9] Cén fáth a raibh difríocht idir cléir an tuaiscirt agus cléir an deiscirt ar an ábhar sin? Is amhlaidh gurbh é an fáth ba mó ná nach raibh siad ag iarraidh go dtarraingeodh a gcuid tuataí 'scannal' orthu féin os comhair a gcuid comharsan Protastúnach, a bhí sa tromlach; measadh nár chóir na cluichí sin a imirt dá mba rud é go ndéanfaí masla don Chaitliceachas agus dochar do chaidrimh phobail.[10] Ag an am sin bhí tuairim na cléire iontach cumhachtach: chloígh roinnt mhaith daoine lena gcuid moltaí agus dhiúltaigh siad na cluichí a imirt as sin amach.

D'oibrigh an sabóideachas in éadán CLG ó thaobh na poiblíochta de fosta. Bhíodh dearcadh aontachtach ag formhór na nuachtán mór sa chúige – seachas an *Belfast Morning News, Irish News,* an *Anglo-Celt,* an *Derry Journal* agus an *Dundalk Democrat.* Ní raibh nuachtán áitiúil náisiúnach ar bith i gcontaetha Thír Eoghain, Fhear Manach, Ard Mhacha agus An Dúin. Rinne na nuachtáin aontachtacha cáineadh láidir ar chluichí Domhnaigh CLG.[11] Dhiúltaigh an chuid is mó de na nuachtáin aontachacha tuairiscí ar chluichí Domhnaigh a fhoilsiú. Gan phoiblíocht dá gcluichí, ní raibh deis ag oifigigh CLG mórán dul chun cinn a dhéanamh maidir le suim a chothú sna cluichí i measc an phobail.

As siocair go raibh bunús an talaimh sa tuaisceart i seilbh Phrotastúnach, bhí deacrachtaí móra ag CLG páirceanna imeartha a fháil do chluichí Domhnaigh. Fiú amháin dá mba rud é nár mhiste le feirmeoir Protastúnach páirc a thabhairt ar iasacht le haghaidh cluiche Domhnaigh, thiocfadh sabóidigh chuige go luath lena insint dó nach raibh lucht a chomhchreidimh sásta leis as ucht é bheith ag cuidiú le milleadh an Sabóide.[12] Gan mórán áiseanna imeartha fóirsteanacha a bheith ar fáil, ní raibh CLG i gCúige Uladh ábalta sluaite móra a mhealladh go dtí na cluichí; dá bharr sin, ní raibh mórán airgid á thógáil ag geataí na gcluichí; agus gan airgead ag teacht isteach mar sin, ní raibh CLG ábalta forbairt sa tuaisceart. Ó ba rud é go raibh

THE MORNING NEWS, SATURDAY, FEBRUARY 14, 1885.

THE ARCHDIOCESE OF DUBLIN

DUBLIN, Friday.

The Right Reverend Dr. Walsh, President of St. Patrick's College, Maynooth, was, at the meeting of the Chapter to-day, elected Vicar-Capitular of the Archdiocese of Dublin.

THE EXTRAORDINARY CASE.

NOLAN AGAINST NOLAN.

DUBLIN, Friday.

To-day, in the Exchequer Court, before the Lord Chief Baron and a special jury, the hearing of the case of Nolan v Nolan was resumed. The action was brought by Patrick Nolan to establish his title and recover the rents of a small property in county Roscommon. The plaintiff claimed under a provision in the will of his father, which gave him the property on the death of his brother James Nolan without issue. He alleged that his brother died without issue. The defendant, James Nolan, aged about eleven years, who appeared by Philip Maher, his guardian *ad litem*, disputed the plaintiff's title; denied that James Nolan had died without issue, and said that he was the lawful child of a marriage between James Nolan and Margaret Marie Cronin, which took place in Dublin in 1867. The question of legitimacy was the question to be decided by the jury. Evidence had been given by Mrs Nolan that the defendant was not her child. She had by bandaging herself pretended to be *enciente*, and had passed off the defendant (whom she bought for £2 from a soldier's wife, in the Coombe Hospital) as her child. Medical evidence was given by Drs Purefoy and Madden that in their opinion

DUNGANNON.

(FROM OUR CORRESPONDENT.)

DUNGANNON, Friday.

A STUPID HOAX.

The dead walls of this borough were placarded with the following manifesto last night :—" Relief of General Gordon. Dungannon to the rescue. A voice from the City of the Volunteers. A monster meeting will be held in Dungannon on Saturday, the 14th February, 1885. Men of Dungannon, awaken ! Our nation is becoming a by-word to the world, through the bungling and thimbling of the so-called G O M. Arouse that spirit which once prevailed in you. Show that the historic borough is yet worthy of the name of 100 years ago. Once more enroll yourselves on the side of justice, liberty, and true Nationalism. Let us once again raise the banner of 1782, and make our town once more worthy of the name of the Volunteers. Honour the Union Jack of Old England. Three cheers for the red, white, and blue. England, Ireland, and Scotland. United we stand and divided we fall." Generally the placard is looked upon as a hoax.

GAELIC ATHLETIC ASSOCIATION.

A branch of the above Association has been formed in Dungannon in connection with the Catholic Reading Room. About forty members have been enrolled. Mr James Collins was appointed treasurer.

MR VAUGHAN MONTGOMERY, LATE J P, OF AUGHNACLOY.

At the conclusion of the business of the Board

There had been several attempts to organise the GAA in various areas of Ulster in the year or so prior to Ballyconnell's affiliation. Here is a report of a meeting to form a club in Dungannon, in February 1885. This effort did not result in an affiliation with the Central Council, however.

an cumann ag iarraidh deis a thabhairt d'oiread imreoirí agus ab fhéidir spórt a imirt, ní dhearna siad mórán machnaimh ar lá imeartha eile a roghnú – d'oibrigh formhór na n-imreoirí faoin tuath ar feadh sé lá sa tseachtain, agus ba é an Domhnach an t-aon lá amháin a bhí saor acu.[13]

Ní mór a rá nach raibh baill CLG féin saor ó locht maidir le cuid mhór de na fadhbanna a bhí acu in Ultaibh. Tharla raiceanna foréigneacha ag na dosaenacha de chluichí mar thoradh ar dhrochiompar na n-imreoirí agus an lucht féachana, a bhí faoi thionchar an alcóil go minic. Bhí na raiceanna sin i measc na dtosca sin a chuir isteach go mór ar an chléir Chaitliceach.[14] Lean na hargóintí ar aghaidh sna cruinnithe boird agus i gcolúin litreacha na nuachtán ó am go chéile.[15] B'iomaí ball a bhí rodhílis dá chlub féin agus is amhlaidh nár thug go leor aon aird ar shochar CLG. Ba léir go raibh ganntanas de thaithí riaracháin ag oifigigh CLG sa chúige agus ar fud na tíre; roimh Acht an Rialtais Áitiúil i 1898, ba bheag an ról a bhí le himirt ag an chosmhuintir i dtaca le riarachán de chineál ar bith.[16]

Tá dóthain fianaise ann fosta nach raibh oifigigh sna cúigí eile, agus an Ardchomhairle mar sin, tuisceanach go leor ar na fadhbanna troma a bhí ag a gcomhghleacaithe in Ultaibh. Tionóladh an chéad chruinniú sa bhliain 1884 i nDúrlas Éile, i gcúige na Mumhan, an cúige is faide ó dheas agus an cúige is faide ó Ultaibh; agus ba sa Mhumhain a tionóladh a lán de na cruinnithe Ardchomhairle sna chéad fiche bliain. Ní raibh sé praiticiúil d'oifigigh Uladh taisteal go dtí cruinnithe i nDúrlas Éile agus i nGabhal Luimnigh; ghlacfadh an turas sin cúpla lá sa dá threo, agus mar sin de ní dheachaigh siad go dtí na cruinnithe sin go hiondúil.[17] Is léir ó nuachtáin na linne sin go raibh naimhdeas millteanach idir oifigigh Laighean agus oifigigh na Mumhan sna 1880idí agus sna 1890idí.[18] Ní dhearnadh mórán smaointe ar spreagadh a thabhairt d'Ultaibh nó do Chonnachtaibh, na cúigí laga. Cé go ndeachaigh clubanna Ultacha ar thurais go Baile Átha Cliath le haghaidh cluichí dúshláine, ní dhearna clubanna Bhaile Átha Cliath an turas sa treo eile sna blianta tosaigh.[19] Ba mhór an cailleadh sin d'Ultaibh, toisc go raibh taispeántais imeartha agus spreagadh de dhíth sa tuaisceart.

De réir na dtuairiscí comhaimseartha, bhí muintir CLG i gcúige Uladh measartha aineolach faoi rialacha na gcluichí Gaelacha, mar a bhí leagtha síos ag CLG, anuas go dtí tús an fhichiú haois. Déantar cur síos san alt 'From Cú Chulainn to Cusack' (sa leabhar seo) ar an fhéidearthacht gur cheap CLG rialacha a bhí níos claonta i dtreo stíleanna imeartha an deiscirt, agus gur tháinig na rialacha sin salach ar na stíleanna imeartha *camán* nó *commons* a bhí beo in áiteanna sa tuaisceart go dtí na 1880idí. Bhí míthuisicintí i gCúige Uladh maidir le rialacha na peile Gaelaí fosta. Mar shampla, shocraigh Coiste CLG Chontae Dhoire i 1890 nach gceadófaí 'use of the hands in football' as sin amach.[20] Is léir go raibh an 'pheil Ghaelach' a bhí á himirt in áiteanna sa thuaisceart (ach chan i ndeisceart Chúige Uladh) cosúil le sacar,[21] agus is dócha go léiríonn sé sin go raibh an sacar láidir sa réigiún sular bunaíodh CLG. Is iomaí sampla atá againn ó stair an spóirt go ginearálta gurb é an chéad chluiche coitianta a éiríonn coitianta in aon cheantar ar bith an spórt is ansa le bunadh an cheantair as sin amach. Is eol dúinn go ndearna foirne iománaíochta agus peile Uladh cuid mhór imeartha ar an talamh chomh déanach leis na 1920idí,[22] agus níos déanaí is dócha.

Tá sé furasta a fheiceáil go raibh CLG ag dul i laige in Ultaibh (agus ar fud na tíre) ó 1890 i leith mar gheall ar na tosca thuasluaite. Rinne scoilt Pharnell i 1891 cinnte de go scriosfaí é. Níor chruthaigh scoilt Pharnell aon deighilt i gCLG ó thuaidh, ach bhris sé spiorad na gluaiseachta náisiúnaí agus tharraing a lán daoine siar as eagraíochtaí náisiúnacha ina dhiaidh sin. Timpeall an ama céanna, d'éirigh an imirce níos measa arís, agus d'fhág na mílte fear óg an tír. Ó 1892 go 1898 bhí CLG tite as ord in Ultaibh: ní raibh coiste chontae ar bith ag feidhmiú sa tréimhse sin, agus ní raibh níos mó ná ceithre chlub cleamhnaithe go hoifigiúil leis an Ardchomhairle ag aon am ar bith.[23] Tá fianaise ann áfach gur lean cluichí peile ar aghaidh go neamhoifigiúil, idir foirne neamhchleamhnaithe, i ndeisceart an chúige.[24]

Thosaigh athbheochán CLG Chúige Uladh sa bhliain 1898. Ba i mBéal Feirste a thosaigh sé. D'eagraigh Club Iománaíochta na gCraoibhe Rua ('Red Branch Hurling Club') ócáid mhór lúthchleasaíochta mar aon le cluiche iománaíochta i mí na Samhna. Tháinig na mílte daoine a amharc ar na himeachtaí agus bhí

The Antrim football team of 1908 that won the first of five Ulster championships in a row between then and 1913, playing most of their games at considerable distances away from home. This was not a six-in-a-row, despite what some sources have claimed; no championships were organised in 1911 as the Ulster secretary was ill (see records section of this book for the revised roll of honour). The players did not get any medals for winning these five consecutive championships until they got a combined medal each in 1927; yet when Monaghan claimed the title in 1914 its players were rewarded with medals soon afterwards. (*Michael Hasson*)

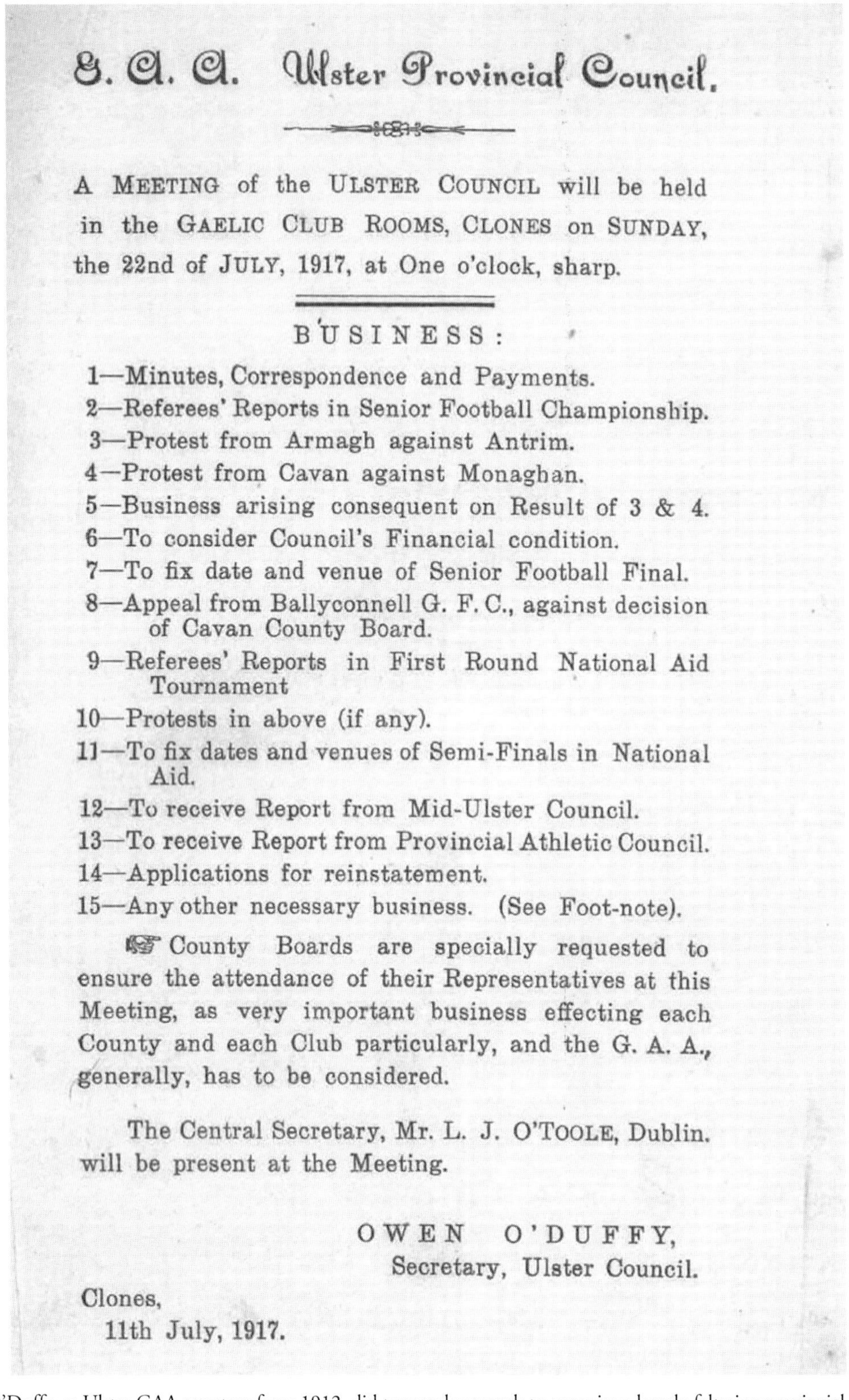

G. A. A. Ulster Provincial Council.

A MEETING of the ULSTER COUNCIL will be held in the GAELIC CLUB ROOMS, CLONES on SUNDAY, the 22nd of JULY, 1917, at One o'clock, sharp.

BUSINESS:

1—Minutes, Correspondence and Payments.
2—Referees' Reports in Senior Football Championship.
3—Protest from Armagh against Antrim.
4—Protest from Cavan against Monaghan.
5—Business arising consequent on Result of 3 & 4.
6—To consider Council's Financial condition.
7—To fix date and venue of Senior Football Final.
8—Appeal from Ballyconnell G. F. C., against decision of Cavan County Board.
9—Referees' Reports in First Round National Aid Tournament
10—Protests in above (if any).
11—To fix dates and venues of Semi-Finals in National Aid.
12—To receive Report from Mid-Ulster Council.
13—To receive Report from Provincial Athletic Council.
14—Applications for reinstatement.
15—Any other necessary business. (See Foot-note).

☞ County Boards are specially requested to ensure the attendance of their Representatives at this Meeting, as very important business effecting each County and each Club particularly, and the G. A. A., generally, has to be considered.

The Central Secretary, Mr. L. J. O'TOOLE, Dublin. will be present at the Meeting.

OWEN O'DUFFY,
Secretary, Ulster Council.

Clones,
11th July, 1917.

Eoin O'Duffy, as Ulster GAA secretary from 1912, did tremendous work to organise a largely faltering provincial council. This neatly printed *clár* for a council meeting in 1917 indicates improvements in correspondence. But the document, containing as it does listings for two protests and an appeal, also proves the struggle that the council and the association in general had to move away from petty disputes over the results of games.

Micheál Cíosóg ann mar aoi speisialta.[25] Tháinig an Cíosógach ar ais go Béal Feirste d'imeachtaí CLG sna blianta 1899[26] agus 1903.[27] Idir an dá linn tharla athfhorbairt an chumainn sa chúige, ach próiseas mall a bhí ann. Cuireadh Coiste Chontae Aontroma ar bun i 1901, agus sula raibh 1903 thart bhí coistí contae ag feidhmiú fosta i gcontaetha Dhoire, an Chabháin agus Ard Mhacha. De bhreis air sin, cuireadh Comhairle Uladh de CLG ar bun den chéad uair in Ard Mhacha i 1903. Ar an lá céanna in Ard Mhacha tosaíodh Craobh Peile Uladh arís agus imríodh an chéad chluiche ceannais de Chraobh Iománaíochta Uladh riamh.[28] Bhí na comórtais idirchlub sa dá spórt ag teacht le chéile laistigh de na contaetha fosta. Sa bhliain 1904 bunaíodh coistí An Dúin, Thír Eoghain agus Fhear Manach. B'é Dún na nGall an contae deireanach le bheith eagraithe go foirmiúil, ach cuireadh é sin ina cheart sa bhliain 1905.[29] As sin amach, bhí struchtúr éifeachtach i bhfeidhm i gCúige Uladh agus bhí na cluichí Gaelacha in ann dul i bhfeabhas sa tuaisceart. Mealladh tacaíocht ó dhaoine suntasacha sa phobal; fuarthas coirn do chraobhacha idirchlub ó bheirt Chomhaltaí Parlaiminte i gcontaetha Ard Mhacha (Liam Mac Philip) agus an Dúin (Diarmaid Mac An Bheatha). Bhí tionchar Chonradh na Gaeilge sofheicthe i gCLG sa chéad nua: rugadh roinnt clubanna CLG ó chraobhacha an Chonartha, agus d'eagraigh siad céilithe, ranganna Gaeilge agus staire chomh maith le cluichí ar a gcláir imeachtaí.[30]

Ní scéal dul chun cinn simplí a bhí ann áfach. I roinnt contaetha – Tír Eoghain, Doire agus Dún na nGall go háirithe – thit CLG as a chéile anois agus arís anuas go dtí na 1920idí. Chaill foirne Uladh go trom gach bliain i gcluiche leath-cheannais iománaíochta na hÉireann, agus ó thaobh na peile de ní raibh na hUltaigh in ann dul in iomaíocht le curaidh na gcúigí eile, ach amháin Aontroim i gcraobhacha Uile-Éireann 1911 agus 1912 (nuair a shroich siad an cluiche ceannais faoi dhó). Ní raibh cúrsaí riaracháin rathúil ach oiread. Tharla sé i mbliain nó dhó nár tionóladh craobhacha Uladh ar chor ar bith. Ó bhliain go bliain bhí Comhairle Uladh agus bunús na mbord chontae briste le bochtanas.[31]

Cad a bhí cearr mar sin? Ar dtús, bhí na fadhbanna céanna ann agus a bhí ann sa tréimhse roimhe. Cuireadh in éadan cluichí an Domhnaigh arís agus arís eile. I 1903 agus 1904 d'fhógair easpaig Chaitliceacha Dhoire agus an Chlochair go raibh siad in éadán na gcluichí Domhnaigh. Chuir na ráitis sin isteach ar na cluichí Gaelacha i nDoire Cholmcille, i bhFear Manach[32] agus i Muineachán[33] ar feadh tamaill – ach ní raibh

Patrick Whelan of Co. Monaghan, Ulster GAA president, on parade in Irish Volunteer uniform. By 1919, he had to step down from his provincial presidency due to a ban on oath-taking civil servants in the association. (*Aogán Ó Fearghail*)

The construction of Corrigan Park, Belfast, in the 1920s. This was the GAA's second 'county ground' in Ulster, after Bréifne Park was opened in Cavan in 1923. (*Anna Harvey*)

an tionchar chomh holc agus a bhí freasúra na cléire timpeall 1888–91 agus i ndiaidh 1905 níor chualathas mórán cáinte ó na heaspaig Chaitliceacha maidir le cluichí Domhnaigh.

Seans maith gurbh iad na húdaráis iarnróid na sabóidigh ba mhó a rinne dochar do CLG sa tuaisceart le linn na 1900idí. Dhiúltaigh an comhlacht Great Northern Railway – a raibh monaplacht iomlán acu nach mór i dtrátha an ama sin – traenacha a chur ar fáil do chluichí CLG ar an Domhnach, de bharr (arsa an GNR) an drochiompair a bhain le sluaite peile.[34] Cúis mhór díospóide idir oifigigh CLG agus na boic mhóra traenacha ab ea an polasaí seo. B'éigean cluiche ceannais peile Uladh a chur siar i 1905 mar thoradh air.[35] D'fhreastail Pádraig Ó Faoláin, Uachtarán Chomhairle Uladh CLG, ar an Choimisiún Leasríogach um Iarnróid in Éirinn, i Londain i 1908, agus chuir sé in iúl dóibh cad é mar a bhí polasaí an GNR ag cur isteach ar chúrsaí CLG in Ultaibh.[36] Thóg an GNR an cosc faoi dheireadh i 1910,[37] ach bhí cuid mhór oibre le déanamh ag Comhairle Uladh próifíl a gcraobhacha a thógáil agus a n-ioncam a mhéadú tar éis na mblianta casta roimhe sin.

I gcuideachta na bhfadhbanna sin rinne dílseoirí 'sabóideacha' ionsuithe foréigneacha ar imreoirí CLG. Mar shampla, tharla círéibeacha móra sa cheantar idir Blaris agus Lios na gCearrbhach i 1904 nuair a thosaigh club iománaíochta áitiúil a imirt ar an Domhnach.[38] Rinneadh ionsuithe chomh maith ar fhoirne ar a mbealach go dtí na cluichí ó am go chéile.[39] Ardaíodh na hábhair seo i dTeach na dTeachtaí i Westminster de bharr ceisteanna ó Chomhaltaí Parlaiminte Náisiúnacha agus Aontachtacha idir 1904 agus 1906. Ag éirí as na díospóireachtaí sin, d'fhógair Ard-Rúnaithe na Breataine – George Wyndham ar dtús i 1904, agus a chomharbaí ina dhiaidh sin – den chéad uair riamh go raibh sé de cheart ag saoránaigh an Domhnach a chaitheamh mar ba mhian leo ó thaobh an spóirt de; ach dúirt siad go raibh dualgas ar imreoirí Domhnaigh a chinntiú nach mbrisfidís an ciúnas i gceantair (Phrotastúnacha) nach raibh fáilte rompu iontu.[40]

De réir a chéile d'eirigh an ghéarchoimhlint idir sacar agus na cluichí Gaelacha níos tromchúisí sa tuaisceart. Ba é Béal Feirste croílár an tsacair in Éirinn agus bhí deis ag an sacar scaipeadh go tapa ó shin timpeall an iarthuaiscirt. Le linn na tréimhse deich mbliana (*c.* 1891–*c.* 1901) nach raibh CLG in ord nó in eagar sa tuaisceart d'fhás an sacar go mór, sna cathracha agus i mbailte móra ar leith. Ba sna blianta sin a cuireadh Belfast Celtic F.C. agus Derry Celtic F.C. ar bun – dhá chlub sacair a bhí iontach mór i measc na gCaitliceach. Ní raibh an Irish Football Association, an cumann sacair a bhí bunaithe i mBéal Feirste, sásta glacadh le hathfhás CLG. Idir 1898 agus 1904 chum an IFA rialacha chun coisc a chur ar chlubanna sacair a bpáirceanna a thabhairt ar iasacht do chluichí Domhnaigh;[41] agus ceapadh riail eile a chuir cosc ar imreoirí sacair cluiche ar bith a imirt ar an Domhnach.[42] Cé nach raibh tagairt dhíreach do chluichí Gaelacha sna rialacha sin, níl aon amhras ann ach gur buille in éadán CLG a bhí ar intinn an IFA. I 1903 chuir CLG cosc arís ar a gcuid ball bheith ag imirt nó ag amharc ar shacar, rugbaí, cruicéad agus haca; bhí riail mar sin i bhfeidhm roimhe idir 1887 agus 1896.[43] Creid é nó ná creid é, ba é cúige Uladh an cúige ba laidre in éadán an choisc sin i 1903.[44]

Cuireadh uafás ar oifigigh CLG in Ultaibh nuair a bhronn an IFA deontais chun sacar a scaipeadh agus a neartú i gceantair ina raibh sé lag – in iarthar Uladh go háirithe. Rinne oifigigh CLG Fhear Manach agus Uladh gearáin go poiblí gur 'breabanna' a bhí iontu.[45] Chlóigh oifigigh CLG níos dlúithe lena gcosc ar chluichí 'gallda' i ndiaidh eachtraí mar sin. D'fhéadfadh sé go raibh an cosc sin éifeachtach do CLG faoin tuath cionn is gur chuidigh sé leis na cluichí Gaelacha an lámh in uachtar a fháil sna paróistí éagsúla sula raibh deis ag sacar éirí 'bunaithe' iontu. Sna cathracha agus sna bailte móra áfach, d'oibrigh an cosc in éadán rath CLG bunús an ama, de bhrí go raibh sacar roláidir sna háiteanna sin roimh ré agus bhí na clubanna CLG ansin ag tarraingt ar imreoirí a tógadh le sacar ar na sráideanna, sna scoileanna agus i gclubanna sacair thart timpeall. Faoin tuath fiú ní raibh CLG slán sábháilte ó thionchar an tsacair. Ó thus an chéid ar aghaidh go dtí na 1920idí ar a laghad ba ghnách le go leor clubanna / foirne aistriú ón pheil Ghaelach go sacar nó a mhalairt – in amanna mar ágóid in éadán chinneadh éigin a rinne an bord contae.[46]

Níl dóthain spáis againn anseo chun fiosrú iomlán a dhéanamh ar na cúiseanna ar chaill foirne ón tuaisceart cluichí leathcheannais chraobh na hÉireann go rialta, ach is léir go raibh ganntanas eagair acu go ginearálta, agus easpa féinmhuiníne. Thairis sin tuigtear nach raibh scileanna na gcluichí cleachtaithe chomh maith acu agus a bhí ag foirne an deiscirt, ceapadh ard an liathróid go hiondúil;[47] agus dúradh gur fhorfheidhmigh na réiteoirí deisceartacha na rialacha ní ba liobrálaí ná mar a rinneadh i gcúige Uladh.[48]

Bhí fadhbanna ollmhóra ag CLG sa tuaisceart go fóill rochtain a fháil ar pháirceanna agus ar áiseanna eile. Cé go raibh teacht acu ar níos mó páirceanna idir na 1900idí agus na 1920idí ná mar a bhí roimhe, bhí go fóill corr áit nach raibh CLG ábalta faiche mhaith a fháil inti chun cluichí a imirt. I 1906 shocraigh Bardas Bhéal Feirste cúlphoist Ghaelacha a chur suas i bPáirc Bhóthar na bhFál, ach ní raibh CLG ábalta a lán úsáide a bhaint as sin de bhrí nach raibh imirt ar an Domhnach ceadaithe ar pháirceanna poiblí.[49] Choinnigh cúpla cumann talmhaíochta i gcontaetha an Chabháin agus Mhuineacháin páirceanna siar ó chluichí Domhnaigh freisin.[50] Chuir na comhairlí áitiúla bacanna eile roimh fhás CLG. Sa bhliain 1906

A line-up of the Monaghan team that played in the All-Ireland football final of 1930, before the pre-match parade. This match is renowned in local folk memory as 'the last battle of the Civil War', due to the perceived associations of the Kerry and Monaghan teams with the Republican and Free State sides respectively, and the number of Monaghan players injured in the game! Up to now, remarkably, no known photograph of this team – the only Monaghan team ever to reach a senior championship final – has survived or been reproduced. (*Fabian Murphy*)

A street scene of dignitaries and crowd members at a Feis event organised jointly by the GAA and Conradh na Gaeilge in Dungannon, *c.* 1934. Lord Ashbourne is the kilt-wearer, and Pádraig Mac Conmidhe, Uachtarán Chomhairle Uladh CLG (and later national GAA president) is pointing. Co-operation between the two cultural organisations was greater in Ulster than in the other Irish provinces. (*Helen and Art McRory*)

dhiúltaigh Comhairle Bhaile Chluain Eois cead do Chomhairle Uladh halla an bhaile a úsáid fá choinne cruinnithe[51] – is fíric íorónach í, anois go bhfuil clú agus cáil ar Chluain Eois mar lárionad CLG i gcúige Uladh le blianta fada anuas.

Ar ndóigh, bhí aonaid CLG i gCúige Uladh róbhocht chun a n-áiseanna féin a cheannach. Bhí roinnt ball (go háirithe sna cúigí eile) den bharúil go raibh na riarthóirí ó thuaidh neamhhinniúil ó thaobh an ghnó de.[52] Shíl lear mór daoine in Ultaibh nach raibh tuiscint ar bith ag na hoifigigh náisiúnta ar na constaicí a bhí rompu sa tuaisceart.[53] Fuair Comhairle Uladh deontas £20 ón Ardchomhairle i 1904, ach tada eile ar feadh blianta ina dhiaidh sin, cé gur dhúirt na hUltaigh gur tugadh gealltanas ar airgead breise dóibh.[54] Ualach trom a bhí ann d'oifigigh CLG – fir óga de gnáth – agus iad i bpoist lánaimseartha i rith an lae chomh maith. Bhí a lán dualgas ag brath ar oifigeach nó beirt. Níor eagraíodh craobhacha Uladh i 1911 ó ba rud é go raibh an rúnaí tinn.

Bhí muintir CLG sa tuaisceart ciontach as cuid mhór den chruachás a chruthú dóibh féin. Bhí a lán teannais ann idir contaetha agus idir clubanna. Chaith Comhairle Uladh agus na coistí contae na céadta uair ar dhíospóireachtaí faoi ionaid imeartha na gcluichí agus faoi ionaid na gcruinnithe toisc gur bhain go leor buntáistí leis na cinntí sin. Mar a tharla i gCúige Uladh, ba iad na contaetha inar tionóladh an méid is mó cruinnithe móra agus cluichí móra – an Cabhán, Muineachán agus Aontroim – na contaetha céanna ba rathúla ar pháirc na himeartha. Bhí na dosaenacha díospóidí ann faoi thorthaí cluichí chomh maith. Is dócha go ndearnadh níos mó ágóidí in éadán thorthaí chluichí CLG ná a rinneadh in aon eagras spóirt eile ar domhan, agus b'iomaí agóid fhoirmiúil a cuireadh faoi bhráid Chomhairle Uladh agus faoi bhráid na gcoistí contae. In ainneoin go raibh Comhairle Uladh ag éirí níos proifisiúnta ag an leibhéal riaracháin thart fán am sin, phléasc conspóid mhór inmheánach i 1914. Shocraigh Comhairle Uladh boinn a bhronnadh ar Mhuineachán, curaidh pheile agus iománaíochta Uladh na bliana sin, cé nár bronnadh boinn ar bhuaiteoirí chomórtas an chúige sna blianta roimhe sin mar gheall ar bhochtannas na comhairle; níor mhó ná sásta a bhí Aontroim, a bhuaigh cúig chraobh peile as a chéile idir 1908 agus 1913 gan aon bhonn ar bith a fháil![55] Shíl oifigigh ó chontaethe eile go raibh barraíocht cumhachta ag Muineachán laistigh de Chomhairle Uladh. D'éirigh an t-aighneas nimhneach eatarthu tar éis cinnidh eile i 1917. Bhuaigh an

Cabhán in éadán Mhuineacháin sa chraobh peile ach rinne Muineachán agóid agus aisiompaíodh an toradh. Bhí muintir an Chabháin chomh feargach faoi na himeachtaí sin gur rith siad rún go dtí Comhthionól CLG Uladh 1918 a raibh sé de chuspóir aige briseadh ó Chúige Uladh go glan agus 'cúige' úr darbh ainm 'Tara' a bhunú le haghaidh cúiseanna CLG, in éineacht leis an Longfort, Lú, an Mhí agus an Iarmhí.[56] Ní hiontas é nár éirigh leis an rún sin ag an chomhthionól cúige, ach léiríonn sé cé chomh teann agus a bhí cúrsaí an chumainn sa chúige sa tréimhse sin.

Roimh 1916 ní raibh mórán fianaise de phoblachtachas réabhlóideach i gCLG Uladh, ach d'éirigh an cumann níos radacaí in iarmhairt gach aon chinnidh leatromaigh a rinne rialtas na Breataine. Bhí Rúnaí Chomhairle Uladh, Eoghan Ó Dufaigh, lárnach sa phróiseas sin. I 1916, mar shampla, nuair a fuarthas éilimh ó na húdaráis cáin siamsaíochta a íoc ar ioncam na gcluichí agus cuireadh roinnt seirbhísí traenach ar ceal fosta, chuir Ó Dufaigh cuma ar an scéal (ina chuid óráidí agus scríbhínní) go raibh an rialtas ag díriú a n-iarrachtaí ar CLG a scrios.[57] Mhúnlaigh sé an chomhairle chúige mar mheán neamhoird i gcoinne údarás na Breataine, go háirithe tar éis dó clárú le hÓglaigh na hÉireann i 1917.[58] Mhaígh sé gurbh eisean agus cúige Uladh a bhí freagrach fosta as ucht 'Domhnach Gaelach' a cheapadh i mí Lúnasa 1918 – an ócáid chinniúnach sin nuair a imríodh na céadta de chluichí ag an am céanna ar fud na tíre ionas go mbrisfí cosc de chuid an stáit. Ó toghadh Séamas Ó Doibín (Aontroim) – ball sinsearach de Bhráithreachas Phoblacht na hÉireann – mar Uachtarán Chomhairle Uladh CLG i 1919, bhí an chomhairle chúige faoi stiúir réabhlóideach. I rith Chogadh an Neamhspleáchais d'éirigh CLG sa tuaisceart iontach dlúth le gluaiseacht na poblachta, agus chaith ardoifigigh Chomhairle Uladh (Ó Doibín agus Ó Dufaigh) cuid mhór den chogadh i bpríosún nó ar a dteitheamh ó fhórsaí slándála na Breataine.[59] Dá bharr sin tháinig gníomhaíochtaí Chomhairle Uladh ar stad iomlán idir Iúil 1920 agus Deireadh Fómhair 1921[60] agus cuireadh cúrsaí an chumainn ar fionraí ag am éigin i mbeagnach gach aon chontae eile ina theannta sin.

Cruthaíodh fadhb mhór úr do CLG i gCúige Uladh le tabhairt isteach na críochdheighilte ag deireadh 1920 agus teorainn á tarraingt idir an dá stat nua in Éirinn. Sna sé chontae san oirthuaisceart bhí an t-athrú coinníollacha olc ar fad. Bhí fórsaí slándála Thuaisceart na hÉireann níos naimhdí le CLG agus le náisiúnaithe go ginearálta ná mar a bhí a réamhtheachtaithe. Roimh an Chonstáblacht Speisialta 'B' ach go háirithe a bhí eagla ar imreoirí agus tacaithe na gcluichí Gaelacha. Dá ndéanaidís baill CLG a stopadh, bhí seans maith ann go gcuiridís faoi dhianscrúdú iad agus go n-úsáidfidís foréigean orthu. Ba í an eachtra ba chlúití gabhadh 'pheileadóirí Mhuineacháin' ar an Droim Mhór (Co. Thír Eoghain) ar a mbealach chuig cluiche ceannais chraobh Uladh i nDoire Cholmcille i mí Eanáir 1922. Fuarthas gunnaí agus urchair ina seilbh agus is léir go raibh siad ag dul a chuidiú le hiarracht éalaithe triúr cime ó Phríosún Dhoire. Ar an láimh eile, is dócha go raibh sé beartaithe acu imirt sa chluiche ina dhiaidh sin.[61] D'éirigh achrann idir na ceannasaithe stáit, James Craig, Michael Collins agus Winston Churchill, as coinneáil na n-imreoirí sin i bpríosún ach cé gur scaoileadh saor iad tar éis roinnt seachtainí d'eascair sraith eachtraí foréigneacha as a ngabhadh.[62] Seachas an ócáid sin tharla sé go minic (go háirithe ag tús na bhfichidí) go bhfuair gnathbhaill CLG nach raibh nasc ar bith acu le paraimíleatachas drochíde ó na fórsaí stáit.[63] Bhí páirt mhór ag na fórsaí stáit fosta in olltionscamh idir 1922 agus 1924 a rinne a lán dochair do CLG sna sé chontae – imtheorannú. I measc na gcéadta fear náisiúnach a tógadh gan choinne bhí cathaoirleach agus rúnaí Bhord Chontae an Dúin agus go leor ball eile de chuid CLG.[64] Ba bheag duine acu a bhí ina óglach; roghnaíodh d'imtheorannú iad mar gur measadh gur cheannasaithe náisiúnacha áitiúla iad a raibh tionchar acu sa phobal.[65] A mhalairt ón suíomh roimh 1920, bhí an stát sa tuaisceart cumhachtach go leor chun brú a chur ar aonaid CLG cáin siamsaíochta a íoc; glacadh club amháin os comhair na cúirte agus fuarthas ciontach é as neamh-íocaíocht.[66]

Bhain na míbhuntaistí ba mhó do CLG sna sé chontae le polasaithe na bpolaiteoirí Aontachtacha. Cé go raibh níos mó comhairlí ag cur áiseanna imeartha ar fáil sna páirceanna poiblí de réir a chéile, ní raibh aon teacht ag CLG orthu – cuireadh poist sacair ar an tromlach acu agus coinníodh cosc ar chluichí Domhnaigh i bhfeidhm. Ba é an cás is measa an Brandywell, an staid a bhí i seilbh Bhardas Dhoire Cholmcille. Den chéad uair riamh fuair na Náisiúnaigh tromlach na suíochán ar bhardas na cathrach i 1920 agus mar cheann de na hathruithe a d'eascair as sin, tógadh an cosc ó chluichí Domhnaigh sa Brandywell. Idir 1920 agus 1923 mar sin, tharla athbheochán mórthaibhseach do na cluichí Gaelacha sa chathair, agus tionóladh cluichí móra fiú i gcraobhchomhórtais Uladh sa staid.[67] Ach shocraigh an pharlaimint i mBéal Feirste fáil réidh leis an chóras vótála 'ionadaíocht chionmhar' i 1923. De réir mar a bhí beartaithe ag an rialtas, fuair na hAontachtaithe an chumhacht ar ais i nDoire Cholmcille. As sin amach thacaigh an bardas leis an sacar go mórmhór. Ba comhairleoirí den chuid is mó a chuir club sacair Derry City F.C. ar bun i 1928[68] agus rinne siad an pháirc Brandywell níos lú ionas go mbeadh sí ní b'fhóirsteanaí don sacar – agus robheag do na cluichí Gaelacha, mar a tharla sé.[69] Is féidir a rá go raibh 'gerrymandering' ag dul ar aghaidh ar pháirc na himeartha chomh maith le cúrsaí toghcháin. In áiteanna eile rinne comhairlí áitiúla a lán socruithe in éadán CLG agus na gcluichí Gaelacha. Ní raibh na socruithe sin i gcónaí iontach cinniúnach ach go ginearálta rinne siad atmaisféar neamhthorthúil do na cluichí Gaelacha.

Sna trí chontae Ultacha ar an taobh eile den teorainn bhí coinníollacha i bhfad níos fearr ar ndóigh. Le bunú an tSaorstáit i 1922 tháinig go leor buntáistí do CLG i gcontaetha Mhuineacháin, an Chabháin agus Dhún na nGall. Saolaíodh fórsaí nua stáit, an Garda Síochána agus Arm na hÉireann, agus seoladh na scór dá mbaill chuig na trí chontae Ultacha sin a bhí ar taobh ó dheas den teorainn. B'as an Mhumhain agus Laighin ó dhúchas do go leor de na gardaí agus na saighdiúirí sin (agus fostaithe sa tseirbhís poiblí, de leithéid oifigigh custaim fosta), agus imreoirí den chéad scoth a bhí i gcuid mhaith acu. Neartaigh siad foirne na gcontaetha sin, agus mar sin de chonacthas feabhas mór sna taispeántais a rinne foirne peile Mhuineacháin agus foirne iománaíochta Dhún na nGall agus an Chabháin, mar shampla.[70] Mhothaigh roinnt ball de chuid CLG ar an taobh thuaidh den teorann gur bhain Coimisinéir na nGardaí, Eoghan Ó Dufaigh, úsáid mhíchothrom as a oifig chun imreoirí oilte a cheapadh do Mhuineachán.[71] Ar aon nós, bhí timpeallacht i bhfad níos caoithiúla do na cluichí Gaelacha go ginearálta sna trí chontae sin ná mar a bhí ann sna sé chontae eile.

D'ainneoin an mhoill thuasluaite in imeachtaí CLG ag tús na bhfichidí nuair a bhí pobal náisiúnach na sé gcontae faoi scamall dorcha, níorbh fhada go raibh na cluichí á n-imirt arís i mbeagnach gach ceantar sa chúige. Roimh dheireadh 1924, bhí ocht gcinn de na naoi gcontae atheagraithe faoi limistéar bhord chontae agus na comhairle cúige; ba é Doire an t-aon eisceacht a bhí ann agus níor ghlac siad páirt go leanúnach go dtí luath sna tríochaidí. Sna hocht gcontae sin chuaigh CLG ó neart go neart. Atógadh clubanna ar fud an chúige agus – idir 1924 agus 1929 dúblaíodh méid na gclubanna (ó 128 go 257)[72] – de réir a chéile d'éirigh siad níos buaine ná na clubanna a bhí ann rompu. D'oscail an cumann a chéad chúpla staid i gCúige Uladh sna fichidí – Páirc Bhréifne i mBaile an Chabháin i 1923, agus Páirc Uí Chorragáin i mBéal Feirste i 1927. Ar a laghad bhí dhá ionad réasúnta nua-aimseartha fá choinne na gcluichí móra a tionóladh. Faoi dheireadh fosta bhí duaiseanna fóirsteanacha á dtabhairt do bhuaiteoirí na gcomórtas. Sa bhliain 1925 bhronn an nuachtán *Anglo-Celt* corn le haghaidh curaidh pheile Chúige Uladh, agus bhronn Easpag Chlochair, Dr Mac Cionnaith, corn do chomórtas peile eile sa chúige.[73] Sna blianta a bhí le teacht gheobhadh Comhairle Uladh agus na boird chontae coirn eile. Den chéad uair riamh foilsíodh clár chuimhneacháin do chluichí ceannais peile Uladh i 1923. Ar pháirc na himeartha bhí feabhas céimseach le sonrú chomh maith. Bhuaigh Ard Mhacha Craobh Peile Sóisear na hÉireann 1926 – an chéad chraobh náisiúnta a fuair foireann ar bith as Ultaibh. Ba é an Cabhán is mó a rinne dul chun cinn áfach. Bhuaigh contae Bhréifne Craobh Peile Sóisear na hÉireann i 1927, shroich siad cluiche ceannais sinsearach na hÉireann i 1928 agus bhuaigh siad Craobh Peile Sinsearach na hÉireann i 1933 agus i 1935. Mar dhuaiseanna do na buanna sin chuaigh peileadóirí an Chabháin ar trí turas go Meiriceá sna 1930idí. Gan amhras bhí stádas níos airde bainte amach ag na cluichí Gaelacha i gCúige Uladh. Cibé nár bhuaigh foirne Ultacha tuilleadh onóracha, bhí an cúige rannpháirteach i gcomórtais uile-Éireann (mar aon le comórtais nua: na Sraitheanna Náisiúnta, comórtais Chorn an Iarnróid agus craobhacha na mionúr) níos leanúnaí ná roimhe. Bhí an rannpháirtíocht sin iontach tábhachtach do náisiúnaigh sna sé chontae: b'iad na cluichí náisiúnta CLG a thug deis dóibh a náisiúntacht a chur in iúl – deis nach raibh acu ó lá go lá i stát a bhí iontach tugtha do struchtúir agus do shiombailí na Breataine.

Ar an drochuair do CLG in Ultaibh, ní raibh an caighdeán iománaíochta sa tuaisceart ag dul i bhfeabhas chomh mór agus a bhí deisceart. Cén fáth? Tá go leor freagraí ann, ach go bunúsach is féidir a rá go raibh na ceantair ab fhearr ó thaobh na hiománaíochta de (Aontroim go háirithe) scoite ó na contaetha láidre sa deisceart agus níor cothaíodh 'traidisiún' d'iománaíocht iomaíoch sa chúige. Ní raibh tíreolaíocht amháin taobh thiar de sin. De bharr chríochdheighilte, níor tháinig státseirbhísigh ón Mhumhain agus ó Laighin

The Brantry GAA sports-day, Co. Tyrone, in the 1930s. This was typical of the sports-days held in most rural areas – significant highlights of the year in the parish, and also events which attracted participants from much further afield. The presence of Fr Alexander Connolly in the centre of the photograph exemplifies the ubiquity of parish priestsabout local GAA affairs in this period. (*Nora Donnelly*)

aneas mar ba ghnách, Ina theannta sin bhí easpa múinteoirí scoile a raibh tuiscint acu ar an iománaíocht agus ba mhinic go mbíodh deacrachtaí go leor ann camáin a fháil.

Ba chúis mhór bhróid do mhuintir CLG Uladh gur choinnigh siad an cúige le chéile mar aonad naoi gcontae sa chumann, cé go raibh teorainn tarraingte tríd an chúige ó thaobh na polaitíochta de.[74] Le fírinne, ní raibh sé chomh doiligh sin aontacht an tseanchúige a chaomhnú; chloígh na heagraíochtaí rugbaí, haca, dornálaíochta agus spóirt eile le cúige naoi gcontae in ainneoin na críochdheighilte polaitiúla. Chruthaigh an teorainn deacrachtaí úra do CLG i gCúige Uladh – mar shampla, díospóidí faoi íocaíocht cháin siamsaíochta, ionaid imeartha na gcluichí agus rudaí eile[75] – ach rinne na naoi gcontae iarrachtaí níos láidre cur le chéile in aghaidh na críochdheighilte.

B'fhéidir go raibh oifigigh Chomhairle Uladh ag díriú go hiomarcach ar cheisteanna náisiúnta sna 1920idí agus sna 1930idí áfach. Beagnach gach bliain chaill an chomhairle airgead cé go raibh na sluaite a bhí ag freastal ar chluichí ag méadú. Is féidir cuid den locht sin a chur ar éifeachtaí na críochdheighilte, ach le fírinne bhí an chomhairle ag déileáil lena gcuid cúrsaí gnó go míchúramach. Ceapadh Eoghan Ó Dufaigh mar chisteoir onórach na comhairle i 1925 agus atoghadh é sa phost sin gach bliain go dtí 1934 cé go raibh sé ag cónaí i mBaile Átha Cliath agus é rófhada ón chúige le bheith in ann cuntais na comhairle a láimhseáil.

Thosaigh réabhlóid i riarachán an chúige i 1934 nuair a ceapadh Gearóid Mac Airt (Ard Mhacha) mar rúnaí Chomhairle Uladh. Bhí dushlán mór roimhe airgeadas an chúige a chur in ord ach rinne sé é go gasta. Ó shin amach ní raibh Comhairle Uladh i bhfiacha arís. De réir a chéile tháinig feabhas ar na háiseanna imeartha agus ar mhéid na sluaite. Osclaíodh páirceanna 'contae' úra in Ard Mhacha (1936), i Leitir Ceanainn (1937) agus sa Chaisleán Nua (1939). Ba é tógáil Pháirc Thighearnaigh, Cluain Eois, an fhorbairt ba mhó sa chúige. Osclaíodh an staid sin i 1944 agus gan mhoill aithníodh í mar lárionad na gcluichí Gaelacha in Ultaibh. Ní amháin go raibh coire nadúrtha ann leis 'an Cnoc' clúiteach ag amharc anuas ar an pháirc; buntáiste eile a bhain leis ná gur acomhal iarnróid lárnach don chúige ab ea Cluain Eois, agus d'fhéadfaí sluaite os cionn tríocha míle duine a mhealladh agus a óstáil.

A poster advertising the Ulster Football Championship final of 1952 and the trains going to the game through dozens of stations all over the province. This typifies the importance of the railways to the development of Clones as the annual Ulster football final venue. Yet by the end of the 1950s, rail-tracks around the province were being stripped away, and bus and car were preferred methods of transport to the big games. The referee for this game was Seán Óg Ó Ceallacháin, who, fifty-seven years later, still broadcasts the Gaelic games results nationwide on RTÉ radio on Sunday nights. (*Micheál Greenan*)

Lean an monaplacht iomlán a bhí ag an Cabhán agus Muineachán i gCraobh Peile Sinsear Uladh ó 1913 go dtí 1946, ach clúdaíonn an liosta gradam an dul chun cinn a bhí ar siúl sna contaetha eile. D'imir Ard Mhacha, mar shampla, ina lán cluichí ceannais agus ní raibh an t-ádh leo. Chuidigh an t-ardú caighdeáin go ginearálta le deiseanna an chúige i gcomórtas peile Chorn an Iarnróid, agus bhuaigh Ulaidh an chraobh sin faoi dheireadh i 1942 agus arís i 1943. Bhí clú ar na foirne Ultacha sin mar gheall ar stíl imeartha 'lámhphasála' iontach glic a d'úsáid siad.[76] Tharla roinnt 'briseadh tríd' don iománaíocht sa tuaisceart fosta i rith an Dara Cogadh Domhanda. Shroich Aontroim cluiche ceannais Chraobh Iománaíochta Mionúr na hÉireann i 1940 agus an cluiche ceannais sinsearach i 1943, agus bhain Ulaidh cluiche ceannais Chorn an Iarnróid amach i 1945. Cé gur bualadh go trom iad sna cluichí ceannais sin agus cé go raibh siad ag brath go mór ar imirt i bPáirc Uí Chorragáin (Béal Feirste) chun deis a fháil na deisceartaigh a shárú, ba mhór na gaiscí sin dul ní b'fhaide ná foirne ar bith ó Ultaibh roimhe.

Bhí i bhfad níos mó ná cluichí i gceist le CLG i gcónaí dá gcuid ball i gCúige Uladh, agus bhí an taobh cultúrtha den chumann ní ba láidre ansin ná áit ar bith eile. Tharla athbheochán mór sa náisiúnachas cultúrtha mall sna 1920idí agus luath sna 1930idí, go háirithe sa tuaisceart. Ó shin i leith chloígh clubanna CLG Uladh go dílis leis an dualgas a cuireadh orthu céilithe a reáchtáil in ionad 'damhsaí gallda'. De réir tuairiscí agus tuairimí oifigigh na gcúigí eile, níorbh fhéidir an rud céanna a rá faoi na clubanna sa deisceart.[77] D'eagraigh roinnt clubanna ranganna Gaeilge agus staire fosta. Is dócha gurbh é an cinneadh ba radacaí cruinnithe Chomhairle Uladh a thionól trí mheán na Gaeilge amháin ó 1942. Cé gur phléigh an Ardchomhairle agus na comhairlí cúige eile moltaí dá leithéid ó am go chéile, ba é cúige Uladh an t-aon chúige CLG a bhí dáiríre go leor faoin teanga dul an míle bhreise ar son na teanga.

Ón léirmheas gairid seo, is léir go raibh fadhbanna speisialta ag Cumann Lúthchleas Gael i gCúige Uladh idir 1884 agus 1945 (agus ina dhiaidh sin) a bhí taobh thiar den íoschaighdeán imeartha, chomh maith leis an bhochtannas airgid agus drochstádas na gcluichí sa tuaisceart ar feadh bhunús na tréimhse sin. Is féidir na deacrachtaí áirithe sin a chur in dhá chatagóir – freasúra seachtrach agus laige inmheánach. Bhí na fadhbanna sin chomh tromchúiseach do CLG sa tuaisceart anuas go dtí na 1920idí gur féidir ceist lárnach an ailt seo a chasadh thart: cén fáth a raibh cúige Uladh ábalta imeachtaí CLG a choinneáil chomh gníomhach sin chomh fada sin, agus é ag imirt in aghaidh na gaoithe i gcónaí? Is doiligh an cheist sin a fhreagairt go cruinn, ach tchítear gur bhain sé le spiorad dochloíte bhaill an chúige; bhí CLG rothábhachtach dóibh lena ligean dó bás a fháil, go háirithe in iarmhairt chríochdheighilt an náisiúin. Idir na 1920idí agus na 1940idí d'éirigh an cumann níos stuama sa tuaisceart agus bhí Cúige Uladh ag teacht suas leis na cúigí eile. Bhí an bhunsraith tógtha do níos mo ratha sna blianta a bhí le teacht.

Armagh players Jack Bratten, Mick O'Hanlon and
John McBreen in training at their camp at Maghery before
the 1953 All-Ireland football final. (*Jack Bratten*)

Section 3: The Expansion and Modernisation of Gaelic Games

The Civilising of Gaelic football
John Connolly and Paddy Dolan

**An Overview of the Playing Rules of
Gaelic Football and Hurling, 1884–2010**
Joe Lennon

Irish Republican attitudes to sport since 1921
Brian Hanley

The Gaelic Athletic Association and Irish-America
Paul Darby

**American Gaels and Cavan Heroes:
The 1947 All-Ireland Gaelic Football Final in New York**
Aogán Ó Fearghail and Paul Darby

The Emergence and Development of the GAA in Britain and Europe
David Hassan and Stephen Moore

The GAA in a Global Sporting Context
Alan Bairner

The Civilising of Gaelic football

John Connolly and Paddy Dolan

The issue of violence within Gaelic football has been a recurring theme for GAA administrators and journalists for some time now.[1] Implicit in this commentary is the suggestion that the scale and level of violence within contemporary Gaelic football is either a considerable problem or is on the increase. In this chapter, we address this specific issue through the application and interpretation of the work of sociologists Norbert Elias and Eric Dunning.[2] We use the word 'civilising'[3] as a technical term. The characteristics of a civilising trend, or process, include: a movement along a continuum between social and self regulation towards the latter – the internalisation of rules and less reliance on other people for their enforcement; an advance in the threshold of repugnance for engaging in and witnessing violent acts; and enhanced feelings of anxiety and shame over such behaviour. These developments occurred because of a complementary process of increasing social interdependency within Ireland. This means that more and more people of different class dispositions became mutually dependent on each other for the fulfilment of their needs, such as the provision of food, work and protection.

Gaelic football is not civilised in any absolute sense, but we argue that it has become more civilised over the last 125 years.[4] However, this process has been in no way linear. Violent transgressions still occur for several reasons, namely, the structure of the on-field game contests and Ireland's specific state-formation processes and its international relations with Britain. Nevertheless, there has been a transformation in the type of the transgressions from spontaneous violent displays towards aggressive behaviour of a more instrumental form.

When the GAA was established in 1884, no national standardised game of 'Gaelic' football existed; instead local and regional variations of 'Gaelic' football predominated.[5] To complicate matters further, many teams and clubs that had switched their allegiance to the nascent GAA from either association football or rugby continued to exhibit elements of these sports during Gaelic football matches.[6] This was often a factor in the many disputes which arose concerning how the game should be played.[7] Gaelic football at that time has been described as a sport of 'rough-and-tumble … [where the] go-for-the-man system pertained'.[8] Handigrips or wrestling was allowed until 1886,[9] although they appear to have remained an aspect of the game for some time thereafter. For instance, a match report from 1887 stated: 'There were a few good wrestling matches during the progress of the game. It was quite impossible to keep some of the players from a having a tussle. But I must say they wrestled very honestly, and helped to enliven the proceedings a little. Two or three men were put out for short periods for infringing on the rules.'[10]

Newspaper reports of matches in the late 1880s frequently refer to enhanced levels of excitement by players and supporters when outbursts of fighting occurred.[11] Such emotional volatility was not merely characteristic of the sport of Gaelic football, but was also related to the general volatility of life at the time.[12] Expressive violence, often enacted through faction fights, which were still a feature of Irish life,[13] overlapped with Gaelic football matches,[14] many of which were particularly violent affairs. For example, in 1893 following a violent disturbance during a football match in Limerick, a player was stabbed to death as he ran from the field.[15] Although violence of this nature clearly became less prevalent,[16] we cannot be absolutely certain of an overall decline in violence. However, we are confident that a civilising process has occurred in the sport of Gaelic football and is empirically demonstrable. This is evident in both a movement from social control to greater self-control and in the advance in the threshold of repugnance toward violent displays. Over the last 125 years, the sport of Gaelic football has undergone a process of sportisation, meaning that formal written rules governing the sport have become more precise and comprehensive,[17] which itself is evidence of a civilising trend in a specific direction.[18]

In the formative years of the GAA, the level of self-control and restraint exercised by players was fairly volatile and individuals were prone to spontaneous and emotional outbursts. There was an understanding, indeed, an expectation, that players were prone to losing their tempers. For instance, in an account of a

Letter from Séamus Ó Brogáin, *rúnaí* of Mullagh club in Co. Cavan, predicting a rough game the following weekend, in June 1937. (*Micheál Greenan*)

match in 1887, the journalist, most probably, Michael Cusack, asks, in a clearly frustrated tone, 'When will players learn to control tempers and play in a friendly way with one another? … One hot player is enough to get a bad name for a team, and, surely, men can play vigorously enough, in fact, much better, without losing their self-control than when they are in a state of uncontrollable excitement.'[19] Although players and teams were criticised, referees, in particular, were castigated for their failure to impose the rules, illustrating the emphasis placed upon social control for curbing indiscipline. It reflected the normative belief of the time that external constraint was the primary means to deal with player transgressions. For example, in a game characterised as involving 'strong rough play, with an occasional push from behind, and a free indulgence in handigrips', the journalist goes on to emphasis how 'natural' it was for players to become aggressive:

> The toleration of this kind of play by the referee in charge is a thing that cannot be too strongly deprecated. It has the effect of stirring up the passions and jealousy of men who are naturally hot-tempered, and individual manly pride will endeavour to assert itself, in some instances, by the use of knuckles.[20]

At this time, the control of matches remained a considerable problem for referees. In part this was probably due to a lack of knowledge of the rules by some referees and a failure on the part of others to impose them. For example, during a match in 1887, it was reported that, 'Many of the members of the home team committed fouls, but no notice was taken of them.'[21] The level of precision in the initial set of rules published in 1884 was rudimentary – the referee and umpires had the power to disqualify any player 'for any act they may consider unfair.'[22] Gradually the rules became more precise; 'Pushing, tripping, kicking, catching, holding, or jumping at a player, or butting with the head' were 'deemed fouls' under the 1895 rules.[23] In addition, the sanctions available to referees increased and became more varied, when the penalty of a free-kick was introduced in 1888.[24] Yet, even where referees sought to apply the rules, players often refused to accept their decision,[25] and in such cases matches would often finish prematurely owing to a player or team refusing to continue.[26] Thus, in 1895, the GAA authorities added the sanction of suspension and forfeit of the match for teams leaving the field of play without the permission of the referee.[27]

The desire to ensure discipline and curb violent and aggressive play through the rules occurred at the same time as the sport and players were valorised for their manly strength and physicality. From the outset, the playing of Gaelic games was conflated with physical preparation for war.[28] Matches were described in military metaphors[29] and both players and teams were commended on their manly play and physical prowess. Within this portrayal, Gaelic players were conceived as unaccustomed 'to rigid discipline'[30] and to that extent were more dangerous than those who played 'English' games. This desire to portray Gaelic players as physically dangerous and, indeed, volatile in nature moderated the contradictory desire to curb violence within the game. At one level, this ambivalence towards violence meant those who committed transgressions were labelled 'ungaelic',[31] while at same time GAA players and officials were, paradoxically, within a short few years, training with the Irish Volunteers[32] and attempting to establish rifle clubs.[33]

Attempts to exert greater control over player behaviour through the imposition of more rules and sanctions did not lead to immediate changes in this regard. This emphasises the fragile nature of the internalisation process towards socially acceptable behaviour of the time. For instance, the rule-changes of 1908 were considered by one Gaelic commentator and prominent GAA official of the time to 'impose a very considerable constraint on players as compared with former times.'[34] Yet, in the same year, the *Gaelic Athletic Annual* claimed that 'Many hot-headed players have time and again spoiled a good game by refusing to conform to the rulings of the referee, when he orders them to the side line for breaches of the rules. They refuse to go unless after much persuasion.'[35] Gradually players began to exert greater levels of self-steering and specific practices were internalised and 'became second nature'. The well-known Gaelic games journalist of the day, 'Carbery', writing in the *Gaelic Athletic Annual* of 1927, claimed that 'malpractices and displays of temper on the playing fields have disappeared'[36] – perhaps indicative of an overall improvement in player behaviour. A civilising process, of course, is not absolute, but processual, and Carbery's contention must be judged in this context. Even by the late 1920s and 1930s, there were regular reports of players refusing to accept the decisions of referees leading, on occasion, to a further escalation of events involving spectators.[37] Both referees and players were often the victims of such disturbances.[38] For instance, in 1938, during a club match in Cavan, it was reported that 'a player was assaulted with ash-plants.'[39]

A further indication of a movement toward greater self-restraint amongst players is evident from both changes in the structure of on-field play and in the punctuality of players. In the early years of the GAA, physical strength was a critical component of the sport of Gaelic football with 'scrimmages'[40] and 'scrummages'[41] a regular feature of play. It appears from newspaper descriptions at the time that this involved large numbers of players attempting to move the ball in a particular direction, while simultaneously being resisted by players from the other team. As such, the 'weight' and strength of players counted immeasurably.[42] The larger number of players allowed on a team, up to twenty-one aside until 1895 and seventeen per side until 1913, and the congregating of all players with the exception of the goalkeepers at the centre of the pitch in two lines for the throw-in, contributed to this specific structure of Gaelic football at this time. Gradually, the rule-changes facilitated more open play through a reduction in numbers and the prescription of player positions.[43] The structure and pattern of play changed not only as a result of the rules, although that clearly facilitated these changes, but also because players demonstrated greater foresight and self-restraint as evidenced by the fact that they began to maintain specific on-field positions and developed patterns of combination play. Tardiness was regularly reported by administrators as a particular problem even by the early 1900s.[44] For example, in 1908 the *Anglo-Celt* reported that '… a football match, timed to start at 2 p.m. sharp, which 4 p.m. barely saw commenced.'[45] Noticeable improvements in time keeping were noted by a journalist in the1930s.[46] By 1943, the rules stated that should a match be postponed for some unavoidable cause, it may be re-fixed for a date seven days later,[47] indicating that teams were more certain of being able to turn up. Again these were relative improvements as even during the late 1960s concerns were

Cavan Slashers G. F. Club.

Plunkett Street,

Cavan,

12th May, 1937.

A chara,

       I am directed by the Committee of above Club
to call the attention of the County Committee to the conduct
of certain Playing members and Supporters of Crubany Club,
who made an uncalled for attack on two of our Players (John
Coyle and Louis Blessing) at the Tournament in Breffni Park
on Sunday 9th Inst.

       Our Players, as they were entitled to do,
attended as Spectators on this occasion and apparently it
had been arranged to avail of the opportunity to give one of
them (Louis Blessing) what might be regarded as a "hiding".
Without any justification whatever he was set upon by Players
and members of the Crubany Club and would probably have been
seriously assaulted were it not for the interference of other
members of the County Team, who can give you full particulars
of the attack.

       Our Club protests in the strongest manner
possible against such unseemly conduct and feels sure that
the County Committee will take such steps as may be necessary
to prevent a recurrence of it. We are satisfied that
the attack was an organised one and we think that the

Cavan Slashers letter from 1937 highlighting the dangers faced by players – inter-county players (such as Louis Blessing and Jackie Coyle) in particular – from spectators as well as opposing players. It also points up the tendency of some urban-rural contests to give rise to friction. (*Micheál Greenan*)

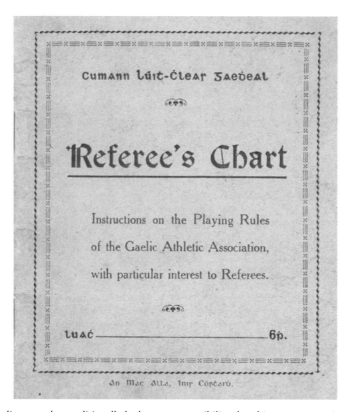

The referee in Gaelic games has traditionally had more responsibility than his counterparts in some other sports. Over the decades the GAA administration at Croke Park has produced increasingly voluminous publications of advice to referees. Debate has often focused on whether outbreaks of violence in Gaelic games have been caused by bad refereeing or ambiguity in the playing rules.

raised about punctuality.[48] We emphasise improvements in time-keeping[49] as they are indicative of greater self-restraint, reflection and foresight. These improvements in punctuality occurred across Irish society and were reflected not only within the sport of Gaelic football, but in all spheres of life, such as, in personal and work relationships.

The GAA authorities also sought to widen the social observation on players by increasing the responsibilities and power of linesmen and umpires, which by the 1950s remained limited – indicating a score and when and where the ball was out of play.[50] Essentially, referees were seen as the primary mechanism for dealing with player transgressions. In 1906, for example, during a heated debate at an Ulster Council meeting, one official claimed 'that a lines man could no more interfere with the referee than could the spectators.'[51] Such a belief persisted for some time. In 1955 a congress motion to amend the rules so that linesmen and umpires were empowered to report any serious breaches of the rules were rejected. One delegate opposing the motion suggested: 'This is a dangerous motion I would not like to be the linesman in a serious championship [match] who would call over the referee when the ball was up the field. Suppose the referee did not see the signals of the linesman? There would be civil war on the grounds if you had such a rule.'[52] This potential rule was clearly envisaged by the delegate as likely to cause more serious incidents arising and it indicates that players viewed the referee as the sole functionary responsible for deciding on a transgression of the rules. While the delegate in question may have exaggerated the potential consequences, it is indicative of the lack of co-operation that existed up to that time between match officials. Over time this progressively changed.

In 1973, umpires and linesmen had the power to bring 'incidents of rough tactics or deliberate striking, hitting and kicking' to the notice of the referee.[53] These surveillance duties were further extended in 1978, when they were given authority to bring notice of incursions by team officials onto the field of play.[54] Since then co-operation and co-ordination between officiating functionaries became even more cohesive. Infringements by players are regularly identified, and players are dismissed, based on the advice of linesmen and umpires.[55]

The use of technological surveillance removed spatial and temporal constraints particularly at inter-county level and facilitated more comprehensive levels of observation in relation to offenders, who escaped on-field punishment. By the 1990s, GAA players were regularly subjected to sanction by the GAA's disciplinary systems based on video evidence.[56] The social pressure on the referee and his officials to strictly enforce the rules was gradually accompanied by a greater social pressure on players, their officials and the GAA authorities to address indiscipline and outbreaks of violence. For instance, the section on discipline in the GAA's first published strategic review, in 1971, stated:

> There is, we fear, an increasing tendency to depend on the Referee to impose proper standards of sportsmanship and good behaviour on players. This should not be so … In our view the *primary* responsibility for ensuring good conduct and sportsmanship rests not on the Referee but on the officials of the Association who are in close contact with the players and who are able to influence them. It is they who must teach discipline – by exhortation, by training and by example. Ideally, it is only as a last resort that it should be necessary to impose it.[57]

This sentiment – that players could and should learn to control themselves – is increasingly perceptible within media reports and commentary. Violence was now no longer considered solely the outcome of overexcited and hot tempered players as it was in the past, when 'excited partisans and fever heat enthusiasm are the elements that give rise to spontaneous outbursts of temper, [and where] no blame can be attributed to the Gaelic Athletic Association for the incidents.'[58] The GAA authorities and players increasingly became a focus of criticism for failing to address violent displays illustrating the change in the expectations of journalists and the public at large concerning control of violence.[59] This movement in the direction of greater self-restraint was also accompanied by an advance in the threshold of repugnance towards violence.

Certainly by the 1930s match officials were still prone to physical assault by players even at inter-county level.[60] While such incidents were condemned, the moral denunciation of this violence remained relatively muted in comparison to later years, indicating a higher tolerance for such displays of violence. For example, in 1936, the then GAA president, speaking in response to some of these incidents, argued that players 'might not have adverted to the extreme gravity of their conduct.'[61] At the same time, the authorities were increasingly adopting a tougher stance in relation to player violence. Following the striking of an umpire and referee by players in the 1943 All-Ireland football final, one player later received a twelve-month suspension while another was banned for life.[62] In the *Irish Independent* report of that particular match,[63] none of the players involved were named, which was common practice at that time and reflects less of a willingness to identify and specifically allocate blame to individual players.

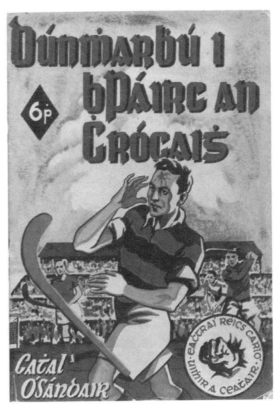

Although a work of fiction, the title of this novella (translating as *Murder in Croke Park*) from 1944 clearly depicts hurling as a dangerous game.

Dick Fitzgerald, in his book, *How to Play Gaelic Football* (1914), demonstrating a particular foul that was more common to that time than to the present day, owing to the greater amount of ground-play in Gaelic football in the early twentieth century.

Moreover, while the actions of players involved were condemned this was, to an extent, subdued in comparison to contemporary analysis and commentary. This can be contrasted with later journalistic accounts from the 1970s onwards, where, for example, players were more overtly criticised for violent behaviour.[64]

The tone and sentiment within contemporary accounts is more judgmental and disapproving. Individual players are now named, reflecting a less forgiving attitude to violent transgressions. The sense of shame is also more discernible. For example, a journalist commenting on the Leinster football final of 1993, during which no player was sent-off, wrote 'I was utterly appalled at what was offered up as sport … It is now a game from which normal standards of decency and acceptable behaviour have gone walk about.'[65] This illustrates a change in the public attitude towards displays of violence, where the sense of moral outrage is more palpable than in the past. The recent commentary surrounding the hitting of a notebook from a referee's hand by an inter-county player,[66] illustrates how offences of this nature are now viewed with a far greater sense of outrage than in the past. Such journalistic accounts are, in fact, a reflection of a higher threshold of repugnance; violent or aggressive displays, which in previous decades went unnoticed as part of a manly game, are 'nowadays regarded as abhorrent'.[67]

An examination of the rules also illustrates an increasing concern with player safety, which is symptomatic of a heightening sensitivity to violence and injury. For instance, since the 1880s goalkeepers had been particularly vulnerable to physical assault with the result that, in 1908, the small parallelogram was introduced in an effort to protect the goalkeeper from being 'charged' before the ball arrived in the goalmouth area.[68] The increasing sensitivity towards violence is also perceptible in other rule-changes, such as the decision to add greater precision to the rule concerning the practice of 'charging'. For example, in 1966, 'a charge' was defined specifically as 'shoulder to shoulder'[69] and by 1975 as 'side to side with at least one foot on the ground.'[70]

The number of 'frees' awarded during a match was increasingly looked upon in a negative light by commentators.[71] Here was evidence of a general transformation in the nature of player transgressions, that is, away from spontaneous expressive violence towards more instrumental transgressions – to impede the progress of an opponent in an effort to win both individual on-field contests and, thereby, the match. This was a reflection of the growing competitiveness of Gaelic football, which began to be articulated by GAA administrators as the 'win-at-all-costs-approach.'[72] In response the GAA authorities created the category of 'persistent fouling' in 1975 in an effort to address this.[73]

Yet, even by the early 1970s, as referee John Gough recounts, 'hitting a guy a punch was reasonably acceptable,'[74] demonstrating that the tendency to control oneself and the inculcation of socially acceptable standards remained fragile. Player self-control could break down during the competitive pressure of a match. None of this is to suggest that violent assaults on either players or referees no longer occur. In 1985, a referee in Wicklow was seriously assaulted by a player[75] and similar incidents have been reported since then.[76]

However, when these incidents do occur, they are now viewed in a harsher light and the sense of shame and moral outrage is decidedly greater[77] than in the past indicating an increase in the threshold of distaste towards violence.

These changes – the movement in the balance between social and self-restraint in favour of the latter, and the advancing threshold of repugnance – reflect changes in the personality structure of Gaelic players, and people in general in Ireland, as no sport is detached from the wider society in which it exists.[78] In the latter part of this chapter, we explain why such changes occurred.

Over the course of the last 125 years, Irish people became more dependent on one another, and also on people from other nation-states.[79] This was both a gradual and uneven process. Industrialisation in Britain during the nineteenth century had the unplanned effect of involving more Irish people in more specialised, agricultural functions through the production, distribution and exchange of food, as Irish producers competed with other European nations for British consumers. This had the corresponding, and related, effect of expanding centres of administration and commercial exchange within Ireland as more extensive transport networks were built. This growing interdependency between Irish producers and British consumers, and indeed other competitors, led to the compelling process of larger and more mechanised farms and the subsequent migration of displaced farm-workers to towns and cities within Ireland and, of course, abroad through emigration. While increased social interdependency can initially exacerbate tensions,[80] increasing awareness of mutual interdependence, the dependence of each individual or group on different functions provided by others, leads to a compelling process, whereby most sectors of society are under considerable, though class- and gender-specific, social pressure to exert greater foresight concerning their actions and behaviour.

The decline in the agricultural labour force is particularly significant as life, in general, on farms is less immediately and consistently reliant on many other people (especially strangers) compared to industrial or post-industrial urban conurbations, in which people are subjected to more varied social pressures. According to selected Census of Population statistics (1861 to 2002), the proportion of the male labour force engaged in agricultural occupations remained as high as sixty per cent up to the 1940s. Since then, there has been a steep decline; falling to forty-three per cent in 1963 and to just eight per cent by 2002. The process of urbanisation, a further example of expanding social interdependencies, increased significantly over this same period. Between 1900 and 1971, the proportion of people who lived in towns of more than 1,500 people, rose from thirty-two per cent to fifty-two percent[81] and to sixty-one percent by 2006.[82] Increasing urbanisation means more people become functionally dependent on one another. Simply put, they rely on one another for a range of requirements, the simplest to the most complex – transport, food provision and employment. As people come to depend on others for more and more of their needs, they are compelled to attune their behaviour to that of others. They must control and regulate their conduct in a more even and stable manner. By the 1960s, Ireland's economic and political situation became more expansive and outward-looking in order to address high levels of emigration and unemployment, through the attraction of foreign investment. This was both an indication of expanding social interdependencies and an impetus for further expansion. For example, in 1951, only sixteen per cent of manufacturing output was exported; yet by 1988, this had increased to sixty-four per cent with foreign firms accounted for seventy five per cent of this.[83] Accession into the European Economic Community (EEC) in 1973 brought new social pressures and opportunities to those involved in the Irish industrial and farming sectors.[84] Ireland's integration in the EEC and later European Union was not only economic of course, but also political and cultural. As a result of being enmeshed in these international competitive networks, the pressure for more specialised and differentiated social functions (occupations) increased. This process of increasing social interdependence set in motion a further civilising spurt, as people were further compelled to control and regulate their conduct more evenly. Over time this conscious effort to control oneself becomes internalised and a matter of habit. Greater social pressure to exercise more consistent self-restraint advanced in Irish society[85] and this is reflected in the sport of Gaelic football.

This process went hand in hand with the gradual, but uneven, development of the state control over and monopolisation of violence, and the creation and maintenance of a pacified social space in Ireland. We

Paul Donnelly (Tyrone) throws away the boot of James McCartan (Down) during the 1994 Ulster football final. The behaviour of players has come under increasing scrutiny by the media in recent decades, and accordingly transgressions have been subjected to more publicity and greater expression of repugnance.

emphasise here the formation of a monopoly of force, because under such conditions the threat, which individuals or groups represent for each other, is subject to stricter controls and becomes more calculable. Violence is generally pushed behind the scenes and only breaks out in cases of extreme social tension or war. The state monopolisation of physical violence means people have to restrain their own aggressive tendencies; it imposes a greater degree of self-control.[86] By the 1880s, Ireland had undergone an agrarian class transformation and tension and conflict between farmers, landholders and labourers was superseded by disputes mainly between landowners and tenants (farmers).[87] A decline in violence and greater enmity between 'native' Catholic agrarian classes meant a relatively pacified space, which in turn facilitated attempts to pursue the regular 'organisation' of games and the formation of the GAA. Yet, the growing tensions along religious and ethnic lines overlapped class tensions culminating in the outbreak of violence between these various groupings in the early twentieth century; between the predominantly urban working classes and the representatives of Irish industrial, capitalist classes; between Irish and British military forces, in 1916 and later 1919–21; and during the Civil War. These latter conflicts caused delays in the GAA championships, with matches postponed for over a year; teams withdrew from the Championship due to the imprisonment and involvement of players during the war; transport lines were destroyed, which unintentionally hampered the travel of players and spectators.[88] This demonstrates how the pursuit of leisure practices depends upon the relative pacification of social relations, which in turn depends on the state monopolisation of the means of physical violence within a given territory.[89] However, violent confrontations within Ireland did not disappear and continued to be a feature of Irish society well into the twentieth century. For instance, violent altercations between members of the opposing groups in the Civil War persisted into the 1930s.[90] There was also sporadic violence over the status of the Irish nation-state; groups differed on the means to complete or reunite the nation. Gradually violence became increasingly pushed 'behind the scenes' as the Irish state strengthened its hold on the monopolisation of violence over its jurisdiction (the Republic of Ireland), although this was not the case for the six counties (Northern Ireland), where the monopoly of violence exercised by the British state remained particularly fragile throughout the 1970s and 1980s. This also, to a degree, extended to the twenty-six counties (the Republic of Ireland), where the Irish state's police and armed forces were required to contain the violent actions of armed nationalist factions and their sympathisers. Gradually, nationalists and unionists in general became more trustful of each other and of the British and Irish governments. In addition, the main armed factions gave up relying on violence by the mid 1990s, although some groups remained committed to violence, as a means of achieving their aims. Despite this, the monopoly over violence became more stable.

In conclusion, it is our contention, that it is only in conjunction with these overlapping social processes – the relationship between Ireland and Britain; the increasing social interdependencies enmeshing Irish people – that a more stable mechanism of self-restraint developed within Irish people. This is consistent with the Elias and Dunning[91] theory of civilising processes and violence in sport generally, but with some qualifications due to Ireland's specific history. As outlined in this chapter, this process was uneven and non-linear, due, in particular, to the fragile nature of the monopoly of violence, which existed in Ireland. The symbolic alignment between Gaelic players and the 'Irish nation' and conflation of GAA players as warriors, as 'true Gaels' ready for military conflict in the cause of nationhood, embodied an ambivalence toward violence within the game and moderated the progressive social constraints imposed. Indeed, Gaelic football's symbolic association with manliness remains.

Alongside the advancing threshold of repugnance towards violence and the shift in balance towards greater self-control, was a process of increasing competitiveness and seriousness of involvement within the sport. Over the decades, players resorted to deliberately breaking the rules and/or to instrumental forms of violence in their efforts to win matches and these incidents, on occasion, led to further violence. To re-confirm, we are not arguing that violence no longer occurs in Gaelic football matches; rather the nature of the violence has changed and is, generally, of a more muted and calculating form.

An Overview of the Playing Rules of Gaelic Football and Hurling, 1884–2010

Joe Lennon

When the Gaelic Athletic Association was founded in 1884, one of the first tasks undertaken by Michael Cusack and Maurice Davin was to draft sets of rules for each game – ten for football and twelve for hurling. These sets of rules were adopted at the second meeting of the new association, held in Cork in December 1884, and first published in *United Ireland* newspaper on 7 February 1885. Since forms of football and hurling had been played for centuries before 1884, why was there an urgency to publish these playing rules so soon after the GAA was founded? As Davin explained in a previous letter to *United Ireland* in October 1884, 'I may say there are no rules and therefore the games are dangerous'.[1] Evidently he realised that rules were necessary for the safety of the players as well as for the good of the games.

These 1884 rules were not unusual for their time. Rules for various sports had been codified previously.[2] Indeed, five sets of rules for Irish hurling were published before 1884.[3] Likewise, between 1859 and 1884, seven sets of playing rules were published for what later became known as Australian rules football – all prior to the GAA.[4] Hence the suggestion that the Australian code owes its origin or some of its genes to Gaelic football is fanciful.[5] The earliest full sets of playing rules broadly relative to the GAA are probably those for Cornwall's 'Hurling to Goales' and 'Hurling to the Countrie', published in 1602.[6] However, this Cornish game of 'hurling' more closely resembled modern rugby; in both games the ball was hurled by hand – not by a stick.

Athletics had a higher priority than Gaelic football and hurling in the first couple of years of the GAA. In addition, the young association soon developed an extensive portfolio of other activities, with printed rules such as for handball, cycling, tug-of-war, rounders and wrestling.[7] Nonetheless, this chapter will focus on the evolution of the playing rules of football and hurling, as these have been the principal sports of the GAA since the late 1880s. It will examine what were the rationales and influences behind rule-changes, how the relevant legislation was introduced and maintained, and how these changes shaped the games. It is not intended to record every single rule-change or to assess how the rules have been implemented by referees. Rather, the aim is to give a concise insight into the legislation that has produced the indigenous Irish games of football and hurling in their present forms.

Analysis of the 125-year period is divided into three eras: first, 1884–1950, when the playing rules of football and hurling were in separate sections of the *Official Guide* (*O.G.*); second, 1950–90, when the rules of the two games were 'co-ordinated', (amalgamated); and finally, from 1991 to the present time, in which the rules of the two games have been detailed separately from each other and, significantly, published in a separate book of the *Official Guide*.

Turning to the initial time period outlined here and, as indicated earlier, the first sets of playing rules drafted in 1884 contained ten rules for football and twelve for hurling. Of the ten football rules, four dealt with the actual playing of the game; the penalty for aggressive fouls was dismissal; the dress for both games was knee-breeches and stockings and boots or shoes. Dangerous boots were banned in football. Of the twelve hurling rules, three dealt with set play and two dealt with aggressive fouls. It is also clear that there were many unwritten rules observed at this time. This reflects the former practice of agreeing the rules for the matches on the morning[8] of the games and perhaps confirms that these 'rules' were in fact well known.

Despite the existence of the various sets of rules mentioned above, there is little evidence that any copying between associations took place, beyond a couple of small exceptions.[9] More tellingly, it is clear that the rules for football and hurling were written by different people, if not different committees.[10] It was also clear that the founding fathers were determined to design a game of football quite different from all other football games. For example, the rules forbade throwing and carrying as in rugby.

The changes made to the goal area were among the most salient developments in the playing rules in the first three decades of the GAA. This montage of photographs from the 1903 All-Ireland football final shows how the point-posts used to be on either side of the goal-posts employed until 1910. (*Eoghan Corry*)

Initially, playing rules were changed as the leading officials thought fit. Cusack proposed four rule-changes of his own a few months after the founding of the GAA.[11] The Kerry County Board adopted its own set of playing rules for football in November 1889, and the Meath County Board adopted a set of rules for football in 1894.[12] These latter rules were proposed by the county secretary, R. T. Blake, who, a year later, was appointed secretary of the GAA. During his tenure in the mid 1890s, the Central Council introduced many rule changes without recourse to congress. The proliferation of sets of playing rules had the potential to damage the games and the association itself. By the 1900s it was established that the annual convention was the primary forum for rule-changing. It was subsequently decided that playing rules could be changed only at every other annual congress; and, at the 1903 Annual Convention, it was decided that playing rules could only be changed every three years.

In the 1896/97 *O.G.*, the number of rules for football had almost trebled to twenty-seven, and hurling rules had almost doubled to twenty-two. In the *Official Guide* for the years 1907–09, football and hurling each had twenty-four rules of play and specifications, and there were a further seventeen 'Rules of Control' that applied to both games. Because of the level of disagreement on and off the field, the need to write down the rules had become accepted, and these additional rules helped to define the games more clearly.

Dick Fitzgerald, the Kerry captain who pioneered writing about how to play Gaelic games. This contemporary cartoon reflects his high public profile, and in the image on the right (from 1914) he demonstrates the over-the-shoulder 'screw kick', which was an admired skill at that time. The author of the present chapter, Joe Lennon, followed his lead by bringing out books about coaching and fitness for Gaelic football while still playing at the top level in the 1960s.

Towards the end of the first era, it was clear that the association was experiencing great difficulty in administering the existing playing rules. As each crisis in the rules developed, the association simply appointed a rules revision committee to deal with it. In fact, no fewer than six such committees were set up during this era.

A further problem was caused by the fact that motions to annual conventions and congresses did not always appear on a printed *clár* or agenda. Imagine the chaos at convention and congress as motions or amendments were proposed without a written version of it being available to the executive or the delegates! This appeared to be still the case as late as the 1930s. The then secretary Pádraig Ó Caoimh appealed in his annual report of 1933 to congress delegates to write down motions for rule changes on a piece of paper and submit them.[13]

One of the biggest changes in the playing rules in the first era was the reduction of team sizes from a maximum of twenty-one with a minimum of fourteen (as they were from 1884), to seventeen 'not more not less' in 1896.[14] Some flexibility was introduced in 1901, when a team could begin a match with thirteen players but seventeen were required to start the second half. From 1907, club championship and league games 'may be 13 a side'.[15] In 1915, the inter-county team size was reduced to fifteen. Curiously, Rule 5, relating to 'Number of Players', stated that 'the second half hour cannot be resumed unless there are 15 players on each side'.[16] Given that a player who was sent off could not be replaced, this rule was anomalous for many years.

The second visible change arising from these rules was the adjustment to the size of the playing field. Initially, the hurling field was 200 yards x 150 yards or (30,000 square yards), whereas the football field was 120 yards x 80 yards (9,600 square yards) – less than one third the area of the hurling field. The dimensions were gradually reduced until 1910, when each field of play had the same dimensions – 140 to 170 yards long, by 84 to 100 yards wide. In 1937 the maximum length for each field was reduced to 160 yards.

Another big visible change at this time was the configuration of the goal-posts. Initially there were only goal-posts and crossbars. The football posts were fifteen feet apart and eight feet high. The hurling goals were twenty feet by ten feet. Point-posts were introduced in 1886, and these were placed twenty-one feet on either side of the goal-posts, which were both now twenty-one feet apart; but the hurling crossbar was raised to ten feet by six inches. In 1896 the distance between all four posts was twenty-one feet and both crossbars were now positioned eight feet off the ground. In 1907 the distance between all four posts was reduced to fifteen feet. H-shaped posts were introduced in 1910, with the uprights twenty-one feet apart, and the crossbar at eight feet. This configuration has lasted until today.[17]

In the early years, forfeit points were part of the scoring system. A forfeit point was awarded against a team that played the ball over its own end line outside all the posts. Five forfeit points equalled a goal. Forfeit points were abolished at convention of 1886 and replaced by a forty-yard free-kick or -puck.

The first square marked in front of goal was introduced in 1895. This was a seven-yard square that remained for hurling till 1907. A ten-yard line replaced the seven-yard square on the football field in 1901, but in 1907, three five-yard squares were marked outside the point-posts and the goal-posts for both games. In 1910, when the H-shaped goals were adopted, an area measuring fifteen yards by five yards was marked outside the goalposts; so what was originally a square came to be referred to in Rule 4 as a parallelogram, and still to this day, is often referred to as 'the square' or 'the parallelogram' even though it is, strictly speaking, a rhombus.[18]

In the first decade of the twentieth century, during the early years of Luke O'Toole's secretaryship of the GAA, a determined effort to abolish the skill of catching in football was evident. A motion to the 1903 convention designed to abolish catching in football was defeated by just eleven votes. In 1911, a senior official, Thomas Hoey Redmond, set out the reasons in an article, 'Catching: A Plea for its Abolition', which appeared in the association's official annual.[19] Football continued to evolve naturally, most notably with development of the skill of the solo-run in the 1920s by a Mayo player, Dr Seán Lavan. This beautiful and technical skill added a new dimension to football. It gave the skilful player opportunities to demonstrate his ability, and it helped to counteract the disadvantage of the smaller players.

Legislating for the solo-run exemplified the problems of the GAA at central level in using terminology for definition. The rule on 'The Play' stated that the ball 'may not be carried', before clarifying that 'Carrying shall be taking more than four steps while holding the ball, which must not be held longer than is necessary to hop it, kick it or fist it away.' Apart from the errant use of 'carrying' instead of 'overcarrying', this statement was inherently contradictory: a player was required to dispose of the ball immediately, yet he could take up to four steps with the ball. The rule then stated that the ball could be 'hopped *once* with either one or both hands against the ground';[20] this was a mis-defined reference to bouncing the ball, which in fact players could do repeatedly in the course of a solo-run.

Although the 1935 congress decided to extend from three years to five years the period between congress at which playing rules could be changed, this decision was not implemented. Not only were there some playing-rule changes made in 1937;[21] an extraordinary set of rules was produced in 1939, entitled *Playing Rules of Hurling and Football*, in which a set of rules common to both codes appeared in the opening section, under the heading, 'Hurling and Football'.[22] This attempt to combine the rules of the two games provided a preview of what was to come in 1950.

Towards the end of this era, the open-hand pass in football (though not in hurling) became a very contentious issue. Some members, including senior officials, wanted it replaced by a more restrictive fist-pass. A motion to effect this change was defeated at congress in 1945. However, the minutes of this debate were written up by secretary Ó Caoimh as though the motion had been carried.[23] This led to a challenge at the 1946 congress by Armagh delegate, Alf Murray (later to become president of the association). He succeeded in having the erroneous minute corrected even though Ó Caoimh argued that the fisted pass was not a change.[24] At this time, Ó Caoimh had planned to circulate an instructional booklet for referees In Rule 11 of this booklet ('The Play'), clause (h), it was stated in bold print:

An extract from a programme for a GAA sports-day at Derrymacash, Co. Armagh, in 1921. Up to the following year, the GAA legislated for and governed much of the track-and-field athletics in Ireland, as well as football, hurling and a range of other sports. (*Michael Anderson*)

> Referees must be exceedingly vigilant so as to detect "throwing" the ball – a not so infrequent occurrence when a player attempts to pass the ball with his hand to one of his colleagues. NOTE. – In hand-passing the ball must be fisted.[25]

Some two thousand booklets containing this had been printed.[26] It was full of rule interpretations and contained many rule-changes. The first section of this booklet opens with the first statement of the policy of 'speeding up the game' for the sake of spectator enjoyment, which was to become a dogma of the GAA. To achieve this, referees were instructed to insist that free-kicks and -pucks 'should be taken at once'; in the event of an injury to a player (regardless of how serious), 'see that the game resumes inside 2 minutes'; and '[d]o not hold up the game by whistling petty infringements'.

Despite the fact that Antrim and Ulster inter-provincial teams had made the hand-pass an important feature of their play, and had achieved success by exploiting this skill, a motion from Antrim to congress in 1950 to abolish the hand-pass succeeded against all expectations.

Although the first era saw the games develop and mature, the legislation was far from perfect or properly managed and, periodically, descended into chaos. By 1935, when the GAA was just fifty years in existence, at least forty sets of playing rules had been produced, and at least six special committees had been appointed by convention to 'revise and clarify the rules for the guidance of clubs'.[27] It was clear that the association could not control the quality of playing-rule legislation. There was neither an overall plan nor a philosophy for legislation. Despite this, the games survived this lack of management expertise and the attempts to delete the skills of catching and hand-passing from football but not from hurling.

In the second era of the playing rules, broadly speaking from 1950 until 1990, the GAA appointed three general secretaries (or directors-general), and each had an important impact on the playing rules. Between 1950 and 1990, the rules of Gaelic football and hurling were 'co-ordinated'. This was the term used to explain the extraordinary decision to combine the rules of play of these two essentially different games. Additionally, the playing rules lost their position of prominence in separate sections of the *O.G.* as they were submerged and dispersed amongst the other rules of the association.

Prior to 1950 the playing rules of football and hurling each had a section of their own, in which the rules were numbered 1–20 in each case. Post 1950, the competitions rules were numbered 116 to 122; then a section on 'Travelling and Hotel Expenses', in Rules 123 to 126. The section on 'Playing Rules' (applicable to football and hurling) were Rules 127 to 150. Their presentation was anything but user-friendly. This was Ó Caoimh's solution to the problems that the playing rules were causing. He made no attempt to manage the process of legislation. Instead, he dispersed them. This 'solution' was to cause very serious problems later in this era.

The new *O.G.* of 1950 fudged important rules even more. Although it was previously specified (since 1895) that footballers could hold the ball for four steps,[28] without a change at congress Rule 140 now stated that 'carrying shall be taking more than three steps while holding the ball'.[29] This error persisted for ten years, despite the opportunity to correct it at the congress of 1955. An attempt to re-define the reference to bouncing the football caused yet greater confusion by stating (in error) that 'only one hop' was allowed (even though solo-runs typically contained more than one bounce). There was also fudging in the rules with respect to charging the goalkeeper, bad language, the taking of free-pucks, and the fourteen-yard line in hurling.

After two decades of 'co-ordinated' rules, members became frustrated with the difficulty of processing and steering motions on the playing rules through congress. Unsurprisingly, little new legislation was introduced. This led to the policy of publishing sets of playing rules with accompanying written interpretations, which often clearly changed the intent of the rules. The policy apparently became, 'if we can't change them, we'll interpret them!' For example, in 1973, the GAA published *Lámhleabhar do Réiteoirí agus Imreoirí*, a little green booklet in which decisions on interpretations were inserted opposite the rules. In the foreword, Seán Ó Siocháin, the *Ardstiúrthóir* (Director-General), wrote, 'instructions, interpretations and playing rules must themselves be interpreted and a very necessary requirement for each referee is common sense to make this interpretation acceptable.' Alas, commonsense was not as common as he thought. From 1976 to 1981, several editions of a booklet entitled, *Rules for Gaelic Football and Hurling: Referees' and Players' Guide*, were published by the National Referees' Advisory Council. The legal status of

In Play it is permitted to strike or catch the ball when it is off the ground, kick or fist it away, or hop it once **only** with one or both hands (89—11).

A ball not caught may be hopped repeatedly with one or both hands; not otherwise (91—11, Note).

A ball on the ground must not be touched with the hand; but a player knocked down in possession may fist it away, though it is grounded.

The goal-keeper can touch the ball on the ground, but only within the limits of the parallelogram (89—11).

Forbidden. Carrying—that is, taking more than four strides while holding the ball—is prohibited, and the ball must not be thrown.

Ball must not be held longer than is necessary to hop, kick, or fist it. Tipping on the hand is "carrying" (89—11).

Foul Play. The following are deemed foul tactics:—

Pushing, tripping by means of legs or body, kicking, catching, holding or obstruction by hand or arm in any way;

Jumping at or butting with head, charging from behind, or interfering in any manner with a player unless he is about to play or in the act of playing the ball (93—16; 95—16, Note 4).

Frees for such offences are taken:—

(a)—From where the foul occurred if it prevented the ball being played; or if the ball went over the side-line or end-line; and

(b)—From where the ball landed if foul followed or did not prevent delivery. If a score was made it is valid and no free is awarded. (95—16;, Note 3).

This extract from a rulebook of 1939 includes some of the confusing and occasionally contradictory definitions of aspects of play which complicated the rules for many years. The presentation of the rules then also lacked a logical format or clear numerical sequence.

these little yellow booklets was not made clear; they included almost as many paragraphs of interpretations of the playing rules as paragraphs for the rules themselves. These interpretations effectively changed eight of the ten playing rules, without reference to congress.[30] To a large degree, the rules became what the referees wanted them to be because there was ambivalence as to which set of rules the referees should apply – those in the *O.G.* or those in the various booklets of rules-interpretations issued by Central Council or the National Referees' Advisory Council. The circulation of two contradictory sets of playing rules – one in the *Official Guide*, the other in booklets of interpretation – led to a twelve-year period of chaos in rules and refereeing, caused by the carelessness of the association's executive.

Even when a rule was changed by congress without ambiguity, and without the need for interpretation, it could take some time to be reflected in the published rules of the association, or to be taken on board fully by members. The metric system, originally proposed in 1915, was approved by congress in 1975, but reference to the imperial system of weights and measures was retained in rules interpretation booklets. Around the same time, the term 'side-to-side' charge replaced the anatomically incorrect term 'shoulder charge', but the latter term was still more widely used (and is still today). This shows how long it can take for the public, journalists and commentators in particular, to adopt new terminology. And in 1974, after twenty-four years of the fisted-pass restriction, the open hand-pass option was restored, although it soon had to be re-defined.[31]

After a successful motion tabled by Co. Down in 1980 to modernise and upgrade the *O.G.* in time for the centenary of the GAA, congress appointed yet another rules revision committee.[32] This committee reported to congress in 1985, which in turn decided to call a special congress in Cork later that year to deal with the report, which was essentially a new *Official Guide* in all but name. The special congress ended in frustration when delegates were refused permission to debate motions that were on the agenda. They were told by then president, Dr Mick Loftus they could either accept the report or go home. The delegates stayed.

An analysis of this set of playing rules showed that it contained over forty errors. It lasted just four years. At Congress in 1988, it was pointed out that these little yellow booklets of playing rules effectively meant that there were two contradictory sets of playing rules in operation.[33] Then, after nearly four decades of amalgamation, it looked as if the playing rules of the very different games of football and hurling would be separated once again. An edition of the *Playing Rules of Football* was published by Central Council in 1988, and a year later a similar booklet, entitled *Rules of Hurling* 1989. This turned out to be a sign of things to come for the new format of presentation.[34] The legal standing of these separate published 'Rules of Play' was not established, however. Once again there were conflicting sets of playing rules in circulation, between *Official Guides* and advisory booklets Their publication was the nadir of a decade in which the process of legislation deteriorated markedly.

The introduction of an experimental rules programme for the National Leagues was to cause major upset for a decade. 1988 was an unusual year, as three separate editions of the *Official Guide* were published by Central Council. In each of these, Rule 77 in relation to 'Motions', deals with the submission and processing of motions through annual congress. However, in one of these three editions of the *Official Guide*, Rule 77 (c) states:

> Motions to revise playing Rules may be tabled only in years divisible by five, and in such years they shall take precedence in motions on Annual Congress Agenda.
> In the year prior to the revision of Playing Rules, motions with proposed rule changes for experiment in national and county league may be tabled.

This second paragraph did not appear in either of the other two 1988 editions of the *O.G.* Nor did it appear in the 1986 edition of the *O.G.*, which contained the full revised text of the *Rules of the Official Guide* as sanctioned by special congress, in 1985. There is no record of a motion for such an amendment to Rule 77 (c) in the congress booklets for 1986, 1987 or 1988! Moreover, Rule 122 of the 1988 edition of the *Official Guide* deals with the 'Organisation of League Competitions'. In just one of the three 1988 editions of the *Official Guide*, the following statement was added:

> Playing Rule changes recommended by Ard-Chomhairle may be experimented with in national and county Leagues of the year prior to the Congress at which motions for revisions of playing rules are tabled.

This demonstrates that the whole experimental rules programme of that period was illegal, and that Ardchomhairle [Central Council] had usurped the power reserved to congress to make rule changes. On the downside, this second era ended with the first 'Experimental Playing Rules' in the 1989/90 National (Hurling and Football) Leagues season. On the upside, this second era ended with the rejection of the revamped but very short-lived edition of the *O.G.* that had been railroaded through the special congress held in Cork in December 1985. Furthermore, congress of 1990 accepted a Co. Meath motion that the playing rules of football and hurling be set down separately, in a framework of presentation designed by the author.[35]

A special committee was set up to transfer all the playing rules of both games out of the 'co-ordinated' form into the new simplified format of rule presentation.[36] This committee reported to a special delegate congress comprised only of Central Council delegates. This report[37] was passed on 12 December 1990 with only one dissenting voice, and became the format of rule presentation with effect from January 1991. The *O.G.* was divided into two parts with the playing rules in Part Two. This was a very important and useful change. At last the playing rules had a home of their own. But, as predicted, they were now much more vulnerable to those seeking, for any reason, to change the playing rules. The policy of introducing 'experimental rules' posed an obvious threat to the extant skills of Gaelic football.

This is the new format of rule presentation that came into operation in January 1991.

FLOWCHART OF THE PLAYING RULES

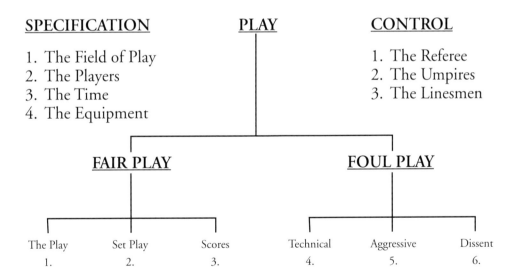

SPECIFICATION	PLAY	CONTROL
1. The Field of Play		1. The Referee
2. The Players		2. The Umpires
3. The Time		3. The Linesmen
4. The Equipment		

FAIR PLAY			FOUL PLAY		
The Play	Set Play	Scores	Technical	Aggressive	Dissent
1.	2.	3.	4.	5.	6.

From this it can be seen that each rule of play is both totally inclusive and mutually exclusive. This means that no part of any of the six rules of play is or can be duplicated in any other rule. Hence, anyone looking for a rule or part of a rule can locate it quickly, be sure that it is all there and is not replicated or contradicted elsewhere. This removed many of the difficulties in using previous sets of playing rules.

Up to 1991, only one or two key terms were defined, and even then poorly and in the body of the text of the rule. Now all the key definitions were set out clearly in a section of their own and, importantly, were now an integral part of the playing rule legislation. This put an end to the decades-old squabbles and

Seán O'Neill performs a solo run and Joe Lennon moves in to tackle in one of the demonstration photographs from the latter's book, *Coaching Gaelic Football for Champions* (1964). The solo run and other aspects of play, such as bouncing the ball, were poorly defined in the GAA playing rules for several decades. (*Joe Lennon*)

debilitating arguments about what the true definitions of terms like the hand-pass and 'the tackle' were.[38] Crucially, this format facilitated the comparative analysis of different sets of playing rules of the same game and of different games.[39] It can be used to monitor developments in any part of the rules of any game.

The large rectangle, 13 x 19 metres, was introduced in 1992, and the exclusion zone – a semi-circle of thirteen-metre radius – was introduced in 1995. These were the only changes to the markings on the field of play since 1910. Perhaps the biggest visual change in hurling was the increase in the number of players wearing a helmet. The first step was to require all minor hurlers to wear helmets with faceguards. Then in 1995, a successful Dublin motion to congress resulted in requiring all hurlers up to and including under-21 grade to wear a helmet with a facial guard. Although senior hurlers are not required by rule to wear a helmet, the numbers who do not appears to be very small. This was a very significant improvement in the safety of players.

Much attention was drawn away from the importance of this unique and historic breakthrough in rule-presentation by the advent of the 'experimental rules' campaign. There were three such experiments in football in the 1990s, and the proposed rule changes in football were clearly intended to change it into a game very similar to Australian rules.[40] Just two of the proposed changes were adopted: the free-kick from the hands (optional), and the sideline-kick from the hands. Only the first two 'experimental rules trials' applied to hurling, and in any case they did not seek to change the game fundamentally; rather, they sought to enhance the game as a ball-and-stick game only, by reducing the use of the hand and foot to play the ball.

The third 'experimental rules' trial, in 1998, only applied to football, and contrary to the rule that specified that these experiments were to be applied only in national and county leagues, they were used in provincial competitions, three of which had a championship or knock-out format. These experimental rules caused havoc, as players, spectators, commentators and referees all struggled to come to terms with them because overnight they had to change their thinking about how to play the game, referee the game and understand the game. This required considerable concentration from the footballers in the heat of the games.

While hurling would be exempt from further experiments, football was still exposed to extraordinary proposals to change its nature. An objective reading of these experiments would lead to the conclusion that they were intent on changing Gaelic football for reasons that did not appear to seek improvement so much as changing it. The skills of Gaelic football were being deliberately eroded *seriatim*. The policy to make Gaelic football more similar to Australian rules was now clearly exposed. The membership of the GAA did not wish for such fundamental changes to the game. The 1998 experimental rules programme for football collapsed and was discontinued before the planned end of the trial period. The adverse comments mounted until breaking point was reached, and the organisers of the experiment had to admit defeat and failure. These drastic ill-fated changes were all endorsed by the *Ardstiúrthóir*.[41]

In this twenty-year period, the aptly named 'compromise rules'[42] games against the professional footballers from Australian rules was a further distraction from the proper development of our indigenous football game. The international games against the Shinty Association paled into insignificance by comparison with the amount of publicity and 'no expense spared' approach to the 'International Rules' games between Ireland and Australia. Inevitably, comparisons were made – many of which were unfair criticisms. For example, it was claimed repeatedly that 'there is no high catching in Gaelic football' or that 'the high catch could not be made because the catcher was immediately surrounded by opponents.' Apart from the fact that no figures or comparative analyses were produced to substantiate such claims, there is no reason why opponents should not surround the catcher.[43] Another mantra of the critics is that there is no tackle in Gaelic football, and this despite the fact that the skill of the tackle is referred to in several rules[44] and listed as one of the important definitions common to both football and hurling

In 2000, a Co. Tyrone motion, seeking that there be no revision of playing rules in 2005, nor experiment with the rules in the years immediately preceding 2005, was passed. This would have given the playing rules a breathing-space and time to recover. However, this motion was never included in the *O.G.* nor put into practice by Central Council. This cavalier approach to legislation showed that Central Council has practically usurped the paramount role of congress in legislation. In 2005 and 2007 the 'runner' and the water official were introduced. Both are features of Australian rules and are unnecessary distractions for spectators. From 2007, football goalkeepers were allowed to use a tee for the kick-out. This tee was not introduced in hurling, although it might have improved the game by restricting the length of puck-outs.

One of the central tenets of a philosophy for legislation in games can be stated simply thus. The rules are the game and the game is its rules; if you change the rules, you change the game. This idea is set out very clearly by Michael Oriard. In his book he showed that American football was born from rugby football just by changing two rules to begin with: the forward-pass and the 'five-yard rule'.[45] But for the collective wisdom of congress, Gaelic football would surely have perished. The policy of proponents of the agenda for change seems to have been, 'propose a lot of rule changes and congress will not have the nerve to reject them all'.[46] Inevitably, congress did not fend off all the arrows. The sideline-kick from the hands is now mandatory; the free-kick from the hands is the preferred option; and these, with kick-outs off a tee, have combined to reduce the opportunities for performing the age-old basic skill of kicking a stationary ball from the ground – a considerable loss to the game. Despite all the disruption caused by them, the changes to football rules have been more cosmetic than structural. Yet the game has been shaken by a massive amount of unfair criticism.

In recent years, the process of legislation[47] in the GAA has been increasingly centralised by changes to how motions making, amending or rescinding playing rules, are submitted and reviewed. Up to 1997, motions could only originate at club level. Since then, motions can also originate from county committees, provincial councils, and Central Council.[48] These motions go to the Motions Committee in Croke Park, for ratification. This committee effectively controls what legislation, if any, is debated at annual congress. It can strike out motions, even if legal and valid, on the basis of perceived expediency.[49] There is no appeal (within the association's ordinary structures) against decisions of the Motions Committee. It is comprised of the president, the Ardstiúrthóir and the past-presidents. Since at least two (and sometimes three) of these are members of Central Council, they are 'judges in their own court'. The potential for conflict of interest has become a reality at times.[50] A motion can surmount all of these hurdles, but the president still has the

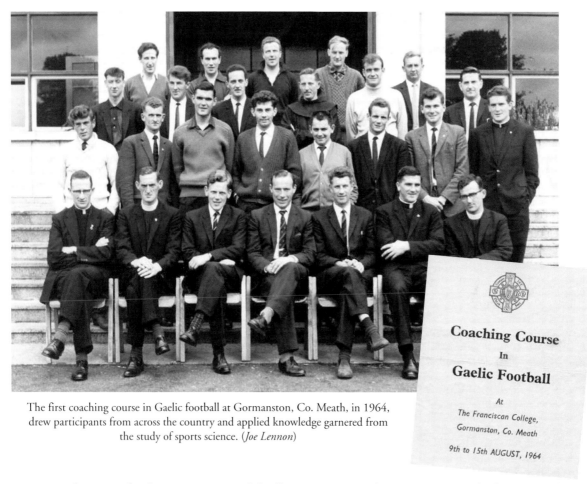

The first coaching course in Gaelic football at Gormanston, Co. Meath, in 1964, drew participants from across the country and applied knowledge garnered from the study of sports science. (*Joe Lennon*)

Coaching Course
In
Gaelic Football

At
The Franciscan College,
Gormanston, Co. Meath

9th to 15th AUGUST, 1964

power to rule it out of order at congress. And finally, a Motions Drafting Committee, which reviews all passed motions, may question the compatibility of a motion with existing rules, and thus stop it from ever reaching the rulebook. This growth of executive paternalism in the GAA has resulted in ever more motions being passed in the name of Central Council, and relatively fewer from clubs.

This process is completely undemocratic and, since it is at the heart of the legislative process of the GAA, leaves the association open to the criticism that its most important powers have been corrupted. The frequent convocation of special congresses as a process of legislation for making changes to the playing rules is an additional source of grave concern about where the association is headed.

Although not as widely played as Gaelic football, the game of hurling has survived and prospered in this 125-year period. Football has proved to be a very robust species that has survived the regular attempts from within the association to degrade it by changing the major skills of the games. It should, however, have an ombudsman who will defend it from these irrational and unfair attacks on its rules of play. At present the game does not have anyone to take its part and defend its integrity. If, as it is argued, the tackle in Gaelic football is not well performed by some players, it should be remembered that it is not a function of the rules to correct poor play. It is wrong to change a rule to try to correct faulty coaching techniques. The symbiotic relationship between the game and its rules should be foremost in the minds of our legislators. A good working knowledge of the functions and the characteristics of rules should be prerequisite for membership of any committee set up to revise playing rules.[51]

The primary and most important function of the playing rules is to preserve the essential characteristics of the game. The GAA has failed to recognise this. Both Gaelic football and hurling are important parts of our cultural heritage – equally important, it should be stressed. Hopefully they will be cherished equally in the remainder of this century.

Irish Republican attitudes to sport since 1921

Brian Hanley

In May 1943, in the midst of a dispute concerning the status of Gaelic games within the Irish Army, the Central Council of the Gaelic Athletic Association (GAA) reminded Fianna Fáil's Minister for Defence Oscar Traynor that during the War of Independence the IRA had been recruited 'almost exclusively' from the ranks of the GAA.[1] The Central Council's view that there was a natural link between Gaelic games and revolutionary activity has been taken as read by many republicans. During 1982 the journal *Iris* claimed that 'historically … [the GAA] has aligned itself with the cause of full sovereignty.'[2] Observers such as W. F. Mandle have also concluded that 'no other organization had done more for Irish nationalism than the GAA – not the IRB, the Gaelic League or even Sinn Féin.'[3] Many members of the GAA continue to highlight this perception, particularly during contentious debates such as those over Rules 21 or 42. That many republicans have played, followed and organised Gaelic sports from the 1880s to the present day is beyond doubt. That many GAA members regard themselves as Irish nationalists and see their support for Gaelic games as an integral part of this is also self-evidently the case. However even at the highpoint of the independence struggle from 1919–21 there were republicans who either had little interest in the GAA or who followed what it considered 'foreign' games. In the modern era this is even more apparent. Like all aspects of republican politics, attitudes to sport have been heavily influenced by questions of class and region and by changing trends in Irish society itself.

Marcus de Búrca suggests that the phrase 'almost exclusively' used by the GAA in 1943 was a barbed reference to Oscar Traynor himself, a former commander of the IRA's Dublin Brigade whose sporting career had included spells as a soccer goalkeeper for Belfast Celtic and Shelbourne football clubs.[4] Traynor was not defensive about his support for soccer and refused to be 'banned as a good Irishman' because of this, though on occasion he claimed that it was a 'Celtic game, pure and simple, having its origins in the Highlands of Scotland.' Traynor stated in 1928 that that he could 'give a long list of patriotic Irishmen who either played Rugby, Soccer or Cricket', singling out among others, Kevin Barry and Cathal Brugha. He mischievously suggested that these men's association with non-Gaelic sports made them no less Irish then the fact that 'hundreds of Gaels fought in the British Army' during the Great War. He provocatively claimed that when interned in Frongoch after the Easter Rising of 1916 that he was 'amazed at the number of old soccer colleagues who were daily appearing there' and that some of his fellow internees were disappointed that the same could not be said of their Gaelic clubs.[5] Was there any basis for Traynor's claims?

When giving a statement to the Bureau of Military History during the 1940s, Sean Clifford, a former commander of the 4th battalion, Mid Limerick Brigade of the IRA, claimed that 'men who spoke only English and who never had much time for Gaelic games met, attacked and beat the enemy whereas those who claimed a monopoly on Irish patriotism, namely the Gaelic Athletic Association and the Gaelic League, were nowhere to be seen when it came to a fight.'[6] This suggests some tension between republicans and Gaels in this area at least. In Limerick City after 1917 the Irish Volunteers were divided into two battalions, with one, the 1st battalion recalled as being 'nearly confined to the rugby clubs.'[7] Remarking on the high level of physical fitness among his fellow prisoners at Knutsford camp after 1916 Robert Holland speculated that there was the makings of an all-Ireland Gaelic football team in the camp; but he also noted the 'good sprinkling' of Strandville, Distillery and St James' Gate soccer players among the internees.[8] There were certainly a number of prominent republicans who were devotees of 'foreign' sports. Gerald Boland, brother of Harry and from an old Fenian family would claim that 'more than half of the Dublin Brigade of 1918–21 were soccer men.'[9] Kevin Barry was secretary of Belvedere rugby club and also played cricket.[10] Cathal Brugha was a 'first class' cricketer who bowled for Belvedere and Pembroke cricket clubs. He also lined out at half-back for Belvedere, Clontarf and Santry in rugby.[11] Todd Andrews, a member of the Dublin IRA from 1917–23, was a supporter of Bohemians football club and a regular at Dalymount Park, before becoming an accomplished soccer player himself with University College Dublin. However during the War of

An extract from the Comhairle Uladh CLG minute-book in relation to the adjourned provincial convention of 17 April 1920. The meeting was in session at the home of Charles O'Neill, Armagh, when 'armed aliens' entered and arrested the provincial secretary, Eoin O'Duffy who was taken to Crumlin Road prison in Belfast. O'Duffy was then a leading member of both the GAA and the IRA in Ulster, and his entangling of some aspects of Gaelic games with republican activity accentuated the republican image of the GAA in Ulster, particularly in the eyes of unionists, for years to come.

Independence Andrews found himself interned in Rath with mainly rural prisoners, many of them Cork IRA men. There soccer and rugby were not tolerated and Andrew's dislike of Gaelic games 'didn't help' his initial relations with his comrades. Later during the Civil War he was again interned in Newbridge camp, where Dubliners constituted a majority, and he found that both soccer and rugby were played, with Gaelic football ranked only third in terms of popularity. Rugby in the camp was organised by a Dublin bank clerk, Jack Callanan.[12] A notable example of a republican who actually excelled at several codes was Joe Stynes. Stynes, originally from Kildare, was a member of 'C' Company of the 2nd Battalion, Dublin Brigade. He was an accomplished Gaelic footballer for Dublin. He fought on the anti-treaty side in the Civil War and was interned but after his release played soccer for Shelbourne F.C. and then spent two seasons at Bohemians F.C. before emigrating to the United States. In New York he played Gaelic football for Kildare and returned to Ireland in 1928 with the New York team for the Tailteann Games.[13] These examples illustrate that there were at least some within the revolutionary movement who were certainly fighting for an Ireland free but not necessarily, or only, Gaelic as well. What is interesting is that for the next five decades there is little or no acknowledgement by republicans of this diversity. Publicly at least Gaelic games were celebrated as the *only* field-sports that a republican could support or play and those who argued otherwise were denounced as 'traitors.'[14]

In the post-Civil War period some republicans hoped that they could enlist the GAA in the struggle against the Free State. For a brief period the IRA even thought seriously about attempting to 'gain control of the GAA.' It was encouraged by the decision of the Kerry and Limerick teams to refuse to play in the 1923 All-Ireland finals in protest at the continuing imprisonment of over 10,000 republicans. IRA volunteers were ordered to approach all members of county teams and county boards 'for the purpose of obtaining resolutions' calling for the release of the republican prisoners. Teams were to be asked to withdraw from competition in protest. If they refused then republicans were to threaten them with a boycott. The IRA leadership felt that if control of the GAA was secured that it would be possible to severely embarrass the Free State by organising a complete boycott of the Tailteann Games planned for August 1924.[15] However from an early stage problems with these ambitious plans were apparent. As one IRA officer noted, 'there had been a great deal of talk about the GAA … but very little was done.'[16]

Seamus Dobbyn, Ulster GAA president, 1919–23. A leading IRB man in Belfast, he was imprisoned several times during that period. He also travelled to the United States to raise funds for the Tailteann Games and returned to live in Dublin after the Irish Civil War. (*Brídín Uí Mhaolagáin, née Dobbyn*)

The problem for the organisation was that while its own propaganda portrayed the GAA as the embodiment of nationalist Ireland (which in the sense of including a wide spectrum of opinion it was) this meant that the IRA as a relatively small organisation was likely to be a minority. There were recurring complaints from republicans about the fact that Garda and Free State soldiers were prominent in the association. In 1927 a senior IRA officer outlined several problems with the GAA from his organisation's point of view. Firstly many prominent Gaels were 'arrant hypocrites' and 'traitors' because they allowed clubs to be controlled by 'policemen' or the 'little pimp and tout of the Peeler.' While the GAA complained about foreign games it contained men within it who upheld 'foreign rule.' These included *gardaí* and soldiers who, despite their membership of the GAA, spent their time 'raiding, arresting, harassing and spying' on republicans. The IRA officer noted that the Royal Ulster Constabulary were precluded from playing Gaelic games but asked just what was the difference between the 'Peelers in the "North" and those in the "South?"' He even suggested that the Free State sought 'deliberately' to divert young men from the IRA by encouraging them into GAA clubs.[17]

The reality was that the IRA could only be a small component of the much more diverse nationalist constituency within the GAA, where *gardaí*, soldiers, Fianna Fáil, Fine Gael and Labour supporters, along with Hibernians and Foresters in the north, were likely to be represented. A good example of this diversity can be seen in the Mayo football team that visited New York during 1932, the make-up of which the local IRA described for its American allies. Of twenty one players listed, just one was an IRA member, one was described as 'republican labour', five were Fianna Fáil supporters, four Cumann na nGaedheal, three were *gardaí*, four were 'neutral' and one was described as an 'Imperialist', a term which presumably covered a multitude of sins![18] Depending on location the local GAA could be either reasonably sympathetic to republicans, as in Sligo and Donegal, or hostile as in Leitrim or Roscommon.[19] Hundreds of IRA members of course played Gaelic games in this era some gaining prominence for a variety of reasons such as Seán McCool (or Mac Cumhaill) of Donegal, John 'Nipper' Shanley of Leitrim, John Egan of Dungarvan or Stephen Hayes of Wexford.[20] But for most IRA members the playing of Gaelic sports was probably a choice born of a desire to represent their parish or county and take part in competition with their friends and neighbours rather than one rooted purely in ideology. Where support for the GAA still represented a form of opposition to the state as in Northern Ireland more political reasons would also have contributed.

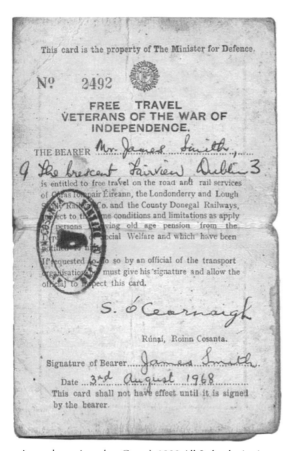

A travel-pass issued to Cavan's 1933 All-Ireland winning captain, Jim Smith, as a veteran of the Irish War of Independence. Many prominent GAA players and officials from the 1920s onwards had some involvement in that war, and retained republican sympathies of one sort or other. (*Gearóid Mac Gabhann*)

During the late 1920s Irish republican *émigrés* had some success in gaining influence in New York GAA circles and were to organise a tour during 1927 by the Kerry football team. In January 1927 the IRA's main American representative Connie Neenan was elected, along with two other republicans to the New York Board. Neenan promoted the idea of a Kerry tour, with the aim of raising funds for the republican movement and in so doing was somewhat successful, though in the end and after much wrangling, only some of the money from Kerry's tour went to the IRA.[21]

Back in Kerry, where senior IRA figures such as John Joe Sheehy and John Joe Rice were GAA officials and at various stages held positions on the county board, the IRA became embroiled in major controversy during 1934. J. J. Sheehy of course was also a former captain of the county, an outstanding footballer and holder of four All-Ireland medals. Some accounts have stressed the positive impact of Gaelic games on alleviating Civil War bitterness in Kerry.[22] But the picture was more complex than this. The IRA's attempts to make the GAA in Kerry a weapon in its struggle for legitimacy with the Fianna Fáil government caused major disruption to the county's sporting calendar and did damage to the IRA's image. During 1934 and 1935 dozens of Kerry IRA members were jailed after clashes with Blueshirts and other opponents. In response the IRA pushed for clubs to stand down and for Kerry to withdraw from inter-county competition.

Clubs such as John Mitchel's and Austin Stack's refused to play in protest. There was initially some support for the IRA's position and sympathy for its prisoners. Even some rugby clubs in Tralee reportedly refused to play matches in support of their cause.[23] The boycott did cause a great deal of disruption to the games in Kerry but rather than force the government to concede to IRA demands it created something of a backlash against the organisation. Members of the county board claimed that the IRA had reduced Gaelic games in Kerry to 'below zero' and that youngsters were taking up soccer and rugby as a result. When the IRA complained of ill-treatment, one delegate to the Munster Council argued that it was ill-treatment for them to 'hammer young boys on the street' too. The Kerry IRA itself divided over the issue with J. J. Sheehy arguing for a conciliatory policy whilst younger men such as Eugene Powell of John Mitchel's wanted even more militant tactics. The IRA prisoners in the Curragh also expressed disquiet over the disruption. During 1935 the boycotts were abandoned amid much recrimination. In a county where the IRA had real influence in the GAA it failed to use it effectively.[24]

During the 1930s the republican movement promoted the view that only 'hybrids', 'mongrels' or 'traitors' played 'foreign' sports.[25] *An Phoblacht*, the IRA's newspaper from 1925–1936 was at its narrowest in its sporting coverage, verging on the hysterical at times. This was unusual, because in terms of literature, music or culture the paper was often and generally quite open to international trends. There is no hint that any IRA members during the 1930s played or even watched soccer or rugby, even though the organisation had hundreds of members in Dublin and Belfast, where soccer had a strong working-class base. For *An Phoblacht* Gaelic games were 'factors in the maintenance of our national consciousness and well being.' By 'keeping in touch with native games … we keep in touch with the soul of Ireland.'[26] Therefore the paper gave extensive coverage to Gaelic sports, both reports on the games themselves and on broader issues. Both its sport correspondents 'Mutius' and 'Cimarron' agreed that Gaelic games were far more than just examples of sport. Without a patriotic sense sport was 'merely an amalgam of personal vanity, personal prowess, demoralised rivalry and commercialised ambition.'[27] Furthermore the appeal of the GAA, they argued, should be kept uniquely Irish. Efforts to spread its appeal abroad would only make it lose its distinctiveness.[28] The GAA was urged to celebrate its nationalist mission and dedicate itself to the 'extermination of all forms of Foreignism.'[29] There was no question that a republican could also enjoy soccer or rugby; 'there can be no flirting with foreignism. You cannot be true to Caitlin ni Houlihan and carry on an amour with Dame Britannia … these were the games imported here by those who raped and robbed and ruined those whose blood flows in our veins.'[30] This was not simply the view of the IRA. When the left-wing Republican Congress was formed in 1934 its newspaper too stressed that Gaelic Games were 'part of our racial inheritance … more then a contest of skill and strength … [they are] a manifestation of national spirit.'[31] When Peadar O'Donnell suggested a 'soccer notes' column for the left wing *Irish Democrat* newspaper he was opposed in no uncertain terms by his colleague Frank Ryan.[32] There is no record of internees in the Curragh camp during the Second World War playing anything other than Gaelic games and the camp held at various stages five All-Ireland medal winners, from Kerry, Cork and Wexford.[33] Hurling and football were both played by republican prisoners in Belfast's Crumlin Road gaol during the 1956–62 campaign, though eventually only football was allowed by the IRA's staff because of the number of injuries that occurred while prisoners played hurling.[34] Indeed, it was largely due to such safety concerns that prison authorities rarely allowed hurling among internees.

Similar views to those of the 1930s *An Phoblacht* also informed republican attitudes to sport for the next two decades. The *United Irishman,* the newspaper of the republican movement during the 1950s and 1960s, continued to support Gaelic games while denouncing their foreign rivals. Given the cultural ethos of the paper, which called for more rather than less censorship of foreign films, books and newspapers during the 1950s, this is not altogether surprising.[35] As late as 1964 the paper was contrasting the 'virility and manliness' of traditional music with unhealthy 'sensuality that is part and parcel of the 'pops' craze.'[36] Again the fact that many of those active in the GAA did not adhere to republican politics caused anguish. Commenting on a report that a Garda football team had been composed of members of the force on border duties the paper asked that if 'members of the British forces in Ireland are officially banned from the GAA … what of those who have collaborated with them?'[37] The paper was clear that the GAA ban on members playing 'foreign' sports had to be retained as it was the 'last bulwark against foreign influence.'[38] In October 1964 the *United Irishman* explained in greater detail why 'the Ban' was a 'bulwark against colonialism.' The paper reminded its readers where 'the Tans went on Bloody Sunday' it was not in 'Landsowne Road or Dalymount Rd [sic] they popped their machine guns? No, not likely! They knew where to find the Fíor Gael. They went to where the soul of Ireland's boyhood was being thrilled by the élan of stick against stick.' Despite a disappointing lack of knowledge of what game was actually played on Bloody Sunday the writer's main point was that he had seen 'so-called Irishmen' who had been 'reared in a rural environment with a caman and sliotar in their hands … scamper for tickets to Lansdowne Rd' after they settled in Dublin and become west Britons over night. This proved that more, not less, bans were needed, on the 'putrescent British press' and 'propaganda films' as well as foreign games.[39] The article was not unrepresentative of the *United Irishman's* coverage during either

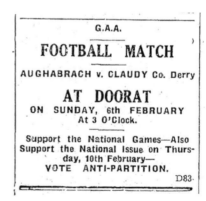

Notice for a GAA match in the parish of Donagheady in north Tyrone, in 1949, with an obvious political message for election time. (*Dungannon Observer*)

The official programme for the opening of Casement Park, Belfast in June 1953. The venue was named after Roger Casement, the Protestant nationalist who was executed for his role in the 1916 Easter Rising. The ground has been the leading GAA venue in the city since its opening, though it was taken over by the British army for some time in the early 1970s. Subsequently the grounds became a focal point for many republican rallies. Some Unionist politicians – notably the Minister for Culture, Arts and Leisure in 2009, Nelson McCausland – have made an issue of the naming of such a prominent GAA ground after a republican martyr.

the 1950s or 1960s. There is no indication in the paper of the popularity of either League of Ireland soccer during the 1950s or 1960s or the interest among thousands of Irish people in English or Scottish football in the same period. That it was perfectly possible to share at least some of the opinions expressed by the *United Irishman* while supporting Shamrock Rovers, Bohemians or Waterford United football clubs never seemed to have struck any of the writers who dealt with sport in the paper as likely.

Where republicans did play both an active and innovative role during these decades however was in the promotion of athletics and cycling. Republicans were active in both the National Athletic and Cycling Association and the especially in the National Cycling Association after it was expelled from the international cycling body, the UCI, in 1948 for refusing to recognise a separate Northern Ireland cycling association. A new internationally recognised 26-county association was formed but the NCA was kept alive by republican activists like its president Jim Killeen, a former IRA Army Council member.[40] A great deal of attention was given over to NCA activities in the *United Irishman*. The NCA's constitution made it clear that the object of the association was to 'promote Irish nationality and Amateur Cycle Racing in the thirty two counties of Ireland (but) at all times the promotion of Nationality shall be considered more important than the promotion of cycle racing'. Furthermore the NCA forbade membership to members of the British Army, Royal Ulster Constabulary, B Specials, Orange Order, 'Amateur Athletic Union of "Eire", the "Northern Ireland" Cycling Federation or Cumann Rothaidheachta na hEireann.' When the Cork Cycling Board of the NCA allowed a former member of St Finbarr's Cycling Club who had joined the British Army, to attend a convention of the association it provoked a heated debate and condemnation from the *United Irishman*.[41]

During the 1950s young republican NCA members such as Joe Christle and Phil Clarke helped create a new 'cycling craze' and left a lasting impact on Irish sport. In 1953 Christle organised the first Rás Tailteann, as a two-day event, which became an eight-day round-Ireland race in 1958. By 1972 when Christle retired from its organisation the Rás had become a major event, attracting foreign participation and hundreds of competitors. Christle, Clarke and a number of other key NCA activists were members of the IRA, taking part in the famous Armagh and Omagh raids of 1954, for which Clarke was jailed for ten years and later elected as an abstentionist MP for Fermanagh / South Tyrone. The 1956 Rás saw clashes along its route through Northern Ireland because of the display of the tricolour, culminating in a serious riot outside Cookstown, Co. Tyrone. By this point Christle had left the IRA and was active with independent republican military groupings.[42] Christle was himself jailed in 1957 but organisation of the Rás continued. During the 1960s it became more popular, attracting the participation of a Polish team in 1963 and remained extremely political in nature. Programmes for the Rás during the 1960s included articles on Roger Casement, the Fenians, apartheid and colonialism. In 1970 the programme was dedicated to James Connolly and V. I. Lenin, in honour of the visiting Soviet team.[43] Christle was active in its organisation after his release from internment, while he also continued more secretive republican activities.[44] Among the Rás organisers during the 1960s was Seamus Ó Tuathail, who became the editor of the *United Irishman* in 1967.

The NCA was very much the most successful of the national athletics bodies. In 1967 the NACA suffered another split when Bord Lúthchleas na hÉireann (BLÉ) was formed to represent athletes in the twenty-six counties. For the *United Irishman* the split was the result of an effort by 'shoneens' to destroy the NACA. For several years republicans refused to recognise BLÉ, supporting cross-country, track and field, long jump and other events organised by the NACA, holding events in counties Louth, Kerry, Clare and Cork. In November 1968 some 434 athletes took part in the NACA cross-country races.[45] The fact that after four decades of absolute GAA support for the NACA, the majority of the GAA Central Council now did not oppose the setting up of BLÉ, and took a neutral stance in this new athletics dispute, suggested to republicans that a sell-out on the issue of the 'ban' on 'foreign games' was in the offing, if not also a general weakening of nationalist sentiment.[46] In the aftermath of the eruption of violence during August 1969, a special 'Free Belfast Grand Prix' was organised, with a cycle race around the barricaded area of the Lower Falls.[47] That Rás Tailteann continued to be a success, with 600 riders taking part in 1970 was an encouraging sign for Sinn Féin of resistance to 'Hibernianism' and 'Free Statism'.[48] In 1971 the Rás was dedicated to the growing number of Irish republican prisoners held in British jails and the 'age old struggle for Irish independence.'[49]

Perhaps surprisingly little attention was given to the debate on the deletion of the GAA's ban in the republican press. Then again, given the split in the republican movement and the growing crisis in Northern Ireland its importance may well have been overshadowed. The re-launched *An Phoblacht*, the organ of Provisional Sinn Féin, did address the issue in March 1971 arguing that the GAA should 'uphold that Ban!' because 'foreign games and pastimes constitute a serious source of disunion, particularly among young people … the playing of foreign games brings with it the reading of foreign newspapers- corroding sources of national and social weakness.'[50] The *United Irishman*, now the paper of Official Sinn Féin, continued to promote the NACA and NCA but made no comment on the debate with the GAA. However, Tom Mitchell, a veteran republican associated with the Officials did attack the removal of the 'Ban' in his Easter address at Carrickmore, Co. Tyrone in 1971.[51] The Rás remained very much the centre of the *United Irishman's* sporting calendar and the paper

The cover of the programme for the pageant held to commemorate the golden jubilee of the 1916 Easter Rising, at Croke Park and Casement Park in 1966. The GAA nationally, like the Irish nationalist political establishment, became less overtly republican in expression after that anniversary year. (*Síghle Nic An Ultaigh collection, CÓFLA / Feargal McCormack*)

Republican slogans written on adjacent rooftops are clearly visible to both players and spectators at a game in Lurgan in 1984. On many occasions republicans have attempted to exploit popular GAA events to publicise their messages. (*Irish News*)

complained bitterly about RTÉ's devotion of coverage to English sport in comparison to its neglect of the Rás.[52] The transformation of Official republican politics during the 1970s would mean that by the 1980s its successor organisation, Sinn Féin the Workers Party, had no difficulty covering soccer and rugby as well as GAA and athletics in its publications. The SFWP magazine *Workers Life* reported on League of Ireland, Irish League and Scottish and English football as well as having informed commentary on boxing and athletics.[53] An indication of the political shift was the attention given in *Workers Life* to condemnation of what it alleged was a 'covert and overt relationship' between the GAA and the 'Provisional terrorist organisation.' *Workers Life* in contrast supported those in the GAA like Tom Woulfe and John O'Grady who condemned any links between the association and republican paramilitary organisations.[54] Woulfe, an official of the Civil Service club in Dublin, was best known for spearheading the campaign against the 'foreign games' ban during the 1960s.

But the eruption of the northern 'troubles' had changed much about republicanism, in a cultural sense as well as in other ways. The upsurge in support for militant republicanism in Belfast and Derry city and other urban areas saw a distinct working-class dimension emerge and, very crudely, it also meant that thousands of young people who supported Glasgow Celtic, Manchester United or Liverpool football clubs saw no contradiction between that and being members of the IRA.[55] As early as 1972 soccer was being played along with Gaelic football in Crumlin Road gaol.[56] Despite these cultural shifts it would be a mistake not to acknowledge the impact that the conflict after 1969 had in solidifying identification between the GAA in the north and nationalism.[57] Firstly the GAA as an organisation and more especially its ordinary members faced routine harassment by the British Army and police from the early 1970s onwards. Quite apart from the high profile sequestration of Crossmaglen Rangers' ground and the occupation of Casement Park in the early 1970s, players, officials and match-goers all experienced low-level harassment on a regular basis.[58] Particularly shocking was the killing of Aidan McAnespie on his way to a match in February 1988. Club premises were also targeted for attacks by loyalist paramilitaries, ranging from vandalism to gun and bomb attacks. A significant number of players, officials and club members were murdered in sectarian attacks.[59] At various stages Unionist politicians condemned the GAA as a 'sectarian' organisation, claiming that it discriminated against Protestants and insinuated that it was, in Sammy Wilson of the DUP's words, simply 'the IRA at play.'[60] The assumption that the GAA was a republican organisation has been used by Unionist politicians – including a recent Minister for Culture, Arts and Leisure – to continue to sneer at the association up the present day.[61] Of course it has been the case that members of both the Provisional and Official IRAs, and the INLA have been footballers or hurlers, among them hunger-striker Kevin Lynch, who won an All-Ireland under-16 medal for Co. Derry in hurling. But given political divisions between supporters of the SDLP and Sinn Féin (and in the early 1970s the Republican Clubs) and the fact that the GAA is an all-Ireland body, the assumption that its members were uniformly sympathetic to militant republicanism does not hold water. Indeed the involvement of large numbers of *gardaí* in the GAA probably ensured that there were in fact a large body of Gaels hostile to republicanism as represented by the IRA.[62] While many GAA clubs and dozens of individuals within the association in the North were drawn into republican politics in one way or another the 32-county nature of the organisation and the wide variety of views within it meant that it could not function as a support group for any branch of the republican movement. Indeed on occasions republicans were harshly critical of the organisation's perceived lack of support for them, with one group of IRA prisoners in 1974 writing that 'with deep regret' they found it 'necessary at this stage to re-examine and justify our continued membership and support for the GAA' because of its 'tame protests' and 'puny manifestations of public indignation' over conditions in Long Kesh.[63]

Neither was republican interest in sport confined to the GAA. During the 1980s *An Phoblacht* (*An Phoblacht/Republican News* since 1979) began to feature soccer, hesitatingly and only at international level to begin with. Fittingly the exploits of the Northern Ireland team in Spain during 1982 brought (tongue-in-cheek) recognition that while the team represented a 'political unit we do not recognize' traditional republican antipathy to soccer was 'misplaced and too introverted' as soccer was an international game. The Northern Ireland World Cup campaign was described as 'real fairytale stuff' and the 'Irishness of the team was never in doubt', with Gerry Armstrong from Belfast's Falls Road among the team's heroes.[64] In 1984 the paper speculated that republicans should support the idea of a 32-county team, though the writer felt that while only three Northern Ireland players were good enough to make the all-Ireland first eleven, Billy Bingham of Belfast should certainly be its manager.[65] *An Phoblacht*'s sports coverage during the 1980s, often by the iconoclastic 'John Joe King' continued to mainly focus on GAA and was sometimes very funny, especially his sustained baiting of the 1984 Dublin team –, 'the real heavy gang … all Ireland brawling champions' – which produced outraged responses from Dublin readers who accused the paper of aping the 'British gutter press'.[66] The outrage over the brawling during the first International (Compromise) Rules series drew the comment from King that it was 'GAA backroom boys who actually advocate this stuff in pre-match dressing rooms and then deny it takes place in Gaelic Football at all.'[67] An occasional nostalgia for more simple days surfaced in the belief of one contributor to *Iris* magazine that the initiation of a 'campaign for a re-implementation of the "Ban" rule' might have real popular support.[68] However *An Phoblacht* did not regularly feature coverage of soccer or rugby except for international games. Therefore any debate on the subject was limited. Occasionally a reader expressed disappointment about any coverage of 'foreign' games, as in 1986 when a correspondent from Cork complained that the publicity given to the fortunes of Derry City F.C. was making Derry resemble a 'north of England town' and causing rejection of 'our own national games.' Readers' replies warned that inferring that those who followed soccer were less

Irish than GAA supporters was racist and that the GAA had only itself to blame if it was losing ground to other sports.[69]

The 1990 and 1994 World Cups further normalised soccer coverage within the pages of *An Phoblacht*. Initially the paper contended that Jack Charlton's 'ugly predictable' style based entirely on 'work rate and sweat … rather than skill or vision' meant the Republic of Ireland were 'dreadful to watch.' Indeed the long-ball game had produced two of the 'worst' games in the competition against England and Egypt.[70] However, within a few weeks *An Phoblacht* too was caught up in the wave of euphoria as the Irish team reached the quarter-finals and delighted in the explosion of 'National Pride!'[71] Some critics complained that they had never seen 'such coverage' in *An Phoblacht* for a GAA match and questioned why 'an English game' and a team 'run by an Englishman' should be featured in a republican newspaper.[72] These opinions were dismissed as 'laughable' by other correspondents who countered that 'soccer is a world game.'[73] By 1994 almost any hint of controversy in the coverage of the Republic of Ireland team in *An Phoblacht* had disappeared with NORAID in New York even selling Sinn Féin 1994 World Cup 'put em under pressure!' t-shirts.[74]

Increasingly, by the late 1990s, the affairs of Glasgow Celtic F.C. were featured regularly in *An Phoblacht*, reflecting both its genuine popularity in Ireland and historic links to the diaspora.[75] But Celtic also had a status among at least some Sinn Féin supporters as the politically correct choice for republican soccer fans, in a way in which Manchester United or Liverpool football clubs could never be. Indeed *An Phoblacht* tended to presume 'real football fans' followed Celtic.[76] There seemed a stubborn reluctance to acknowledge that republicans, including members of Sinn Féin were watching and travelling to Liverpool, Manchester and London to follow English teams as well. But coverage of GAA matters remained constant and there was a tendency to see the GAA as superior, because of its local roots and amateur status and because it was played by 'real heroes' as opposed to millionaires.[77] Some argued too that most GAA supporters were 'nationalist or at least nationally minded', a concept that might not withstand serious examination.[78] Unlike the early 1980s the Northern Ireland team and Irish League now tended to be presented as inherently sectarian. The Republic of Ireland was accepted as the team that all nationalists should identify with, despite some evidence to the contrary.[79] On one level these were never key issues for Sinn Féin, which could accommodate all manner of sporting choices and indeed none within its ranks. But some lingering resentment of 'English soccer' did lead to discussions about coverage of sport that saw much of the paper's soccer coverage, including that of Celtic, curtailed.[80]

The increased visibility of Gaelic sports during the 1990s and the success of northern teams, coinciding with the 'peace process' and the political rise of Sinn Féin tended to produce coverage that merged all these events into a vision of nationalist resurgence. In a rather obvious way the GAA and support of its games continued to mean something different north and south of the border. On any given summer's day on the Falls Road in Belfast men and women can be observed wearing Dublin, Kerry, Offaly and Cork GAA jerseys among others. There are few hurling or football fans in Dublin or Kerry, Limerick or Tipperary who would wear a rival county's colours. Therefore the GAA remains for many Northern nationalists a way to express 'Irishness'. Yet the fact that Martin McGuinness, one of the two most prominent Sinn Féin figures of recent decades, can happily (and without controversy) announce that he has been a supporter of Manchester United F.C. since the 1960s, and indeed of cricket as well, also points to other changes in modern Irish republican culture.[81]

The Gaelic Athletic Association and Irish-America

Paul Darby

In December 2008, during her speech to mark the official opening of Páirc na nGael, the San Francisco Gaelic Athletic Association's first permanent home in the city, Uachtarán na hÉireann, Mary McAleese, spoke effusively of her 'absolute joy' at witnessing first hand the fruits of the 'enthusiasm, energy and civic spirit of the Irish community of San Francisco and the love that they have for Gaelic heritage'.[1] She went on to aptly capture the significance of the GAA for Ireland's worldwide diaspora by asserting that '… our sports are at the heart of our Gaelic heritage. There is nothing that connects us more to one another wherever we are in the world than our Gaelic games'.[2] This chapter builds on President McAleese's contention by sketching the history of the GAA in the United States of America and analysing the socio-economic, political and cultural import of Gaelic games for Irish immigrant communities there. The arguments presented in this chapter are rooted in empirical evidence collected as part of a broader study examining the development of Gaelic games in four of the key focal points of Irish immigration and main centres of GAA activity in the US, namely Boston, New York, Chicago and San Francisco.[3]

Uncodified versions of Gaelic football and hurling were played in America long before the establishment of the GAA in 1884. For example, Abbott and McGinn provide details of documentary evidence concerning the existence of rudimentary forms of hurling in New York as early as the 1780s.[4] The emergence of Gaelic sports clubs in the city though, had to wait until the 1850s with the establishment of the Irish Hurling and Football Club in 1857.[5] Early versions of Gaelic football and hurling were also played on the Pacific coast at this time with *Alta California*, one of the city's earliest newspapers, reporting in May 1853 on the establishment of San Francisco's first hurling club.[6] By the late 1870s and early 1880s Gaelic games were also taking place on a somewhat regular basis in Boston and Chicago. However, it was not until the mid 1880s, following the inception of the GAA following that famous meeting in Thurles, that codified, organised versions of Gaelic games began to be played on American shores. Beyond the inauguration of clubs and the efforts of some notable individuals, the most significant development in the emergence of Gaelic games in America at this time was the 'Gaelic Invasion' of 1888, which saw over fifty Irish athletes tour the country's north-eastern seaboard as part of an initiative aimed at helping to revive the Tailteann games, an athletic and cultural festival which had last taken place in Ireland in the twelfth century. This tour did much to raise awareness of and help popularise Gaelic games and this ensured that by the turn of the century hurling and particularly Gaelic football were well established in parts of Irish America.

While the spread of Gaelic games in Boston, New York, Chicago and San Francisco may not have matched the pace and pervasiveness of the GAA's growth in Ireland, the association quickly established itself as an important sporting, cultural and socio-economic resource for those Irish immigrants who had journeyed to the 'New World' in the latter decades of the nineteenth century. The motivation of immigrants to get involved in and help to preserve Gaelic games on American shores was clearly rooted in the fact that their involvement in these games allowed them to experience excitement, pleasure and fun in what could otherwise be a drab and difficult, urban existence. High skill levels as a player or organisational abilities as an administrator were likely to have conferred a degree of kudos on individuals and it may have been this that encouraged some to take part. For others, simply being outdoors and engaging in or watching robust physical endeavour may explain the appeal of hurling and Gaelic football in this period. The fact that Gaelic games were so intimately connected to and resonant of 'home' also undoubtedly piqued a primordial passion in enthusiasts and as will be revealed later in this chapter, this was particularly important in cementing the place of the GAA amongst sections of the Irish diaspora in America.

During the opening decades of the twentieth century, the GAA experienced varying levels of growth. The inauguration of a number of governing bodies and a co-ordinated approach to the promotion of Gaelic games was hugely influential in this regard. For example, the inception of the 'Gaelic Athletic Association of the United States' in New York in 1914 was described by Byrne as being 'to New York what the Thurles

The 'Cavan' team of New York in the 1900s. Many of the players were natives of Co. Cavan who had emigrated. The tradition of clubs being aligned with certain Irish counties still continues in many American cities. This may in part explain the difficulty experienced by the GAA in the USA in attracting substantial numbers of second- and third-generation Irish Americans into Gaelic games. (*Gearóid Mac Gabhann*)

meeting was to Ireland'.[7] While the progress of Gaelic games in this period was rooted in these sorts of internal initiatives, the health of the association became increasingly susceptible to external influences, particularly fluctuations in levels of Irish immigration into the USA. Thus, the outbreak of the Great War, America's decision to enter hostilities in 1917 and a subsequent decline in rates of Irish immigration, impacted on the Association significantly, not least through a decrease in the complement of GAA clubs.

The conclusion of the First World War did much to revive levels of immigration and replenish depleted GAA stocks. Buoyed by this revival organisational bodies began to form elsewhere, most notably in Boston, where the Massachusetts Gaelic Athletic Association was instituted in 1923. The GAA's Dublin-based administration looked favourably on these developments, and in 1926 it sanctioned regular tours of the USA by All-Ireland winning inter-county teams in both hurling and football, a move which did much to further embed these sports in the consciousness of the Irish *émigré*. However, the Wall Street crash of 1929 and a resultant global depression heralded a period of stagnation and decline in the GAA's fortunes in America. The Great Depression of the 1930s, keenly felt as it was in areas of heavy industrialisation, had a devastating impact on America's Irish community, most of which depended for their livelihood on unskilled labour and as such were victims of the worst economic ravages of the era. In such a difficult environment, identifying ways of alleviating socio-economic hardship as opposed to seeking to preserve the sports and games of the 'old country', became the priority for many. Dramatically reduced levels of immigration also fed into this decline.

Some units of the association were better prepared for the challenges of depression-era America than others though. For example, while the GAA in New York and San Francisco were progressive enough to initiate what became very successful youth programmes amongst an American-born pool of talent, the failure to do the same in Boston and Chicago quickly saw Gaelic games there go into freefall. However, the creation of a youthful, locally based grassroots that had been developed in New York and San Francisco could do little to prevent the virtual disappearance of Gaelic games across America once the United States government took the decision to enter the Second World War. It became patently clear to those with aspirations to rebuild the GAA in post-war America that its revival would have to be organised around an event of considerable import.

Thus whilst there were palpable signs of recovery in the immediate aftermath of the war, the historic decision by the GAA's Annual Congress in 1947 to grant New York the right to host the All-Ireland Gaelic football final was undoubtedly the cornerstone of the Association's renewal.[8] Although the turnout was disappointing,[9] the event provided a massive boost for Gaelic games throughout America. Of particular significance was the fact that the 1947 final did much to improve the relationship between the GAA in America and its counterparts in Ireland. Tangible evidence of this was quickly apparent in the following year when the association's Central Council agreed to set aside an international fund of £2,000 to facilitate closer relations with the New York GAA and institute more regular playing contact.[10] This level of support for 'international' fixtures was matched across the Atlantic and just three years later, New York was taking part in the finals of the GAA's National League competitions.

A resumption of healthy levels of immigration during the 1950s rapidly restocked GAA clubs and new ones were established to cope with the increased demand for Gaelic games. This growth encouraged America's Gaels to turn their attentions to the establishment of a nationwide governing body to oversee the development of Gaelic games and provide opportunities for inter-city competition. While a number of attempts were made to bring this aspiration to reality during the 1950s, it was not until the establishment of the North American County Board (NACB) in 1959 that this plan became a reality. The establishment

A pictorial representation of some of the skills of Gaelic football for the benefit of an American audience, so as to be able to follow Cavan's matches with New York in 1934. This 'International' match was preceded by a hurling match and a minor football game. The drawing of Jim Smith's high kick is a surprisingly accurate depiction of a real photograph, which provided one of the match-programme covers. The American press were quick to promote such games as 'world championship' series. (*Gearóid Mac Gabhann*)

of the NACB, along with continued healthy rates of Irish immigration into the USA, in light of economic stagnation in Ireland, did much to ensure that Gaelic games enthusiasts entered the 1960s with considerable optimism. However, the passing of legislation through the US Congress in 1965, which led to the Immigration Act (1965), seriously curtailed Irish immigration to the USA. The appointment of Seán Lemass as Irish *Taoiseach* in 1959 and his role in Ireland's economic recovery, one built on expansionist policies and membership of the European Economic Community (1973), also fed into the sharp reduction in Irish migration.[11] By 1969 the effect of these developments on American units of the GAA were being felt and Gaelic games once again began to struggle.

With increasing numbers of clubs folding, some within the NACB and the New York board began to feel that youth programmes, targeted at American-born children with Irish lineage, would help preserve Gaelic games and hence, a number of divisional boards began to invest more time in nurturing young talent. Before this work could come to fruition however, rising levels of unemployment in Ireland, following an economic downturn in the late 1970s and 1980s, revived the flow of Irish migrants seeking opportunities in the USA. This did much to regenerate the association in this period and most senior clubs, eager for championship honours, had little space for American-born players. In such circumstances, youth-player development and the building of a talent pool to sustain Gaelic games for the longer term was increasingly neglected.

With the granting of Donnelly and Morrison visas in 1986 and 1990 respectively and a continued rise in the numbers of undocumented Irish in the USA in the early 1990s, the GAA returned to a healthy position. However, with the economic upturn in Ireland (commonly referred to as the 'Celtic Tiger') persuading more young Irish people to remain at home, anxieties about the preservation of Gaelic football, hurling and camogie on American soil began to resurface around this time. The NACB's clubs were able to play down their concerns and veil the impact of slowing immigration by continuing to import high-profile players from Ireland for at least part of the regular season and the play-off stages of their competitions. However, from around the mid 1990s, some local Gaels began to question whether this strategy was likely to bring long-term benefits for Gaelic games in North America. In addition, the number of complaints from Irish-based clubs and counties who were effectively losing their most talented players to clubs in the USA rose steadily, necessitating a revamp and tightening of the sanction or transfer system by Central Council in 1998.[12] Further restrictions on immigration into the USA following the terrorist attacks of 11 September 2001 upon New York and Washington (commonly referred to as 9/11) led to some clubs calling for a liberalisation of the rules governing transatlantic transfers and an increase in the number of 'sanction players' permitted to play. However, those within the higher echelons of the NACB and the New York County Board have gradually come to the realisation that the future of Gaelic games will be best sustained by nurturing an American-born grassroots, one which embraces children from a range of ethnic groups. Significant steps have been taken down this road, not least the

The Cavan team that visited New York and Philadelphia in 1934 were presented with this trophy by their hosts. Note the spelling of 'Caven CBS society'. (*Gearóid Mac Gabhann*)

A photograph from the gala dinner at the Plaza Hotel, New York, for the Cavan team who travelled to the United States of America in 1934. Such banquets were held every year for the visiting All-Ireland champion teams, who were treated as heroes for the duration of their lengthy tours. (*Gearóid Mac Gabhann*)

appointment of a number of games development officers in the USA, who are funded as part of a partnership agreement between the GAA and the Irish government's Department of Foreign Affairs, signed off in 2008, aimed at promoting Gaelic games abroad.[13]

Of course the fact that the GAA has survived many challenges in the USA over the course of its almost 125-year history and appears to be entering a new, exciting period in its growth and development, raises questions about why a whole host of GAA officials, adherents and benefactors have sought to promote and preserve Gaelic games. The presence of organised versions of Gaelic games in America from the mid 1880s through to the current day has clearly been dependent on their ability to satisfy a number of crucial socio-economic, cultural and political functions for the Irish *émigrés*. For those of a sporting disposition, the significance of the Gaelic football or hurling club in smoothing their transition from rural Ireland to sprawling, noisome and inhospitable urban centres cannot be overstated. Put simply, the GAA in the USA provided a comforting home away from home for thousands of Irish immigrants. It allowed them the opportunity to associate with like-minded individuals and in doing so helped to alleviate the feelings of alienation and dislocation that the Irish *émigrés* often felt. Involvement with a GAA club or attendance at a match or function also provided entrance into the social networks that enabled newly arrived immigrants to find work, accommodation, make friends and of course, experience the excitement of competitive sports. The functioning of the GAA in these respects have been evident in the USA since the 1880s and it is these same forces and dynamics that have done so much to sustain Gaelic games there right through to the current day.

NEW YORK

T. Sheehan
(Kerry)

D. O'Connor   T. Gallagher   J. Foley
(Cork)   (Philadelphia)   (Kerry)

J. Redican   W. Carlos   E. Kenny
(Offaly)   (Roscommon)   (Carlow)

P. McAndrew   F. Driscoll
(Mayo)   (Cork)

M. O'Sullivan   J. Hughes   P. Ryan
(New York)   (New York)   (Galway)

E. Deady   J. McElligott   F. Quinn
(Kerry)   (Kerry)   (Galway)

Only three of the New York football team that lined out against Cork in 1957 were not from Ireland.

The fact that Gaelic games have also allowed Irish immigrants and their offspring to mark themselves out as ethnically distinctive and express their affinities for Ireland has also been crucial in allowing the GAA to retain a place in Irish America. In much the same way that the inception of the GAA in Ireland in 1884 was rooted in an Irish nationalist agenda, the emergence of Gaelic football and hurling clubs in a range of American cities at this time was also linked to the broader groundswell of support for Irish nationalism. This manifested itself in a number of ways. The pioneering figures behind the inception the GAA in America were mostly staunch nationalists who saw in Gaelic games an opportunity to not only get involved in and promote healthy, physical activity amongst the Irish diaspora but as a vehicle for building the vibrant Gaelic culture in America upon which support for the political objectives of Irish nationalism may be built. John Boyle O'Reilly, a former member of the Irish Republican Brotherhood and a key figure in the early promotion of Gaelic games in Boston certainly interpreted the GAA in this way, as did John F. Finerty, the firebrand Irish nationalist newspaper publisher, who played a major role in helping to popularise hurling and football in Chicago and Father Peter Yorke, one of Irish America's leading churchmen and a committed nationalist, who did likewise in San Francisco.[14] Beyond these individuals, the founders of America's earliest Gaelic football and hurling clubs also sought to align their activities to the cause of Irish independence and they did this most visibly by following the trend evident in Ireland, of naming their clubs after historical and popular nationalist personalities and organisations.[15] Thus, appellations such as Emmet's, Redmond's, Parnell's, Wolfe Tone's, Young Ireland, Davitt's, O'Connell's, Emeralds and Shamrocks were adopted by clubs across America.

The place of the GAA in the psyche of Irish nationalists in America at this time was also cemented and broadened by the fact that a range of nationalist organisations, of both the physical force and parliamentary kind, turned to Gaelic games as a way of attracting adherents and promoting their cultural and political agenda. In New York, Boston and Chicago for example, organisations such as the Irish National League, the Hibernian Rifles, the Advanced Irish Nationalists and Clan na Gael harnessed the mobilising power of Gaelic games to recruit members, fundraise and encourage the Irish immigrant population to view and express themselves as Irish nationalists. This pattern was repeated on America's Pacific coast where groups such as the Knights of the Red Branch (KRB), the Gaelic League and the Ancient Order of Hibernians (AOH) all ardently got behind Gaelic games and were more than happy to be closely associated with the GAA. The ties between Gaelic games and Irish nationalism were also reinforced amongst the broader Irish community through evocative, rousing and intensely nationalistic reporting on GAA activities in the Irish-American press. For example, the accounts in the *Irish Echo* and *The Gael* of GAA field-days in Boston in the early 1880s routinely described them as 'patriotic', imbued with the 'spirit of freedom' and part of a practical drive for 'Irish emancipation'.[16]

The portrayal of Gaelic games as emblematic of Irish identity and aspirations for independence did much to bolster the strength of the GAA in the late nineteenth century. Those who took up the baton of promoting these sports in America at the outset of the twentieth century were well aware of their significance as important markers of Irish ethnic identity. However, the extent to which they specifically sought to link their activities to overtly politicised expressions of Irish nationalism became largely dependent on the ebb and flow of the nationalist struggle in Ireland. It should come as little surprise then to note that the association between the GAA in America and a more hostile, belligerent Irish nationalism gathered strength in the period leading up to the Easter Rising in 1916 as GAA members sought to demonstrate their patriotism by

The goals at the Polo Grounds, New York, in 1957. These are much shorter than those generally used for Gaelic games. Indeed the playing area was also much smaller than that normally used for football and hurling. The GAA in the USA and elsewhere abroad often had to improvise and adapt unsuitable playing grounds. (Jim McQuaid).

Iggy Jones, a star Tyrone player, at the Polo Grounds before the county's game against a New York select in 1957.
(*Jim McQuaid*)

backing the Irish nationalist cause in very tangible ways. This was done specifically through fund raising activities in Boston, Chicago, San Francisco and particularly New York, aimed at arming the Irish National Volunteers. The Irish-American press did much to ensure a healthy turn out at fundraising matches, field-days and social events organised by the GAA, not least by using evocative, rousing and intensely nationalistic language. One editorial in the New York Irish paper, *The Advocate* was typical:

> The Gaelic athlete here never forgets his national honour. Today Ireland is undergoing a trying ordeal. Thousands of Irishmen have volunteered to defend IRELAND FOR IRELAND, and in this way they must be armed. The Irishmen of Greater New York can show their appreciation of Ireland's National Volunteers by turning out in their thousands at Celtic Park on Labor Day … . It's an occasion that the Gael should make the most of and show the hated Saxon that at least there are a few Irishmen in New York who are not willing to 'hold Ireland for England'.[17]

In the aftermath of the failed Rising in 1916, the GAA in America continued to promote a virulent, revolutionary Irish nationalism. For example, during the War of Independence between 1919 and 1921, fundraising and expressions of support for the IRA were commonplace at GAA events. However, from the mid to late 1920s this trend began to decline largely as a consequence of the fact that for many Irish-Americans partition had effectively resolved the 'Irish question'. As they became more assimilated into American society, the Irish gradually lost interest in Irish politics and as a corollary to this, the GAA became significantly less politicised than it had been in previous years.

This changed though with the onset of the 'Troubles' in Northern Ireland in the late 1960s. Reflecting Irish-American anger at what was transpiring in Northern Ireland, the GAA in the USA once again adopted an overtly nationalist persona. For example, in the early 1970s a close relationship developed with Irish Northern Aid (NORAID),[18] particularly in New York. This was hardly surprising given that the men who were instrumental in establishing NORAID, Michael Flannery, Matthew Higgins, Jack McCarthy and John McGowan, were also influential figures in the Gaelic games fraternity.[19] Beyond New York, there were other notable examples of a close relationship between republicanism and the GAA. One particularly stark case in point is the Ulster Gaelic Football Club (GFC) in San Francisco. This club was established in 1986 by a group of individuals who hailed mainly from the north of Ireland and who were republican in their political outlook. Their intentions for the club extended beyond sporting concerns and they were eager to ensure that it reflected their politics. This was perhaps most visible in the club's constitution, article two of which states that:

> The objectives of the club shall be to preserve and defend the democratic principles enshrined in the Declaration of Independence, and the Proclamation of the Irish Republic, declared on Easter Week 1916.[20]

The extent to which the club functioned as a vehicle for the expression of republicanism was further amplified through a number of other practices. For example, the club established a 'political wing committee'. It aligned itself with the activities of the San Francisco chapter of NORAID, with significant cross-membership between both organisations.[21] It regularly celebrated remembrance masses for IRA volunteers killed in the conflict in Northern Ireland, while the highpoint of the club's year, off the field of play, was its annual Easter brunch, organised to commemorate and celebrate those who had taken part in the 1916 Easter Rising.

During the course of the 'Troubles' in the north of Ireland**,** there were many other examples of GAA members in the USA accommodating a strong republican component within their broader promotion of Gaelic games. However, since the mid 1990s there have been a number of developments that have diluted the GAA's nationalist persona in the US. The peace process in Northern Ireland has been central in this regard. This process has strongly influenced the nature of Irish nationalist expression in the USA. While a small minority remains opposed to the provisions of the Belfast (Good Friday) Agreement,[22] the vast majority of those living in America who would consider themselves Irish republicans have either adopted a

Irish-American politician Bobby Kennedy greeting spectators at one of the Cardinal Cushing games in New York in 1964. Appearing at a Gaelic game in the USA was a useful method of courting the Irish vote. Derry footballer Jim McKeever and his wife Teresa were captured inadvertently in the background. (*Jim McKeever*)

position broadly in keeping with that of the mainstream republican movement in Ireland or have at least become increasingly circumspect and cautious about publicly expressing support for a more hard-line stance. The events of 9/11 and the response of the US authorities in their aftermath have fed into this process. Since 9/11 Irish republicans have been worried about how their political position might be perceived by their American neighbours and they have concerns that a public espousal of this stance might be misconstrued as being supportive of terrorism in its broadest sense and hence, insensitive to the loss of life that occurred on 9/11. These fears are magnified for Irish republicans living in the USA illegally, who are worried about deportation should their political position bring them under the radar of the US Department of Homeland Security. This has led to a situation where Irish republicans are increasingly keeping their political views to themselves.[23]

This process has also been played out within the GAA fraternity and since the signing of the Belfast-Good Friday Agreement and the events of 9/11 there has been a decline in the extent to which Gaelic games have functioned as a space for producing and reproducing overtly politicised versions of Irishness. This has manifested itself in a whole host of ways. For example, the NACB took a much softer position on the debate over the GAA's Rule 42 than it did on Rule 21,[24] while members of the Ulster GFC in San Francisco have observed a decreasing interest in the more politicised aspects of their club over the last five to ten years.[25] Perhaps the clearest indication of a shift in the relationship between the GAA and Irish nationalist expression though can be seen in the association's response to dwindling rates of Irish immigration to the USA post '9/11'. With immigration from Ireland into the USA now at a trickle, a whole range of Irish social and cultural organisations have felt the pinch and many are struggling to survive. In recent years GAA clubs have been able to sustain themselves through the sanction system. However, as noted earlier, there is a growing consensus that this is a short-term approach to a problem that is unlikely to be resolved any time soon and a range of initiatives have been established aimed at creating an American-born grassroots. As part of this strategy, there has been an implicit acceptance of the limitations of promoting Gaelic games solely to a shrinking Irish constituency and of the need to embark on a more cosmopolitan recruitment drive. Increasingly, the focus is shifting to selling Gaelic games as exciting sports to a broader ethnic audience rather than packaging them as 'national' pastimes to an exclusively Irish or Irish-American constituency. As the second half of this chapter has shown, this is a radical departure in terms of how the GAA has operated in the past. In light of this, some have expressed concerns that something of the essence, tradition and ethnic purity of Gaelic games in the USA is being lost by following this approach to securing the future of the GAA. However, in a context where a significant influx of long-term Irish immigrants is unlikely, it seems that this is the only way to preserve Ireland's sporting heritage in America.

American Gaels and Cavan Heroes:
The 1947 All-Ireland Gaelic Football Final in New York

Aogán Ó Fearghail and Paul Darby

The hosting of the 1947 All-Ireland Gaelic football final at New York's Polo Grounds was, at the time, and remains, one of the most momentous events in the 125-year history of the Gaelic Athletic Association (GAA). It represented the first and, indeed, only occasion that an All-Ireland senior final has been hosted outside the island of Ireland. The match was fundamental in the post-war revival of Gaelic games in the United States of America (USA) and did much to reinvigorate an enthusiasm amongst Irish-Americans in the games of the 'old country'. It also heralded in a period of unparalleled success in All-Ireland competition for Cavan's footballers and has since acquired almost mythical status in the folklore of Gaelic football in Cavan, and, of course, New York. The import of the 1947 All-Ireland final in the history of Gaelic games is recognised within the hierarchy of the GAA, a fact exemplified by the presence of a sizeable exhibit recalling the event, at the association's museum in Croke Park. In the broader historiography of Gaelic games, the game at the Polo Grounds has also featured prominently in a number of books and articles, both populist and academic.[1] This chapter builds on this historiography by undertaking a detailed analysis of the circumstances surrounding the decision to award New York the hosting rights for the All-Ireland football final. Beyond examining the discussions and machinations that brought the match to New York, this chapter accounts for its significance in reconnecting Irish-Americans with the GAA at a time when Gaelic games were on the verge of extinction in the USA. It also details the significance of the final for 'Gaeldom' in Cavan and highlights the fact that those who represented the county on that September day in New York subsequently acquired hero status within local GAA circles. The chapter draws on primary source material collected from archives in New York, Dublin and Co. Cavan and also utilises interview research conducted with some of those who featured prominently in this event.

Aside from its significance for the GAA in New York, the 1947 final stands out as a high-point in the history of Gaelic football in Cavan and Kerry, but it was not an entirely unique expedition for either county. Due to their long and distinguished histories in the game – by the start of that year Kerry topped the All-Ireland football roll of honour, with sixteen senior titles; Cavan had only claimed the national senior honours twice (in 1933 and 1935), but reigned supreme in Ulster, having won twenty-seven of the fifty-odd provincial senior titles up to then – both counties had sent previous champion teams to America: Kerry on several occasions since 1927, including the 1931 trip (in which a crowd of sixty thousand spectators at Yankee Stadium set a world-record for a Gaelic game),[2] and Cavan teams visited the USA three times in four years – 1934, 1936 and 1938. For the young men involved, mostly from modest agricultural backgrounds in largely rural counties, who had been playing football merely as a parochial pastime a few short years earlier, it was an experience that they could never have imagined the sport bringing to them. To have an all-expenses-paid trip to America; to be treated to one banquet after another; to be feted everywhere as heroes and ambassadors of their county and country – these were extraordinary exploits that would otherwise have remained beyond their means.

Cavan's previous tours had proven especially memorable. On the seven-week tour of 1934, Cavan travelled by boat from Galway in the month of May. The team played a draw (1-7 each) with New York before forty thousand spectators at Yankee Stadium; and moved on to play challenge games in New Jersey, Philadelphia and Boston, before contesting the return game against New York. Towards the end of this last game, a large number of spectators rushed onto the field, a melee ensued, and police and firemen intervened to restore order.[3] New York won this game, although Cavan did not return home empty-handed – the team was presented with a grand trophy by the Cavan Men's C.B.S. Society of Philadelphia (see Darby in this section). On the 1936 tour, however, Cavan beat New York by a point in the aggregate score over two games, to win the Bill Dolan Cup and gold medals. The players were hailed as world champions on their

Cavan players discuss the skills of the game on the boat journey to the United States in 1947.
(*Cavan County Museum*)

return home, before two thousand supporters in the county town.[4] Cavan got on the 1938 tour as All-Ireland runners-up, but champions Kerry declined the invitation to join them, in protest at comments made to the press by Bréifne players, officials and supporters about Kerry's 'questionable methods' in their encounter in the 1937 final replay. Laois joined Cavan on tour instead.[5] Two figures connected Cavan's three previous tours and that of 1947: Hughie O'Reilly, who played up to 1936, and trained the team thereafter; and 'Big' Tom O'Reilly, who won a record thirteen Ulster football medals between 1933 and 1947 (see the records section), and was an older brother of 1947 captain, John Joe O'Reilly. Thankfully, by 1947 the former Cavan-Kerry enmity of yore was a fading memory.

As revealed elsewhere in this collection (see Darby above),[6] prior to 1947 the fortunes of the GAA in America waxed and waned according to fluctuations in emigration from Ireland, the strength of the resolve and organisational acumen of leading Irish-American Gaels, and the inclination of Irish immigrants to patronise their 'national' pastimes. By the late 1930s, the Great Depression had virtually devastated branches of the GAA across America and the ending of tours by All-Ireland final teams after 1939 deprived the American GAA calendar of its showcase fixtures. The onset of the Second World War did little to help the flagging fortunes of the association in America and while there were pockets of GAA activity, by the conclusion of the war it became clear to those who had aspirations to rebuild a vibrant GAA culture in the country that dedication, resolve, persistence and perhaps most of all, a signature event aimed at regenerating Gaelic games, were required. The acquisition of an agreement from the GAA Congress and Central Council in Ireland to host the final of the 1947 All-Ireland football championship in New York provided this signature event and ultimately acted as a catalyst for the renewal of sustained GAA activity in Irish-America.

But how did what seemed to many at the time a preposterous idea actually come to fruition, and who were the key individuals who worked to turn it into reality? It is to these questions that this chapter now turns.

The key individual responsible for getting the 1947 decider to New York was undoubtedly the legendary John 'Kerry' O'Donnell who was at that time the most influential figure in the New York GAA (NYGAA). He was born in Co. Kerry and left Ireland in 1918. Following a period in Montreal, he moved to New York where he worked in construction before exhibiting shrewd business sensibilities as owner of a number of bars in the city. O'Donnell's involvement in the affairs of the association in New York began in 1929 when he joined the Kerry club as a player.[7] Thereafter, he acted in various administrative capacities, including president of the NYGAA in 1940. As a staunch advocate of the association, O'Donnell was dismayed at the demise of Gaelic games in the early 1940s, particularly the threat of losing the lease to Innisfail Park, the chief venue for Gaelic games in the city. The city's Gaels were struggling to raise the finances necessary to meet the rental costs on the venue. By 1942, the NYGAA was no longer in a position to afford regular payments and the lease was taken up by a local soccer group and renamed. Gaelic games did still feature at the park but only on an intermittent basis and only when the fixture was likely to cover the requisite rental costs. In November 1944, the situation worsened when some of the soccer clubs that had been using the venue sought the lease on a permanent basis.

This potentially disastrous development was averted though by O'Donnell, who raised the funds necessary to purchase a longer term lease and allow him to become the sole proprietor. Indeed, in 1952, the then GAA president, Vincent O'Donoghue, remarked at a Central Council meeting, that had it not been for O'Donnell's actions in securing a base for Gaelic games in the city, 'there would not be any GAA in New York now'.[8] Although O'Donnell's proprietorship of Gaelic Park is perhaps the contribution that he is best remembered for, his role in bringing the 1947 All-Ireland final to New York was equally, if not more, important. While the NYGAA had begun to make small strides in reviving interest in Gaelic football and hurling in the city,[9] O'Donnell recognised that an event of some significance was needed to revitalise these sports. Hosting an All-Ireland final on New York soil quickly became the main pillar in his ambitious plans for the GAA in the city. O'Donnell recognised in the drawn 1946 All-Ireland football final between Roscommon and Kerry an opportunity, and using his links with the GAA in Kerry he floated the idea of bringing the replay to New York.[10] Whilst this proposal was quickly dismissed by Central Council, the idea of using the association's showpiece event to arrest the marginalisation of Gaelic games in the USA re-emerged on the GAA's agenda in the following year. Chief amongst those who began to canvass to turn what had seemed a year earlier an outlandish proposition into a reality was the influential Clare official, Canon Michael Hamilton, who proposed a motion at the Association's Congress in 1947 to allow Central Council to consider the possibility of New York hosting the 1947 All-Ireland football final.[11]

That Canon Hamilton took this step on behalf of New York's Gaels was hardly surprising. He had acted as an advocate of the association in the USA since 1937 when he accompanied the Mayo Gaelic football team on their tour of New York, Boston and Philadelphia. His affection for New York's Gaels was particularly marked and was evidenced in a belated Christmas greeting that he sent them via *The Advocate* in January 1939. Recalling a previous visit to the city, he spoke warmly about the hospitality he had been accorded and of his impression of the city's GAA fraternity:

> I was intensely impressed with the ardour and enthusiasm with which our Irish exiles have preserved in the land of their adoption, the grand traditions of their forefathers in the matter of Gaelic pastimes, national ideals, the community of brotherhood of the Gael, and above all in their ardent loyalty to faith and the banner of St Patrick.[12]

Canon Hamilton's words reveal that he was a man sensitive to the efforts of those who had not only worked tirelessly to preserve and promote Gaelic games overseas but had also made many financial contributions to a whole range of charitable, educational, social and, of course, nationalist institutions in Ireland. However, this sensitivity was lacking in others within the GAA's Central Council. They were largely unmoved by the plight of the association in the USA and felt little inclination to cater for the sporting needs of the Irish abroad,[13] a fact that can be partly explained in terms of persistent concerns about elements of professionalism in Gaelic games in the USA which had led to 'an unwillingness (on the part of the Dublin-based GAA) to accept the Gaels in America as totally sincere about the promotion of the games'.[14] That the motion was passed was due in large part to the strength of the arguments that were put forward, chiefly by Canon Hamilton, but it is also possible that the successful outcome was also based partly on the unusual circumstances within which the Congress was conducted.

The Congress began in Dublin City Hall and was adjourned at lunchtime to allow the delegates to go to Croke Park to watch the Railway Cup hurling final, which had previously been postponed due to heavy snowfall. The Congress was reconvened under the old Hogan Stand much later in the day and with snow falling heavily, many delegates had decided to forgo the remainder of the Congress and begin their journeys home. Furthermore, those remaining were anxious for proceedings to draw to a close. As Maurice Hayes, the Down delegate who was present recalls in his earlier chapter in this collection, most delegates would have voted for anything in order to bring proceedings to a speedy close to allow them to set out on their journeys for home.[15] While the delegates were eager for the Congress to end in such circumstances, Canon Hamilton clearly felt that there was still much convincing to be done when he presented his case on behalf of the NYGAA. He began by stressing that the future of Gaelic games amongst the exiled Gaels in New York was dependent on the success of his motion. After detailing the decline in Gaelic games since the early 1940s, Canon Hamilton suggested that the granting of the right to host the All-Ireland final would be 'epoch-making' and akin to a 'blood transfusion to save the life of the association'.[16] As he continued, Canon Hamilton's address became more emotive and he appealed to the delegates' sense of shared kinship with those across the Atlantic by eulogising about what witnessing an All-Ireland final live would mean for the New York Irish:

> chords will be touched in the hearts of that Irish throng that nothing else in this world could touch. Tears of joy and pride will glisten in the eyes of thousands of men and women and strong hearts will throb with an emotion that only those who have been in exile can appreciate or understand.[17]

Cavan players and officials pictured at a reception in New York.

Canon Hamilton brought his speech to a close with more of the same sentiment, arguing that the gift of hosting the final in the centenary of the worst year of the Great Famine would be an appropriate gesture to America's 'exiled' Gaels. Seconding the motion, a fellow Clare delegate, Bob Fitzpatrick, read what he claimed was an impassioned letter from an Irish immigrant in New York.[18] These eloquent and evocative arguments clearly touched many of the Congress delegates, who duly voted in favour of the motion to allow Central Council to consider the feasibility of taking the final to New York.

Following the decision of Congress, a party that included the GAA's General Secretary, Pádraig Ó Caoimh and Tom Kilcoyne, Secretary of the Connacht Council, were dispatched to New York to carry out their feasibility study. During their month-long visit they met with local GAA officials, including John O'Donnell and potential sponsors, and they appeared to have been convinced about the logistics of moving the final to New York and of the benefits that would accrue in terms of both reviving Gaelic games in the USA and bolstering the GAA's coffers at home. Upon their return, a meeting of the GAA's Central Council was convened for 23 May to consider their report and make a final decision about where the game would be played. Stern opposition, described by de Búrca, was very evident at the meeting:

> To many the idea of playing what had become the biggest national sports event of the year outside the country bordered on the unthinkable. Some also wondered if the sponsors of the idea had given any thought to the possible effects on the average Gaelic spectator, who would be deprived of the customary climax to his seasonal championship fare.[19]

Some delegates, and even the president, Dan O'Rourke of Roscommon, thought the proposal simply unfeasible. Hence the Central Council, in private session, voted to reject the plan. But in the public session, in front of pressmen, some delegates changed side.[20] The motion to host the All-Ireland final in New York was carried by twenty votes to seventeen.[21] The date for the match was fixed for 14 September and the venue was to be the Polo Grounds, home to the New York Giants baseball club. The venue, which was in an area (formerly known as 'Coogan's Hollow') with strong Irish connections had hosted a wide range of major sporting events since its opening in 1876,[22] but it was smaller than the regulation size for a Gaelic field. Nonetheless it was the best stadium available, and the final would be played on a pitch that was a mere seventy-one yards wide at one end.[23]

There was much to be done in the months leading up to the game and it was decided that Ó Caoimh would need to move to New York to oversee preparations. The overseas hosting of the finale of the GAA's season necessitated a number of unique organisational provisions. For example, a number of receptions and banquets had to be arranged, along with travel and hotel reservations, ticketing and radio coverage of the event for those in Ireland. An advance party of GAA officials, including the former president, Pádraig McNamee,[24] travelled to New York to make preliminary arrangements and work closely with the local organising committee, led by John O'Donnell and ably assisted by the Mayo-born Mayor of New York, William O'Dwyer.[25] In a move that signalled the potential of the match to reinvigorate Gaelic games elsewhere in the USA, assistance was also provided by a number of individual members of the association in Boston, San Francisco and Los Angeles.[26] This group made good headway and Ó Caoimh's organisational contribution following his arrival in New York in late July ensured that final preparations went smoothly.

An advance party of GAA officials, substitutes from both teams and county officials set sail for New York from An Cóbh in Cork on 3 September 1947 on board the *S.S. Mauritania*. Most of the starting players of both teams flew to New York from Rineanna (later re-named Shannon Airport) on 8 September, via Santa Maria in the Azores, Gander Airport and Boston, in what was a gruelling twenty-nine-hour journey.[27] One of the Cavan first-team players, Bill Doonan, refused to fly, however. He opted instead to travel on board the *Mauritania* along with several of his colleagues.[28] When the Kerry and Cavan parties arrived in New York on 9 and 10 September, they were taken into Manhattan in a cavalcade of thirty cars escorted by eighteen New York police motorcyclists. Both teams were welcomed to New York with a reception, hosted by Mayor O'Dwyer at City Hall.[29] This welcome set the tone for a series of receptions, gala dinners and parades which did much to promote the game amongst the city's Irish. On the morning

CAVAN

COLORS: BLUE

1. V. Gannon (Goal)

2. W. Doonan   3. B. Reilly   4. P. Smith

5. P. J. Duke   6. Comdt. J. J. O'Reilly   7. Lt. S. Deignan
(Capt.)

8. C. McDyer   9. P. Brady

10. T. Tighe   11. M. Higgins   12. T. P. O'Reilly

13. J. Stafford   14. P. Donohue   15. E. Carolan

SUBSTITUTES

16. J. Wilson   17. T. Sheridan   18. O. R. McGovern   19. J. J. Cassidy   20. D. Donagher   21. T. O'Reilly   23. E. Tiernan

The Cavan and Kerry teams from the 1947 final programme. (*Jim McDonnell*)

KERRY

COLORS:
GREEN & GOLD

1. D. O'Keeffe (Goal)

2. D. Lyne (Capt.)   3. Lt. J. Keohane   4. P. Brosnan

5. T. Lyne   6. W. Casey   7. E. Walsh

8. E. Dowing   9. E. O'Connor

10. G. O'Sullivan   11. W. O'Donnell   12. B. Garvey

13. F. O'Keeffe   14. T. O'Connor   15. D. Kavanagh

SUBSTITUTES

16. T. Brosnan 17. T. O'Sullivan 18. M. Finucane 19. T. Long 20. S. Keane 21. G. Teehan 22. P. Kennedy (Injured)

of the match, Cardinal Spellman, the Archbishop of New York, said Mass for the touring party at St Patrick's Cathedral and wished both teams well. Following the Mass, both teams went up to the altar to shake hands with the archbishop before being presented with a holy medal. Despite what was a significant gesture on the part of Cardinal Spellman, the thoughts of some of the players were clearly focused on what was to follow, with Bill Doonan remarking to his team-mate Mick Higgins, 'I hope we get a better one (medal) later on'.[30] With all of the preliminaries completed, all that was left was to play the match in front of what the organisers hoped would be a sell-out crowd of 54,000.

Despite the months of meticulous planning and promotion that went into the event, heavy rain on the evening before the final convinced many New York Irish to stay away and the actual attendance fell almost twenty thousand short of the capacity of the Polo Grounds. Ó Caoimh noted in his report to Central Council that the arrangements for the sale of tickets may also have had a negative impact on the attendance. In their desire to prevent the tickets being bought by black-marketeers and sold on at inflated costs, the organising committee had decided not to use the services of the city's ticketing agencies and instead only sold tickets from a single location in Manhattan, controlled by the GAA.[31] The 34,941 spectators who attended the final witnessed an event that has since gone down in the annals of the GAA history. The import of the event in terms of its potential to reinvigorate the association in America and cement ties between Gaels on both sides of the Atlantic resonated around the Polo Grounds in the immediate pre-match rituals. In the official programme, on sale at fifty cents, GAA President Dan O'Rourke expressed his wishes for the match: 'May it strengthen further the bonds between us! May it bring to hearts a joy and a pride in the heritage that is yours!'[32] Mayor O'Dwyer echoed these sentiments remarking that:

> The coming of these envoys of good-will to our shores manifests a great sacrifice on the part of the people of Ireland, in that they yield for our enjoyment their supreme sporting events a token of their appreciation of the friendship which has always existed among Americans of every racial background for old Erin.[33]

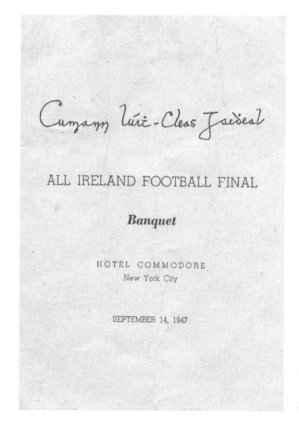

Cumann Lúit-Cleas Jaedeal

ALL IRELAND FOOTBALL FINAL

Banquet

HOTEL COMMODORE
New York City

SEPTEMBER 14, 1947

Prior to the game the teams were paraded around the pitch perimeter by the New York Police Brass Band and two pipers' bands, and the two national anthems – *Amhrán na bhFiann* and *The Star-Spangled Banner* – were played, as well as *Faith of our Fathers* and several Irish tunes.[34] The crowd was reportedly 'a mass of white' shirts and dresses, while many players were handed white long-peaked baseball caps to protect them from the sun. The solar impact was also seen in the partially burnt ground, which was 'hard and brown in spots'. These conditions, coupled with fresh advances in playing equipment – 'twelve new white balls pumped and laced' were on hand – caused the ball to bounce to a remarkable height.[35]

The game itself began at a frenetic pace and Kerry tore into an early lead. Within ten minutes Cavan were eight points down and many observers foresaw 'a complete wipe-out'.[36] *Irish Press* reports of the match pinpointed the key influence of Kerry's Batt Garvey, who created huge problems in the Cavan defence.[37] Gradually though, Cavan began to rein in Kerry and soon enraptured the watching crowd. A tactical switch by Cavan trainer, Hughie O'Reilly,

The Cavan team of 1947

putting P. J. Duke onto Garvey was significant, as was the increasing influence of the Cavan players, Tony Tighe, Mick Higgins, P. J. Duke and free-taker, Peter Donohoe.[38] Goals from Higgins and Stafford left Cavan with a narrow 2-5 to 2-4 lead at half time. In the second half Cavan quickly extended their lead, thanks to Peter Donohoe's marksmanship, which earned him singular acclaim in the American press as the 'Babe Ruth of Gaelic football'.[39] The contrast of playing styles, often a feature of Kerry-Ulster clashes, was equally highlighted: 'Kerry acted as if they never heard of Dr James Naismith, who invented basket-ball. Cavan must have heard all about him, as hand-passing was the deciding factor which brought about a smashing unexpected victory.'[40] When the final whistle was blown by the referee, Martin O'Neill of Wexford, Cavan had claimed their third All-Ireland football title by a score of 2-11 to 2-7. The celebrations for Cavan were wild, and in some instances over-exuberant; hundreds of exiles swarmed around the dressing-rooms, and at least one Cavan player (John Wilson) reputedly returned from the shower to find that all his playing gear had been lifted as souvenirs.[41] American reporters lauded the game as robust but fair, and embellished their accounts in their distinctive colourful style:

> There was more violence than you would find in a game between Army and Notre Dame, yet ... [t]he teams, after knocking the stuffing out of each other, rushed over, not to throw a final punch, but to shake hands ... . There was not one punch tossed during the afternoon and not one temper lost. The first Hibernian to get belted into Dream Street was 'Tom' [sic] Tighe of Cavan. He got the most vicious block since last time Nello Falaschi, the Football Giants, mousetrapped the enemy guard. That fellow Tighe was continually in trouble. After the match the crowd milled about the field, not heading for the exits like sports crowds here. They held re-unions talking about the great match. Outside the field, with the 'elevated' rattling on top and the subway underneath, crowds made rings and danced Irish dances to the music of fiddles and mouth-organs.[42]

Although the turn-out was disappointing, the final provided a massive boost for Gaelic games in New York and indeed, throughout America. The night before the game, the *Gaelic American* had suggested that '[w]hatever the outcome of the game ... the contest will mark a great victory for Irish Americans who are interested in the promotion of the Irish race'.[43] This certainly proved to be the case and those present not only witnessed an enthralling match. but also saw the next generation of New York Gaels showcasing their skills in a series of minor and intermediate level games, played before the main event.[44] It was even speculated that the success of the final might lead to the game being introduced into American schools and universities.[45] Crucially for the future of Gaelic games in the USA, the 1947 final did much to improve the relationship between the GAA in America and the association in Ireland. The manner in which the players and officials were received in New York both before and after the final, and the fact that the match generated a healthy profit of just over £10,200, were significant in this regard.[46]

The 1947 final also encouraged the association's grassroots membership in Ireland to view their counterparts in America with a little more empathy. While some may have remained disgruntled at missing out on their annual September 'pilgrimage' to Croke Park, Michael O'Hehir's vivid radio commentary which was broadcast live on Raidió Éireann and brought the sounds and voices of Irish America into Irish homes,[47] reminded those in the 'old country' of the commitment of their counterparts in the 'New World' to Ireland's sporting and cultural heritage. As Puirséal observed, 'the game had cemented ties of friendship between the GAA at home and the Gaels in New York and renewed the bonds between thousands of Irish-Americans and the land of their fathers'.[48] Tangible evidence of these bonds and ties of friendship were quickly evident at the GAA's Congress the following Easter when the Central Council agreed to set aside an 'international fund' of £2,000 to facilitate closer relations with the New York GAA and institute more regular playing contact. This gesture was matched by their counterparts across the Atlantic and just three years later, New York made an historic step into the parent body's National League competitions,[49] and laid the foundations for what was to become a 'golden era' in the history of the NYGAA.[50]

Beyond the impact of the final on Gaelic games in New York and indeed, throughout the USA, Cavan's success was also lauded in Ireland, particular, of course, in Co. Cavan. Almost all of the county's supporters followed the game on the radio. In Maudabawn, outside Cootehill, for example, Aidan Farrell removed the kitchen window as crowds gathered outside his home on the roadway to listen to the game.[51] Such scenes were replicated nationwide. 'In Dublin groups of people gathered in restaurants and cafes, where radio sets were tuned in … .The most popular men in the city, however, were those motorists with car radios.'[52] The final whistle resounded to sheer ecstasy in Cavan:

> The listeners sent up a crescendo of cheers and dashed into the streets or on to the roadways or laneways congratulating each other in a most enthusiastic manner. Such scenes were never before witnessed in the towns, villages and rural districts, and people who might have had some little differences about local matters smothered them up with hearty handshakes, and hospitality of various kinds was liberally dispensed. Bonfires were lighted and the hillsides of Breffni were ablaze.[53]

The resonance and significance of Cavan's victory and the pride that it generated throughout the county was clearly evident in the days, months and indeed, years following the match. The manner in which the Cavan players were feted on their return to Ireland spoke volumes in this regard. The Cavan-Kerry entourage travelled home by ship and arrived in Dún Laoghaire on 3 October 1947. They were welcomed by the Chairman of Dún Laoghaire Borough Council, H. M. Dockrell, and were guests of the council at breakfast in the Salthill Hotel, Monkstown. From there, they travelled to the Mansion House where they were welcomed by Lord Mayor of Dublin, P. J. Cahill. A further reception followed at Árás an Uachtaráin where both teams and officials met the then President of Ireland, Séan T. O Kelly, Taoiseach Éamonn de Valera, and Cavan man and Minister for Agriculture, Paddy Smith.[54] Following the Áras reception both teams ended a busy day with the official banquet at the Gresham Hotel. In the course of many speeches both teams were praised as worthy ambassadors of Ireland and of Gaelic football. Both team-captains, Dinny Lyne of Kerry and Cavan's John Joe O'Reilly received special presentations.[55] It was only at this point that the Cavan players were presented with the Sam Maguire Cup; it had not made the journey to America, with remarkably 'no remarks' being passed about its absence on final day.[56] The following day, the teams went their separate ways back to their respective counties, all that is except for one player, Cavan captain John

CAVAN'S MARCH OF TRIUMPH

THE CHAMPIONS ARRIVE HOME

MEMORABLE SCENES OF WELCOME

15,000 AT RECEPTION IN FARNHAM GARDENS

An *Anglo-Celt* headline on the occasion of the team's victorious return.

Joe O'Reilly. In many senses O'Reilly's actions encapsulated the ethos of the association and did much to further endear him to Cavan Gaels at that time. Rather than have the honour and personal kudos of leading the team back into Cavan with the Sam Maguire trophy, O'Reilly instead travelled alone to Kildare to play a championship match for his adopted club.[57]

Cavan returned by bus to their native Bréifne in glorious sunshine on Sunday 4 October 1947. Receptions, addresses of welcome and bands greeted them along the route in Navan and Kells. When they arrived at Cavan's borders at Maghera outside Virginia, they were greeted with a banner that proclaimed; 'Bréifne welcomes her Victors'.[58] Fr Michael O'Rourke welcomed the team to Virginia, where the *Anglo-Celt* recorded that they were accompanied by approximately one hundred cars. In a clear indication of the hero-status that the team had acquired, the *Celt* estimated that fifteen thousand people awaited the team in Cavan Town.[59] A huge procession headed through the town led by the Cootehill Brass Band from the home club of the team coach, Hughie O'Reilly. The team were led onto a platform in Farnham Street by vice-captain Joe Stafford from Killinkere before Bishop of Kilmore, Dr Lyons, and local dignitaries welcomed their heroes home. At a reception in the Farnham Hotel that night John Joe O'Reilly returned to join his team-mates. Further functions and welcomes followed as the team toured the county over the following weeks. In one particularly memorable function in Ballyconnell, the team were welcomed by eight survivors of the first affiliated GAA team in Ulster, the Ballyconnell First Ulsters.[60] Most fans finally got a chance to see the highlights of the game when a twelve-minute film of it was shown at cinemas over the next month.[61]

The nature of the welcome that the Cavan team received when they returned from New York and the respect that they were accorded by dignitaries, public figures and the association's rank-and-file in the county revealed much about what their success meant to the people of Cavan. The team went on to experience further success, winning All-Ireland titles in 1948 and 1952 which further cemented their place in Cavan's football folklore. Even when many of those who played in 1947 and subsequent successes retired from the game their status as household names remained and they were much sought-after throughout the county and beyond as team-trainers and for presentations and functions. A further but unwelcome reminder of the significance of the Cavan players to the local popular psyche became evident in 1950 and 1952 with the untimely deaths of two of the team's most prominent members. On 1 May 1950, P. J. Duke, a star of the Polo Grounds and three other All-Ireland finals, died aged just twenty-five. During the funeral, Captain John Joe O'Reilly led his team-mates and cortege on a huge procession through Dublin, where Duke had died, before he was taken to his final resting place in his native Stradone. A lament, later published to commemorate him (as cited by Cardinal Brady earlier in this collection), pointed up his status in Cavan and Ulster GAA circles.[62]

Further tragedy befell the Cavan team just two years later when John Joe O'Reilly died in the Curragh Military Hospital on 21 November 1952, aged thirty-three years old. A three-mile funeral cortege brought his remains along the same route from Dublin that P. J. Duke had travelled and that O'Reilly himself had travelled with many Cavan teams. The cortege paused at St Patrick's College, Bréifne Park and in Cornafean. His coffin was carried by his team-mates to his grave in Killeshandra where the army rendered full military honours. The lament published to commemorate his untimely passing spoke of his significance nationally, within Ulster, in his county and finally in his parish.

> They will grieve for him in Kerry, throughout Mayo, Louth and Cork,
> While his comrades go in mourning through the sidewalks of New York,
> Where the Yankees they did cheer him on that never forgotten day,
> When victory was found with high renown three thousand miles away.
> God rest you John Joe O' Reilly, that's the prayer of Royal Meath,
> But his loss his felt the keenest on his native Ulster heath,
> Through the length and breath of Bréifne they are singing one refrain,
> God rest you John Joe O Reilly you were the pride of Cornafean.[63]

The fact that this lament, published thirty years after the 1947 All-Ireland final, makes reference to O'Reilly's 'comrades' in New York highlights the enduring importance and resonance of the 1947 final in Ireland, but particularly in Cavan. The presence today of a strong New York County Board and the participation of New York teams in All-Ireland competition is due in no small measure to the efforts of Cavan Gaels such as O'Reilly, Duke and their colleagues who have since passed away. There is one remaining member of that epic event at the Polo Grounds over sixty years ago. Mick Higgins, possessor of ten Ulster championship medals and three All-Ireland medals, and captain of the victorious 1952 team, has kept the memory of 1947 alive. Subsequently, he served the GAA as a volunteer coach, official, referee and ambassador. In March 2009, he attended the conference from which this collection of articles emanated. His presence enriched the proceedings and continued to remind those present and those who read this collection of the significance of the 1947 All-Ireland football final.

The Emergence and Development of the GAA in Britain and Europe

David Hassan and Stephen Moore

The significance of Europe for the Irish nation is widely appreciated and understood. Ireland is both a part of Europe and remains partially dependent upon it. Irish men and women have migrated to various destinations throughout the continent, including Britain, in search of employment, greater opportunities and social enlightenment. In many cases they have held dear the cultural practices of their homeland, foremost amongst these being support for and the playing of games belonging to the Gaelic Athletic Association (GAA). For the purposes of this chapter, which examines the development of the GAA, its games and cultural mores throughout the continent, the discussion will demarcate Britain from the remainder of Europe, only because the former location has witnessed the highest concentration of Irish *émigré* and therefore, not surprisingly, represents a fruitful site for the study of cultural and sporting practices associated with the GAA.

While this chapter deals with the GAA in Britain and mainland Europe it would be wrong to conclude that there are a great many similarities between these two settings in terms of migrant experiences. If anything a study of this nature serves to highlight the different ways in which discourses surrounding racial discrimination, colonialism and mass immigration are unpacked within different national settings. It is possible to draw distinctions in terms of the socio-economic status of the migrant groupings, their willingness to assimilate to their new environments and the degree to which they are received by the host community. For instance, it is interesting to note that the treatment afforded Irish immigrants in mainland Europe was considerably more sympathetic than that experienced by their fellow migrants in Britain. Even in terms of the success of the GAA, whilst its breadth and depth on the continent is modest in comparison to Britain, there are also some compelling differences in terms of ethnic spread, the organisation and playing of the games and their support base. It is also appropriate to state that individual experiences remain variable and so one must guard against generalisations, even if on occasions they can prove helpful when highlighting broad trends and patterns of behaviour.

The early part of this chapter examines the formative years of the GAA in Britain. It accepts that, perhaps much more readily that might even be the case in Ireland, the GAA was a central aspect of life for Irish men and women on the island from the late nineteenth century onwards. Inevitably it was couched in a broader and fractious relationship between Britain and Ireland and its activities occasionally fell foul of this animosity. Ultimately, the history of the GAA in Britain is the story of Irish emigration, of solidarity between the migrant population and of a desire to retain an Irish identity amid unfamiliar and occasionally hostile surroundings.

As far back as 1861 there existed an Irish population of 805,717 in Britain, a figure that continued to rise, albeit at a relatively slower rate, throughout the late nineteenth and early twentieth centuries.[1] Irish migration was concentrated on Britain's dense urban centres of Liverpool, Glasgow, Manchester, Birmingham and London, and this often proved to be 'a harsh and disorientating experience' as the Irish encountered social deprivation, poverty and prejudice.[2] Their Catholic faith and the indigenous cultural baggage that they brought with them were anathema to the largely conservative Anglo-Protestant host population and they became social outcasts on the basis of 'class, nationality, race and religion.'[3] To combat this negative cultural stereotyping the Irish tended to congregate together in enclaves where manual work in the shipyards and its associated industries was available. For example, in London and Liverpool, Irish men gained employment as labourers or dock-hands while the Irish women worked as domestic servants or sweated labour in the garment trade. The Railway and canal construction provided Irish settlers with further low-paid manual labour. The Irish were, therefore, employed on the bottom level of the employment sector and could only afford to live in the poorest parts of the expanding urban cities in which they existed. The

The London Gaelic football team from 1909. Sam Maguire after whom the All-Ireland senior football trophy
is named is seated on the extreme right-hand side of the middle row.

Irish in these neighbourhoods resided amid impoverished settings and suffered from inadequate housing,
overcrowding, disease, high levels of crime and poor sanitation. However, rather than attempt to assimilate
many chose to preserve their sense of Irish identity through the Catholic Church, Irish pubs and a range of
cultural and sporting organisations.[4] This enabled the Irish to become increasing assertive and empowered
as their sheer number in areas such as London's East End, Liverpool or Birmingham produced a milieu of
solidarity and security which was centred around such institutions.

Evidence of Gaelic sports in England can be located as far back as 1775 when a large group of Irish
people gathered together and played a 'hurling match on a sports field near to Camden Town'[5] in north
London. Although the diffusion and popularisation of a codified version of the games did not occur in
Britain until the 1890s there is substantial evidence of Gaelic games being organised on an *ad hoc* basis in
parts of Britain in previous decades – even if we regard reports of 'hurling' in south-west England as referring
to the sport of Cornish 'hurling' (throwing, rather than stick-and-ball), which was essentially different from
its Irish namesake.[6] In 1856, the *Morning Chronicle* newspaper in London reported on how 'the ancient
game of hurling was played under the direction of Mr W. S. Treleaven and a committee at ten o'clock.'[7] By
1876 *The Graphic* newspaper revealed how, for St Patrick's Day, 'the Irish residents of London postponed
their rejoicings until Saturday, when they met in force at Muswell Hill, and took part in the sport of
"hurling", and listened to the concert of Irish music, and the popular *Colleen Bawn*.'[8] In fact Liam
MacCarthy, a famous figure in the GAA's history, wrote in 1922 of having 'played hurling on Clapham
Common 50 years ago'.[9]

Thus, even before the formation of the GAA in 1884, Gaelic games performed a vital role for the Irish
diaspora in Britain, albeit in an impromptu and sporadic fashion. The organisation of infrequent games of
hurling or football and other Irish activities was underpinned by a desire to recreate leisure and social pursuits
from home that would contribute to and help migrants psychologically adjust to their new surroundings.
However, despite the significance of these annual festivals and occasional matches all of which were well
attended, the absence of a governing body to regulate fixtures, leagues and venues continued to hamper any
future development of the games in Britain. This was rectified by the turn of the twentieth century when
the GAA made steady inroads amongst the Irish population in Britain.

In 1885, Britain's first GAA club was founded in Wallsend near Newcastle-upon-Tyne, but there was little or no activity elsewhere. A decade later the *Irish Tribune*, pointing to the fondness of Irishmen in Scotland for Glasgow Celtic Football Club, remarked that 'the Irish in England have until now been somewhat behind their fellow countrymen at home and abroad in the cultivation of athletic sports'.[10] In that same year (1895), however, GAA clubs began to emerge in London. Although there were some tensions between Irish Republican Brotherhood (IRB) and Irish National League elements the GAA's Central Council commended the new clubs for 'working on non-political' lines and reiterated that it would not recognise 'any clubs or body run under political auspices'.[11] In 1896, following a showcase event for Gaelic games – held at Stamford Bridge, the home of archetypal English soccer club, Chelsea F.C. – an official GAA board was eventually founded in London. By 1897 ten clubs were affiliated to the board. The Irish concerts and dances held by these clubs, and the hurling tournament prizes ('seventeen Histories of Ireland'), provided evidence of their cultural nationalism.[12] The influx of athletic young Irishmen into the civil service in the city was noted as a key factor.[13] In Scotland, the GAA first emerged in 1897, when 'a large and enthusiastic meeting of your Irishmen of the city' resulted in the formation of Red Hugh O'Neill GAA club, Glasgow.[14] By 1903 the city had five affiliated units and a newly established county board.[15]

The designation of England as a province for GAA purposes in 1900, and the organisation of a GAA provincial council for Britain, confirmed some significant progress. British champion teams were accordingly accommodated in the final stages of competitions in Ireland. This produced the anomaly of London winning the All-Ireland Hurling Championship of 1901; similarly, Glasgow beat Antrim in the 1910 hurling quarter-final in Belfast.[16] This progress was wiped out, however, by the advent of World War One, which brought the GAA in Britain to a standstill for several years.

Politics was an intricate part of the GAA in Ireland and it was inevitable that this would be mirrored in Britain. The involvement of the IRB was to become a central component of the GAA in Britain in the 1900s and 1910s. Two of the most renowned figures in the IRB, Michael Collins and Sam Maguire, were prominent in the GAA in London. Collins was secretary of Geraldines GAA club and became treasurer of London County Board. Maguire excelled as both a London player and as county board chairman. Both men played pivotal roles in the struggle for Irish independence: Collins utilised his position in the post office in London to transfer intelligence back to Ireland; and Maguire later became a chief intelligence officer of the IRA in Britain during the War of Independence.

The Sam Maguire Cup (for the All-Ireland football title) was presented to the GAA in 1928 by a special committee set up to commemorate Maguire. Five years earlier, Liam MacCarthy donated £50 for the purchase of an All-Ireland hurling cup, and it was duly named after him. Hence, ironically, the two most famous trophies in Irish sport have commemorated men whose part in the GAA was centred almost entirely in London.

Many of Britain's earliest clubs were named after nationalist or mythical Irish figures. This was a common trend amongst the GAA fraternity in Ireland; according to Cronin, it acted as a vehicle through which the Irish could construct an identity 'that stresses and publicises their links as sportsmen to the nationalist mission, the embrace of things Irish and the rejection of West Britonism.'[17] Throughout the decades that followed, clubs in Britain were named in honour of leading nationalist icons of modern times such as Robert Emmet, Charles Stewart Parnell, William Rooney, Tomás MacCurtain and Seán Treacy, and others drew names from earlier Irish historical figures and legend, such as Cuchulainn's, Shamrocks, Brian Boru, Granuaile, Rapparees, Clann na nGael and Móindearg. Likewise, camogie clubs in British cities (many of which preceded the establishment of camogie in some Irish counties) adopted female names from Irish history and mythology, such as Emer, Tara, Granuaile, Eithne Cairbre and Róisín Dubh.[18]

For the most part, however, the GAA in Britain was dependent on the association in Ireland, and the umbilical cord was never cut. Officials in Britain always held onto a degree of expectation, or at least hope, that their counterparts in Ireland would have sufficient sympathy for their position to lavish some of their more bountiful resources across the Irish Sea. This was very evident when efforts were made to revive the scene in Britain in the early 1920s. When a new county board was set up in south Wales *c.* 1920, with eight affiliated hurling clubs and three football clubs, it wrote to Ireland for assistance in providing cups for its own competitions. Back then, the debt-ridden and trophy-less Ulster Council was unable to help.[19] Over time, the GAA at central level began to provide more funding, though often not to the extent desired in Britain.

The success of the GAA in Britain remained dependent on the depth of immigration from Ireland. Following the imposition of an immigrant quota system to the United States of America in 1921, Britain became the primary destination for Irish migrants once again. During this period, the growth of the GAA in Britain was often restricted by the reluctance of the native population to give its approval or support to Gaelic games. The GAA was regularly refused local government assistance in its quest for facilities and grounds.[20] However, the association remained resolute in the face of what it perceived to be blatant prejudice and continued to organise club, inter-city and provincial games and tournaments with the support of the growing Irish communities. The formation of the Provincial Council of Britain in 1926 brought a new level of organisation to activities. The Central Council in turn recognised Britain as the fifth (and only non-Irish) 'province' of the GAA, and gave assistance to bolster the emerging profile of Gaelic games there. In 1927 the Cork and Tipperary hurling teams travelled to play in London and Liverpool, and thus began an annual series of leading Irish county teams travelling to the English capital for exhibition games at Whitsuntide. In addition, from the 1920s to the 1990s the All-Ireland finals proper of inter-county junior championships were frequently hosted (and periodically won) by the British champions.

The turn of the 1930s also witnessed an economic depression throughout Britain and this had a profound impact upon the GAA. Having left Ireland in search of work only a short time earlier, many members now found themselves out of a job in Britain. For example, twelve of the Brian Ború hurling team that contested the 1929 London county final were unemployed. It is claimed that these players were training collectively every two days and 'signing on at the London Exchange in Camden Town two days a week', and therefore possibly 'the only club to be state subsidised while training for a championship.'[21] Similarly, the London hurling and football teams that crossed the Irish Sea for the 1932 All-Ireland junior finals included fourteen unemployed players.[22] There is a palpable sense that the GAA served as a solid support network for such men, enabling them to overcome their adverse personal circumstances. The association in Britain soldiered on anyhow. By 1934, the London County Board reported seven football clubs and six hurling clubs in existence, and by 1936 this had increased again to eleven football clubs and seven hurling clubs. This indicates a steady increase from only four functioning units in 1923, as the GAA in the English capital began to gain a solid foothold. During the same period, Manchester reported four football clubs and one hurling club, Liverpool catered for two hurling and two football clubs, Warwickshire had six clubs and Oxfordshire and Yorkshire had a combined total of eight clubs.[23]

There continued to be a nationalist element behind the ongoing growth of the association and it became a tool in the GAA's recruitment process. For example, in his 1936 report Paddy Costello, the secretary of the Provincial Council of Britain, attempted to reach out to the Irish in Britain by employing what was by now familiar rhetoric. He appealed 'to all our exiles in Britain to join the GAA. The colour of our flag is neither red, (nor) black nor blue and we stand by the principles of an Ireland, united, Gaelic and free.'[24] Such statements were aimed at resonating with nationalist-minded Irish immigrants in Britain. By doing so, the GAA hoped that these migrants would reconnect with the main Irish cultural organisation from home whilst living in Britain. In the same report, however, Costello suggested that 'the county committees get in touch with Catholic schools in their areas with a view to organising minor hurling and football teams'.[25] This was an early recognition that if the games were to survive and prosper in Britain and should migration from Ireland decline, that the association needed to open up to a wider community – specifically the second- and third-generation Irish. Such visionary thinking was not widely adopted by the association in Britain until some years later. Incidentally Costello was a strong Labour Party activist,[26] and several other GAA officials got involved in politics in Britain: Liam MacCarthy was a local councillor in London; and Frank Short, a president (1943–45) of the Provincial Council of Britain, became prominent in the Anti-Partition League (and his daughter Clare Short was later elected as an MP in Birmingham for Labour).[27]

The GAA in Britain enjoyed quite a post-war boom. More facilities became available to play Gaelic games, and at last a permanent site was obtained in London: 'Croke Park', Eltham, was blessed and opened

The GAA's hopes of developing international hurling-shinty compromise games were shattered by the decision in 1934 of the Camanachd Association to cease contact, upon advice from government officials in Whitehall and Edinburgh. No official working relationship existed between the bodies from then until the early 1970s. Individual universities continued to play exchange games, however. Edinburgh University and Queen's University Belfast were frequent contestants, such as in the above match in 1947. (*Anna Harvey*)

by the Catholic Archbishop of Westminster, Cardinal Bernard Griffin, in 1948.[28] On the same day the ground hosted the All-Ireland junior hurling final between London and Meath, watched by over three thousand spectators. The expansion of the GAA in Britain was fuelled by increasing immigration from Ireland. By 1951 the British census revealed a population of '627,021 Irish-born' in England and Wales.[29] Emigration to Britain continued to accelerate dramatically during economic downturns in the Irish economy, especially during the 1960s and 1980s. The GAA made strenuous efforts to encourage these first-generation Irish to engage with its games. The annual exhibition games between Irish county teams were held at Mitchum Stadium in south London, before crowds of up to 30,000, until the venue was demolished in 1955.[30] From 1958 to 1975 the exhibition matches were held at Empire Stadium, Wembley, on Whit Saturdays; the series peaked in 1962, when over 40,000 spectators attended.[31] The importance of the exhibition matches to the Irish diaspora was accurately captured by the *Munster Express* in 1960. It stated that they were:

> A mammoth undertaking by the exiles and one reflecting great pride on their attachment and aspirations to the games of the motherland. Because of circumstances beyond their control, thousands upon thousands of our kith and kin have been forced to seek employment across the waves, and now annually, under the patronage of the London County Board, they gather on common ground to pay tribute to a heritage that can never be forgotten.[32]

In fact the successful staging of these matches leads to the conclusion that the significant point about the relationship between Britain and Ireland is not an administrative one but one of the games themselves. The 'Wembley experiment' indicates that it might have been possible to hold a major game, such as an All-Ireland semi-final or final, in Britain, albeit this was a proposal that was never seriously considered. Obvious

Tony Casey, Liam O'Neill and Billy Kiely lead the way for Cuchulainn's Hurling Club in south London, prior to a match at New Eltham in the 1960s.

locations like Parkhead, the home ground of Glasgow Celtic F.C., or even Villa Park in Birmingham, were eminently capable of hosting such games, certainly more easily than was the case for the 1947 Polo Grounds final featuring Kerry and Cavan. The absence of such matches may indicate only a passing commitment on the part of the GAA's central administration to the promotion of Gaelic games abroad. Yet some initiatives by the GAA at central level were thwarted by factors beyond its control. The staging of hurling-shinty internationals between Irish and Scottish teams in the 1930s ended abruptly when Home Office officials in Edinburgh and Whitehall warned the Camanachd Association about the 'anti-British political flavour' of the GAA, and thus the two sports bodies did not resume official contact again until the 1970s[33] – though some universities did arrange hurling-shinty games among themselves.

It was during the 1950s–70s period that the association reached its pinnacle in Britain with new clubs forming on a regular basis. Indeed, by the end of the 1960s the GAA in London alone had nearly eighty fully functional clubs. New county boards were also formed in growing Irish areas which included Derby, Gloucester and Hertfordshire. Of course Britain's gain was also Ireland's loss and many of those who migrated to the near island left behind much-weakened GAA clubs, many of which struggled to sustain a presence during these migrant waves.

Again the Irish *émigré* were engaged in hard manual labour, the building sites of Britain's major urban centres being their chosen workplace. Whilst the rewards were considerable the experience was unforgiving, and some migrants struggled to come to terms with their new locales. According to Tom Denning, who migrated to London from Co. Cavan in 1957, the reception from the English population was often harsh and unwelcoming. He stated that 'the reception wasn't nice. The Irish weren't wanted here. I went to places where you would see signs in windows saying 'no dogs, no blacks, no Irish'. When the 'Troubles' came along in the 1960s we were all treated as terrorists. It wasn't easy to be Irish in Britain.'[34] This social, economic and racial discrimination encouraged the Irish to congregate together and they were sustained by a range of Irish institutions with the Catholic Church and the GAA often to the forefront. The GAA in Scotland occasionally encountered discrimination, partly of a sectarian nature, until relatively recently;

unionist elements in the Scottish media sometimes ridiculed the games as a 'daft' Irish sport, and depicted it as supporting republican paramilitaries.[35]

As emigration patterns continued to fluctuate throughout the late 1960 and 1970s, the GAA in Britain soon became aware that the long-term survival of the association lay with the second- and third-generation Irish diaspora. The establishment of several initiatives at minor level by the Provincial Council of Britain was supplemented by the formation of a minor board in London in the 1970s. This was a significant step towards the promotion of Gaelic games amongst Britain's youth, and a number of clubs and provinces followed this lead throughout the 1980s and 1990s. Meanwhile, in an attempt to raise the profile of the games, London took a fuller participation in major inter-county

Emerald GAA Grounds, South Ruislip, the headquarters of the GAA in London. The flying of the Irish national flag at grounds regardless of their location in the world is a constant reminder of the sense of national identity that the GAA has help to preserve among the Irish diaspora. For players and supporters the association is one of their few direct links with their native or ancestral country.

competitions. London has played annually in the Connacht Senior Football Championship since 1975, the Ulster Senior Hurling Championship since 1998, and the National Leagues since 1993, but with few real successes. There was also a steady increase in the number of Irish students migrating to Britain during this period. This 'temporary diaspora' were attracted to Britain by the increased opportunities open to them in the higher-education sector and by the possibility of well-paid future employment.[36] Although their participation in Gaelic games was initially slow, by 1992 the Provincial Council of Britain had added its support to the establishment of a British colleges competition. This represented a major change in attitudes of the traditional GAA hierarchy in Britain who previously viewed Irish students as something of an administrative nuisance in that they came and left in a short period of time, causing eligibility problems for their own county championships and contributing little else to the established structures. The formation of a formal governing body, the British Universities GAA (BUGAA) finally gave Gaelic games the platform to cater for the rapid growth in participation throughout the 1990s.

With the economic upturn of the 1990s and solid advancements in the Irish peace process, emigration to Britain dwindled and the GAA again struggled to survive in cities such as Manchester, Liverpool and Birmingham. According to an official of the Irish Department of Foreign Affairs, this forced the association in Britain to radically alter its recruitment policy:

> The GAA in Britain has had to look beyond new arrivals from Ireland for its future, as all the regions in Britain are suffering in terms of GAA players. There has been a fall in playing numbers and clubs in Sheffield and Liverpool, for example, but there is recognition now that the GAA must work and build on what is here and not just hope that the economy struggles in Ireland. That is not a sustainable way to keep an organisation going. The aim is to keep the games alive with second and third generation (Irish) and the benefit lies with allowing the second and third generations to stay in touch with their identity and find a way of expressing that identity.[37]

So along its difficult pathway the GAA in major British cities began to realise during the early twenty-first century the need for a sustainable future reliant on the indigenous communities to promote the games and administer the clubs. Indeed the development of an appetite for Gaelic games amongst groups of young British children and in turn their role in the future development of the GAA in England and elsewhere, has been prioritised accordingly. Towards this end, since the turn of the millennium ambitious initiatives to

Down players defending their goal at one of the major Gaelic games in Wembley Stadium.

A Gaelic football match between teams from Dundee University and Napier University, Edinburgh. The growth of Gaelic games in British universities in the last two decades is one of the most outstanding areas of development for the GAA in recent times. Formal inter-varsity competitions only began in Britain in 1989, and today there are approximately forty universities in Great Britain playing annually. Many of the student players in Britain retain affiliation with home clubs in Ireland throughout their university education, and therefore do not integrate into the traditional British GAA club scene, which declined during Ireland's economic boom years. Some graduates, however, have pioneered the introduction of Gaelic games in British schools, even among non-Irish pupils. (*Peter Mossey*)

promote Gaelic games in schools of multi-ethnic pupil enrolment have been remarkably successful, particularly in the English midlands region.

In a similar vein the European County Board (ECB), or at least GAA units located on the near continent, having already arrived at this realisation, could be readily defined by its youthful profile and by its particular appeal for ethnic groups dotted throughout various parts of the continent. In contrast to Britain, however, tracking Irish emigration to mainland Europe is problematical. There is a dearth of research in this field compared to studies into Irish migration to North America or Britain.[38] The most reliable measures are intercensal estimates of net emigration, which provide aggregate data for a five- or ten-year period.[39] At several points over the last two decades the numbers of Irish emigrants moving to mainland Europe have exceeded those settling in North America.[40] In 1988 approximately 2,800 Irish people migrated to mainland Europe, and 7,900 to North America; but in 1992 the numbers emigrating to Europe had risen to 7,500 people, whilst those moving to North America had more than halved to 3,500 individuals.[41] It is not possible to state definitively that Irish people were opting to emigrate to Europe rather than North America, but there was a clear transformation in migrant activity. Whereas the trend towards Irish emigration to Britain and the USA has been in decline over the last fifteen years, the numbers relocating to mainland Europe have remained consistent. These are now more than thirty per cent higher than the figures for Irish emigration to North America, whilst over the same period there has been a remarkable decline in the numbers of Irish emigrants to Britain, from a peak of 48,400 in 1989 to 6,300 in 2000.[42]

Thus one feature of the most recent 'wave' of Irish emigration, from its pinnacle in the mid 1980s, was the greater variety of destinations.[43] Mainland Europe received considerable numbers of young Irish people.

In 1992 almost a quarter of the total annual outflow of Irish men and women made its way to mainland Europe.[44] That said, only a small number of countries, primarily in the north-central part of the continent, have received sizeable numbers of Irish migrants,[45] and the figures have oscillated somewhat in more recent times, confirming the less predictable aspect of Irish migration to the near continent. The peak of the early 1990s was attributable to the Single European Act of 1987 and other treaties providing for the free movement of labour within the E(E)C / European Union;[46] and also to the greater emphasis being placed on European languages in Irish schools and universities from the mid 1980s onwards.[47]

It is also noteworthy that whereas most other European migrant flows have been dominated by single males, the Irish flow was not.[48] Indeed Kennedy (1973) argues that in 'normal' circumstances – that is, without a European war – a higher rate of female emigration from Ireland was the established pattern since the mid nineteenth century. Since the turn of the millennium levels of emigration between the sexes have been broadly even. Where there is inequality is between the emigrant profiles based on age;[49] those who left twentieth-century Ireland were relatively more youthful than their predecessors[50]

To begin with Gaelic games were played informally throughout Europe from the early 1970s. No official league or championship was in operation but players met periodically, especially in large cities throughout the Benelux region, to participate in Gaelic football and hurling.[51] At present GAA clubs are spread throughout the Benelux countries, France, Germany, Scandinavia, Switzerland and southern Europe. Membership is currently running in excess of one thousand people, but this does not account for the great many others who are not officially attached to the association. In 2005 a raft of new clubs were formed, most notably Maastricht, alongside the continued growth of units based in Budapest, Copenhagen and Vienna. Northern European cities with a strong commercial and economic base attract most Irish migrants in search of work, with major international corporations located in the central business districts being their typical employers.[52] This rapid expansion, not least in ladies' Gaelic football and camogie, is the product of excellent work on the part of individual clubs, a partnership between the ECB and the GAA's Leinster Council and a general enthusiasm on the part of the diaspora to promote the association's games and culture during its 125th anniversary year (2009). The ECB receives some financial support from Croke Park, commensurate it appears with an evolving if still modest level of development within the region.

When examining the Gaelic games scene in Europe two main themes emerge. The first is the increasing numbers of young, well-educated and confident Irish men and women to be found in major cities throughout north-central Europe. Their Irish identities are a more modern construct and are unburdened

L'équipe de football Gaelique d'Institut National des Sciences Appliquées (INSA), Rennes, 2007.
These Breton students are among the more diverse groups now being drawn to Gaelic games as a means of expression of their national and Celtic identity. (*Peter Mossey*)

by the often negative image of the Irish *émigré*, which existed as recently as the mid 1980s. Whilst some are very accomplished Gaelic games players most use the GAA scene as an opportunity to meet fellow Irishmen and women and to engage in mutually shared social, cultural and sporting interests. Second, and the other pertinent issue in any study of the GAA in Europe, is the strong local presence within certain clubs; for instance, among those based in Brittany and Barcelona. This is because people from the Breton and Catalan regions are able to relate to and appreciate the value of indigenous games and choose to engage with Gaelic sports on this basis. One example is the very successful GAA club in Rennes, in Brittany in the north-west region of France. This city has a population slightly in excess of 215,000 people, but its GAA team contains not one player born or brought up in Ireland; it is an entirely local affair.

Indeed for the Breton people of France the ancient Irish sport of hurling is particularly popular, with several representative sides composed exclusively of those born in the region. In fact the Breton enthusiasts of Gaelic games have even instigated their own body, *Fédération Française de Football Gaelique*, to help promote and gain national recognition for Gaelic sports within France. Coaching structures have been established, and co-operation with some twenty schools in the Rennes district has resulted in Gaelic games activity in the region continuing to grow in popularity annually. The *Championnat de Bretagne* (Brittany Club Championship) is administered under the auspices of the *Association Française des Sports Gaelique* and features almost exclusively French-born players. The well-established clubs in Brest and Rennes have been supplemented in recent years with sides from other parts of the region, and they act as a timely reminder of the internationalisation of the GAA without its integrity being compromised.

In a fascinating account of Celtic revivalism in Europe, Jarvie (1999) highlights the case of Breton ethnic identity. In doing so he also makes a broader point about submerged nationalisms that has relevancy to this discussion. Referring to the specific role of sport in the celebration of Celtic 'nations' he hails its contribution to 'the conviviality and solidarity, resistance and struggle, and sheer accessibility within and between the configuration and development of Celtic cultures'.[53] He claims the survival and vibrancy of Celtic cultures is 'a triumph of popular memory over the kind of forgetting that suits the powerful',[54] and it is amid this sort of conception that the success of the GAA in Europe, specifically its appeal to the locals, can be understood.

Whilst the Bretons' interest in GAA may appear unique, in fact the same is broadly true of the Zurich Inneoin Hurling and Camogie Club in Switzerland. What is even more remarkable, in light of this, is that the latter is widely regarded as amongst the leading hurling clubs on mainland Europe, despite the almost total absence of any Irish nationals on the team. Whilst this may indicate that the level of competition on show is not particularly high, the tournaments are in fact fiercely contested, albeit not to the same extent as in the North American championships. Zurich has only a nominal Irish involvement and is instead viewed as a 'Swiss' club, served by a mixture of physical-education teachers and active sportsmen who possess the necessary dexterity to play the game. In both cases the fact that it is hurling again, not Gaelic football, which is adopted as the sport of choice, is interesting on two levels. First, for many hurling is viewed as the quintessential Irish sport, and second, compared to Gaelic football, the skills of hurling are difficult to master and have only limited transference from other codified sports.

In dealing with the development of hurling throughout Europe the growth of the sport in the Netherlands, specifically The Hague, owes much to the interest shown in it by a hockey club in Amsterdam called, appropriately enough, 'Hurley Club'. The latter, as part of its centenary celebrations, approached the GAA to arrange two hurling teams from Ireland to provide a demonstration of the game for its members. It followed that Clare and Wexford played an exhibition match, which was attended by the First Secretary at the Irish Embassy in The Hague at the time, Noel Kilkenny. It also served as a meeting-point for several Irish exiles, whose conversations led to the formation of the first ever GAA team from The Hague to play Brussels and Luxembourg in a triangular tournament held in Cambrai, France. These developments constituted the formative years of what is now recognized as the Den Haag Club, so called because it grew out of informal meetings between Irish exiles interested in Gaelic sports in Zulder Park, the home of the renowned soccer club FC Den Haag. The growth of hurling in the Netherlands has been unprecedented in European GAA circles. During the summer of 2006 some ninety secondary school physical-education teachers attended coaching sessions overseen by leading Irish hurling coaches. Since then another club,

Amsterdam GAC, has formed, catering for Irish exiles in the city who share a mutual interest in GAA activities. Previously the Irish Club Netherlands (*De Ierse Vereniging Nederland*) was founded in 1984 to provide a focal point for Irish people living in the Netherlands.

The playing of Gaelic games in Europe is not without its difficulties, however. The distance between clubs has had a profound impact upon the ability to offer regular games, meaning that occasional GAA tournaments rather than regular single-fixture matches are the preferred option for most teams. Whilst there are strong clubs in Paris, Munich and Barcelona, travelling to Luxembourg or The Hague places a considerable strain upon the finances of the competing clubs not to mention the capacity of individual members to commit to what are, after all, amateur pastimes. Typically the numbers actively competing in the games are small, so seven-a-side or eleven-a-side matches are the norm; this is perhaps convenient, as finding larger pitches to facilitate fifteen-a-side matches is problematical. Finally, playing Gaelic games in Europe is unlikely ever to be as attractive for young Irish men and women as doing so in North America. Thus the development and long-term sustainability of the games on the continent appear to owe more to the people of the regions in which they are played than the Irish *émigrés*. The migratory patterns of Irish people to Europe may indeed prove short-term but it seems that the people of the countries and cities in which they reside are more interested than most in sustaining and playing Gaelic games long after their visitors have moved on.

In summary, the cultural critic Terry Eagleton once wrote that while, on the one hand, Ireland signifies 'roots, belonging, tradition', at the same time it also spells 'exile, diffusion, globality [sic], Diaspora.'[55] This chapter has examined the latter through a focus on the place of Gaelic games activity in Britain and the remainder of Europe. In part, what it has demonstrated is that the ethos underpinning the GAA in Ireland – 'roots, belonging, tradition' – resonates with a great many people outside of Ireland too. Hence the apparent fascination the sports of Gaelic football (male and female forms) and hurling hold on the near continent, particularly amongst those communities familiar with the need to preserve an ethnic identity so often threatened by more dominant forms.

When examining the GAA scene in both Britain and Europe it is appropriate to highlight certain commonalities as well as point to issues of disparity between these two locations. First, as mentioned at the beginning of this chapter, there are considerable differences in the types of migrants settling in both regions and the manner in which they were, and in some cases are, received by the indigenous communities. Second, by its very definition the migrant population is transitory and so the vibrancy of the GAA in different settings depends upon the forms of available employment. Nonetheless some Irish men and women have made London, Manchester, Paris and Amsterdam their new homes and have lived there for many years. Thus typically one finds it is a small number of older, indeed elderly, men and women who are the driving forces behind certain clubs. It highlights the final issue, common indeed to both settings, which is the vexed question of sustainability. There are signs that members of indigenous communities, especially in Europe, have an appetite and interest in Gaelic games and with similar moves in Britain it is conceivable that we are witnessing the first concerted approach to ensuring the long-term survival and development of GAA activities outside of Ireland. Whilst it may take a generation of young local enthusiasts to embed the GAA in the lives of local people, there are grounds for optimism surrounding the future development of the sports throughout Europe, including Britain, and with that a very real potential for their sustained and meaningful internationalisation.

Examples of GAA club badges from across Europe.

The GAA in a Global Sporting Context

Alan Bairner

> Once in a blue moon, a team considered "no hopers" reaches a county final. 1996 was one of those years when a breakaway parish called Gurteen got such a head of steam up that the sum of their combined efforts on the field of play was many times greater than that of the individual parts. But that's the beauty of playing for your own and bringing honour on the houses around which you grew up.[1]

This chapter outlines and examines those aspects of the GAA's history and current standing that are particularly relevant for an understanding of the wide range of roles that sport can and does play in the contemporary world. The chapter focuses on three main issues – the relationship between sport and national identity, the role of sport in the community, and the commodification of sport – all of which are reflected in the development of the GAA and are also prominent in the world of sport more generally. This chapter asks what can be learned by the wider sporting community from the experiences of the GAA and what the GAA can learn from the historical development of other sports and their governing bodies.

Writing about and lecturing on the GAA for an Irish and, more specifically, a Northern Irish, audience presents its own challenges. Many students and others are very much part of the Gaelic games movement. They bring with them their own insights and experiences as insiders. Other members of the nationalist community have less direct knowledge of Gaelic games but almost certainly understand something of the GAA's wider role as a vitally important community resource. One does not have to have played Gaelic games to have attended a range of social activities in Gaelic athletic clubs – including, ironically, watching English Premiership and Scottish Premier League soccer on large screens in club bars and lounges. As for the unionist community, knowledge of and attitudes towards the GAA tend to range from indifference through distrust to downright hatred. The general point is though that most of those who attend one's lectures and read one's work have opinions – often based on ignorance (and this applies to those who play Gaelic games as well as to those who demonise the GAA) but strongly held nevertheless. This was my experience whist lecturing for twenty-five years at the University of Ulster at Jordanstown (formerly the Ulster Polytechnic) and also whilst conducting classes from 1996 until 1999 with loyalist and republican prisoners in the Maze prison, where only one loyalist prisoner, the late Billy Wright, founder of the Loyalist Volunteer Force, admitted to having played Gaelic football as a boy. My 'innocent' inquiry as to whether he had retained an interest in Gaelic games was met with a silent but nevertheless tangible rebuke. Having moved, in 2003, to Loughborough University in the English east midlands, my challenge is now very different.

Loughborough is well known throughout the United Kingdom and almost certainly further afield for its sporting connections. Alumni include Sebastian Coe, Paula Radcliffe, Clive Woodward, Monty Panesar, and former Northern Ireland soccer team manager, Lawrie Sanchez. In 2007–8, the men's and women's combined sports teams won the British universities overall championship for the twenty-eighth and thirtieth times respectively. The university is also home to a well-respected School of Sport and Exercise Sciences, and to a highly regarded sport technology research group. All in all, it is a relatively easy place to teach students about sport. However, despite having fifty-five separate sports clubs, including ones for freestyle kickboxing, skydiving and cheerleading; there is no Gaelic football club at Loughborough, unlike many English and Scottish universities. This is scarcely surprising when one realises how few Irish students or students with Irish ancestry attend the university. Most are from the south of England and only a few from the major cities where Irish immigrants have tended to settle. In sum, most of my sociology of sport students know little about Gaelic games and are no doubt initially disinclined to believe that the history of the GAA might have some direct relevance not only to their studies but also to their own sporting experience.

To engage students with no previous knowledge of the GAA and also to stimulate interest amongst an even broader audience, it is important to set some of the main characteristics of the association in a global

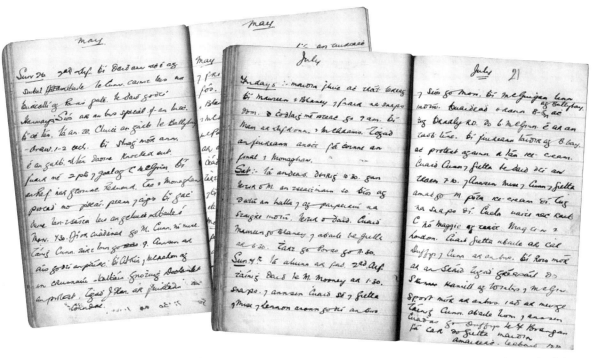

A diary for 1935 written by P. S. Ó Dufaigh (Patsy Duffy, or the 'master'), a player of the Cremartin Shamrocks club (formed a year earlier) in Co. Monaghan. These accounts, written largely *trí Ghaeilge*, give a clear flavour of the level of interest in local games at that time, the forms of transport used, the frequency of violence at club games (a lot of people being 'knocked out') and the propensity to protest against results. They evoke a remarkable resonance with accounts of the poet Patrick Kavanagh playing for Inniskeen in the south of the county a few years earlier. (*Patrick Duffy*)

sporting context. The most appropriate themes in this respect are the relationship between sport and national identity, the commodification of sport, and the role of sport in relation to community.

Most people are aware, albeit to greatly varying degrees, that sport is a useful tool for promoting national interest and establishing national self-esteem. Thus, 'at the most basic level of analysis, it is easy to see the extent to which sport, arguably more than any other form of social activity in the modern world, facilitates flag-waving and the playing of national anthems, both formally at moments such as medal ceremonies and informally through the activities of fans'.[2] That said, it is important to recognise that the precise relationship between sport and nationalism varies dramatically from one political context to another. Thus, far fewer commentators are conscious of the ways in which sport can be harnessed to political struggle in situations where nationhood has either been lost or has never previously be granted constitutional legitimacy. There is no better example than that provided by the GAA to show the extent to which a sporting organisation can contribute to nationalist politics.

Gaelic games, according to Cronin, 'have played a central role in definitions of Irish nationalism'[3] Indeed the GAA's contribution in this regard has been twofold – first, to provide cultural ballast to the efforts of a constitutionally submerged nation to achieve statehood and, second, since partition to help to consolidate and support the Irish Free State (and, subsequently, the Republic of Ireland). This aspect of the GAA's history allows for wider debate concerning the relationship between sport and the construction and reproduction of national identities in other parts of the world. As David Daiches wrote, in a different context, 'there are two ways in which a baffled and frustrated nation can attempt to satisfy its injured pride'.

It can attempt to rediscover its own national traditions, and by reviving and developing them find a satisfaction that will compensate for its political impotence; or, accepting the dominance of the culture of the country which has achieved political ascendancy over it, it can endeavour to beat that country at its own game and achieve distinction by any standard the dominant culture may evolve.[4]

221

In challenging the emerging hegemony of British games, the GAA clearly eschewed the latter course of action. But it went further than the former by its insistence that political independence rather than compensation was one of its key objectives. To that end, not only were most of its activities to be distinctively Irish, its approach to sport would also differ from the British model.

Traditional games and sports have seldom been commodified to the same extent as their global counterparts. This was certainly true of Gaelic games until relatively recently. Yet most of us are conscious of the fact that, in capitalist societies, particularly those in which consumerism has largely replaced production as the dominant mode of profit making, sport sells. It sells itself. It sells its key celebrities. It sells its merchandise. According to Crawford, 'in line with wider changes within late-capitalist societies, the nature of sport (being a significant and constituent part of most contemporary societies) has likewise witnessed considerable change and development in recent years'[5] However, as Horne points out, 'the relationship of sport to commodification and commercialisation has been a constituent feature of debates about modern professional sport since its inception at the end of the 19th and the beginning of the 20th century'.[6]

For most of its history, the GAA has managed to successfully resist the commercialisation of its sporting practices. Only Irish-made products were used. Commercial sponsorship was minimal. Above all, players were amateurs, not for the same reason that amateurism was much vaunted in English sport as evidence – if any was needed – that some people did not have to earn a living from playing sport, but in order to ensure democratic access to Gaelic games. In a world in which sport and money seem so closely interwoven, even at the grassroots level, this aspect of the GAA's development never ceases to amaze the uninitiated.

What is also surprising is the extent to which the GAA remains an essentially community-based organisation. English students and Japanese academics alike are surprised to learn that it is theoretically possible for the best Gaelic footballer in Ireland to be playing for one of the weakest club sides and for a county with no real expectations of winning a major trophy – the 'no-hopers', if you like. Only when the relationship between the player, his community and parish, and his Gaelic club is explained does this make any sense. Also unfamiliar to a non-Irish audience is the extent to which Gaelic clubs are more than places where sports are played. Birthday parties are held in them, concerts, engagement parties and so on. Indeed in Belfast, and other towns in the north of Ireland during the 'Troubles', Gaelic clubs were widely regarded (erroneously, in some cases, as tragic events were to prove)[7] in nationalist communities as safer and more easily accessed leisure spaces than downtown bars and clubs.

The relationship between sport and community is, of course, by no means confined to the GAA. In England, for example, many professional football clubs were formed by churches, eager to strengthen the bond between religion and the people who lived in a particular town or city district. As Brown, Crabbe and Mellor note, 'many of today's most successful clubs and particularly the longest established clubs have their origins in "community organisations" such as churches, social clubs or work's teams'[8] Furthermore, until relatively recently, most clubs continued to draw the overwhelming bulk of their support from the local area. Today, just as the concept of community has itself evolved, so too has the direct spatial relationship between football clubs and their immediate locality.[9] So-called internet communities have their sporting counterparts in the worldwide support base for clubs such as Manchester United and Liverpool. As a result, according to Brown et al, 'our supporter communities can never become "real communities" in a traditional sense because "traditional" community bonds are no longer possible (if they ever were)'[10] Nevertheless, not only these global enterprises but also numerous smaller clubs do work 'in the community' as self-conscious outsiders rather than as the organic products of the communities involved. The GAA, on the other hand, has never acted self-consciously in relation to local communities. Gaelic clubs have been and remain integral parts of their respective communities and, as such, have provided an example that clubs in other sports have seldom, if ever, been able to emulate. Perhaps this is the feature of the GAA's history that students outside Ireland can learn from most as they contemplate careers in the sports industries and especially in sport development. They should be warned, however, that successful as it has been, the GAA now faces challenges relating to each of the main aspects of its life that have been identified here as globally relevant.

Cumann Lúit-Cleas Gaedeal

coisde connvae muineacáin

Cataoipleac:
Séamur Ó Catáil.

coll an bille,
Dún Dealgan,
co. muineacáin

Rúnaióe:
León Ó Bpoin.
Telepón—Coll an bille 1.

14/6/ 19 51.

A Chara,

You have been selected to play for Monaghan in Ulster S.F. Championship versus Derry on 24th inst. There is no need to stress the importance of this game which is on Derrys home ground.

For the past few years Monaghan have been defeated in the first round of the Ulster Senior Championship. This year we have to win the first round and in order to do this each and every selected player must pull his weight. I request you for the honour of your county to be a fit as possible for this test, please do any training you can within the next week and should you require anything please communicate with me immediately.

You will be notified about travelling arrangements early next week.

Good luck and best wishes.

Do chara,

Runaidhe.

Unlike many other sports in which a season-long league is regarded as the main competition, the GAA mentality has always focused on winning 'the championship' in knock-out format. Failure in a GAA championship was usually equated with failure for the season, regardless of success in subsidiary competitions. This letter indicates the determination of the Monaghan County Board to improve the county's fortunes in the Ulster Senior Football Championship of 1951. Note the instructions for training before the game. Players were reminded of their obligation to do their utmost for the sake of their county.
(*Rose O'Rourke and family*)

A postcard sent to Armagh minor goalkeeper Gerry Murphy informing him that he had been selected to play in the 1951 All-Ireland final against Kerry at Croke Park. The idea of a regular team 'panel' was quite nebulous back then; one was a county player as long as one received a letter of notification for each match. Only the county jersey was supplied and even this would be reused after the match.
(*Gerry Murphy*)

Cumann Lúit-Cleas Gaedeal

coisde connvae árd maca

81, NORTH STREET,
LURGAN.

a Cara,   16 - 9 - 1951

You have been selected to play for Armagh Co. Minor Team

versus   Kerry   at   Croke Park

on   next Sunday

Bring boots, togs and stockings.

If unable to travel please notify me by return.

p. Ó muireadaig, Rúnaióe.

Local heroes. Monaghan players being carried from the field following their victory over Kildare in the 1956 All-Ireland Junior Football Championship 'home' final at Carrickmacross. The attachment of inter-county players to their place and county of origin has underpinned the popularity of Gaelic games, while also doing much to secure their amateur and voluntary status. *(Rose O'Rourke and family)*

The GAA's promotion of wider cultural activities is quite unique among organisations catering for sport worldwide. The growth of GAA *Scór* competitions since 1969 has helped the association to continue its commitment to traditional Irish music and culture.

According to Tom Humphries, 'ties between Irish nationalism and the playing of Gaelic games have never been broken. Nor will they be'[11] This presupposes, however, that there exists a single Irish nationalist perspective, something that is wholly at odds with the historical evidence.[12] Furthermore, it can also be taken to imply that nationalism itself is safe from the challenge posed by the homogenising tendencies of globalisation.[13] Even if one does not subscribe to the more extreme versions of the globalisation thesis, one cannot ignore the major developments that constantly redefine the ways in which nations and national identities are narrated.[14] Migration alone renders meaningless attempts to link the nation to a single ethnic group. Thus, Miller, Lawrence, McKay and Rowe argue that the global exchange of sporting bodies 'has made it increasingly difficult for the nation-state to be represented by conventional corporeal symbols'.[15] Meanwhile the global reach of diaspora populations brings into question any idea that the Irish nation is territorially bounded. As Darby and Hassan observe, since Mary Robinson's presidency, 'there has been a growing acceptance of the status of the diaspora as "authentically" Irish'.[16] In time, moreover, the so-called 'new Irish' will simply become 'the Irish', an even more ethnically diverse people than in the past. The GAA has already reached out to this new constituency but how effective will its overtures be compared with those made by the once vilified 'foreign' games?

Having for many years adopted an essential defensive stance towards other sports as evidenced by the ban on foreign games, the GAA's growing confidence that Gaelic games were and remain secure has resulted in a more inclusive approach to Irish sporting nationalism. This is embodied in the athletic performances of those who have chosen to play not only football and hurling but also 'foreign' games such as soccer and rugby union, thereby expressing pride in the uniqueness of Irish culture and also a desire to take on the world. It is an interesting balance and one that was impossible to achieve in the old days when players and even supporters were forced to choose between Irish games and English ones. The challenge for the GAA today is that its own defences have been dropped and English games are now no longer English but global with an appeal that, at least in the case of soccer, extends to every corner of the inhabited world. It is also highly marketable and its leading players can expect to earn vast sums of money. This brings us to another challenge confronting the GAA in the twenty-first century.

Whilst outsiders are fascinated by the strength of the relationship between players and their local clubs, they are arguably even more surprised when they learn that even leading players are amateurs. The GAA has, of course, been transformed in recent years in relation to the commodification of its games. Replica shirts and the development of Croke Park are perhaps the most visible signs of that. Yet, amateurism still rules despite increasingly regular demands from some players that the hours that are devoted to preparing for and competing in the major competitions deserves to be recognised not by the reimbursement of related expenses and favours done, but by upfront, officially sanctioned payment. To most outsiders, the case for professionalism is open and shut. Elite sport requires elite performers and elite performers must be paid. Indeed, it is interesting to note how the use of the words 'amateur' and 'professional' has evolved over time. In the past, as D. J. Taylor notes, '"amateur" was defined as someone who did what he did for the sheer love of doing it; the modern notion of "cack-handed novice" lay far across the horizon'.[17] The word 'professional', on the other hand, scarcely existed as a noun. People were employed in the professions but 'a *professional* meant someone who did something (usually, but not exclusively sporting) for money'.[18] Thus, as Taylor underlines, 'both words came weighed down with a solid freight of insinuation'. But, he asks, a century later, 'who ... would care to be described as an "amateur"'?

> If there is one state to which the average twenty-first century worker aspires it is the glossy, cast-iron prestige of the "professional", with its imputations of expertise, competence and status.[19]

Is it any wonder then that many Gaelic footballers aspire to the status of 'professional'? However, those who follow other sports that have gone down the road towards professionalism (and rugby union's experience is probably the best example, given that it happened relatively recently) will be only too aware that such a change comes at a price. Discussing Richmond Football Club in the 1997, a year after rugby union officially renounced its amateur status, Ian Malin wrote, 'they have a business rather than a rugby mentality and the idea of a sporting empire does sound vainglorious in the eyes of rugby people, but the club realises that it has to produce and not just buy talent'.[20] Founded in 1861 and having embraced the professional era more than most in the English game, Richmond signed a number of players on lucrative contracts, and at the end of season 1996–97 gained promotion to the English Premiership. After temporarily overcoming financial problems in the following years, the club finally went into administration in 2000 and for season 2000–01 were relegated eight leagues to the Hertfordshire / Middlesex 1st Division. The club's first team currently plays in the National Third Division (South).[21] It is a salutary tale of how professionalism can damage, if not an entire sport, certainly some of its traditional protagonists. In the same vein, it is worth noting that the Scottish borders, so long the heartland of Scottish rugby union, has been unable to sustain a professional club, arguably with significantly damaging repercussions for the overall strength of the national game.[22]

As long ago as 1997, D. J. Carey, the famed Kilkenny hurler, remarked, 'the GAA will sooner or later have to grasp the nettle of professionalism'.[23] Indeed, no less a Gaelic games luminary than Micheál Ó Muircheartaigh has written, 'there are times when I think it is almost inevitable that the GAA will embrace professionalism, and that the association must be prepared to grapple with the problems that would ensue from such a course'.[24] To that end, he suggested that 'the GAA could do worse than engage in serious discussions with the Irish Rugby Football Union on the merits and drawbacks of professionalism in that sport'.[25] Ó Muircheartaigh was only too aware himself, however, of the specific problems that professionalism would pose for the GAA. 'If a move to professionalism were dependent on commercial sponsorship', he argued, 'that would quickly lead to a championship for no more than a dozen teams, with others falling by the wayside'.[26] In addition, and arguably at least as importantly, 'the onset of professionalism could erode real community involvement'. 'Loyalty', according to Ó Muircheartaigh, 'would be the first casualty; in the new era small clubs could no longer expect to hold on to their star players'.[27] With this would go not only one of the most unusual aspects of Gaelic games but arguably also the association's main *raison d'être* in the modern era.

Some may feel that, in a supposedly post-nationalist age, the GAA's contribution to cultural nationalism is now far less important than in the past. This might, of course, be disputed in the six north-eastern counties of Ireland where analysis might suggest that there remains unfinished nationalist business regardless of the current involvement in the governance of Northern Ireland by nationalist and republican politicians. It could also be argued that the GAA has managed to deal with the challenge posed so far by the commercialisation of sport in a sensible and, indeed, highly profitable manner and that the organisation will cope with the issue of professionalism just as adroitly. But as other sports have found in the past, professionalism can have massive and often unforeseen consequences. For the GAA, these could include a genuine threat to the strong bond between player, club and community which has until now been the bedrock of the Gaelic games movement.

If professionalism is introduced it will be difficult indeed to prevent the emergence of a transfer system, whether informal or officially sanctioned. Simon Mason, an Irish rugby international who was later to play his part in Ulster's European Cup triumph in 1999, left Orrell, the Lancashire club which had nursed his talents, for Richmond in 1996.[28] The move was prompted by a lucrative contract, itself a reflection of his

Action from an inter-county match of women's Gaelic football. The growth of women's football is one of the most striking aspects of the last two decades of Gaelic games. The sport was formally organised in 1974, but it was not until the early 1990s that it began to achieve widespread popularity. Since then it has diffused rapidly and has led to the creation of hundreds of clubs in Ireland and other countries. The proportion of the Irish female population who are playing members of Gaelic football clubs is one of the highest per capita rates for any sport in any country in the world. (*Irish News*)

new club's ambition. Unless professionalism could be very carefully handled, it is difficult to see what would prevent the emergence of ambitious county and club sides in Gaelic football, the Richmond equivalents, and the movement of players from their local parishes and counties to the big spenders.

In such circumstances, who are the local heroes, the role models whom the young will wish to emulate not least because they went to the same school or are to be seen each Sunday morning at Mass? Needless to say, Gaelic games will continue to have their star performers. But how quickly will they become remote from the fans?

Furthermore, the impact of such developments will not only be seen on the field of play. Scottish rugby club members consistently bemoan the fact that there is little or no socialisation with the players. The club is still a place for these supporters to meet and drink but much of its meaning as a distinctive social space has been lost. Without that sense of common purpose and belonging which in the past united players and supporters, the club becomes just another place to drink and arguably a place that has less and less appeal for the young who are looking for far more in the way of décor than black-and-white photographs of the teams of yore.

Such concerns do not of course spring wholly from developments within sport. They are also fundamentally linked to broader changes in Irish society and beyond. For example, it would be remiss to ignore the extent to which the GAA has traditionally been embedded in rural Irish society. Indeed, in the words of Marcus de Búrca, the GAA 'helped to regenerate Irish rural life and gave rural Ireland a separate, defiant, self-reliant and democratic culture with a strong nationalist base'.[29] The legacy remains. A sense of place, and more particularly of small towns and rural communities, is common to the majority of evocations of Gaelic games in Ireland even today. For example, as King points out, 'predominantly a rural game, hurling has not transplanted to the cities'.[30] But in Ireland, as in almost every other part of the world, we are now confronted with what Lefebvre described as 'the urban phenomenon'.

> Today, the urban phenomenon astonishes us by its scale; its complexity surpasses the tools of our understanding and the instruments of practical activity. It serves as a constant reminder of *complexification*, according to which social phenomena acquire increasingly greater complexity.[31]

Part of that complexification is an increasing diversity of belief systems, partly resulting from migration but also from easier access to the world's religions and various new-age philosophies. This is not to imply that Ireland has ceased to be a Christian country. Indeed, as Inglis notes, 'being Catholic or Protestant has been fundamental to what Irish people have done and said over the past two hundred years'.[32] Thus, 'being religious – that is, identifying with and belonging to a church, accepting its beliefs and engaging in its practices – has been, and still remains, a major feature of modern social life'.[33] But secularisation is also a fact of Irish life and, as Inglis observes, 'the decline in the importance of religious capital in the Republic (of Ireland) can be linked to the demise of Ireland's status as a chiefly rural society dominated by farming and agriculture'.[34] The end result is that two traditional pillars of the Gaelic games movement are considerably less sturdy than they once were with inevitable implications for the GAA's relationship with its communities. So what of the future?

It is a pleasure to teach the uninitiated about the fascinating, and at times, bewildering history of the GAA. It allows great scope for

Handball is the only Gaelic game in which regular world championships are held, and the Irish participants are far from guaranteed success. Here we see Paul Brady of Cavan who in 2009 became the first man to win three consecutive world handball titles. (*Damien Eagers / Sportsfile*)

examining various aspects of the social significance of sport in general – its relationship with nations and nationalism, its response to increased commercialism and commodification, its importance for community life and social well-being. It is particularly useful, of course, that the GAA can so often be invoked for the purposes of providing some contrast with other sports and their historic trajectory.

Of course, it would be easy to assume that the GAA will inevitably go the same way as other sporting organisations, with ties between sport and nation and between sport and community being gradually weakened if not wholly severed in the face of economic pressures to change. It would be dangerous, however, to jump to premature conclusions. After all, the GAA has survived major challenges in the past not least in the aftermath of the Irish Civil War, when 'a shattered people needed some reason and some extraordinary heroes to reunite them in a common purpose';[35] and during and immediately after the republican hunger strikes of 1981, when the leadership performed 'a perilous balancing act meeting the demands for action and protest from the members on the ground, while at the same time working to prevent the Association as a whole from getting sucked into the trench warfare of the political crisis'.[36] Yet, these were moments in time when social agency had a greater degree of purchase and the difficulties facing the GAA could be negotiated internally. The question remains whether the organisation is now confronted by inexorable and perhaps insurmountable challenges from outside – the demise of the nation as the most significant form of human association, the economic demands of late capitalism and the fundamental transformation of what is meant by community in an age of urbanisation, secularism and time-space compression. The end result may be 'a kind of tsunami that overwhelms local imperatives and traditions'.[37] If the GAA can survive with its most cherished values intact, it will be a remarkable achievement, one which my English students and I will follow with great interest.

The then Fr Tomás Ó Fiaich presents a trophy at the annual internal 'house' competition at St Patrick's College, Maynooth, while he was a lecturer there. (*CÓFLA collection*)

*Section 4: The Cardinal Ó Fiaich
Library and Archive and the GAA*

Cardinal Tomás Ó Fiaich and the GAA: an appreciation
Roddy Hegarty

The Search for John McKay:
The Ulsterman at the first meeting of the GAA
Kieran McConville and Dónal McAnallen

Cardinal Tomás Ó Fiaich and the GAA: an appreciation

Roddy Hegarty

For many of those who knew the late Cardinal Tomas Ó Fiaich, and for many others who never met him, his memory will forever be closely associated with Crossmaglen, Armagh and the GAA. He was regularly to be seen in the crowd at GAA events, whether in Crossmaglen, Armagh, Clones or Croke Park. Indeed it has been claimed that he rarely missed a GAA function to which he was invited in his home terrain.[1] Close friends have described how sport was almost like a second religion to 'Father Tom', as he was affectionately known. If so, then his particular denomination was the GAA. With his untimely passing in 1990 it was generally agreed that the GAA had lost one of its most steadfast supporters and greatest advocates. This short chapter will attempt to explore that relationship and to examine why that association remains so powerful two decades after his death.

Tomás Ó Fiaich was born in the townland of Anamar, in the parish of Cullyhanna (Lower Creggan), in south Armagh on 3 November 1923, and received his early education in Cregganduff – where his father was the schoolmaster – and at St Patrick's College in Armagh City. In the absence of formal club competitions for minors at that time, is most likely that he first played organised Gaelic football in the then black-and-white jersey of St Patrick's College in the 1930s, on the playing fields that are overlooked today by his late residence as Cardinal, the library subsequently built in his memory, and St Patrick's Cathedral. The extent of his sporting involvement at the school remains largely undocumented, however.

'Sometime in the early 1930s I was brought to see Armagh play a Dublin selection in Jackson's field up the Monug Road outside Crossmaglen', he recounted on the occasion of the GAA's centenary in 1984. 'It was my first experience of an Armagh County team in action and the beginning of a love-affair which has blossomed over half a century.'[2] His first trip to Croke Park came in 1937, when he watched Cavan play against Kerry. So dedicated an Armagh supporter did Tomás soon become that at the age of seventeen he cycled from Cullyhanna to Coalisland and back to watch Armagh take on Tyrone in the first round of the Ulster championship in 1941. The round trip was about eighty miles and Armagh were well beaten, scoring just one point in the game.[3] His enthusiasm for football and for Armagh was undiminished, however.

For several reasons, Tomás got to play in senior club football for only a short period in the 1940s, with St Patrick's club in his native Cullyhanna and then with Crossmaglen. Cullyhanna, he wrote later, 'was the first local selection which gave me a chance to play the game that has remained a great love of mine to this day'.[4] Cullyhanna footballers were not pampered then. He described how 'the hedge furthest from the road was our "changing rooms" and a bike was excellent transport to our "away" games in Cross, Newtown or Oram'.[5] Due to wartime restrictions in the main, the Cullyhanna club folded in 1943 and there was no club operating in the parish. Thus, by default, he came to play for neighbouring Crossmaglen Rangers. He recognised his own limitations as a footballer, but he was selected to play for the Rangers in the 1943 Armagh Senior Football Championship final. 'We lost that day but it's certainly the nearest thing I ever came to winning a senior championship medal. It was more or less a one-off thing'.[6]

1943 was also the year in which Tomás received his B.A. degree with first-class honours, from St Patrick's College, Maynooth. His bout of serious illness, with pleurisy and pneumonia, in 1944,[7] combined with his continued studies for the priesthood, probably put an end to his football career. There is no evidence that he played after that, either at home or at St Peter's College, Wexford, where he was ordained in 1948. From there he went in turn to University College Dublin, where he obtained a Masters degree in 1950, and to the Irish College in Louvain, Belgium, where he stayed until he was appointed to his first parish in June 1952.

Fr Tom's first appointment was to Clonfeacle, where the parish priest was the redoubtable Fr Tom Soraghan, who did much work to propagate camogie in Armagh and Louth. Unsurprisingly, the young energetic curate soon became involved with the local GAA. He organised the first GAA week in An Port

Mór in 1953[8] and he chauffeured the local camogie team to various venues across the province for games.[9] In appreciation of his support, the camogie team presented him with an electric razor upon his departure from the parish that September.[10]

He left to take up the position of lecturer in Modern History at Maynooth, but he maintained a keen interest Gaelic games. In 1954 he accepted an invitation to accompany the Armagh camogie team on a playing tour of Cork and Tipperary.[11] Passionate as he was about all aspects of Irish culture, Tomás was happy to travel around the country and impart his encyclopaedic knowledge and endless enthusiasm. When Alf Ó Muirí, Pádraig Mac Floinn and others in Comhairle Uladh established its own *cúrsa Gaeilge* at Ros Goill in 1959, with the aim of training GAA administrators in the use of the Irish language, they requested *An tAthair* Tomás to deliver a lecture at the inaugural course, and in spite of his heavy workload, he did so.[12]

Even though he was living outside of Ulster, the relationship between Tomás and Crossmaglen Rangers strengthened in the 1950s, principally because his family had moved to the parish of Upper Creggan. From then on he was a fervent supporter and unofficial mentor of Crossmaglen teams. Gene Larkin, a Rangers player of that time, believed that 'many a closely contested game was swung our way by his pre-match visit to

The young Tomás with his father and older brother, Patrick, in the 1920s. (*Irish News*)

the dressing-room and his words of encouragement'.[13] Ó Fiaich was even a committee member for a spell, and became an honorary president of the club in the 1950s. The opening of Blessed Oliver Plunkett Park as the Crossmaglen club pitch in 1959 gave him particular pleasure. For the souvenir booklet, he wrote a short but insightful preface, praising the enterprise. He stated that it was not just an act of veneration but one that would ensure that Oliver Plunkett's name would be kept on the lips of the people of south Armagh for years to come.[14] At the official opening ceremony, he delivered an oration on the life and times of Plunkett. His association with Crossmaglen Rangers remained strong over the next thirty years. During his time in Maynooth he remained a member of the Rangers club and always made an effort to attend its annual general meeting and, in later years, its annual dinner. In 1971 he even hosted the club's team and officials for a *céilí mhór* at the college.

In his support of his county team Tomas Ó Fiaich exemplified the loyal GAA follower. As early as 1953 he was known to give words of support and advice to Armagh minor and senior football teams before big games,[15] and in that year, as if partly inspired by him, the county reached the All-Ireland senior final. Despite the pain of that narrow defeat, and many more to come, from then on his 'team' of supporters (friends and family) travelled with him in his car, a little Morris Minor – known as 'Tin Lizzie' – to as many Armagh games as possible in the Ulster Senior Football Championship.[16] Year after year he stood on 'the Hill' at Clones. When other counties won out of Ulster, he was happy to transfer his allegiance to them in the All-Ireland semi-final. In her tribute to him after he died, his sister-in-law, Deirdre Fee, provided further details of his match-going rituals:

> Football was the love of Tom's life and his diary would always have the main matches marked in as early in the year as possible. He tried, even as Cardinal, to keep these days free. For over twenty years, Tom and his team of football-fans attended practically every match in the Ulster Football Championship series and many All-Ireland Football Semi-Finals. … This was serious work and everybody concerned took it that way. If Armagh was playing, they would discuss the likely outcome of the game and the form of every member of the football team. They would set off from

In later years Cardinal Ó Fiaich watched the big games at Croke Park with the dignitaries. Here he is pictured in conversation with the *Ardstiúrthóir* (Director-General) of the GAA, Liam Mulvihill; the President of Ireland, Dr Patrick Hillery; and the GAA President, Dr Mick Loftus. (*Irish News*)

Crossmaglen, with the appropriate flag flying, after Mass on the Sunday morning. They would arrive back on Sunday night to see the highlights on TV. This would always end with a post-mortem on the match. Win, lose or draw, a great day was had by all.[17]

His own 'team' would inevitably disband each September, however, upon his return to Maynooth to teach. During his time at Maynooth, the college changed dramatically. From the late 1960s lay students were admitted as well as clerical. As a consequence the college began to participate in external sporting competitions at last. In previous decades undergraduates at Maynooth had played Gaelic games in internal 'house' competitions – in which Ó Fiaich took a keen interest – but from 1969 the college entered its own teams in the new inter-varsity leagues. Swiftly after gaining admission to the inter-varsity championships (in 1972), Maynooth went on to win the Fitzgibbon Cup (in 1973 and 1974) and to host the Sigerson Cup finals of 1974. There was further success after Fr Ó Fiaich was appointed president in 1974: Maynooth won the Sigerson Cup in 1976, and hosted the Fitzgibbon Cup finals in 1977.

Fr Ó Fiaich's elevation to the archbishopric of Armagh in 1977, becoming Primate of All Ireland, brought him back to his native county. This allowed him to become a familiar sight at the Athletic Grounds when Armagh played at home. Two years later he was made cardinal, and on the day of his consecration in Rome, in August 1977, he demonstrated once more the importance of the GAA in his life. Returning from St Peter's Basilica to the Irish College, he addressed those who had travelled from home for the occasion. 'I will start with the good news. The Rangers won this afternoon and are through to the second round of the championship.'[18] No matter what the setting, a reference to the GAA in a sermon, lecture or article was never out of bounds. When Pope John Paul II came to Ireland in 1979, Cardinal Ó Fiaich wrote, 'I could easily imagine him playing centre-half in an All-Ireland in Croke Park.'[19] And in 1989, when addressing a congregation at St Killian's Cathedral, Wurzburg, he remarked: 'We in Ireland do not venerate St Killian as you in Germany do, but we have a football team [Whitecross] in my archdiocese, named in his honour … [but] there is not a Beckenbauer among them!'[20]

As an historian, Fr Ó Fiaich broke new ground in scholarship on the history of Gaelic games and the GAA, helping to pave the way for a greater body of writing on these subjects. He used his academic skill and knowledge to bring a fresh approach to these subjects. This was most evident in his article about the names of Armagh clubs, for the *Armagh GAA Year Book* of 1968. These club names, he pointed out, covered the whole course of Irish history, and could be used to introduce GAA members to historical events and figures.[21] He divided the club names into six types: those derived from pre-Christian legends; those adopting a saint's name; those from the medieval period; those taken from the period after the Flight of the Earls; those inspired by the United Irishmen and nineteenth-century nationalists; and those named after twentieth-century patriots. He advised that a 'well-chosen name should be an aid to discipline and devotion among club members and supporters'. Cognisant of the GAA's role within the nationalist community of the north, he added: 'Let the club name be not only one of historical significance in the district but one which will inspire patriotism, loyalty, courage and fair play, a reminder to be generous in victory, unbending in defeat and always to play the game'. This article remains possibly the most impressive piece published to date on the naming of GAA clubs at local level.

At the Merriman Summer School in 1969, he delivered a comprehensive lecture on 'Michael Cusack and the tradition of rural sports in Ireland'. His parochial wit, as well as his great knowledge, was to the fore, as ever. Addressing an audience from Michael Cusack's home county, he described himself as 'a northerner from the non-hurling backwoods of Armagh', but claimed that Cú Chulainn, an Ulsterman, had performed 'the first great "solo-run" in Irish history'.[22] In 1974, in an article for the Sigerson Cup programme, he examined the history of football in Ireland. He noted that a century earlier, in the mid 1870s – a decade before the GAA – the Maynooth College authorities had confiscated a football, lest it cause inter-diocesan rivalries.[23] During the 1970s he was a member of the advisory committee that oversaw the compilation of the first official history of the GAA, by Marcus de Búrca. Ó Fiaich's accession to high office in the Catholic Church precluded him from undertaking further significant study into the history of the GAA and its games, but the short pieces that he did write were invariably valuable contributions. He had prodigious powers of recall of games as far back as the 1930s, and could reel off lists of former players from various clubs and counties in an instant.[24] He commended the flurry of research and publication of GAA history books that took place

Ó Fiaich was a regular at Clones on Ulster final day. He is pictured here sharing a joke with
Paddy McFlynn and Vincent McAviney of Ballybay. *(Martin McAviney)*

Con Murphy (Uachtarán CLG 1976–79), Tomás Ó Fiaich, Con and Celia Short.
This was probably Ó Fiaich's first visit to Croke Park after he was made cardinal.

in the 1980s in connection with the centenary, and he indeed he penned the foreword for several club and county histories. He lamented the fact that greater effort had not been made to chronicle the association's early history when many of the pioneer members were still alive.[25]

One foreword in particular was less pleasant to write, however. From 1971 onwards, British army incursions onto (and part occupation of) Oliver Plunkett Park, were a major grievance for the GAA in Crossmaglen and at all levels. To highlight the issue, the club published a booklet in 1977, and naturally it turned to its honorary president, Tomás Ó Fiaich, for support. He wrote of how 'saddened' he was by his recent visit to the ground, and detailed the many ways in which soldiers had reduced it to a 'shambles'. 'But the affair of St. Oliver Plunkett Park is also symbolic of something deeper,' he concluded. 'Crossmaglen's loyalty to Gaelic games, despite all the obstacles put in its way, is but one facet of its allegiance to the Irish nation.'[26] His overtly nationalist identity probably endeared him all the more to GAA members in Ulster at that time, but not to some 'loyalists'. It was on his way to open the Whitecross pitch in 1978 that his car was pursued by two others at high speed for twenty minutes, in what appeared to be an attempted ambush.[27]

The Cardinal was the archetypal Gael to the core. He recognised instinctively the role of the GAA in local communities. As a priest he knew well the association's parallel parish structures and the parochial rivalries that underpinned them. He cherished the sense of identity associated with the GAA, and its cultural impact. 'No organisation,' he wrote in 1984, 'has made a greater contribution to Irish life and to the national revival. Its members are spritely, noisy, unselfish, idealistic. I hope they never become materialistic, soft or self-centred.'[28] He would hardly have approved of the increasing drive towards commercialism and professionalism in some circles of late but, a quarter of a century on, he would surely recognise that unselfish idealism within clubs and county boards, particularly in his native Ulster.

Cardinal Ó Fiaich also realised the critical role played by the association in providing focus for the cultural expressions of the minority community in the north of Ireland, from partition to the present day. 'In the North,' he wrote in 1984, 'the GAA is now our strongest link with the rest of Ireland. For GAA men, Ulster has still nine counties and Ireland thirty-two. Clones, Breifne Park and Ballybofey are as well known to us as Armagh, Newry and Dungannon. There are still bridges to be built with people with the tradition of

The Cardinal demonstrating his skill with both foot and hand on the occasion of his visit to St Malachy's College Belfast in 1984. (*Irish News*)

Cardinal Ó Fiaich blessing the pitch at the official opening of
Tír na nÓg Park in Portadown, 3 August 1986. (*CÓFLA*)

McCracken and Munroe, Mitchel and Casement.'[29] This challenge to the association to develop its cross-community relations, has been taken up enthusiastically by the Ulster Council in the much-changed political and social environment of recent years. Cardinal Ó Fiaich's only apparent disappointment with the GAA related to the standard of play in latter years, especially the constant stoppages due to free-kicks. He thought the inter-county games of the 1980s inferior to those of the 1950s and 1960s, although he also wondered if it was 'just a case of getting on in years and losing one's youthful enthusiasm'.[30]

Becoming Archbishop of Armagh and Cardinal brought with it a place in the seated enclosures of major grounds, although many who knew Tomás suspected that he would rather be among his friends and ordinary fans than with the special guests. The days of a bishop throwing in the ball at the start of a game were no more, but his ceremonial introduction to the rival captains and the referee on the field became part of Ulster final day pageantry right through the 1980s.[31]

To the end Tomás kept his close link with Crossmaglen Rangers. He provided counsel to the club in the ongoing dispute over Oliver Plunkett Park, and raised its case with prominent political authorities.[32] He also did a great deal to restore some of the diminished prestige of the venue, by instigating the Ó Fiaich Cup tournament. He presented the club with this trophy in memory of his late brother, Dr Patrick, in 1983. The competition was contested by the four county football teams within the Archdiocese of Armagh, and it reintroduced inter-county football to the town for the first time since 1969. He received Rangers' ultimate honour, the club 'hall of fame' award, in 1987.[33] Being highly esteemed among ordinary GAA members, he was sought out often to speak at the opening of facilities or at a function. His command of any subject, whether history, religion, language or the GAA, coupled with his famous common touch, made him both accessible and acceptable to a wide audience. On one Sunday he had to attend important engagements in Dublin and one in Belfast, both involving government ministers or representatives, but he made sure to get the first one finished early so that he could be present at the opening of a handball alley in Cregganduff.[34] He extended his patronage to clubs outside his own area too. It has also been suggested that his decision to transfer Fr Sean Hegarty, the former Armagh football manager, to the parish of Errigal Kerrogue in Co. Tyrone in 1989 was done in the interest of solving the Ballygawley-Glencull football split. By the following year Fr Hegarty and others had succeeded, and a new, united club, Errigal Ciaran, was born.

Cardinal Ó Fiaich making a presentation to a young Oisin McConville, who would later play a major role in securing Armagh's first senior All-Ireland football title in 2002. (*Irish News*)

His sudden death in Toulouse while on pilgrimage to Lourdes in May 1990 stunned Ireland. It left a void in the GAA in Armagh, in Ulster and nationally. At his funeral Mass in St Patrick's Cathedral in Armagh, the former Crossmaglen and Armagh player Joe Kernan carried the black-and-amber Rangers jersey in the offertory procession.[35] He would later, of course, manage the county to All-Ireland success. The Ó Fiaich Cup that he presented continued to be contested into the early 1990s, but his name has not been perpetuated within GAA nomenclature in the manner of some of his predecessors (like Cardinals MacRory and D'Alton). For some time after his death the idea of erecting a stand dedicated to Ó Fiaich's memory was talked about in Armagh but it has never come to pass. As the Athletic Grounds has undergone extensive refurbishment in recent years, with the installation of new floodlighting in 2009, perhaps the idea of an 'Ó Fiaich Stand' might be revisited.

He would surely have cherished Crossmaglen's four All-Ireland club titles from 1997, and the sight of Armagh lifting the Sam Maguire Cup in 2002. Surely too he would have enjoyed the victories of Ulster neighbours Down, Derry and Tyrone, even when they beat the men of Armagh along the way. Indeed one can imagine him celebrating the fact that all four counties in the Archdiocese of Armagh have now won All-Ireland senior titles, as opposed to just one twenty years ago.

Tomás Ó Fiaich was an inspired patriot whose loyalty to the parish, club, county, province and country – *Pobal, Club, Contae, Cúige agus Tír* – was undeniable. His wit, intellect and passion for the GAA and Gaelic games left an indelible mark on all who met him and many who did not. He was courageous and fair, generous but unbending and always there for the games. He was part of the GAA and the GAA was part of him.

Ar dheis Dé go raibh a anam uasal.

The Search for John McKay:
The Ulsterman at the first meeting of the GAA

Kieran McConville and Dónal McAnallen

The historic meeting to found 'the Gaelic Athletic Association for the preservation and cultivation of our national pastimes', on Saturday 1 November 1884 in Hayes's Hotel, Thurles, brought into being an organisation that went on to have an immense influence on the social, cultural, political and sporting life of the Irish people. Many events were organised to commemorate the GAA's 125th anniversary, not least in the Cardinal Ó Fiaich Library. The library also does much work in the increasingly popular field of genealogy, and we were able to combine our knowledge and resources relating to GAA history and genealogy in a 125th anniversary research project to trace the story of John McKay, a pioneering but largely forgotten member of the GAA.

Much of the story of how Michael Cusack and Maurice Davin set about founding the GAA is well documented, and their motives of reviving Irish sports, and prising Irish athletics from the increasing dominance of a perceivably pro-British, upper-class elite who sought to exclude working-class participants, are well known. It has often been recounted too that seven men attended that fateful first meeting in Thurles, namely: Davin, Cusack, John Wyse Power, John McKay, Joseph P. Ryan, Thomas St George McCarthy and J. K. Bracken. As well as Davin and Cusack, the attendance of most of the other five can be explained quite easily: Ryan (a Carrick-on-Suir native, working in Callan), Bracken and McCarthy (both Templemore) were all Co. Tipperary men, convenient to the place of meeting; and Wyse Power (Naas) and McKay (*Cork Examiner*) were both journalists, who provided reports of the meeting for newspapers. In addition, most if not all knew Cusack or Davin or both, and some were members of the Irish Republican Brotherhood (IRB), who may have wanted to infiltrate the new body. Some accounts claimed that several other men also attended. Cusack's original account, for one, added 'etc, etc' after the seven names;[1] he may have been disappointed at the actual turnout on the day and added the etceteras to suggest that more people had attended.[2] Yet it is only the seven named above whose attendance is beyond question.

While Cusack and Davin are well known and memorialised by having sections of Croke Park named in their honour, the other five are less famous. A few played little or no part in the subsequent history of the association after attending that historic meeting. Nonetheless all of the seven deserve to be remembered for their part in the creation of the premier sporting organisation in Ireland to date. The GAA centenary celebrations in 1984 brought back into focus the story of the founding fathers and prompted initiatives to honour them, even if only by placing memorials on their graves. Up to 2009, however, one of these graves could not be found – that of John McKay. Indeed, unlike the other six men,[3] nobody seemed to know for certain where he came from and what became of him. It was simply stated in various sources that he was either 'a Belfast man'[4] or 'a Cork man',[5] an obviously wide disparity; and yet in neither of these places did the GAA fraternity appear to know anything about him. The information provided by the first historian of the GAA, Thomas F. O'Sullivan (who almost certainly knew McKay and published the only known photograph of him) in 1916 – that he 'afterwards became connected with journalism in Belfast, Dublin and is at present residing in London.'[6] – was scarcely added to since in any published work. This is all the more remarkable given that McKay was one of the first honorary secretaries of the association, along with Cusack and Wyse Power, from 1884 to 1886, and indeed Marcus de Búrca asserts that his 'role in the successful launching of the GAA may well have been secondary only to that of Cusack and Davin.'[7] Hence the present authors embarked on a search to find John McKay and unravel the many mysteries surrounding him.

So how would we track down this elusive man? The first port of call, as usual with deceased figures, was newspaper obituaries. Alas for anyone who sought McKay previously, when and where he died had long been a mystery. In 2009, however, the sports historian Eoghan Corry provided us with information relating to the time of McKay's death, which he found on newly provided online digital newspaper archives, and this enabled us to pursue his obituaries. When he got the exact date of his death, we were able to order his death certificate. From these sources we discovered some basic details of his life. He died in December 1923 in London, but his age was not specified. The obituaries indicated that he was 'an Ulster man by birth',[8] but nothing more explicit. These obituary details also provided information which enabled us to go further in our search for McKay's grave and other aspects of his family background, but first this chapter will outline what we discovered about the chronology of his career in journalism and the GAA.

McKay's journalistic career began in the early to mid 1870s with the *Belfast Morning News*, a nationalist daily newspaper. One source claims that he was 'also associated with' the *Northern Whig*, a liberal unionist daily organ in Belfast, around that time.[9] In April 1878 he left to join the reporting staff of the *Cork Examiner*, a nationalist daily paper. He reported primarily on political events, principally those of the Parnellite Irish National League (INL). Over the next decade he reported on at least two hundred meetings of the INL and Land League, held in every county in Munster. He was not merely an impartial observer; he was a member of the INL and, he later professed, a 'strong

The only known image of John McKay.

sympathiser' of the Land League.[10] His work for the *Examiner*, an obituary relates, brought him into 'close contact with the Nationalist leaders of the period' and with many 'stirring events' connected with the Land League and the INL.[11] He also attended some of these events and meetings in a non-reporting capacity. A similar source imparts that McKay 'played a prominent part in Southern public life during his long connection with the *Cork Examiner*'; and that '[a]s a leading reporter he was on friendly terms with all the leaders of the Irish people since the days of Parnell'. He was still working for this paper in 1884, when he was listed as representing Cork Athletic Club at the first meeting of the GAA. The *Examiner* carried the longest report of the meeting, which gave special attention to his contribution:

> He (Mr McKay) had at first intended to oppose any business being done at that meeting on account of the small attendance; but he had changed his mind when he found what the nature of the propositions were. Who, he asked, could offer any opposition to their association being placed under the patronage of Archbishop Croke, Mr Parnell, and Mr Davitt, three names that went straight to the heart of every true son of the Green Isle (applause) – and as to their selection of Mr Maurice Davin as president, then was no meeting of athletes and friends of athletics that would not rejoice to have the opportunity of ratifying such a selection (hear, hear!!). … the club he represented looked with favour on any such movement as the present provided it was properly carried out; but he thought that the formation of the Gaelic Association should only form one step researching the goal they were all anxious to arrive at – namely, the formation of a general athletic association for Ireland – composed of representatives from all the leading clubs – to regulate the management of all meetings, to frame rules of their own for the government of such meetings, and put an end once and for ever to their being bound by the rules of the English A. A. Association (hear, hear!!)[12]

It seems clear enough that McKay was present primarily as a representative of the Cork Athletic Club but presumably he also made use of his presence in his professional capacity as a journalist to report on the meeting. It is also obvious from what he says that the poor attendance made him initially doubt the viability of the new movement. His contribution and endorsement of the project and his promise of support from his club may have been of some significance in the decision to hold the second meeting of the GAA in

GAELIC ASSOCIATION FOR NATIONAL PASTIMES.

A MEETING of athletes and friends of athletics was held on Saturday, at three o'clock, in Miss Hayes' Commercial Hotel, Thurles, for the purpose of forming an association for the preservation and cultivation of our national pastimes.

Mr. Michael Cusack, of Dublin, and Mr. Maurice Davin, Carrick-on-Suir, had the meeting convened by the following circular :—" You are earnestly requested to attend a meeting, which will be held at Thurles on the 1st of November, to take steps for the formation of a Gaelic Association for the preservation and cultivation of our national pastimes, and for providing rational amusements for the Irish people during their leisure hours. The movement, which it is proposed to inaugurate, has been approved of by Mr Michael Davitt, Mr Justin M'Carthy, M P, Mr W O'Brien, M P, Mr T Harrington, M P, and other eminent men, who are interested in the social elevation of our race." The meeting was but poorly attended, and several important athletic clubs in the south did not send a representative, but perhaps this was owing to the fact that the notice given was very short. Another meeting will be held in the course of a month or so, and it is to be hoped that all who take an interest in the revival of ancient Irish pastimes, carried out under strict and proper rules, will lend a hand in the good work which Mr Cusack and Mr Davin have originated. Amongst those present at the preliminary meeting on Saturday were—Mr Cusack, Mr Davin, Mr Bracken, Mr O'Ryan (Thurles), Mr Wise Power (Naas and Kildare Club), Mr Ryan, sol., Callan ; Mr John M'Kay (Cork Athletic Club), &c.

Mr. Davin was called to the chair, and Mr. Cusack read the circular convening the meeting.

The Chairman then said that many of the good old Irish games had been allowed to die out in the country, which he and many others would like to see revived.

Mr Cusack then detailed the steps he had taken to get real Irish athletic events put in the programme of athletic meetings throughout the country, and how when he suggested to the promoters of the Caledonian Association games (which came off in Dublin on last Easter Monday) to introduce the high jump, the long jump, throwing the hammer, slinging the 56lbs, and putting or throwing the 16lbs, that they at once consented to do so. The Caledonian Association expended £300 on their meeting, and it resulted in their having a balance of £200 on their hands at the close. He (Mr Cusack) thought they should be able to have the Gaelic Association meeting in 1885, but Mr Michael Davitt thought it would be too soon—that it should be put off until 1886—because it would require £1,000 to carry out such a meeting, and a general election was at present impending. Mr Davitt guaranteed that £500 of the £1,000 would be got from the Irish in America. Mr Wm O'Brien also promised his support, but cautioned him (Mr Cusack) against the movement being political in any sense.

Mr Cusack went on to say that he did not send circulars to the members of Parliament, so that, accordingly, he had no replies from them to read. Two clergymen—Father Keran, of Carron, County Clare, and Father Cantwell, of Thurles—wrote expressing their approval of the movement, and Mr Morrison Little, the Secretary of the Caledonian Association, also wrote in terms of warm approval. Mr C Crowley, of Bandon ; Mr George Liston, solicitor, Bruff ; and Mr John Hargrave, Six-mile-bridge, County Clare, promised every assistance to the movement.

On the motion of Mr Cusack, seconded by Mr Power, Archbishop Croke, Mr Parnell, and Mr Davitt were appointed patrons of the new association ; and on the motion of the same gentlemen, the title of the new association was fixed as " The Gaelic Association for the Preservation and Cultivation of National Pastimes."

Mr Cusack then proposed that Mr Maurice Davin—an athlete who had distinguished himself so much both in Ireland and England—should be the president of the association.

Mr M'Kay (Cork) seconded the motion, and in doing so bore testimony to the appropriate selection of a president for the association. The name of Davin was one respected by all Irish athletes, and of that distinguished family in the arena of athletics, it was but meet that the Gaelic Association of Ireland should select the senior representative of it as their head. He (Mr M'Kay) had at first intended to oppose any business being done at that meeting on account of the small attendance ; but he had changed his mind when he found what the nature of the propositions were. Who, he asked, could offer any opposition to their association being placed under the patronage of Archbishop Croke, Mr Parnell, and Mr Davitt—three names that went straight to the heart of every true son of the Green Isle (applause)—and as to their selection of Mr Maurice Davin as president, there was no meeting of athletes and friends of athletics that would not rejoice to have the opportunity of ratifying such a selection (hear, hear). While he was now speaking, he wished to avail of the occasion to say that the club he represented looked with favour on any such movement as the present provided it was properly carried out ; but he thought that the formation of the Gaelic Association should only form one step in reaching the goal they were all anxious to arrive at—namely, the formation of a general athletic association for Ireland—composed of representatives from all the leading clubs—to regulate the management of all meetings, to frame rules of their own for the government of such meetings, and put an end once and for ever to their being bound by the rules of the English A. A. Association (hear, hear).

Mr M. Davin was then unanimously elected president of the association, while

Mr Cusack, Mr Power, and Mr M'Kay were appointed hon secretaries of the association.

The meeting soon after terminated. Due notice will be given of the next meeting to be held in connection with the matter.

The *Cork Examiner* report of the inaugural report of the GAA, almost certainly written by John McKay.

Cork City in December 1884. McKay almost certainly made good use of his position as a reporter to make sure that the fledgling organisation got plenty of positive publicity in the *Cork Examiner*.[13] As a prominent member of the Cork Athletic Club he was also in a position to help persuade that organisation and similar ones to throw their allegiance behind this new movement in Irish sport. An important decision was taken at the Cork meeting to elect the organising committee of the INL automatically *en bloc* onto the Central Council of the GAA.[14] As Ó Riain points out, 'the decision amounted to an alignment of the new association with the National League and gave rise to the charge that the GAA was founded on political lines'.[15] As a member of the INL John McKay may have had an input into this decision, which was in keeping with Cusack's policy of identifying the newly founded association with the major nationalist leaders and organisations existing at that time in Ireland.

At any rate, from the start track-and-field athletics seem to have been McKay's primary interest in the GAA, and in the two years of his secretaryship athletics was the dominant sporting facet of the association, more so than hurling or football. The GAA's success in the athletics sphere, despite many obstacles in these early years, owed in no small part to McKay's work. Established sporting bodies such as the Amateur Athletic Association were strongly opposed to a new organisation which sought to usurp its position as the controlling body for Irish athletics. To counter the GAA, a new and unionist-dominated organisation, the Irish Amateur Athletic Association, was founded in February 1885 at a meeting in Dublin. Cusack and McKay attended, and naturally opposed this new institution. McKay denied that the GAA was a politically inspired body and assured the meeting that it had room for all Irish athletes. Nonetheless the IAAA pressed on with efforts to destroy its GAA rival. The gauntlet had been thrown down. McKay was particularly prominent during 1885 in travelling around the country winning recruits for the GAA, and officiating as a timekeeper at athletics meetings.[16] By 1886 it was obvious that the GAA was by far the most popular of the new sporting authorities and the IAAA now asked for a merger of the two organisations. This application was made to McKay, because he was seen to be more approachable than his abrasive colleague, Cusack. McKay, however, soon made it plain that the GAA was interested only in absorption and not amalgamation.[17] In subsequent months, nonetheless, McKay showed a willingness to improve relations with the IAAA, and in April 1886 he proposed the motion (which was carried) to abolish the rule that allowed money-prizes at GAA sports[18] – which had been a bugbear for the IAAA for some time.

While he must take the primary credit for the GAA's sudden growth, Cusack was by nature combative and volatile with a knack of making enemies on all sides. His erratic and offensive behaviour prompted a majority of the executive of the GAA to come to the conclusion that their founding father had in effect become a hindrance to the prosperity and future growth of the organisation. When Cusack fell out with GAA patron Archbishop Croke in 1886 it was a step too far even for such as McKay who had worked alongside him since the first meeting. In a letter to his own paper, the *Cork Examiner*, McKay stated:

> I desire to take the earliest opportunity of both repudiating and condemning the action of Mr Cusack in writing an offensive letter to the patriotic Archbishop of Cashel, one of the patrons of our Association. Mr Cusack had no authority from the Association to write such a letter and I feel certain every member of our Executive will condemn his action as heartedly as I do.[19]

At a special meeting held on 4 July in Hayes's Hotel, McKay was among the strong critics of Cusack, accusing him of being dictatorial in manner and offensive to any officer who was unfortunate enough to disagree with him on any point. By a vote of 47 to 13 Cusack was forced to resign his position as secretary of the GAA. His part in the overthrow of Cusack was almost John McKay's last act as secretary of the GAA. He resigned from the position in August of that year. We do not know why he did so. Perhaps he abhorred the growing influence of the IRB in the association. A problem with this theory is the fact that his replacement as secretary, Timothy O'Riordan, like McKay, held apparently constitutional Parnellite views; so much so indeed, that McKay could almost have handpicked him. O'Riordan (1856–99) was a native of Tralee who worked for the *Cork Daily Herald* in the 1880s and covered Parnell party meetings. He served as a secretary of the GAA up to 1889, when he joined the *Freeman's Journal*, and then moved to London as its parliamentary correspondent.[20] The Fenian influence did not become truly pronounced until 1887. Alternatively, McKay's resignation may have been linked to the relatively demoted position of athletics in the GAA; after he left office in 1886 athletics went from being the association's primary sporting activity to its third most important.

Above all though, we must consider McKay's domestic circumstances. It is likely that as a married man with a young family he was unable to meet the workload involved in the running of a rapidly expanding countrywide organisation. His frequent changes of address while living in Cork suggest that he was not financially comfortable. In 1883 he and his family lived at 7 Upper Panorama Terrace, in the Sunday's Well area;[21] in 1886, at 4 Elizabeth Place;[22] in 1887, at 9 Frankfield Terrace;[23] and in 1889, at 10 Ardilea Terrace.[24] He was still working for the *Cork Examiner* in 1889, and probably into the early 1890s. He remained a Parnellite in sympathy, if not a party activist. In May 1889 he appeared before the Parnell Commission at the Royal Courts of Justice, London, to give evidence as a reporter who had attended INL meetings. The main thrust of his evidence was that the INL never condoned violence, and that its events were always marked by good behaviour, except when 'interfered with unduly' by the police.[25] He was reportedly also a vice-chairman of the Cork National Society for a time.[26]

After this it becomes difficult to keep tabs on McKay's movements. It has been claimed that he continued to serve as an athletics official for thirty years after 1886,[27] but evidence of any consistent participation in the GAA on his part thereafter is scarce. What we know about the rest of his life concerns mainly his journalistic career and family. Around 1896 McKay moved back to Belfast to work for the daily *Irish News*, which had superseded his former paper, the *Belfast Morning News*, at the start of the decade. For how long he worked there we do not know, but at some stage he left the *Irish News* to work for the *Freeman's Journal* in Dublin.[28] Owing to this uncertainty we have been unable to locate him on any 1901 census to date. The next clue we have of his whereabouts is the fact that 'J. MacKay' was appointed as a Cork delegate to the GAA's annual congress at Thurles in November 1902,[29] and duly attended.[30] De Búrca suggests that McKay had recently returned after spending some years living in London, but corroborative evidence is hard to come by. He is not to be found in England in the 1901 census. Even if, as one suspects, he lived in Ireland throughout these years, a coherent chronology is still not apparent. The appearance of 'J. MacKay' – presumably the man we are pursuing – as a Cork delegate in 1902 suggests that he was back living by the Lee, though two obituaries indicate that he did not return to Cork from the *Freeman's Journal* until 1910. Anyhow, his nomination as a Cork GAA delegate in 1902 was apparently a one-off gesture (possibly instigated by the chairman),[31] for he seems not to have attended any meetings of the county board beforehand or afterwards.[32] There is no evidence that he was involved in GAA activity while he lived in Belfast or Dublin either. However, as his interest seems to have been primarily in athletics perhaps he was still involved in this area and has not been noticed as most historians of the GAA have concentrated on the stories of Gaelic football and hurling.

By 1911 at least McKay was back living in Cork, and working as chief reporter for the *Cork Free Press*,[33] an evening radical newspaper published by William O'Brien MP and the All-For-Ireland League from 1910. The AFIL was a Munster-based moderate nationalist party, which sought conciliation with the Irish Protestant and unionist community. The *Free Press* was a direct commercial and political rival to the Redmondite *Cork Examiner*, and the two organs expressed their enmity in print.[34] By 1916, however, McKay had moved to London. One may surmise that his departure was caused directly or indirectly by the decline of the *Free Press*; in summer 1915 it was operating at a significant loss and reduced to weekly issues, and in 1916 it was suppressed by the British censor[35] and it collapsed soon after that. The last *Free Press* editor, Frank Gallagher, was formerly its London correspondent.[36] It is possible that McKay crossed the sea to act as London correspondent for the *Free Press*, due to its changed situation. One source states that 'on his retirement' he moved to London,[37] but otherwise it is indicated that he continued to engage in work in journalism,[38] and as a 'press agent' up to the time of his death,[39] which could simply be a term for a freelance reporter who was not attached to any particular publication.

About the rest of the life of McKay we know little else, up to the point of his death in London on 2 December 1923. The first Irish newspaper to report his death was the *Irish Independent*, in a small item

ÉIRE IRELAND

Acht um Clárú Pósadh, 1863. Foirm A.   Registration of Marriages Act, 1863. Form A.

1883	Pósadh a Sollúnaíodh i Marriage Solemnized at the Catholic	Chapel of St Peter + Paul	i gCeantar in the Registrar's District of	Cork No 5				

Uimh. 78

Pósadh
Marriage
Uimh.
No. 164

A Cláraíodh
Registered
by me, this
26th

lá de
day of
June
19 1883

P.J.Hayes

Cláraitheoir
Registrar.

i gCeantar Chláraitheora Maoirseachta   Cork   i gContae   Cork
in the Superintendent Registrar's District of   in the County of

Uimh. No. 1	Dáta an Phósadh When Married 2	Ainm agus Sloinne Name and Surname 3	Aois Age 4	Staid Condition 5	Gairm Bheatha Rank or Profession 6	Ionad Cónaithe Residence at the time of Marriage 7	Ainm agus Sloinne an Athar Father's Name and Surname 8	Gairm Bheatha an Athar Rank or Profession of Father 9
164	19th April 1883	John McKay Ellen Browne	full full	Single spinster	Reporter —	7 Upper Panorama terrace Munster Hotel	Joseph McKay Deceased James Browne	labourer turner

Arna bPósadh i   Chapel   of St Peter + Paul   do réir Uird agus Gnáthaí na hEaglaise Caitilicighe.
Married in the Catholic   according to the Rites and Ceremonies of the Catholic Church by me.

James Canon Hegarty

Sollúnaíodh an Pósadh
so Eadrainn-ne
This Marriage was
Solemnized between us,
{ John McKay
Ellen Browne }

In ár bhFianaise
in the Presence of us
{ John D Collins
Katie Lombard

Is fíor cóip í seo de thaifid atá i gClár-leabhair na bPósadh i nOifig an Ard-Chláraitheora i mBaile Átha Cliath.
Certified to be a true copy taken from the Certified Copies of Entries of Marriages in Oifig an Ard-Chláraitheora, Dublin.

Tugtha fé Shéala Oifige an Ard-Chláraitheora
Given under the Seal of Oifig an Ard-Chláraitheora   an }
this }   twenty second   lá so de }
day of }   September   2009

Ath-Scríofa D.D   Scrúdaithe B.Q.
Copied   Examined

Is cion trom é an teastas seo a athrú nó é a úsáid taréis a athraithe.

TO ALTER THIS DOCUMENT OR TO UTTER IT SO ALTERED IS A SERIOUS OFFENCE

Marriage certificate of John McKay and Ellen Browne.

CENSUS OF IRELAND, 1911.

Two Examples of the mode of filling up this Table are given on the other side.

FORM A.

RETURN of the MEMBERS of this FAMILY and their VISITORS, BOARDERS, SERVANTS, &c., who slept or abode in this House on the night of SUNDAY, the 2nd of APRIL, 1911.

No. on Form B.____

No.	NAME AND SURNAME		RELATION to Head of Family.	RELIGIOUS PROFESSION.	EDUCATION.	AGE (last Birthday) and SEX.		RANK, PROFESSION, OR OCCUPATION.	PARTICULARS AS TO MARRIAGE.				WHERE BORN.	IRISH LANGUAGE.	If Deaf and Dumb; Dumb only; Blind; Imbecile or Idiot; or Lunatic.
	Christian Name.	Surname.				Age of Males	Age of Females		Whether "Married," "Widower," "Widow," or "Single."	Completed years the present Marriage has lasted.	Total Children born alive.	Children still living.			
1	John	McKay	Head of Family	Roman Catholic	Read & write	56		Journalist	Married				Co Down		
2	Ellen	McKay	Wife	Roman Catholic	Read & write		55		Married	28	6	3	Co. Cork		
3	Joan	McKay	Daughter	Roman Catholic	Read & write		23		Single				Cork City		
4															
5															
6															
7															
8															
9															
10															
11															
12															
13															
14															
15															

I hereby certify, as required by the Act 10 Edw. VII., and 1 Geo. V., cap. 11, that the foregoing Return is correct, according to the best of my knowledge and belief.

D McCarthy
Signature of Enumerator.

I believe the foregoing to be a true Return.

John McKay
Signature of Head of Family.

The household return form of John McKay and family at 80 Western Road, Cork, in the 1911 census.

on 6 December. The *Irish News* was the first to print an obituary, on 8 December. Two days later, the *Freeman's Journal*, *Irish Times* and *Irish Independent* published obituaries, the last being the most substantial and based on information from 'a colleague' – presumably a fellow reporter who knew him well and provided reasonably accurate details. The only Co. Down local newspaper that published an obituary was the *Newry Reporter*, which replicated the details contained in other papers.[40] Strangely enough, the *Cork Examiner*, with which he worked for many years, made no mention of his death;[41] perhaps he left that job on bad terms, or his joining the rival *Cork Free Press* was not forgiven.

Despite his exile in later years McKay was obviously still remembered by some of his Irish journalistic colleagues. A number of points stand out from their articles. First, McKay was identified as a journalist first and foremost – as 'for many years one of the best known members of the Irish Press'.[42] He was described as 'a genial and kindly Irishman popular amongst a host of friends including all the members of the profession to which his life was devoted,'[43] 'versatile and hard-working', and 'helpful towards the younger journalists with whom he came in contact'.[44] All of the articles were vague about his place of origin, describing him simply as 'a native of Ulster',[45] or 'an Ulster man by birth'.[46] Remarkably, none of the newspapers seemed to know the place or county of origin of such a supposedly well-known journalist. Equally conspicuous is the lack of significance placed on his GAA career: some obituaries did not mention it at all, others merely briefly in passing, and only the *Freeman's Journal* emphasised his role as a founder.[47] The association, moreover, appeared to have forgotten him: no reference was made to his death at any GAA meeting or event around the time of his death – not even at the Cork County Board or the Central Council.[48]

Many GAA histories describe McKay as a Belfast man but there is no evidence from the obituaries to support this contention; perhaps his two early stints working for Belfast newspapers inspired this assumption. His origins soon became further confused. In 1934, only eleven years after his death, the *Irish Press GAA Golden Jubilee Supplement*, published in 1934, referred to McKay as 'a Corkman'.[49]

After his appearance at the 1902 Congress John McKay seems to have slipped back into relative obscurity. Now in the GAA's 125th year it is timely to highlight his contribution and seek more information about him, particularly in Ulster, as he represents the only solid link that this historic province has with that memorable day in Thurles in 1884. As we set out on our mission of research the most important fact to ascertain was where exactly he was buried, so that, if thought fitting, a memorial could be put on his grave to commemorate his part in the GAA's establishment. In addition we were keen to find out as many facts about him as possible and in particular where in Ulster he was from, as no doubt any GAA unit would be very proud to claim such a distinguished son as one of their own.

The vagueness of the information about McKay's origins coupled with his peripatetic life was always likely to make tracing him a difficult assignment. Our first purpose was to find his last resting place. Armed with his date of death the first fact to ascertain was his residence. Having contacted the General Register Office in London, soon we were issued with a death certificate which indicated that he had been living at 20 Dumbarton Road, Brixton Hill. His age was given as 72 and he died of acute pneumonia.[50] John McKay's age at death suggested that he was born in 1851, which meant that we would have to look exclusively for Roman Catholic Church records to find his date and place of birth, as civil records did not start until 1864. Equally important was the fact given that his death was reported by his son Patrick Joseph McKay, as we knew nothing about his children.

Being a Catholic it was likely that John McKay would be buried in a Catholic cemetery although in a major city like London burial in a municipal cemetery was equally likely. Having looked up a list of Catholic cemeteries in London we first tried St Patrick's on Langthorne Road, which was the closest to where he lived. When contacted by telephone a quick search of their computerised records revealed no John McKay, but they suggested that we contact the next closest Catholic cemetery, St Mary's, Kensal Green. Within a minute of contacting St Mary's we had the exciting information that, yes, a John McKay of 20 Dumbarton Road was buried there on 6 December 1923. Without doubt this was him. Buried with him were his wife, Ellen, who died in 1949 at 6 Gunterstone Road, Fulham, at the grand old age of 95; his son, Patrick Joseph, who died at Chislehurst, Bromley, Kent, in 1929, aged only 42; and a child, Patrick Joseph junior

Death certificate of John McKay.

(presumably a grandson of John), who died in 1917, aged ten days.[51] This information was very useful in our search for more details of the family. The most striking news of all was that the grave was not marked with any form of memorial. It would appear that John and the family who survived him in London were not very wealthy, and that in the immediate aftermath of his death the newspapers and GAA officials with whom he had worked or who knew of him were not hugely concerned that he should be honoured.

Having established the place where his life concluded the task remained to establish where it had begun. McKay is a common name in Ulster and John was one of the most commonly used Christian names in the nineteenth century. Fortunately, during the course of our search the 1911 census for Ireland was made available on the internet. We were quickly able to find McKay on the Irish National Archives census website. It turned out the vitally important information that McKay, then living at 80 Western Road (an eight-room private dwelling) in Cork City, was born in Co. Down; that he was married to Ellen for twenty-eight years; that they had six children, but only three of whom surviving; and that of these, only Joan, aged 23 still lived with the parents. The census return unfortunately throws up an anomaly about McKay's age – an important fact when his birth details are being sought. His age on his death certificate would have made around 1851 his year of birth but in 1911 his age is given as 56[52] which would mean he was born around 1855. Which is correct?

Now that we knew he was from Co. Down, we wanted to find out where exactly in the county. There was a good chance that numerous John McKays would appear in church records of the same general period, so it was important to find out his father's name, in order to distinguish him. It was safe to assume, based on the 1911 census information, that he married around 1883, and that a civil record of his marriage would carry the name of his father. From the General Register Office in Roscommon we obtained a copy of John McKay's marriage certificate, which shows that he married Ellen Browne in the Church of St Peter and St Paul, in Paul Street, Cork City, on 19 April 1883. This document carried the important information that John's father was named Joseph. Ellen was born in Co. Cork and her father was James Browne, a farmer. Her address was given as the Munster Hotel where presumably she worked. Joseph McKay's occupation was listed as labourer,[53] so John probably came from a relatively humble background which may have precluded any chance of him attending a college. It is more likely, however, that the extent of his formal education was at a national school. In some areas the local national teacher had knowledge of and perhaps a qualification in subjects such as shorthand and typing. They earned extra income by coaching students who were interested in a career in the civil service or organisations like the Royal Irish Constabulary.

Armed with this much additional information, finding the exact whereabouts of John McKay's place of birth seemed on the face of it to be a fairly straightforward piece of work. However the task was to prove a more difficult one than was initially imagined. We should perhaps have been ready to face considerable difficulties, given that neither the eminent historian of the GAA in Down Síghle Nic An Ultaigh nor indeed any club historian of the GAA in that county seem to have been aware of his local connection, which no doubt would be a great honour to the club and locality that could claim him as a distinguished son of their community.

Griffith's Valuation seemed an obvious place to look for John's father, Joseph, as this survey of householders was carried out around 1860, a few years after John was born. But the Co. Down records show not a single Joseph McKay as a head of a household at that time. John's marriage certificate states that Joseph was deceased by 1883 so he may have died relatively young and before Griffith's was compiled. Attempts to find a civil record of his death also failed. If he died before 1864 there would be no such record. The obvious next place to look in the RC parish records for a John McKay, a son of Joseph, baptised in the 1850s. This search was unavailing despite trawling through many parish records.

It is possible that our search has been obstructed by the various spellings and pronunciations of the name McKay. In many cases, it was spelt 'MacKay' or 'Mackay'. 'McCay' is another common version in the north, and some people with similar-sounding names in Co. Down spell it 'McKey'. Many records, especially in the nineteenth century, contained anomalies in spelling of names, ages and other details. Some records of John McKay's family were listed under different spellings; for example, one son's name was spelt as 'McKey' in a civil record.[54] If some of the other children were recorded under similar variant spellings, it might explain why certain details have remained elusive.

The other matter worth investigating was what became of John's family, through which we might find out more about the man himself. By checking Catholic records in Cork City we were able to find that four children of John and Ellen McKay were baptised in St Finbarr's (South) parish: Joseph James, born 1884; John Paul, born 1885; Johanna Teresa, born 1886; and Maurice Henry, born 1889.[55] Johanna Teresa is presumably one and the same as 'Joan', the daughter who lived with John and Ellen in 1911, although in fact a year older than the 23 listed on her census record. Patrick Joseph, who was mentioned previously, could not be found in Catholic baptismal records in Cork, but the civil register of births confirms that he was born in 1887.[56] We could not find any baptismal records for the sixth child. Maurice Henry died after just six months in 1889.[57] We could not find in Irish records any notice of the other two deaths before 1911; their deaths might not have been formally registered, particularly if they died very young, or outside of the country. It is likely that Joseph James, the first-born who was given the names of his two grandfathers, died as an infant; the fact that Joseph was also the second name given to Patrick at birth in 1887 suggests that Joseph James had already died.

Before concluding, it is only right to acknowledge the part of several people in helping us through our exhaustive search. Jarlath Burns (the chairman, from Armagh) and John Arnold (Cork) of the GAA's national 125 Years Events Committee led a general effort to commemorate the seven men from Hayes's Hotel and they highlighted the need to find John McKay. Previously, Jim Cronin, also of Co. Cork, started off the pursuit of McKay when vital information was less accessible. Danielle Carroll, who works in St Mary's Cemetery, Kensal Green, located McKay's grave, upon our request. The General Register Office, Roscommon, furnished us with his civil marriage record; his Catholic marriage record was provided by Paddy Walsh of St Peter and St Paul parish, Cork; and Joe Riley of St Finbarr's (South) parish, Cork, located the baptismal records of the McKay children. The keepers of records in numerous other parishes also aided us along the way by perusing their records for relevant information.[58] Throughout the process, our library colleagues Roddy Hegarty and Joe Canning rendered much valuable assistance too.

Descendants of Joseph McKay

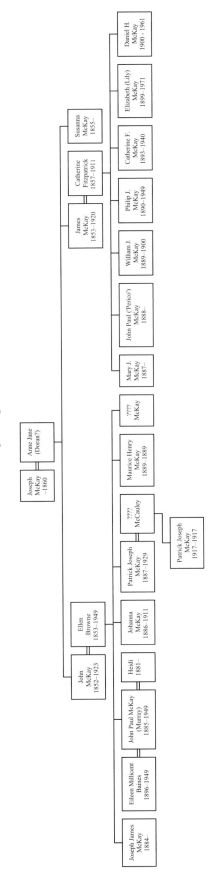

This truncated family tree of the McKay family includes the known details of John's parents, his two known siblings, his six children and his one known grandson. It also includes the details of his brother James McKay's children, but not their spouses, their children or subsequent generations. Danny McKay, who contacted the authors to confirm the family connection, is a grandson of Daniel H. McKay (1900–61).

So what new information did our search for John McKay yield? There are seven notable findings, quite aptly for one of the seven men at the first GAA meeting. First, contrary to some previous belief, he was a native of Co. Down and Ulster. Ironically, considering that the organisation he helped to create tended to promote a sense of loyalty to one's home-place, he lived in four cities and at least ten different addresses (even more than the nomadic Michael Cusack). Third, whereas the Fenian connections or sympathies of several of the GAA founders have been emphasised, McKay was clearly a moderate, constitutional nationalist. Fourth, of the seven men who met in Thurles on 1 November 1884, he had apparently the narrowest specific interest in athletics. Fifth, being a GAA founder did not carry with it the degree of kudos that one might expect today, for he was largely a forgotten man within the association long before and after his demise. Consequently, we found that (sixth) he and some of his family were buried in an unmarked grave in London. And finally (or seventh), bearing in mind that this search arose from an aspiration to honour John McKay and that it has led to a gravestone being erected on his grave, it is clear that in more recent times the GAA has become more conscientious about remembering its founders.

Appendix

Where exactly in Co. Down did John McKay come from?

The preceding article was completed before the following additional information became known. The exact whereabouts of John McKay's birthplace in Co. Down had not been discovered, and as no-one in the county seemed to be aware of his local link, it was likely that his wider family circle had moved away from his native place several generations ago and the memory of the connection had been lost. But with the GAA's 125th anniversary day and the erection of a gravestone to McKay imminent, it was decided to make a last-ditch attempt to find the missing details. Somewhere in Ireland or further afield, we hoped, might be a relative whose family might have retained a memory of their connection with this historic figure. It was not implausible that if John had brothers and sisters, their great-grandchildren or great-great-grandchildren would be around today, and with the recent upturn in interest in genealogy, someone might know of a family tie with him or a McKay with links to Co. Down might be stirred into researching his or her family tree until it linked up with that we had drawn up.

Hence the *Irish News* was asked to carry a feature on McKay, and it gladly obliged, being proud that a founding member of the GAA had worked for the newspaper. The paper carried a full-page article on Friday 23 October which also asked for anyone who had any additional information to contact us. The first few replies did not give great promise as it was soon obvious that they could not be referring to what we can now call 'our John McKay'. A week passed, and it seemed too late to solve our mystery in this anniversary year.

Then on Friday 30 October we received a phone-call from Mr Danny McKay of Belfast, and everything changed. Danny intimated that his great-grandfather, James McKay, was a brother of John McKay, journalist and founding member of the GAA, and he provided us with enough initial facts to confirm that this was the breakthrough we were looking for. He had a letter written in the late 1970s by a grand-uncle, Jimmy McKay, to Philomena (an aunt of Danny) which clearly outlined the relationship.[1] Unfortunately, however, Danny did not know the exact place in Co. Down where his ancestors originated, understandably given that his great-grandfather James had moved to Belfast as a young man and the family had now lived there for five generations.

All was not lost, however. Knowing that his great-grandfather had lived in east Belfast in the early part of the twentieth century we immediately consulted the 1911 online census database, hoping against hope for a clue there. Fortune favoured us this time. We found the McKay family living at 70 Eliza Street, Cromac and in the box which asked, 'state which county or city where born', James McKay wrote 'Downpatrick, Co. Down'. It was a significant stroke of luck, as strictly speaking he was only required to enter the name of the county; indeed, he had initially written 'Belfast', and then scribbled it out and wrote 'Downpatrick'. From the details supplied by his descendant Danny – i.e. that he had been an insurance agent and had seven children – we knew that this James McKay was definitely the correct ancestor. The census return also indicated that James' wife, Catherine (née Fitzpatrick), was also from Downpatrick,[2] and this raised the possibility that they were married in that town or area. An enquiry for their civil marriage certificate brought the information that they were married in St Malachy's Catholic Church, Ballykilbeg, near Downpatrick, in 1885; James lived in Belfast prior to the wedding, while Catherine lived in the townland of Lisnamaul.[3] Ballykilbeg and Lisnamaul were separated by the adjoining townland of Cargagh.[4]

These details corroborated references to the townlands of Cargagh and Bonecastle in the letter of Jimmy McKay,[5] which was proving remarkably accurate in most aspects. He wrote that the father of John and James McKay, who was officially recorded as Joseph, died suddenly at the age of 39, and the family sold whatever property or land they had and moved to Belfast soon afterwards.[6] If so, it was likely that Joseph died between 1855 (when Susanna was born) and the compilation of the Griffith Valuation around 1860. We now had enough information to revisit the Valuation, where we found Anne Jane McKay (possibly a widow) as one of only two female heads of household of the surname in Downpatrick union, and the only one in Cargagh. By way of further proof of the family's roots, it emerged that extracts from the 1841 and 1851 censuses list McKay as the chief family name in the townlands of Cargagh and Bonecastle, along with Doran and Smith.[7] For this and the final amazing revelation about the place of John McKay's origin we are indebted to John Devaney, a Co. Longford native now resident in Downpatrick, who volunteered to help us complete our search. On 4 November 2009 he established from Griffith Valuation maps, the exact location of the house headed by Anne McKay around 1860 and in which John McKay almost certainly grew up. On visiting the townland, he found that no building remains where that house once stood. The plot of land in question is on a corner where the Buckshead Road branches off from the Ballydougan Road (between Downpatrick and the village of Clough). The field is owned today by a Mrs Hamilton, and immediately next to it lives John Smith, the half-back who played on Down's All-Ireland-title winning football team of 1961!

Having ascertained where John McKay came from, we wanted to establish when exactly he was born and what became of his parents and siblings. We proceeded to look for baptismal records of John and James in the parish of Downpatrick. Luckily for us, such records are available from 1851, and it was with much further good fortune that we found the records of baptism of both of them, and Susanna, a sister about whom we had not previously heard, all under the name 'McKee'.[8] John was baptised in October 1852 (and almost certainly born in the same month) – so both burial and census records were inaccurate about his age – and his sponsors were James Drake and Susan Doran. James and Susanna were baptised in December 1853 and February 1855 respectively.[9] Despite the anomalous spelling of their surname every other detail fitted in (such as their parents' names being Joseph and Anne) and we could state for certain that we had located the birth of John McKay and siblings. There are a number of other interesting local aspects. One of the sponsors of James' baptism was Mary Crolly. William Crolly (1780–1849), Catholic Archbishop of Armagh, 1835–49, and his family also came from Ballykilbeg.[10] So too did the (in)famous Orangeman and MP, William Johnson (1829–1902) – also known as 'Johnston of Ballykilbeg'.[11] James McKay died in Belfast some time before 1920. We do not know what became of Susanna, but presumably she died young or moved away from the family in her youth, for she did not feature in the detailed letter of Jimmy McKay or the collective memory of the family.

A few more important details about John McKay and his family arose out of this late flush of information from the letter Danny McKay read to us. It was revealed that Mallow was the town in Co. Cork from which his wife Ellen hailed. It appears also that in his second period living in Belfast, after his return from Cork (around 1896, when he reputedly joined the *Irish News*), John kept close to his brother and family. We can surmise this because Jimmy McKay, in his aforementioned letter, referred to how John's son, John Paul, 'used to write little shows and charge Dad [Paul, James' son], uncle Danny and the rest of the family a halfpenny to see the performance!'[12] These family members listed lived in Belfast throughout this period, and it appears that John Paul (who turned eleven years of age in 1896) attended St Malachy's College in the city around this time.[13] This information raises the possibility that John's return north was somehow connected to his children's education, and that perhaps also his second stint in the northern city lasted

Danny McKay of Belfast reads the old family letter confirming that John McKay was his great-grand-uncle, at an event at the Cardinal Ó Fiaich Library on the GAA's 125th anniversary day, on 1 November 2009. A public appeal through the *Irish News* had helped to make the connection with the McKay family. The letter was written to Danny's aunt Philomena (a grandniece of John McKay), who also attended the event. (*John Merry / Comhairle Uladh*)

several years. Jimmy McKay, in a similar letter to another relative, imparted that the family of James McKay (John's brother) were involved in athletics; his sons Paul and Philip were apparently 'very keen harriers'.[14] This tends to increase the likelihood John McKay retained an interest in athletics when back in Belfast, although no longer an active GAA member.

The new information further revealed that John Paul and Johanna (his sister) went to London in their youth. They, along with Patrick Joseph, were the three children of John and Ellen McKay who survived to adulthood. The story of John Paul is most fascinating and worthy of outline. It was reported that he ran away from school (presumably St Malachy's, Belfast) to become a journalist[15] (perhaps in his father's footsteps). At the age of seventeen, around 1902, he got a job in the booking office of a Cardiff theatre.[16] He attempted to become an actor but he fluffed his debut appearance.[17] From then on he worked as a manager, agent and producer. He adopted the name 'Paul Murray' for career purposes, and under this name he was recorded in the 1911 English census, at the age of 25, as a 'general manager of circuit of vaudeville theatres', and as being married for two years to Hedi [sic – Heidi?], a 30-year-old native of Prussian Poland (and German subject).[18] He was soon appointed a manager of one of Sir Oswald Stoll's theatres in London and he 'became very influential in the theatre world'.[19] His rapid success probably explains why John and Ellen McKay and all three children had gone to London by the 1910s. He went on to co-present several revues, such as *All French* (1915),[20] *Pot Luck* (1921), *Midnight Follies* (1922), *Snap* (1922),[21] *Lido Lady* (1926), *The Blue Train* (1927) and *The House that Jack Built* (1930).[22] He travelled widely around Britain with these shows, and internationally too; he visited Chicago in 1922, for example.[23] In 1927 he went into partnership with the famous musical comedy star Jack Hulbert – who was married to actress Cicely T. Courtneidge – and they formed 'Jack Hulbert and Paul Murray Ltd'. Some of these shows achieved notable success on their tours. In 1930 Paul Murray (McKay) even co-directed a film – one of the first British films with sound – named *Elstree Calling*, in which his fellow directors included a young Alfred Hitchcock, and the musical composer Ivor Novello wrote music and Hulbert and Courtneidge starred. It has been described as 'a lavish musical film revue' and Britain's response to the recent revues produced by the major American studios in Hollywood.[24]

Then, however, things began to go badly wrong for Paul Murray (McKay). Since the mid 1920s at least he had financial troubles, and in 1925, when his liabilities amounted to almost £6,000, he arranged a repayment scheme for his creditors.[25] After the Wall Street crash of 1929, economic depression set in worldwide, and the introduction of sound to film in the late 1920s also ate into the theatre market, but he and Hulbert still launched more ambitious shows. In August 1930 they produced the revue, *Follow a Star*, at the Winter Garden Theatre, and in December 1930 they also produced *Folly to be Wise* – reportedly a 'spectacular musical cocktail', with no expense spared[26] – at the Piccadilly Theatre. Both productions were failures. Paul's share of the losses amounted to £3,369 for one show, and £2,119 for the other show. In 1931 he produced various music-hall acts and turns which flopped and a year later he directed a company that carried on business as cinema agents. In 1933 he filed for bankruptcy,[27] and his theatrical career never returned to its previous heights, despite a new musical partnership (with Mr Robert Nesbitt) from 1937.[28] At some stage he remarried – we do not know what became of Heidi – to Eileen Millicent Baines (whose

The authors of this chapter, Comhairle Uladh CLG officials and a relative of John McKay, at the ceremony for the unveiling of the headstone on the grave in St Mary's Catholic Cemetery, Kensal Green, London, on 7 November 2009. Left to right: Michael Hasson, Aogán Ó Fearghail, Kieran McConville, Philip Byrne (a great-grandnephew of John McKay), Tom Daly, Dónal McAnallen and Oliver Galligan.

brother Gilbert was manager of the Empress Theatre), and they lived in Earls Court. Paul's later ventures continued to meet with failure, and they sold all their furniture and possessions for creditors. They were found dead in their house in tragic circumstances in October 1949. Their inquest reported that they died from asphyxia due to carbon monoxide poisoning – a joint suicide.[29] To the end Paul had entertained friends at his residence, and, the *Daily Express* recorded, 'offered sherry to one and all and ordered flowers to grace his hospitality'.[30] He was remembered as 'a charming and buoyant character'.[31]

At the time of writing we do not know whether any direct descendants of GAA founding member John McKay are alive today. We have not yet found evidence of John Paul (Murray) having a child by either of his wives. It seems that his sister Johanna (Joan) also lived in London until the late 1940s at least,[32] but we do not know whether she married. There also remain unanswered questions about what family, if any, Patrick Joseph left behind. He married a woman named McCauley in London in the early part of 1914, but we do not know if they had any children who survived to adulthood. If there are direct descendants alive today, they are unlikely to be in Ireland, and the search for them will focus primarily on British records.

There is no such problem in finding relatives through the line of James McKay, John's brother. Within days of Danny McKay's phone-call, we had established that surviving today are at least four grandnieces of John McKay, one grandnephew, and twenty-five great-grandnieces and -grandnephews. Two of the grandnieces, Maeve and Philomena McKay of Belfast, and two great-grandnephews of John McKay who had never met, Danny McKay (Belfast) and Philip Byrne (Bray) attended a lecture on our 'search for John McKay' in the Cardinal Ó Fiaich Library, on 1 November 2009, the GAA's 125th birthday. Philip Byrne, and the present authors, also went to London for a ceremony in St Mary's Catholic cemetery, Kensal Green, on 7 November, at which a gravestone was at last unveiled for GAA founding member John McKay and family. Hopefully this monument and the other fruits of our research will ensure that this previously obscure figure will be remembered well into the future.

In an Ulster Senior Football Championship semi-final at Clones in 1983, Peter McGinnity of Fermanagh attempts to block the kick of Jim McAweeney of Cavan. (*Irish News*)

Section 5: Ulster Senior Championship Records, 1888–2009

Ulster Senior Football Championship results 1888–2009

Ulster Senior Football Championship final teams 1888–2009

Ulster Senior Football Championship winning captains 1888–2009

Ulster Senior Hurling Championship results 1902–2009

Ulster Senior Hurling Championship final teams 1902–2009

Ulster Senior Championship Records, 1888–2009

Dónal McAnallen

The following section comprises the most comprehensive set of Ulster Senior Football and Hurling Championship records published to date. It provides the key details of almost every single match played in these championships from 1888 to 2009 – the dates, the venues and the results and then the full line-outs of the teams that played in each final. The equivalent records of provincial championship matches and final teams have already been researched and published in the other three Irish provinces, by Jim Cronin (Munster), Tom Ryall (Leinster) and Tomás Ó Móráin (Connacht).

The foundation for these Ulster records was built by Eoghan Corry and Jerome Quinn, who researched and published most of the football results back to the start in *High Ball* magazine (July 1999) and various Ulster GAA publications (1993–2003) respectively. The list in this section collates their records, fills in remaining gaps and corrects inadvertent errors that appeared therein. The lists of Ulster football final teams published herein owes much to both writers also. Jerome published lists of Ulster final teams from 1950–2003 inclusive in his Ulster GAA publications, while Eoghan provided us with many of the team-lists from the pre 1950 period. We are very grateful to both men for allowing us to use their research data.

The additional information in the updated records was obtained through research of the following sources in the main: Comhairle Uladh minutes, 1917–72; Con Short's files of research notes on Ulster GAA history; Síghle Nic An Ultaigh's research notes on GAA history of An Dún; lists of An Cabhán teams, 1920–39, compiled by Gearóid Mac Gabhann; the county GAA histories of Tír Eoghain (Joseph Martin), An Dún (Síghle Nic An Ultaigh) and Muineachán (Séamus McCluskey and John P. Graham); the club histories of Armagh Harps (Phil McGinn), Cornafean (George Cartwright) and Burt (Campbell, Dowds and Mullen); and various newspapers, chiefly *Anglo-Celt*, *Irish News*, *Derry People*, *Frontier Sentinel*, *Dundalk Democrat*, *Dungannon Democrat*, *Fermanagh Herald*, *Newry Reporter* and *Ulster Herald*.

Part 1 (a) of these records provides the key details of almost every single match played in the Ulster Senior Football Championships from 1888 to 2009 – the dates, the venues and the results. Part 1 (b) contains a list of team line-outs from every Ulster SFC final from 1888 to 2009. In Part 1 (c) there appears a newly researched and near-complete list of football championship winning captains from the start.

Part 2 (a) comprises the dates, venues and results of Ulster Senior Hurling Championship matches back to 1902. Although some research work was done on this championship by the above-named authors, this book provides much more detail on the early history of the competition, between 1902 and 1946. Likewise, Part 2 (b), which provides lists of Ulster SHC final teams back to 1902, was largely unresearched previously. These records unlock the hidden history of the Ulster hurling championships, in which all counties participated in the 1900s.

By far the most difficult aspect of this research has been to put the records in order for the years 1900–16. The problems are caused by the unavailability of Comhairle Uladh minutes for this period, the paucity of newspaper reports of games in many instances, and the sheer irregularity of the championships – often running late, by up to a year or more, and sometimes not contested at all.

One of the consequences of the new research presented here is that some of the important details of previously published records have to be revised. Most notably, this book advocates changes to the hitherto accepted rolls of honour for the Ulster senior championships, for the years 1900–12. Previously, the sequencing was predicated on an (arbitrary but understandable) assumption that each Ulster championship should be attributed to the championship season or 'year' in which the Ulster champion team played in the All-Ireland Semi-final – which was usually late. For example, the 1902 Ulster SFC was ascribed to Ard Mhacha, because the county then went on to play in the All-Ireland Semi-final of 1902, which was running late and played in 1904. Yet this logic overlooks the fact that Comhairle Uladh was not formed and

The Antrim football team that contested the 1911 All-Ireland final.

organising championships until spring 1903. Although the Central Council had organised the Ulster football championships of 1888 to 1891, there were no further Ulster championships from then until 1903 when it was under the aegis of Comhairle Uladh. Moreover, this method of predating Ulster championship leaves an unexplained gap in the roll of honour; up to now the records have said 'No Championship' for football in 1907, but in fact an entire championship was played from first round to final between April and August 1907, and indeed the next football championship began in December 1907.

Having considered this and other aspects of the championships in this period, I argue that the Ulster roll of honour should apportion each championship only to the year(s) in which it was played, or the winter-spring season straddling two years – for example, 1903/04 – as was commonly in vogue in the GAA at that time – unless contemporary evidence emerges to indicate that the Ulster Council described one of its championships played in 1904, for example, as the championship of 1902. At the time of writing, no such evidence is known to exist.

ULSTER SENIOR FOOTBALL CHAMPIONSHIP RESULTS 1888–2009

ROLL OF HONOUR:

AN CABHÁN (36): 1891, 1904/05, 1905/06, 1915, 1918, 1919, 1920, 1923, 1924, 1925, 1926, 1928, 1931, 1932, 1933, 1934, 1935, 1936, 1937, 1939, 1940, 1941, 1942, 1943, 1944, 1945, 1947, 1948, 1949, 1952, 1954, 1955, 1962, 1967, 1969, 1997.

ARD MHACHA (14): 1890, 1903/04, 1950, 1953, 1977, 1980, 1982, 1999, 2000, 2002, 2004, 2005, 2006, 2008.

MUINEACHÁN (14): 1888, 1906/07, 1914, 1916, 1917, 1921, 1922, 1927, 1929, 1930, 1938, 1979, 1985, 1988.

AN DÚN (12): 1959, 1960, 1961, 1963, 1965, 1966, 1968, 1971, 1978, 1981, 1991, 1994.

TÍR EOGHAIN (12): 1956, 1957, 1973, 1984, 1986, 1989, 1995, 1996, 2001, 2003, 2007, 2009.

AONTROIM (8): 1902/03, 1907/08, 1909, 1910, 1912, 1913, 1946, 1951.

DOIRE (7): 1958, 1970, 1975, 1976, 1987, 1993, 1998.

DÚN na nGALL (5): 1972, 1974, 1983, 1990, 1992.

1888

19 Aug	Drogheda	Muineachán 0-2 An Cabhán 0-2
9 Sept	Drogheda (replay)	Muineachán 0-3 An Cabhán 0-1

1890

12 Oct	Blaris, Lisburn	Ard Mhacha 3-7 Aontroim 0-1
Final:		
12 Oct	Blaris	Ard Mhacha 2-8 Tír Eoghain 1-2

1891

24 Aug		Ard Mhacha 3-17 Aontroim 0-0
Final:		
1 Nov	Bailieborough	An Cabhán beat Ard Mhacha (abandoned – re-fixture ordered)
6 Dec	Smithborough (re-fixture)	An Cabhán 1-11 Ard Mhacha 0-0

[1892–1901: No Ulster championships were organised during this period. An Cabhán played in the Leinster Football Championship in 1895.]

1902/03

Aontroim w.o.

(The Ulster Council billed the Antrim SFC final at Belfast on 4 Apr 1903 (Tír na nOg 3-5 Red Hand 2-5) as the 'Championship of Ulster' football match – *Irish News*, 4 April 1903.)

1903/04

3 Jan 1904	Armagh	Ard Mhacha 0-2 Tír Eoghain 0-3 (abandoned – re-fixture ordered)
24 Jan 1904	Dungannon (re-fixture)	Ard Mhacha 1-6 Tír Eoghain 0-3
7 Feb 1904	Seaghan's Park, Belfast	Aontroim 1-4 An Cabhán 0-1
Final:		
3 Apr 1904	Seaghan's Park, Belfast	Ard Mhacha 2-2 Aontroim 1-4

1904/05

1 Jan 1905	Dungannon	Tír Eoghain w.o. Doire
6 Jan 1905	Enniskillen	Muineachán 0-4 Fear Manach 0-1 (objection – re-fixture ordered)
22 Jan 1905	Newry	Ard Mhacha 2-9 An Dún 0-1
22 Jan 1905	Cavan	An Cabhán 0-5 Aontroim 0-2 (objection – re-fixture ordered)
19 Feb 1905	Carrickmacross (re-fixture)	Muineachán w.o. Fear Manach
26 Feb 1905	Cavan (re-fixture)	An Cabhán 0-5 Aontroim 0-3
Semi-finals:		
19 Feb 1905	Coalisland	Ard Mhacha 0-12 Tír Eoghain 0-3 (objection – re-fixture ordered)
12 Mar 1905	Armagh (re-fixture)	Ard Mhacha 7-4 Tír Eoghain 0-1
17 Mar 1905	Newbliss	An Cabhán 1-8 Muineachán 0-3
Final:		
24 Apr 1905	Armagh	An Cabhán 0-5 Ard Mhacha 0-5
28 May 1905	Cavan (replay)	An Cabhán 0-5 Ard Mhacha 0-5
11 June 1905	Newbliss (2nd replay)	An Cabhán 0-8 Ard Mhacha 0-5

1905/06

22 Oct 1905	Derrylin	An Cabhán 0-4 Fear Manach 0-1
26 Nov 1905	Muineachán	Muineachán 1-13 Ard Mhacha 1-2
3 Dec 1905	Banbridge	Aontroim 1-11 An Dún 1-1
4 Feb 1906	Strabane	Doire 1-3 Tír Eoghain 0-2
17 Mar 1906	Derry	Doire 20 pts Dún na nGall 0-1
Semi-finals:		
11 Feb 1906	Cavan	An Cabhán 0-10 Aontroim 0-1 (objection – re-fixture ordered)
15 Apr 1906	Clones (re-fixture)	An Cabhán 1-6 Aontroim 0-1
6 May 1906	Baile na Lorgáin	Muineachán w.o. Doire
Final:		
20 May 1906	Clones	An Cabhán 0-7 Muineachán 0-3

1906/07

21 Apr 1907	Cootehill	Muineachán 2-4 An Cabhán 0-5
5 May 1907	Newry	An Dún 1-6 Ard Mhacha 0-4
2 June 1907	Belfast	Aontroim w.o. Tír Eoghain
16 June 1907	Newry	Aontroim 1-8 An Dún 0-9
23 June 1907	Derry	Doire 0-18 Dún na nGall 0-2
Semi-finals:		
5 July 1907	Newbliss	Muineachán 0-10 Fear Manach 1-4
18 Aug 1907	Belfast	Aontroim 1-14 Doire 0-4
Final:		
25 Aug	Clones	Muineachán 2-10 Aontroim 1-2

1907/08

15 Dec 1907	Newry	Aontroim 0-4 An Dún 0-4
26 Jan 1908	Clones	Fear Manach w.o. Muineachán
2 Feb 1908	Newry (replay)	Aontroim 0-9 An Dún 0-5
16 Feb 1908	Newbliss	An Cabhán w.o. Tír Eoghain
Semi-finals:		
6 June 1908	Armagh	Aontroim 0-12 Ard Mhacha 0-6
21 June 1908	Enniskillen	An Cabhán 0-7 Fear Manach 0-2
Final:		
13 Sept 1908	Clones	Aontroim 1-8 An Cabhán 0-4

1909

28 Mar	Castleblayney	Muineachán v Ard Mhacha (abandoned)
1 Aug	Castleblayney (replay)	Muineachán 1-7 Ard Mhacha 0-3
22 Aug	Clones	Fear Manach 2-4 Tír Eoghain 1-6
29 Aug	Newry	An Cabhán w.o. An Dún

Semi-finals:

12 Sept	Clones	Aontroim 0-10 Muineachán 0-6
17 Oct	Belturbet	An Cabhán 0-6 Fear Manach 0-1

Final:

28 Nov	Clones	Aontroim 1-9 An Cabhán 0-5

1910

1 May 1910	Castleblayney	Muineachán 0-10 Ard Mhacha 1-7
15 May	Belfast	Aontroim w.o. An Dún
15 May	Belturbet	An Cabhán v Fear Manach (abandoned)
3 July	Belturbet (re-fixture)	An Cabhán 1-9 Fear Manach 0-5
3 July	Dungannon	Tír Eoghain w.o. Doire
3 July [?]	Crossmaglen (replay)	Muineachán 1-5 Ard Mhacha 0-4

Semi-finals:

17 July	Bundoran	An Cabhán 1-9 Tír Eoghain 1-4
4 Sept	Armagh	Aontroim 1-4 Muineachán 1-3 (objection - re-fixture ordered)
27 Nov	Dundalk (re-fixture)	Aontroim 1-2 Muineachán 0-3

Final:

18 June 1911	Dundalk	Aontroim 3-4 An Cabhán 0-1

1911

No championship

1912

Armagh		Ard Mhacha w.o. An Dún
26 May	Wattlebridge	An Cabhán 2-2 Fear Manach 0-2

Semi-finals:

12 May	Clones	Aontroim 3-1 Muineachán 0-5
14 July	Newbliss	An Cabhán 0-1 Ard Mhacha 0-1
4 Aug	Newbliss (replay)	An Cabhán 1-2 Ard Mhacha 1-1 (objection; awarded to Ard Mhacha)

Final:

10 Nov	Castleblayney	Aontroim 2-2 Ard Mhacha 0-1

1913

15 June	Belfast	Aontroim 1-6 An Dún 0-3
22 June	Monaghan	Fear Manach 1-3 Ard Mhacha 1-1
4 Aug	Dungannon	Aontroim 5-1 Tír Eoghain 1-1

Semi-final:

15 June	Cavan	An Cabhán 1-3 Muineachán 2-0
20 July	Cootehill	Muineachán 0-3 An Cabhán 0-2
31 Aug	Clones	Aontroim 1-4 Fear Manach 1-3

Final:

21 Sept	Newbliss	Aontroim 2-1 Muineachán 1-2

1914

24 May	Newry	Ard Mhacha 11 pts An Dún 0-0
21 June	Derry	Muineachán 3-2 Doire 0-3
21 June	Clones	Fear Manach 2-4 Tír Eoghain 1-2
4 July	Clones	An Cabhán 2-3 Aontroim 1-2

Semi-finals:

26 July	Clones	Fear Manach 2-1 An Cabhán 0-4
7 Aug	Carrickmacross	Muineachán 0-0 Ard Mhacha 0-0
16 Aug	Culloville (replay)	Muineachán 1-1 Ard Mhacha 0-2

Final:

23 Aug	Newbliss	Muineachán 2-4 Fear Manach 0-2

1915

30 May	Wattlebridge	An Cabhán 1-3 Aontroim 0-2 (objection – re-fixture ordered)
13 June	Clones	Fear Manach 1-2 Muineachán 1-1
11 July	Newry	Ard Mhacha 1-7 An Dún 1-3
18 July	Wattlebridge (replay)	An Cabhán 0-3 Aontroim 0-1
8 Aug	Belturbet (re-fixture)	Muineachán 5-2 Fear Manach 2-0

Semi-finals:

1 Aug	Newbliss	An Cabhán 0-9 Ard Mhacha 0-4

Final:

22 Aug	Belturbet	An Cabhán 2-5 Muineachán 3-2
2 Sept	Clones	An Cabhán 0-4 Muineachán 0-3

1916

25 June	Wattlebridge	An Cabhán 2-3 Fear Manach 0-1
2 July	Clones	Muineachán 2-5 Doire 0-1
23 July	Camlough	Aontroim 4 pts Ard Mhacha 0-1

Semi-finals:

20 Aug	Belturbet	Muineachán 4-3 An Cabhán 1-5
27 Aug	Portaferry	Aontroim 1-3 An Dún 1-0

Final:

24 Sept	Clones	Muineachán 2-3 Aontroim 0-2

1917

13 May	Derry	An Cabhán 3-5 Doire 2-1
13 May	Wattlebridge	Muineachán 1-2 Fear Manach 1-0
20 May	Downpatrick	Aontroim 0-22 An Dún 0-4
20 May	Armagh	Ard Mhacha 2-3 Tír Eoghain 1-3

Semi-finals:

17 June	Armagh	Aontroim 2-4 Ard Mhacha 1-5 (objection – re-fixture ordered)
1 July	Cootehill	Muineachán 3-1 An Cabhán 0-2
12 Aug	Belfast (re-fixture)	Ard Mhacha 0-5 Aontroim 0-3

Final:

28 Oct	Clones	Muineachán 4-2 Ard Mhacha 0-4

1918

28 Apr	Belfast	Aontroim 4-1 Doire 2-4
5 May	Ard Mhacha	w.o. An Dún
26 May	Belturbet	An Cabhán 1-4 Fear Manach 1-2
10 June	Armagh	Muineachán 4-4 Tír Eoghain 1-0

Semi-finals:

30 June	Armagh	Aontroim 1-2 Muineachán 0-3
7 July	Cootehill	An Cabhán v Ard Mhacha postponed
17 Aug	Cootehill (re-fixture)	An Cabhán 2-4 Ard Mhacha 0-0

Final:

15 Sept	Belturbet	An Cabhán 3-2 Aontroim 0-0

1919

18 May	Castleblayney	Ard Mhacha 0-4 Muineachán 0-3
25 May	Strabane	Dún na nGall 4-4 Tír Eoghain 2-0
25 May	Wattlebridge	Doire 2-4 Fear Manach 0-3
1 June	Cavan	An Cabhán 0-10 An Dún 1-0
1 June	Derry	Aontroim 1-4 Doire 1-1
Semi-finals:		
22 June	Armagh	Aontroim 2-4 Ard Mhacha 1-4
7 July	Bundoran	An Cabhán 3-10 Dún na nGall 2-2
Final:		
31 Aug	Clones	An Cabhán 5-5 Aontroim 0-2

1920

9 May	Newcastle	An Dún 0-10 Aontroim 0-5
16 May	Dungannon	Ard Mhacha 2-1 Tír Eoghain 0-0
23 May	Clones	An Cabhán 2-2 Muineachán 1-3
23 May	Derry	Doire 0-11 Dún na nGall 1-2
13 June	Wattlebridge	An Cabhán 8-3 Fear Manach 2-1
Semi-finals:		
20 June	Camlough	Ard Mhacha 0-4 An Dún 0-3
23 July	Belturbet	An Cabhán 3-4 Doire 0-1
Final:		
8 Aug	Cootehill	An Cabhán 4-6 Ard Mhacha 1-4

1921

6 Nov	Clones	Muineachán 0-3 Ard Mhacha 0-1
27 Nov	Newcastle	Aontroim 1-5 An Dún 1-2
13 Nov	Strabane	Doire 2-1 Dún na nGall 0-3
Semi-finals:		
11 Dec	Brandywell, Derry	Doire 1-4 Aontroim 0-3
11 Dec	Clones	Muineachán 2-1 An Cabhán 2-1
1 Jan 1922	Clones (replay)	Muineachán 2-1 An Cabhán 0-2
Final:		
28 Oct 1923	Clones	Muineachán 2-2 Doire 0-1

1922

7 May	Clones	Muineachán 1-4 Aontroim 1-3
7 May	Moygannon	Ard Mhacha 2-4 An Dún 0-1
11 June	Bundoran	An Cabhán 0-8 Dún na nGall 1-1
Semi-finals:		
16 July	Ballybay	Muineachán 2-9 Ard Mhacha 0-2
13 Aug	Cavan	An Cabhán 4-4 Doire 1-1
Final:		
22 April 1923	Clones	An Cabhán 2-3 Muineachán 2-3
20 May 1923	Belturbet (replay)	Muineachán 2-7 An Cabhán 2-6

1923

10 June	Belturbet	An Cabhán 1-5 Aontroim 0-4
17 June	Letterkenny	Doire 1-3 Dún na nGall 1-2 (Doire disqualified)
8 July	Ballybay	Muineachán 4-1 Ard Mhacha 1-4
Semi-finals:		
12 Aug	Bundoran	An Cabhán 4-10 Dún na nGall 3-1
19 Aug	Clones	Muineachán 2-6 Tír Eoghain 0-3
Final:		
2 Sept	An Cabhán	An Cabhán 5-10 Muineachán 1-1

1924

18 May	Cootehill	An Cabhán 5-6 Ard Mhacha 1-6
18 May	Letterkenny	Tír Eoghain 0-2 Dún na nGall 0-1

25 May	Clones	Muineachán 4-6 Fear Manach 2-1
1 June	Downpatrick	Aontroim 1-6 An Dún 1-2
Semi-finals:		
22 June	Ballybay	Muineachán 1-5 Aontroim 1-4 (objection – re-fixture ordered)
24 Aug	Belturbet	An Cabhán 1-6 Tír Eoghain 0-7
31 Aug	Carrickmacross (re-fixture)	Muineachán 1-4 Aontroim 1-1
Final:		
21 Sept	Belturbet	An Cabhán 1-3 Muineachán 0-6
2 Nov	Ballybay (replay)	An Cabhán 2-3 Muineachán 1-3

1925

3 May	Castleblayney	Muineachán 1-3 Ard Mhacha 0-5 (objection - re-fixture ordered)
10 May	Newry	Aontroim 3-7 An Dún 0-1
24 May	Dungannon	An Cabhán 1-5 Tír Eoghain 1-3
14 June	Ballyshannon	Dún na nGall 3-6 Fear Manach 0-1
21 June	Castleblayney (re-fixture)	Muineachán 2-2 Ard Mhacha 1-4
Semi-finals:		
5 July	Newry	Aontroim 2-5 Muineachán 0-4
19 July	Ballyshannon	An Cabhán 6-2 Dún na nGall 0-2
Final:		
2 Aug	Monaghan	An Cabhán 2-3 Aontroim 3-0
16 Aug	Belturbet (replay)	An Cabhán 3-6 Aontroim 0-1

1926

9 May	Omagh	Tír Eoghain 3-8 Fear Manach 2-1
9 May	Camlough	Aontroim 3-6 Ard Mhacha 1-8
16 May	Hilltown	Muineachán 0-4 An Dún 0-1
16 May	Cavan	An Cabhán 4-7 Dún na nGall 1-5
6 June	Dungannon	Tír Eoghain 3-2 Doire 1-3
Semi-finals:		
27 June	Belturbet	An Cabhán 0-7 Muineachán 0-7
5 July	Omagh	Aontroim 2-5 Tír Eoghain 0-3
1 Aug	Ballybay (replay)	An Cabhán 0-7 Muineachán 1-3
Final:		
22 Aug	Cavan	An Cabhán 5-3 Aontroim 0-6

1927

22 May	Belfast	An Cabhán 7-7 Doire 4-3
22 May	Armagh	Ard Mhacha 0-8 Dún na nGall 1-1
22 May	Belfast	Aontroim 1-9 Tír Eoghain 0-11
22 May	Newry	Muineachán 2-5 An Dún 1-2
Semi-finals:		
19 June	Castleblayney	Muineachán 2-6 An Cabhán 1-6
26 June	Newry	Ard Mhacha 3-6 Aontroim 0-4
Final:		
31 July	Armagh	Muineachán 3-5 Ard Mhacha 2-5

1928

27 May	Dungannon	Tír Eoghain 7-3 Doire 2-3
27 May	Castleblayney	Muineachán 3-5 An Dún 1-3
10 June	Ballyshannon	Ard Mhacha 1-8 Dún na nGall 1-4
10 June	Enniskillen	Muineachán 6-3 Fear Manach 1-7
17 June	Belturbet	An Cabhán 1-5 Aontroim 0-2
Semi-finals:		
1 July	Carrickmacross	Ard Mhacha 0-4 Muineachán 0-1
8 July	Dungannon	An Cabhán 4-3 Tir Eoghain 0-3
Final:		
29 July	Cavan	An Cabhán 2-6 Ard Mhacha 1-4

1929

19 May	Newry	Ard Mhacha 5-4 An Dún 3-2
19 May	Enniskillen	Tír Eoghain 0-8 Fear Manach 0-2
26 May	Belfast	An Cabhán 1-11 Aontroim 0-2
2 June	Bundoran	Muineachán 2-8 Dún na nGall 0-1

Semi-finals:

16 June	Monaghan	Muineachán 3-7 Tír Eoghain 1-2
30 June	Belturbet	An Cabhán 4-10 Ard Mhacha 0-2

Final:

28 July	Cavan	Muineachán 1-4 An Cabhán 1-4
11 Aug	Carrickmacross (replay)	Muineachán 1-10 An Cabhán 0-7

1930

25 May	Dungannon	Ard Mhacha 2-3 Tír Eoghain 2-3
1 June	Enniskillen	Aontroim 3-3 Fear Manach 2-5 (objection – Aontroim eliminated)
8 June	Armagh (replay)	Ard Mhacha 1-8 Tír Eoghain 1-3
8 June	Newry	Muineachán 7-8 An Dún 1-6
22 June	Belturbet	An Cabhán 2-3 Fear Manach 1-0

Semi-finals:

29 June	Armagh	Muineachán 2-2 Ard Mhacha 0-5
6 July	Corrigan Park	An Cabhán 1-5 Aontroim 1-2

Final:

27 July	Carrickmacross	Muineachán 4-3 An Cabhán 1-5

1931

10 May	Letterkenny	Dún na nGall 2-4 Aontroim 0-2 (objection - Dún na nGall eliminated)
17 May	Dungannon	Muineachán 3-9 Tír Eoghain 1-3
24 May	Newry	Ard Mhacha 0-6 An Dún 0-4
14 June	Belturbet	An Cabhán 2-5 Fear Manach 1-2

Semi-finals:

21 June	Carrickmacross	Ard Mhacha 1-9 Muineachán 0-4
5 July	Corrigan Park	An Cabhán 4-9 Aontroim 2-3

Final:

2 Aug	Dundalk	An Cabhán 0-8 Ard Mhacha 2-1

1932

10 Apr	Ard Mhacha	Ard Mhacha 1-5 Tír Eoghain 1-4
17 Apr	Monaghan	Muineachán 1-7 Fear Manach 1-3
17 Apr	Corrigan Park	Aontroim 4-10 An Dún 0-1
24 Apr	Cavan	An Cabhán 8-7 Dún na nGall 1-6

Semi-finals:

8 May	Corrigan Park	Ard Mhacha 2-6 Aontroim 0-6
29 May	Belturbet	An Cabhán 8-8 Muineachán 2-6

Final:

19 June	Monaghan	An Cabhán 2-4 Ard Mhacha 0-2

1933

11 June	Coalisland	Tír Eoghain 0-3 Aontroim 0-3
18 June	Warrenpoint	Ard Mhacha 1-4 An Dún 1-3
25 June	Corrigan Park (replay)	Tír Eoghain 3-5 Aontroim 3-5
25 June	Belturbet	Fear Manach 2-3 Muineachán 0-3
9 July	Omagh (2nd replay)	Tír Eoghain 1-8 Aontroim 1-2

Semi-finals:

2 July	Cavan	An Cabhán 1-8 Ard Mhacha 0-2
16 July	Bundoran	Tír Eoghain 1-4 Fear Manach 1-3

Final:

6 Aug	Cavan	An Cabhán 6-13 Tír Eoghain 1-2

1934

29 Apr	Omagh	An Cabhán 2-5 Tír Eoghain 2-4
3 June	Newry	Muineachán 4-7 An Dún 2-6
3 June	Corrigan Park	Ard Mhacha 0-12 Aontroim 0-5
3 June	Carrickmacross	Fear Manach 2-5 Dún na nGall 1-3

Semi-finals:

1 July	Armagh	Ard Mhacha 1-6 Muineachán 1-3
15 July	Belturbet	An Cabhán 3-4 Fear Manach 1-3

Final:

29 July	Castleblayney	An Cabhán 3-8 Ard Mhacha 0-2

1935

9 June	Armagh	Ard Mhacha 2-4 An Dún 0-5
9 June	Bundoran	An Cabhán 1-11 Dún na nGall 1-9
1 6 June	Omagh	Fear Manach 0-5 Tír Eoghain 1-2
16 June	Castleblayney	Muineachán 3-8 Aontroim 2-2
30 June	Irvinestown (replay)	Fear Manach 1-11 Tír Eoghain 2-6

Semi-finals:

30 June	Cavan	An Cabhán 2-12 Muineachán 0-1
8 July	Enniskillen	Fear Manach 0-9 Ard Mhacha 1-6
14 July	Armagh (replay)	Fear Manach 3-4 Ard Mhacha 2-2

Final:

28 July	Belturbet	An Cabhán 2-6 Fear Manach 2-1

1936

14 June	Belfast	Ard Mhacha 0-11 Aontroim 2-1
14 June	Warrenpoint	An Dún 4-5 Tír Eoghain 2-3
21 June	Enniskillen	Dún na nGall 1-8 Fear Manach 0-7
28 June	Carrickmacross	Muineachán 3-5 An Dún 2-8
12 July	Newry (replay)	Muineachán 4-8 An Dún 0-4

Semi-finals:

19 July	Armagh	An Cabhán 1-8 Ard Mhacha 2-1
26 July	Carrickmacross	Muineachán 2-8 Dún na nGall 0-11

Final:

9 Aug	Castleblayney	An Cabhán 1-7 Muineachán 0-7

1937

6 June	Bundoran	Dún na nGall 3-8 Aontroim 0-6
6 June	Coalisland	Muineachán 4-12 Tír Eoghain 0-8
13 June	Enniskillen	An Cabhán 3-11 Fear Manach 2-6
13 June	Armagh	Ard Mhacha 4-14 An Dún 2-7

Semi-finals:

27 June	Cavan	An Cabhán 2-12 Dún na nGall 1-4
4 July	Castleblayney	Ard Mhacha 2-12 Muineachán 1-3

Final:

25 July	Castleblayney	An Cabhán 0-13 Ard Mhacha 0-3

1938

19 June	Corrigan Park	Ard Mhacha 2-5 Aontroim 1-4
19 June	Omagh	Muineachán 3-3 Tír Eoghain 0-6
3 July	Belturbet	An Cabhán 3-10 Fear Manach 1-4

Semi-finals:

10 July	Carndonagh	Muineachán 0-7 Dún na nGall 0-6
17 July	Armagh	Ard Mhacha 2-7 An Cabhán 1-4

Final:

31 July	Armagh	Muineachán 2-5 Ard Mhacha 2-2

1939

25 June	Omagh	An Cabhán 4-11 Tír Eoghain 1-2
25 June	Corrigan Park	An Dún 1-6 Aontroim 1-5

2 July	Magheragallon	Dún na nGall 0-6 An Dún 1-1
16 July	Castleblayney	Muineachán 1-6 Ard Mhacha 1-6
Semi-finals:		
23 July	Castleblayney	Ard Mhacha 1-6 Muineachán 0-2
23 July	Cavan	An Cabhán 5-12 Dún na nGall 0-4
Final:		
6 Aug	Castleblayney	An Cabhán 2-6 Ard Mhacha 2-4 (abandoned)
13 Aug	Croke Park (re-fixture)	An Cabhán 2-3 Ard Mhacha 1-4

1940

23 June	Corrigan Park	Aontroim 3-3 An Cabhán 0-12
23 June	Armagh	Dún na nGall 0-6 Ard Mhacha 0-5
30 June	Newcastle	An Dún 4-4 Tír Eoghain 2-5
7 July	Cavan (replay)	An Cabhán 6-13 Aontroim 0-4
Semi-finals:		
14 July	Bundoran	An Cabhán 0-12 Dún na nGall 2-3
14 July	Castleblayney	An Dún 2-3 Muineachán 2-3
21 July	Newcastle (replay)	An Dún 0-8 Muineachán 1-3
Final:		
28 July	Cavan	An Cabhán 4-10 An Dún 1-5

1941

15 June	Corrigan Park	An Dún 5-4 Aontroim 0-4
6 July	Coalisland	Tír Eoghain 3-13 Ard Mhacha 0-1
6 July	Cavan	An Cabhán 3-7 Muineachán 3-2
Semi-finals:		
13 July	Bundoran	An Cabhán 1-6 Dún na nGall 0-7
13 July	Newcastle	Tír Eoghain 1-10 An Dún 1-7
Final:		
3 Aug	Armagh	An Cabhán 3-9 Tír Eoghain 0-5

1942

31 May	Armagh	Ard Mhacha 3-4 Tír Eoghain 0-0
14 June	Newcastle	An Dún 4-4 Aontroim 3-7
14 June	Castleblayney	An Cabhán 1-4 Muineachán 0-6
21 June	Corrigan Park (replay)	An Dún 2-11 Aontroim 1-5
Semi-finals:		
28 June	Cavan	An Cabhán 7-10 Dún na nGall 4-6
5 July	Newcastle	An Dún 0-7 Ard Mhacha 0-6 (abandoned)
12 July	Newcastle (replay)	An Dún 1-12 Ard Mhacha 2-5
Final:		
19 July	Dundalk	An Cabhán 5-11 An Dún 1-3

1943

20 June	Omagh	Tír Eoghain 1-8 Dún na nGall 0-7
27 June	Armagh	Muineachán 3-8 Ard Mhacha 3-4
27 June	Corrigan Park	Aontroim 0-13 An Dún 1-8
Semi-finals:		
4 July	Enniskillen	An Cabhán 4-10 Tír Eoghain 1-3
11 July	Armagh	Muineachán 1-10 Aontroim 1-5
Final:		
1 Aug	Cavan	An Cabhán 2-3 Muineachán 0-5

1944

2 July	Monaghan	Muineachán 3-7 Ard Mhacha 3-3
2 July	Corrigan Park	An Dún 3-4 Tír Eoghain 0-4

2 July	Corrigan Park	An Cabhán 1-4 Aontroim 1-2
Semi-finals:		
9 July	Corrigan Park	Muineachán 1-5 An Dún 1-4
16 July	Omagh	An Cabhán 5-9 Dún na nGall 2-3
Final:		
30 July	Clones	An Cabhán 1-9 Muineachán 1-6

1945

17 June	Cavan	An Cabhán 2-11 Aontroim 3-3
10 June	Letterkenny	Dún na nGall 3-7 Doire 2-3
24 June	Enniskillen	Fear Manach 4-13 Muineachán 0-5
24 June	Armagh	Ard Mhacha 3-13 Tír Eoghain 0-2
1 July	Armagh	An Cabhán 0-14 An Dún 1-3
Semi-finals:		
8 July	Clones	Fear Manach 2-4 Ard Mhacha 1-6
15 July	Clones	An Cabhán 6-12 Dún na nGall 2-4
Final:		
29 July	Clones	An Cabhán 4-10 Fear Manach 1-4

1946

9 June	Magherafelt	Doire 4-6 Fear Manach 0-4
23 June	Omagh	An Cabhán 8-13 Tír Eoghain 3-2
23 June	Clones	Dún na nGall 4-5 Muineachán 1-9
23 June	Newcastle	Ard Mhacha 1-10 An Dún 0-4
30 June	Corrigan Park	Aontroim 1-11 Doire 0-10
Semi-finals:		
7 July	Omagh	An Cabhán 5-8 Dún na nGall 0-3
14 July	Armagh	Aontroim 1-12 Ard Mhacha 0-6
Final:		
28 July	Clones	Aontroim 2-8 An Cabhán 1-7

1947

8 June	Irvinestown	Tír Eoghain 0-7 Fear Manach 1-4
15 June	An Cabhán	An Cabhán 0-9 Muineachán 1-6
15 June	Coalisland (replay)	Tír Eoghain 3-5 Fear Manach 2-6
15 June	Lurgan	An Dún 2-11 Doire 2-5
22 June	Clones (replay)	An Cabhán 1-11 Muineachán 1-9
22 June	Armagh	Tír Eoghain 1-6 Ard Mhacha 1-6
29 June	Dungannon (replay)	Tír Eoghain 2-5 Ard Mhacha 1-4
Semi-finals:		
6 July	Lurgan	Aontroim 3-13 An Dún 1-7
6 July	Dungannon	An Cabhán 4-5 Tír Eoghain 0-2
Final:		
20 July	Clones	An Cabhán 3-4 Aontroim 1-6

1948

6 June	Clones	Muineachán 2-9 Doire 2-6
6 June	Corrigan Park	Aontroim 1-3 Dún na nGall 0-1 (unfinished)
13 June	Dungannon	Tír Eoghain 5-9 Fear Manach 0-4
13 June	Newcastle	An Dún 4-10 Ard Mhacha 2-3
20 June	Lurgan	An Cabhán 2-9 An Dún 2-4
20 June	Corrigan Park (replay)	Aontroim 4-5 Dún na nGall 1-4
Semi-finals:		
4 July	Lurgan	Aontroim 0-12 Tír Eoghain 1-3
11 July	Cavan	An Cabhán 1-9 Muineachán 0-7
Final:		
25 July	Clones	An Cabhán 2-12 Aontroim 2-4

1949

4 June	Magherafelt	Aontroim 5-9 Doire 1-6
4 June	Lurgan	Ard Mhacha 3-6 Muineachán 1-8
12 June	Cavan	An Cabhán 7-10 Tír Eoghain 1-7
12 June	Letterkenny	Dún na nGall 2-6 An Dún 0-8
Semi-finals:		
26 June	Corrigan Park	An Cabhán 3-7 Aontroim 2-6
3 July	Dungannon	Ard Mhacha 0-14 Dún na nGall 1-4
Final:		
31 July	Clones	An Cabhán 1-7 Ard Mhacha 1-6

1950

4 June	Corrigan Park	Aontroim 5-10 Doire 0-5
11 June	Coalisland	An Cabhán 8-7 Tír Eoghain 0-3
18 June	Newcastle	An Dún 2-8 Dún na nGall 3-5
25 June	Clones	Ard Mhacha 0-14 Muineachán 1-5
25 June	Letterkenny (replay)	An Dún 4-3 Dún na nGall 1-7
Semi-finals:		
2 July	Clones	An Cabhán 1-12 Aontroim 2-6
9 July	Dungannon	Ard Mhacha 1-8 An Dún 1-7
Final:		
23 July	Clones	Ard Mhacha 1-11 An Cabhán 1-7

1951

3 June	Letterkenny	Aontroim 2-7 Dún na nGall 2-7
17 June	Armagh	Ard Mhacha 1-13 Tír Eoghain 2-3
17 June	Corrigan Park (replay)	Aontroim 1-6 Dún na nGall 1-5
17 June	Kingscourt	An Cabhán 2-9 An Dún 0-7
24 June	Magherafelt	Doire 1-3 Muineachán 0-5
Semi-finals:		
1 July	Coalisland	Aontroim 1-8 Ard Mhacha 0-5
8 July	Lurgan	An Cabhán 1-6 Doire 1-4
Final:		
29 July	Clones	Aontroim 1-7 An Cabhán 2-3

1952

15 June	Newcastle	An Cabhán 3-10 An Dún 1-3
15 June	Dungannon	Ard Mhacha 1-8 Tír Eoghain 1-6
22 June	Clones	Muineachán 2-12 Doire 0-12
29 June	Corrigan Park	Aontroim 1-7 Dún na nGall 2-3
Semi-finals:		
6 July	Dungannon	Muineachán 1-8 Ard Mhacha 1-5
13 July	Clones	An Cabhán 3-6 Aontroim 2-6
Final:		
27 July	Cavan	An Cabhán 1-8 Muineachán 0-8

1953

30 May	Magherafelt	Doire 1-11 An Dún 2-5
14 June	Ballybofey	Tír Eoghain 0-12 Dún na nGall 0-6
21 June	Lurgan	Ard Mhacha 1-8 Aontroim 1-4
21 June	Cavan	An Cabhán 2-7 Muineachán 0-2
Semi-finals:		
5 July	Clones	An Cabhán 2-10 Tír Eoghain 2-4
12 July	Casement Park	Ard Mhacha 4-11 Doire 1-5
Final:		
26 July	Casement Park	Ard Mhacha 1-6 An Cabhán 0-5

1954

13 June	Dungannon	Tír Eoghain 1-7 Dún na nGall 1-5
13 June	Newcastle	Doire 4-11 An Dún 3-4
10 July	Casement Park	Ard Mhacha 1-8 Aontroim 1-6
27 June	Clones	An Cabhán 3-8 Muineachán 2-5
Semi-finals:		
4 July	Casement Park	Ard Mhacha 1-12 Doire 1-6
11 July	Castleblayney	An Cabhán 3-10 Tír Eoghain 2-10
Final:		
25 July	Clones	An Cabhán 2-10 Ard Mhacha 2-5

1955

5 June	Magherafelt	Doire 0-13 Tír Eoghain 1-5
5 June	Bundoran	Dún na nGall 3-8 Muineachán 2-8
12 June	Lurgan	Ard Mhacha 1-8 An Dún 0-5
19 June	Cavan	An Cabhán 1-10 Aontroim 2-1
Semi-finals:		
3 July	Casement Park	Doire 3-4 Ard Mhacha 0-2
10 July	Clones	An Cabhán 2-5 Dún na nGall 1-6
Final:		
31 July	Clones	An Cabhán 0-11 Doire 0-8

1956

3 June	Dungannon	Tír Eoghain 3-7 Doire 2-4
10 June	Carrickmacross	Muineachán 0-14 Dún na nGall 1-5
17 June	Casement Park	An Cabhán 3-15 Aontroim 2-4
24 June	Newry	Ard Mhacha 2-5 An Dún 0-6
Semi-finals:		
8 July	Lurgan	Tír Eoghain 2-9 Muineachán 0-7
15 July	Castleblayney	An Cabhán 1-9 Ard Mhacha 1-5
Final:		
29 July	Clones	Tír Eoghain 3-5 An Cabhán 0-4

1957

9 June	Ballinascreen	Doire 4-14 Aontroim 0-8
16 June	Ballyshannon	Dún na nGall 3-2 An Dún 0-3
16 June	Cavan	An Cabhán 1-12 Muineachán 1-5
30 June	Lurgan	Tír Eoghain 2-9 Ard Mhacha 3-5
Semi-finals:		
7 July	Dungannon	Doire 1-10 An Cabhán 1-9
14 July	Cavan	Tír Eoghain 3-5 Dún na nGall 2-3
Final:		
28 July	Clones	Tír Eoghain 1-9 Doire 0-10

1958

1 June	Casement Park	Doire 0-8 Aontroim 0-5
15 June	Clones	An Cabhán 0-7 Muineachán 0-7
15 June	Newry	An Dún 3-11 Dún na nGall 3-5
22 June	Dungannon	Tír Eoghain 1-9 Ard Mhacha 0-10
29 June	Cavan (replay)	An Cabhán 1-5 Muineachán 1-5
6 July	Casement Pk (2nd replay)	An Cabhán 0-14 Muineachán 1-6
Semi-finals:		
6 July	Lurgan	An Dún 1-9 Tír Eoghain 0-2
13 July	Clones	Doire 4-7 An Cabhán 3-6
Final:		
27 July	Clones	Doire 1-11 An Dún 2-4

1959

31 May	Lurgan	Ard Mhacha 1-6 Doire 0-5
7 June	Ballybofey	An Cabhán 2-9 Dún na nGall 0-4
14 June	Newcastle	An Dún 4-9 Aontroim 1-3
21 June	Castleblayney	Tír Eoghain 1-9 Muineachán 0-7
5 July	Castleblayney	An Cabhán 0-13 Ard Mhacha 2-7

Semi-finals:

12 July	Casement Park	An Dún 1-6 Tír Eoghain 1-6
19 July	Clones (replay)	An Cabhán 1-9 Ard Mhacha 1-7
26 July	Casement Park (replay)	An Dún 1-12 Tír Eoghain 0-4

Final:

9 Aug	Clones	An Dún 2-16 An Cabhán 0-7

1960

5 June	Cavan	An Cabhán 1-10 Dún na nGall 1-0
5 June	Magherafelt	Doire 3-10 Ard Mhacha 1-9
12 June	Casement Park	An Dún 0-14 Aontroim 1-4
19 June	Irvinestown	An Cabhán 3-4 Fear Manach 2-7
26 June	Dungannon	Muineachán 3-11 Tír Eoghain 3-6
26 June	Cavan (replay)	An Cabhán 3-9 Fear Manach 2-2

Semi-finals:

10 July	Dungannon	An Dún 2-11 Muineachán 0-7
17 July	Casement Park	An Cabhán 3-6 Doire 0-5

Final:

31 July	Clones	An Dún 3-7 An Cabhán 1-8

1961

28 May	Ballybofey	Doire 2-10 Dún na nGall 0-4
4 June	Lurgan	Ard Mhacha 2-7 An Cabhán 0-8
4 June	Castleblayney	Muineachán 1-10 Aontroim 0-6
11 June	Newry	An Dún 0-12 Fear Manach 0-7
11 June	Ballinascreen	Doire 1-9 Tír Eoghain 0-10

Semi-finals:

25 June	Dungannon	Ard Mhacha 5-9 Muineachán 0-5
2 July	Belfast	An Dún 2-12 Doire 1-10

Final:

23 July	Belfast	An Dún 2-10 Ard Mhacha 1-10

1962

3 June	Magherafelt	Doire 2-10 Dún na nGall 2-7
10 June	Casement Park	Aontroim 2-7 Muineachán 0-2
21 June	Dungannon	Tír Eoghain 1-9 Doire 2-2
24 June	Cavan	An Cabhán 3-8 Ard Mhacha 2-2
1 July	Irvinestown	An Dún 4-10 Fear Manach 1-8

Semi-finals:

8 July	Casement	An Cabhán 1-6 Aontroim 0-5
15 July	Casement Park	An Dún 1-12 Tír Eoghain 1-6

Final:

29 July	Belfast	An Cabhán 3-6 An Dún 0-5

1963

2 June	Belfast	Aontroim 2-9 Tír Eoghain 0-3
9 June	Newry	An Dún 6-11 Muineachán 1-3
16 June	Lurgan	Ard Mhacha 1-8 Aontroim 2-3
16 June	Ballybofey	Dún na nGall 2-12 Fear Manach 1-6
23 June	Ballinascreen	An Cabhán 3-9 Doire 2-8

Semi-finals:

7 July	Belfast	An Dún 0-9 Ard Mhacha 0-5
14 July	Clones	Dún na nGall 4-5 An Cabhán 0-6

Final:

28 July	Cavan	An Dún 2-11 Dún na nGall 1-4

1964

31 May	Dungannon	Aontroim 1-9 Tír Eoghain 0-8
7 June	Irvinestown	Dún na nGall 1-10 Fear Manach 0-7

14 June	Cavan	An Cabhán 3-9 Doire 2-3
14 June	Belfast	Aontroim 2-6 Ard Mhacha 1-8
21 June	Ballybay	An Dún 2-9 Muineachán 1-6

Semi-finals:

28 June	Irvinestown	An Cabhán 1-9 Dún na nGall 0-7
5 July	Clones	An Dún 2-8 Aontroim 1-9

Final:

19 July	Belfast	An Cabhán 2-10 An Dún 1-10

1965

30 May	Ballinascreen	Aontroim 2-9 Doire 1-6
6 June	Irvinestown	Muineachán 2-12 Fear Manach 1-5
13 June	Newry	An Dún 3-13 Tír Eoghain 1-6
20 June	Ballybofey	An Cabhán 1-8 Dún na nGall 1-8
20 June	Lurgan	Ard Mhacha 3-7 Muineachán 1-9
4 July	Cavan (replay)	An Cabhán 0-14 Dún na nGall 2-8
11 July	Cavan (replay)	An Cabhán 0-9 Dún na nGall 0-8

Semi-finals:

4 July	Newry	An Dún 0-10 Aontroim 1-5
18 July	Clones	An Cabhán 1-10 Ard Mhacha 0-4

Final:

1 Aug	Clones	An Dún 3-5 An Cabhán 1-8

1966

5 June	Clones	Fear Manach 3-8 Muineachán 0-12
5 June	Belfast	Aontroim 2-7 Doire 0-6
12 June	Dungannon	An Dún 2-9 Tír Eoghain 0-4
19 June	Cavan	Dún na nGall 5-6 An Cabhán 1-11
26 June	Irvinestown	Fear Manach 3-8 Ard Mhacha 0-8

Semi-finals:

10 July	Belfast	An Dún 0-9 Aontroim 0-5
17 July	Dungannon	Dún na nGall 4-17 Fear Manach 1-8

Final:

31 July	Belfast	An Dún 1-7 Dún na nGall 0-8

1967

4 June	Armagh	Dún na nGall 2-13 Ard Mhacha 1-8
11 June	Newry	An Dún 3-9 Doire 1-10
11 June	Dungannon	Tír Eoghain 0-13 Fear Manach 3-2
18 June	Belfast	An Cabhán 2-12 Aontroim 2-8
25 June	Dungannon	Tír Eoghain 1-13 Muineachán 1-7

Semi-finals:

2 July	Clones	An Dún 2-8 Dún na nGall 2-5
9 July	Irvinestown	An Cabhán 1-13 Tír Eoghain 3-3

Final:

23 July	Clones	An Cabhán 2-12 An Dún 0-8

1968

2 June	Irvinestown	Fear Manach 2-8 Tír Eoghain 0-8
9 June	Ballinascreen	An Dún 1-8 Doire 1-6
16 June	Cavan	An Cabhán 5-9 Aontroim 1-12
16 June	Ballybofey	Dún na nGall 2-10 Ard Mhacha 1-3
23 June	Irvinestown	Muineachán 0-12 Fear Manach 1-9
30 June	Irvinestown (replay)	Muineachán 2-12 Fear Manach 2-5

Semi-finals:

30 June	Cavan	An Dún 2-14 Dún na nGall 0-8
7 July	Clones	An Cabhán 1-11 Muineachán 0-5

Final:

28 July	Belfast	An Dún 0-16 An Cabhán 1-8

1969

1 June	Dungannon	Doire 2-8 Tír Eoghain 0-8
8 June	Belfast	Aontroim 2-10 Dún na nGall 0-14
15 June	Armagh	Muineachán 1-9 Ard Mhacha 0-8
15 June	Irvinestown	An Cabhán 1-9 Fear Manach 2-4
22 June	Newry	An Dún 0-8 Ard Mhacha 0-4
Semi-finals:		
29 June	Clones	An Cabhán 2-3 Doire 0-9
6 July	Armagh	An Dún 2-15 Muineachán 1-7
13 July	Clones (replay)	An Cabhán 1-8 Doire 0-6
Final:		
27 July	Belfast	An Cabhán 2-13 An Dún 2-6

1970

7 June	Ballybofey	Aontroim 3-8 Dún na nGall 2-6
7 June	Cavan	An Cabhán 3-13 Fear Manach 1-3
7 June	Ballinascreen	Doire 3-12 Tír Eoghain 0-7
14 June	Castleblayney	Muineachán 3-7 Ard Mhacha 1-7
21 June	Casement Park	Aontroim 2-9 An Dún 1-6
Semi-finals:		
28 June	Irvinestown	Doire 1-8 An Cabhán 1-5
5 July	Newry	Aontroim 2-10 Muineachán 1-8
Final:		
26 July	Clones	Doire 2-13 Aontroim 1-12

1971

6 June	Ballinascreen	Doire 4-10 Fear Manach 1-10
6 June	Lurgan	Ard Mhacha 4-9 Tír Eoghain 2-10
13 June	Casement Park	Doire 0-8 Aontroim 0-4
13 June	Ballybay	An Cabhán 2-10 Muineachán 1-12
20 June	Newry	An Dún 3-14 Doire 3-6
Semi-finals:		
4 July	Casement Park	Doire 3-12 Ard Mhacha 1-10
11 July	Castleblayney	An Dún 0-11 An Cabhán 2-3
Final:		
25 July	Casement Park	An Dún 4-15 Doire 4-11

1972

4 June	Dungannon	Tír Eoghain 0-13 Ard Mhacha 1-7
4 June	Irvinestown	Doire 5-7 Fear Manach 0-7
11 June	Cavan	An Cabhán 3-9 Muineachán 0-6
18 June	Ballybofey	Dún na nGall 1-8 An Dún 0-8
25 June	Ballinascreen	Doire 2-9 Aontroim 2-5
2 July	Irvinestown	Dún na nGall 0-12 An Cabhán 2-6
Semi-finals:		
9 July	Dungannon	Tír Eoghain 1-8 Doire 0-9
16 July	Clones (replay)	Dún na nGall 2-11 An Cabhán 1-9
Final:		
30 July	Clones	Dún na nGall 2-13 Tír Eoghain 1-11

1973

3 June	Castleblayney	Doire 1-7 Muineachán 0-5
10 June	Newry	An Dún 2-10 Ard Mhacha 2-9
17 June	Irvinestown	Fear Manach 3-9 Aontroim 4-4
24 June	Ballybofey	Tír Eoghain 0-12 Dún na nGall 1-7
24 June	Newry	An Dún 1-7 An Cabhán 0-8
Semi-finals:		
8 July	Clones	Tír Eoghain 1-15 Fear Manach 0-11
15 July	Lurgan	An Dún 1-12 Doire 0-9
Final:		
29 July	Clones	Tír Eoghain 3-13 An Dún 1-11

1974

2 June	Casement Park	Aontroim 2-7 Fear Manach 1-8
9 June	Ballinascreen	Doire 3-6 Muineachán 0-8
9 June	Lurgan	An Dún 1-10 Ard Mhacha 0-6
16 June	Omagh	Dún na nGall 1-9 Tír Eoghain 0-8
23 June	Cavan	An Dún 2-8 An Cabhán 0-12
Semi-finals:		
7 July	Clones	Dún na nGall 5-9 Aontroim 1-7
14 July	Lurgan	An Dún 1-12 Doire 0-7
Final:		
28 July	Clones	Dún na nGall 1-14 An Dún 2-11
4 Aug	Clones (replay)	Dún na nGall 3-9 An Dún 1-12

1975

1 June	Castleblayney	Muineachán 0-13 Tír Eoghain 1-5
1 June	Irvinestown	Ard Mhacha 4-6 Fear Manach 0-10
8 June	Ballybofey	An Cabhán 0-15 Dún na nGall 0-13
15 June	Newcastle	An Dún 3-12 Aontroim 0-7
22 June	Omagh	Doire 2-15 Ard Mhacha 1-7
Semi-finals:		
29 June	Castleblayney	An Dún 1-13 An Cabhán 1-10
6 July	Dungannon	Doire 1-11 Muineachán 1-11
13 July	Dungannon (replay)	Doire 0-14 Muineachán 1-6
Final:		
27 July	Clones	Doire 1-16 An Dún 2-6

1976

23 May	Armagh	Ard Mhacha 1-13 Fear Manach 1-12
30 May	Cavan	An Cabhán 1-9 Dún na nGall 0-8
6 June	Casement Park	An Dún 0-14 Aontroim 2-6
6 June	Dungannon	Tír Eoghain 2-10 Muineachán 1-10
13 June	Omagh	Doire 1-19 Ard Mhacha 2-1
Semi-finals:		
20 June	Castleblayney	An Cabhán 1-18 An Dún 0-10
27 June	Clones	Doire 0-12 Tír Eoghain 0-8
Final:		
18 July	Clones	Doire 1-8 An Cabhán 1-8
25 July	Clones (replay)	Doire 0-22 An Cabhán 1-16 (a.e.t.)

1977

29 May	Ballybofey	Doire 1-12 Dún na nGall 0-12
29 May	Castleblayney	Muineachán 0-10 Aontroim 0-6
5 June	Armagh	Ard Mhacha 2-14 An Cabhán 1-12
12 June	Newry	An Dún 3-9 Fear Manach 0-7
19 June	Lurgan	Doire 3-10 Tír Eoghain 1-11
Semi-finals:		
26 June	Dungannon	Ard Mhacha 2-12 Muineachán 3-5
3 July	Clones	Doire 0-10 An Dún 0-8
Final:		
24 July	Clones	Ard Mhacha 3-10 Doire 1-5

1978

21 May	Casement Park	Aontroim 4-6 Muineachán 2-4
28 May	Ballinascreen	Doire 3-12 Dún na nGall 0-7
11 June	Cavan	An Cabhán 0-16 Ard Mhacha 0-9
11 June	Irvinestown	An Dún 0-14 Fear Manach 2-7
18 June	Lurgan	Doire 3-11 Tír Eoghain 0-9
Semi-finals:		
2 July	Casement Park	An Dún 1-14 Doire 2-8
9 July	Castleblayney	An Cabhán 2-13 Aontroim 1-10

Final:
23 July   Clones   An Dún 2-19 An Cabhán 2-12

1979
20 May   Dungannon   Tír Eoghain 2-9 Aontroim 2-5
27 May   Castleblayney   Muineachán 0-14 An Dún 0-10
3 June   Lurgan   Ard Mhacha 5-3 Fear Manach 1-7
10 June   Cavan   Doire 2-12 An Cabhán 1-13
17 June   Ballinascreen   Dún na nGall 1-11 Tír Eoghain 1-9
Semi-finals:
24 June   Cavan   Muineachán 2-10 Ard Mhacha 2-8
1 July   Omagh   Dún na nGall 2-9 Doire 0-14
Final:
22 July   Clones   Muineachán 1-15 Dún na nGall 0-11

1980
18 May   Casement Park   Tír Eoghain 1-8 Aontroim 1-7
25 May   Newry   Muineachán 0-13 An Dún 1-4
1 June   Irvinestown   Ard Mhacha 3-8 Fear Manach 1-4
8 June   Ballinascreen   An Cabhán 2-9 Doire 2-7
15 June   Irvinestown   Tír Eoghain 1-17 Dún na nGall 0-9
Semi-finals:
22 June   Cavan   Ard Mhacha 0-12 Muineachán 0-5
29 June   Clones   Tír Eoghain 2-12 An Cabhán 1-9
Final
20 July   Clones   Ard Mhacha 4-10 Tír Eoghain 4-7

1981
17 May   Castleblayney   Muineachán 2-9 Tír Eoghain 0-6
24 May   Casement Park   Aontroim 2-13 An Cabhán 2-12
31 May   Armagh   Ard Mhacha 2-15 Dún na nGall 0-13
7 June   Ballinascreen   Doire 0-12 Fear Manach 0-10
14 June   Newry   An Dún 0-10 Muineachán 0-10
28 June   Castleblayney
             (replay)   An Dún 3-4 Muineachán 1-9
Semi-finals:
21 June   Castleblayney   Ard Mhacha 4-7 Aontroim 1-3
5 July   Clones   An Dún 0-12 Doire 0-9
Final:
19 July   Clones   An Dún 3-12 Ard Mhacha 1-10

1982
16 May   Dungannon   Tír Eoghain 1-9 Muineachán 0-9
23 May   Cavan   Aontroim 1-7 An Cabhán 0-8
30 May   Ballybofey   Ard Mhacha 1-11 Dún na nGall 0-13
6 June   Irvinestown   Fear Manach 1-9 Doire 1-8
13 June   Newry   Tír Eoghain 1-12 An Dún 0-11
Semi-finals:
20 June   Clones   Ard Mhacha 1-20 Aontroim 1-6
27 June   Cavan   Fear Manach 1-8 Tír Eoghain 0-10
Final:
18 July   Clones   Ard Mhacha 0-10 Fear Manach 1-4

1983
22 May   Ballinascreen   An Cabhán 1-12 Doire 0-11
29 May   Irvinestown   Fear Manach 0-10 An Dún 0-8
5 June   Castleblayney   Muineachán 2-18 Aontroim 0-4
13 June   Ballybofey   Dún na nGall 1-10 Ard Mhacha 0-7
20 June   Cavan   An Cabhán 0-11 Tír Eoghain 0-10

Semi-finals:
28 June   Irvinestown   Dún na nGall 1-14 Muineachán 1-9
3 July   Clones   An Cabhán 2-12 Fear Manach 1-7
Final:
24 July   Clones   Dún na nGall 1-14 An Cabhán 1-11

1984
20 May   Newry   An Dún 3-6 Fear Manach 0-8
27 May   Casement Park   Muineachán 2-17 Aontroim 1-6
27 May   Cavan   Doire 1-13 An Cabhán 0-14
3 June   Armagh   Ard Mhacha 1-10 Dún na nGall 0-12
10 June   Ballinascreen   Tír Eoghain 1-13 Doire 3-4
Semi-finals:
17 June   Cavan   Ard Mhacha 2-8 Muineachán 0-9
24 June   Casement Park   Tír Eoghain 0-10 An Dún 0-5
Final:
15 July   Clones   Tír Eoghain 0-15 Ard Mhacha 1-7

1985
19 May   Ballybofey   Dún na nGall 2-12 An Dún 2-8
26 May   Cavan   An Cabhán 0-9 Aontroim 0-5
2 June   Ballinascreen   Doire 1-9 Tír Eoghain 1-8
9 June   Armagh   Ard Mhacha 2-13 Fear Manach 0-5
16 June   Castleblayney   Muineachán 1-14 Dún na nGall 0-7
Semi-finals:
23 June   Armagh   Doire 0-11 An Cabhán 0-7
23 June   Cavan   Muineachán 0-10 Ard Mhacha 0-10
7 July   Cavan
             (replay)   Muineachán 1-11 Ard Mhacha 2-7
Final:
21 July   Clones   Muineachán 2-9 Doire 0-8

1986
18 May   Newcastle   An Dún 2-8 Dún na nGall 1-10
25 May   Casement Park   An Cabhán 1-8 Aontroim 0-7
1 June   Omagh   Tír Eoghain 2-6 Doire 1-7
8 June   Irvinestown   Ard Mhacha 1-11 Fear Manach 0-7
15 June   Castleblayney   An Dún 1-10 Muineachán 0-13
22 June   Newcastle
             (replay)   An Dún 2-11 Muineachán 0-11
Semi-finals:
22 June   Irvinestown   Tír Eoghain 2-16 An Cabhán 1-12
29 June   Castleblayney   An Dún 3-7 Ard Mhacha 0-12
Final:
20 July   Clones   Tír Eoghain 1-11 An Dún 0-10

1987
17 May   Armagh   Ard Mhacha 2-9 Fear Manach 0-9
24 May   Cavan   An Cabhán 0-12 Muineachán 0-10
31 May   Newry   Doire 1-12 An Dún 2-7
7 June   Casement Park   Tír Eoghain 0-9 Aontroim 0-9
14 June   Omagh
             (replay)   Tír Eoghain 2-6 Aontroim 2-5
14 June   Ballybofey   Ard Mhacha 1-8 Dún na nGall 0-6
Semi-finals:
21 June   Omagh   Doire 2-7 An Cabhán 1-10
28 June   Irvinestown   Ard Mhacha 5-9 Tír Eoghain 1-9
5 July   Omagh (replay) Doire 2-11 An Cabhán 2-8
Final:
19 July   Clones   Doire 0-11 Ard Mhacha 0-9

1988

15 May	Irvinestown	Ard Mhacha 2-12 Fear Manach 1-13
22 May	Clones	Muineachán 0-16 An Cabhán 0-14
29 May	Ballinascreen	An Dún 1-11 Doire 0-7
5 June	Omagh	Tír Eoghain 3-13 Aontroim 2-4
12 June	Armagh	Ard Mhacha 2-10 Dún na nGall 0-8

Semi-finals:

19 June	Cavan	Muineachán 1-11 An Dún 0-9
26 June	Irvinestown	Tír Eoghain 0-15 Ard Mhacha 1-8

Final:

17 July	Clones	Muineachán 1-10 Tír Eoghain 0-11

1989

14 May	Casement Park	Muineachán 0-8 Aontroim 0-5
21 May	Cavan	Dún na nGall 3-12 An Cabhán 0-14
28 May	Irvinestown	Doire 4-15 Fear Manach 1-7
4 June	Omagh	Tír Eoghain 1-11 Ard Mhacha 2-7
11 June	Castleblayney	An Dún 1-14 Muineachán 0-9

Semi-finals:

18 June	Clones	Dún na nGall 2-8 Doire 1-9
25 June	Castleblayney	Tír Eoghain 1-12 An Dún 1-7

Final:

16 July	Clones	Tír Eoghain 0-11 Dún na nGall 0-11
23 July	Clones (replay)	Tír Eoghain 2-13 Dún na nGall 0-7

1990

13 May	Castleblayney	Muineachán 3-17 Aontroim 0-8
20 May	Ballybofey	Dún na nGall 0-13 An Cabhán 0-9
27 May	Derry	Doire 4-14 Fear Manach 1-7
3 June	Ard Mhacha	Ard Mhacha 0-12 Tír Eoghain 0-11
10 June	Newry	An Dún 3-11 Muineachán 1-12

Semi-finals:

17 June	Clones	Dún na nGall 1-15 Doire 0-8
24 June	Casement Park	Ard Mhacha 1-13 An Dún 2-10
1 July	Casement Park (replay)	Ard Mhacha 2-7 An Dún 0-12

Final:

15 July	Clones	Dún na nGall 0-15 Ard Mhacha 0-14

1991

19 May	Omagh	Doire 1-9 Tír Eoghain 1-8
26 May	Casement Park	Fear Manach 3-12 Aontroim 1-8
2 June	Ballybofey	Dún na nGall 2-14 An Cabhán 0-12
9 June	Newry	An Dún 1-7 Ard Mhacha 0-8
16 June	Derry	Doire 0-13 Muineachán 0-8

Semi-finals:

23 June	Omagh	Dún na nGall 1-18 Fear Manach 0-13
30 June	Armagh	An Dún 0-13 Doire 1-10
14 July	Armagh (replay)	An Dún 0-14 Doire 0-9

Final:

28 July	Clones	An Dún 1-15 Dún na nGall 0-10

1992

17 May	Derry	Doire 1-10 Tír Eoghain 1-7
24 May	Cavan	Dún na nGall 1-15 An Cabhán 1-15
31 May	Ballybofey (replay)	Dún na nGall 0-20 An Cabhán 1-6
31 May	Irvinestown	Fear Manach 1-9 Aontroim 1-8
7 June	Armagh	An Dún 1-12 Ard Mhacha 0-9
14 June	Castleblayney	Doire 1-14 Muineachán 3-8
21 June	Derry (replay)	Doire 2-9 Muineachán 0-7

Semi-finals:

21 June	Omagh	Dún na nGall 2-17 Fear Manach 0-7
28 June	Casement Park	Doire 0-15 An Dún 0-12

Final:

19 July	Clones	Dún na nGall 0-14 Doire 1-9

1993

16 May	Irvinestown	Ard Mhacha 1-9 Fear Manach 1-9
23 May	Armagh (replay)	Ard Mhacha 4-8 Fear Manach 1-16
23 May	Castleblayney	Muineachán 2-9 An Cabhán 0-15
30 May	Cavan (replay)	Muineachán 3-10 An Cabhán 2-8
30 May	Newry	Doire 3-11 An Dún 0-9
6 June	Ballybofey	Dún na nGall 0-12 Aontroim 0-9
13 June	Armagh	Ard Mhacha 0-13 Tír Eoghain 1-10
20 June	Omagh (replay)	Ard Mhacha 2-8 Tír Eoghain 0-12

Semi-finals:

20 June	Casement Park	Doire 0-19 Muineachán 0-11
27 June	Cavan	Dún na nGall 0-15 Ard Mhacha 1-12
4 July	Cavan (replay)	Dún na nGall 2-16 Ard Mhacha 1-7

Final:

18 July	Clones	Doire 0-8 Dún na nGall 0-6

1994

15 May	Armagh	Ard Mhacha 1-6 Fear Manach 0-6
22 May	Cavan	Muineachán 3-10 An Cabhán 1-12
29 May	Derry	An Dún 1-14 Doire 1-12
5 June	Casement Park	Dún na nGall 1-12 Aontroim 1-9
12 June	Omagh	Tír Eoghain 3-10 Ard Mhacha 1-10

Semi-finals:

19 June	Armagh	An Dún 0-14 Muineachán 0-8
26 June	Cavan	Tír Eoghain 1-15 Dún na nGall 0-10

Final:

17 July	Clones	An Dún 1-17 Tír Eoghain 1-11

1995

21 May	Clones	Dún na nGall 1-12 An Dún 0-9
28 May	Armagh	Doire 1-17 Ard Mhacha 0-10
4 June	Irvinestown	Tír Eoghain 1-15 Fear Manach 1-11
11 June	Cavan	An Cabhán 2-11 Aontroim 0-8
18 June	Ballybofey	Muineachán 1-14 Dún na nGall 0-8

Semi-finals:

25 June	Clones	Tír Eoghain 0-11 Doire 0-10
2 July	Clones	An Cabhán 1-9 Muineachán 0-10

Final:

23 July	Clones	Tír Eoghain 2-13 An Cabhán 0-10

1996

26 May	Clones	An Dún 1-9 Dún na nGall 0-11
2 June	Derry	Doire 1-13 Ard Mhacha 1-6
9 June	Omagh	Tír Eoghain 1-18 Fear Manach 0-9
16 June	Casement Park	An Cabhán 1-15 Aontroim 1-11
23 June	Clones	An Dún 0-14 Muineachán 0-9

Semi-finals:

30 June	Clones	Tír Eoghain 1-13 Doire 1-8
7 July	Clones	An Dún 1-13 An Cabhán 0-13

Final:

28 July	Clones	Tír Eoghain 1-9 An Dún 0-9

1997

18 May	Clones	Tír Eoghain 0-15 An Dún 2-9
25 May	Clones (replay)	Tír Eoghain 3-8 An Dún 1-11
25 May	Ballybofey	Dún na nGall 2-12 Aontroim 1-13
1 June	Clones	Doire 1-11 Muineachán 2-8
8 June	Derry (replay)	Doire 2-15 Muineachán 0-10
8 June	Clones	An Cabhán 1-12 Fear Manach 1-12
15 June	Clones (replay)	An Cabhán 0-14 Fear Manach 0-11
15 June	Omagh	Tír Eoghain 1-12 Ard Mhacha 0-12

Semi-finals:

22 June	Clones	An Cabhán 2-16 Dún na nGall 2-10
29 June	Clones	Doire 2-15 Tír Eoghain 2-3

Final:

20 July	Clones	An Cabhán 1-14 Doire 0-16

1998

17 May	Omagh	An Dún 0-15 Tír Eoghain 2-7
24 May	Casement Park	Dún na nGall 1-11 Aontroim 0-11
31 May	Derry	Doire 3-13 Muineachán 0-11
7 June	Cavan	An Cabhán 0-13 Fear Manach 0-11
14 June	Clones	Ard Mhacha 0-16 An Dún 0-11

Semi-finals:

21 June	Clones	Dún na nGall 0-15 An Cabhán 0-13
28 June	Clones	Doire 2-13 Ard Mhacha 0-12

Final:

19 July	Clones	Doire 1-7 Dún na nGall 0-8

1999

30 May	Clones	Fear Manach 2-12 Muineachán 1-10
6 June	Ballybofey	Ard Mhacha 1-12 Dún na nGall 2-9
13 June	Clones (replay)	Ard Mhacha 2-11 Dún na nGall 0-12
13 June	Casement Park	Doire 2-15 An Cabhán 2-15
20 June	Cavan (replay)	Doire 2-14 An Cabhán 0-5
20 June	Newry	An Dún 1-15 Aontroim 0-14
27 June	Clones	Tír Eoghain 0-18 Fear Manach 0-8

Semi-finals:

4 July	Clones	Ard Mhacha 1-10 Doire 0-12
11 July	Casement Park	An Dún 2-14 Tír Eoghain 0-15

Final:

1 Aug	Clones	Ard Mhacha 3-12 An Dún 0-10

2000

14 May	Enniskillen	Fear Manach 3-12 Muineachán 1-10
14 May	Cavan	Doire 2-13 An Cabhán 1-5
28 May	Casement Park	Aontroim 0-13 An Dún 1-7
4 June	Celtic Park	Ard Mhacha 0-12 Tír Eoghain 0-8
11 June	Ballybofey	Fear Manach 1-12 Dún na nGall 0-13

Semi-finals:

18 June	Casement Park	Doire 0-14 Aontroim 2-8
25 June	Clones	Ard Mhacha 0-13 Fear Manach 0-12

2 July	Casement Park (replay)	Doire 1-17 Aontroim 2-5

Final:

16 July	Clones	Ard Mhacha 1-12 Doire 1-11

2001

13 May	Ballybofey	Fear Manach 2-13 Dún na nGall 1-16
19 May	Enniskillen (replay)	Fear Manach 1-9 Dún na nGall 0-11
20 May	Clones	Tír Eoghain 1-14 Ard Mhacha 1-9
27 May	Casement Park	An Dún 2-10 An Cabhán 1-14
3 June	Celtic Park	Doire 1-11 Aontroim 0-9
10 June	Enniskillen	Muineachán 2-10 Fear Manach 0-14

Semi-finals:

17 June	Clones	Tír Eoghain 3-7 Doire 0-14
24 June	Clones	An Cabhán 0-13 Muineachán 0-11

Final:

8 July	Clones	Tír Eoghain 1-13 An Cabhán 1-11

2002

12 May	Cavan	Dún na nGall 1-17 An Cabhán 0-15
12 May	Clones	Fear Manach 4-13 Muineachán 2-11
19 May	Clones	Ard Mhacha 1-12 Tír Eoghain 1-12
26 May	Clones (replay)	Ard Mhacha 2-13 Tír Eoghain 0-16
2 June	Casement Park	Doire 0-16 Aontroim 0-6
2 June	Ballybofey	Dún na nGall 3-12 An Dún 1-6

Semi-finals:

9 June	Clones	Ard Mhacha 0-16 Fear Manach 1-5
16 June	Clones	Dún na nGall 1-9 Doire 0-10

Final:

7 July	Clones	Ard Mhacha 1-14 Dún na nGall 1-10

2003

11 May	Clones	Muineachán 0-13 Ard Mhacha 0-9
18 May	Clones	Tír Eoghain 0-12 Doire 1-9
24 May	Casement Park (replay)	Tír Eoghain 0-17 Doire 1-5
25 May	Casement Park	Aontroim 2-9 An Cabhán 1-10
1 June	Enniskillen	Fear Manach 0-10 Dún na nGall 0-6
8 June	Casement Park	An Dún 1-12 Muineachán 0-13

Semi-finals:

15 June	Casement Park	Tír Eoghain 1-17 Aontroim 1-9
22 June	Clones	An Dún 2-10 Fear Manach 0-11

Final:

13 July	Clones	Tír Eoghain 1-17 An Dún 4-8
20 July	Clones (replay)	Tír Eoghain 0-23 An Dún 1-5

2004

9 May	Omagh	Tír Eoghain 1-17 Doire 1-6
16 May	Casement Park	An Cabhán 1-13 An Dún 1-13
23 May	Clones	Ard Mhacha 2-19 Muineachán 0-10
30 May	Ballybofey	Dún na nGall 1-15 Aontroim 1-9
30 May	Cavan (replay)	An Cabhán 3-13 An Dún 2-12
6 June	Clones	Tír Eoghain 1-13 Fear Manach 0-12

Semi-finals:

13 June	Clones	Ard Mhacha 0-13 An Cabhán 0-11

20 June	Clones	Dún na nGall 1-11 Tír Eoghain 0-9
Final:		
11 July	Croke Park	Ard Mhacha 3-15 Dún na nGall 0-11

2005

15 May	Clones	Ard Mhacha 2-12 Fear Manach 1-7
22 May	Omagh	Tír Eoghain 1-13 An Dún 1-6
29 May	Cavan	An Cabhán 0-11 Aontroim 0-11
4 June	Casement Park (replay)	An Cabhán 1-15 Aontroim 2-6
5 June	Clones	Doire 1-17 Muineachán 2-8
12 June	Clones	Ard Mhacha 0-12 Dún na nGall 0-12
18 June	Clones (replay)	Ard Mhacha 3-11 Dún na nGall 1-10
Semi-finals:		
19 June	Clones	Tír Eoghain 0-10 An Cabhán 1-7
25 June	Clones (replay)	Tír Eoghain 3-19 An Cabhán 0-7
26 June	Casement Park	Ard Mhacha 1-11 Doire 0-10
Final:		
10 July	Croke Park	Ard Mhacha 2-8 Tír Eoghain 0-14
23 July	Croke Park (replay)	Ard Mhacha 0-13 Tír Eoghain 0-11

2006

7 May	Casement Park	An Dún 1-13 An Cabhán 0-11
14 May	Clones	Ard Mhacha 0-10 Muineachán 0-10
20 May	Clones (replay)	Ard Mhacha 1-13 Muineachán 0-10
21 May	Enniskillen	Fear Manach 1-9 Aontroim 0-9
28 May	Omagh	Doire 1-8 Tír Eoghain 0-5
4 June	Ballybofey	Dún na nGall 1-12 An Dún 1-11
Semi-finals:		
11 June	Clones	Ard Mhacha 0-11 Fear Manach 2-5
18 June	Clones	Dún na nGall 1-13 Doire 0-11
25 June	Clones	Ard Mhacha 0-16 Fear Manach 1-8
Final:		
9 July	Croke Park	Ard Mhacha 1-9 Dún na nGall 0-9

2007

13 May	Cavan	An Dún 3-8 An Cabhán 2-11
20 May	Newry (replay)	An Dún 0-15 An Cabhán 0-11
20 May	Clones	Tír Eoghain 0-13 Fear Manach 1-9
27 May	Ballybofey	Dún na nGall 1-9 Ard Mhacha 1-8
10 June	Newry	Muineachán 2-15 An Dún 1-15
10 June	Casement Park	Doire 1-13 Aontroim 0-10
Semi-finals:		
17 June	Clones	Tír Eoghain 2-15 Dún na nGall 1-7
24 June	Casement Park	Muineachán 0-14 Doire 1-9
Final:		
15 July	Clones	Tír Eoghain 1-15 Muineachán 1-13

2008

18 May	Casement Park	An Cabhán 1-19 Aontroim 1-14
25 May	Enniskillen	Fear Manach 2-8 Muineachán 0-10
1 June	Ballybofey	Doire 1-14 Dún na nGall 1-12
8 June	Omagh	An Dún 2-8 Tír Eoghain 2-8
14 June	Newry (replay)	An Dún 1-19 Tír Eoghain 0-21 (a.e.t.)
15 June	Cavan	Ard Mhacha 0-17 An Cabhán 0-13
Semi-finals:		
21 June	Omagh	Fear Manach 1-11 Doire 1-9
29 June	Clones	Ard Mhacha 1-12 An Dún 0-11
Final:		
20 Jul	Clones	Ard Mhacha 2-8 Fear Manach 1-11
27 Jul	Clones (replay)	Ard Mhacha 1-11 Fear Manach 0-8

2009

17 May	Enniskillen	Fear Manach 0-13 An Dún 0-10
24 May	Celtic Park	Doire 1-10 Muineachán 0-10
31 May	Clones	Tír Eoghain 2-10 Ard Mhacha 1-10
6 June	Cavan	An Cabhán 0-13 Fear Manach 1-9
14 June	Ballybofey	Aontroim 1-10 Dún na nGall 0-12
Semi-finals:		
21 June	Casement Park	Tír Eoghain 0-15 Doire 0-7
27 June	Clones	Aontroim 0-13 An Cabhán 1-7
Final:		
19 July	Clones	Tír Eoghain 1-18 Aontroim 0-15

ULSTER SENIOR FOOTBALL CHAMPIONSHIP FINAL TEAMS, 1888–2009

The following records represent the most comprehensive list of teams that played in Ulster senior championship finals from 1888 to 2009.

Beyond 1950, numerous problems were encountered in research. In some instances, particularly in the early years, the match was scarcely reported at all, and in many more cases no team-lists were published in the newspapers.

Where team-lists were provided, there were still a large number of obstacles to compiling accurate records. Sometimes the first names of players were completely omitted, or often just their initials provided. On many occasions names were reported mistakenly, or too few names listed. Different reports of the same game occasionally contained divergent details of names and scores.

A further drawback is the fact in the early decades teams were not always listed in line-out formation from goalkeeper to full-forwards. Up to the 1920s it was more common for the captain to be named first on the list, and it was quite common for teams to be listed on the basis of a pre-match panel in which players from each club were grouped together.

Where there is conflict between different sources, I have attempted to ascertain the more accurate one, and use these details accordingly. Some of the first-names of players from the early years up to the 1940s have proven unobtainable thus far.

KEY

In these records, players' Christian names are given where possible for their first listed appearance, and only the initial(s) thereafter. Where there are two players from the same county with the same surnames and initials in the same period of time, their full Christian names are listed.

Where a final went to a replay, the team that lined out in the first game is provided, with notes underneath about any changes to the starting line-up for the replay listed underneath.

Where a team-list cannot be obtained from subsequent reports of the game, the team as named in advance of the game (where available) is provided. If final team-lists are unobtainable either in preview or review, the team from that county that played in the previous or subsequent round of that year's championship is given – either from the provincial semi-final or first round, or the All-Ireland semi-final – and in each case where such a (non-Ulster final) team-list is provided here, it will appear in italics.

For most of the history of the provincial championships, defeat in the final was a devastating finish to the season. Here Donegal football manager Brian McEniff is captured in a dressing-room at Clones, after his team lost to Derry in the Ulster final of 1993 and there ended their effort to retain the All-Ireland championship. Since the inception of the qualifier system in the new millennium, however, several defeated provincial finalists have gone on to win All-Ireland titles. (*Irish News*)

1888

MUINEACHÁN: [Ulster final and replay team-lists not available; the team was drawn from the following group of players]: *Peter Finnegan (goal), Patrick Finnegan (capt), Terry 'Red' Kieran, John Kieran, Mickey Carroll, Mickey Louth, James Meegan, Owen Meegan, Paddy Daly, Larry Tuite, M Tuite, Hopkins McGahon?, Michael Martin, Patrick Martin, ? Moore, ? McBride, John Rafferty, Peter Kelly, Pat Quigley, Bill Agnew.*

AN CABHÁN: [Ulster final and replay team-lists not available; the team was drawn from the following group of players]: *Tom Carroll, Tom McCabe, John Duffy, Paddy Boylan, Tom Clarke, James E Mulvaney, Peter Cahill, James Brady, Tim McCann, George Yore, Michael Fitzsimon, Pat Kane, Phil Daly, Patrick Fitzsimmons, Paddy Neary, Matt Fitzsimmons, Andy Cumiskey, William Mulvaney (capt), Matt Mulvaney, Pat Mulvaney.*

1890

ARD MHACHA: [Ulster final team-list unavailable; the following team played v. Corcaigh in All-Ireland semi-final]: *Joe Donnelly, James McGerrigan, Patrick Knipe, Hugh O Neill, Patrick Molloy, Thomas J Allen (capt), Jack Mullen, James Deegan, James Lennon, Jack Fitzpatrick, John Vallely, Henry Thomas, William Thomas, James Corr, William Slevin, Owen McKenna, John Mulholland, Charles O Neill, Hugh Carbery, Ned Mallon, Barney Corr.*

TÍR EOGHAIN: [team-list unavailable].

1891

AN CABHÁN: [Ulster final and replay team-lists not available; the team was drawn from the following group of players]: *Mick McGurk (capt), James Martin, Hughie O Reilly, Paddy Reilly, Frank Matthews, Dan Taggart, John Taggart, John 'Scotty' Brady, John Gilcreest, James Gilcreest, P O Connor, P Gaffney, J O Donoghue, J O Carroll, John Clarke, F Meyers, Joe Smith, Tommy Brady, John Ritchie, Pat Boylan, Peter O Reilly.*

ARD MHACHA: [final and replay team-lists unavailable].

1892–1901

No Ulster Football Championships organised.

1902/03

No Ulster Football Championship was held. The Aontroim SFC final was advertised as the Ulster final, and the following team selected by Tír na nÓg club won:

AONTROIM: F Johnston, D Clarke, Dan Dempsey, P Mitchell, Owen McKernan, Jimmy Gallen, D Campbell, H Toal, A King, J Murphy, Peter Gallen, Eddie Trainor, O'Donoghue, Denis McCullough, Neil McFarlane, Orange, J Bonnar.

1903/04

ARD MHACHA: J Cartmill, W Slevin, Thomas Rafferty, Dan McKeown, John Harvey, Patrick Corr, John McKenna, Patrick Cleary, J Bermingham, Francis Malone, Patrick McAvinchey, P Rafferty, Bernard Corr, Neil McVeigh, D Marrinan, Patrick O'Neill, Patrick Cullen.

AONTROIM: Dobbin, D Dempsey, Hugh O'Toole, O McKernan, Joe Dunne, Jack Hughes, George McCausland, William Manning, Tom Madden, Frank McIlvenny, Pat McGinley, H Sheehan, Joe Sweeney, Boyd, McCann, Donnellan, Leith.

1904/05

AN CABHÁN: John O Reilly (goal), Terence Maguire (capt), Owen Maguire, John Maguire, Hugh Maguire, John Fitzpatrick, Hugh Fitzpatrick, John Brady, T P Mulligan, Philip McEnroe,

William J Carolan, Patrick J McGovern, John Smith, Matthew Smith, J McFadden, Patrick Gilronan, P J O Keeffe.
Changes for replay: John McCabe and P Cahill started, instead of J Fitzpatrick and Mulligan.
Changes for 2nd replay: J Fitzpatrick, Mulligan, J Drury and J Stokes started, instead of McFadden, Cahill, M Smith and O Keeffe.

ARD MHACHA: B Corr (capt), John Farrell (goal), P Rafferty, N McVeigh, J McKenna, W Slevin, Thomas McAleavey, P Kearney, Frank McAleavey, E Kearney, Jim Brawley, P Kennedy, Jack Woods, John Corrigan, J Breen, Jim Kearney, P O'Neill, James McGerrigan. [18 players listed.]
Changes for replay: J Murtagh, James O'Malley, J Bermingham, Owen Martin and P Cleary started; they replaced Corrigan, Woods, Breen, McGerrigan and F McAleavey.
Changes for 2nd replay: none.

1905/06

AN CABHÁN: T Maguire, O Maguire, H Maguire, J Maguire, J Brady, John McCabe, Peter O Reilly, H Fitzpatrick, John Fitzpatrick, James Reilly, P Gilronan, Joe Gilronan, Joseph Reilly, Joseph Fitzpatrick, P Fitzpatrick, Thomas Boland.

MUINEACHÁN: Costello (goal), John Ward, Joe Kirk, P McCabe, Connor, H Kirk, Cunningham, Daly, Murphy, Finnegan, Owen 'Buttney' Callan, Dan Coyle, Keenan, McMahon, Ignatius McCaffrey, Brady, Peter Martin.

1906/07

MUINEACHÁN: William McGrath (capt), J Ward, J Costello, J Kirk, J Smyth, P McCabe, P Toal, Jess Connolly, T Pettigrew, T McKeown, J Meegan, D Coyle, O Callan, P Kelly, I McCaffrey, P Martin, Patrick Markey.

AONTROIM: James McManus, Joe Fegan, William Clay, Hugh Kane, W Manning, T Murphy, Hugh Sheehan, Patrick Kelly, Harry Sheehan, T Hamill, Dunn, D Dempsey, McAleavey, Marcus Clarke, P McGinley.

1907/08

AONTROIM: Phil Gallagher, Hugh Mallaghan, J Fegan, Patrick Downey, P Kelly, Michael Hughes, Martin McDonagh, James Hamill, H Kane, William J Donnelly, Tom Murphy, John Mitchel Darby, Tim Sheehan, Harry Sheehan, Charles McCurry, Pat Hayes, Will Manning.

AN CABHÁN: Terence Maguire, Owen Maguire, John Maguire, Hugh Maguire, Michael Maguire, John Fitzpatrick, John Reilly, T Quinn, J McCabe, P Cahill, Jack Lee, T Young, Joe Fitzpatrick, T Boland, Michael McKeon, Patrick Gilsenan, J Reilly.

1909

AONTROIM: Harry Sheehan (capt), John Healy, Seán Coburn, J Fegan, H Kane, Lynch, Patrick Barnes, W Manning, William McAreavey, Fred Vallely, P Kelly, J H Mulvihill, J Hamill, J M Darby, Tim Sheehan, P Downey, Murphy.

AN CABHÁN: Young (capt), T Maguire, J Maguire, J McCabe, J Fitzpatrick, Hugh Fitzpatrick, John Reilly, Paddy Gilronan, Joe Gilronan, J McCormack, R McHenry, T Boland, Bernard Briody, Matt McCabe, Joe Fitzpatrick, Patrick McMahon, Owen McKiernan.

1910

AONTROIM: J Healy, Peter Moylan, Harry Sheehan (capt), S Coburn, P Kelly, W Manning, H Kane, P Meaney, J Hamill, J H Mulvihill, Louis Waters, P Barnes, J M Darby, Joseph Mullan, James Murphy, William Lennon, C McCurry.

AN CABHÁN: Mat Gilcreest (goal), 'Black' Benny Reilly,
Jack Smith, O Maguire, T Fitzpatrick, T Maguire, P Gilronan,
Benny Reilly ('The Lane'), Dick McClean, Seán McCormack,
M McCabe, P Smith, T Young, T Boland, M Donohoe, Patrick
Meehan, T Corr.

1911
No championship.

1912
AONTROIM: J Monaghan, P Burns, P Meaney, S Coburn (capt),
H Sheehan, P L Kelly, W Manning, William Mulholland,
L Waters, J H Mulvihill, Edward Ward, J Mullan, Eddie Gorman,
P Barnes, Joe Gallagher, William Wright, Brennan.
ARD MHACHA: Pat Morris (goal), Michael McCaine, Owen
Harvesy, Paddy Maguire, Paddy Hearty, James Morgan, Mick
Duffy, John McKeown, Reb Maguire, John Boyle, James Boyle,
Tommy Chambers, Frank Rooney, Patrick McConville, Francie
Carroll, J O Kane (Camlough), R McAleavey, Frank McArdle,
J Kearney.

1913
AONTROIM: P Henry, P Moylan, Peter Meaney, S Coburn
(capt), H Kane, P L Kelly, W Manning, Jim McCrealey, P Barnes,
L Waters, J Gallagher, E Ward, E Gorman, J Murphy, H Sheehan.
MUINEACHÁN: Keynes, J Ward, J Cumiskey, F Ward, Frank
O Duffy, Marren, Corrigan, John Flanagan, James 'Jess' Connolly,
James Downey, Ignatius McCaffrey, Michael Keelan, P McIvor,
Con Ward, J J Connolly.

1914
MUINEACHÁN: James Costello (goal), J Downey, Ward, 'Jess'
Connolly (capt), I McCaffrey, George McEneaney, J McCarville,
P Cassidy, Cumiskey, F O Duffy, Patrick Gartlan, John McKenna,
Owen Marray, J Flanagan, Joe Kiely.
FEAR MANACH: Felix Curry, Pat Curry, Owen 'Munroe'
McManus, Tommy (T P) Clarke, Pat Clarke, Pat Fitzpatrick,
Owen McAloon, Peter Reilly, Jim (J P) Dunne, Pat Cassidy, Frank
Meehan, J Crudden, Tom McGarvey, Mick McGarvey, J O Kane.

1915
AN CABHÁN: J Mitchell (goal) (capt), D McClean, J Malone,
James Brady, Joe McKeever, P J Farrelly, T McGovern, Paudge
Masterson, Ernie McDonnell, Felix McGovern, P Rogers, Patsy
Fay, Pee McCormack, Andrew Quinn, W Neary.
Changes for replay: None. P Reilly came on as a sub for
McDonnell.
MUINEACHÁN: J Costello (goal), J Downey (capt), T King,
G McEneaney, I McCaffrey, J Connolly, Syl Califf, Jim Farrelly,
F O Duffy, P Gartlan, Standish O Grady, J Kiely, J Reilly, J Smith,
J McKenna.
Changes for replay: James Burns for Farrelly.

1916
MUINEACHÁN: Larry O Reilly (goal), J Downey (capt),
George McEneaney, S O Grady, F O Duffy, S Califf, John Marray,
J Connolly, Jim Farrelly, P Gartlan, Owen Marray, I McCaffrey,
J Kiely, John McKenna, James Marron.
AONTROIM: Hugh Ward (goal), Jim Best, Edward Carabine,
S Coburn, Dan Ahearne, E Gorman, Owen Brennan, Pat Murray,
John Hale, William Rea, Dan Campbell, Seán McKeown,
T Diamond, Joe Gallagher, Dinny Quinn.

1917
MUINEACHÁN: L O Reilly (goal), J Downey (capt),
James Connolly, J Farrelly, James Burns, O Marray, John Marray,
Willie Fleming, John Corrigan, Jim Cooney, Frank Cooney,
James Cumiskey, J McKenna, G McEneaney, S O Grady, J Kiely.
ARD MHACHA: Gordon Houlahan, Frank Chambers, Frank
Rooney, J Morgan, Packie McCabe, Pat McNulty, T Chambers,
P Morris, Mick McCann, Pat Murphy, Barney Donnellan, John
Reilly, Edmund Cunningham, Arthur McAleavey, Harry Murphy.

1918
AN CABHÁN: Andy Donohoe, Pat Cahill, Paul Brady, J J Clarke,
John Malone, Phil Sheridan, John McKeown, P Reilly, Paudge
Masterson, Tom McEneaney, Pat Smith, P Fay (capt), John P
Murphy, T Young, T Kilroy.
AONTROIM: Jack McQuaid (goal), Barney Vallely (capt),
J Gallagher, J Best, D Ahern, J Duffy, Mick McGovern,
Jack McGoran, J Mullroney, James Poynter, P Fox, Joe Mullan,
A Mitchel, E Gorman, S McKeown.

1919
AN CABHÁN: A Donohoe (goal), Phil Sheridan, P Fay (capt),
John Sexton, J J Clarke, J Malone, Pat Carolan, Pat Conway,
J Heerey, John Cullen, P Masterson, P Smith, J P Murphy,
T Young, James Cahill.
AONTROIM: James O Neill, Barney Vallely, Joe Gallagher,
Jim Best, T Byrne, J Duffy, Aloysius P Fox, W Rea, Joe McDonald,
Joe Mullan (capt), T McNally, W Higgins, F Lavery, Tom Fox,
Eddie Gorman.

1920
AN CABHÁN: J Heslin, P Cahill, Jack Tiernan, J Masterson,
P Carolan, Tom Flood, J J Clarke, P Masterson, J Cullen (capt),
P Conway, J Cahill, John McGahern, Jim Smith, J P Murphy,
W O'Byrne.
ARD MHACHA: P McKenna (goal), J Cowan, M McGerrigan,
Jim Cooney, J E O'Hanlon, Joe Luckie, B Young, James Kernan,
Arthur McAleavey, P McKeever, John Joseph Crossey, J Killeen,
J O'Reilly, F Rocks, 'Phil McCabe'.

1921
MUINEACHÁN: Mick Farmer, James Carroll, Packie Daly,
Jimmy Murphy, Dan Hogan, Paddy Cosgrave, J Bishop,
Willie McMahon, Tom Mason, Michael Deery, Joe Brannigan,
P McNally, J McKenna, Frank Tummins, Joe Shevlin, Tom Shevlin.
DOIRE: [No team-list available.]

1922
MUINEACHÁN (as played in drawn game): P Cosgrove,
F Tummins, Edward Bishop, J Kierans, T Allen, J Brannigan,
Jack McCabe, Tommy Bradley, Jack 'Rock' Treanor, J Boylan,
Packie Daly, John Logan, J McGee, S Malcolmson, T Shevlin.
Changes for replay: Sherlock, Mick Farmer, Nulty, James Murphy,
Kirk, Ben Hand, Mickey McAleer and Connors started instead of
Cosgrove, Kierans, Allen, McCabe, Bradley, Treanor, Logan,
Malcolmson.
AN CABHÁN (as played in drawn game): J P Murphy (capt),
John Boyd (goal), John McKeown, J J Clarke, Standish O Grady,
Patrick Carolan, Patrick Leonard, Patrick Murray, James Jermyn,
Patrick Masterson, John McGahern, Vincent Dunne, Thomas Fox,
John Carolan, Thomas Donohoe.
Changes for replay: Joe Cullivan, J Sexton, R H Mulligan,

Paul Doyle, Tom Egan started instead of Boyd, McKeown, Leonard, Murray and Donohoe.

1923

MUINEACHÁN: Tommy Duffin (goal), P Jones, Paddy Cosgrove, M Farmer, Patrick Coyle, Bishop, Patrick Kellett, Daly (capt), P McNulty, J Murphy, John Logan, Shevlin, John 'Jack' Comiskey, John Treanor, Daly.
AN CABHÁN: J Heslin (goal), S O Grady, J Jermyn, P J Masterson, P Carolan, J J Clarke, Pat Kangley, P Masterson, Dan Brady, P Conway, T Egan, J Smith, O'Reilly, V Dunne, Robert Mulligan.

1924

AN CABHÁN (as played in drawn game): Robert Black, J J Clarke (capt), Paddy Murray, Pat McGee, J Murphy, Mick Brown, Bernard O Reilly, Brian Comiskey, M Campbell, Patrick Masterson (Gowna), J Jermyn, Joe Maguire, M Donohoe, S O Grady, D Brady.
Changes for replay: J Tiernan for Brown, P Carolan for Comiskey, Tom Egan for Campbell, Owen Leggett for Maguire, Tom Hegarty for Donohoe, T Mullally for Brady.
MUINEACHÁN (as played in drawn game): John J McCann (goal), Gerry Gillanders, J Treanor, James Murphy, Peter Deery, P Daly, Christy Fisher, J Comiskey, Frank Coyle (capt), P Coyle, James Carroll, Kirke, James McGowan, J Logan, Thomas Wilson.
Changes for replay: Owen Byrne, P Kellett, Mick Keenan and Bernard McElroy started instead of Murphy, Deery, Daly and Kirke.

1925

AN CABHÁN (as played in drawn game): P Fay, Tom Campbell, Patrick J Masterson (Gowna), Patrick Sheridan, J Jermyn, J Sexton, S O Grady, J Smith, Pat Murray, P Conway, Paddy Kirwan, P J Murphy, Harry Mulvanny, Paudge J Masterson (Cornafean), John Murphy (Slashers).
Changes for replay: J F Kiernan for Fay, J Tiernan for Campbell, T Mullally for P J Murphy, Phil Smith for John Murphy.
AONTROIM (as played in drawn game): P Hughes, Dick Sadlier, John Gibbons, W Mulvenna, T Murphy, William Ludlow, John McDonnell, Patsy McGuckian, James Murray, P Fox, Leo Madden, John McFerran, Joe Gallagher, Joe Brannigan, Paddy Cunning.
Changes for replay: John Myles for Mulvenna, John Fox for McGuckian, Rev Francis Cullen for Murphy.

1926

AN CABHÁN: J F Kiernan, Patrick Leddy, Tom Campbell, H Mulvanny, Patrick J Masterson (Gowna), Peter Reilly, Phil McCabe, Jim Smith (capt), Seán Farrelly, W A Higgins, P Conway, Patrick McGee, Jimmy Murphy, John P Murphy.
AONTROIM: S Murphy, D Sadlier, J Cosgrove, J Gibbons, Jim Brogan, J McFadden, J McDonnell, P McGuckian, J Murray, R McCamphill, Eugene Mackin, P Cunning, Leo Madden, Joe McDonnell, Neal Donnelly.

1927

MUINEACHÁN: Tom Bradley, J Slevin, Joe Farrell, Packie Daly, Benny Leavy, Michael McShane, Jimmy Duffy, Paddy Kilroy (capt), Christy Fisher, Mickey McAleer, Billy Mason, Thomas J Weymes, Jack Trainor, P Kellett, Joe Shevlin (Killanny).
ARD MHACHA: Charlie Morgan, John Vallely, Eugene Hanratty, Jim Cooney, Joe Harney, Jim Maguire, Owen Connolly, Jack Corrigan, Mick McCreesh, Francis Toner, Patrick 'Poppy' Fearon, James Kernan, Harry Comiskey, John Donaghy, John McCusker.

1928

AN CABHÁN: John Morgan, Herbie Clegg, T Campbell, J J Clarke (capt), George Malcolmson, Patsy Lynch, P Leddy, P Carolan, P Fox, Hugh O'Reilly, John Murphy, Patrick Devlin, Andy Conlon, Patrick J Masterson, J P Murphy. N.B.: Jim Smith, team captain for the rest of the season, did not play in the Ulster final due to illness.
ARD MHACHA: C Morgan, H Comiskey, E Hanratty, Hugh Arthurs, J Cooney, J Harney, J Maguire, O Connolly, J Corrigan, F Toner, P Fearon, J Kernan, J Donaghy, P Donaghy, J McCusker.

1929

MUINEACHÁN (as played in drawn game): J Duffy (Ballybay), Tom Shevlin, Joe Farrell, Joe Brannigan, Paddy Heeran, Peter Lambe, Seán O Carroll, Paddy Kilroy, T Kirwan, Mickey McAleer, Billy Mason, P J Duffy (Loughegish), Fr P/J McDonald, H Brannigan, C Fisher.
Changes for replay: T Bradley, T J Weymes, J Treanor and Peter Duffy (Ballybay) started instead of J Duffy, P J Duffy, McDonald and Brannigan.
AN CABHÁN (as played in both games): Willie Young, J J Clarke, T Campbell, Rev P Leddy, John P Dolan, P Lynch, Frank Fitzpatrick, J Smith (capt), Paddy Colleran, H O Reilly, P Devlin, John Murphy, P Hennessy, J P Murphy, S Farrelly.

1930

MUINEACHÁN: T Bradley, T Shevlin, J Farrell, Harry Owens, P Hearon, P Lambe, J Sexton, B Mason, P Kilroy, M McAleer, Jimmy Fitzsimons, Peter Duffy, Charlie McCarthy, C Fisher, P J Duffy.
AN CABHÁN: Ben Reilly (goal), T Campbell, Mick Dinneny, Peter Briody, F Fitzpatrick, James Sheridan, Benny 'Red' Fay, H O Reilly, Larry 'Mocksheen' Galligan, Michael J 'Sonny' Magee, Jack Smallhorn, P Devlin, W Young, Packie Joe O Reilly, John Young.

1931

AN CABHÁN: W Young, P Lynch, Tom Crowe, M Dinneny, John Molloy, J Smith (capt), F Fitzpatrick, P Colleran, H O'Reilly, Paddy McNamee, P Devlin, J Smallhorn, S Farrelly, Thomas J Weymes, M J Magee.
ARD MHACHA: Joe Houlahan, Jim McCullough, J Vallely, H Comiskey, J Harney, F Toner, Leo Collins, Benny Evans, J Corrigan, Richie Conlon, P 'Poppy' Fearon (capt), Jack McCreesh, Paddy Quinn, Peter Lambe, J McCusker.
Sub.: Eddie McCreesh for Harney.

1932

AN CABHÁN: W Young, Willie Connolly, Tom Crowe, M Dinneny, J Molloy, P Lynch, Vincent McGovern, Jim Smith (capt), H O'Reilly, Patrick Devlin, P McNamee, J Smallhorn, M J Magee, Louis Blessing, Terry Coyle.
ARD MHACHA: J Houlahan, H Comiskey, J McCullough, J Vallely, J Harney, L Collins, E McCreesh, E McMahon, B Evans, T Toner, P Fearon, Frank McAvinchey, P Quinn, John Donaghy, J McCusker.

1933

AN CABHÁN: W Young, W Connolly, T Crowe, M Dinneny, T Coyle, Jim Smith (capt), Packie Phair, H O'Reilly, Tom O'Reilly, Donal Morgan, P Devlin, J Smallhorn, M J Magee, E Briody, V McGovern.

TÍR EOGHAIN: Seamus Bonner, Willie McElroy, Joe Henry Campbell, Jim Hughes, Joe Kilpatrick, Ned McGee, Peter Mulgrew, Mick O'Neill, James McMahon, Frank Devlin, Jim McLernon, Frank Fullen, Peter Campbell, Seamus Campbell, John McNamara.

1934
AN CABHÁN: W Young, W Connolly, P Lynch, M Dinneny, J Molloy, T Coyle, P Phair, H O'Reilly (capt), Tom O'Reilly, D Morgan, Patrick Boylan, J Smallhorn, V McGovern, L Blessing, M J Magee.
ARD MHACHA: J Houlahan, Tommy McAvinchey, Jim McCullough, Hugh Cassidy, Hugh McConville, Peter Quinn, Leo Collins, John Vallely, Ed McMahon, Joe Harney, Dick Conlan, William McKnight, Patrick Quinn, James McSherry, J Donaghy.

1935
AN CABHÁN: W Young, W Connolly, M Dinneny, P Phair, J Molloy, Brian Reilly, V McGovern, Tom O Reilly, H O Reilly, P Boylan, P Devlin, J Smallhorn, P McNamee, L Blessing, M J Magee.
FEAR MANACH: Patrick Donohoe, Eugene Lennon, Willie Carty, Paddy Burns, Hugh D'Arcy, Eamon McDonnell, Frank McAuley, Jim McCullough, Tom McDonnell, Pat McGrane, Charlie McDonnell, Johnny Monaghan, Eugene Collins, Frank Johnston, Billy Maguire.

1936
AN CABHÁN: W Young, Tom O'Reilly (Mullahoran), M Dinneny, Bill Carroll, Terry Dolan, T O'Reilly (Cornafean), P Phair, H O'Reilly (capt), Jim White, D Morgan, P Devlin, Vincent White, P Boylan, L Blessing, M J Magee.
MUINEACHÁN: Bill Redmond, Pat Hughes, P Lambe, Billy Mason, Terry Clerkin, Joe McElroy, Jack Crawley, Terry Lennon, Hugh Lennon, J McGuinness, Brendan Quigley, C Fisher, Enda McCormack, Packie Boylan, John Loughman.

1937
AN CABHÁN: W Young, Paddy Smith, Eugene Finnegan, M Dinneny, W Carroll, Tom O'Reilly (capt), John Joe O'Reilly, J White, V White, D Morgan, P Devlin, J Smallhorn, P Boylan, L Blessing, M J Magee.
ARD MHACHA: J Houlahan, Eddie McMahon, J Vallely, J Murphy, Mickey McCone, J McCullough, L Collins; Peter Quinn, Owen Quinn; Paddy Duffy, Alf Murray, Austin Colohan, Jimmy Kelly, Jim Pat MacSherry, Dan McGeown.

1938
MUINEACHÁN: A 'Wishie' Lynn, Rory Johnson, Pat Hughes, P F 'Rex' Keelaghan, Terry Clerkin, Peter Finnegan, Jack Crawley, Hugh Lennon, Frank Kelly, Frank Rock, Pat McGrane, Vincent O Duffy, Packie Boylan, Jack Burns, Enda McCormack.
ARD MHACHA: Joe Houlahan, Eddie McMahon, John Vallely, Eddie McLaughlin, Con Short, Hugh Cassidy, Austin Colohan, Tom Clarke, Jim McCullough (capt), Andy Judge, Alf Murray, Jim Pat McSherry, Joe Fitzpatrick, Jackie Reid.

1939
AN CABHÁN (as played in drawn game): Joe Mitchell, W Carroll, E Finnegan, M Dinneny, Gerry Smith, Tom O Reilly, John William Martin, J J O'Reilly, Paddy Smith, T P O'Reilly, P Devlin, Paddy Conaty, Tom Maguire, P Lynch, V White.

Changes for replay: M J Magee and J White started instead of Lynch and Maguire. Sub.: Patsy Clarke for J White.
ARD MHACHA (as played in drawn game): J Houlahan, E McMahon, E McLoughlin, F Carragher, Paddy Crilly, G Shortt, L Collins, Tom Clarke, J McCullough, T Corrigan, A Murray, A Colohan, Patsy Devlin, J Kelly, Frank Arthurs.
Changes for replay: Gerry McGarvey, D McGeown, O Quinn and J Reid started instead of Carragher, Corrigan, Colohan and Arthurs.

1940
AN CABHÁN: W Young, E Finnegan, Bill Carroll, M Dinneny, G Smith, Tom O'Reilly (Cornafean) (capt), P Clarke, J J O'Reilly, T P O'Reilly, D Morgan, P Smith, P Conaty, P Boylan, Joe Stafford, Vincent White.
AN DÚN: Jimmy McLoughlin, Tom McCann, Joe Kane, John McClorey, Gerry 'Joker' Carr, Terry McCormack (capt), John Shields, Mickey King, Dan Morgan, John Carr, Tom O'Hare, Bro. William O'Boyle, Danny McConville, Mick Lynch, Charles McConville.

1941
AN CABHÁN: Brendan Kelly, E Finnegan, Barney Cully, Peter Paul Galligan, Gerry Smith, Tom O Reilly (Cornafean) (capt), J W Martin, J J O Reilly, T P O Reilly (Slashers), D Morgan, Mick Fallon, P Conaty, Simon Deignan, P Boylan, M J Magee.
TÍR EOGHAIN: Cathal Poyntz, Gerry Rice, Joe Herron, Michael Toal, Paddy Donnelly, Peter Crozier, Leo McGrath, Pearse O Connor, Mick Keenan, Dermot Devlin, Packie Begley, Brendan Devlin, Brian Cullen, Thomas Corrigan, John Rafferty. Sub: Frank Comac for Rafferty.

1942
AN CABHÁN: J D (Des) Benson, P Finnegan, B Cully, T O Reilly, T Cahill, G Smith, J W Martin, J J O Reilly, Andy Comiskey, D Morgan, Paddy Smith, T P O Reilly, P Boylan, S Deignan, Bill Doonan.
AN DÚN: John O Hare, T McCann, J Kane, John McClorey, G Carr, Séamus D'Arcy, Joe Fegan, M King, D Morgan, Liam O Hare, A McLean, T McCormack, Willie McKibbin, J Garvey, Tommy McParland.

1943
AN CABHÁN: J D Benson, J W Martin, B Cully, Peter Paul Galligan, G Smith, Tom O Reilly (capt), T Cahill, S Deignan, A Comiskey, Mick Higgins, P Smith, T P O Reilly, P Boylan, Joe Stafford, P Doyle. Sub.: D Morgan for Higgins.
MUINEACHÁN: Seán Mulligan, George Hughes, Pat Hughes, Paddy Burns, Paddy 'Yank' McMahon, Eugene McDonald, Mick Finnegan, Eddie O'Connor, Tom Agnew, Charlie McGrath, Peter McCarney, Tommy McCarville, Leo Burns, Dan Traynor, Seán McCormack.

1944
AN CABHÁN: Seamus Morris, E Finnegan, P P Galligan, J W Martin, Paddy Coyle, S Deignan, J J O Reilly (capt), T P O Reilly, A Comiskey, Tony Tighe, M Higgins, L Murphy, Jack Boylan, B Cully, G Smith.
MUINEACHÁN: S Mulligan, Michael Moore, M Finnegan, Mervin McCooey, E O'Connor, E McDonald, Percy McCooey, Donal Rice, V O Duffy, Charlie Brennan, P McCarney, Eamonn Murphy, C McGrath, Pat McCarville, Macartan McCormack.

1945

AN CABHÁN: B Kelly, Tom O Reilly (capt), P P Galligan, P Smith, John J Wilson, S Deignan, J Boylan, M Higgins, A Comiskey, P A O Reilly, T Tighe, T P O Reilly, J Stafford, Peter Donohoe, P J Duke. Sub.: J W Martin for Comiskey.
FEAR MANACH: Jim Gallagher, Eric McQuillan, Brian Gallagher, Mick O'Grady, Phil Keenan, Redmond Shannon, Tommy Duffy, Tommy Durnien, Bertie Cassidy, Brendan Lunny, Paddy Fox, Paddy Clarke, Christy Creamer, Alph Breslin, Garret O'Reilly.

1946

AONTROIM: Harry Vernon, Mal McMahon, Frank Hamill, Jim O'Hare, Billy Feeney, George Watterson (capt), Paddy 'Cocker' Murray, Harry O'Neill, Seán Gallagher, Seán Gibson, Kevin Armstrong, Frank McCorry, Paddy O'Hara, Brian McAteer, Joe McCallin.
AN CABHÁN: B Kelly, Brian O Reilly, B Cully, 'P Sheridan', T Tighe, J J O Reilly, P Smith, P Donohoe, S Deignan, T P O Reilly, M Higgins, P J Duke, J Boylan, J Stafford, John Joe Cassidy. Sub: Tom O Reilly for Cassidy

1947

AN CABHÁN: Val Gannon, Bill Doonan, B O Reilly, Paddy Smith, P J Duke, J J O Reilly (capt), S Deignan, Columba McDyer, T Tighe, Terry Sheridan, M Higgins, T P O Reilly, J Stafford, P Donohoe, Edwin Carolan. Subs.: Tom O Reilly for Cassidy; Owen Roe McGovern for Doonan.
AONTROIM: Joe Heenan, M McMahon, Seán McAleavey, Ray Beirne, W Feeney, G Watterson, P Murray, H O'Neill, S Gallagher, S Gibson, K Armstrong, F McCorry, P O'Hara, Frank Dunlop, J McCallin. Sub.: B McAteer for Armstrong.

1948

AN CABHÁN: J D Benson, Bill Doonan, B O Reilly, P Smith, P J Duke, J J O Reilly (capt), S Deignan, T Tighe, Phil 'the Gunner' Brady, J J Cassidy, M Higgins, Victor Sherlock, J Stafford, P Donohoe, E Carolan.
AONTROIM: Raymond Flack, Harry McPartland, G Watterson, W Feeney, F McCorry, S Gallagher, P Murray, H O'Neill, R Beirne, S Gibson, K Armstrong, Gerry Fegan, P O'Hara, B McAteer, J McCallin. Sub: M McMahon for McCorry.

1949

AN CABHÁN: S Morris, R O Connor, P Smith, O R McGovern, P J Duke, J J O Reilly (capt), S Deignan, P Brady, V Sherlock, E Carolan, T Tighe, J J Cassidy, J Stafford, P Donohoe, T P O Reilly. Subs: Dessie Maguire for O'Connor, Brian McNamara for Cassidy.
ARD MHACHA: Willie McVeigh, Gerry McStay, Hugh O'Hanlon, Peter McGleenon, Eugene Morgan, Pat O'Neill, Seán Quinn, John McCarron, Bill McCorry, Gerry O'Neill, Art O Hagan, Mal McEvoy, Gerry Fegan, Frank Feighan, Seán McBreen. Sub: Seamus O'Rourke for McCarron.

1950

ARD MHACHA: W McVeigh, G McStay, H O'Hanlon, P McGleenon, E Morgan, P O Neill (capt), S Quinn, A O'Hagan, W McCorry, G O'Neill, M McAvoy, S McBreen, Bertie Regan, F Feighan, Des Slevin. Sub.: Ray McGibbon for Regan.
AN CABHÁN: S Morris, Liam Maguire, D Maguire, P Smith, Paddy Carolan, J J O'Reilly, J J Cassidy, P Brady, V Sherlock, T Tighe, M Higgins, Tom Hardy, E Carolan, P Donohoe, John Cusack.

1951

AONTROIM: Mickey Darragh, Jimmy Roe, Paddy Duggan, Joe Hurley, Brian O'Kane, R Beirne, P Murray, Peter O'Hara, S Gallagher, H O'Neill, K Armstrong, Tony Best, Paddy O'Hara, Donough Forde, J McCallin. Sub: Bobby Cunningham for Murray.
AN CABHÁN: S Morris, Paul Fitzsimmons, P Brady, James McCabe, P Carolan, J J O'Reilly, D Maguire, V Sherlock, L Maguire, T Tighe, M Higgins, Peadar Doyle, J J Cassidy, P Donohoe, E Carolan.

1952

AN CABHÁN: S Morris, J McCabe, P Brady, P Fitzsimmons, T Hardy, L Maguire, D Maguire, V Sherlock, P Carolan, Seamus Hetherton, M Higgins, Brian Gallagher, J J Cassidy, T Tighe, E Carolan.
MUINEACHÁN: P McCooey, Pat McQuaid, Ollie O'Rourke, Mickey McCaffrey, Brendan O'Duffy, John Rice, Mackie Moyna, Tommy Moyna, Tony Prunty, Hughie McKearney, Joe Smith, Paddy O'Rourke, Pat Clarke, Jimmy Brannigan, Eamonn McCooey.

1953

ARD MHACHA: Eamon McMahon, G Morgan, Jack Bratten, John McKnight, Frank Kernan, P O'Neill, S Quinn, Mick O'Hanlon, M McAvoy, Joe Cunningham, Brian Seeley, W McCorry, Pat Campbell, A O'Hagan, G O'Neill. Sub: Joe O'Hare for Campbell.
AN CABHÁN: S Morris, P Fitzsimmons, L Maguire, D Maguire, P Carolan, T Hardy, Noel O'Reilly, B Maguire, V Sherlock, S Hetherton, E Carolan, B Gallagher, J Cusack, S Deignan, M Higgins. Sub: M Keyes for Deignan.

1954

AN CABHÁN: S Morris, P Fitzsimmons, P Brady, J McCabe, J Cusack, T Hardy, B Reilly, Tom Maguire, V Sherlock, B Gallagher, P Carolan, Gerry Keyes, S Hetherton, S Deignan, Brian Deignan.
ARD MHACHA: Brian Daly, Mickey McKnight, J Bratten, J McKnight, F Kernan, P O'Neill, S Quinn, M O'Hanlon, M McAvoy, John McBreen, Patsy Kieran, B McCorry, P Campbell, A O'Hagan, John Hanratty.

1955

AN CABHÁN: S Morris, P Fitzsimmons, P Brady, N O'Reilly, Hubert Gaffney, P Carolan, Jim McDonnell, V Sherlock, T Maguire, B Gallagher, T Hardy, Colm Smith, J Cusack, P Donohoe, E Carolan.
DOIRE: John Murphy, Eddie Kealey, Hugh Francis Gribben, Tommy Doherty, Mickey Gribben, Harry Cassidy, Frank Stinson, Jim McKeever, Patsy Breen, Francie Niblock, Tommy J Doherty, Emmett Fullen, Charlie Higgins, Roddy Gribbin, Colm Mulholland.

1956

TÍR EOGHAIN: Thady Turbett, Brian McSorley, Jim Devlin, Pat Donaghy, Sean Donnelly, Paddy Corey, John Joe O'Hagan, Jody O'Neill, Pat Devlin, Iggy Jones, Jackie Taggart, Frankie Donnelly, Mickey Kerr, Frank Higgins, Donal Donnelly.

Sub: Hugh Kelly for Kerr.
AN CABHÁN: S Morris, N O'Reilly, P Brady, B Reilly,
H Gaffney, J McDonnell, Donal Kelly, Con Smith, B Gallagher,
T Hardy, P Carolan, Charlie Gallagher, Sean Keogan, V Sherlock,
Tommy White. Subs: G Keyes for Smith, James Brady for White.

1957
TÍR EOGHAIN: T Turbett, B McSorley, J Devlin, P Donaghy,
Pat Devlin, Eddie Devlin, Joe O'Hagan, J O'Neill, Mick
Cushnahan, D Donnelly, J Taggart, Mick McIlkenny, S Donnelly,
F Higgins, F Donnelly.
DOIRE: Patsy Gormley, Patsy McLarnon, H F Gribbin,
T Doherty, Gabriel Muldoon, J McKeever, Peter Smith, P Breen,
Owen Gribbin, Sean O'Connell, R Gribben, E Fullen, Willie
Cassidy, T J Doherty, Seamus Young.

1958
DOIRE: P Gormley, P McLarnon, H F Gribbin, T Doherty,
P Breen, C Mulholland, P Smith, J McKeever, Phil Stuart,
S O'Connell, Brendan Murray, Denis McKeever, Leo O'Neill,
O Gribbin, C Higgins.
AN DÚN: Eamon McKay, Kevin O'Neill, Leo Murphy, Pat Rice,
Patsy O'Hagan, Jim McCartan, Kevin Mussen, Jarlath Carey,
Tony Hadden, Kieran Denvir, Paddy Doherty, Ronnie Moore,
Sean Fearon, Jim Fitzpatrick.

1959
AN DÚN: E McKay, George Lavery, L Murphy, P Rice,
K Mussen, J McCartan, K O'Neill, Joe Lennon, P O'Hagan,
Sean O'Neill, J Carey, P Doherty, K Denvir, T Hadden, Brian
Morgan. Subs.: Dan McCartan for S O'Neill, S O'Neill for Denvir.
AN CABHÁN: Brian O'Reilly, N O'Reilly, Gabriel Kelly, Mickey
Brady, H Gaffney, T Maguire, J McDonnell, Hugh Barney
O'Donoghue, K McIntyre, Con Smith, B Gallagher, J Conaty,
Jimmy Sheridan, C Gallagher, J Brady. Subs: Jimmy Meehan for
N O'Reilly, Tommy Galligan for Maguire, Maguire for Galligan.

1960
AN DÚN: E McKay, G Lavery, L Murphy, P Rice, K Mussen,
D McCartan, K O'Neill, P J McElroy, J Lennon, S O'Neill,
J McCartan, P Doherty, T Hadden, P O'Hagan, B Morgan.
Subs: J Carey for McElroy, Eamon Lundy for Lennon.
AN CABHÁN: B O'Reilly, J Meehan, D Kelly, M Brady,
H Gaffney, T Maguire, T Galligan, H B O'Donoghue,
J McDonnell, J Sheridan, Mal Shiels, Con Smith, Seamus Conaty,
J Brady, C Gallagher. Sub: P Carolan for Sheridan.

1961
AN DÚN: E McKay, G Lavery, L Murphy, P Rice, K Mussen,
D McCartan, John Smith, P J McElroy, J Lennon, S O'Neill,
J Carey, P Doherty, T Hadden, P O'Hagan, B Morgan.
Sub: J McCartan for Mussen.
ARD MHACHA: E McMahon, Hughie Casey, Felix McKnight,
Brendan Donaghy, Des Harney, Dan Kelly, Harry Hoy, John
McGeary, Gene Larkin, Jimmy Whan, Danny McRory, Kevin
Halfpenny, Bertie Watson, Pat Campbell, Harry Loughran.
Subs: J McKnight for Harney, Pat McKenna for Campbell,
Campbell for Loughran.

1962
AN CABHÁN: Seán Óg Flood, G Kelly, P J McCaffrey,
M Brady, Tony Morris, T Maguire, J McDonnell, Ray Carolan,
Tom Lynch, C Smith, H B O'Donoghue, Jimmy Stafford, Seamus

McMahon, C Gallagher, J Brady. Sub.: P J O Gorman for Kelly.
AN DÚN: E McKay, G Lavery, L Murphy, P Rice, Pat Hamill,
D McCartan, P O'Hagan, J Carey, J Lennon, S O'Neill,
J McCartan, P Doherty, T Hadden, P J McElroy, B Morgan.
Subs: K O'Neill for Hamill, K Mussen for Carey.

1963
AN DÚN: Patsy McAlinden, G Lavery, L Murphy, P Rice,
P O'Hagan, D McCartan, J Smith, J Lennon, T Hadden,
S O'Neill, J McCartan, P Doherty, B Morgan, B Johnston,
Val Kane.
DÚN na nGALL: Séamus Hoare, Finn Gallagher, Bernard Brady,
Brendan McFeely, Sean O'Donnell, John Hannigan, Paul Kelly,
Frankie McFeely, P J Flood, Donal Breslin, Sean Ferriter,
Des Houlihan, Cormac Breslin, Mick Griffin, Harry Laverty.

1964
AN CABHÁN: P J O Gorman, G Kelly, P J McCaffrey, T Morris,
Frank Kennedy, T Maguire, J McDonnell, R Carolan, T Lynch,
J J O'Reilly, H B O Donoghue, C Gallagher, Mattie Cahill,
Jimmy O'Donnell, J Stafford. Sub: Peter Pritchard for
O Donoghue.
AN DÚN: P McAlinden, G Lavery, L Murphy, K O'Neill,
P O'Hagan, Tom O'Hare, P Hamill, Larry Powell, D McCartan,
B Johnston, J Lennon, P Doherty, S O'Neill, J McCartan, V Kane.
Subs: Jackie Fitzsimmons for Lavery, B Morgan for O'Hare.

1965
AN DÚN: P McAlinden, Seamus Doyle, L Murphy, T O'Hare,
J Lennon, D McCartan, P O'Hagan, George Glynn, L Powell,
Felix Quigley, V Kane, P Doherty, J Fitzsimmons, S O'Neill,
B Johnston. Sub: Colm Curtis for Powell.
AN CABHÁN: John Reilly, G Kelly, Tony Keyes, T Morris,
Brian Kennedy, T Maguire, Donal O'Grady, R Carolan, T Lynch,
John Joe O'Reilly, J O'Donnell, C Gallagher, S McMahon,
Danny Brady, Phil Murray.

1966
AN DÚN: P McAlinden, S Doyle, L Murphy, T O'Hare,
Tom Morgan, D McCartan, J Lennon. F Quigley, G Glynn,
J Fitzsimmons, L Powell, B Johnston, P Doherty, J McCartan,
S O'Neill. Subs: Colm McAlarney for Quigley, Francie Doherty
for Fitzsimmons.
DÚN na nGALL: S Hoare, F Gallagher, B Brady, P Kelly,
S O'Donnell, P J Flood, Anton Carroll, Declan O'Carroll, Sean
Ferriter, Mickey McLoone, F McFeely, M Griffin, D Houlihan,
J Hannigan, Pauric McShea. Subs: B McFeely for Gallagher,
Brian McEniff for O'Donnell.

1967
AN CABHÁN: Seamus Gallagher, Andy McCabe, G Kelly,
P Pritchard, Pat Tinnelly, R Carolan, Brendan Murtagh,
Brendan Donoghue, T Lynch, Steve Duggan, J J O'Reilly,
Micheál Greenan, J O'Donnell, C Gallagher, P Murray.
AN DÚN: P McAlinden, Brendan Sloan, L Murphy, T O'Hare,
Ray McConville, D McCartan, L Powell, G Glynn, J Lennon,
John Murphy, C McAlarney, John Purdy, J McCartan, S O'Neill,
V Kane. Subs: Ray Carville for Murphy, J. Fitzsimmons for Kane,
Brian McVeigh for Sloan.

1968
AN DÚN: Danny Kelly, B Sloan, D McCartan, T O'Hare,
R McConville, Willie Doyle, J Lennon, C McAlarney, Jim

Milligan, Mickey Cole, Dickie Murphy, J Murphy, P Doherty, S O'Neill, J Purdy.
AN CABHÁN: Pat Lyons, G Kelly, B Donoghue, P Pritchard, P Tinnelly, T Lynch, A McCabe, Fergus McCauley, Hugh Newman, M Greenan, J J O'Reilly, P Murray, J O'Donnell, C Gallagher, S Duggan. Sub: B Murtagh for Newman.

1969

AN CABHÁN: Paddy Lyons, G Kelly, B Donoghue, A McCabe, P Tinnelly, T Lynch, Enda McGowan, R Carolan, H Newman, S Duggan, J J O'Reilly, Hugh McInerney, Gene Cusack, Declan Coyle, C Gallagher. Sub.: P Murray for McInerney.
AN DÚN: D Kelly, B Sloan, D McCartan, T O'Hare, R McConville, W Doyle, J Lennon, C McAlarney, J Milligan, M Cole, J Murphy, J Fitzsimons, Peter Rooney, S O'Neill, P Doherty. Sub: James Morgan for Doyle.

1970

DOIRE: Seamus Hasson, Mick McGuckin, Henry Diamond, Tom Quinn, Malachy McAfee, Colm Mullan, Gerry O'Loughlin, Larry Diamond, Seamus Lagan, S O'Connell, Mickey Niblock, Eamonn Coleman, Adrian McGuckin, Brian Devlin, Hugh Niblock. Subs: Anthony McGurk for Mullan, Seamus Gribben for H Niblock.
AONTROIM: Ray McIlroy, Eamonn Grieve, John Burns, Jimmy Ward, Seamus Killough, Billy Millar, Des McNeill, Tony McAtamney, Frank Fitzsimmons, Gerry McCann, Gerry McCrory, Terry Dunlop, Andy McCallin, Owen Ruddy, Aidan Hamill. Subs: Alistair Scullion for Killough, Gerry Dillon for Millar.

1971

AN DÚN: D Kelly, B Sloan, D McCartan, T O'Hare, R McConville, Maurice Denvir, Cecil Ward, Dan Connolly, Donal Gordon, J Murphy, C McAlarney, J Morgan, Mickey Cunningham, S O'Neill, Donal Davey. Sub: M Cole for Morgan.
DOIRE: S Hasson, M McGuckin, H Diamond, T Quinn, Peter Stevenson, H Niblock, G O'Loughlin, L Diamond, S Gribben, S O'Connell, A McGurk, Johnnie O'Leary, A McGuckin, M Niblock, E Coleman. Subs: M McAfee for H Niblock, Mickey P Kelly for Quinn, Tom McGuinness for Gribben.

1972

DÚN na nGALL: Alan Kane, Donal Monaghan, P McShea, John Boyce, B McEniff, Anthony Gallagher, A Carroll, Seamus Bonner, F McFeely, Martin Carney, Mick McMenamin, D O'Carroll, Seamie Granaghan, Mick Sweeney, Joe Winston. Subs: J Hannigan for O'Carroll, Andy Curran for Boyce.
TÍR EOGHAIN: Kieran Harte, Ollie Nugent, Peter Mulgrew, Jackie Duffy, Michael John Forbes, Gerry Taggart, Mickey Hughes, Brendan Dolan, Seamus Donaghy, Patsy Hetherington, Sean McElhatton, Paddy McMahon, Hugh Crawford, Kevin Teague, John Early. Subs: Paddy Parke for Teague, Frank McGuigan for Crawford.

1973

TÍR EOGHAIN: Liam Turbett, G Taggart, P Mulgrew, Barney McAnespie, Joe McElroy, Michael Jordan, M Hughes, F McGuigan, Aidan McMahon, S Donaghy, Pat King, P Hetherington, S McElhatton, Brendan Donnelly, K Teague. Subs: J Early for McMahon, P McMahon for Early, H Crawford for Donaghy.
AN DÚN: Macartan Bryce, Peter Hamill, D McCartan, T O'Hare, John Brown, W Doyle, R McConville, C McAlarney,

D Gordon, D Davey, P Rooney, M Cole, Eugene Cole, S O'Neill, Willie Walsh. Subs: J Murphy for M Cole, Colm Shields for Walsh, B Sloan for Gordon.

1974

DÚN na nGALL: A Kane, D Monaghan, P McShea, A Curran, B McEniff, A Gallagher, Finian Mac An Bhaird, Michael Lafferty, M Carney, S Granaghan, Hugh McClafferty, Neilly Gallagher, J Winston, S Bonner, Kieran Keaney. Subs: Paul McGettigan for Granaghan, P J McGowan for Lafferty.
Replay Changes: Naul McCole for Kane, Michael Carr for Keaney. Subs: P McGettigan for Lafferty, Gerry McElwee for McClafferty, Keaney for Carr.
AN DÚN: Joe O'Hare, B Sloan, D McCartan, P Hamill, Cathal Digney, Mark Turley, Martin Slevin, Clem Stewart, P Rooney, C McAlarney, M Cunningham, C Ward, Peter McGrath, S O'Neill, W Walsh. Subs: Bill Gardner for Stewart, Eugene Grant for Walsh.
Replay Changes: D Gordon for Stewart. Subs: Gardner for Walsh, Grant for McGrath, Stewart for McAlarney.

1975

DOIRE: John Somers, M McAfee, T Quinn, Gabriel Bradley, P Stevenson, A McGurk, G O'Loughlin, Eugene Laverty, T McGuinness, Brendan Kelly, Mickey Lynch, Gerry McElhinney, J O'Leary, S O'Connell, Mickey Moran. Subs: Seamus Lagan for McAfee, Kevin Teague for Lagan, H Niblock for McElhinney.
AN DÚN: Lawrence McAlinden, B Sloan, D McCartan, Paddy Galbraith, P Hamill, C Digney, M Slevin, C McAlarney, Dan Connolly, J Murphy, P Rooney, J Morgan, M Cunningham, S O'Neill, W Walsh. Subs: M Turley for Walsh, D Gordon for Connolly, Barry Fitzsimmons for Digney.

1976

DOIRE: J Somers, Liam Murphy, T Quinn, P Stevenson, G O'Loughlin, A McGurk, M Moran, T McGuinness, Colm McGuigan, B Kelly, M Lynch, J O'Leary, Fintan McCluskey, A McGuckin, G McElhinney. Subs: L Diamond for McGuigan, Christy Grieve for McCloskey.
Replay changes: L Diamond for McGuigan, Grieve for McGuckin. Subs: E Laverty for Diamond, S O'Connell for Grieve, G Bradley for O'Loughlin.
AN CABHÁN: Aidan Elliott, P Tinnelly, Dermot Dalton, E McGowan, Sean Leddy, Frankie Dolan, Pat McGill, Ollie Leddy, Donal Meade, Noel Smith, Ollie Brady, Owen Martin, G Cusack, Kieran O'Keeffe, S Duggan. Sub: Adge King for Smith.
Replay changes: John Dwyer for Smith. Subs: Garrett O'Reilly for Dalton, John Joe Martin for McGill, Jimmy Carroll for S Leddy, Adge King for Cusack.

1977

ARD MHACHA: Brian McAlinden, Denis Stevenson, Jim Finnegan, Jim McKerr, Kevin Rafferty, Tom McCreesh, Joey Donnelly, Colm McKinstry, Joe Kernan, Larry Kearns, Jimmy Smyth, Noel Marley, Peter Loughran, Paddy Moriarty, Peter Trainor. Subs: Eamon O'Neill for Trainor, Sean Daly for Marley, Frank Toman for Rafferty.
DOIRE: J Somers, L Murphy, Frank Trainor, Gerry Forrest, G O'Loughlin, A McGurk, G Bradley, E Laverty, C McGuigan, T McGuinness, M Lynch, Terence McWilliams, Gerry Keane, G McElhinney, P Stevenson.

1978

AN DÚN: Martin McCabe, B Sloan, M Turley, Michael Sands,

C Digney, Brendan Toner, John McCartan, C McAlarney, Liam Austin, B Gardner, M Cunningham, Ronnie Matthews, Joe Byrne, P Rooney, Jarlath Digney. Subs: Emmett McGivern for Matthews, Tommy McGovern for Toner, Pat Murtagh for McCartan.
AN CABHÁN: A Elliott, F Dolan, D Dalton, J J Martin, D Meade, O Brady, E McGowan, A King, O Martin, Tony Brady, Paddy McNamee, Ray Cullivan, O Leddy, Donal Donohue, Mark Goldrick. Subs: K O'Keeffe for King, S Leddy for Cullivan.

1979
MUINEACHÁN: Paddy Linden, Eugene 'Nudie' Hughes, Sean Hughes, Fergus Caulfield, Paddy Kerr, Sean McCarville, Eamonn Tavey, Gerry McCarville, Hugo Clerkin, Gene Finnegan, Dessie Mulligan, Kevin Trainor, Kieran Finlay, Tom Moyna, Brendan Brady. Subs: Anthony McArdle for Finnegan, P J Finlay for Trainor.
DÚN na nGALL: N McCole, Michael Heuston, Martin Griffen, Sandy Harper, M Carr, F Mac An Bhaird, Martin Sweeney, M Lafferty, Michael Gallagher, K Keaney, S Bonnar, Brendan Dunleavy, Jim Brennan, Fionn McDonnell, Seamus Flynn. Subs: Eugene Sharkey for Dunleavy, H McCafferty for Gallagher, Seamus Reilly for Brennan.

1980
ARD MHACHA: B McAlinden, Brian Canavan, J McKerr, K Rafferty, P Moriarty, Jim McCorry, J Donnelly, C McKinstry, J Kernan, N Marley, J Smyth, Fran McMahon, Sean Devlin, Brian Hughes, P Loughran. Subs: Hank Kernan for Devlin, Denis McCoy for Marley.
TÍR EOGHAIN: Barry Campbell, Ciaran McGarvey, Frank Rafferty, Kieran McRory, Kevin McCabe, Sean Donnelly, P King, Patsy Kerlin, Kevin Toner, P Hetherington, G Taggart, Damien O'Hagan, Paul Donnelly, Eugene McKenna, Mickey Harte. Subs: Seamus Daly for P Donnelly, Willie McKenna for Toner.

1981
AN DÚN: Pat Donnan, Adrian McAulfield, Paddy Kennedy, T McGovern, Ned King, B.Toner, M Turley, L Austin, Paddy O'Rourke, Damien Morgan, Ambrose Rodgers, Greg Blaney, Brendan McGovern, John McCartan, Jim McCartan. Subs: C McAlarney for Jim McCartan, Ned Toner for McAlarney.
ARD MHACHA: B McAlinden, Denis Stevenson, J McKerr, Joe Murphy, P Moriarty, Des Mackin, J Donnelly, C McKinstry, F McMahon, S Devlin, J Smyth, Peter Rafferty, Jim Loughran, B Hughes, P Loughran. Subs: J McCorry for Murphy, Martin Murphy for Devlin, J Kernan for Mackin.

1982
ARD MHACHA: B McAlinden, D Stevenson, J McKerr, J Murphy, N Marley, P Moriarty, P Rafferty, C McKinstry, F McMahon, Dermot Dowling, B Hughes, Aidan Short, S Devlin, John Corvan, Mickey McDonald. Subs: J Donnelly for Murphy, J Kernan for McDonald, P Loughran for Short.
FEAR MANACH: Peter Greene, Donald Fee, Ciaran Campbell, Niall Corrigan, John Mohan, Pat McCann, Michael Sheridan, Peter McGinnity, Philip Courtney, Arthur McCaffrey, Aidan Jones, Brendan O'Reilly, Paul McKenna, Dominic Corrigan, Arthur Mulligan. Subs: Gerry McIlroy for Mulligan, Ken McPartland for O'Reilly.

1983
DÚN na nGALL: N McCole, Des Newton, M Griffen, Tommy

McDermott, B Dunleavy, M Lafferty, M Carr, P McGettigan, Anthony Molloy, Donal Reid, Martin McHugh, Joyce McMullan, Pauric Carr, S Bonnar, K Keaney. Sub: Frank Rushe for McHugh.
AN CABHÁN: Damien O'Reilly, Eugene Kiernan, Jim McAweeney, F Dolan, T Brady, Joe Dillon, Jim Reilly, A King, Danny Finnegan, D Donohue, Michael Faulkner, R Cullivan, Martin Lynch, Derek McDonnell, P McNamee. Subs: Brian O'Grady for Brady, Stephen King for A King.

1984
TÍR EOGHAIN: Aidan Skelton, F Rafferty, C McGarvey, S Donnelly, K McCabe, Hugh O'Hagan, Noel McGinn, E McKenna, Plunkett Donaghy, Colm Donaghy, D O'Hagan, P Kerlin, S Daly, F McGuigan, Paddy O'Neill. Sub: John Lynch for C Donaghy.
ARD MHACHA: B McAlinden, J Donnelly, Thomas Cassidy, J McCorry, Kieran McNally, Colin Harney, B Canavan, C McKinstry, F McMahon, Tommy Coleman, J Kernan, Ger Houlahan, J Corvan, P Moriarty, P Rafferty. Subs: J McKerr for McKinstry, D Stevenson for Cassidy, B Hughes for Rafferty.

1985
MUINEACHÁN: P Linden, Gene Sherry, G McCarville, F Caulfield, Brendan Murray, Ciaran Murray, Declan Flanagan, David Byrne, H Clerkin, Ray McCarron, Michael O'Dowd, B Brady, Eamon McEneaney, Eamonn Murphy, E Hughes.
DOIRE: John Mackle, Ciaran Keenan, Tony Scullion, Hugh Martin McGurk, Paddy Mackle, Brendan McPeake, Joe Irwin, Plunkett Murphy, Damien Barton, Dermot McNicholl, Eddie McElhinney, Declan McNicholl, Damien Cassidy, Brian Kealey, Terence McGuckian. Subs: Tom Doherty for McElhinney, Eunan Rafferty for Cassidy, Paul McCormack for Declan McNicholl.

1986
TÍR EOGHAIN: A Skelton, S Donnelly, C McGarvey, J Lynch, K McCabe, N McGinn, Joe Mallon, P Donaghy, Harry McClure, Mickey McClure, E McKenna, Sean McNally, Stephen Rice, D O'Hagan, Mickey Mallon. Subs: Pat McKeown for Donnelly, Stephen Conway for Lynch, Enda Kilpatrick for Rice.
AN DÚN: P Donnan, A McAulfield, P Kennedy, Barry Breen, Peter Walsh, P O'Rourke, Ross Carr, L Austin, John McCartan, Mickey Linden, G Blaney, Tony McArdle, John 'Shorty' Treanor, A Rodgers, Brendan Mason. Subs: Brian Conlon for McArdle, Francie McKibben for Treanor, Treanor for O'Rourke.

1987
DOIRE: Damien McCusker, H M McGurk, Danny Quinn, T Scullion, P McCormack, J Irwin, Paul McCann, P Murphy, Brian McGilligan, Enda Gormley, Dermot McNicholl, D Barton, D Cassidy, B Kealey, Kevin McWilliams. Sub: John McGurk for McWilliams.
ARD MHACHA: B McAlinden, Vinny Loughran, T Cassidy, J McCorry, B Canavan, K McNally, A Short, Kieran McGurk, Martin McQuillan, Neil Smyth, Paul Grimley, G Houlahan, Shane Skelton, Denis Seeley, Jim McConville. Subs: J McKerr for Grimley, D McCoy for Smyth, J Kernan for Seeley.

1988
MUINEACHÁN: P Linden, Gerard Hoey, G Sherry, Brendan Murray, C Murray, Declan Loughman, D Flanagan, Bernie Murray, D Byrne, R McCarron, G McCarville, Owen Hamilton, E Hughes, E McEneaney. Sub: E Murphy for Hamilton.

TÍR EOGHAIN: A Skelton, S Donnelly, C McGarvey, Raymond Munroe, J Lynch, N McGinn, Paddy Ball, P Donaghy, H McClure, K McCabe, E McKenna, S Conway, D O'Hagan, P Kerlin, Paudge Quinn. Subs: Paul Byrne for Munroe, S McNally for Quinn, M McClure for Kerlin.

1989
TÍR EOGHAIN: A Skelton, J Mallon, C McGarvey, R Munroe, Seán Meyler, E Kilpatrick, John McGoldrick, P Donaghy, H McClure, Ciaran Corr, D O'Hagan, S Conway, K McCabe, E McKenna, P Quinn. Subs: N McGinn for Meyler, M McClure for Quinn, P Kerlin for McCabe.
Replay Changes: S McNally for McCabe, S Donnelly for Quinn (Meyler switched to forwards). Subs: K McCabe for Conway, P Ball for Mallon.
DÚN na nGALL: Gary Walsh, John Joe Doherty, John Connors, Brian Tuohy, D Reid, Martin Gavigan, Martin Shovlin, A Molloy, Michael Gallagher, Charlie Mulgrew, M McHugh, J McMullan, Tommy Ryan, Brian Murray, Marty Carlin. Sub: Leslie McGettigan for Carlin.
Replay Changes: B Dunleavy for J J Doherty. Subs: L McGettigan for Carlin, Paddy Gavigan for Murray.

1990
DÚN na nGALL: G Walsh, J J Doherty, M Gavigan, Matt Gallagher, D Reid, John Cunningham, M Shovlin, A Molloy, B Murray, James McHugh, M McHugh, J McMullan, Declan Bonnar, T Ryan, Manus Boyle. Subs: Tony Boyle for Ryan, John Bán Gallagher for Murray, Barry McGowan for Bonnar.
ARD MHACHA: B McAlinden, Pádraig O'Neill, Gareth O'Neill, B Canavan, Leo McGeary, John Grimley, A Short, Mark Grimley, N Smyth, Ollie Reel, John Toner, Martin Toye, J McConville, K McGurk, G Houlahan. Sub: Shane Skelton for Toye.

1991
AN DÚN: Neil Collins, Brendan McKernan, Conor Deegan, Paul Higgins, John Kelly, P O'Rourke, D J Kane, B Breen, Eamonn Burns, R Carr, G Blaney, Gary Mason, M Linden, Peter Withnell, James McCartan. Sub: Michael Quinn for Higgins.
DÚN na nGALL: G Walsh, J J Doherty, Sean Bonnar, Matt Gallagher, D Reid, M Gavigan, B McGowan, B Murray, Michael Gallagher, M McHugh, C Mulgrew, J McMullan, D Bonnar, T Boyle, M Boyle. Subs: Noel Hegarty for S Bonnar, Pauric Brogan for Murray, J McHugh for Mulgrew.

1992
DÚN na nGALL: G Walsh, J Cunningham, Matt Gallagher, N Hegarty, D Reid, M Gavigan, M Shovlin, A Molloy, B Murray, J McHugh, T Ryan, J McMullan, M McHugh, T Boyle, D Bonnar. Sub: B McGowan for Boyle.
DOIRE: D McCusker, Kieran McKeever, D Quinn, T Scullion, J McGurk, Henry Downey, Gary Coleman, B McGilligan, Dermot Heaney, Anthony Tohill, Dermot McNicholl, D Cassidy, Declan Bateson, Seamus Downey, E Gormley. Subs: D Barton for Tohill, John McErlean for Quinn, Joe Brolly for Bateson.

1993
DOIRE: D McCusker, K McKeever, T Scullion, J McGurk, Fergal McCusker, H Downey, G Coleman, A Tohill, B McGilligan, Brian McCormack, D Barton, D Cassidy, Stephen Mulvenna, D Heaney, E Gormley. Subs: Dermot McNicholl for Heaney, J Brolly for Mulvenna, Karl Diamond for McNicholl.
DÚN na nGALL: G Walsh, J J Doherty, Matt Gallagher, B McGowan, Mark Crossan, Paul Carr, M Shovlin, Michael

Gallagher, B Murray, J McHugh, M McHugh, J McMullan, D Bonnar, M Boyle, John Duffy. Subs: Mark McShane for Bonnar, A Molloy for J McHugh, M Gavigan for Michael Gallagher.

1994
AN DÚN: N Collins, Micheál Magill, Brian Burns, P Higgins, E Burns, B Breen, D J Kane, Gregory McCartan, C Deegan, R Carr, G Blaney, J McCartan, M Linden, Aidan Farrell. G Mason. Sub: P Withnell for Farrell.
TÍR EOGHAIN: Joe Cassidy, Gareth McGirr, Chris Lawn, Fay Devlin, Paul Donnelly, Fergal Logan, Aidan Morris, C Corr, P Donaghy, Adrian Cush, Adrian Kilpatrick, Stephen Lawn, Brian Gormley, Peter Canavan, Ciaran Loughran. Subs: Pascal Canavan for Loughran, Paul Devlin for F Devlin, Mattie McGleenan for Gormley.

1995
TÍR EOGHAIN: Finbarr McConnell, P Devlin, C Lawn, F Devlin, Ronan McGarrity, Seamus McCallan, Sean McLaughlin, Jody Gormley, F Logan, C Corr, Pascal Canavan, C Loughran, Ciaran McBride, Peter Canavan, S Lawn. Subs: A Cush for McBride, M McGleenan for McBride.
AN CABHÁN: Paul O'Dowd, Aidan Watters, Damien O'Reilly, John Donnellan, Gerry Sheridan, Aidan Connolly, Bernard Morris, S King, Tommy Smyth, Dermot McCabe, Peter Reilly, Ronan Carolan, Adrian Lambe, Fintan Cahill, John Brady. Subs: Fergal Hartin for Lambe, Anthony Forde for Brady.

1996
TÍR EOGHAIN: F McConnell, P Devlin, C Lawn, F Devlin, Ronan McGarrity, Seamus McCallan, Sean McLaughlin, J Gormley, Pascal Canavan, Brian Dooher, Gerard Cavlan, A Cush, C McBride, Peter Canavan, B Gormley. Subs: F Logan for McCallan, Damien Gormley for B.Gormley.
AN DÚN: Michael McVeigh, Finbar Caulfield, B Burns, P Higgins, G Mason, M Magill, D J Kane, C Deegan, G McCartan, R Carr, J Treanor, J McCartan, M Linden, P Withnell, G Blaney. Subs: Cathal Murray for Kane, A Farrell for Treanor, Ciaran McCabe for Deegan.

1997
AN CABHÁN: P O'Dowd, Philip Kermath, Ciaran Brady, G Sheridan, Terry Farrelly, B Morris, Patrick Sheils, S King, D McCabe, P Reilly, R Carolan, Raymond Cunningham, Larry Reilly, F Cahill, D O'Reilly. Subs: Jason Reilly for Cahill, Phil Smith for King, Mickey Graham for L Reilly.
DOIRE: D McCusker, K McKeever, David O'Neill, Johnny McBride, Sean Martin Lockhart, H Downey, G Coleman, A Tohill, D.Heaney, F McCusker, Dermot Dougan, Gary Magill, J.Brolly, S Downey, Joe Cassidy. Subs: Gary Doyle for McGill, Karl Diamond for Dougan.

1998
DOIRE: Eoin McCloskey, K McKeever (capt), S M Lockhart, G Coleman, D O Neill, H Downey, Paul McFlynn, A Tohill, Enda Muldoon, G Magill, D Dougan, Eamon Burns, J Brolly, S Downey, J Cassidy. Subs.: D Heaney for Burns, E Gormley for S Downey, Geoffrey McGonigle for Cassidy.
DÚN na nGALL: Tony Blake, M Crossan, J J Doherty, B McGowan, Damien Diver, Martin Coll, Noel McGinley, Jim McGuinness, N Hegarty, J Duffy, Adrian Sweeney, John Gildea, M Boyle, T Boyle, Brendan Devenney. Subs.: James Ruane for Crossan, J McHugh for Sweeney, Brian McLoughlin for M Boyle.

1999
ARD MHACHA: Brendan Tierney, Enda McNulty, Gerard Reid, Justin McNulty, Kieran Hughes, Kieran McGeeney, Andrew McCann, Jarlath Burns (capt), Paul McGrane, Paddy McKeever, John McEntee, John Rafferty, Cathal O Rourke, Diarmaid Marsden, Oisin McConville. Subs.: Tony McEntee for Rafferty, G Houlahan for O Rourke.
AN DÚN: M McVeigh, F Caulfield, Seán Ward, Pádraig Matthews, P Higgins, M Magill, Simon Poland, B Burns, Alan Molloy, R Carr, Shane Mulholland, Gerard Deegan, M Linden, C McCabe, Shane Ward. Subs.: G McCartan for Molloy, A Farrell for Deegan, J McCartan for Linden.

2000
ARD MHACHA: B Tierney, E McNulty, G Reid, J McNulty, K Hughes, K McGeeney, A McCann, J McEntee, P McGrane, P McKeever, Barry O Hagan, C O Rourke, O McConville, T McEntee, Steven McDonnell. Subs.: Alan O Neill for McKeever, James Byrne for O Hagan.
DOIRE: E McCloskey, S M Lockhart, K McKeever, G Coleman, Niall McCusker, H Downey, P McFlynn, A Tohill, D Heaney, E Burns, D Dougan, J Cassidy, Patrick Bradley, E Muldoon, Johnny McBride. Subs.: J Brolly for Bradley, Ronan Rocks for Burns, S Downey for Dougan, F McCusker for Cassidy.

2001
TIR EOGHAIN: F McConnell, Ciarán Gourley, Colin Holmes, Michael McGee, Ryan McMenamin, Seán Teague, Declan McCrossan, Cormac McAnallen, Kevin Hughes, B Dooher, Stephen O Neill, Pascal Canavan, Owen Mulligan, Peter Canavan, G Cavlan. Subs.: C Lawn for Teague, Brian McGuigan for Mulligan, Eoin Gormley for Dooher, D Gormley for McGuigan.
AN CABHÁN: Aaron Donohoe, Michael Brides, Thomas Prior, Rory Donohoe, James Doonan, A Forde, Edward Jackson, D McCabe, Barry McCrudden, Peter Reilly, Paul Galligan, John Tierney, L Reilly, J Reilly, Finbar O Reilly. Subs.: Gerry Sheridan for R Donohoe, M Graham for Tierney, Hubert Smith for Jackson, B Morris for Galligan.

2002
ARD MHACHA: B Tierney, Francie Bellew, E McNulty, J McNulty, Aidan O Rourke, K McGeeney (capt), K Hughes, John Toal, P McGrane, P McKeever, J McEntee, O McConville, S McDonnell, Ronan Clarke, D Marsden. Subs.: B O Hagan for McKeever, Philip Loughran for Toal.
DÚN na nGALL: T Blake, Shane Carr, M Crossan, N McGinley, Raymond Sweeney, Barry Monaghan, Kevin Cassidy, John Gildea, J McGuinness, Christy Toye, Michael Hegarty, Paul McGonigle, A Sweeney, B Devenney, Brian Roper. Subs.: D Diver for S Carr, Eamonn Doherty for Crossan, Colm McFadden for Toye, Kevin Rafferty for McGonigle, Brendan Boyle for Roper.

2003
TIR EOGHAIN (as played in drawn game): John Devine, Dermot Carlin, C Lawn, R McMenamin, Conor Gormley, D McCrossan, Philip Jordan, C McAnallen, Seán Cavanagh, B Dooher, B McGuigan, K Hughes, Enda McGinley, Peter Canavan (capt), O Mulligan. Subs: Gourley for McCrossan, Brian Robinson for Lawn.
Changes for replay: Pascal McConnell for Devine, C Gourley for Lawn, Séamus Mulgrew for McCrossan. Subs.: G Cavlan for Dooher, Frank McGuigan Jr for McGinley, Michael Coleman for B McGuigan.

AN DÚN (as played in drawn game): M McVeigh, John Clarke, Brian Burns, Martin Cole, John Lavery, Aidan O Prey, A Molloy, Seán Ward, Gregory McCartan, Liam Doyle, Michael Walsh, Brendan Coulter, Ronan Sexton, Dan Gordon, Ronan Murtagh. Subs: J McCartan for Murtagh, Shane King for Sexton, M Linden for Seán Ward, Patrick Pearse McCartan for Walsh.
Changes for replay: Brendan Grant for G McCartan, J McCartan for Sexton. Subs.: Colm McCrickard for Walsh, Declan Sheeran for Burns, Adrian Scullion for Molloy, Glen McMahon for Coulter.

2004
ARD MHACHA: Paul Hearty, E McNulty, F Bellew, Andy Mallon, K Hughes, K McGeeney (capt), A O Rourke, P Loughran, P McGrane, P McKeever, T McEntee, O McConville, S McDonnell, R Clarke, D Marsden. Subs.: Brian Mallon for Clarke, J Toal for Loughran, A McCann for McGeeney, J McNulty for Bellew, J McEntee for Marsden.
DÚN na nGALL: Paul Durcan, Niall McCready, R Sweeney, D Diver, Éamonn McGee, B Monaghan, S Carr, B Boyle, Stephen McDermott, C Toye, M Hegarty, B Roper, C McFadden, A Sweeney, B Devenney. Subs.: J Gildea for McDermott, Rory Kavanagh for Toye, P McGonigle for Roper, John Haran for A Sweeney, Karl Lacey for McGee.

2005
ARD MHACHA (first game): P Hearty, A Mallon, F Bellew, E McNulty, Aaron Kernan, K McGeeney (capt), A O Rourke, J Toal, P McGrane, M O Rourke, T McEntee, O McConville, S McDonnell, R Clarke, B Mallon. Subs used in drawn game: P McKeever for M O Rourke, Loughran for Toal, J McEntee for T McEntee, Malachy Mackin for B Mallon, Ciaran McKeever for Kernan.
Changes for replay: P Loughran for Toal, C McKeever for M O Rourke, J McEntee for T McEntee. Subs.: P McKeever for Mallon, A McCann for A O Rourke, T McEntee for Loughran.
TIR EOGHAIN (first game): J Devine, R McMenamin, C Lawn, Shane Sweeney, David Harte, Gavin Devlin, P Jordan, C Gormley, S Cavanagh, B Dooher, B McGuigan, Martin Penrose, Peter Canavan, S O Neill, E McGinley. Subs: Mulligan for Penrose, Mark Harte for Canavan, Joe McMahon for D Harte, Brian Meenan for McGinley.
Changes for replay: P McConnell for Devine, Ryan Mellon for Canavan. Subs.: Canavan for Penrose, O Mulligan for McGuigan.

2006
ARD MHACHA: P Hearty, A Mallon, F Bellew, E McNulty, A Kernan, C McKeever, Paul Duffy, K McGeeney (capt), P McGrane, M O Rourke, J McEntee, M Mackin, S McDonnell, R Clarke, O McConville. Subs.: P McKeever for Mackin, A O Rourke for Duffy.
DÚN na nGALL: P Durcan, Neil McGee, Paddy Campbell, K Lacey, E McGee, B Monaghan, Barry Dunnion, Neil Gallagher, B Boyle, C Toye, M Hegarty, Ciarán Bonner, Rory Kavanagh, Conall Dunne, A Sweeney. Subs.: Colin Kelly for Dunne, D Diver for Boyle, S McDermott for Sweeney.

2007
TIR EOGHAIN: J Devine, C Gormley, C Gourley, R McMenamin, D Harte, D Carlin, P Jordan, Joe McMahon, K Hughes, B Dooher (capt), Raymond Mulgrew, S Cavanagh, Colm McCullagh, G Cavlan, O Mulligan. Subs.: S O Neill for Cavlan, Justin McMahon for Harte, E McGinley for Mulgrew, M Penrose for McCullagh, Damien McCaul for Carlin.

MUINEACHÁN: Shane Duffy, Vincent Corey, Dessie Mone, Dermot McArdle, John Paul Mone, Donal Morgan, Gary McQuaid, Eoin Lennon, Dick Clerkin, Stephen Gollogly, Damien Freeman, Ciarán Hanratty, Paul Finlay, Tomás Freeman. Subs.: Ciarán McManus for Hanratty, Colm Flanagan for Morgan, Paul Meegan for Gollogly, Shane Smith for J P Mone.

2008
ARD MHACHA (drawn game): P Hearty, A Mallon, F Bellew, Finian Moriarty, A Kernan, A O Rourke, C McKeever, P McGrane, Kieran Toner, Charlie Vernon, B Mallon, M O Rourke, S McDonnell, R Clarke, Stephen Kernan. Subs: P McKeever for M O Rourke, O McConville for S Kernan, M O Rourke for Vernon, David McKenna for B Mallon.
Changes for replay: Tony Kernan for S Kernan. Subs.: Paul Kernan for Mallon; S Kernan for T Kernan; P Duffy for Vernon; Brendan Donaghy for Bellew.
FEAR MANACH (drawn game): Ronan Gallagher, Shane Goan, Shane McDermott, Peter Sherry, Damien Kelly, Ryan McCluskey, Tommy McElroy, Mark Murphy, Martin McGrath, Ciaran McElroy, James Sherry, Ryan Keenan; Eamon Maguire, Shane McCabe, Mark Little. Subs: Barry Owens for McCabe, Shane

Lyons for Kelly, Tom Brewster for J Sherry, Declan O Reilly for Goan, Shaun Doherty for McElroy.
Changes for replay: Matthew Keenan for J Sherry, Liam McBarron for McCabe. Subs: Brewster for M Keenan, Owens for McBarron, McCabe for C McElroy, J Sherry for Owens, Doherty for R Keenan.

2009
TÍR EOGHAIN: John Devine, P J Quinn, Justin McMahon, R McMenamin, D Harte, C Gormley, P Jordan, K Hughes, S Cavanagh, B Dooher, Tommy McGuigan, Joe McMahon, M Penrose, Stephen O Neill, O Mulligan. Subs used: E McGinley for T McGuigan, Colm Cavanagh for Dooher, C Gourley for McMenamin, B McGuigan for Penrose, C McCullagh for O Neill.
AONTROIM: Peter Graham, Colin Brady, Andy McClean, Kevin O Boyle, Tony Scullion, Justin Crozier, James Loughrey, Michael McCann, Aodhán Gallagher, Terry O Neill, Kevin Brady, Niall McKeever, Paddy Cunningham, Seán Burke, Tomás McCann. Subs used: Kevin Niblock for K Brady, Conor Murray for Burke, Ciarán Close for McKeever, Déaglán Ó Hagan for O Neill, Seán McGreevy for Graham.

ULSTER SENIOR FOOTBALL CHAMPIONSHIP WINNING CAPTAINS 1888–2009

1888 Patrick Finnegan (Muineachán)	1937 Tom O Reilly (An Cabhán)	1973 Frank McGuigan (Tír Eoghain)
1890 Thomas Allen (Ard Mhacha)	1938 Jack Crawley (Muineachán)	1974 Pauric McShea (Dún na nGall)
1891 Unavailable (An Cabhán)	1939 Tom O Reilly (An Cabhán)	1975 Peter Stevenson (Doire)
1902/03 Unavailable (Aontroim)	1940 Tom O Reilly (An Cabhán)	1976 Peter Stevenson (Doire)
1903/04 Barney Corr (Ard Mhacha)	1941 Tom O Reilly (An Cabhán)	1977 Jimmy Smyth (Ard Mhacha)
1904/05 Terence Maguire (An Cabhán)	1942 Tom O Reilly (An Cabhán)	1978 Colm McAlarney (An Dún)
1905/06 Terence Maguire (An Cabhán)	1943 Tom O Reilly (An Cabhán)	1979 Brendan Brady (Muineachán)
1906/07 William McGrath (Muineachán)	1944 John Joe O Reilly (An Cabhán)	1980 Paddy Moriarty (Ard Mhacha)
1907/08 Harry Sheehan (Aontroim)	1945 Tom O Reilly (An Cabhán)	1981 Tommy McGovern (An Dún)
1909 Harry Sheehan (Aontroim)	1946 George Watterson (Aontroim)	1982 Colm McKinstry (Ard Mhacha)
1910 Harry Sheehan (Aontroim)	1947 John Joe O Reilly (An Cabhán)	1983 Michael Lafferty (Dún na nGall)
1911 No competition	1948 John Joe O Reilly (An Cabhán)	1984 Eugene McKenna (Tír Eoghain)
1912 Seán Coburn (Aontroim)	1949 John Joe O Reilly (An Cabhán)	1985 Gene Sherry (Muineachán)
1913 Seán Coburn (Aontroim)	1950 Pat O Neill (Ard Mhacha)	1986 Eugene McKenna (Tír Eoghain)
1914 Jess Connolly (Muineachán)	1951 Kevin Armstrong (Aontroim)	1987 Plunkett Murphy (Doire)
1915 J Mitchell (An Cabhán)	1952 Mick Higgins (An Cabhán)	1988 Ciarán Murray (Muineachán)
1916 James Downey (Muineachán)	1953 Seán Quinn (Ard Mhacha)	1989 Plunkett Donaghy (Tír Eogghain)
1917 James Downey (Muineachán)	1954 Simon Deignan (An Cabhán)	1990 Anthony Molloy (Dún na nGall)
1918 Patsy Fay (An Cabhán)	1955 Phil 'the Gunner' Brady (An Cabhán)	1991 Paddy O Rourke (An Dún)
1919 Patsy Fay (An Cabhán)	1956 Jody O Neill (Tír Eoghain)	1992 Anthony Molloy (Dún na nGall)
1920 John Cullen (An Cabhán)	1957 Eddie Devlin (Tír Eoghain	1993 Henry Downey (Doire)
1921 Unavailable (Muineachán)	1958 Jim McKeever (Doire)	1994 D J Kane (An Dún)
1922 P Daly (Muineachán)	1959 Kevin Mussen (An Dún)	1995 Ciarán Corr (Tír Eoghain)
1923 J J Clarke (An Cabhán)	1960 Kevin Mussen (An Dún)	1996 Peter Canavan (Tír Eoghain)
1924 J J Clarke (An Cabhán)	1961 Kevin Mussen (An Dún)	1997 Stephen King (An Cabhán)
1925 Standish O Grady (An Cabhán)	1962 Jim McDonnell (An Cabhán)	1998 Kieran McKeever (Doire)
1926 Jim Smith (An Cabhán)	1963 George Lavery (An Dún)	1999 Jarlath Burns (Ard Mhacha)
1927 Paddy Kilroy (Muineachán)	1964 Jim McDonnell (An Cabhán)	2000 Kieran McGeeney (Ard Mhacha)
1928 J J Clarke / Jim Smith (An Cabhán)	1965 Seán O Neill (An Dún)	2001 Seán Teague (Tír Eoghain)
1929 Paddy Kilroy (Muineachán)	1966 Dan McCartan (An Dún)	2002 Kieran McGeeney (Ard Mhacha)
1930 Paddy Kilroy (Muineachán)	1967 Charlie Gallagher (An Cabhán)	2003 Peter Canavan (Tír Eoghain)
1931 Jim Smith (An Cabhán)	1968 Joe Lennon (An Dún)	2004 Kieran McGeeney (Ard Mhacha)
1932 Jim Smith (An Cabhán)	1969 Charlie Gallagher (An Cabhán)	2005 Kieran McGeeney (Ard Mhacha)
1933 Jim Smith (An Cabhán)	1970 Seán O Connell (Doire)	2006 Paul McGrane (Ard Mhacha)
1934 Hugh O Reilly (An Cabhán)	1971 Colm McAlarney (An Dún)	2007 Brian Dooher (Tír Eoghain)
1935 Hugh O Reilly (An Cabhán)	1972 Frank McFeely (Dún na nGall)	2008 Paul McGrane (Ard Mhacha)
1936 Hugh O Reilly (An Cabhán)		2009 Brian Dooher (Tír Eoghain)

ULSTER SENIOR HURLING CHAMPIONSHIP RESULTS 1902–2009

ROLL OF HONOUR:

AONTROIM (43): 1902, 1904, 1905, 1907, 1909/10, 1913,
   1916, 1924–31 all, 1933–40 all, 1943–46 all, 1989–91 all,
   1993, 1994, 1997–99 all, 2002–09 all.
DOIRE (4): 1903, 1908/09, 2000, 2001.
AN DÚN (4): 1941, 1992, 1995, 1997.
DÚN na nGALL (3): 1906, 1923, 1932.
MUINEACHÁN (2): 1914, 1915.

1902

22 Mar 1903	Armagh	Aontroim 6-6 Ard Mhacha 2-2
5 Apr 1903	Belfast	Aontroim 41 pts Doire 12 pts

1903

28 June 1903	Seaghan's Park, Belfast	Aontroim 4-9 Ard Mhacha 3-5
9 July 1903	Rosemount, Derry	Doire 6-13 Tír Eoghain 0-1
22 Aug 1903	Derry	Doire w.o. Dún na nGall
20 Sept 1903	Armagh	Aontroim 1-3 An Dún 0-6
27 Sept 1903	Belfast (replay)	Aontroim 3-11 An Dún 1-4
18 Oct 1903	Seaghan's Park, Belfast	Doire 2-7 Aontroim 2-5

1904

30 July 1904	Corrody, Derry	Dún na nGall 2-7 Doire 1-3
7 Aug 1904	Abbey Park, Armagh	Ard Mhacha 5-5 Tír Eoghain 0-1
21 Aug 1904	Newry	Aontroim 19 pts An Dún 6 pts
11 Sept 1904	Derry	Dún na nGall w.o. Fear Manach
18 Sept 1904	Seaghan's Park, Belfast	Aontroim 4-13 Ard Mhacha 2-8 (objection – re-fixture ordered)
23 Oct 1904	Armagh (re-fixture)	Aontroim 5-6 Ard Mhacha 0-3
Final:		
30 Oct 1904	Seaghan's Park, Belfast	Aontroim 2-4 Dún na nGall 0-5

1905

25 June 1905	Derry	Dún na nGall 16 pts Doire 16 pts
16 July 1905	Seaghan's Park, Belfast	Aontroim 2-9 An Dún 8 pts
23 July 1905	Omagh	Tír Eoghain 30 pts Fear Manach 6 pts
13 Aug 1905	Burt (replay)	Dún na nGall 13 pts Doire 6 pts
20 Aug 1905	Crossmaglen	Ard Mhacha beat Muineachán
20 Aug 1905	Derry	Dún na nGall 3-9 Tír Eoghain 3-7 (objection - re-fixture ordered)
10 Sept 1905	Abbey Park, Armagh	Aontroim 6-6 Ard Mhacha 1-9
24 Sept 1905	Derry (re-fixture)	Dún na nGall 2-13 Tír Eoghain 1-0
Final:		
1 Oct 1905	Belfast	Aontroim beat Dún na nGall – no result available.

[*It is unclear whether the game took place, but Aontroim was recognised as winning the championship.*]

1906

17 June 1906	Enniskillen	Tír Eoghain 1-3 Fear Manach 0-2
1 July 1906	Letterkenny	Dún na nGall 4-6 Doire 0-6
5 Aug[?]1906	Baile na Lorgáin	Ard Mhacha w.o. Muineachán
19 Aug 1906	Newcastle	Aontroim 0-11 An Dún 1-7
21 Oct 1906	Seaghan's Park, Belfast	Aontroim 33 pts Ard Mhacha 12 pts
28 Oct? 1906	Strabane	Dún na nGall v. Tír Eoghain – no result available
Final:		
14 July 1907	Burt	Dún na nGall 5-21 Aontroim 0-1

1907

11 Aug 1907	Derry	Doire 12 pts Tír Eoghain 5 pts
11 Aug 1907	Bundoran	Fear Manach w.o. Dún na nGall
18 Aug 1907	Keady	Ard Mhacha w.o. Muineachán
8 Sept 1907	Newcastle	Aontroim 5-9 An Dún 3-4
22 Sept 1907	Omagh	Doire 22 pts Fear Manach 10 pts
29 Sept 1907	Keady	Aontroim 4-15 Ard Mhacha 5-3
Final:		
25 Oct 1907	Seaghan's Park, Belfast	Aontroim 4-17 Doire 1-6

1908/09

6 Sept 1908	Seaghan's Park, Belfast	Aontroim 2-12 Ard Mhacha 1-10
13 Sept 1908	Bundoran	Fear Manach 0-3 Dún na nGall 0-3

[This game was not replayed. Instead the fixtures were redrawn, with new pairings.]

25 Oct 1908	Belfast	Aontroim 4-21 An Dún 3-8
15 Nov 1908	Burt	Doire 0-6 Dún na nGall 0-4
22 Nov 1908	Belturbet	An Cabhán 3-6 Fear Manach 1-0
12 Apr 1909	Brandywell, Derry	Doire 13 pts Aontroim 5 pts
Final:		
9 May 1909	Cluain Eois	Doire 2-8 An Cabhán 0-2

1909/10

19 Sept 1909	Newry	Aontroim 3-13 An Dún 1-5
26 Sept 1909	Newbliss	Muineachán 4-3 An Cabhán 0-2
26 Sept 1909	Omagh	Doire 4-10 Tír Eoghain 0-2
17 Oct 1909	Belfast	Aontroim w.o. Ard Mhacha
28 Nov 1909	Derry	Dún na nGall 3-3 Doire 2-0
17 Apr 1910	Baile na Lorgáin	Aontroim 4-16 Muineachán 2-3
Final:		
3 July 1910	Belfast	Aontroim v. Dún na nGall – no result available.

[*It is unclear whether the game took place, but Aontroim was recognised as winning the championship.*]

1911–12
No championships.

1913

7 Sept	Ardglass	Aontroim 29 pts An Dún 20 pts
Final: 9 Nov	Monaghan	Aontroim 3-3 Muineachán 0-0

1914

8 Nov	Downpatrick	Aontroim 5-2 An Dún 2-4
Final 6 Dec	Belfast	Muineachán 2-0 Aontroim 2-0

Replay:

31 Jan 1915	Clones	Muineachán 4-3 Aontroim 1-0

1915

20 June	Ardglass	Aontroim 5-1 An Dún 2-2

Final:

12 Sept	Clones	Muineachán 1-5 Aontroim 1-2

1916

27 Aug	Ardglass	Aontroim 6-2 An Dún 2-2

Final:

28 Oct	Carrickmacross	Aontroim 3-1 Muineachán 1-1

1917–19

No championships.

1920

6 June 1920	Cavan	An Cabhán 4-1 Muineachán 1-0
1 Aug	Wattlebridge	Fear Manach 2-0 An Cabhán 1-0

Championship not completed.

1921–22

No championships

1923

19 Aug 1923	Clones	Muineachán 3-3 An Cabhán 3-0
30 Sept	Clones	Aontroim 5-4 Muineachán 2-3
14 Oct	Lifford	Dún na nGall 6-4 Doire 1-3

Final:

6 Apr 1924	Clones	Dún na nGall 7-1 Aontroim 2-0

1924

22 June	Ballybay	Aontroim 4-4 Muineachán 1-0
12 Oct	Cavan	Dún na nGall 7-2 An Cabhán 2-1

Final:

2 Nov 1924	Lifford	Aontroim 5-3 Dún na nGall 4-0

1925

16 Aug [?]	Clones	An Cabhán 5-2 Muineachán 2-3
23 Aug	Portaferry	Aontroim 5-5 An Dún 3-2
11 Oct	Clones	Dún na nGall 6-7 An Cabhán 4-3
Final: 25 Oct	Clones	Aontroim 5-4 Dún na nGall 4-5

1926

16 May	Cavan	An Cabhán 5-7 Dún na nGall 5-2
4 July	Clones	Aontroim 12-3 Muineachán 2-3
29 Aug	Newry	Aontroim 8-3 An Dún 2-2
Final: 31 Oct	Belfast	Aontroim 4-3 An Cabhán 3-1

1927

7 July	Newry	Ard Mhacha 5-3 An Dún 2-2
31 July	Armagh	Aontroim 4-8 Dún na nGall 4-1
7 Aug	Clones	An Cabhán 11-7 Muineachán 4-4
11 Sept	Cootehill	An Cabhán 8-6 Ard Mhacha 1-4
Final: 2 Oct	Cavan	Aontroim 5-4 An Cabhán 3-3

1928

27 May	Carrickmacross	An Dún 4-1 Muineachán 2-1
17 June	Belturbet	Aontroim w.o. An Cabhán
7 Oct	Letterkenny	Aontroim 4-1 Dún na nGall 3-1
Final: 21 Oct	Castlewellan	Aontroim 4-5 An Dún 1-1

1929

19 May	Newry	An Dún 4-6 Ard Mhacha 3-5
26 May	Belfast	Aontroim 6-3 An Cabhán 2-6
7 July	Belfast	Aontroim 7-3 An Dún 3-1
21 July	Omagh	Dún na nGall 7-5 Tír Eoghain 3-0

(Both Dún na nGall and Tír Eoghain were disqualified for arriving late, so Aontroim was awarded the title.)

1930

18 May	Letterkenny	Dún na nGall 7-1 Doire 1-5
1 June	Enniskillen	Aontroim 8-7 An Cabhán 4-4
8 June	Newry	An Dún 8-9 Muineachán 1-0
22 June	Armagh	Aontroim 8-3 Ard Mhacha 2-0
29 June	Armagh	An Dún 4-4 Dún na nGall 0-4

Final:

27 Oct	Newcastle	Aontroim 10-4 An Dún 2-0

1931

10 May	Letterkenny	Aontroim 6-2 Dún na nGall 1-7
24 May	Newry	An Dún 7-1 Ard Mhacha 3-3
14 June	Belturbet	Doire 3-2 An Cabhán 2-3
21 June	Newry	Aontroim 4-8 An Dún 0-8

Final:

5 July	Belfast	Aontroim 4-10 Doire 0-1

1932

17 April	Newry	Ard Mhacha 4-4 An Dún 3-3
8 May	Letterkenny	Dún na nGall 8-4 Doire 2-0
15 May	Keady	Aontroim 4-1 Ard Mhacha 3-0

Final:

5 June	Ballycastle	Dún na nGall 5-4 Aontroim 4-5

1933

9 July	Bessbrook	An Dún 5-2 Ard Mhacha 3-5
23 July	Newcastle	Aontroim 6-4 An Dún 2-3

Final:

20 Aug	Ballycastle	Aontroim 1-7 Dún na nGall 2-1

1934

3 June	Corrigan Pk, Belfast	Aontroim 5-6 Ard Mhacha 1-1
10 June	Carndonagh	Dún na nGall 9-9 Doire 2-2
15 July	Belturbet	Dún na nGall 3-5 An Cabhán 0-5
8 July	Castlewellan	Aontroim 2-5 An Dún 1-2

Final:

5 Aug	Letterkenny	Aontroim 3-4 Dún na nGall 2-2

1935

9 June	Armagh	An Dún 4-6 Ard Mhacha 1-2
9 June	Bundoran	Dún na nGall 7-7 An Cabhán 3-1
16 June	Castleblayney	Aontroim 11-9 Muineachán 0-0
14 July	Corrigan Park	Aontroim 8-3 An Dún 0-2
14 July	Letterkenny	Dún na nGall w.o. Doire

Final:

4 Aug	Belfast	Aontroim 7-9 Dún na nGall 1-2

1936

7 June	Cavan	An Cabhán 5-3 Ard Mhacha 5-2
7 June	Ballycastle	Aontroim 4-6 Dún na nGall 1-3
5 July	Toomebridge	Aontroim 3-10 Doire 2-2
12 July	Newry	An Cabhán 3-1 An Dún 2-2

Final:
| 26 July | Breifne Park | Aontroim 2-10 An Cabhán 3-2 |

1937
13 June	Armagh	An Dún 5-5 Ard Mhacha 2-2
13 June	Newbridge	Aontroim 6-5 Doire 2-2
18 July	Letterkenny	Dún na nGall 4-4 An Cabhán 2-2
18 July	Corrigan Park	Aontroim 7-5 An Dún 3-6
Final:
1 Aug	Ballycastle	Aontroim 6-7 Dún na nGall 3-2

1938
12 June	Carndonagh	Dún na nGall 6-3 Doire 3-0
19 June	Belfast	Aontroim 4-10 Ard Mhacha 0-0
19 June	Cootehill	An Cabhán 4-0 Muineachán 2-3
3 July	Kilclief	Aontroim 5-4 An Dún 2-2
10 July	Bundoran	Dún na nGall 8-3 An Cabhán 0-0
Final:
24 July	Letterkenny	Aontroim 3-5 Dún na nGall 2-2

1939
2 July	Clones	Muineachán 6-5 Fear Manach 0-4
2 July	Ballinascreen	An Dún 8-4 Doire 1-1
16 July	Ballycastle	Aontroim 7-7 Dún na nGall 3-2
16 July	Kilkeel	An Dún 9-10 Muineachán 2-2
Final:
30 July	Kilclief	Aontroim 9-8 An Dún 4-2

1940
[Only two counties entered.]
Final:
| 21 July | Newcastle | Aontroim 4-4 An Dún 1-3 |

1941
[Only two counties entered.]
Final:
| 3 Aug | Armagh | An Dún 5-3 Aontroim 2-5 |

1942
No championship.

1943
[Only two counties entered]
Final:
| 13 June | Belfast | Aontroim 8-6 An Dún 2-0 |

1944
9 July	Derry	Aontroim 9-7 Dún na nGall 0-3
16 July	Monaghan	Muineachán 3-7 An Dún 1-10
23 July	Monaghan	Aontroim 5-7 Muineachán 6-4
Final:
6 Aug	Belfast	Aontroim 7-3 Muineachán 0-1

1945
13 May	Newry	An Dún 6-7 Ard Mhacha 3-1
20 May	Clones	Muineachán 7-2 Doire 3-2
3 June	Derry	Dún na nGall 8-3 Doire 2-4
8 July	Belfast	Aontroim 7-7 Muineachán 2-4
15 July	Derry	Dún na nGall 9-9 An Dún 4-5
Final:
22 July	Derry	Aontroim 8-2 Dún na nGall 2-4

1946
| 2 June | Derry | Ard Mhacha 5-1 Doire 3-1 |
| 9 June | Belfast | An Dún 4-2 Dún na nGall 4-1 |
(objection – An Dún eliminated; Dún na nGall reinstated)
16 June	Enniskillen	Muineachán 8-6 Fear Manach 7-4
7 July	Belfast	Aontroim 7-15 Muineachán 2-8
7 July	Omagh	Ard Mhacha 4-4 Dún na nGall 3-6
Final:
21 July	Belfast	Aontroim 6-3 Ard Mhacha 2-1

1947–88
No Ulster Senior Hurling Championship. Instead an Ulster Junior Hurling Championship was organised during this period. The senior championship was revived in 1989, with the Liam Harvey Cup as the prize.

Brendan Harvey presents the Liam Harvey Cup, in honour of his father, to Antrim captain Ciarán Barr, after the 1989 Ulster Senior Hurling Championship final at Armagh. This was the first such championship since 1946. (*Anna Harvey*)

1989
| 25 June | Casement Park | An Dún 6-7 Doire 1-13 |
Final:
| 8 July | Casement Park | Aontroim 2-16 An Dún 0-9 |

1990
| 23 June | Casement Park | An Dún 1-23 Doire 1-5 |
Final:
| 8 July | Casement Park | Aontroim 2-16 An Dún 0-9 |

1991
| 24 June | Casement Park | An Dún 6-13 Doire 2-10 |
Final:
| 7 July | Casement Park | Aontroim 3-14 An Dún 3-10 |

1992
| 5 July | Casement Park | An Dún 9-18 Doire 0-10 |
Final:
| 5 July | Casement Park | An Dún 2-16 Aontroim 0-11 |

1993
[Only two counties entered.]
Final:
| 4 July | Casement Park | Aontroim 0-24 An Dún 0-11 |

1995

[Only two counties entered.]
Final:

9 July	Casement Park	An Dún 3-7 Aontroim 1-13

Replay:

16 July	Casement Park	An Dún 1-19 Aontroim 2-10

1996

[Only two counties entered.]
Final:

14 July	Casement Park	Aontroim 1-20 An Dún 2-12

1997

22 June	Casement Park	An Dún 1-15 Doire 1-10

Final:

6 July	Casement Park	An Dún 3-14 Aontroim 0-19

1998

14 June	Casement Park	Aontroim 0-19 Londáin 0-19
21 June	Casement Park (replay)	Aontroim 6-28 Londáin 1-7
21 June	Casement Park	Doire 2-17 An Dún 0-18

Final:

5 July	Casement Park	Aontroim 1-19 Doire 2-13

1999

19 June	Casement Park	Doire 4-17 An Dún 4-8
19 June	Casement Park	Aontroim 3-23 Londáin 1-6

Final:

10 July	Casement Park	Aontroim 2-19 Doire 1-9

2000

3 June	Casement Park	An Dún 3-14 Nua Eabhrach 1-10
11 June	Casement Park	Doire 2-15 An Dún 0-8
11 June	Casement Park	Aontroim 2-23 Londáin 0-12

Final:

9 June	Casement Park	Doire 4-8 Aontroim 0-19

2001

10 June	Gaelic Park, New York	Doire 1-16 Nua Eabhrach 2-12
1 July	Casement Park	Doire 1-24 Londáin 0-12
1 July	Casement Park	An Dún 2-14 Aontroim 1-10

Final:

15 July	Casement Park	Doire 1-17 An Dún 3-10

2002

12 May	Casement Park	An Dún 3-22 Londáin 1-9
25 May	Casement Park	An Dún 0-12 Doire 1-9
26 May	Gaelic Park, New York	Aontroim 5-19 Nua Eabhrach 2-11
1 June	Casement Park (replay)	An Dún 2-12 Doire 1-12

Final:

9 June	Casement Park	Aontroim 3-16 An Dún 1-18

2003

11 May	Casement Park	Aontroim 8-27 Londáin 1-5
11 May	Gaelic Park, New York	Doire 0-15 Nua Eabhrach 1-10
18 May	Casement Park	Aontroim 0-21 An Dún 2-12

Final:

14 June	Casement Park	Aontroim 3-21 Doire 1-12

2004

16 May	Ruislip	Doire 2-14 Londáin 1-12
23 May	Gaelic Park, New York	An Dún 1-19 Nua Eabhrach 1-9
23 May	Casement Park	Aontroim 2-14 Doire 0-12

Final:

6 June	Casement Park	Aontroim 1-19 An Dún 1-19
13 June (replay)	Casement Park	Aontroim 3-14 An Dún 0-18

2005

15 May	Casement Park	An Dún 4-25 Londáin 1-17
22 May	Gaelic Park, New York	Aontroim 2-20 Nua Eabhrach 2-14
22 May	Casement Park	An Dún 1-12 Doire 2-9
29 May	Casement Park (replay)	An Dún 3-19 Doire 4-9

Final:

5 June	Casement Park	Aontroim 2-22 An Dún 1-18

2006

7 May	Ruislip	Aontroim 2-16 Londáin 1-14
21 May	Gaelic Park, New York	Nua Eabhrach 1-18 Doire 1-12
21 May	Casement Park	Aontroim 2-23 An Dún 0-12

Final:

22 May	Boston	Aontroim 2-20 Nua Eabhrach 1-14

2007

13 May	Casement Park	Doire 1-14 Ard Mhacha 0-16
13 May	Casement Park	Aontroim 4-16 Londáin 3-8
20 May	Casement Park	An Dún 1-13 Doire 0-16
26 May	Casement Park	An Dún 5-16 Doire 1-15

Final:

3 June	Casement Park	Aontroim 2-24 An Dún 0-4

2008

11 May	Cavan	Muineachán 2-15 An Cabhán 1-16
11 May	Enniskillen	Tír Eoghain 1-11 Fear Manach 2-7
18 May	Clones	Muineachán 1-15 Dún na nGall 1-14
18 May	Omagh	Londáin 2-13 Tír Eoghain 1-6
24 May	Newry	Londáin 2-23 Ard Mhacha 4-16
25 May	Derry	Doire 7-23 Muineachán 3-13
1 June	Casement Park	An Dún 4-16 Londáin 1-16
1 June	Casement Park	Aontroim 2-17 Doire 1-12

Final:

15 June	Casement Park	Aontroim 3-18 An Dún 2-16

2009

9 May	Enniskillen	Fear Manach 0-13 An Cabhán 1-9
9 May	Letterkenny	Dún na nGall 1-21 Tír Eoghain 0-6
9 May	Keady	Ard Mhacha 1-22 Muineachán 1-8
17 May	Letterkenny	Ard Mhacha 3-24 Dún na nGall 2-12
23 May	Ruislip	Londáin 1-23 Fear Manach 0-7
30 May	Casement Park	Doire 4-10 Londáin 3-12
30 May	Casement Park	An Dún 5-20 Ard Mhacha 0-13
14 June	Casement Park	An Dún 2-17 Doire 1-18

Final:

28 June	Casement Park	Aontroim 3-20 An Dún 4-15

ULSTER SENIOR HURLING CHAMPIONSHIP FINAL TEAMS 1902–2009

1902
AONTROIM: Tom Madden, Frank Lowe, Dan Dempsey, Jimmy Langtry, Hugh O Toole, Bob Pimley, Alex Donnelly, Jimmy Laverty, Jack Hughes, H Crosgry, Harry Laverty, Neil McFarland, H McVeigh, Jimmy Brady (capt), Cathal McComb, H McKay, G McCausland.
DOIRE: James Crossan, Bradley, Browley, Frank Carlin, Bradley, Bradley, J Barr, James MacGill, Charles McGill, Hugh Elliott, Alexander Keys, James Lawrence Elliott, M Hampsey, J O Donnell, McGill, Patrick Heaney, Storey.

1903
DOIRE: Alphonsus Cowley (goal), D McLaughlin (capt), J L Elliott, Peter Bonner, Thomas Mellon, M Cannon, Patrick McCallion, J McCallion, Henry Patton, Hugh Coyle, Andrew Coyle, Daniel Coyle, H Brown, J Duffy, Peter McCallion, J Crossan, P Heaney.
AONTROIM: T Madden (goals), William Kearney, C McComb, Paddy Orr, McCann, Donnelly, F Lowe, Mallon, H O Toole, John McGinley, O Malley, H Laverty, [H?] McVeigh, Clarke, McMahon, N McFarland, J Hughes. Sub.: William Manning for McFarland.

1904
AONTROIM: [No team-list contained in reports; team listed as selected beforehand]: T Madden (goal), D Dempsey (capt), Harry Sheehan, H O Toole, P Orr, B Pimley, Frank McIlvenny, Art McGann, Brian Donnelly, F Lowe, Eddie Trainor, Frank McCotter, Dick McDaniel, Joe Fegan, [W] Kearney, Denis McCullough, H McVeigh. D Maguire is recorded in a match-report as having played.
DÚN na nGALL: [No report or team-list available.]

1905
AONTROIM: [No report available; team listed as selected beforehand]: D Dempsey (capt), Phil Gallagher, Joseph McKay, Owen McKernan, A McGann, E Trainor, D McCullough, H Sheehan, F McIlvenny, W Manning, Pat McGinley, J McGinley, Sheppard, F Lowe, Pat McKeown, Joe McCann, John Magowan.
DÚN na nGALL: [Ulster final team-list unavailable; the following team played in the Ulster SHC semi-final v. Tír Eoghain on 24 Sept 1905]: *Charlie Dowds, James Gallagher, William Kennedy, D Coyle, J Moody, J Dowds, John Gallagher, James Kennedy, M Coyle, Tom Coyle, John Burns, J Campbell, E O Donnell, D Gill, John Whoriskey, James Whoriskey.*

1906
DÚN na nGALL: Jamie McLaughlin, James Gallagher, C Dowds, George Dowds, John Gallagher, J Burns, Willie Gallagher, John Whoriskey, James Whoriskey, Willie Kennedy, Willie Moody, T Coyle, Manus Coyle, Willie Sheering, Joseph Campbell, Peter McCafferty.
AONTROIM: Dan McCarry, J Black, Patrick Butler, Hugh McCormack, Tom Hernon, Archibald McKay, J McKeegan, John O Neill, Willie McGavock, Arthur Harvey, Henry McKee, John McAleese, John Magowan, H Sheehan, Justin Ralph, [H?] Gallagher, W Manning, D Dempsey.

1907
AONTROIM: Pat Robinson, J Dobbyn, H Sheehan, J McCann, Patrick Dealliott, J Bartley, J Ralph, James Hamill, Tim Sheehan, John McManus, Peter Clarke, W J Donnelly, James McVeigh, John Magouran, Joe Devlin, J Magowan, Daniel Jarvis.
DOIRE: Barney McCafferty, Robert Harte, Patrick McCallion, John McCallion, D Coyle, T Mellon, James McGrory, S McCallion, John C Porter, J Mearns, Alla Cowley, H Elliott, Joseph McCallion, Peter McCallion, Denis Ferry, A Coyle, P Heaney.

1908/09
DOIRE: Harte (capt), Patrick McCallion, Robert Harte, Peter McCallion, Joseph Gallagher, T Mellon, Thomas McCallion, John McCallion, A Cowley, J McDermott, H Elliott, A Coyle, P Heaney, B McCafferty, J McGrory, Lennon, Jeremiah Meenan.
AN CABHÁN: Eddie Reilly (goal), Pat Anglim, James Fitzpatrick, Pat Reilly, Pat Farrelly, Joe Sweeney, Joe McGuigan, Patrick J Small, Peter Small, Vincent Quinn, Loughran, Pat Rafferty, John Fitzpatrick, Bob Farrell, Séamus Donohoe, Steve O Mara, Charlie Smith. Sub.: Dick Copeland for McGuigan.

1909/10
AONTROIM: [as played in All-Ireland SHC quarter-final v. Glasgow on 31 Sept 1910]: *Patrick McFadden, Harry Sheehan, Dan Dempsey, Dan Ahern, Frank Kelly, Louis Watters, W Manning, Fred Vallely, Denis Maguire, Pat McKeown, Dan Cahill, Pat McGinley, Tom Rogan, Ed Gorman, J Magowan (capt), D McCullough, Patrick McGoey.*
DÚN na nGALL: [as played v. Doire in Ulster semi-final]: *J Devenny (goal), W McDaid, John Gallagher, James Dougal, J Burns, J Black, W Robb, John McDaid, J Kelly, D McDaid, N Devenny (capt), John Dougal, Hugh Dougal, T Robb, H Snodgrass, D Devenny, P Devenny.*

1911–12
No championships.

1913
AONTROIM: Frank McGoey (goal), John Dobbyn, D Ahern, F Vallely, F Kelly, J Gaynor, J Saunders, Séamus Dobbyn, Patrick McKeown, W Manning, Patrick Ahern, Robert Bateson, Thomas Ferris, E Gorman, P McGoey.
MUINEACHÁN: P Maguire (goal), F Macklin, George McEneaney, Power, Joe Kiely, McKenna, Monaghan, Cooney, John McDonald, Dunn, William McMahon, Gunn, Standish O Grady, M Ryan, Mackin.

1914
MUINEACHÁN (as played in drawn game): Dan Costello (goal), Patrick Lonergan, Michael Mulvey, Joe Boylan, Peter Reilly, G McEneaney, Larry Reilly, J McDonald, J Kiely, Joe Clinton, Tom O Brien, F Macklin, Standish O Grady, Michael Keogh (capt), James O Brien.
Changes for replay: Frank Reilly for Macklin. Subs.: Macklin for McDonald.
AONTROIM (as played in drawn game): Patrick McFadden (goal), Louis Watters, William Rea, D Ahern, A McBride, Séamus Dobbyn, Fred Vallely, Patrick Barnes, P McKeown, Frank J McCarragher, Frank McGoey, Kennedy O Brien, A N Other, J Saunders, H Sheehan (capt).
Changes for replay: Frank Kelly for McFadden, William Gaynor for Watters, Robert Best for Barnes, Hugh Smith for McKeown, Hugh Colligan for McGoey, Francis Dobbyn for Sheehan, Hugh McNally for Saunders.

The Derry (Sarsfield's) team that won the second Ulster Senior Hurling Championship, at Belfast in 1903. The player standing in the middle of the second row from the back is 20-year-old Louis O'Kane, who was a draper's assistant and the first secretary of the Ulster Council of the GAA.

1915
MUINEACHÁN: M Keogh (capt), D Costello (goal), Reddin, Abbott, Reilly, J Clinton, M Ryan, S O Grady, G McEneaney, Mulroy, F Reilly, L Reilly, P Lonergan, O Brien, McCabe.
AONTROIM: [No report available; team listed as selected beforehand.] P McFadden (goal), F Kelly, D Ahern, W Rea, W Gaynor, P McKeown, F McGoey, P King, Seán McKeown, S Dobbyn (capt), J McCusker, K O Brien, E Gorman, R Bateson, P Ahern. *Dundalk Democrat* report mentions McBride, Gallagher and Barnes as playing.

1916
AONTROIM: P McFadden (goal), Frank McCarry, W Rea (capt), P McKeown, Jimmy Best, S McKeown, F McGoey, P Barnes, E Gorman, S Dobbyn, T McMahon, Joe Gallagher, J Magauran, 'T. Maley', Joe McCarry.
MUINEACHÁN: M Mulvey (goal), J Daly, J Kiely, S O Grady, J Clinton, J O Brien, M Cremin, P Lonergan, J Keogh (capt), Dan Hogan, T O Brien, W McMahon, B Maguire, Feely, F Reilly.

1923
DÚN na nGALL: Paddy Rooney, M Ryan, Dan Lenihan, Michael Doherty (capt), James Clooney, P McMahon, J Carroll, M Kelly, M Mulhall, P Tobin, Lynch, Dan Taylor, M Killiher, Twomey, E White.
AONTROIM: [No report available; team listed as selected beforehand]: George Fitzsimmons (goal), Dick Sadlier, J Gallagher (capt), G Fields, D Ahern, J Brennan, McDonnell, Paddy Fleming, S McKeown, Tom O Brien, [Turley?], Frank Montague, Alf Fox, J McCarry, J Best.

1924
AONTROIM: James Kelly, James Connolly, D Sadlier, P Nolan, Frank Feeney, J McDonnell, A Butler, P Fox, S McKeown, P Fleming, Willie McMullan, James P McAllister, Charles McCormick, J McCarry, Eddie Connolly.
DÚN na nGALL: Willie Gallagher (goal), J Clooney, D Lenihan, M Kelly, M Ryan, M Kelleher, N Mulhall, E White, B Keating, D J O Sullivan, Jack James Sadlier, D Taylor, J Tuohy, P Tobin. [14 names listed.] Sub.: D Doherty for Keating.

1925
AONTROIM: [No report available; team listed as selected beforehand]: J Meighan, D Sadlier, Jim Connolly, D Ahern, P Fox, S McKeown, Seán 'Skinner' Osborne, P Fleming, T O Brien, Duffin, Alf Fox, W Mulvenna, J P McAllister, Alex Butler, C McCormick.
DÚN na nGALL: [No report available; team listed as selected beforehand]: W Gallagher (goal), D Lenihan, J Daly, J Clooney, Bro Cassin, N Mulhall, D Taylor, B Keating, J Tuohy, E White, M Ryan, W Sheerin, P McLaughlin, J Callaghan, J Gallagher, M Kelleher, J Fahy, P Smith, A Reilly. [19 names listed.]

1926
AONTROIM: Tom Gillen, Dick Sadlier, J Connolly, Pat Butler, P Fleming, S McKeown, Alex Butler, J Doherty, E Connolly, C McCormick, Alf Fox, Art Thornberry, J P McAllister, P Duffin, J McCarry.
AN CABHÁN: J McKeever (goal), P Moroney, H Semple, F Rehill, J Clarke, Michael Aherne, M Duffy, J Ryan, Seán Farrelly, T Murphy, Michael Daly, P Flynn, C Kelly, J Coyle, J J Walsh.

1927
AONTROIM: J Hunter, R Sadlier, J Connolly, P Butler, C McCormick, S McKeown, Hugh Reid, Pat Boomer, A Thornbury, A Butler, Gerard Connolly, A Fox, C Duffin, J McCarry, Pat Cunning.
AN CABHÁN: O Connolly, G Burke, J O Dwyer, H Semple, P Moroney, M Aherne, J Lynch, M Daly, E O Riordan, B Farrelly, B Flynn, Jim Smith, M Ryan, S Flynn, J Walsh.

1928
AONTROIM: J Hunter, Gerry McDermott, P Butler, Dan Armstrong, Joe Dowd, S McKeown, H Reid, John McNally, Alex McCollum, M Mulvenna, Paddy Fleming, Hugo Hill, J Tuohy, P Cunning, D McCarry.
AN DÚN: Thomas Gilmore, H Magee, P McCann, John McCullough, Rev Frank McKenna, Gerry O Donoghue, M Quinn, John Emerson, H McCusker, T Fitzmaurice, Pat McGrady, Barney Owens, Pat Owens, V O Keeffe, F McCavitt.

1929
[No final. Aontroim declared champions, after Dún na nGall was disqualified for turning up late for semi-final.]
AONTROIM: [as played v. An Dún in Ulster semi-final]:
J Hunter, Eddie McHenry, J McDonnell, J Connolly, M Mulvenna, A Thornbury, H Reid, Eugene Mackin, J McNally, C McCormick, S McKeown, A Butler, J Harvey, P Cunning, J McCarry.
DÚN na nGALL: [as played v. Tír Eoghain in Ulster semi-final]:
James Daly, John Sadlier, James Sullivan, John Clooney, J Daly, Patrick Liddy, Patrick McMahon, E O Riordan, James Canton, John Carroll, P Hurley, Jim Hehir, John McLaughlin, Denis Smith, Dan Taylor (capt), John Stewart, Peter Lambe.

1930
AONTROIM: Patrick J Elliman, John McDonnell, E Mackin, D Armstrong, H Hill, P Fleming, J McKeown, H Reid, P Boomer, George O Connell, J McNally, Peter Meegan, Alex McDonnell, A Smith, P Cunning.
AN DÚN: T Gilmore, J McCullough, G O Donoghue, C Miller, P Curran, H Cummins, H McCusker, E Fox, P Owens, P Curran, J Mason, P O Hare, John Smith, M Quinn, C McCavitt.

1931
AONTROIM: P Elliman, Dan McElgorm, G McDermott, D Armstrong, John Butler, S McKeown, H Reid, E McHenry, A Thornbury, H Hill, George O Connell, J McNally, A McDonnell, P Cunning, J Maguire.
DOIRE: Willie Gallagher, Andy McGeady, Denis McLaughlin, M Lynch, Charlie McLaughlin, J Sadlier, James McLaughlin, Paul Carthy, P Stewart, J Hurley, E Boland, E White, M Connellan, John Crawford, Tommy McLaughlin.

1932
DÚN na nGALL: John Ward, J Clooney, John Mullin, J Campbell, Dubhghlas C Mac Fhionnlaoich, A Gallagher, Michael Walsh (capt), Pat J Mulcahy, M O Sullivan, Dan O Donnell, A Varilly, Aidan Sweeney, John McDermott, C Gilmartin.
AONTROIM: P Elliman, G McDermott, J O Donnell, Andy Smith, A O Donnell, Daniel McCormick, W Mulvenna, J Butler, S McKeown, Alex Butler, E McHenry, G O Connor, Denis McKeegan, P Cunning, Jimmy Walsh.

1933
AONTROIM: Gerard Connolly, D Armstrong, G McDermott, A Butler, Robert Graham, J Butler, Arthur Gibson, E McHenry, S McKeown, Pat Quinn, G O Connell, J Kavanagh, G Phillips, P Cunning, J Walsh.
DÚN na nGALL: Willie Gallagher, Joseph Duff, M McLaughlin, J Mullin, J Farren, A Gallagher, D C Mac Fhionnlaoich, Pat J Mulcahy, M Walsh, D O Donnell, Hugh Doherty, Paul Carthy, Jim McDevitt, Tommy McLaughlin, Stephen Butler. Subs.: D Gallagher for Walsh, James J Doherty for A Gallagher. Willie Gallagher, J Duff, J Mullin, W Gallagher, Jim McDevitt, Hugh Doherty, D C Mac Fhionnlaoich, Pat J Mulcahy, M Walsh, D O Donnell, Tommy McLaughlin, J Farren, Denis McLaughlin, Paul Carthy, Stephen Butler.

1934
AONTROIM: P Elliman, D Armstrong, G McDermott, A Butler, Robert Graham, S McKeown (Sr), A Gibson, Robert Sloan, John Clarke, G O Connell, J McNally, J Walsh, Willie Lenaghan, Jim Higgins, H Devlin.
DÚN na nGALL: J J Doherty, D McLaughlin, J Duff, C O Doherty, J Clancy, A Gallagher, D C Mac Fhionnlaoich, Pat Mulcahy, M Walsh, J Farren, J Mullin, D O Donnell, T McLaughlin, P Butler, P Carty.

1935
AONTROIM: P Elliman, D Armstrong, G McDermott, Gerry Connolly, John McFall, J Butler, A Butler, Gene Thornbury, J Clarke, R Graham, G O Connell, A Gibson, Seán Óg McKeown, J Higgins, Harry Devlin.
DÚN na nGALL: Joe Doherty, J Clooney, D McLaughlin, Joe Farren, A Gallagher, J Mullan, D C Mac Fhionnlaoich, P J Mulcahy, Tom McLoughlin, P Carthy, Jim Farren, Patrick P Doherty, J Sadlier, J Duff, S Butler.

1936
AONTROIM: Dan McKillop, E Mackin, T Maguire, A Butler, J McFall, J Butler, J McNally, H Gallagher, John Clarke, P Farrelly, S McKeown, Eddie Regan, Pearse Murphy, Charlie Jolly, Harry Devlin.
AN CABHÁN: J Boyle, P McGee, Thomas O Donnell, J McGinn, J Molloy, J Coogan, J Donohoe, P Dunne, H O Reilly, J McCabe, James Murphy, M Daly, Thomas Meehan, A Breslin, Andrew McEntee.

1937
AONTROIM: P Elliman, Paddy Adams, Charles McAllister, Alex Butler, John McFall, John Butler, J Walsh, J McNally, S McKeown, Jack Donnelly, Robert Sloan, E Regan, P Murphy, C Jolly, H Devlin.
DÚN na nGALL: Tom Farren, J Grimes, James Clooney, Owen Doherty, D C Mac Fhionnlaoich, J Doherty, John Lynch, Joe Farren, Jim Farren, Con McLaughlin, Dermot Bury, James Grimes, J McDevitt, Denis Farren, James J Reid.

1938
AONTROIM: John Hurl, Jack Donnelly, Malachy McDonnell, D McAllister, J Walsh, J Clarke, Tom Rice, G Thornbury, J McNally, Dan Gibson, Seán McKeown, William Graham, John McAteer, Tommy Walsh, H Devlin.
DÚN na nGALL: T Farren, Seán Ruth, Seán Boyle, D C Mac

Fhionnlaoich, Denis McGlynn, Seán Walsh, Joseph Doyle, Jim McGlynn, Joe Farren, Anthony McBrearty, Jim Farren, James Diver, J J Reid, Denis Farren, Seán Mullan.

1939
AONTROIM: J Hurl, Mal McDonald, Pearse Murphy, Dan Gibson, Dan McKillop, J Walsh, Tom Rice, Seán McKeown, Seán McNally, Pat Poland, Charlie Jolly, Hugh Mulholland, John Reddicks, Tommy Walsh, Jim Sheehan.
AN DÚN: C Convery, J Hynds, D McCusker, Seán Southwell, J Swail, R Fitzsimmons, Eddie Smith, J McMullan, J Denvir, Peadar McArdle, Gerry Murphy, Anthony King, John Blaney, John White, W Curran.

1940
AONTROIM: Charlie Jolly, Pat McKeown, P Maguire, Pat McGarry, Kevin Murphy, Jimmy Walsh, Gregory Donnelly, Tom McAllister, John McNally, Sam McHugh, Kevin Armstrong, Hugh Mulholland, P Boylan, Tommy Walsh, Harry Devlin.
AN DÚN: Oliver Keenan, J Hynds, F McEvoy, Harry Faloona, Tommy Swail, Phil Gunn, J Kearney, Brian Denvir, J Denvir, Gerry Murphy, D McCusker, S Southwell, P McArdle, John White, T McMullan.

1941
AN DÚN: Oliver Keenan, Jim Campbell, Phil Gunn, Willie Small, Tommy Swail, Barney McCusker, Brendan Murray, Tony King, Greg Donnelly, Gerry Murphy, Danny O Hare, John White, Joe Marshall, Danny Doran, John Doran.
AONTROIM: J Maguire, Pearse Bradley, McAllister, Edwin Leddy, Noel Campbell, D Boyle, T Rice, D McKillop, D Gibson, Kevin Armstrong, K Murphy, Charlie Vernon, J Quinn, T Walsh, H Devlin.

1943
AONTROIM: John Hurl, John Currie, K Murphy, P McGarry, Mick Butler, J Walsh, Paddy McKeown, John Butler, D McKillop, Séamus Quinn, T Walsh, Joe Mullan, K Armstrong, Jackie Bateson, Sam Mulholland.
AN DÚN: D McCusker, Richard Mullan, J Hynds, Brian O Rourke, W Swail, B McCusker, T Swail, W Kerr, J Denvir, J White, B Denvir, J King, John Swail, Jim Swail, B Cashen.

1944
AONTROIM (as played in replay): Mick McKeown, W Feeney, Pearse Murphy, Jimmy Butler, P McKeown, Joe Mullan, H Mulholland, Kevin Armstrong, Noel Campbell, Tom Phillips, P Murphy, Larry McGrady, Willie Best, Dan McAllister, Sam Mulholland. Sub.: Gerry McAteer for Campbell.
Drawn game: Séamus 'Stout' McDonald, J McNeill and McAteer started, and were replaced by McKeown, Butler and P Murphy (forward).
MUINEACHÁN (as played in replay): Paddy Callan, L Nugent, Joe Butler, Eamon O Toole, Pat Smyth, Paddy Hudson, M Bowers, Gerry Dwyer, Con Ahern, T Lavery, J Lillis, C McGlynn, Pat Nugent, Jim Cahill, P Dwan.
Drawn game: Seán Kennedy, Jack Clerkin, Seán Lally, Paddy O Brien and Frank Lane were listed as starting; Seán Óg Ó Ceallacháin who attended the game recalls that some of those names were pseudonyms for Seamus O Callaghan, Gerry Glenn, Joe Hickey and Tom Shortall, who played. In their places Bowers, Lavery, Lillis, McGlynn and Dwan started the replay.

1945
AONTROIM: Mannix McAllister, J Butler, B Feeney, Brendan Donnelly, Mick Butler, T Tiernan, J Mullan, S McKeown, N Campbell, John Murray, S McDonald, L McGrady, Des Cormican, Chris McMullan, S Mulholland.
DÚN na nGALL: S Mullan, W Doherty, E Casey, D Horgan, John Doherty, D Fitzgerald, J Diver, H Doherty, John Giles, John J Doherty, J McGlynn, J O Connell, M Guilfoyle, D McDaid, C King.

1946
AONTROIM: M McAllister, M McDonald, B Feeney, Jimmy Woods, M Butler, J Mullan, G Brady, Jack Loughead, N Campbell, D Cormican, H Mulholland, J Murray, Dan Butler, Danny MacRandal, S Mulholland.
ARD MHACHA: Harry McGeough, S McAteer, Tom Fitzgerald, Frank Trainor, Thomas Keenan, Patsy Murray, Paddy McCormack, Gerry Lenagh, Oliver Keenan, Hugh Holywood, Sean Devlin, Charlie Vernon, Pat Woodgate, P J Keenan, Pat Dolan.

1947–88
No championships.

1989
AONTROIM: Niall Patterson, Ger Rogan, Terence Donnelly, Dessie Donnelly, James McNaughton, Dominic McKinley, Gary O Kane, Paul McKillen, Terence 'Sambo' McNaughton, Brian Donnelly, Aidan McCarry, Sean Paul McKillop, Donal Armstrong, Ciaran Barr, Danny McNaughton. Subs: Ger Holden for O Kane, Dominic McMullan for McKillen, Aidan Murray for Rogan.
AN DÚN: Noel Keith, Kevin Coulter, Paddy Dorrian, Séamus Fay, Paul Coulter, Martin Mallon, Paddy Braniff, Danny Hughes, Philbin Savage, Noel Sands, Gerard Coulter, Chris Mageean, Barry Coulter, Hugh Gilmore, Brendan Coulter. Subs.: Martin Bailie for Barry Coulter, Paul McMullan for P Coulter.

1990
AONTROIM: N Patterson, G Holden, D Donnelly, D McKinley, John Carson, Declan McKillop, A Murray, Jim Close, P McKillen, B Donnelly, A McCarry, S P McKillop, Alistair McGuile, C Barr, Olcan McFetridge. Subs: Noel Murray for McGuile, Gary O Kane for D McKillop, Mickey Sullivan for McKillen.
AN DÚN: N Keith, K Coulter, P Dorrian, P Braniff, M Mallon, G Coulter, C Mageean, John McCarthy, M Bailie, D Hughes, N Sands, Barry Coulter, Michael Blaney, Philbin Savage, P Coulter. Sub.: Hugh Gilmore for B Coulter.

1991
AONTROIM: N Patterson, Paul Jennings, D McKinley, D Donnelly, G Rogan, J McNaughton, D McKillop, S P McKillop, P McKillen, J Carson, C Barr, D Armstrong, A McCarry, T McNaughton, J Close. Sub: Gary O Kane for Close.
AN DÚN: N Keith, K Coulter, P Dorrian, P Braniff, M Mallon, G Coulter, P McMullan, M Bailie, J McCarthy, D Hughes, C Mageean, P Coulter, M Blaney, Pearse McCrickard, N Sands.

1992
AN DÚN: N Keith, K Coulter, G Coulter, P Braniff, M Mallon, Paul McMullan, Dermot Woods, D Hughes, Gary Savage, Gerard McGrattan, Greg Blaney, P Coulter, M Blaney, M Bailie, N Sands. Subs: C Mageean for M Blaney, P Savage for P Coulter.
AONTROIM: N Patterson, Ronan Donnelly, D McKinley,

J McNaughton, D McKillop, Gary O Kane, P Jennings, P McKillen, T McNaughton, S P McKillop, A McCarry, D Armstrong, Alistair Elliott, C Barr, J Close. Subs.: Séamus McMullan for Jennings, J Carson for T McNaughton, D Donnelly for Armstrong.

1993
AONTROIM: Pat Gallagher, Séamus McMullan, D McMullan, Eoin McCloskey, R Donnelly, D McKinley, J McNaughton, P McKillen, P Jennings, A Elliott, Gary O'Kane, S P McKillop, J Close, T McNaughton, Gregory O Kane.
AN DÚN: N Keith, Stephen McAree, G Coulter, P Braniff, M Mallon, P McMullan, D Woods, D Hughes, G Savage, G McGrattan, M Bailie, Dermot O Prey, M Blaney, Jerome McCrickard, N Sands. Sub.: B Coulter for McCrickard.

1994
AONTROIM: Brendan Prenter, S McMullan, D McKinley, Frankie McMullan, S P McKillop, P Jennings, Joe McCaffrey, P McKillen, Jim Connolly, J Carson, Gary O'Kane, Paddy Walsh, Conor McCambridge, Gregory O'Kane, A Elliott. Subs: T McNaughton for Gary O'Kane, Aidan McAteer for McCaffrey, Brendan McGarry for Gregory O'Kane.
AN DÚN: N Keith, K Coulter, G Coulter, P Braniff, M Mallon, P McMullan, D Woods, D Hughes, J McCarthy, B Coulter, C Mageean, D O Prey, P Coulter, H Gilmore, N Sands. Sub.: P Savage for P Coulter.

1995
AN DÚN: N Keith, K Coulter, G Coulter, P Braniff, M Mallon, P McMullan, D Woods, D Hughes, G Savage, M Blaney, P Coulter, Dermot O Prey, Conor Arthurs, Hugh Gilmore, N Sands. Subs: Seán Mallon for Blaney, Michael Braniff for McMullan, G McGrattan for Arthurs.
Replay: John McCarthy replaced O'Prey. Subs: B Coulter for Woods, M Braniff for McMullan, S Mallon for Gilmore.
AONTROIM: Shane Elliott, Eoin Colgan, E McCloskey, Seán McElhatton, S McMullan, Gary O Kane, R Donnelly, S P McKillop, Nigel Elliott, Conor McCambridge, J Carson, Paul Donnelly, Gregory O Kane, T McNaughton, A Elliott. Subs.: Joe Boyle for Carson, Jimmy Wilson for McCambridge, P McKillen for P Donnelly. No changes for Replay. Replay subs: J Wilson for McKillop, Colm McGuckian for McCambridge, F McMullan for A Elliott.

1996
AONTROIM: B Prenter, E McCloskey, E Colgan, S McElhatton, P Jennings, T McNaughton, R Donnelly, J Connolly, P McKillen, Aidan McCloskey, Gary O'Kane, Gregory O'Kane, Paul Graham, S P McKillop, A Elliott. Subs: S McMullan for Donnelly, J Carson for McKillop, P Donnelly for R Donnelly.
AN DÚN: N Keith, K Coulter, P Braniff, P McMullan, M Mallon, G Savage, Martin Coulter Snr, J McCarthy, D O Prey, G McGrattan, M Braniff, Brian Braniff, P Coulter, N Sands, C Arthurs. Subs.: D Hughes for B Braniff, S Mallon for McCarthy, Martin Coulter Jnr for Arthurs.

1997
AN DÚN: Graham Clarke, Barry Smith, Stephen Murray, Barry Milligan, M Braniff, M Mallon, Tom Coulter, N Sands, P Coulter, B Coulter, M Bailie, G Savage, Martin Coulter, J McCrickard, G McGrattan. Sub: B Braniff for McCrickard.
AONTROIM: S Elliott, Ciaran McCambridge, E Colgan,

S McElhatton, S P McKillop, Gary O Kane, P Jennings, J Connolly, P McKillen, Conor McCambridge, Gregory O Kane, Aidan Mort, Aidan Delargy, J Carson, A Elliott. Subs.: T McNaughton for Jennings, J Close for Delargy, J Boyle for Gregory O Kane.

1998
AONTROIM: S Elliott, R Donnelly, E Colgan, F McMullan, Séamus McMullan, Gary O Kane, Kieran Kelly, P McKillen, C McGuckian, J Carson, Gregory O Kane, J McIntosh, A Elliott (capt), Joe O Neill, Liam Richmond. Subs.: Ciarán McKiernan for O Neill, O Neill for McKieran, Jarlath Elliott for McIntosh.
DOIRE: Kieran Stevenson, Adrian Hickey, Conor Murray, Niall Mullan, Benny Ward, Colm McGurk, Ronan McCloskey, Oliver Collins, Gary Biggs, Michael Conway, Michael McCormick, Paddy McEldowney, Geoffrey McGonigle, John O Dwyer. Subs.: Gregory Biggs for Conway, Michael Collins for McCormick, Adrian McCrystal for O Dwyer.

1999
AONTROIM: S Elliott, Ciarán McCambridge, Owen McCloskey, Seán Mullan, S McMullan, Gary O Kane (capt), Ronan Donnelly, Conor Cunning, Jim Close, J Carson, C McGuckian, Brendan McGarry, A Elliott, Gregory O Kane, L Richmond. Subs.: S P McKillop for McGarry, F McMullan for Carson, John Flynn for Elliott.
DOIRE: K Stevenson, Emmett McKeever, C McGurk, N Mullan, B Ward, Declan Cassidy, Barry Kelly, R McCloskey, M Conway, P McEldowney, Gregory Biggs, C Murray, M Collins, G McGonigle, Dermot Doherty. Subs.: J O Dwyer for Doherty, Damien Kearney for Ward, Shane McCartney for McGonigle.

2000
DOIRE: K Stevenson, C McGurk, C Murray (capt), N Mullan, B Ward, Colin McEldowney, D Cassidy, Oliver Collins, M Conway, Kevin McCloy, Kieran McKeever, R McCloskey, Gary Biggs, M Collins, J O Dwyer. Sub.: Gregory Biggs for Conway.
AONTROIM: S Elliott, Emmett O Hara, C McCambridge, Declan McKillop, Michael McCambridge, Malachy Molloy, Kieran Kelly, Jim Connolly, C Cunning, Conor McCambridge, Gary O Kane, R Donnelly, Aidan Delargy, Gregory Kane, A Elliott. Subs.: Chris Hamill for O Hara, Aidan Mort for Donnelly.

2001
DOIRE: K Stevenson, C McEldowney, E McKeever, Ryan Lynch, B Ward, M Conway, C Murray, R McCloskey, O Collins, Gary Biggs, K McKeever, Gregory Biggs, M Collins, G McGonigle, J O Dwyer. Subs.: Pádraig Kelly for Lynch, Séamus Downey for Gary Biggs, Fergal McEldowney for M Collins.
AN DÚN: G Clarke, Jerome Trainor, S Murray, Simon Wilson, Tom Coulter, G Savage, Gabriel Clarke, Paddy Monan, Gerard Adair, G McGrattan, Barry Coulter, Gary Gordon, Martin Coulter Jr, Paul Braniff, N Sands. Subs.: Peter Mallon for B Coulter, John McGrattan for Monan, Liam Clarke for Trainor, Martin Craig for Mallon, Trainor for T Coulter.

2002
AONTROIM: Damien Quinn, Michael Kettle, K Kelly, Eoin McCloskey, Karl McKeegan, R Donnelly, Ciarán Herron, C Cunning, J Connolly, Liam Watson, C McGuckian, L Richmond, A Delargy, Gregory O Kane, Conor McCambridge. Subs.: Brian McFall for A Delargy, M McCambridge for McCloskey, Seán Delargy for McFall, John Campbell for Donnelly.

AN DÚN: Graham Clarke, S Wilson, S Murray, L Clarke, Gabriel
Clarke, G Savage, M Coulter Snr, Tom McMahon, P Monan,
G McGrattan, Michael Braniff, J Trainor, J McGrattan, Paul
Braniff, N Sands. Subs.: Paddy Coulter for McMahon, G Adair
for J Trainor, G Gordon for M Braniff, Emmett Trainor for
J McGrattan.

2003
AONTROIM: D D Quinn, M Kettle, K Kelly, J Campbell,
M McCambridge, K McKeegan, C Herron, C Cunning, J
Connolly, Paddy Richmond, C McGuckian (capt), L Richmond,
L Watson, Gregory O Kane, B McFall. Subs.: Aidan Delargy for
Gregory O Kane, S Delargy for McFall, Paul Gillen for
P Richmond.
DOIRE: K Stevenson, Paul McVeigh, E McKeever,
C McEldowney, Dominic Magill, M Conway, Peter O Kane,
Ruairi Convery, Paul Carton, Gregory Biggs, O Collins, Réamann
Kennedy, J O Dwyer, M Collins, Danny McGrellis. Subs.:
B Ward for McVeigh, Adrian McCrystal for Carton, Gary Biggs
for Kennedy, Cathal McKeever for McGrellis, Kevin Hinphey for
McEldowney.

2004
AONTROIM (as played in drawn game): D D Quinn, Gerard
Cunningham, K Kelly, Brendan Herron, M McCambridge,
K McKeegan, J Campbell, C Herron, J Connolly, Michael Herron,
C McGuckian (capt), L Richmond, Darren Quinn, P Richmond,
Brian McFall. Subs.: L Watson for L Richmond, M Kettle for
Cunningham, J McIntosh for Connolly.
Changes for replay: Kettle and Watson started instead of
Cunningham and Watson. Replay subs.: L Richmond for
McCambridge, McIntosh for Watson, Gareth Ward for Darren
Quinn, Michael Magill for Connolly.
AN DÚN (as played in drawn game): Graham Clarke, L Clarke,
S Murray, James Henry Hughes, S Wilson, G Savage, Gabriel
Clarke, G Adair, Andy Savage, G McGrattan, John Convery,
Brendan McGourty, Martin Coulter Jr, Gareth Johnson, Michael
Braniff. Subs.: Stephen Clarke for Braniff, Emmett Dorrian for
J H Hughes, Emmett Trainor for G McGrattan, Eoin Clarke for
G Johnson.
Changes for replay: Emmett Dorrian and S Clarke started in place
of J H Hughes and M Braniff. Replay subs.: J H Hughes for
Wilson, Paddy Hughes for Murray, Andrew Bell for J H Hughes.

2005
AONTROIM: D D Quinn, M Kettle, Gavin Bell, Chris Hamill,
Gerard Cunningham, J Campbell, M McCambridge, P Richmond,
Martin Scullion, K McKeegan, K Kelly, M Herron, J McIntosh,
J Connolly (capt), Joe Scullion. Subs.: Karl Stewart for Kelly,
C Herron for M Herron, Brian McFall for Scullion, C McGuckian
for Cunningham.
AN DÚN: Graham Clarke, L Clarke, S Murray, Paddy Hughes,
Gabriel Clarke, G Savage, S Wilson (capt), G Adair, A Savage,
B McGourty, P Monan, Eoin Clarke, Martin Coulter, G Johnson,
Jonathan McCusker. Subs.: Ciarán Coulter for Hughes, John
Convery for Monan, E Trainor for McCusker.

2006
AONTROIM: D D Quinn, Bernard McAuley, Jim McKernan,
J Campbell, K McKeegan, C Herron, M Molloy, C Cunning,
M Scullion, Joe Scullion, K Kelly, M Herron, J McIntosh,
P Richmond, Brian McFall. Subs.: G Bell for Molloy, Brian
Delargy for Kelly, Paddy McGill for McIntosh, Malachy Dallas
for M Scullion.
NUA EABHRACH: Alan Gleeson, Philip Wickham, Richie
Gaule, Matthew Mitchell, Hugh O Leary, Tom Moylan, Adrian
Guinan, Liam O Connor, Tomás Maher, Michael Kennedy, John
Madden, Paul Murray, Kieran Bergin, Martin Finn, Kevin
Kennedy. Subs.: Trevor Fletcher for Maher, Colin White for
Madden, K McHale for O Leary.

2007
AONTROIM: Ryan McGarry, M Kettle, M McCambridge,
S Delargy (capt), M Molloy, J Campbell, C Herron, B Herron,
K McKeegan, P McGill, Neil McManus, M Herron, Simon
McCrory, J McIntosh, Paul Shiels. Subs.: Neil McAuley for
Campbell, Brian McFall for Shiels, P Richmond for McGill,
Séamus McDonnell for McIntosh, Barry McFall for Kettle.
AN DÚN: Graham Clarke, L Clarke, S Murray, Fintan Conway,
Gabriel Clarke, Paddy Hughes, Michael Ennis, A Savage,
B McGourty, E Trainor, Kieran Courtney, Jerome Trainor, Eoin
Clarke, G Johnson, Paddy Coulter. Subs.: Andy Bell for E Trainor,
Aaron Dynes for E Clarke.

2008
AONTROIM: R McGarry, Aaron Graffin, Neil McGarry,
S Delargy, C Herron, K McKeegan, J Campbell, K Stewart, Eddie
McCloskey, M Herron, Cormac Donnelly, P McGill, P Richmond,
L Watson, Paul Shiels. Subs.: P J O Connell for Donnelly,
S McCrory for McGill, M Kettle for Herron.
AN DÚN: Graham Clarke, L Clarke, S Murray, F Conway,
S Wilson, K Courtney, Gabriel Clarke, A Savage, Ruairí
McGrattan, Paul Braniff, B McGourty, Conor Woods, E Clarke,
E Trainor, Stephen Clarke. Subs.: Conor O Prey for L Clarke,
Kevin McGarry for Trainor, Brendan Ennis for S Clarke, P Hughes
for Conway.

2009
AONTROIM: R McGarry, Kieran McGourty, N McGarry,
S Delargy, J Campbell, A Graffin, N McAuley, B Herron,
K McKeegan, N McManus, C Donnelly, K Stewart, P Richmond,
Shane McNaughton, J Scullion. Subs.: Eddie McCloskey for
Stewart, M Herron for B Herron.
AN DÚN: Graham Clarke, Seán Ennis, S Murray, F Conway,
K Courtney, R McGrattan, M Ennis, A Savage, C Woods, C O
Prey, Paul Braniff, S Wilson, James Coyle, G Johnson, S Clarke.
Subs.: Martin Coulter for Coyle, K McGarry for O Prey, Alan
Higgins for S Clarke.

SELECT BIBLIOGRAPHY
from the Gaelic Games Collection at CÓFLA

This select bibliography has been compiled from the Gaelic games collection of the Cardinal Tomás Ó Fiaich Memorial Library and Archive in Armagh. It is intended to provide a useful guide to the wide range of publications of historical relevance to the GAA that are available at the library for consultation or research. The list does not include the full extent of the library's Gaelic games collection; items such as biographies of current or recent players and managers are generally omitted due to considerations of space.

In keeping with the theme of this collection, and to aid research, the bibliography is divided into the different layers of the GAA – national, provincial, county and club – as they feature in published histories, and then individual sections are devoted to each Gaelic game and different types of source for further research.

The library has an active acquisitions policy in respect of Gaelic games manuscripts, publications and ephemera, and this extends to all material relating to the GAA and Gaelic culture in general. The majority of the items listed in this select bibliography have been received through kind donation and the library would like to acknowledge and thank these benefactors for their continuing generosity.

1. NATIONAL AND INTERNATIONAL HISTORY
Bairner, Alan (ed.), *Sport and the Irish: histories, identities, issues*. Dublin, 2005.
Bradley, Joseph M., *The Gaelic Athletic Association and Irishness in Scotland*. Glendaruel, 2007.
'Carbery' [Mehigan, P. D.], *Hurling: Ireland's national game*. Dublin, 1940.
Carey, Tim, *Croke Park: a history – updated edition*. Cork, 2007.
Corry, Eoghan, *Catch and kick: great moments of Gaelic football 1880–1990*. Dublin, 1989.
—, *An illustrated history of the GAA*. Dublin, 2005.
Cronin, Mike, *Sport and nationalism in Ireland: Gaelic games, soccer and Irish identity since 1884*. Dublin, 1999.
—, Murphy, William, Rouse, Paul (eds), *The Gaelic Athletic Association 1884–2009*. Dublin, 2009.
—, Duncan, Mark and Rouse, Paul, *The GAA: A People's History*. Dublin, 2009.
Cumann Lúthchleas Gael, *A century of service*. Dublin, 1984.
Darby, Paul, *Gaelic Games, Nationalism and the Irish Diaspora in the United States*. Dublin, 2009.
—, and Hassan, David (eds), *Emigrant players: sport and the Irish diaspora*. London, 2008.
De Búrca, Marcus, *The GAA: a history*. Dublin, 1980.
—, *The GAA: a history* (2nd ed.). Dublin, 1999.
—, *Céad bliain ag fás: Cumann Lúthchleas Gael, 1884–1984*. Baile Átha Cliath, 1984.
Devlin, P. J., *Our Native Games*. Dublin, [1935].
Holt, Richard, *Sport and the British: a modern history*. Oxford, 1992.
King, Seamus J., *A History of Hurling* (2nd ed.) Dublin, 2005.
King, Seamus J., *The clash of the ash in foreign fields: hurling abroad*. Cashel, 1998.
Mac Lua, Brendan, *The steadfast rule: a history of the G.A.A. ban*. Dublin, 1967.
Mahon, Jack, *A history of Gaelic football*. Dublin, 2000.
Mandle, W. F., *The Gaelic Athletic Association & Irish nationalist politics 1884–1924*. London, 1987.
Ó Caithnia, Liam P., *Báirí cos in Éirinn*. Baile Átha Cliath, 1984.
—, *Scéal na hIomána: ó thosach ama go 1884*. Baile Átha Cliath, 1980.
Ó Ceallaigh, Séamus, *The story of the G.A.A.: a book of reference for Gaels*. Limerick, 1977.
Ó Maolfabhail, Art, *Camán: 2,000 Years of Hurling*. Dundalk, 1973.
O'Sullivan, Thomas F., *Story of the GAA*. Dublin, 1916.
O'Toole, Pádraig, *The glory and the anguish*. Loughrea, 1984.
Puirséal, Pádraig, *The G.A.A. in its time*. Dublin, 1982.
Sugden, John and Bairner, Alan, *Sport, sectarianism and society in a divided Ireland*. Leicester, 1995.

2. PROVINCIAL
Cronin, Jim, *Munster G.A.A. story*. Ennis, 1985.
—, *Munster G.A.A. story. Vol. II: 1985–2001*. Cork, 2001.
Cullen, Tom (ed.), *Beart de réir ár mbriathair: a history of the GAA in Ulster*. Armagh, 2003.

De Búrca, Marcus, *Comhairle Laighean 1900–1984: forbairt agus fás*. Dublin, 1984.
Ó Móráin, Tomás (eag.), *Stair CLG Chonnacht: history of Connacht GAA 1902–2002*. Carrick-on-Shannon, 2002.
Short, Con, *The Ulster GAA Story*. Monaghan, 1984.

3. COUNTY AND DIVISIONAL HISTORIES
Cúige Uladh / Ulster
Brock, Gabriel M., *The Gaelic Athletic Association in County Fermanagh*. Enniskillen, [1984].
Corry, Eoghan, *Oakboys: Derry's football dream come true*. Dublin, 1993.
Cullen, Tom (ed.), *A Gaelic Graduation: a history of the G.A.A. in Fermanagh*. Enniskillen, 2004.
Davies, Anthony, *Iubhaile Órga: stair Coiste Deisceart an Dúin*. Newry, 1981.
Deery, Leo and O'Kane, Danny (eds), *Doire: a history of the G.A.A. in Derry*. Derry, 1984.
Gallogly, Daniel. *Cavan's Football Story*. Cavan, 1979.
Nic An Ultaigh, Síghle. *Ó Shíol go Bláth: An Dún – the G.A.A. story*. Newry, 1990.
Graham, John P., *The GAA in Monaghan 1887–1999: some account of its progress*. Monaghan, 1999.
McBride, Máire, 'The G.A.A. in Belfast 1885–1921'. Unpublished dissertation, Queen's University Belfast, 1976.
Short, Con, Murray, Peter and Smyth, Jimmy, *Ard Mhacha 1884–1984: a century of GAA progress*. Armagh, 1985.
McCaughey, Michael, *The West Tyrone Board of the G.A.A. (1931 to 1974)*. Omagh, 1998.
McCluskey, Seamus, *The Monaghan Gael: eighty years a growing, 1887 to 1967*. Emyvale, 1967.
—, *The G.A.A. in Co. Monaghan: a history*. Monaghan, 1984.
Martin, Joseph, *The GAA in Tyrone 1884–1984*. Omagh, 1984.
—, *The GAA in Tyrone: the long road to glory* (2nd ed.). Omagh, 2003.
—, *The GAA in Tyrone: the road to greatness*. Omagh, 2005.
Ó Gallchóir, Seán. *The 'Donegal Democrat' Book of Donegal G.A.A. Facts* (2nd ed.). Ballyshannon, 1989.
—, *The Raidió na Gaeltachta Book of Donegal GAA Facts* (4th ed.), 2000.

Cúige Chonnacht / Connacht
Conboy, Tony, *Ros Comáin: 101 years of Gaelic games in County Roscommon 1889–1990*. Roscommon, 1990.
Cusack, J. P. (ed.), *Galway's hurling glory: a pictorial record 1923–2000*. Galway, 2000.
McTernan, John C. (ed.), *Sligo G.A.A.: a centenary history*. Sligo, 1984.
Mahon, Jack, *Galway GAA in old photographs*. Dublin, 2002.
Ó Laoi, Padraic, *Annals of the G.A.A. in Galway. Vol. 1: 1884–1901*. Galway, 1983.
—, *Annals of the G.A.A. in Galway. Vol. 2: 1902–1934*. Galway, 1992.
Reilly, Terry and Neill, Ivan, *The Green above the Red: a compilation of Mayo's All-Ireland triumphs at all levels*. Ballina, 1985.

Cúige Laighean / Leinster
Bourke, Martin, *Mid Tipperary GAA 1884–2007: a photographic History* (2007).
Brophy, Jim, *The Leather's Echo: a story of hurling, football, handball and camogie in Co. Wicklow from 1884 to 1984*. Wicklow, 1984.
Corry, Eoghan, *Kildare G.A.A.: a centenary history*. Newbridge, 1984.
Courtney, Sean. *Ten decades of glory: a pictorial history of Kilkenny in Senior championship hurling*. Graiguenamanagh, 1996.
Fennelly, Teddy, *100 years of G.A.A. in Laois: centenary year book*. Portlaoise, 1984.
Hunt, Tom, *Sport and society in Victorian Ireland: the case of Westmeath*. Cork, 2007.
Mulligan, John, *The G.A.A. in Louth: an Historical Record*. Dundalk, 1984.
—, *The G.A.A. in Louth: an Historical Record, The Century-The Millennium*. Dundalk, 2000.
Murphy, Phil (ed.), *Centenary tribute to G.A.A. in Wexford*. Wexford, 1984.
Nolan, William (ed.), *The Gaelic Athletic Association in Dublin 1884–2000* (3 vols). Dublin, 2005.
O'Neill, Gerry. *The Kilkenny GAA Bible (*2nd ed.). Kilkenny, 2005.
Ryall, Tom, *Kilkenny: the GAA story 1884–1984*. Kilkenny, 1984.
Wicklow Millennium Committee, *Moments of history*. Wicklow, 2000.
Williams, Dominic, *The Wexford hurling & football bible 1887–2008: a complete statistical history of Wexford GAA*. Wexford, 2008.

Cúige Mumhan / Munster
Byrnes, Ollie, *Against the Wind: memories of Clare hurling*. Cork, 1996.
Cronin, Jim, *Making connections: a Cork G.A.A. miscellany*. Cork, 2005.

Fogarty, Philip, *Tipperary's G.A.A. story*. Thurles, 1960.
Honohan, Bob, *Rebels with a cause: 120 years of Cork football*. Dublin, 2007.
Horgan, Tim, *Cork's Hurling Story*. Dublin, 1977.
King, Seamus J., *A history of the GAA in the North Tipperary Division*. [Nenagh], 2001.
Ó Ceallaigh, Seamus and Murphy, Sean, *One hundred years of glory: a history of Limerick G.A.A. 1884–1984*. Limerick, 1987.
—, *Tipperary's G.A.A. story 1935–84*. Thurles, 1988.
—, *Tipperary's G.A.A. story 1985–2004*. Thurles, 2005.
O'Meara, Micheál, *South Tipperary G.A.A. 1907–2007*. Kilkenny, 2007.

4. CLUB HISTORIES

Aontroim / Antrim

Anon., *Ar Mhaithe Leis An Spórt: Scéal Cumainn Tír-na-nÓg CLG Baile Raghnaill Chontae Aontroma 1919–1985*. [Randalstown, 1986].
Anon. [Macaulay, Ambrose], *Queen's GFC: A Souvenir History*. Belfast, 1982.
Anon., *Stair Cumainn na Seamróg 1915–1980*. Loughgiel, 1980.
Campbell, Marty, *The Pearse's Story*. Belfast, 1997.
Lavery, Joe, *Ard-Eoin Club History 1907–1985*. Belfast, 1985.
McKillop, Felix, *St Joseph's Glenarm*. Ballycastle, [1984].
Ritchie, Paddy and Lamb, Tommy (eds), *A History of the GAA in Glenavy 1910–1984*. Glenavy, 1987.

Ground opening programmes: Aghagallon (1947), Casement Park (1953 and 1999 reopening), Con Magee's, Glenravel (1977), Cushendall (1980), Lámh Dhearg, Hannahstown (1984), St Enda's, Glengormley (1998), Glenavy (1990), Rasharkin (1983) and St Paul's, Belfast (1979).

Corrigan Park GAA Week Programme: 1946 and 1947.

Ard Mhacha / Armagh

Anon., *St Oliver Plunket Park Crossmaglen: saga of a sportsfield*. 1977.
Boyle, B. *et al*, *The Village Story: A History of Forkhill G.F.C. 1888–1985*. Forkhill, 1985.
Donegan, Michael, *Life on the Ridge: Gaelic Games and Culture of Dromintee, Co. Armagh*. [Dromintee, 1993].
McCann, Sean, *A Local History of the GAA*. Mullaghbawn, 1978.
McCorry, Francis, *St Paul's GFC Lurgan 1971–1996*. [c. 1996].
McDonald, Stephen, *Middletown GAA: A History*. Middletown, 1994.
McGinn, Phil, *Armagh Harps GFC 1888–2008: Celebrating 120 Years*. Armagh, 2008.
Mackle, Colin, *An Port Mór O'Neill's GFC 1934–1994*. 1994.
Murphy, Louis, *St Killian's G.A.C. Whitecross: A History*. Whitecross, 1996.
Murtagh, Oliver, *The History of Lissummon*. Lissummon, 1992.
O'Callaghan, Michael, *The Culloville GAA Story 1888–1992*. Culloville, 1994.
Short, Con, *The Crossmaglen GAA Story 1887–1987*. Crossmaglen, 1987.

Ground opening programmes: Annaghmore (1998), Armagh Athletic Grounds (1984), Ballymacnab (1981), Carrickcruppen (2003), Clady (1989), Clann Éireann, Lurgan (1990 and 2008), Collegeland (1998), Crossmaglen (1959), Culloville (1992), Cullyhanna (1988), Davitt Park, Lurgan (1947), Derrytrasna (1962), Derrynoose (1983 and 2001), Fr. Dan McGeown Park (1996), Granemore (1984), Grange (1980), Keady (1977), Middletown (1992), Mullaghbawn (1978), An Port Mór (1978), Tullysaran (1997), Grange (1980), Belleek (2002), St Patrick's, Cullyhanna (2008), St Peter's, Lurgan (1990), Silverbridge (1980, 1995 and 2007), Tír na nÓg, Portadown (1986), Whitecross (1978) and Wolfe Tone's, Derrymacash (1977).

An Cabhán / Cavan

McKeown, Noel (ed.), *Lurgan Hearts of Erin: Gaelic Games in Lurgan Parish 1884–2005*. Lurgan (Cavan), 2005.
O'Brien, Hugh, *The Celtics 1894–1994: A Centenary History of the GAA in Cootehill*. Cavan, 1994.
Reilly, J. J. (ed.), *Come on the Gaels! 1957–2007*. Cavan, 2007.

Ground opening programmes: Bréifne Park, Cavan (1952 and 1979), and Cavan Gaels (1970).

Doire / Derry

Anon., *Mitchel's GFC 1925–1975*. [c. 1975].

Anon., *St Matthew's GAC*. [Drumsurn], 1988.
Anon., *The Shores of Traád*. [Ballymaguigan], 1985.
Anon., *Watty Graham's Gaelic Athletic Club Glen, Maghera 1933–1984*. Maghera, 1984.
Johnston, G., Diamond, B., Gunning, T., McKenna, J. and Quigg, P., *1946–1977 Michael Davitt's GAC Swatragh*. 1977.
McLaughlin, Jim, *O'Donovan Rossa Gaelic Football Club Magherafelt: The First Fifty Years*. Magherafelt, 1998.
Mullan, Colum and Mullan, Bernie (eds), *Ballerin GAC 1944–84 Centenary Memento*. 1984.
O'Kane, Seán, *O'Connor's Glack Co. Derry Gaelic Athletic Club*. 1987.
Walsh, Rev. J. R., Bradley, P., O'Kane, L. and O'Kane, Danny, *Glenullin John Mitchel's 1925–1975*. [*c*. 1975].

Ground opening programmes: Ballinascreen (1974), Ballinderry (1979), Ballerin (1997), Claudy (1973), Desertmartin (1984 and 1993), Glenullin (1978, 1987 and 1991), Glack (1994), Kilrea (1979), Lavey (1979), Loup (1981), Magherafelt (1960). Ógra Colmcille, Littlebridge (2000) and Swatragh (1988).

An Dún / Down
Anon., *Féile 50 Cloch Fhada CLG 1945–1995*. [1995].
Anon., *Glenn John Martin Golden Jubilee 1931–1981*. [1981].
Anon., *Newry Shamrocks 1931–2006*. [2006].
Conlan, Aidan (ed.), *Celebrating 75 Years of Gaelic Games and Culture in Glenn 1931–2006*. [2006].
Gilmore, Teresa, *St Joseph's Ballycran GAC 1939–1989*. 1991.
Dougherty, Gerry and Crilly, Ciaran, *'The Town': A History of Castlewellan Town, The Parish of Kilmegan and 100 Years of the Castlewellan GAA Club 1905–2005*. Castlewellan, 2006.
Gordon, Donal, Madine, Michael and McLeigh, Tommy, *Ár Scéal Féin: Stair CLG Loch An Oileáin / Our Story: The History of Loughinisland GAC*. [2007].
Kearns, P. D., Scéal *Chluain Dáimh: The Clonduff Story 1887–1984*. Newry, 1984.
Leitrim Fontenoys, *Fontanóigheannaí Liatroma – Céad Blain D'fhás agus D'fhobairt na gCluichí Gaelacha* 1888–1988. Newry, 1988.
McAteer, Seán Óg (ed.), *John Mitchel GFC 1956/1981*.
McCarthy, Gerard, *Saval's Gaelic Tradition*. Newry, 1986.
McEvoy, Paddy, *The Russell Chronicles: A History of Gaelic games in Downpatrick*. Downpatrick, 1984.
Magee, S., Murray, M., Treacy, E. and McNabb, N., *Carryduff GAC 1972–1982*. [Carryduff], 1982.
O'Neill, Gerard, Leckey, Bertie and Stewart, Jimmy, *The Aghaderg Story: A History of Gaelic Games and Culture in the Parish of Aghaderg 1903–1984*. 1984.
Travers, A., Gribben, D., Walls, M. and McGilligan, G., Scéal *Chluain Daimh: The Clonduff Story 1985–2007*. [2007].

Ground opening programmes: Aghaderg GFC and Ballyvarley Hurling Club (1984), An Ríocht (1993), Attical (1975), Ballela (2007), Ballycran (1966), Ballyholland (1984), Ballymartin (1995), Burren (1968 and 1975), Carryduff (1997), Castlewellan (1978), Clonduff (1968 and 1998), Dromara (1995), Drumaness (1981 and 1987), Drumgath (1994), St John's, Drumnaquoile (1990), Killyleagh (1970), Mayobridge (1978), Saul (1997).

Dún na nGall / Donegal
Anon., *Club na gCeithre Máistir CLG 1932–2007*. [*c*. 2007].
Campbell, D., Dowds, D. and Mullan, D., *Against the Grain: a History of Burt, its people and the GAA*. Burt, 2000.
Mac Conaill, Seán (ed.), *Idir Peil agus Pobal: History of the GAA in the Parish of Ardara 1921–2003*. Ardara, 2004.
Ground opening programmes: Killygordon (1996), Four Masters, Donegal (1992), Naomh Bríd, Ballintra (1992) and St Michael's, Dunfanaghy (1984).

Fear Manach / Fermanagh
Corrigan, Paul, *Belnaleck Art Mac Murrough's GFC: A History*. 1985.
Conway, Mark and Cauldwell, Gareth, *Glory days: the story of Fermanagh GAA's journey 2004*. Enniskillen, 2004.
Mulligan, Marius, *Roslea Shamrocks GFC 1954–1958: The Glorious Fifties*. 1998.
Ground opening programmes: Derrygonnelly (1962), Enniskillen Gaels (1982), Roslea (1996) and St Joseph's, Ederney (1989).

Muineachán / Monaghan
Anon., *1905–2005 Centenary Year of Castleblayney Faughs GFC*. [*c*. 2005].
Anon., *Clontibret O'Neills 1949–1952: The Glorious Years*. [1991].
Gilsenan, Michael, *The Hills of Magheracloone 1884–1984*. Magheracloone, 1985.
McKenna, Peter, *A History of Rockcorry in The Emetresse*. [1991].

Meegan, Larry, *The Inniskeen Story: A History 1888–1988*. Inniskeen, 1988.
Ó Mórdha, Pilib, *Cumann Peile Thiarnaigh Naofa Cluain Eois 1886–1993*. [1994].

Ground opening programmes: Aghabog, Monaghan (1996), Aughnamullen (1980), Carrickmacross (1953 and 1989), Clontibret (1973), Cremartin (1987), Currin (2002), Gavan Duffy Park, Monaghan (1958), Inniskeen (1960), Killanny (1994), Latton (1992), Magheracloone (1997), Ballybay (1951), Oram (1983) and Seán McDermott's, Threemilehouse (1961 and 1979) and Toome (1996).

Tír Eoghain / Tyrone
Anon., *A History of the GAA in Ard Bó*. [*c*. 1988].
Anon., *Cora Criche Fr. Rock's GAA 1889–1989: Centenary Souvenir Booklet*. 1989.
Anon., *Na Fianna 1904–1984: A History of Coalisland Fianna GFC*. [1985].
Clancy, Leo and Keogh, Michael (eds), *'Glorious Clonoe': the story of O'Rahilly GFC (1916–1986)*. Clonoe, 1986.
Connolly, Tom, *Eochair Naomh Macartáin: A Club History 1908–2000*. [*c*. 2000].
Fintona Pearse's, *Ceiliúradh Céad Bliain: A Century of Gaelic Games in the Donacavey parish*. Fintona, 2007.
Fitzgerald, Malachy, *Derrytresk Fir an Chnoic 1903–2003: The Little Club with the Big Heart*. Derrytresk, 2006.
Harkin, Brendan, *Years to Remember: An outline of the development of the GAA in the parish of Cappagh 1904–1979*. Omagh, 1980.
Healy, Sean (ed.), *Fifty Years Onward 1932–1982: A History of Omagh St Enda's Gaelic Athletic Club*. Omagh, 1982.
McCann, Dermot and Traynor, Tommy, *The Gaelic Fields of Errigal Kerrogue*. 2006.
McCaughey, Michael, *The Spirit of The Reds: Trillick St Macartan's, Co. Tyrone*. Trillick, 1985.
McLernon, Brian, *A Kick on the Shore*. [Derrylaughan, 2005].
Mooney, Francis (ed.), *The First Fifty Years: A History of St Malachy's Gaelic football club 1932–1982* [Edendork, *c*. 1982].
Quinn, Paul (ed.), *A Club for all Ages: 100 Years of Gaelic Games and Culture in Donaghmore 1903–2003*. Donaghmore, 2004.
Rodgers, Alan, *Forever Young on the Fields of Moy. A 100 Year History of An Mhaigh*. Moy, 2008.
—, *Down from the 'Cross: A GAA Journey*. Beragh, 2006.
St Colmcille's GAC, Carrickmore, *The Carrickmore Tradition 1932–1982*. [Carrickmore, 1982].
Various authors, *The Carrickmore Tradition 1982–2002*. Carrickmore, 2003.

Ground opening programmes: An Charraig Mhór (1982 and 2000), Clogher (1987), Coalisland (1949 and 1988), Cookstown (1972), Derrytresk (1997), Edendork (2002), Eskra (1992), Fintona (2007), Kildress (1984), Loughmacrory (2006), Moortown (1972), Moy (1998), Naomh Colum Cille [Coalisland/Clonoe] (2006), O'Neill Park, Dungannon (1947), Pomeroy (1948 and 1998) and Rock (1998).

Gaillimh / Galway
Conwell, John Joe, *Hearts of Oak: The Rise of Portumna GAA Club*. Portumna, 2008.
Cloherty, Gerry, *The Story of Rahoon Hurling 1889–2002*. [Galway], 2004.
Fahy, Michael (ed.), *A History of Kilconieron GAA Club 1885–2005: Rich in Hurling Tradition*. Kilconieron, 2006.
McGann, D. (ed.), *For the Pride of the Parish: a History of Gaelic Games in New Inn and Bullaun*. 2003.
Ground opening programmes: Pearse Stadium, Galway (2003) and St Brendan's, Loughrea (1977).

Liatroim / Leitrim
Kelly, Liam, *Kiltubrid*. Carrick-on Shannon, 1984.
Ground opening programmes: Cloone (1980), Melvin Gaels, Kinlough (1995), Sean MacDermott Park (1964).

Maigh Eo / Mayo
Anon., *Ballyhaunis GAA Past & Present*. [1981].
Reilly, Terry, *The Goal of Victory: History of Ballina Stephenites 1886–1986*. Ballina, 1986.

Ros Comáin / Roscommon
Anon., *Michael Glavey's: The First Roscommon Intermediate Champions*.
Anon., *Cúpla Focail: 50 Years of Michael Glavey's GAA Club 1956–2006*. [2007].
Mullaney, Thomas, *Shannon Gaels GAA Club Croghan/Drumlion 1884–1984: A History*. [*c*. 1985].
Ground opening programmes: Clann na nGael (1994), Fuerty (2006), Kilmore (1982), Michael Glavey's (1986), St Faithleach's (1981), St Michael's (1996) and Shannon Gaels (2002).

Sligeach / Sligo
Ground opening programmes: Enniscrone / Kilglass (1989).

Baile Átha Cliath / Dublin

Anon., *Cumann Iománaíochta agus Peile Naomh Uinsinn: A record of St Vincent's Hurling and Football Club 1931–1953.* Dublin, 1953.

Campbell, John & Casey, Liam, *A History of Erin's Isle GAA Club Finglas.* Dublin, 2000.

Vaughan, D. J., *Liffey Gaels: A Century of Gaelic Games.* 1984.

Wren, Jimmy, *Saint Laurence O'Toole GAA Club Dublin 75th Anniversary Record 1901–76.* Dublin, [1976].

Ground opening programmes: Hogan Stand (1959), Áras Daimhín, Páirc an Chrócaigh (1984), St Brigid's, Blanchardstown (1979).

Cill Chainnigh / Kilkenny

Ground opening programmes: Glenmore (1981).

Cill Dara / Kildare

Anon., *Mágh Núadhat.* [Maynooth], 1966.

Ground opening programmes: Athy, 1984.

An Iarmhí / Westmeath

Farrell, E., Seery, O., Ryan, J., Ó hAnluain, E. and Jordan, K., *Southern Gaels Hurling Club 1973–1998.* [1998].

Ground opening programmes: Ballinagore (1993), Maryland (1993).

Longfort / Longford

Ground opening programmes: Dromard (1976), Kenagh (1978).

Lú / Louth

Boyle, Sean, *Cooley Kickhams GFC 1887–1987* (1987).

Mulligan, John, *Dundalk Young Irelands GFC: An Historical Record of the Green and Blacks.* Dundalk, 2004.

Powderly, T., Brennan, B., Bellew, P. and Mackin, N., *A History of St Kevin's GFC Philipstown 1949–99.* [*c.* 2000].

Ground opening programmes: Naomh Fionnbarra (1984), Cooley (1969), Dowdallshill (1959), Hunterstown Rovers (1984), St Patrick's, Lordship (1976) and Naomh Malachi (2000) and Stabannon (1989).

An Mhí / Meath

Ground opening programmes: Drumconrath (1991), St Peter's, Dunboyne (1993), Ratoath (2004).

Uibh Fhailí / Offaly

Ground opening programmes: Ballinamere (1980), Clara (1980), St Carthage's (1993).

Ciarraí / Kerry

Anon., *A Legion of Memories 1929–1979.* [Killarney Legion GAA].

Ground opening programmes: Kilcummin (1985), Rathmore (1984), Tarbert (1983).

An Clár / Clare

Anon., *A Proud Past: Highlights of the Newmarket-on-Fergus Hurling and Football Story 1885–1973.* Newmarket-on-Fergus, 1974.

Ground opening programmes: Crusheen (1984), Cusack Park, Ennis (1980), Teach Mhichíl Chíosóg, Carn (1986).

Corcaigh / Cork

Arnold, John, *Bride Rovers Abú: The Story of Gaelic Games in Rathcormac Parish.* Bartlemy, 1999.

Cronin, Jim, *Millstreet's Green and Gold.* [Tralee, *c.* 1977].

Lyons, Tom, *Clonakilty GAA 1887–1987.* [Clonakilty], [1987].

O'Connor, Michael, *Ballinora GAA Under the Dropping Ball: How the GAA creates belonging in Ballinora.* Ballinora, 2006.

Ring, W. J., *History of Cloyne GAA* [Midleton, *c.* 1977].

Ground opening programmes: St Finbarr's (1970), Páirc Uí Chaoimh (1976), Russell Rovers (1980) and Sam Maguire Memorial, Maulabracka, Dunmanway (1984).

Luimneach / Limerick

Harrold, John, *The Contests of Athletic Youth: A History of Gaelic Games in Bruree and Rockhill.* Bruree, 2003.

Various authors, *Ballinacurra Gaels / Gael Baile Na Corra CLG 1979–2004.* [*c.* 2005].

Ground opening programmes: Galtee Gaels (1981) and Gerald Griffin's (1985).

Port Láirge / Waterford
Various authors, *Dún na Mainistreach / Baile na Cúirte: The Growth and Development of a GAA Club*. 1980.
Ground opening programmes: Tramore (1980).

Tiobraid Árann / Tipperary
Anon., *Moycarkey-Borris GAA Story*. 1984.
Hannon, Jackie, *A History of Gaelic Games in Lattin and Cullen 1886–2000*. [2001].
King, Seamus J., *Cashel King Cormac's GAA History 1985–2005*. 2006.
—, *Lothra agus Doire 1884–1984 Iomáint agus Peil*. 1984.
Molloy, Dick, *Ballingarry 100 years of Gaelic Games 1887–1987*. [*c*. 1987].
O'Dwyer, Michael (ed.), *The Parish of Emly: History of Gaelic Games and Athletics*. Emly, 2000.
Ground opening programmes: Aherlow (1979) and Glen Rovers (1998).

Loch Garman / Wexford
Culleton, Edward, *St Martin's GAA Club 1932–1982*. Wexford, 1982.

Thar Saile / Overseas
Beatty, Tom (ed.), *Brian Ború GAA Club (London) Centenary Story*. [*c*. 2000].
John Mitchel's GFC, *The Story of the GAA in Liverpool*. [1984].
Various authors, *Clan na Gael London 1951–1998*. [1998].
Ground openings: Gaelic Park, Melbourne (1985).

5. REFERENCE BOOKS

Buckley, Gerry, *Fifty five years of the Croke Cup: All-Ireland Colleges 'A' hurling competition, 1944–1948 and 1957–2006*. Naas, 2007.
Breheny, Martin and Keenan, Donal, *The ultimate encyclopedia of football and hurling*. Dublin, 2001.
Carthy, Brian, *The Championship*. Dublin. Editions: 1995, 1996, 1997, 1998, 1999, 2000, 2001, 2002, 2003, 2004, 2005, 2006, 2007.
Corry, Eoghan. *Kellogg's book of G.A.A. facts: a young person's guide*. Dublin, 1985.
Donegan, Des (ed.), *The complete handbook of Gaelic games: a comprehensive record of results and teams (1887–2005)*. Dublin, 2005.
Guiney, David and Puirséal, Pádraig, *Guinness book of hurling records*. [*c*. 1967]
Lennon, Joe, *The playing rules of football and hurling 1602–2010*. Gormanstown, 2001.
—, *A comparative analysis of the playing rules of football and hurling 1884–1999*. Gormanstown, 1999.
McCann, Owen, *Greats of Gaelic Games*. Vols 1 (1977), 2 (1980), 3 (1982), 4 – centenary edition (1984), 5 (1985).
—, *Recordmakers of Gaelic games* (1996).
—, *The Shell book of the McCarthy Cup: All-Ireland hurling championship finals down the years*. Dublin, 1993.
McManus, Darragh, *GAA confidential: everything you never knew you wanted to know about Gaelic games*. Dublin, 2007.
Morrison, Tom. *For the record: a history of the National Football and Hurling League finals*. Cork, 2002.
Ó Droighneáin, Muiris, *An Sloinnteoir Gaeilge agus An tAinmneoir*. Belfast and Dublin, n.d.
Smith, Raymond, *A century of Gaelic games: a comprehensive record of results and teams*. Dublin, 1987.
—, *The Sunday Independent / ACC Bank complete handbook of Gaelic games: a comprehensive record of results and teams (1887–1993)*. Dublin, 1993.
—, (ed.), *The Sunday Independent / ACC Bank complete handbook of Gaelic games: a comprehensive record of teams and results (1887–1999)*. Naas, 1999.
Sportsfile, *A Season of Sundays*. Dublin. 1998, 2000, 2004, 2005, 2007 editions.

6. HURLING

Downey, Paddy, *Hurling at the Crossroads: a survey*. Dublin, 1965.
Freeman, Norman, *Classic Hurling Matches 1976–91*. Dublin,1993.
Fullam, Brendan, *The Wolfhound Guide to Hurling*. Dublin, 1999.
Furlong, Nicholas, *The Greatest Hurling Decade: Wexford and the epic teams of the '50s*. Dublin, 1993.
Hutchinson, Roger. *Camanachd!: the story of shinty*. Edinburgh, 2004.
Morrison, Tom, *Cork's glorious years*. Cork, 1975.
King, Seamus, *Classic Munster Hurling Finals*. Dublin, 2007.
MacLennan, Hugh Dan. *Shinty!* Nairn, 1993.

—, *Not an Orchid … .* Inverness, 1995.

Riegel, Ralph, *Three kings: Cork, Kilkenny, Tipperary: the battle for hurling supremacy.* Dublin, 2008.

Ryan, Martin, *3 by the Lee: the making of the Cork hurlers' 3-in-a-row 1976–78.* Cork, 2006.

Smith, Raymond, *Decades of Glory: a comprehensive history of the national game.* Dublin, 1966.

—, *Player's no. 6 Book of Hurling: a popular history of the national game (1884–1974).* Dublin, 1974.

—, *The Clash of the Ash: a popular history of the national game 1884–1981* (2nd ed.). Dublin, 1981.

—, *The Hurling Immortals: a popular history of the national game 1884–1984.* Dublin, 1984.

Walsh, Denis. *Hurling: the revolution years.* Dublin, 2005.

7. FOOTBALL

Anon., *The Derry Heirs: 1993 All-Ireland Champions.* Derry, 2004.

Barrett, J. J., *In the name of the game.* Bray, 1997.

Barry, John and Horan, Eamon, *Years of Glory: the Story of Kerry's All-Ireland Senior Victories.* Tralee, 1977.

Campbell, Dónal and Dowds, Damian, *Sam's for the Hills: Donegal's All-Ireland Odyssey.* Burt, 2003.

Canny, Richard and Heagney, Liam, *Into the West '98: Galway's Road to Success.* Roscommon, 1998.

Corry, Eoghan. *Kingdom Come.* Dublin, 1989.

Duggan, Keith, *House of pain: through the rooms of Mayo football.* Edinburgh, 2007.

Dunne, Mick, *The Star Spangled Final: the story of the 1947 All-Ireland football final in New York.* Dublin, 1997.

Fitzgerald, Dick, *How to Play Gaelic Football.* Cork, 1914.

Foley, Michael, *Kings of September: the day Offaly denied Kerry five in a row.* Dublin, 2007.

Guiney, David, *Gaelic Football.* Dublin, 1976.

Lennon, Joe, *Coaching Gaelic Football for Champions.* Poyntzpass, 1964.

—, *Fitness for Gaelic Football.* Alba House, 1969.

McDermott, Peter, *Gaels in the Sun: a detailed account of Meath's historic trip to Australia, March 1968.* Drogheda, 1968.

McGee, Eugene, *Classic Football Matches.* Dublin, 1993.

Mahon, Jack, *Twelve Glorious Years.* Galway, 1965.

—, *Three in a row: Galway 1964-65-66.* Galway, 1966.

Maloney, Seamus. *The Sons of Sam: Ulster's Gaelic Football Greats.* Belfast, 2004.

Mooney, Francis, *Sam: the story of Tyrone's first All-Ireland.* Monaghan, 2003.

O'Grady, Seamus (ed.), *Coiste Peil na nÓg [Gaillimh], 1976–2006.* Galway, 2006.

O'Sullivan, E. N. M., *The Art and Science of Gaelic Football.* Tralee, 1958.

Quinn, Jerome, *Sam Comes Home.* Belfast, 2003.

Smith, Raymond, *The Football Immortals: a popular history of Gaelic football (1884–1984).* Dublin, 1983.

Tighe, Anton, *The American All-Ireland: a GAA classic.* Newry, 1997.

Tormey, Roland, *Summertime Blues: Dublin's epic journey to a historic All-Ireland.* Edinburgh, 2007.

Whelan, Daire, *A Year with the Dubs.* Dublin, 2008.

Whyte, Eunan, *Heroes of '57: the complete story of Louth's All-Ireland victory.* Dublin, 1997.

8. CAMOGIE

Cumann Camoguidheachta na nGaedheal, *Treoraí Oifigiúil.*

Conway, Marion, *A history of camogie in Roscommon.* Boyle, [2004].

Moran, Mary, *Camogie champions: a complete handbook of camogie.* Cork, [1998].

—, *A resounding success: thirty years of All-Ireland colleges camogie.* Cork, [1998].

—, *Munster's camogie story 1904–2004.* Cork, [2004].

—, *Cork's camogie story 1904–2000.* Cork, [2000].

—, *Gymfrocks to Headbands: Thirty Years of Munster Colleges Camogie.* [n.d.]

Anon., *Scéal na Camógaíochta.* Kilkenny, 1984.

[Toner, P. J.], *The Armagh camogie story: fifty years of earnest endeavour.* Armagh, [1978].

9. HANDBALL AND ATHLETICS

Doherty, Ray, *Handball,* Dublin, 1970.

Griffin, Pádraig, *The politics of Irish athletics 1850–1990.* Ballinamore, 1990.

McElligott, Tom, *The Story of Handball: the Game, the Players, the History.* Dublin, 1984.

Ó Loinsigh, Seosamh, *Handball: fás agus forbairt.* Dublin, 1984.

Vallely, Brian, *There Are No Boundaries in Sport: The story of 92 Years of Struggle by the GAA and NACAI to Represent Ireland in International Competition*. Lurgan, 1976.

10. GAELIC GAMES GENERAL

Anon., *Dublin Primary Schools League: golden jubilee commemorative book*. Dublin, 1978.

Bellew, Ronnie, *GAA: the glory years of hurling and football*. Dublin, 2005.

Breheny, Martin and Keys, Colm, *The Chosen Ones: celebrating 1000 GAA All Stars*. Dublin, 2004.

Burke, Frank, *All-Ireland Glory: a Pictorial History of the Senior Football Championship 1887–2005*. Galway, 2005.

—, *All-Ireland Glory: a Pictorial History of the Senior Hurling Championship 1887–2004*. Dublin, 2004.

Coiste na nÓg, *Highlights of the GAA Story*. Dublin, 1984.

Duggan, Keith, *The Lifelong Season: at the heart of Gaelic games*. Dublin, 2004.

Dunne, Aaron, *Around the World in GAA Days*. Edinburgh, 2009.

Fahy, Desmond, *How the GAA survived the troubles*. Dublin, 2001.

Fullam, Brendan, *The Throw-in: the GAA and the men who made it*. Dublin, 2004.

Humphries, Tom, *Green Fields: Gaelic sport in Ireland*. London, 1996.

King, Seamus, *Tipperary's Bord na nÓg story*. Thurles, 1991.

King, Seamus, Ó Donnchú, Liam and Smyth, Jimmy, *Tipperary's GAA Ballads*. Thurles, 2000.

Lennon, Joe, *Towards a philosophy for legislation in Gaelic games*. Gormanstown, 2000.

McGahon, Arthur, *Hours of Glory: Recalling great moments in the story of the GAA*. Dublin, [*c.* 1954].

Mahon, Jack, *Action Replay*. Galway, 1984.

—, *For love of town and village*. Dublin, 1997.

Mehigan, P. D., *Vintage Carbery*, Dublin, 1984.

Mendlowitz, Andy, *Ireland's Professional Amateurs: a sports season at its purest*. Lincoln (USA), 2007.

Ó Ceallacháin, Seán Óg, *The Dubs: Dublin GAA since the 1940s*. Dublin, 2007.

Ó Coigligh, Pádraig, *Gaelic Games*. Dublin, 1977.

O'Connor, Gerard, *Ready to Play: a GAA guide to coaching and planning nursery programmes*. Dublin, 2007.

Ó Faoláin, Dómhnall, Ó Bruain, Aodh agus Ó Riain, Micheál, *Cumann Lúthchleas Gael na nGairm Scol 1960–1985*. Baile Átha Cliath, 1985.

O'Hehir, Michael, *The GAA 100 years*. Dublin, 1984.

Ó hEithir, Breandán, *Over the Bar: a personal relationship with The GAA*. Dublin, 1984.

Smyth, Jimmy, *In Praise of Heroes: ballads and poems of the GAA*. Dublin, 2007.

Sweeney, Eamonn, *The Road to Croker: a GAA fanatic on the Championship trail*. Dublin, 2004.

—, *O'Brien pocket history of Gaelic sports*. Dublin, 2004.

Quinn, Jerome, *Ulster football and hurling: the path of champions*. Dublin, 1993.

—, *Ulster sports 1995*. Belfast, 1995.

—, *The Mirror book of Ulster Gaelic games*. Belfast, 1997.

—, *Jerome Quinn's Championship*. Belfast, 2000.

Smyth, Jimmy, *Ballads of the Banner*. 1998.

11. BIOGRAPHIES.

Anon., *Eamon Coleman memorial, 1947–2007*. Magherafelt, [2008].

Anon., *Mattie McDonagh: 'fathach i measc na bhfear' / a giant among men*. Ballygar, 2007.

'Carbery', *Famous Captains: Pen Pictures of Eight Gaelic Football Leaders*. Dublin [*c.* 1947].

Carthy, Brian, *Football Captains: The All-Ireland winners*. Dublin, 1993.

Clan na Gael, Lurgan, *Ómós do Aonraí Mac Garaidh*. Lurgan, 1993.

Codd, Martin, *The way I saw it: Nickey Rackard leads Wexford to hurling Glory*. Enniscorthy, 2005.

De Búrca, Marcus, *Michael Cusack and the GAA*. Dublin, 1989.

De Paor, Seán Óg agus de Paor, Aoife, *Lá an Phaoraigh*. Indreabhán, 2007.

Dorgan, Val, *Christy Ring: a personal portrait*. Dublin, 1980.

Doyle, Tommy, *A lifetime in hurling as told to Raymond Smith*. London, 1955.

Fogarty, Weeshie, *Dr Eamonn O'Sullivan: a man before his time*. Dublin, 2007.

Fullam, Brendan, *Hurling Giants*. Dublin, 1998.

—, *Legends of the Ash*. Dublin, 1998.

—, *Captains of the Ash*. Dublin, 2002.

Grimes, Pat (ed.), *Patrick Tobin: Everything Bright and Fair*. Cookstown, 2007.

Guckian, Des, *The life and times of Fr. Sean Manning (a Gaelic leader)*. Longford, 1979.

Horgan, Tim, *Christy Ring: hurling's greatest*. Cork, 2007.

Kavanagh, Dermot, *Ollie: the hurling life and times of Ollie Walsh*. Dublin, 2006.

Keane, Colm. *Hurling's top 20*. Edinburgh, 2002.

Keher, Eddie. *Hurling heroes*. Dublin, 2000.

Looney, Tom, *Dick Fitzgerald: king in a kingdom of kings*. Dublin, 2008

McAlinden, Eithne, *Alf Ó Muirí 1914–1999*. Lurgan, 2009.

McGarry, Fearghal, *Eoin O'Duffy: A Self-Made Hero*. Oxford, 2005.

McNamara, Seán, *The man from Carron*. Ennis, 2005.

McRory, Seamus, *The voice from the sideline: famous GAA managers*. Dublin, 1997.

—, *The Road to Croke Park: great GAA personalities*. Dublin, 1999.

—, *The All-Ireland dream: over 25 interviews with GAA greats*. Dublin, 2005.

Mahon, Jack, *Memories*. Galway, 2004.

—, *The game of my life: Jack Mahon in conversation with the giants of the GAA past and present*. Dublin, 1993.

Meaney, Sean, *Our name is on the cup: the stories of Liam MacCarthy and Sam Maguire*. London, 2008.

Morrissey, Mick, *Hurling and my hurling stars past and present*. [Waterford, 1977].

Murphy, Seán, *The life and times of Jackie Power, "the prince of hurlers"*. Limerick, 1996.

Ó Baoighill, Pádraig, *Nally as Maigh Eo*. Baile Átha Cliath, 1998.

Ó Caithnia, Liam P., *Micheál Cíosóg*. Baile Átha Cliath, 1982.

O'Ceallaigh, Seamus and Murphy, Sean, *The Mackey Story*. Limerick, 1982.

O'Connell, Mick, *A Kerry Footballer*. Cork, 1975.

O'Connor, Christy, *Last man standing: hurling goalkeepers*. Dublin, 2006.

Ó Muircheartaigh, Joe and Flynn, T. J., *Princes of the Pigskin: a Century of Kerry footballers*. Cork, 2007.

Ó Muircheartaigh, Micheál, *From Borroloola to Mangerton Mountain*: *travels and stories from Ireland's most beloved broadcaster*. Dublin, 2006.

O'Neill, Dan, with Horan, Liam, *Divided Loyalties: The life and times of a Mayo man who won an All-Ireland title with Louth in 1957*. Galway, 2008.

Ó Riain, Séamus, *Maurice Davin (1842–1927): first president of the GAA*. Dublin, [1995].

O'Sullivan, Jim, *Men in Black*. Dublin, 2002.

Ó Tuama, Liam, *Where we sported and played: Jack Lynch: a sporting celebration*. Dublin, 2000.

Rafferty, Eamonn, *Talking Gaelic: leading personalities on the GAA*. Dublin, 1997.

Scally, John, *All-Ireland Ambitions*. Dublin, 2001.

—, *The Best of the West: GAA greats of Connacht*. Cork, 2008.

—, *The Earley Years: official biography*. Dublin, 1992.

Sweeney, Eamonn, *Munster Hurling Legends: seven decades of the greatest teams, players and games*. Dublin, 2003.

Tierney, Mark, *Croke of Cashel: the life of Archbishop Thomas William Croke, 1823–1902*. Dublin, 1976.

Walsh, Margaret, *Sam Maguire: the enigmatic man behind Ireland's most prestigious trophy*. Cork, 2003.

Williams, Tom, *Cúchulainn's Son: the story of Nickey Rackard*. Dublin, 2006.

12. OFFICIAL GAA PUBLICATIONS

Anelius, Josephus, *National Action: A Plan for the National Recovery of Ireland*. Dublin, 1942.

Gaelic Athletic Annual: 1932–33, 1936–1937, 1951.

Cumann Lúthchleas Gael, *An Treoraí Oifigúil / Official guide* [rulebook, after 1988 divided into *Part 1* and *Part 2*.] Editions: 1934, 1938, 1939 (abridged), 1943, 1950, 1956, 1961, 1966, 1973, 1978, 1988 (2 eds), 1991, 1994, 1995, 1997, 1998, 2001 and 2007.

Playing Rule Books (otherwise *Part 2*): 1992, 2003 and 2008.

Lámhleabhar do Réiteoirí agus Imreoirí. Dublin, 1966.

Rules of Gaelic football and hurling. 1976.

Referees' guide to the playing rules of hurling and football. 1988 & 1991 editions.

Rules of football. 1991.

Rules of hurling. 1989, 1991.

Refereeing Matters. [Dublin], 2006.

Notes for hurling Coaches. Dublin, 1962.

An Action Plan for GAA Coaching. Dublin, 1979.

Best Practice guidelines to GAA Clubs.

Céim sa Teanga.

Dressing Rooms & Social Centres for GAA Clubs. Dublin, 1975.
Handbook on Club Management. [Dublin].
Ó Cochláin, P. S., *Know Your Rules: Hurling*. [Dublin].
Wanted: More men for the whistle! Dublin, 1987.

Commission on the GAA, *Report of the Commission on the GAA*. Dublin, 1971.
Strategic Review Committee, *Enhancing Community Identity*. [Dublin, 2002].

Commission on the G.A.A. in Galway, *Report of the Commission*. Galway, 1974.
O'Hara, Patricia and Kelleher, Carmel, *The GAA in County Wexford: a report on organisational structure*. Dublin, 1980.

13. MANUSCRIPT SOURCES

Annual Congress booklets: 1943, 1947–1949, 1952, 1955–1959, 1961, 1962, 1964–1967, 1969–2003, 2005, 2006.
Annual Congress minutes: 1943, 1947, 1948, 1969, 1971, 1979–1982, 1984–1992, 1994–1996, 1998–2002. Special
        Congress minutes: 1997, 1998, 2000, 2002.

Ulster Council minute books: 1917–39, 1950–72.
Ulster Convention booklets: 1943–1948, 1950, 1955–1957, 1962, 1967, 1969, 1970, 1972–2009.
Ulster Convention minutes: 1943, 1944, 1946–1948, 1951–1982, 1984–1993, 1997–1999, 2001–2008.

Armagh County Board minute books: 1933–79.
Armagh Hurling Board papers: 1945–64, 1971–77 and 1994–94.
Armagh Athletic Grounds minute book: 1936–84.
Miscellaneous minutes, correspondence and documentation relating to Cavan County Board: *c.* 1933–*c.* 1962.
Miscellaneous minutes, convention papers, correspondence and documentation relating to Down County Board:
        c. 1940–*c.* 1966.
Monaghan County Board annual accounts: 1945–72.
Tyrone County Board accounts book: 1926–32.

Con Short collection: research files on Ulster GAA history, 1884–1984.
Síghle Nic An Ultaigh collection: research files on Ulster GAA history, *c.* 1887–*c.* 1990.
Pádraig Mac Floinn collection: GAA related correspondence and documents, *c.* 1942–2005.

Clann na nGael GAC, Lurgan, minute book: 1944–48.
Armagh Harps GAC minute book: 1903–05.
St Patrick's College, Armagh students' football diary, 1903–19.

Youth and Sports Council for Northern Ireland minutes: 1962–71.

Ó Beoláin, Caoimhghín, 'James Boland 1857–1895'. Unpublished manuscript.
Canning, Joseph, Armagh County Teams, 1974–1988. Unpublished manuscript.

14. NEWSPAPERS & PERIODICALS

Irish Independent GAA Golden Jubilee Congress Record. 12 April 1932.
Irish Press GAA Golden Jubilee supplement, 1934.
Celtic Times: Michael Cusack's Gaelic Games Newspaper. Dublin, 2003.
Book of Gaelic Games (7 magazine issues, *c.* 1984).
Breaking Ball (various issues, 2001–03).
An Camán (various issues, 1931–34).
Croke Park Annual (2003/04, 2006/07, 2007/08, 2008/09).
Cuchulainn Annual (1956, 1960, 1963, 1964, 1968, 1969).
An Cúl (various issues, 1970–78).
Eadrainn Féin: information bulletin for G.A.A. officials (various issues, 1981–2006).
Fios (various issues, 1974–77).
GAA in the Orchard County (all 24 issues, 1990–94).

The Game (various issues, 2004–05)
Gaelic Life (various issues, 2007–09).
Gaelic Games (various issues, 1979, 1980, 2004, 2005).
Gaelic Review (various issues, 1987–88).
Gaelic Sport (various issues, 1960–2002).
Gaelic Stars (various issues, 1967–1989).
Gaelic World (various issues, 1979–2004).
Gaelsport annual (all issues, 1981–1998).
Gaelsport magazine (various issues, 1991–98).
High Ball (various issues, 1998–2005).
Hogan Stand (various issues, 1991–2009).
Hurling and Football Annual (all issues, 1992–98).
Hurling World (2 issues, 2008).
Our Games (all issues, 1958–1979).
An Ráitheachán: the Gaelic quarterly review (all 5 issues, 1936–37).
Solo (various issues, 1973).
Ulster Games Annual: (various issues, 1981–1998).
World of Gaelic Games: 176, 1977, 1979.

15. COUNTY YEARBOOKS
Cúige Chonnacht
Gaillimh: 1984, 1990, 1992, 1993, 1997–1999, 2002, 2003. Leitrim: 1975.
Maigh Eo: 1979–80, 1989.
Ros Comáin: 1972/73, 1978, 1983, 1985, 1986, 1988, 1991, 1993, 1995, 1997, 1998, 2001, 2006/07.
Sligeach: 1969.

Cúige Laighean
BÁC: 1975, 1978, 1982, 1985, 1987, 1989, 1990, 1992–94, 1999, 2000.
Cill Dara: 1974. Cill Chainnigh: 1973, 1982, 1984, 1991, 1992, 1998, 2008.
Cill Mhantáin: 1996, 2002. An Iarmhí: 1974/75, 1977. Laois: 1987.
Longfort: 1990/1991. Lú: 1988/89, 1999, 2000, 2001, 2005, 2008.
Loch Garman: 1982, 1983. An Mhí: 1974, 1976, 1979. Uibh Fhailí: 1971, 2001.

Cúige Mumhan
Ciarraí: 1975/1976, 1977, 1978, 1981, 1982, 1984, 1985, 1987, 1988.
An Clár: 1977, 1982, 1985, 1990. Cork: 1972, 1985, 1987, 1993, 1997, 2000.
Luimneach: 1972, 1975–77, 1979–85, 1998. Port Láirge: 1984, 1986.
Tiobraid Árann: 1973, 1975.

Cúige Uladh
Aontroim: 2006, 2007. Ard Mhacha: 1968, 2002, 2008. An Cabhán: 1994, 2007.
Doire: 1979, 1986, 2006. An Dún: 1981–89, 1991, 1994–2005, 2007, 2008.
Dún na nGall: 1992, 1999, 2008. Fear Manach: 1979, 1986, 1987, 1989, 1992.
Muineachán: 1978–80, 1986–93, 1998, 2004.
Tyrone, 1974, 1975, 1978, 1981, 1983–88, 1992–2002, 2007.

16. MISCELLANEOUS ITEMS
The library collection contains many additional items of historical interest. There is a wide range of match programmes from the 1940s to the 2000s, from All-Ireland SHC & SFC finals, semi-finals and quarter-finals, provincial finals and ordinary championship games, Railway Cup finals, National Hurling and Football Leagues, All-Ireland under-21 finals, county championship finals and tournaments.

There are also numerous county convention booklets, fixture booklets, club newsletters and special publications; reports and strategic plans of the association at national, provincial and county levels; and various additional items such as photographs, video and audio recordings, scrapbooks, newspaper supplements and cuttings, posters, tickets and other ephemera.

ENDNOTES

From Cú Chulainn to Cusack: Ball-Playing, Camán, Shinny and Hurling in Ulster before the GAA

1   A. B. Gleason, 'Hurling in Medieval Ireland' in Mike Cronin, William Murphy and Paul Rouse (eds), *The Gaelic Athletic Association 1884–2009* (Dublin, 2009), pp 1, 9.

2   This chapter, in referring to Ulster, shall deal with the area covered by the modern nine–county province of that name, although previously the region of Ulaidh had different boundaries.

3   For an extensive glossary of the terms used in certain texts from the *Táin*, see John Strachan (ed.), *Stories from the Táin*, ed. Osborn Bergin (3rd edition, Dublin, 1944), pp 39–95.

4   J. P. Mallory offers a probable date for the *Táin* as being no earlier than the fourth century AD, or as he refers to it, the 'pagan' Irish Iron Age. See J. P. Mallory, *Aspects of the Táin* (Belfast, 1992), p. 152.

5   'F–an ópair in cú. No fethed–som a cluiche colléic. Fo–cerded a líathróit 7 fo–cerded a loirg inna diad, co mbenad in líathróit. Níbo móo in band ol–daas a chéle. Ocus fo–ceird a bunsaig inna ndiaid, conda gaibed re tothaim.' This can be roughly translated as: 'The hound attacks him. Meanwhile he attends to the play. Throwing the *líathróit* and throwing the *loirg* after it, he wounds the dog with the *líathróit*. With one stroke not greater than the other. It is often written that he threw his javelin after it until it fell.'

6   John Strachan, *Stories from the Táin* (Dublin, 1908), pp 8–11.

7   See, for example, Pádraig Mac Con Midhe, *Seanchas Sua* (3rd edition, n.p., 1976), p. 11.

8   *Lebor na hUidhre*, eds. R. I. Best and O. Bergin, (Dublin, 1929), p. 157.

9   For a full examination, see Cecile O'Rahilly, *Táin Bó Cuailnge* (Dublin, 1961), pp vii–lxi.

10 Strachan, *Stories from the Táin*, p. 9.

11 Gleason, 'Hurling in Medieval Ireland' in Cronin *et al*, *Gaelic Athletic Association 1884–2009*, p. 9.

12 Michael George Crawford, *Legendary Stories of the Carlingford Lough District* (Newry, 1913), p. 187.

13 Eugene O'Curry, *Lectures on the Manuscript Materials of Ancient Irish History* (Dublin, 1861), p. 328. A. O'Kelleher and G. Schoepperle (eds), *Betha Colaim Chille* (Chicago, 1918; reprinted, Dublin, 1998), pp 178–9, commented as follows: 'It is encrusted with episodes familiar in the lives of other saints, in romances of troubadours and Arthurian knights, of the Fianna, the Ultonian heroes and the gods, in stories of druids and in folk-tales.' (See *ibid*, p. xiii. See also Brian Lacey, *The Life of Colum Cille* (Dublin, 1998).

14 Gleason, 'Hurling in Medieval Ireland' in Cronin *et al*, *Gaelic Athletic Association 1884–2009*, p. 9.

15 P. W. Joyce, *A Social History of Ancient Ireland* (Dublin, 1913), pp 474–7. The Brehon Laws were transcribed, translated and published in a five–volume series, entitled *The Ancient Laws of Ireland*, with an accompanying glossary, between 1865 and 1901, by a specially appointed government commission. For a more recent analysis, see D. A. Binchy (ed.), *Corpus Juris Hibernici*, vols 1–vi, with a separate booklet, *Introductory Matter* (Baile Átha Cliath, 1978). Of the nineteenth-century edition, Binchy says, 'Beware the English translations of the ancient text in the official edition; I might almost say ignore them.' (See *ibid*, p. xx.) See also D. A. Binchy, 'Mellbretha' (Judgements concerning games), *Celtica*, viii (1968), pp 144–154.

16 W. Neilson Hancock *et al, Ancient Laws and Institutes of Ireland* (6 vols, Dublin, 1865–1901).

17 Hancock *et al, Ancient Laws and Institutes*, iii, pp 554–555.

18 Hancock *et al, Ancient Laws and Institutes*, ii, p. 147.

19 Joyce, *Social History*, p. 474.

20 Henry F. Berry (ed.), *Statutes and Ordnances, and Acts of Parliament of Ireland: King John to Henry V* (Dublin, 1907), pp 438–439. The last letter of *horlinge* is unclear; it is possible that the word is actually *horlings*.

21 (Art Ó Maolfabhail, *Camán: 2,000 Years of Hurling in Ireland* (Dundalk, 1973), pp 12–15.

22 John T. Gilbert, 'Archives of the Town of Galway – Queen's College, Galway' in Historical Manuscript Commission 10th report, appendix V: *The Manuscripts of the Marquis of Ormonde, The Earl of Fingall, the Corporations of Waterford, Galway, &c* (London, 1885), p. 402.

23 Gleason, 'Hurling in Medieval Ireland' in Cronin *et al*, *Gaelic Athletic Association 1884–2009*, pp 2–3.

24 Registri Johannis Swayne qui Ecclesiam Armach rexit ab Anno 1418 ad Annum 1439, Public Record Office of Northern Ireland, DIO/4/2/4, p. 556.

25 D. A. Chart (ed.), *Register of Primate John Swayne* (Belfast, 1935), pp 12–13. See also Alan Fletcher, *Drama and the Performing Arts in Pre-Cromwellian Ireland: A Repertory of Sources and Documents from the Earliest Times until c.1642* (Cambridge, 2001), pp 432, 584.

26 Tadhg Ó Donnchadha, *Leabhar Cloinne Aodha Buidhe*, (Dublin, 1931), pp 65–8. Apart from the mention of *iomáin* (in the genitive case, *d'fhios na hiomána*), this poem does not appear to refer to any typical characteristics of stick–and–ball hurling, but the playing of 'cammon or shinny' at Christmas in Carrickfergus was recorded in the early nineteenth century (Ó Maolfabhail, *Camán*, p. 141).

27 Lambert McKenna, *Pilib Bocht Ó hUiginn*, (Dublin, 1931), p. 10.

28 In 1569 Tarlach Luineach Ó Néill, chief of Tír Eoghain, married Agnes Caimbeul from Kintyre in Scotland, a lady who brought a number of *gallóglaigh* (gallowglasses, or mercenary soldiers) with her as part of her dowry. It is possible that there were some competent *camán*-men among them.

29 *Camanachd* in Scotland seems to have survived the Highland Clearances of the eighteenth and nineteenth centuries, but rules varied from place to place, as they did in Ireland. Uniformity of rules could hardly be realised while the social order was changing so much. See Hugh Dan MacLennan, *Not an Orchid …* (Inverness, 1995); and Roger Hutchinson, *Camanachd!: The Story of Shinty* (Edinburgh, 1989).

30 See, for example, a reference to the playing of *Commons* in a poem based in Co. Westmeath in the early nineteenth century (Patrick Fagan, *A Georgian Celebration: Irish Poets of the Eighteenth Century* (Dublin, 1989), pp 34–36; cited in Tom Hunt, *Sport and Society in Victorian Ireland: The Case of Westmeath* (Cork, 2007), p. 197).

31 Eoin Kinsella, 'Riotous Proceedings and the Cricket of Savages: Football and Hurling in Early Modern Ireland' in Cronin *et al, Gaelic Athletic Association 1884–2009*, p. 15, argues that the earliest forms of hurling in Ireland – presumably before the seventeenth century – resembled *camanachd* or shinty. If we accept this argument, which is based on a large degree of assumption, it is possible that the

game evolved more in the southern provinces between the seventeenth and nineteenth centuries, while the *camán / commons* still found in Ulster centuries represented a closer adherence to old Irish hurling traditions.

32 *Cammag* ceased to be played around the year 1900 after the introduction of football, but was revived in the 2000s.

33 Kevin Whelan, 'The Geography of Hurling' in *History Ireland*, vol. 1, no. 1 (Spring 1993), pp 27–8.

34 'This ball they use at the hurlings, which they strike with a stick called with comaan. … At the lower end it is crooked and about three inches broad, and on this broad part you may sometimes see one of the gamesters carry the ball tossing it for 40 or 50 yards … They seldom come off without broken heads in which they glory very much. At this sport one parish sometimes or barony challenges another; they pick out ten, twelve or twenty players of a side, and the prize is generally a barrel or two of ale … This commonly is on some very large plain, the barer of grass the better … At some of these gatherings two thousand have been present together.' See 'John Dunton's description of his tours in Ireland', MS. Rawlinson D 71 in the Bodleian Library, Oxford; reproduced in Edward MacLysaght, *Irish Life in the Seventeenth Century: After Cromwell* (Dublin, 1939), p. 364.

35 Ó Maolfabhail, *Camán*, pp 137–40.

36 *Arthur Young's Tour of Ireland*, ed. A. W. Hutton (2 vols, London, 1892) i, pp 446–7. The young prospective bride was the subject of a competition after Mass on a Sunday, sometimes involving teams from different baronies and as often as not having to be completed over several Sundays.

37 Cited in Ó Maolfabháil, *Camán*, pp 29–30.

38 Angélique Day and Patrick McWilliams (eds), *Ordnance Survey Memoirs of Ireland* [hereafter, *OSM*] (40 vols, Belfast), *Parishes of Co. Down III 1833–8*, (Belfast, 1992), p. 58. Based in part on this Waringstown reference, the nearby townland of Aghacommon – documented from the seventeenth century – was interpreted some time ago as meaning 'hurling field' (Bernard J. Mooney, 'The Place-Names Explained' in anon., *The Parish of Seagoe* (n.p., 1954), p. 15), but a more recent study has questioned this and suggested 'the field of the little bends' as an alternative interpretation (Pat McKay, *A Dictionary of Ulster Place-Names* (Belfast, 1999), p. 1).

39 John Anketell, *Poems on several subjects* (Dublin, 1793), p. 213.

40 *Ibid*, pp 209–18.

41 The Earl of Belmore, *The History of Two Ulster Manors and their Owners* (2nd edition, Dublin, 1903), p. 415.

42 See, for example, Patricia Hughes-Fuller, 'Am I Canadian?: Hockey as a "National" Culture', Library and Archives of Canada (2005), pp 25–39, on www.arts.ualberta.com, on 21 Sept. 2009.

43 Énrí Ó Muirgheasa (ed.), *Dhá Chéad de Cheoltaibh Uladh* (Baile Átha Cliath, 1934), pp 362–8.

44 Conchubhar Ó Cuileanáin, 'Iomáin le Camán agus Iomán le Cois' in *Our Games Annual*, 1960, pp 11–12; Con Short, *The Ulster GAA Story 1884–1984* (Rassan, 1984), pp 15–16; Liam P. Ó Caithnia, *Báirí Cos in Éirinn* (Baile Átha Cliath, 1984), pp 24–29.

45 *The Montgomery Manuscripts*, ed. Rev. George Hill (1869), vol. 1, p. 126.

46 Rev. James O'Laverty, *An Historical Account of the Diocese of Down and Connor, Ancient and Modern* (5 vols, Dublin, 1878–95), i, p. 18.

47 Kinsella, 'Riotous Proceedings' in Cronin *et al*, *Gaelic Athletic Association 1884–2009*, pp 16–18.

48 William Shaw Mason, *Statistical Account or Parochial Survey of Ireland* (3 vols, Dublin, 1814–19).

49 Shaw Mason, *Statistical Account*, iii (Dublin, 1819), p. 207.

50 Shaw Mason, *Statistical Account*, i (Dublin, 1814), p. 157.

51 *Gaelic Journal*, 1 Oct. 1895, pp 108–09. In An t–Athair Eóin Ua Riain (ed.), *Féil-sgríbhinn Eóin Mhic Néill* (Baile Átha Cliath, 1940), p. 140, Éamonn Ó Tuathail recorded an older version of this song, which was originally written down by Roibeáird Mac Ádhaimh (Robert MacAdam) in 1830.

52 Shaw Mason, *Statistical Account*, ii (Dublin, 1816), p. 160.

53 Shaw Mason, *Statistical Account*, i, 124. Samuel Lewis, *A Topographical Dictionary of Ireland* (2 vols, London, 1837), ii, p. 669, mentions 'common' as 'a favourite amusement of the young men' in Co. Tyrone, but it seems that this reference is lifted almost verbatim from the account of Ardstraw in Shaw Mason's survey.

54 *Irish News*, 22 Nov. 1906.

55 Ó Maolfabhail, *Camán*, pp 95–8, 149.

56 P. J. McGill, 'Cross Country Hurling in South-West Donegal' in *Donegal GAA Yearbook*, 1978, pp 9–10. See also Liam P. Ó Caithnia, *Scéal na hIomána: ó Thosach Ama go 1884* (Baile Átha Cliath, 1980), pp 440–3; and Seamus J. King, *A History of Hurling* (Dublin, 1996), p. 221.

57 J. H. Andrews, *A Paper Landscape: The Ordnance Survey in Nineteenth-Century Ireland* (Oxford, 1975), pp 165–7, 175–7.

58 Angélique Day and Patrick McWilliams (eds), *OSM*, xiii, *Parishes of County Antrim IV 1830–8* (Belfast, 1992), p. 65.

59 *Idem*, *OSM*, xvi, *Parishes of County Antrim V 1830–5, 1837–8* (Belfast, 1992), p. 18.

60 *Idem*, *OSM*, xxxvii, *Parishes of County Antrim XIV 1832, 1839–40* (Belfast, 1996), p. 77.

61 *Idem*, *ODM*, viii, *Parishes of County Antrim II 1832–8* (Belfast, 1991), p. 113.

62 Angélique Day, Patrick McWilliams and Nóirín Dobson (eds), *OSM*, xxiii, *Parishes of County Antrim VIII 1831–5, 1837–8* (Belfast, 1993), p. 73.

63 Day and McWilliams (eds), *OSM*, xxi, *Parishes of County Antrim VII 1832–8* (Belfast, 1993), p. 109.

64 Day, Williams and Dobson (eds), *OSM*, xxiv, *Parishes of County Antrim IX 1830–2, 1835, 1838–9* (Belfast, 1994), p. 132.

65 Day and McWilliams (eds), *OSM*, xi, *Parishes of Co. Londonderry III 1831–5* (Belfast, 1991), pp 14 (Aghanloo), 54 (Dunboe).

66 *Idem*, *OSM*, xxii, *Parishes of Co. Londonderry VI 1831, 1833, 1835–6* (Belfast, 1993), p. 52.

67 *Idem*, *OSM*, xxxi, *Parishes of Co. Londonderry XI 1821, 1833, 1836–7* (Belfast, 1995), p. 60.

68 *Idem*, *OSM*, xxvii, *Parishes of Co. Londonderry VIII 1830, 1833–7, 1839* (Belfast, 1994), p. 18.

69 *Idem*, *OSM*, xv, *Parishes of Co. Londonderry IV 1824, 1833–5* (Belfast, 1992), p. 76.

70 *Idem*, *OSM*, vi, *Parishes of Co. Londonderry I 1830, 1834, 1836* (Belfast, 1990), p. 100.

71 *Idem*, *OSM*, xviii, *Parishes of Co. Londonderry V 1830, 1833, 1836–7* (Belfast, 1993), p. 100.

72 Ó Maolfabhail, *Camán*, pp 141–3.

73 *Benbradagh*, no. 5, spring 1975, p. 32. The original source of this poem is not known, so it may have been written some time after 1825. It was preserved by oral tradition

until Pat Kealey of Dungiven recorded it in the 1940s. In terms of authenticity, the poem lists the names of twelve Dungiven players who did live there in the 1820s. However, the date mentioned, 17 January 1825, was a Monday – which, one would imagine, was ordinarily a day of work with short hours of daylight, and hardly conducive to outdoor team-sports.

74 Day and McWilliams (eds), *OSM*, xv, *Counties of South Ulster 1834–8* (Belfast, 1838), p. 128.

75 *Ibid*, pp 109, 133, 140.

76 *Idem*, *OSM*, xxxviii, *Parishes of County Donegal I 1833–5* (Belfast, 1997), p. 17; Ó Maolfabhail, *Camán*, p. 143.

77 *Londonderry Sentinel*, 11 Jan. 1834. The authors are grateful to Mr John Dooher, Leckpatrick, for this reference.

78 W. H. Maxwell, *Wild Sports of the West* (1832; reprint, London, 1915), pp 13–14.

79 William Carleton, *Rody the Rover* (1845), p. 84. Allegations of hurling matches being used as cover for political organisation had been made in the south since the seventeenth century (Ó Maolfabhail, *Camán*, pp 20, 43, 46).

80 *Belfast Morning News*, 23 Dec. 1882.

81 Letter from Cardinal Joseph MacRory, published in *Irish Independent G.A.A. Golden Jubilee Supplement 1884–1934*, p. 10.

82 P. J. Devlin, *Our Native Games* (Dublin, 1935), pp 44–5.

83 Angélique Day, Patrick McWilliams and Lisa English (eds), *OSM*, xxxiii, *Parishes of Co. Londonderry XIII 1829–30, 1832, 1834–6* (Belfast, 1995), p. 164.

84 Day and McWilliams (eds), *OSM*, xi, *Parishes of Co. Londonderry III 1831–5* (Belfast, 1991), p. 137.

85 Irish Folklore Commission Archives, University College Dublin, vol. 1747, p. 438ff; Rev. Daniel Gallogly, *Cavan's Football Story* (Cavan, 1979), p. 17.

86 See, for example, Dónal Campbell, Damian Dowds and Damien Mullan, *Against the Grain: A History of Burt, its People and the GAA* (Burt, 2000), p. 91.

87 A. T. Lucas, *Furze: A Survey and History of its Uses in Ireland* (Dublin, 1960), pp 164–5, records the use of furze or whin for *camáin* in counties Cavan (Scrabby, Bailieborough), Derry (Drumachose), Donegal (Templecrone, Gleann Choilm Cille), Down (Clonallon) and Monaghan (Tydavnet).

88 William Hugh Patterson, *A glossary of words and phrases in use in the Counties of Antrim and Down* (London,1880), p. 89. *Ibid*, p. 23, defines *Common* as follows: '*sb*. Hockey; a game. Same as Shinney. Called in some districts Comun and Kamman, from the Irish name for the game'.

89 *Ibid*, p. 71.

90 *Irish News*, 22 Nov. 1906. It is hard to know whether to take the reference to a trophy literally, as 'Benmore' was prone to write colourful descriptions more so than accurate accounts.

91 Eamon Phoenix, Pádraic Ó Cléireacháin, Eileen McAuley and Nuala McSparran (eds), *Feis na nGleann: A Century of Gaelic Culture in the Antrim Glens* (Belfast, 2005), pp 158–67.

92 'Lurigedan', 'Cushendall: I remember' in *The Glensman*, vol. 1, no. 4 (January 1932), pp 7–8.

93 Charles McAllister, 'Cumann Oisin 1904–2004' in Phoenix, Ó Cléireacháin, McAuley and McSparran (eds), *Feis na nGleann*, pp 163–4.

94 Felix McKillop, *St Joseph's GAC, Glenarm 1903–1984* (Glenarm, 1984), p. 9. On p. 4, it is recorded that the bend in the *camán* was often made by burying it in hot horse–manure.

95 Jeanne Cooper Foster, *Ulster Folklore* (Belfast, 1951), pp 31–2.

96 Campbell *et al*, *Against the Grain*, pp 73–7.

97 P. S. Mac 'Ghoill, 'A Hundred Years of the GAA in Co. Donegal' in *Donegal Annual*, no. 36 (1984), p. 89.

98 Seumas [sic] McManus, *The Bend of the Road* (2nd edition, Dublin, 1906), p. ix.

99 *Idem*, *Through the Turf Smoke: Love, Lore, and Laughter of Old Ireland* (New York, 1899), pp 105–10 *passim*.

100 *Ibid*, p. 105. When the narrator informs Nelly, a female character, that he has to play the next day in 'a caman match between two townlan's', she replies, '"it's no place for the lake of you, that should be doin' for yer sowl, instead of makin' a tom–fool of yerself with a crooked kippeen; an' ye'll lie in yer bed all day the morra!"'

101 *Idem*, *Yourself and the Neighbours* (New York, 1914), p. 20.

102 *Ibid*, pp 35–6.

103 *Idem*, *Bold Blades of Donegal* (New York, 1935), pp 175–83; *idem*, *A Lad of the O'Friels* (London, 1903), pp 30, 90, 189.

104 *Derry People*, 14 Oct. 1905. It should also be noted that in his autobiographical work on his youthful years, McManus makes no mention of *camán*. See Seumas MacManus, *The Rocky Road to Dublin* (Dublin, 1947).

105 *Derry People*, 28 Oct. 1905.

106 McGill, 'Cross Country Hurling in South-West Donegal', pp 9–10.

107 IFCA, vol. 986, p. 170; Ó Maolfabhail, *Camán*, p. 104. Another interesting term was 'goaly-wipe', as identified by P. W. Joyce. 'In Ulster, a goaly-wipe is a great blow on the ball with the *camaun* or hurley: such as will send it to the goal.' See P. W. Joyce, *English as we speak it in Ireland* (London, 1910), p. 351.

108 Anon., 'Derry' in *Irish Independent G.A.A. Golden Jubilee Congress Record*, 12 Apr. 1934, p. 62.

109 'Downman', 'Down' in *ibid*, p. 63.

110 IFCA, vol. 1747, pp 587–592; cited in Gabriel M. Brock, *The Gaelic Athletic Association in County Fermanagh* (Enniskillen, 1984), pp 10–11.

111 IFCA, vol. 1747, pp 593–4; cited in Brock, *G.A.A. in County Fermanagh*, pp 10–11. A contemporary described the playing of *camans* among the youth of Roslea in the 1880s as 'a rather primitive form' of hurling, with 'the caman being taken from the nearest hedge and the ball a lump of any convenient material, like a lump of wool, a large spool or a ball made of straw or hay' ('The Memoirs of Master Hugh Rooney 1880–1970', published on www.rooneys-of-roslea.com, accessed on 27 Aug. 2009). It is also reported that the game was played in the Tempo-Coa area with a wooden ball called a *nig* or *neug* (Brock, *G.A.A. in County Fermanagh*, p. 10. *Kites* was probably a form of *cead na slise*, or *tip-cat*, a game which consisted of striking a short stick that was either thrown or raised from the ground by a sharp blow.

112 IFCA, vol. 986, pp 106; *ibid*, vol. 1161, p. 536; cited in Gallogly, *Cavan's Football Story*, p. 14.

113 Henry McCourt, 'Derrylaughan G.F.C.' in Frank Ó Néill (ed.), Programme for the official opening of Cardinal MacRory Memorial Park, Coalisland, 19 June 1949, p. 19.

114 Patrick J. Campbell (ed.), *The Carrickmore Tradition* (Carrickmore, 1982), pp 15–16.

115 Síghle Nic An Ultaigh, *Ó Shíol go Bláth: An Dún – The GAA Story* (Newry, 1990), pp 17–18; Leitrim Fontenoys GAC, *Glimpses of a hundred years of Gaelic sporting and cultural activities in the Parishes of Upper and Lower Drumgooland* (Leitrim, Co. Down, 1988), p. 48.

116 Edward Marjoribanks, *The Life of Lord Carson*, vol. 1 (London, 1932), p. 13; cited in Trevor West, *The Bold Collegians: The Development of Sport in Trinity College, Dublin* (Dublin, 1991), p. 35.

117 T. S. C. Dagg, *Hockey in Ireland* (Tralee, 1944), p. 37.

118 Neal Garnham, *Association Football and Society in Pre-partition Ireland* (Belfast, 2004), pp 18–21. P. J. Devlin, *Our Native Games*, p. 45, said of the 1880s around Newry: 'The only football in my region was played by British military teams, and these matches were sternly forbidden my patronage by parental decree.'

119 Gallogly, *Cavan's Football Story*, pp 15–16; IFCA, vol. 974, p. 57; *ibid*, vol. 966, p. 144; *ibid*, vol. 1015, p. 30.

120 Shan F. Bullock, *After Sixty Years* (London, 1926), p. 79.

121 Con Short, Peter Murray and Jimmy Smyth, *Ard Mhacha 1884–1984: A Century of GAA Progress* (Armagh, 1985), pp 24–25; Seamus McCluskey, *The GAA in Co. Monaghan … a History* (Monaghan, 1984), pp 2–3.

122 Mr & Mrs S. C. Hall, *Ireland, its Scenery, Character, & c.* (2 vols, London, 1841), p. 256).

123 The tortuous question of the origins of *caid* is discussed in Ó Caithnia, *Báirí Cos in Éirinn*, pp 58–86 *passim*. Maurice Davin, the first GAA president, recognised 'Irish football' as something distinctive from other codes prior to 1884: 'Irish football is a great game and worth going a long way to see, when played on a fairly laid out ground under proper rules.' (*United Ireland*, 18 Oct. 1884).

124 *Shan Van Vocht*, 2 Aug. 1897.

125 Minutes of the Dublin Hurling Club, 3 Jan. 1883, held in the Michael Cusack Archive, National University of Ireland, Galway.

126 *Tyrone Constitution*, 1 Jan. 1886. The authors would like to thank Mr Alan Rodgers, Beragh, for this reference.

127 *Belfast Morning News*, 12 Dec. 1888.

128 Cumann Ruairí Óg Bun an Dála 1900–1980, 'Coisriceadh agus Oscailt Oifigiúil Pháirc Mhuire, 6 Aibreán 1980 [programme for the consecration and official opening of St Mary's Park, Cushendall, on 6 Apr. 1980], pp 11–12. There is a reference to *shinny* and *nag* in the Ballymena Observer in 1892 (Fionnuala Carson Williams, 'Life and Lore – an analysis of Ulster-Scots', in *The Ulster Scot*, 1 Oct. 2003. See also James Fenton, *The Hamely Tongue: A personal record of Ulster-Scots in County Antrim* (Newtownards, 1995), p. 139, for the survival of the word *shinny* – as in the simile, 'as crooked as a shinny' – after 1930.

129 Geo. B. Antrime, 'William Clarke Robinson' in *The Glensman*, vol. 1, no. 5, pp 25–6; *Belfast News-Letter*, 5 Jan. 1932.

130 W. Clarke Robinson, *Antrim Idylls and other Poems* (Belfast, 1907), pp 63–4.

131 See, for example, *Derry People*, 5 May 1906; *ibid*, 12 Jan. 1907; and *Derry Journal*, 26 Apr. 1907. The game was still referred to as *camán* as well in the early days of the GAA in north Antrim – see, for example, *Ballymena Weekly Telegraph*, 9 July 1904.

132 *Derry Journal*, 26 Mar. 1890. See also *ibid*, 2 May 1890.

133 *An Camán*, 22 Deireadh Fóghmhair 1932. The use of the old-style *camán* persisted in Burt until the 1950s. At a Donegal hurling board meeting in 1953, delegates from other clubs called for this old *camán* to be banned as it was 'a museum piece', 'slowed the game' and smashed the lighter hurling sticks (Campbell *et al*, *Against the Grain*, p. 166; *ibid*, p. 147).

134 IFCA, vol. 1747, p. 559; cited in Ó Caithnia, *Scéal na hIomána*, pp 638–9.

135 Campbell, *Carrickmore Tradition*, pp 15–16.

Why the GAA was founded

1 *Cork Examiner*, 3 Nov. 1884; *United Ireland*, 8 Nov. 1884; *Leinster Leader*, 8 Nov. 1884; *The Irish Sportsman*, 8 Nov. 1884 and the *Tipperary Advocate*, 8 Nov. 1884. A further complicating factor is that folk memory in clubs in counties such as Kilkenny and Clare claim that various individuals from their areas also attended the first meeting. This seems highly unlikely and the most probable thing is that what happens is that these individuals attended either the third meeting of the GAA in Thurles on 15 January 1885, or to the first annual convention of the GAA which was also held in Thurles in late 1885.

2 See, for example, Stephen Jay Gould, *Triumph and Tragedy in Mudville: A Lifelong Passion for Baseball* (2003), *passim*.

3 T. F. O'Sullivan, *Story of the GAA* (Dublin, 1916), p. 1.

4 There is considerable dispute over how many people actually attended the meeting. Many more people claimed later to have been present than were actually listed. There is no conclusive proof that more than the seven people who were listed in press reports actually attended. Even allowing for the fact that up to thirteen people might have attended, it does not change the basic fact that members of the IRB were prominent at the meeting.

5 *Sport*, 29 Oct. 1887.

6 See Nancy Murphy, 'Joseph K. Bracken: GAA founder, Fenian and politician', in William Nolan (ed) *Tipperary: History and Society* (Dublin, 1985), pp 379–93.

7 Report by Inspector A. W. Waters, in National Archives of Ireland, CBS 126/S, 11 Nov. 1887.

8 W. F. Mandle, 'The I.R.B. and the beginnings of the GAA', in *Irish Historical Studies*, vol. xx, no. 80 (1977), pp 418–38, p. 420; Meelick GAA Club, *Centenary of the First All–Ireland Hurling Final* (Galway, 1988); Pádraig Puirséal, *The GAA in its Time* (Dublin, 1982), pp 34–6; Caoimhghín Ó Beoláin, 'James Boland (1857–1895)', unpublished manscript, n.d.), Cardinal Ó Fiaich Library and Archive, Armagh, pp 60–73; Pádraig Ó Baoighill, *Nally as Maigh Eo* (n.p., 1998), pp 278–84.

9 Tom Markham, 'It was kindled from the Fenian Fire' in *Irish Press Jubilee Supplement*, 14 Apr. 1934, p. 56.

10 W. F. Mandle, *The Gaelic AthleticAassociation and Irish Nationalist Politics, 1884–1924* (Dublin, 1987), pp 21–3.

11 *United Ireland*, 19 Dec. 1885.

12 *Sport,* 27 Mar. 1886.

13 *Celtic Times*, 15 Oct. 1887.

14 *Celtic Times*, 12 Nov. 1887.

15 *The Shamrock*, 8 July 1882.

16 *The Shamrock*, 8 July 1882.

17 Coimisiún Béaloideasa Éireann, University College Dublin, vol. 921, pp 56–7: interview with Peter Clarke, Killann, Co. Cavan.

18 Séamus Ó Ceallaigh, *A History of the Limerick GAA* (Limerick, 1984).

19 *Sport*, 8 Nov. 1884.

20 *Sport*, 29 Sept. 1883.

21 Tony O'Donoghue, *Irish Championship Athletics 1873–1914* (2005), p. 14.

22 *Irish Weekly Independent and Nation*, 13 Dec. 1902.

23 Maurice Davin Notebook, GAA Museum and Archives, Croke Park; Seamus Ó Riain, *Maurice Davin (1842–1927): First President of the GAA* (Dublin, 1994), p. 19.

24 *Sport*, 6 Aug. 1881.

25 See, for example, *Cork Examiner*, 3 Nov. 1884; and Tipperary *Advocate*, 8 Nov. 1884.

26 *United Ireland*, 18 Oct. 1884.

27   T. S. C. Dagg, *Hockey in Ireland* (1944), pp 30–5.
28   *Sport*, 3 Feb. 1883.
29   *Sport*, 17 Feb. 1883.
30   *Sport*, 3 Feb. 1883. Later, after the founding of the GAA, the game of hurley collapsed and just two clubs remained, King's Hospital and High School. They remained faithful to the game of hurley until it became clear in the early 1890s that the game was not about to grow in strength. By then a Hockey Association had been founded in England and a code of rules developed. In the autumn of 1892 both King's Hospital and High School abandoned hurley and turned to hockey. Then, in February 1893, the two clubs drove the formation of the Irish Hockey Union, with the Rev. Gibson elected President.
31   *Celtic Times*, 2 Apr. 1887.

Parish Factions, Parading Bands and Sumptuous Repasts: The diverse origins and activities of early GAA clubs

1   Marcus de Búrca, *The G.A.A.: A History* (2nd edition, Dublin, 1999), preface.
2   Mike Cronin, William Murphy, Paul Rouse (eds), *The Gaelic Athletic Association 1884–2009* (Dublin, 2009), reviewed the association's history through several new thematic prisms, such as interaction with the Irish language, amateurism, photography and motion pictures; and also reassessed issues surrounding the organisation's foundation and its position in the Irish revolutionary period (1913–23).
3   Tom Hunt, 'The GAA: social structure and associated clubs', in Cronin *et al* (eds), *Gaelic Athletic Association*, pp 183–202.
4   *Cashel Sentinel*, 8 June 1895.
5   Peter Meskell, *Suir View Rangers 1895–1898* (Thurles, 1998), pp 8–10.
6   Rev. Daniel Gallogly, *Cavan's Football Story* (Cavan, 1979), pp 36–7.
7   Noel O'Donoghue, *Proud and Upright Men*, (Indreabhán, 1986), pp 183–8.
8   Tom Hunt, 'The early years of Gaelic football and the role of cricket in County Westmeath' in Alan Bairner (ed), *Sport and the Irish: histories, identities, issues* (Dublin, 2005), p. 24.
9   John G. Maher, *Tubberadora; the Golden Square Mile* (Thurles, 1995), p. 4.
10   Liam Ó Donnchú, *Horse and Jockey: All-Ireland hurling champions* 1899 (Thurles, 1999), p. 6.
11   John Mullingan, S.M., *Dundalk Young Ireland's G.F.C.: an historical record of the green and the black* (Dundalk, 2004), p. 41.
12   Seán Seosamh Ó Conchubair, *Kilmoyley to the rescue* (Kilmoyley, 2000), pp 101–04.
13   See Hunt, 'The GAA: social structure and associated clubs' in Cronin *et al.*, *The Gaelic Athletic Association*, pp 193–7, for a more detailed analysis of this idea
14   Tom Hunt, 'Tipperary hurlers, 1895–1900, a socio–economic profile: part 1' in *Tipperary Historical Journal*, 2009 (forthcoming).
15   Liatroim GAC, *Leitrim Fontenoys 1888–1988: Céad Bliain ag Fás* (Liatroim, 1988), pp 49–56.
16   Felix McKillop, *Cumann Lúthcleas Gael St Joseph's, Glenarm 1913–1984* (Glenarm, 1984), p. 17.
17   Hunt, 'The GAA, social structure and associated clubs', pp 186, 197–8.
18   Mulligan, *Dundalk Young Ireland's,* pp 5–7.
19   *Ibid*, pp 11–13.
20   *Ibid*, pp 7–13.
21   Bernadette Lally, *Print culture in Loughrea, 1850–1900: reading, writing and printing in an Irish provincial town* (Dublin, 2008), pp 29–33.
22   Phil McGinn, *Armagh Harps GFC, 1884–2008: celebrating 120 years* (Armagh, 2008), p. 10.
23   *Ibid*, pp 18, 27; cited from Dónal McAnallen, 'Playing on the fourth green field: the GAA, politics and society in Ulster' (unpublished PhD thesis, Ollscoil na hÉireann, Gaillimh).
24   Joseph Brady, 'The heart of the city, commercial Dublin, *c*.1890–1915' in Joseph Brady and Anngret Simms (eds), *Dublin through space & time* (Dublin, 2001) pp 303–310.
25   William Nolan (ed.), *The Gaelic Athletic Association in Dublin* 1884–2000 (3 vols, Dublin, 2005), iii, p. 1234; *Sport*, 20 Aug. 1887.
26   Dermot Keogh, *The rise of the Irish working class: the Dublin Trade Union movement and labour leadership 1890–1914* (Belfast, 1982), p. 9.
27   Nolan, *GAA in Dublin,* vol. 3, pp 1254, 1276–7.
28   *Ibid*, pp 1220–21.
29   D. J. Vaughan, *Liffey Gaels: a century of Gaelic games*, (Dublin, 1984), p. 138
30   P. J. McEvoy, *They wore the green and white; a history of Stradbally G.A.A. club, 1889–1989* (Stradbally, 1989), p. 15.
31   *Celtic Times*, 17 Dec. 1887.
32   Nolan, *GAA in Dublin*, vol. 1, pp 13–14,
33   Paul Rouse, 'Michael Cusack: sportsman and journalist', in Cronin *et al*, *Gaelic Athletic Association* 1884–2009, p. 53.
34   Nolan (ed.), *GAA in Dublin*, vol. 1, p. 5.
35   *Sport*, 20 Aug. 1887.
36   *Celtic Times*, 23 Apr. 1887.
37   Nolan, *Gaelic Athletic Association*, vol. 3, p. 1226.
38   Jim Cronin, *Making connections: a Cork G.A.A. miscellany* (Cork, 2005), pp 323–325.
39   Neal Garnham, *The Origins and Development of Football in Ireland, being a reprint of R. M. Peter's Irish football annual of 1880* (Belfast, 1999), p. 172.
40   Tom Hunt, *Sport and Society in Victorian Ireland: the Case of Westmeath* (Cork, 2007), pp 201–07.
41   De Búrca, *The G.A.A.*, p. 25; Paul Rouse, 'The politics of culture and sport in Ireland: a history of the GAA ban on foreign games 1884–1971. Part 1: 1884–1921,' in *International Journal of the History of Sport*, x, no. 3 (Dec. 1993), pp 347–8.
42   Hunt, *Sport and Society*, pp 113–40.
43   Patrick Bracken, *'Foreign and Fantastic Field Sports': Cricket in County Tipperary* (Thurles, 2004).
44   Michael O'Dwyer, *The History of Cricket in County Kilkenny – the Forgotten Game* (Kilkenny, 2006).
45   Niamh Carroll and Des Waters, 'When Moore soared in the sky,' in *Journal of the Taghmon Historical Society*, 3, 1999, p. 24.
46   O'Donoghue, *Proud and upright men* (Galway, 1986), pp 23–6.
47   Hunt, *Sport and Society*, pp 200–01.
48   Alan Rodgers, *Down from the 'Cross: a GAA story* (Beragh, 2006), pp 36–7.
49   *The Celtics 1894–1994: a centenary history of the GAA in Cootehill* (Cavan, 1994), pp 25–6.
50   McGinn, *Armagh Harps*, p. 18.
51   Aogán Ó Fearghail and Rev. Daniel Gallogly, *One Hundred Years of Cavan GAA.* (Cavan, 1984), p. 10.
52   Sean Ó Suilleabháin, *Scéal Club Colmcille GAA* (Longford, 1984), p. 12.
53   John Casey, *Rathcline: pathways to the past* (Lanesboro, 1995), p. 202.

54 Phil Murphy (ed), *Centenary tribute to G.A.A. in Wexford, 1884–1984* (Wexford, 1984), p. 19.

55 Ó Fearghail & Gallogly, *One Hundred Years of Cavan GAA.* (Cavan, 1984), p. 10.

56 *Westmeath Nationalist*, 10 Feb. 1893.

57 *The Gael*, 7 Jan. 1888. See also Gillespie and Hegarty, 'Camán and Crozier: The Catholic Church and the GAA' in this book, p. 112.

58 Con Short, *The Crossmaglen GAA story* 1887–1987 (Crossmaglen, 1987), p. 37.

59 Neal Garnham, 'Accounting for the early success of the Gaelic Athletic Association,' in *Irish Historical Studies,* xxiv, no. 133 (May 2004), p. 73.

60 *Westmeath Nationalist*, 22 June 1893.

61 *Celtic Times,* 17 Dec. 1887.

62 *Sport*, 17 Dec. 1898.

63 Nolan, *GAA in Dublin*, vol. 1, p. 59.

64 *Ibid*, p. 41.

65 Vaughan, *Liffey Gaels*, pp 150–51.

66 Paul Quinn, *A club for all ages: 100 years of Gaelic games and culture in Donaghmore 1903–2003* (Donaghmore, 2004), p. 60.

67 *Ibid*, p. 67.

68 Hunt, *Sport and Society*, pp 235–6.

69 *Sport*, 27 Aug. 1887. Similarly, in Longford, Moydow Harpers played their first match against Clough on 26 October 1889 at Moydow. The bands of both parishes played the teams to and from the field (Leo Kenny, 'Longford G.A.A. 1884–1904/5: the beginning … and before' in Seán O Corcora (ed), *C.L.C.G. Chontae Longfoirt 1887–1987* (Longford, 1987), p. 16).

70 McGinn, *Armagh Harps*, p. 14.

71 *Roscommon Herald*, 25 Apr. 1903.

72 It is a far from exhaustive analysis of the origins of clubs. Clubs emerged from temperance clubs, civil servant groups, associations of men from the same county background, workers associated with newspapers, nationalist organisations etc.

73 For the six counties of Northern Ireland the equivalent records can be found under the reference VAL/12B in the Public Record Office of Northern Ireland, Belfast.

The Mass Media and the Popularisation of Gaelic Games

1 *Freeman's Journal*, 2 June 1867, reported an inter-county cricket match between Westmeath and Longford. These county cricket clubs served as a forgotten model for the GAA in the 1880s. County Kildare Cricket Club was founded in 1871 'for the promotion of cricket, football, archery, pigeon shooting, lawn tennis and, if possible, polo.' The club's second pavilion, built in 1906, still serves the Naas Lawn Tennis Club. The County Galway Cricket Club, based in Athenry, took part in representative matches and was open to 'any person who was born in county Galway or resident in it for twelve months and Army or navy officers stationed in the county.' Some of these county clubs survive today: County Carlow survives as the rugby club, and County Limerick as a tennis club.

2 John O'Donovan, *Life By the Liffey: A Kaleidoscope of Dubliners* (Dublin, 1986), p. 118.

3 An example was the letter in the aftermath of the 1803 rebellion, relating that a football match at Donnybrook was arranged between Kildare and Wicklow so that people 'could see and understand strength and numbers of the party.' Evan Nepean to John King, 27 Feb. 1804, The National Archives (UK)?, HO 100/124/76.

4 Some of these references were first sourced by an unnamed prisoner who was researching as part of his supervised work in the late 1960s, and used in Art O Maolfábháil, *Camán: 2000 Years of Hurling in Ireland* (Dublin, 1973). The recent digitalisation of *Finn's Leinster Journal* will be a cause of celebration among historians of early hurling. This is a by no means exhaustive list of eighteenth century newspaper references to hurling: *Dublin Flying Post*, 28 June 1708, 19 June 1708; *London Daily Advertiser*, 28 Sept. 1747; *Dublin Courant*, 21 May 1748, 31 May 1748, 4 June 1748, 20 May 1749; *Faulkner's Journal*, 7 June 1748; *Finn's Leinster Journal*, 19 March 1766; *Cork Evening Post*, 4 Sept. 1769; *Finn's Leinster Journal*, 16 July 1768, 30 July 1768, 3 Sept. 1768, 12 July 1769, 29 July 1769, 27 Oct. 1770, 19 July 1776, 29 Aug. 1780; *Dublin Evening Post*, 12 Aug. 1779; *Hibernian Journal*, 8 Oct. 1792; *Universal Advertiser*, 17 July 1753, 27 Sept. 1757; *Freeman's Journal*, 24 Jan. 1763, 23 Sept. 1766, 21 June 1774, 1 Oct. 1768, 4 Oct. 1768, 19 Aug. 1777, 20 July 1779, 18 Apr. 1793, 9 Sept. 1784, 3 Nov. 1792; *Hoey's Public Journal*, 14 Aug. 1771; *Hibernian Journal*, 8 Oct. 1792, 17 Oct. 1792. Newspaper references to football include the following: *Dublin Courant*, 23 July 1745; *Pue's Occurrences*, 23 Aug. 1746; *Universal Advertiser*, 19 March 1754; *Cork Evening Post*, 3 July 1754; *Slater's Public Gazetteer*, 21 Apr. 1759; *Dublin Gazette*, 28 Apr. 1765; *Faulkner's Dublin Journal*, 15 Apr. 1765 and 12 Feb. 1779; *Hibernian Journal*, 30 Apr. 1774; and *The Observer*, 26 Feb. 1792.

5 'A Carrickman's Diary 1787–1809', published in *Journal of the Waterford Archaeological Society*, xiv, p. 150.

6 *Freeman's Journal*, 19 Aug. 1777.

7 *Ibid*, 20 July 1779.

8 *Ibid*, 3 Nov. 1821.

9 *Ibid*, 1 Apr. 1831.

10 *Ibid*, 3 Mar. 1821, 1 Apr. 1831, 23 Apr. 1844. See also references of 3 Dec. 1803, 4 Aug. 1814 and 13 Apr. 1866.

11 *Dublin University Magazine*, 1761. See also *Dublin Evening Post*, 16 Oct. 1792: 'This is one of the native sports of this country and we would be glad that an English garrison or the family of an English minister should dare to enter into competition with us in this instance, where, and not in an English exercise – cricket – Irishman have a right to excel.'

12 Pádraig Puirséal, *The GAA in its Time* (Dublin, 1982), p. 34. James Hope (1764–1846), a weaver from Templepatrick, led 'the Spartan band' at the battle of Antrim in 1798 and assisted Robert Emmet in his rebellion of 1803. O'Ceallaigh claims, a little optimistically, that his proposal for a revival of athletics on the lines of Rousseau, was supported by Lord Edward Fitzgerald, William McNevin and John Sweetman, see Richard R. Madden, *The United Irishmen: Their Lives and Times*, vol. 1, (3rd ed., Dublin, 1846), pp 229–312. See Seamus O'Ceallaigh, *Story of the GAA* (Dublin, 1977), p. 13.

13 Richard D. Mandell, *Sport: A Cultural History* (New York, 1984), pp 128–9.

14 *Das Deutsches Volkstum* (1810), which translates as 'the German Nationality' unveiled Jahn's theories, and he founded the first centre for gymnastics in Berlin in 1811 to give the young men of Prussia pre-military training. Jahn led the *Lutzovsche Freikorps* in 1813. *Deutsche Turnkunst* appeared in 1816. Its suppression and his imprisonment in 1819 for what would later become revered as pioneering pro-democratic ideals effectively finished his philosophical career. He was granted the Iron Cross in 1840 and elected to the German parliament in 1848. Although the

movement was harmed by Jahn's imprisonment, sportsplatze remained open in at least Sachsen-Weimar, Oldenburg and Braunschweig. See Mandell, *Sport: A Cultural History*, p. 162.

15 *Freeman's Journal*, 15 June 1852. Thomas Francis Meagher attended hurling matches in and around his native Waterford through the years immediately preceding the Young Ireland rising. He constantly exhorted his many followers to 'hold on to the hurling' and rephrased lines from Byron to suit his purpose 'You have the Irish dances yet, Where is the Irish hurling gone?' After an enthusiastic election meeting in February 1848 in Ballybricken, Meagher and Michael Doheny led the hurlers to the playing field, where a huge crowd watched the subsequent game featuring hurlers from Fahastrogeen, a traditional centre of the game, roughly corresponding to the present-day Barrack Street. At the end of the match, Meagher exhorted the young men of the city to go back to the old Irish games that made men, and kept them in Ireland. When departing he expressed the hope that, when he came again, he would see 'hurlers galore from up the roads and around the hill of Ballybricken.' Hurling was revived in the middle 1860s by such Fenian men as Denis B. Cashman.

16 See article on Meagher in *United Ireland*, 10 Jan. 1888, p. 5; anon., 'Meagher of the Sword rousing Waterford GAA' in the *Irish Press Golden Jubilee Supplement* (Dublin, 1934), p. 68; and Séamus Upton / 'Vigilant', 'A Hurried Look Back' in Sean O'Ceallaigh (ed.), *Gaelic Athletic Memories* (Limerick, 1945). In the 1920s–1960s period advocacy of an Irish separatist athletic tradition was traced to the Whiteboys in the south ('who had been organising hurling matches as a cloak for their meetings – and as recruiting centres for their night-riders') and to James Hope (see note 12 above), and it was claimed that Lord Edward Fitzgerald, William McNevin, and John Sweetman were also interested in native games.

17 Grant Jarvie and Graham Walker (eds), *Scottish Sport in the Making of a Nation* (Leicester, 1994).

18 *Freeman's Journal*, 2 Sept. 1867.

19 *Irish Times*, 19 July 1873; *Freeman's Journal*, 4 June 1876.

20 *Freeman's Journal*, 1 Jan. 1883.

21 *Irish Times*, 12 Sept. 1903.

22 In the 'Our Boys' column he started in *The Shamrock* in 1882 Cusack declared that cricket was an Irish game suitable for young Irish men to play, advising readers how to play, how to form a club, how to keep the bat, and urging people to buy Irish stumps, bats and balls.

23 Especially, 'A Word About Irish Athletics' published simultaneously in *United Ireland* and *The Irishman*, 11 Oct. 1884.

24 The inaugural meeting of the Irish Hurley Union applied to Blackheath, Surbiton and Rossall Hurley clubs in England (where a short lived Hockey union was formed in 1876) for copies of their rules for their consideration. Revised rules were published in 1879 and 1882. Trinity Hurley club lapsed in 1884. By 1892 the organisation of hurley had fallen apart and some ex-hurley players formed a club under hockey rules in High School.

25 *Irish Sportsman*, 26 Jan. 1884.

26 *Irish Sportsman*, 9 Apr. 1881, 2 July 1881, 1 Nov. 1881 and 11 Nov. 1882.

27 See Liam P. Ó Caithnia, *Micheál Cíosóg* (Baile Átha Cliath, 1982); Marcus de Búrca, *Michael Cusack and The GAA* (Dublin, 1989).

28 *Daily Telegraph*, 6 Nov. 1884. The paper commented, 'we may be sure that an agrarian offence is no disqualification for a competitor'.

29 These even include the Dublin Amateur Athletics Club of 1867; Henry Dunlop's Irish Champion Athletics Club of 1872, which organised championships; Val Dunbar's Irish National Athletics Committee of 1877, which was to have led to the Irish AAA in 1878 but disappeared without trace; Cusack's 'National Athletics Meeting' of 1880; Henry Dunlop's Amateur Athletics Association of Ireland of 1881; and the Dublin Athletics Club of 1882. The Irish Cross Country Association of 1881 (which involved Cusack) and the Irish Cyclists Association of 1882 had both survived, but with a narrow Dublin base.

30 Hoctor is one of the least understood of the writers who helped build the GAA, reflected in recent scholarship as a malevolent figure through his appearances in the RIC files. No copy of *The Gael* survives, although extracts are included in the RIC files. A cutting from *The Gael*, 3 Sept. 1887, Crime Branch Special 126/S, shows the extent of feeling on the IRB side when it proclaimed the Freeman's Journal AC meeting and threatening suspension from the GAA of competitors and spectators who chose to show 'their preference for a half-day's pleasure to the exclusion of that spirit of true national independence.' An editorial called for action on behalf of 'two hundred thousand true-hearted Irishmen' against a weak-minded, dissentient clique, acting under the control of the worst form of the West British element. On the one side is independence; on the other, treachery. *The Gael*, which published early work by several leading literary figures such as Joyce and Yeats, may have greater significance than the few surviving clippings suggest.

31 Marcus de Búrca was responsible for rescuing the files of *Sport* from the *Irish Independent* library where they were in danger of destruction and their lodging in the National Library. The only surviving record of the *Celtic Times*, a bound volume, was passed to the special collection of Clare County Library in Ennis by Brendan Mac Lua. This file appeared to have been in the possession of de Burca's grandfather and was certainly available to Canon Philip Fogarty in the compilation of his *Tipperary's GAA Story* (Tipperary, 1960). Thanks to CLASP, the local press in Clare, the complete volume of *Celtic Times* is now available to a general readership.

32 *Irish Times*, 12 September 1903.

33 *United Ireland*, 8 Nov. 1884; *The Irishman*, 8 Nov. 1884, *The Shamrock*, 15 Nov. 1884.

34 *Cork Examiner*, 3 Nov. 1884.

35 *Leinster Leader*, 15 Nov. 1888.

36 *Freeman's Journal*, 3 Nov. 1884; *Daily News*, 3 Nov. 1884; *Irish Sportsman*, 8 Nov. 1884.

37 P. Puirséal, *GAA in its Time*, p. 43.

38 *Irish Independent*, 10 Dec. 1923; *Irish Times*, 10 Dec.1923.

39 *Irish Times*, 12 Feb. 1887, 14 Aug. 1890.

40 Among McCarthy's imitators at local level perhaps the most eloquent was R.C. Langran in the pro-colonial *Carlow Sentinel*, which covered cricket and rugby, leaving Gaelic games to the opposition *Nationalist and Leinster Times*.

41 *Irish Sportsman*, 31 Jan. 1885, *Freeman's Journal*, 5 June 1885, *Irish Times*, 5 June 1885.

42 *United Ireland*, 19 Dec. 1885.

43 *The Nation*, 12 Oct. 1889.

44 Cusack's wife died at the age of 35 in 1890, his two daughters went to live with relatives in England, and his sons ended up in Dublin orphanages. He moved address

several times and was financially hard-up after his educational column in *The Shamrock* was ended in 1902. His two attempts to become involved in the GAA once more were short–lived. In 1893 he became secretary of the Dublin Board of the GAA, forcing a split in the body when the result of a ballot was disputed. In 1901 he was also proposed once more for secretary of the GAA at national level but defeated. After his death the *Gaelic Journal* said that he was 'the living embodiment of the GAA'.

45 The *Irish Times*, perceived as a colonial newspaper, which had dismissed the 1920 All-Ireland football final (attendance 25,000) in a report of 230 words, used the heavily stylised reports of *Cork Examiner* GAA correspondent P. D. Mehigan on major matches after 1925. See report by 'Pato' on All-Ireland hurling final, 'Dublin Overwhelmed' in *Irish Times*, 8 Oct. 1925. The report of the football final in *Irish Times*, 12 June 1922, is dwarfed by the report and photographic coverage of yachting at Kingstown. The recent *Irish Times* editor Conor Brady is among those who believe that the perception of the *Irish Times* as a unionist organ in independent Ireland is unjustified.

46 *Freeman's Journal*, 8 Apr. 1912.

47 Tony Farmar, *Ordinary Lives: Three Generations of Irish Middle Class Experience* (Dublin, 1991), p. 45.

48 Gillian McIntosh, *The Force of Culture: Unionist Identities in Twentieth–Century Ireland* (Cork, 1999), pp 82–83; Rex Cathcart, *The Most Contrary Region: The BBC in Northern Ireland 1924–1984* (Belfast, 1984), p. 67.

49 *Sport*, 30 June 1905; *Irish Independent*, 18 June 1923, 8 Oct. 1923, 12 Sept. 1931; *Irish Times*, 6 Sept. 1937, 27 Sept. 1927, and 18 Oct. 1937.

50 Breandán Ó hEithir, *Over the Bar: A Personal Relationship with the GAA* (Dublin, 1984), pp 176–7, describes the confusion of listeners who heard the boos from the crowd when Kerry's Bill Casey and Antrim's Harry O'Neill were both sent off, but were not told what was happening by commentator Micheál O Hehir. At the 'Wireless to Wireless' event in the GAA museum in January 2009 Seán Óg Ó Ceallacháin gave a colourful account of the pressures brought to bear by Pádraig Ó Caoimh on radio journalists not to mention players who had been sent off.

51 *Southern Star*, 22 Aug. 1926; *Irish Independent*, 25 Aug. 1926, 2 Sept. 1929, 6 Sept. 1937. J. J. Walsh told a broadcasting convention in Dublin in late 1926 that the GAA broadcast had been picked up as far away as the Netherlands (*Irish Independent*, 2 Nov. 1926).

52 *Irish Independent*, 18 Mar. 1937, 6 Sept. 1937, 27 Sept. 1937, 15 Aug. 1938, 18 Mar. 1954; Interview by author with Micheál O Hehir, 18 Sept. 1983.

Camán and Crozier: The GAA and the Catholic Church 1884–1902

1 Austin Reid, *Irish History 1851–1950* (Dublin, 1980), pp 97–8.

2 Mark Tierney, *Ireland Since 1870* (Dublin, 1988), p. 112.

3 Marcus de Búrca, *The G AA: A History* (Dublin, 1980), p. 34.

4 For a discussion of this claim, see Marcus De Búrca, 'Was Cusack a Fenian?' in *Our Games: Official Annual of the GAA*, 1967, p. 80.

5 Marianne Elliott, *The Catholics of Ulster: A History* (London, 2000), p. 369.

6 Emmet Larkin, *The Roman Catholic Church and the Plan of Campaign 1886–1888* (Cork, 1978), p. xiii.

7 T. P. Gilmartin, *Bishop of the Land War: Dr Patrick Duggan, Bishop of Clonfert, 1813–1896* (Dublin, 1987), p. 3.

8 *Freeman's Journal*, 2 Nov. 1885; as cited in Pádraig Puirséal, *The GAA in its Time* (Dublin, 1982), p. 36.

9 *United Irishman*, 27 Dec. 1884.

10 T. F. O'Sullivan, *The Story of the GAA* (Dublin, 1916), p. 87.

11 Elizabeth Mahon, *Ireland Sober, Ireland Free: drink and temperance in 19th century Ireland* (Dublin, 1986), pp 327–31.

12 De Búrca, *The GAA: A History*, p. 31.

13 O'Sullivan, *Story of the GAA*, p. 27.

14 *Freeman's Journal*, 19 Mar. 1886. See also Puirséal, *GAA in its Time*, p. 64.

15 Puirséal, *GAA in its Time*, p. 66.

16 De Búrca, *The GAA: A History*, p. 23.

17 *Freeman's Journal*, 26 Aug. 1887.

18 *Ibid*, 11 Nov. 1887.

19 *Ibid*, 12 Nov. 1887.

20 W. F. Mandle, *The Gaelic Athletic Association and Irish Nationalist Politics 1884–1924* (Dublin, 1987), p. 59.

21 Croke to Walsh, 11 Nov. 1887, Walsh Papers, Dublin Diocesan Archives (DDA).

22 Croke papers, Diary, January 1888; as cited in Mark Tierney, *Croke of Cashel: The Life of Archbishop Thomas William Croke, 1823–1902* (Dublin, 1976), p. 204.

23 Pastoral Letter, February 1888, Logue Papers, Cardinal Ó Fiaich Library and Archive Armagh (CÓFLA).

24 Rev. James Mc Gee, Dunleer Parish schedule, 1889, CÓFLA. (Editors' note: some of these parish reports were also included in the original draft of Tom Hunt's chapter for this volume, but are retained only within the present chapter in order to avoid repetition.)

25 Rev. Patrick McGeeney, Upper Creggan Parish schedule, 1889, CÓFLA.

26 See Síghle Nic An Ultaigh, *Ó Shíol go Bláth: An Dún – The GAA Story* [Newry, 1990], p. 35.

27 *Anglo–Celt*, 10 Nov. 1889.

28 *Freeman's Journal*, 31 July 1889.

29 Croke to Walsh, 22 Nov. 1890, DDA.

30 *Freeman's Journal*, 9 Jan. 1891. See also Mandle, *Gaelic Athletic Association and Irish Nationalist Politics*, p. 81.

31 Marcus De Búrca, *John O'Leary* (Tralee, 1967), p. 200; cited in de Búrca, *The GAA: A History*, p. 45.

32 National Archives of Ireland, CBS, Western Division, Secret Society Reports, May 1891; as cited in Mandle, *Gaelic Athletic Association and Irish Nationalist Politics*, p. 83.

33 Croke to Kirby, 21 Jan. 1891, ICA, Rome. See Tierney, *Croke of Cashel*, pp 241–2.

34 NAI, Crime Branch Special Western Division, Secret Society Reports, Feb. 1891. CBS file 2831/S. See Mandle, *Gaelic Athletic Association and Irish Nationalist Politics*, p. 78.

35 MacEvilly to Gilhooly, 14 Mar. 1891, Elphin Diocesan Archives. See Larkin, *Roman Catholic Church*, p. 264.

36 *Freeman's Journal*, 12 Oct. 1891.

37 *Ibid*.

38 De Búrca, *The GAA: A History*, p. 47.

39 Secretary's report to the Annual Convention of the GAA, Jan. 1892; as cited in Mandle, *Gaelic Athletic Association and Irish Nationalist Politics*, p. 93.

40 De Búrca, *The GAA: A History*, p. 47 and O'Sullivan, *Story of the GAA*, p. 102.

41 Mandle, *Gaelic Athletic Association and Irish Nationalist Politics*, pp 101–103.

42 Aisling Walsh, 'Cardinal Michael Logue' Part I in *Seanchas Ard Mhacha*, xvii, no. 1 (1996–97), p. 130.

43   O'Sullivan, *Story of the GAA*, p. 118.
44   De Búrca, *The GAA: A History*, p. 58.
45   O'Sullivan, *Story of the GAA*, p. 155; Mandle, *Gaelic Athletic Association and Irish Nationalist Politics*, p. 132.
46   De Búrca, *The GAA:A History*, p. 64.
47   O'Sullivan, *Story of the GAA*, p. 159.

The Freedom of the Field: Camogie before 1950

1   Richard Holt, *Sport and the British: A Modern History* (Oxford, 1989), pp 74–98 *passim*.
2   *Celtic Times*, 12 Mar. 1887.
3   See Paul Rouse, 'Michael Cusack: sportsman and journalist', in Mike Cronin, William Murphy and Paul Rouse (eds.), *The Gaelic Athletic Association, 1884–2009* (Dublin, 2009).
4   Paul Rouse, '*Sport* and Ireland in 1881' in Alan Bairner (ed.), *Sport and the Irish: Histories, Identities, Issues* (Dublin, 2005), pp 18–19; Tom Hunt, *Sport and Society in Victorian Ireland: The Case of Westmeath* (Cork, 2007), pp 220–221.
5   For example, in 1887, the Chairman of the British Medical Association said: 'In the interests of social progress, national efficiency and the progressive improvement of the human race, women should be denied education and other activities which would cause constitutional overstrain and inability to produce healthy offspring.' (See Jennifer Hargreaves, *Sporting Females: critical Issues in the History and Sociology of Women's Sports* (1997), p. 45.)
6   Holt, *Sport and the British*, p. 117.
7   Hunt, *Sport and Society in Victorian Ireland*, pp 106–11, 112, 250–51.
8   Margaret Ó hÓgartaigh, 'Shedding their 'reserve': camogie and the origins of women's sport in Ireland', in *High Ball* (July, 2003); Tomás Ó Domhnalláin, 'Donlon Family History, 1988', in *Ríocht na Midhe*, vol. xiv, 2003, pp 136–43.
9   The name was devised by Gaelic scholar, Tadhg Ó Donnchadha of Cork. See T. F. O'Sullivan, *Story of the GAA* (Dublin, 1916), p. 167.
10 *Freeman's Journal*, 19 July 1904.
11 O'Sullivan, *Story of the GAA*, p. 167; *Frontier Sentinel*, 22 Oct. 1904, 19 Nov. 1904.
12 *Glasgow Star*, 8 Oct. 1904.
13 Mary Moran, *Cork's Camogie Story 1904–2000* (Cork, 2001), pp 6–7.
14 O'Sullivan, *Story of the GAA*, p. 171.
15 *Irish News*, 19 Aug. 1905.
16 *Derry People*, 7 July 1906. The first affiliated club in Belfast was Banba, formed in 1908 (*Irish News*, 1 Sept. 1908).
17 *Derry People*, 17 June 1905.
18 *Derry People*, 10 March 1906. The first known named and recorded camogie teams in Omagh was Banba in 1908 (*Irish News*, 25 Aug. 1908; Seán Healy, *Fifty Years Onward 1932–1982: A History of Omagh St Enda's Gaelic Athletic Club* (Omagh, 1982), pp 12–13), but it was preceded in Co. Tyrone by Rose Kavanagh's of Fintona in 1907 (Fintona Pearse's GAC, *Ceiliúradh Céad Bliain: A Century of Gaelic Games in Donacavey Parish* (Fintona, 2007), pp 30–31. The game was also taken up in Cloch Cheann Fhaola college (Co. Donegal) in 1907 (*Frontier Sentinel*, 3 Aug. 1907).
19 *Dundalk Democrat*, 26 May 1906.
20 Pádraic Ó Laoi, *Annals of the GAA in Galway, volume II: 1902–1934* (n.p., 1992), p. 36.
21 Louis Murphy, *St Killian's GAC, Whitecross: A History* (Whitecross, Co. Armagh, 1996), pp 15, 35.
22 Anon., *Scéal na Camógaíochta* (*c*. 1984), p. 9. The names of the authors are not specifically listed as such on the

publication, but the introductory article (p. 1) stated that it was 'the work of both Una and her husband Pádraig [Puirséal]', both of whom were deceased when it was published.
23 Joe Lavery, *Cumann Lúthchleas Gael agus Cumann Camoguidheacht Ard-Eoin Club History 1908–1985* (n.p., 1985), p. 82.
24 Seán O'Duffy letter to unnamed newspaper, 5 Nov. 1910 (Seán O'Duffy Collection, Cumann Camógaíochta na nGael).
25 Moran, *Cork's Camogie Story*, p. 6.
26 *Irish News*, 11 June 1910. There were competitions in Belfast each summer from 1910 to the outbreak of World War One.
27 Letter to unnamed newspaper, Apr. 1911. See Seán O'Duffy Collection, Cumann Camógaíochta na nGael.
28 Máire de Buitléir's article, 'Camoguidheacht Association', published on 21 Apr. 1911 in a newspaper (probably the *Evening Telegraph*). The report survives in a scrapbook in the Seán O'Duffy collection, Cumann Camógaíochta na nGael. The full title of the association in English was the 'Irishwomen's National Athletic and Camóguidheacht Association'.
29 This is a 1911 clipping from a newspaper (probably the *Evening Telegraph*), which survives in a scrapbook in the Seán O'Duffy collection, held by Cumann Camógaíochta na nGael.
30 The report survives in a scrapbook in the Seán O'Duffy collection, Cumann Camógaíochta na nGael. The wearing of inadequate footwear was still a problem over a decade later (*FJ*, 11 Dec. 1923).
31 Úna Bean Uí Phuirséal, 'Our Paths Lie Side by Side' in *Our Games Annual*, 1966, p. 77.
32 For example, in Co. Roscommon, where a handful of teams were formed in 1913, but they soon disappeared; apart from one team set up in 1918/19, the game did not return to the county until the 1930s (Anon., *Ceiliúradh an Chéid: A History of Camogie in Roscommon* (Roscommon, 2004), pp 3–4).
33 Madeleine Uí Mhéalóid, 'Agnes O'Farrelly: Crusader for a Gaelic Ireland' in *Breifne: Journal of Cumann Seanchais Bhréifne*, viiii (1998), pp 841–876.
34 Patrick N. Meenan, *St Patrick's Blue and Saffron: A Miscellany of UCD Sport since 1895* (Dublin, 1997), p. 114.
35 Not everyone accepted this at first, however; some of the winning UCG team of 1917 objected to having their names inscribed in Irish, and were duly accused of 'the most glaring piece of Shoneenism … ever witnessed in the College'. See *University College Galway Annual*, 1916–17, pp 48, 59.
36 Moran, *Cork's Camogie Story*, pp 7–8.
37 See, for example, *UCG Annual*, 1915–16, pp 62, 84–7; *National Student*, May 1920, p. 39; *The Quarryman*, Spring 1931, p. 54; *UCG Annual*, 1933–34.
38 One Queen's team, travelling from Belfast to Cork by train, reached Limerick Junction in a famished condition, but, on finding only ham sandwiches available, abstained, because it was a Friday (Interview with Frances Cormican (née Owens), Queen's University camogie player, *c*. 1948–53, conducted by Dónal McAnallen in August 2000).
39 This is a 1911 clipping from a newspaper (probably the *Evening Telegraph*), contained in a scrapbook of the Seán O'Duffy collection, Cumann Camógaíochta na nGael.
40 Jim Connolly, 'The Man in a Female World!' in *Our Games Annual*, 1978, pp 20–21.

41 Helena Duignan, *Keeping the Game Alive: One Hundred Years of Camogie in Britain* (Birmingham, 2004), pp 12–13, relates the story of Rose Anne Murphy, who left Liverpool to take part in the 1916 Easter Rising; a family member said he was 'unsure of whether her playing camogie led her into republicanism, or the other way around'.

42 Pat Rafferty, 'A History of Camogie in Dublin' in William Nolan (ed.), *The Gaelic Athletic Association in Dublin 1884–2000* (3 vols, Dublin), iii, p. 1284. See also Mary Moran, *Munster's Camogie Story 1904–2004* (Cork, 2004), pp 5–6, for the goodwill of the Cork GAA Board to the establishment of camogie.

43 *An Camán*, Deireadh Foghmhair 1931.

44 *Pathé Gazette*, 24 Apr. 1922, accessed on www.britishpathe.com on 22 Sept. 2007.

45 Duignan, *Keeping the Game Alive*, p. 29.

46 For example, in the hurling heartland of Co. Tipperary the game was not being played at all (Martin Bourke and Seamus J. King, *A History of Camogie in County Tipperary* (Tipperary, 2003), p. 15). Similarly, apart from brief manifestations of camogie locally in 1909 and 1913, and again at *feiseanna* in the mid 1920s, hurling-rich Kilkenny made hardly any inroads into the sport before the 1930s (Tom Ryall, *Kilkenny: The GAA Story 1884–1984* (Kilkenny, 1984), p. 245).

47 *Freeman's Journal*, 4 Dec. 1923.

48 *Irish Times*, 4 May 1928.

49 Mary Moran, *Camogie Champions: A Complete Handbook of Camogie* (Cork, 1997), p. 2.

50 *UCG Annual*, 1931–32, p. 73.

51 Dooey family, *The Dooey Twins Recall them Days in Oul' Dunloy 1926–2006* (Dunloy, 2007), pp 25–6.

52 *UCG Annual*, 1923/24, p. 63.

53 For instance, a camogie game played in Armagh City in 1925 reportedly attracted a crowd of over one thousand people, but there was no follow-up organised activity. See P. J. Toner, *The Armagh Camogie Story: Fifty Years of earnest endeavour in the cause of our Gaelic Games* (Armagh, 1978), p. 5.

54 Moran, *Camogie Champions*, p. 170.

55 Anon., *Scéal na Camógaíochta* (c. 1984), p. 12.

56 For the support of nuns in Galway for camogie, see *UCG Annual*, 1924–25, p. 107; and Dónal McAnallen, 'Camógaíocht in UCG' in Tomás Ó Móráin (ed.), *Stair CLG Chonnacht: History of Connacht GAA 1902–2002* (n.p., 2002), p. 253.

57 *An Camán*, Mí na Nodlag 1931.

58 Dónal Mac An Ailín, 'Cluichí Gaelacha sa Roinn Ardoideachais' in Tom Cullen (ed.), *Beart de réir ár mBriathar: A History of the GAA in Ulster* (n.p., 2004), pp 60–61.

59 *Irish News*, 14 Jan. 1930.

60 Anon., 'Camogie: Our Girls' National Game' in *Gaelic Digest*, Oct. 1946, p. 27.

61 Sinéad Nic Aodh, 'Camoguidheacht: How, When and by Whom the Game was instituted: Antrim's Link–up, and the First Clubs' Debut Locally' in *Iris-Leabhar Bliantamhail Chonndae Aondroma* [Co. Antrim GAA Annual], 1948, p. 21.

62 *An Camán*, Samhain 1931.

63 'Agenda for Congress of Affiliated Camoguidheacht Teams', 24 Apr. 1932. Seán O'Duffy Collection, Cumann Camógaíochta na nGael.

64 Seán O'Duffy letter to unnamed newspaper (probably *An Claidheamh Soluis*), 5 Nov. 1910 (Seán O'Duffy Collection, Cumann Camógaíochta na nGael).

65 Moran, *Camogie Champions*, p. 2.

66 *Irish Press*, 18 May 1932.

67 Seán O'Duffy Collection, Cumann Camógaíochta na nGael (unnamed newspaper cutting, 29 June 1932).

68 Seán O'Duffy Collection, Cumann Camógaíochta na nGael (unnamed newspaper cutting, 29 June 1932).

69 See, for example, *Derry People*, 28 July 1934, 6 Oct. 1934.

70 Rev. John Murphy of Tyrone was elected as chairman of the Ulster Council in 1941, and Rev. Tom Maguire (Fermanagh) as its honorary president (*Irish News*, 18 Feb. 1941); and Cardinal Joseph MacRory, the Catholic primate of all Ireland, consented to become a patron of the Camoguidheacht Association in 1940 (*Irish News*, 26 Feb. 1940)

71 *Tipperary Star*, 27 Jan. 1934; cited in Bourke and King, *History of Camogie in County Tipperary*, p. 44.

72 *An Camán*, Lughnasa 1931; Tomás Ó Fiaich, 'Cuimhní Cinn an Ardeaspaig' in Toner, *Armagh Camogie Story*, p. 3; Rev. John Mulligan, *The GAA in Louth: An Historical Record* (Dundalk, 1984), p. 191. Fr Soraghan was actually nominated for the national presidency of An Cumann Camógaíochta in 1933 (*IP*, 1 May 1933).

73 Toner, *Armagh Camogie Story*, pp 36–7.

74 Moran, *Cork's Camogie Story*, pp 35, 38.

75 Mac An Ailín, 'Cluichí Gaelacha sa Roinn Ardoideachais' in Cullen (ed.), *Beart de réir ár mBriathar*, pp 62–3.

76 Rafferty, 'A History of Camogie in Dublin' in Nolan (ed.), *Gaelic Athletic Association in Dublin*, iii, p. 1291.

77 Moran, *Munster's Camogie Story*, p. 11. The clothing company provided a sports-ground, on which the female and male employees played mixed camogie-hurling at lunchtime, and the club drummed up publicity for challenge games against Kerry teams – one of which reportedly attracted some seven thousand spectators.

78 *Irish Press*, 28 Feb. 1935.

79 *Irish News*, 1 June 1934; *Frontier Sentinel*, 2 June 1934; *An Camán*, 2 June 1934.

80 The figures as of Easter 1934 were as follows: Antrim, 24; Derry, 10; Fermanagh, 10; Donegal, 12; Tyrone, 10; Armagh, 9; Cavan, 18 ('Éire Óg', 'Irishwomen's National Game' in *The Irish Independent GAA Golden Jubilee Number*, 12 Apr. 1934, p. 54); and Monaghan, 11 (Gearóidín Ní Chléirigh, 'Camogie: Great Women, Great Men, Great Sport' in John P. Graham (ed.), *The GAA in Monaghan 1887–1999: Some Account of its Progress* (Monaghan, 2000), p. 441). An exact figure for Co. Down has not been obtained, but there were several active clubs then.

81 *Cork Examiner*, 28 Feb. 1933

82 Seán O'Duffy Collection, Cumann Camógaíochta na nGael (unnamed and undated newspaper cutting) (1933).

83 *Irish Times*, 1 May 1933.

84 *Sunday Independent,* 25 Feb 1934.

85 *Irish News*, 2 Mar. 1934.

86 *Irish Press*, 25 Feb. 1935. The latter decision was reported as unanimous, but male delegates did not have a say in it; they were admitted to the meeting, without voting rights. The 1933 congress had already passed a resolution 'that all county boards should be controlled by girls, also refereeing, umpiring and lines, as far as possible' (*Irish Press*, 1 May 1933).

87 Moran, *Cork's Camogie Story*, p. 13. Seán O'Duffy stated that some men were 'a menace to the organisation, for they assumed that girls knew nothing, and that men, therefore, should always lead' (*Irish Times*, 1 May 1933).

88 *Irish News*, 2 Mar. 1936.

89 *Derry People*, 25 Aug. 1934.

90 *Dungannon Observer*, 21 Mar. 1936.

91 Unpublished autobiography of Seán McKeown, Antrim GAA chairman (1939) and Antrim Camogie Board chairman (1940–46), Linen Hall Library, p. 96.

92 Moran, *Munster's Camogie Story 1904–2004*, pp 12–15.

93 See Joseph Martin, *The GAA in Tyrone 1884–1984* (Omagh, 1984), pp 216–221, for an example of how camogie's sudden flourish was petering out by the end of the 1930s.

94 Moran, *Cork's Camogie Story*, p. 34.

95 *Irish Press*, 31 Aug. 1934.

96 Programme for the official opening of Davitt Park, Lurgan, 1 June 1947, p. 7, refers to 'the disastrous attacks of Cupid on the various teams' in camogie in Co. Armagh in the late 1930s. See also *Irish News*, 4 Aug. 1935.

97 Moran, *Cork's Camogie Story*, p. 13; Bourke and King, *History of Camogie in County Tipperary*, p. 98.

98 *Irish News*, 18 Apr. 1939.

99 *IN*, 24 July 1939; *ibid*, 2 Sept. 1939; *ibid*, 5 Sept. 1939; *ibid*, 26 Feb. 1940.

100 Seán O'Duffy Collection, Cumann Camógaíochta na nGael (1939).

101 Seán O'Duffy Collection, Cumann Camógaíochta na nGael (1 Nov. 1941).

102 Anon., *Scéal na Camógaíochta*, pp 14–15.

103 Moran, *Cork's Camogie Story*, pp 42–50; *idem*, *Munster's Camogie Story*, pp 21–27.

104 Anon., *Scéal na Camógaíochta*, p. 15. Even Antrim, in the most successful phase of its history, witnessed sharp divisions over the close relations of its county camogie board with the GAA (see *Irish News*, 13 Jan. 1947).

105 Riobaird A. Bramham, 'Camogie Enthusiasm' in *Gaelic Digest*, Aug. 1948, p. 13.

106 Moran, *Munster's Camogie Story*, p. 23.

107 Nic Aodh, 'Camoguidheacht: How, When and by Whom', p. 17.

108 *Gaelic Digest*, Oct. 1946, p. 27. Antrim had earlier lost to Derry in the 1946 Ulster semi–final, only to be restored by a boardroom decision: the Ulster Camogie Council nullified the result, because it was played on a full–size GAA pitch, and Derry duly withdrew (*Irish News*, 13 Aug. 1946; *ibid*, 3 Aug. 1946).

109 *Irish News*, 10 Nov. 1947.

110 *Tipperary Star*, 11 Oct. 1947; cited in Bourke and King, *History of Camogie in County Tipperary*, p. 84. The journalist even surmised that Ulster 'corncrakes' (that is, hand-rattles) would have intimated the Tipperary players – even though (s)he was apparently not at the game.

111 Moran, *Camogie Champions*, p. 5.

112 Anon., *Scéal na Camógaíochta*, p. 15.

Cén fáth a raibh cúige Uladh chomh lag chomh fada sin?: Deacrachtaí CLG ó thuaidh, 1884–1945

1 Ba mhaith liom buíochas a ghabháil le Gabhán Ó Dochartaigh as ucht dréachtaí an ailt seo a léamh, agus le Gearóid Ó Coirc as a chuidiú fosta.

2 *United Ireland*, 17 Eanáir 1885, 21 Márta 1885, 4 Iúil 1885.

3 Con Short, *The Ulster GAA Story 1884–1984* (Monaghan, 1984), lgh 31–2; Marcus Bourke, 'The Early GAA in South Ulster' sa *Clogher Record*, vii, uimh. 1 (1969), lgh 23–6.

4 Neal Garnham, 'Accounting for the early success of the Gaelic Athletic Association' in *Irish Historical Studies*, xxxiv, uimh. 133 (Bealtaine 2004), lgh 72–4, 78.

5 Daniel Gallogly, *Cavan's Football Story* (Cavan, 1979), lgh 21, 22.

6 *Belfast News-Letter*, 12 Samhain 1898.

7 Bourke, 'Early GAA', lgh 10–11.

8 Con Short, Peter Murray & Jimmy Smyth, *Ard Mhacha 1884–1984: A Century of GAA Progress* (Armagh, 1985), lch 31.

9 Short, *Ulster GAA Story*, lch 31; Gabriel M. Brock, *The Gaelic Athletic Association in County Fermanagh* [Enniskillen, 1984], lch 17; Séamus McCluskey, *The GAA in Co. Monaghan … a history* (Monaghan, 1984), lch 9.

10 Féach ar, mar shampla, *Fermanagh Herald*, 5 Samhain 1904.

11 Amharc ar, mar shampla, *Fermanagh Times*, 8 Samhain 1888; *Armagh Guardian*, 22 Márta 1889.

12 *Frontier Sentinel*, 24 Márta 1906; *Irish News*, 23 Márta 1906.

13 Miontuairiscí, Vice-Regal Commission on Irish Railways (British Parliamentary Papers 1908, lch 157 (13 Márta 1908); *Anglo-Celt*, 21 Márta 1908; Garnham, 'Accounting', *IHS*, xxviii, lgh 71–2.

14 *Newry Telegraph*, 30 Aibreán 1889; Short, *Ulster GAA Story*, lch 260.

15 Amharc ar, mar shampla, *Anglo-Celt*, 17 Samhain 1888, 1 Nollaig 1888, 15 Nollaig 1888, 31 Nollaig 1891.

16 Pádraig Puirséal, *The GAA in its Time* (Dublin, 1982), lch 116.

17 Short, *Ulster GAA Story*, lch 44; *United Irishman*, 28 Eanáir 1905; *IN*, 11 Nollaig 1906; *AC*, 8 Nollaig 1906, 20 Lúnasa 1910.

18 Amharc ar, mar shampla, *Sport*, 16 Samhain 1889, 29 Samhain 1890, 27 Nollaig 1890, 3 Eanáir 1891, 31 Eanáir 1891, 7 Feabhra 1891, 21 Samhain 1891 and 5 Nollaig 1891. Ina theannta sin léigh M. de Búrca, *The GAA*, lgh 52, 53, 56.

19 Short, *Ulster GAA Story*, lch 34; *Sport*, 24 Eanáir 1891, 18 Iúil 1891.

20 *Derry Journal*, 16 Aibreán 1890. Féach fosta ar *Ibid*, 28 Márta 1890, 4 Aibreán 1890, 21 Aibreán 1890, 25 Aibreán 1890, 30 Bealtaine 1890.

21 Féach ar, mar shampla, *Belfast Morning News*, 12 Samhain 1889, 14 Samhain 1889.

22 Short, *Ulster GAA Story*, lch 21; *idem*, Murray & Smyth, *Ard Mhacha 1884–1984*, lch 27.

23 *FJ*, 17 Aibreán 1893, 23 Aibreán 1894, 8 Meitheamh 1895, 11 Bealtaine 1896; Cumann Lúthchleas Gael, *Official Guide*, 1896–97 (Dublin, 1896), lch 38; R. T. Blake, *How the G.A.A. was Grabbed* (gan fhoilsitheoir, 1900), lch 2.

24 Bourke, 'Early G.A.A.', lgh 20–22; Pilib S. Ó Mórdha, *The Story of the G.A.A. in Currin and an Outline of Parish History* (Monaghan, 1986), lgh 14–15; Phil McGinn, *Armagh Harps 120 Years* (Armagh, 2008), lgh 16–17; *Anglo–Celt*, 29 Lúnasa 1896; *ibid*, 21 Deireadh Fómhair 1899.

25 *Irish News*, 14 Samhain 1898; *Northern Whig*, 14 Samhain 1898; *Shan Van Vocht*, 12 Nollaig 1898.

26 *Irish News*, 10 Aibreán 1899; *United Irishman*, 15 Aibreán 1899.

27 *Derry People*, 19 Meán Fómhair 1903.

28 *Irish News*, 6 Aibreán 1903.

29 *Derry People*, 28 Deireadh Fómhair 1905.

30 *Frontier Sentinel*, 22 Deireadh Fómhair 1904.

31 Féach, mar shampla, ar *Anglo-Celt*, 26 Eanáir 1907, 13 Márta 1909.

32 Leo Deery (ed.), *Doire 1884–1984: A History of the GAA in Derry* (Derry, 1984), lch 19.

33 Brock, *Fermanagh*, lgh 23–4; *People's Advocate*, 4 Samhain 1905, 18 Samhain 1905, 25 Samhain 1905.
34 *Belfast News-Letter*, 5 Lúnasa 1905.
35 *Anglo-Celt*, 8 Aibreán 1905.
36 Miontuairiscí, Vice-Regal Commission on Irish Railways (British Parliamentary Papers 1908, lch 157 (13 Márta 1908); *Anglo–Celt*, 21 Márta 1908.
37 *Irish News*, 18 Lúnasa 1910.
38 *Irish News*, 18 Aibreán 1904; *Northern Whig*, 18 Aibreán 1904.
39 *Banbridge Chronicle*, 28 Bealtaine 1904; *Irish News*, 18 Aibreán 1904, 16 Bealtaine 1905; *Armagh Guardian*, 23 Márta 1906.
40 *Hansard* (Commons), sraith 4 iml. 133, col. 853 (21 Aibreán 1904); *ibid*, iml. 146, col 974–975 (22 Bealtaine 1905); agus *ibid*, iml. 154, col 67–68 (19 Márta 1906).
41 Neal Garnham, *Association Football and Society in pre–partition Ireland* (Belfast, 2004), lch 167; *Irish News*, 16 Samhain 1898, 21 Aibreán 1904.
42 Síghle Nic An Ultaigh, *Ó Shíol go Bláth: An Dún – the GAA Story* (Newry, 1990), lch 61.
43 Brendan Mac Lua, *The Steadfast Rule: a history of the GAA ban* (Dublin, 1967), lgh 27–33; Paul Rouse, 'The Politics of Culture and Sport in Ireland: A History of the GAA Ban on Foreign Games 1884–1971. Part One: 1884–1921' san *International Journal of the History of Sport*, x, uimh. 3 (Nollaig 1993), lch 349–51.
44 *United Irishman*, 7 Samhain 1903.
45 Cahir Healy, 'To Combat the Gaelic Games: The Ulster Bribe' sa *Gaelic Athletic Annual & County Directory*, 1907–08, lch 33.
46 *Derry Journal*, 24 Meán Fómhair 1890.
47 *Irish News*, 16 Eanáir 1912, 6 Samhain 1912.
48 *Anglo-Celt*, 24 Meitheamh 1905.
49 Miontuairiscí, Coiste na bPáirceanna, Bardas Bhéal Feirste, 14 Feabhra 1906, PRONI LA/7/11AB/5; *ibid*, 24 Márta 1920, PRONI LA/7/11AB/8; *Irish News*, 9 May 1906, 5 March 1907.
50 *Anglo-Celt*, 4 Aibreán 1908, 25 Aibreán 1908; *Irish News*, 26 Meán Fómhair 1911.
51 *Northern Standard*, 9 Meitheamh 1906.
52 *Irish News*, 23 Lúnasa 1908; *Dundalk Democrat*, 10 Meán Fómhair 1910.
53 *Anglo-Celt*, 20 Feabhra 1909.
54 *Anglo-Celt*, 24 Iúil 1909.
55 *Anglo-Celt*, 3 Deireadh Fómhair 1914, 19 Nollaig 1914, 6 Feabhra 1915; *Irish News*, 1 Deireadh Fómhair 1914, 11 Feabhra 1915.
56 Miontuairiscí Chomhairle Uladh CLG, 13 Aibreán 1918.
57 *Dundalk Democrat*, 2 Nollaig 1916 Fearghal McGarry, *Eoin O'Duffy: A Self-Made Hero* (Oxford, 2005), lch 139; Tuarascáil Rúnaí Chomhairle Uladh CLG don bhliain 1917, i Miontuairiscí Chomhairle Uladh, comhtionól 16 Márta 1918.
58 McGarry, *Eoin O'Duffy*, lch 26; Eoin O'Duffy, 'Days that are Gone' i Séamus Ó Ceallaigh (eag.), *Gaelic Athletic Memories* (Luimneach, 1945), lch 177.
59 Miontuairiscí Chomhairle Uladh, 17 Aibreáin 1920.
60 Miontuairiscí Chomhairle Uladh, 3 Iúil 1920, 22 Deireadh Fómhair 1921.
61 Robert Lynch, *The Northern IRA and the Early Years of Partition* (Dublin, 2006), lch 100; *Freeman's Journal*, 17 January 1922.
62 Peadar Livingstone, *The Fermanagh Story: A Documented History of the County Fermanagh from the Earliest Times to the Present Day* (Enniskillen, 1969), lgh 303–04; Patrick Buckland, *The Factory of Grievances: Devolved Government in Northern Ireland 1921–39* (Dublin, 1979), lch 209.
63 *Derry Journal*, 15 Feabhra 1922; *Frontier Sentinel*, 11 Márta 1922; Nic An Ultaigh, *Ó Shíol go Bláth*, lch 100.
64 Denise Kleinrichert, *Republican Internment and the Prison Ship Argenta, 1922* (Dublin, 2001), lch 62.
65 Kleinrichert, *Republican Internment*, lgh 350, 359.
66 *Tyrone Courier and Dungannon News*, 7 Feabhra 1924.
67 *Derry Journal*, 31 Deireadh Fómhair 1921, 9 Nollaig 1921.
68 *Derry Journal*, 20 Márta 1929, 16 Deireadh Fómhair 1929.
69 *Derry Journal*, 18 Deireadh Fómhair 1929, 15 Samhain 1929.
70 *Derry People*, 12 Aibreán 1924; *Irish News*, 4 Deireadh Fómhair 1927.
71 Short, *Ulster GAA Story*, lch 100; McGarry, *Eoin O'Duffy*, lgh 146–147.
72 Short, *Ulster GAA Story*, lgh 83, 107–108; Marcus de Búrca, *The GAA: A History* (2ú eagrán, Dublin, 1999), lch 161.
73 *Anglo-Celt*, 7 Samhain 1925, 19 Nollaig 1925.
74 Amharc ar, mar shampla, *Irish News*, 4 Marta 1935, 1 Samhain 1935, 24 Feabhra 1936; miontuairiscí Chomhairle Uladh, 22 Feabhra 1936, 25 Feabhra 1939.
75 *Anglo-Celt*, 21 Márta 1925, 11 Iúil 1925.
76 Eithne Nic Giolla Fhiondain, *Alf Ó Muirí 1914–1999* (An Lorgáin, 2009), lch 31.
77 *An Camán*, Meán Fómhair 1931; Art McGann, 'The Place of the Céilidh in the Work of the G.A.A.' in Lorcan O'Toole, *Short History of the G.A.A.* [Baile Átha Cliath, c. 1934], lgh 71–2.

The Civilising of Gaelic football

1 See *Gaelic Sport*, Nov. 1970; *Irish Independent*, 6 Oct. 1996; *Irish Times*, 12 Apr. 1999; *Sunday Independent,* 23 Dec. 2007; *Irish Times*, 22 Apr. 2008.
2 Norbert Elias and Eric Dunning, *Quest for Excitement: Sport and Leisure in the Civilizing Process* (New York, 1986).
3 Norbert Elias, *The Civilizing Process: Sociogenetic and Psychogenetic Investigations* (Oxford, 2000).
4 Our findings on the sport of Gaelic football are similar to our findings in the case of hurling, see Paddy Dolan and John Connolly, 'The Civilizing of Hurling in Ireland', in *Sport in Society,* vol. 12, 2 (2009), pp 193–208.
5 See Tom Hunt, *Sport and Society in Victorian Ireland: The Case of Westmeath* (Cork, 2008), p. 155; Noel O'Donoghue, *Proud and Upright Men* (n.p., 1987), pp 36–7.
6 *Celtic Times*, 16 Apr. 1887, p. 7, 21 May 1887, p. 8, 18 June 1887, p. 7; Hunt, *Sport and Society*, p. 154.
7 *Ibid*, 21 May 1887, p. 8.
8 Dick Fitzgerald, *How to Play Gaelic Football* (Cork, 1914), p. 13; See also Hunt, *Sport and Society*, p. 154.
9 Joe Lennon, *The Playing Rules of Football and Hurling 1602–2010,* (Gormanston, 2001 edition), p. 24.
10 *Celtic Times*, 24 Dec. 1887
11 *Ibid*, pp 46–7.
12 See Carolyn Conley, 'The Agreeable Recreation of Fighting', *Journal of Social History,* Fall 1999, pp 57–72.
13 *Ibid*, p. 67.
14 *Irish Times*, 7 Mar. 1893; *ibid,* 23 July 1890; see also Neal Garnham, 'Accounting for the early success of the Gaelic Athletic Association', in *Irish Historical Studies*, xxxiv, no. 133 (May 2004), p. 77.
15 *Irish Times*, 7 Mar. 1893.

16 Extreme violence and injuries also occurred unconnected with faction fights. For example, there is a report of a player dying from his injuries following a match in Dublin, see William Nolan (ed.), *The Gaelic Athletic Association in Dublin 1884–2000* (3 vols, Dublin, 2005), i, p. 59.

17 See Lennon, *Playing Rules*.

18 See Elias and Dunning, *Quest for Excitement*.

19 *Celtic Times*, 17 Dec. 1887.

20 *Ibid*, 10 Sept. 1887.

21 *Ibid*, 5 Mar. 1887.

22 Lennon, *Playing Rules*, p. 10.

23 *Ibid*, p. 43.

24 *Ibid*, p. 26.

25 *Celtic Times*, 2 Apr. 1887; Hunt, *Sport and Society*, p. 149.

26 *Ibid*, p. 227; Hunt, *Sport and Society*, p. 154.

27 Lennon, *Playing Rules*, p. 45.

28 *Celtic Times*, 19 Feb. 1887, 26 Feb. 1887, 18 June 1887. A similar conclusion was drawn by Patrick McDevitt, 'Muscular Catholicism: Nationalism, Masculinity and Gaelic Team Sports, 1884–1916' in *Gender & History*, 9 (1997), pp 262–84.

29 *Celtic Times*, 2 Apr. 1887.

30 *Ibid*, 5 Mar. 1887.

31 Cited in McDevitt, 'Muscular Catholicism', p. 277.

32 Letter from Robert O'Keeffe to John J. Higgins dated 18 Dec. 1914, in Bailiúchán John J. Higgins, Leix and Ossory GAA, 1914–1917, (The GAA Archive, GAA Museum, Croke Park).

33 W. F. Mandle, *The Gaelic Athletic Association and Irish Nationalist Politics, 1884–1924* (Dublin, 1987), p. 162; Motion from Kerry County Committee at extraordinary general meeting of the Gaelic Athletic Association, 19 Dec. 1914 in 'Bailiúchán John J. Higgins'.

34 Michael Crowe, 'The New Rules and Things in General', in *Gaelic Athletic Annual and County Directory for 1910–11* (Dublin, 1910), p. 58.

35 *Gaelic Athletic Annual* (Dublin, 1908–09 edition), p. 42.

36 *Gaelic Athletic Annual* (Dublin, 1927 edition), p. 8.

37 See, for example, *Connacht Tribune*, 25 June 1927.

38 See, for example, *Meath Chronicle*, 24 Sep. 1938.

39 *Anglo–Celt*, 23 Apr. 1938.

40 *Celtic Times*, 17 Apr. 1887.

41 *Ibid*, 9 July 1887, 3 Sept. 1887.

42 See also McDevitt, 'Muscular Catholicism', p. 276.

43 *Ibid*, pp 94, 239.

44 *Anglo–Celt*, 10 Mar. 1906; *Gaelic Athletic Annual*, 1908, pp 38–9; see also Mandle, *Gaelic Athletic Association*, p. 95.

45 *Anglo–Celt*, 31 Oct. 1908.

46 *Irish Times*, 23 Dec. 1936.

47 Lennon, *Playing Rules*, p. 205.

48 Cumann Lúthchleas Gael, *Report of the Commission on the GAA* (Dublin, 1971), pp 113–14.

49 Norbert Elias, *Time: An Essay* (Oxford, 1993).

50 See Lennon, *Playing Rules*. p. 247.

51 *Anglo–Celt*, 10 Mar. 1906.

52 Minutes of Annual Congress, 10 Apr. 1955.

53 Lennon, *Playing Rules*, p. 289.

54 *Ibid*, p. 341.

55 Jim O'Sullivan, *Men in Black* (Dublin, 2002), p. 92.

56 *Irish Times*, 31 May 1990.

57 C. L. G., *Report of the Commission on the GAA*, p. 107.

58 *Meath Chronicle*, 20 July 1935.

59 See *Sunday Independent*, 1 Aug. 1993.

60 *Connacht Tribune*, 10 Oct. 1931; *Irish Times*, 13 Apr. 1936.

61 *Irish Times*, 13 Apr. 1936.

62 *Anglo-Celt*, 30 Oct. 1943

63 Cited in Pat Courtney (ed.), *Classic All-Ireland finals* (Galway, 2005).

64 *Connacht Tribune*, 1 Sept. 1972; *Irish Press*, 4 July 1977; 4 July 1989.

65 *Sunday Independent*, 1 Aug. 1993.

66 For example, *Irish Times*, 17 June 2008.

67 Eric Dunning and Ken Sheard, *Barbarians, Gentlemen & Players: A Sociological Study of the Development of Rugby Football* (Canberra, 1979), p. 277.

68 Lennon, *Playing Rules*, p. 66.

69 *Ibid*, p. 269.

70 *Ibid*, p. 307.

71 *Gaelic Sport*, 1974; *Irish Press*, 4 July 1977; *Irish Press*, 5 Oct. 1970; *Sunday Independent*, 1 Aug. 1993.

72 C. L. G., *Report of the Commission on the GAA*, p. 108.

73 Lennon, *Playing Rules*, p. 302.

74 O'Sullivan, *Men in Black*, p. 67

75 *Irish Times*, 10 Dec. 1985.

76 *Ibid*, 2 Nov. 2004, for example.

77 *Ibid*, 11 Mar. 2000.

78 Eric Dunning and Ken Sheard, 'The Bifurcation of Rugby Union and Rugby League: A Case Study of Organizational Conflict and Change', in *International Review for the Sociology of Sport* (1976), pp 31–72.

79 For a detailed account of this process see Paddy Dolan, 'The Development of Consumer Culture, Subjectivity and National Identity in Ireland, 1900–1980', Unpublished PhD thesis, Goldsmiths College, University of London, 2005).

80 For example, the violence between workers and employers in the Dublin Lockout of 1913.

81 W. E. Vaughan and A. J. Fitzpatrick (eds.), *Irish Historical Statistics: Population, 1821–1971* (Dublin, 1978).

82 Central Statistics Office (Ireland), 2006.

83 Eoin O'Malley, 'Problems of Industrialisation in Ireland', in John H. Goldthorpe and Christopher T. Whelan (eds) *The Development of Industrial Society in Ireland* (Oxford, 1992).

84 J. J. Lee, *Ireland 1912–1985: Politics and Society* (Cambridge, 1989), pp 491–2.

85 There are differences in the balance between social and self-restraint in terms of social class but in general a movement did occur in a specific direction.

86 Elias, *Civilizing Process*, pp 372–5.

87 Samuel Clark, 'The importance of agrarian classes: Agrarian class structure and collective action in nineteenth-century Ireland', in *British Journal of Sociology*, 29, 1 (1978), pp 22–40.

88 Mandle, *Gaelic Athletic Association*, pp 191–9.

89 Elias and Dunning, *Quest for Excitement*, passim.

90 Lee, *Ireland 1912–1985*, pp 179–82.

91 Our findings generally support the theories of Elias and Dunning (1986), but with some qualifications due to Ireland's specific history as we have explained in this chapter.

An Overview of the Playing Rules of Gaelic Football and Hurling, 1884–2010

1 *United Ireland*, 13 Oct. 1884.

2 The Association Football Rules, 1863; The Lacrosse Rules, 1868; The Laws of Rugby Union Football, 1871; The Rules of Shinty, 1874, 1877; The Glasgow Society Rules (Shinty), 1875; The Argyleshire Shinty Club Rules, 1880.

3 The Killimor Rules, 1869; Laws of Hurley, 1870 and 1879 editions; Dublin Hurling Club Rules, 1883; and 'The Rules

of Hurling' in the early 1880s (exact date unknown). See
Joe Lennon, *The Playing Rules of Football and Hurling
1884–1995* (Gormanston, 1999), pp 1–8.

4   'The Melbourne Football Club Rules', 1859; 'The
Melbourne Rules of Football', 1860; Victorian Rules, 1864,
1874 and 1877; South Australian Rules, 1877 and
Australian Rules, 1883.

5   'The Gaelic Myth' is discussed in a chapter of Geoffrey
Blainey's *A Game of Our Own: The origins of Australian
football* (Melbourne, 1990), pp 88, 89. 'The Gaelic theory
is backed by scant evidence.'

6   These rules were published in Richard Carew, *The first
Booke of the Survey of Cornwall* (1602), V2, V3. Copies of
these rules are reproduced in Joe Lennon, *A Comparative
Analysis of the Playing Rules of Football and Hurling
1884–1999* (Gormanston, 1999), pp 768–75.

7   The *Official Guide* editions of 1889 pp. 40–41; 1896/97,
pp 35–6; and 1907–'08–'09, contain the rules of four types
of wrestling – 'Catch-as-Catch-Can', 'Collar and Elbow',
'Græco-Roman' and 'Catch Hold', as codes in their own
right – even though wrestling was banned from the playing
of Gaelic football and hurling from 1886. Matt
Concannon's 1702 poem, 'A Match at Football', describes
this wrestling in football in former times; some parts of this
poem are reproduced in Lennon, *Playing Rules*, pp xv–xvi.

8   See Pádraic Ó Laoi, *Annals of the G.A.A. in Galway
1884–1901: Volume I, 1884–1901*, p. 6. 'Before the match
began F. J. Lynch captain of the Killimor team and Michael
Cusack settled the rules of the match. They agreed (i) to
play four half-hours; (ii) no tripping or taking holds
(wrestling) were allowed when playing.' The match referred
to was played on 13 April 1884.

9   For example, the first sets of goalposts were similar to those
of association football. Also, the hurling ball was similar in
construction and appearance to the shinty ball!

10   See J. Lennon, *Comparative Analysis,* p. 625.

11   Two and a half months after the publication of the 1884
rules, Cusack sought to expand on some aspects of play
when, in a letter to *The United Irishman,* he urged that:
'*The ball is not to be passed. The ball is not to be carried in
any way. The ball may be caught. When caught, the ball must
be kicked or put on the ground right away. The ball may be hit
with the hand.*' These last two proposals were incorporated
into rule in 1886 and into Rule 10 of 1888.

12   See Lennon, *Playing Rules,* pp 40–41.

13   Report of the *Ard-Rúnaí*, contained in the booklet of the
Annual Congress of the GAA, 1933.

14   Lennon, *Playing Rules*, p. 56.

15   Lennon, *Playing Rules*, p. 79.

16   Gaelic Athletic Association, *Official Guide*, 1913 edition,
p. 37.

17   All these configurations are illustrated in Lennon, *Playing
Rules*, pp 12, 18, 22, 29–30, 39, 47, 56, 79, 93.

18   This situation remained in rule until 1991 when this area
was correctly measured and called a rectangle, after some
uncomplimentary remarks made by the author about the
association's geometry, at a debate in Trinity College.

19   T. H. Redmond, 'Catching: A Plea for its Abolition', in
Gaelic Athletic Annual and County Directory for 1910–1911,
pp. 40–42. 'I desire to direct attention to one aspect (and,
in my opinion, a grave defect) of the game; I mean *the
catching of the ball…* I am convinced this defect is a
grievous one, without any redeeming feature, and one that
calls for immediate remedy … It would, moreover,
constitute no wanton attack upon any peculiar

characteristic of the Gaelic game … it does not propose to
radically alter the Gaelic game.'

20   GAA, *Official Guide*, 1938 edition, p. 89.

21   See, for example, a new paragraph in Rule 4 of the football
rules (Lennon, *Playing Rules*, p. 163).

22   See Lennon, *Playing Rules.* pp 188–193.

23   Minutes of Congress, April 1945.

24   Minutes of Congress, April 1946.

25   Central Council, GAA, *Referees Chart: Instructions on the
Playing Rules of the Gaelic Athletic Association with particular
interest to Referees* – Although this booklet did not have a
printed year of publication, it was probably in 1945; the
owner of one copy signed and dated it in June 1945.
See Lennon, *Playing Rules*, pp 220–36.

26   Central Council, *Referee's Chart*. Although the introduction
(in Irish) recommended that the booklet would 'put an end
to problematic 'interpretations', it was essentially the
interpretations of a committee on the existing rules.
It recommended that referees should 'ignore petty
infringements where same do not impede the course of the
game,' and gave curious advice on 'The Play', such as that
'(f) Referees should bear in mind that once a player catches
the ball he must without delay (1) hop it against the
ground, (2) hop it in the air, (2) kick it, or (3) fist it away
… Players may kick the ball in any direction and either
"drop kicking" or "punting" is allowed. (h) Referees must be
exceedingly vigilant so as to detect "throwing" the ball – a
not too infrequent occurrence when the player attempts to
pass the ball to one of his colleagues. **NOTE. – In hand-
passing the ball must be fisted.**' [The line in bold as it
appeared in original text] See Lennon, *Playing Rules*, p. 228.

27   See, for example, *Official Guide,* 1934–35 edition, p. 77;
Lennon, *Playing Rules*, p. 146.

28   Lennon, *Playing Rules*, p. 44.

29   This rule was in fact mistakenly copied from the equivalent
rule in hurling. Since 1985, hurlers have been allowed to
carry the ball in the hand for four steps.

30   For example, the interpretation of the note at the end of
Rule 143, 'The Kick Out', states that 'the player taking the
kick out shall not at the first or any other attempt take the
ball into his hands'. Whereas the note that is part of this
rule simply states, 'The player taking the kick-out may play
the ball more than once before any other player touches it.'

31   The open hand-pass was tightened somewhat again from
1980, following criticism that some passes were actually
thrown; 'a clear striking action' was necessary from then on.

32   See *Report of the Rules Revision Committee*, March 1985.
The members of this committee were; Dr Mick Loftus,
incoming president of the GAA; Frank Murphy, Cork Co.
Secretary; S. S. Mac Giolla Choilm, Fermanagh; Paddy
Collins, Westmeath; Seán Mac an Ridire, legal advisor to
the GAA; Garret O'Reilly, solicitor; and Liam Ó
Maolmhichíl, *Ard-Stiúrthóir*.

33   The author pleaded with Dr Loftus to withdraw the
spurious set. A few months later, in July 1988, it was
withdrawn.

34   The author had developed a new format of presentation of
the playing rules under three headings – 'The Rules of
Control'; 'The Rules of Play'; and 'The Rules of
Specification'. This demonstrated that only six rules of play
were needed, plus definitions of key terms used in the rules.
The 'Rules of Play' for football had been set out in this
format and submitted to the executive for consideration.

35   The author had drafted a very detailed motion for the Co.
Meath annual convention in 1985, but this was rejected out

of hand by the Motions Committee. Five years later, after much promotion of his ideas, the Meath convention passed a very simple motion to adopt the new format and separate the rules of play, and it was accepted and later succeeded at congress.

36   This committee consisted of President Peter Quinn; *Ardstiúrthóir*, Liam Ó Maolmhichíl; Frank Murphy, Cork Co. Secretary; Dan McCartan, Down's delegate to Central Council; Joe Lennon and referee Paddy Collins (Westmeath) as special advisor to the committee on refereeing issues.

37   The first edition of this report that emerged was based on the statement of the existing rules. When set down in this new format, many errors, duplications, contradictions and inferences stood out. The committee believed that it could not present this to the special delegate congress in December 1990 with any hope of acceptance. The report was rewritten by dispensing with all these mistakes and anomalies. It was this second report that was submitted and accepted by the special delegate congress.

38   It is not uncommon to hear and read statements to the effect that 'There's no tackle in Gaelic football!' Such critics either have not read the definitions or do not accept them. One never hears "There is no tackle in hurling," yet the definition of the tackle is exactly the same for both games.

39   See J. Lennon, *Comparative Analysis*, pp 749, 762.

40   The following elements of Australian rules football were tried out in successive 'experimental rules' trials: the four quarters of fifteen minutes each; the kick-out from the hand inside the small rectangle; the Australian 'mark'; the taking of free-kicks other than the penalty kick from the hand or from the ground; sideline-kicks from the hand; permission for players to lift the ball off the ground; and two referees and the introduction of a 'runner' – as an afterthought and without proper permission. There were also restrictions on the hand-pass; and a bar on the goalkeeper playing the ball away with his hands.

41   See Report of the Ardstiúrthóir, contained in 1997 GAA Annual Congress booklet, pp 12, 13.

42   This was later renamed the 'International Rules' – to avoid the embarrassing 'compromising' title.

43   See *O.G.* 2008, p. 53 (Rule 1.6).

44   See *O.G.* 2008, Rules 1.4 (h); Rule 1.6 that states Player(s) may tackle an opponent for the ball; Rule 1.7 in two provisions and Definition 15 that applies to both games.

45   Michael Oriard, *Reading Football: How the Popular Press created an American Spectacle* (University of North Carolina Press, 1993).

46   See, for example, 2005 Congress booklet, pp 100–10.

47   See Joe Lennon, *Towards a Philosophy for Legislation in Gaelic Games* (Gormanston, 2000), pp 136, 137.

48   The extension of the power (to submit motions to Congress) to County Boards and Provincial Councils was seen as a way of ensuring that this power was also extended to Central Council. The motion to facilitate this was assured of success.

49   For some years now, motions which express an opinion or do not seek to change a rule, have been diverted away from congress, even though there is no provision in rule for such action (Lennon, *Towards a Philosophy*, p. 140).

50   See also Lennon, *Towards a Philosophy*, pp 138–142. More recently, the Motions Committee has – by the admission of one president – thrown out motions that were in order, on the basis that Central Council intended to submit a more comprehensive motion to congress later on the same issue,

without requiring sight of the promised Central Council motion.

51   See Lennon, *Towards a Philosophy*, pp 38–62.

Irish Republican attitudes to sport since 1921

1   Marcus de Búrca, *The GAA: A History* (Dublin, 1999 edition) pp 171–2.

2   *Iris*, no. 4, Nov. 1982.

3   W. F. Mandle, *The Gaelic Athletic Association and Irish Nationalist Politics 1884–1924* (London, 1987), p. 221.

4   Marcus de Búrca, *The GAA: A History* (Dublin,1999) pp 171–2.

5   *Football Sports Weekly,* 11 Feb. 1928. (I am grateful to Conor McCabe for this reference.)

6   National Archives of Ireland (NAI), Bureau of Military History Witness Statement, Sean Clifford, WS 1279.

7   Peter Hart, 'The Social Structure of the IRA' in *idem, The IRA at War, 1916–23* (Oxford, 2003) pp 110–138.

8   NAI, Bureau of Military History Statement, Robert Holland, WS 371. (I am grateful to William Murphy for this reference.)

9   *Irish Times*, 19 Oct. 1968.

10   Donal O'Donovan, *Kevin Barry and His Time* (Dublin, 1989) pp 40–41.

11   Republican Swimming Club, Cathal Brugha Cup Souvenir Programme, 1933. (I am grateful to Frank Bouchier-Hayes for this reference.)

12   C. S. Andrews., *Dublin Made Me* (Dublin, 2001 edition) pp 35–6, 45–6 and 316–17.

13   *An Phoblacht / Republican News, (AP/RN)*, 1 Nov. 1984.

14   *An Phoblacht*, 13 Jan. 1934.

15   University College Dublin Archives, (UCDA), Moss Twomey Papers, 20 June 1924, p. 69/145 (p. 231).

16   UCDA, Moss Twomey Papers, 10 Aug. 1924, p. 69/179 (p. 111).

17   UCDA, Moss Twomey Papers, 1927, p. 69/73.

18   UCDA, Moss Twomey Papers, 28 Apr. 1931, p. 69/52 (p. 199).

19   UCDA, Moss Twomey Papers, May 1932, p. 69/155 (pp 94–97).

20   Sean McCool, an Army Council member was a leading GAA official in Donegal. The GAA grounds in Ballybofey are named after him. John 'Nipper' Shanley, a defendant in the More O'Farrell case, was a former Leitrim footballer. John Egan, the young man shot dead by the IRA as an alleged informer in 1936, played both football and hurling in Dungarvan, Co. Waterford. Stephen Hayes was secretary of the county board in Wexford and later an IRA Chief of Staff.

21   Tom Mahon and James J. Gillogly, *Decoding the IRA* (Dublin, 2008) pp 207–16.

22   J. J. Barrett, *In the Name of the Game* (Bray, 1997).

23   *Kerry Champion*, 24 Feb. 1934.

24   Brian Hanley, *The IRA, 1926–1936* (Dublin, 2002) pp 63–64.

25   *An Phoblacht,* 13 Jan. 1934.

26   *An Phoblacht,* 20 June 1925 and 6 Sept. 1931.

27   *An Phoblacht,* 13 Jan. 1934.

28   *An Phoblacht*, 24 May 1930.

29   *An Phoblacht*, 21 May 1932.

30   *An Phoblacht*, 1 Oct. 1932.

31   *Republican Congress,* 31 Aug. 1934.

32   Sean Cronin, *Frank Ryan: the Search for the Republic* (Dublin, 1979), p. 69.

33 Uinseann MacEoin, *Harry: the Story of Harry White of Belfast* (Dublin, 1985), p. 91.

34 Interview with Art McMillen, former Crumlin Road internee, 15 July 2005.

35 *United Irishman*, Sept. 1953.

36 *United Irishman*, Feb. 1964.

37 *United Irishman*, July 1962.

38 *United Irishman*, Feb. 1962.

39 *United Irishman*, Oct. 1964.

40 Tom Daly., *The Rás: Ireland's Unique Bike Race, 1953–2003* (Cork, 2003), pp 15–57.

41 *United Irishman*, Jan. 1963.

42 Brian Hanley and Scott Millar, *The Lost Revolution: the Story of the Official IRA and the Workers Party* (Dublin, 2009) pp. 11–12.

43 Daly, *The Rás*, pp 118–20.

44 Including organising the blowing up of Nelson's Pillar in 1966. *AP/RN*, 28 Aug. 1998.

45 *United Irishman*, Jan. 1969.

46 *United Irishman*, Feb. 1969.

47 *Irish News*, 9 Sept. 1969

48 *United Irishman*, Jan. 1969.

49 *United Irishman*, July 1971.

50 *An Phoblacht*, Mar. 1971.

51 *Strabane Chronicle*, 17 Apr. 1971.

52 *United Irishman*, Sept. 1970.

53 See any edition, *Workers Life*, 1980.

54 *Workers Life*, Feb. 1971.

55 Conversation with former Provisional IRA prisoner, December 2002.

56 Interview with former Crumlin Road Official IRA prisoner, 14 July 2005.

57 David Hassan, 'Sport, Identity and Irish Nationalism in Northern Ireland' in Alan Bairner, *Sport and the Irish: Histories, Identities, Issues* (Dublin, 2005) pp 123–39.

58 Desmond Fahy, *How the GAA Survived the Troubles* (Dublin, 2001) pp 73, 87–108.

59 Patrick Mulroe, 'Sport and the Northern Conflict: Sport and Conflict in a Divided Society', unpublished MA thesis, Dublin City University, 2007), pp 23–5, refers to the figure of fourteen such murders.

60 *Sunday Tribune*, 18 Jan. 2004.

61 *Belfast Telegraph*, 23 Sept. 2008.

62 Patrick Mulroe, 'Sport and the Northern Conflict', p. 27.

63 *Republican News*, 19 Jan. 1974.

64 *AP/RN*, 1 July 1982.

65 *AP/RN*, 20 Sept. 1984.

66 *AP/RN*, 26 July, 2 and 9 Aug. 1984.

67 *AP/RN*, 25 Oct. 1984.

68 *Iris*, Mar. 1983.

69 *AP/RN*, 22 May 1986.

70 *AP/RN*, 31 May and 21 June 1990.

71 *AP/RN*, 29 June 1990.

72 *AP/RN*, 26 July 1990.

73 *AP/RN*, 2 Aug. 1990.

74 *Irish People*, 4 June 1994.

75 J. M. Bradley., 'Celtic Football Club and the Irish in Scotland' in J. M. Bradley (ed.), *Celtic Minded* (Argyll, 2004), pp 19–86.

76 *AP/RN*, 29 Oct. 1998.

77 *AP/RN*, 19 Aug. 1999.

78 *AP/RN*, 30 Apr. 1998.

79 *AP/RN*, 8 Apr. and 26 Aug. 1999. See Gareth Fulton, 'Northern Catholic fans of the Republic of Ireland soccer team' in Bairner (ed.), *Sport and the Irish*, pp 140–56.

80 *AP/RN*, 16 Sept. 1999.

81 *The Guardian*, 8 Apr. 2001; *Irish Times*, 6 June 2007.

The Gaelic Athletic Association and Irish-America

1 Cited in http://www.sfgaa.org/news/showYear.php?year=2008, accessed on 2 Feb. 2009.

2 *Ibid*.

3 Paul Darby, *Gaelic Games, Nationalism and the Irish Diaspora in the United States* (Dublin, 2009). See also *idem*, 'Gaelic Games and the Irish Diaspora in the United States', in Mike Cronin, William Murphy and Paul Rouse (eds), *The Gaelic Athletic Association 1884–2009* (Dublin, 2009); *idem*, 'Without the Aid of a Sporting Safety Net?: The Gaelic Athletic Association and the Irish Émigré in San Francisco (1888–c.1938)' in *International Journal of the History of Sport*, vol. 26 (1), 2009, pp 63–83; *idem*, 'Emigrants at Play: Gaelic Games and the Irish Diaspora in Chicago, 1884–c.1900' in *Sport in History*, vol. 26 (1), (2006), pp 47–63; *idem*, 'Gaelic Games and the Irish Immigrant Experience in Boston', in A.E.S. Bairner (ed.), *Sport and the Irish: Historical, Political and Sociological Perspectives,* (Dublin, 2005), pp 85–101; *idem*, 'Gaelic Sport and the Irish Diaspora in Boston, 1879–90' in *Irish Historical Studies*, xxxiii, 132 (2003), pp 387–403.

4 Wilbur C. Abbott, *New York in the American Revolution – 1763–1783* (New York and London, 1929); Brian McGinn, 'A Century before the GAA: Hurling in 18th Century New York' in *Journal of the New York Irish History Roundtable,* vol. 11 (1997), pp 12–16.

5 R. C. Wilcox, 'The Shamrock and the Eagle: Irish Americans and Sport in the Nineteenth Century' in G. Eisen and D. K. Wiggins (eds), *Ethnicity and Sport in North American History and Culture* (Westport, CN and London, 1994), pp 54–74.

6 *Alta California*, 4 May 1853.

7 John. Byrne, 'The New York GAA, 1914–1976', in David Guiney (ed.), *The New York Irish* (Dublin, 1976), pp 6–24.

8 GAA Annual Congress minutes, 6 April 1947.

9 The attendance fell some 20,000 short of the 54,000 capacity of the Polo Grounds, the venue for the match.

10 Pádraig Puirséal, *The GAA in its Time* (Dublin, 1982), p. 254.

11 Feargal E. Cochrane, 'The End of the Affair: Irish Migration, 9/11 and the Evolution of Irish America', *Nationalism and Ethnic Politics,* vol. 13 (3), (2007), pp 335–366; David M. Reimers, 'An End and a Beginning', in Ronald H. Bayor and Timothy J. Meagher (eds), *The New York Irish* (Baltimore and London, 1997), pp 275–300.

12 The rules governing the import of players from Ireland to NACB clubs were as follows: Players wishing to play for an NACB club in the regular season had to be registered with that club before a cut off date (normally in early April). These players would be considered 'home-based' and there were no limits on the numbers who could sign for a club. In addition, clubs were permitted to sign 'sanctioned' players from Ireland by a further cut off date (normally in late July). However, only three of these players could be on the field at any one time. These rules were abused by NACB clubs and players. For example, three inter-county Roscommon footballers received lengthy suspensions from the GAA for playing illegally for the Galway club in Boston (Seán Moran, 'McHugh Among 20 Banned by GAC', *Irish Times,* 10 Jan. 1997, p. 15).

13 Irish Department of Foreign Affairs, Press Release, 24 June 2008.

14 Darby, 'Without the Aid of a Sporting Safety Net', *idem*, 'Emigrants at Play'; *idem*, 'Gaelic Games and the Irish Immigrant Experience in Boston', *idem*, 'Gaelic Games, Ethnic Identity and Irish Nationalism in New York City'.

15 Mike Cronin, 'Enshrined in Blood: The Naming of Gaelic Athletic Association Grounds and Clubs' in *The Sports Historian,* vol. 18, 1 (1998), p. 96.

16 *Irish Echo,* July 1888; *The Gael,* May 1887.

17 *The Advocate,* 3 Sept. 1914.

18 NORAID was established ostensibly to collect money in the USA to support the families of republican prisoners in Northern Ireland. However, the American, British and Irish governments came to the conclusion that its primary function was to raise funds to support the IRA, and as such the organisation was proscribed by all three governments.

19 Brian Hanley, 'The Politics of NORAID' in *Irish Political Studies,* vol. 19, no. 1 (2004), pp 1–17.

20 Ulster Gaelic Football Club, Constitution.

21 Interview with Joe Duffy, former Ulster GFC Chairman, San Francisco, CA, 28 Aug. 2006.

22 For example, the anti-Belfast Agreement 32-County Sovereignty Movement has pockets of support in the USA, including the former leader of NORAID, Martin Galvin.

23 Cochrane, 'The End of the Affair'.

24 Perhaps, the clearest evidence of this shifting identity came in April 2005 when an online poll of 120 US clubs on the issue of Rule 42, revealed that ninety per cent favoured the amendment to open up Croke Park, temporarily to rugby union and soccer.

25 Interview with Joe Duffy. UGFC.

American Gaels and Cavan Heroes: The 1947 All-Ireland Gaelic Football Final in New York

1 Sara Brady, 'Playing "Irish" Sport on Baseball's Hallowed Ground: The 1947 All-Ireland Gaelic Football Final' in Matthew J. O'Brien and James Silas Rogers (eds), *After the Flood: Irish America, 1945–1960* (Irish Academic Press, 2009), pp 24–37; Mick Dunne, *The Star Spangled Final: The Story of the 1947 All-Ireland Final in New York* (Dublin, 1997); Anton Tighe, *The American All-Ireland* (Newry, 1997).

2 John Barry and Eamon Horan, *Years of Glory: The Story of Kerry's All-Ireland Senior Victories* (Tralee, 1977), p. 58.

3 Rev. Daniel Gallogly, *Cavan's Football Story* (Cavan, 1979), p. 89.

4 Gallogly, *Cavan's Football Story*, pp 92–3.

5 Gallogly, *Cavan's Football Story*, pp 97–8.

6 Much of this history is accounted for in Paul Darby, *Gaelic Games, Nationalism and the Irish Diaspora in the United States* (Dublin, 2009). See also *idem*, 'Gaelic Games and the Irish Diaspora in the United States', in Mike Cronin, William Murphy and Paul Rouse (eds), *The Gaelic Athletic Association 1884–2009* (Dublin, 2009); *idem*, 'Without the Aid of a Sporting Safety Net?: The Gaelic Athletic Association and the Irish Émigré in San Francisco (1888– *c.* 1938)', vol. 26 (1), 2009, pp 63–83; *idem*, 'Emigrants at Play: Gaelic Games and the Irish Diaspora in Chicago, 1884–*c.*1900', in *Sport in History,* 26 (1), (2006), pp 47–63; *idem*, 'Gaelic Games and the Irish Immigrant Experience in Boston', in Alan Bairner (ed.), *Sport and the Irish: Historical, Political and Sociological Perspectives,* (Dublin, 2005), pp 85–101; *idem*, 'Gaelic Sport and the Irish Diaspora in Boston, 1879–90', in *Irish Historical Studies,* xxxiii, 132 (2003), pp 387–403.

7 *Irish Echo,* 8 Feb. 1964.

8 GAA Central Council minutes, 8 Dec. 1952.

9 Darby, *Gaelic Games, Nationalism and the Irish Diaspora in the United States*, p. 104.

10 John Byrne, 'The Gaelic Athletic Association of Greater New York: Seventy Five Years of Gaelic Sports', in *The GAA Annual Banquet (75th Anniversary) Official Programme* (New York, 1989); Pádraig Puirséal, *The GAA in its Time* (Dublin, 1982), p. 251.

11 GAA Annual Congress minutes, 6 Apr. 1947, Cardinal Tomás Ó Fiaich Library and Archive, Armagh.

12 Cited in *The Advocate,* 8 Jan. 1939.

13 Marcus de Búrca, *The GAA: A History* (2nd edition, Dublin, 1999), p. 181.

14 Fergus Hanna, 'The Gaelic Athletic Association', in Michael Glazier (ed.), *The Encyclopedia of the Irish in America,* (Notre Dame, 1999), p. 353.

15 See Maurice Hayes, 'Down through the Years' in this book.

16 GAA Annual Congress minutes, 6 Apr. 1947.

17 *Ibid.*

18 Dunne, *Star Spangled Final,* p. 17. Questions remain about the veracity of the letter (see Maurice Hayes, 'Down through the Years' in this book. The often confused memories of the decision are not helped by the fact that the official minutes record more than three pages of Hamilton's arguments, and merely lists the other seventeen speakers, with no detail of what they said – a point which probably indicates the level of sway that the cleric had in Croke Park. See GAA Annual Congress minutes, 6 Apr. 1947.

19 De Búrca, *The GAA,* p. 181.

20 Dunne, *Star Spangled* Final, p. 19. It was recounted by some delegates who attended the meeting that a comment by a Roscommon official – that none of his sons would travel by aeroplane, thus insinuating that his county would qualify for the final – may have swung some of the votes, notably from Ulster. See Tighe, *American All-Ireland*, p. 6.

21 GAA Central Council minutes, 23 May 1947.

22 Stew Thornley, *Land of the Giants: New York's Polo Grounds.*

23 Dunne, *Star Spangled Final,* p. 19.

24 McNamee was a teacher and spent his entire summer vacation in New York voluntarily. Interview with Pádraig Mac Floinn, An Dún, *iar-Uachtarán CLG*, February 2009.

25 Mayor O'Dwyer's contribution was noted by Pádraig Ó Caoimh in his report to Central Council in December 1947. Ó Caoimh commented that the Mayor sought frequent updates on what he referred to as 'the great project'. Mayor O'Dwyer also used his official position to secure publicity in the city's principal newspapers. Pádraig Ó Caoimh, Report to GAA Central Council, 13 Dec. 1947.

26 GAA Central Council minutes, 13 Dec. 1947.

27 Gallogly, *Cavan's Football Story*, p. 109.

28 Personal recollections of Mick Higgins, a member of the 1947 Cavan team, conveyed to Aogán Ó Fearghail, Mar. 2009. Doonan's reluctance to fly may have been rooted in his experience as a radio-operator in the British army in southern Italy during the Second World War. A story in circulation, probably apocryphal, claims that Doonan was in a plane shot down during the war, resulting in him injuring his foot.

29 *Gaelic American,* 13 Sept. 1947

30 Personal recollections of Mick Higgins, Mar. 2009.

31 P. Ó Caoimh, Report to Central Council, 13 Dec. 1947.
32 Official Souvenir Programme, All-Ireland Football Championship final, 14 Sept. 1947, p. 2.
33 *Ibid*, p. 1.
34 *Anglo-Celt*, 20 Sept. 1947. Mick Higgins recalls that the anthems 'went on forever'! Personal recollections of Mick Higgins.
35 *Anglo-Celt*, 20 Sept. 1947.
36 *Anglo-Celt*, 20 Sept. 1947. See also Aogán Ó Fearghail and Rev Daniel Gallogly, *One Hundred Years of Cavan GAA* (Cavan, 1984), p. 57.
37 *Irish Press*, 15 Sept. 1947.
38 *Ibid*.
39 He was also described as 'Dead-Eye Dick' and as possessing 'uncanny accurate kicking.' *New York Times*, 15 Sept. 1947, cited in *Irish Press*, 16 Sept. 1947. The *Journal American* picked out another star. Beneath the headline, 'Cop Stars for Cavan', it wrote of the irony of how 'Michael Higgins, a burly, boney man, went against nature', having been born in New York and become a *garda* in Ireland, thus reversing the trend of Irish emigrants becoming New York policemen, 'He and Pete Donohue [sic], a huge farmer, and 13 other assorted amateur athletes with strong lungs and primitive combative instincts, are the toast of County Cavan, today.' (Cited in Tighe, *American All-Ireland*, p. 81.)
40 *New York Times*, c. 15 Sept. 1947; cited in *Anglo-Celt*, 20 Sept. 1947.
41 Tighe, *American All-Ireland*, pp 74–5.
42 *New York Times*, c. 15 Sept. 1947; cited in *Anglo-Celt*, 20 Sept. 1947, and Tighe, *American All-Ireland*, p. 74.
43 *Gaelic American*, 13 Sept. 1947.
44 *Gaelic American*, 20 Sept. 1947.
45 *Anglo–Celt*, 20 Sept. 1947.
46 Pádraig Ó Caoimh, Report to Central Council GAA, 13 Dec. 1947.
47 The broadcast was almost cut short by five minutes. The lines back to Ireland were booked for a specific amount of time and with the pre-match speeches and introductions going on longer than expected, technicians informed O'Hehir that his time was up, with five minutes of the game remaining. Live on air, he famously pleaded for an engineer, 'anyone out there', to extend the broadcast. His plea was answered and the broadcast continued to the end of the game. Eddie Brady, *The Golden Years of Cavan Football 1927–1952* (audio recording, two compact discs, Cavan, 2005), disc two.
48 Puirséal, *The GAA in its Time*, p. 254
49 *Ibid*, pp 260–61.
50 Byrne, 'The Gaelic Athletic Association of New York'.
51 Personal recollection of Aidan Farrell to one of the present authors. For similar accounts elsewhere, see, for example, *Newry Reporter*, 20 Sept. 1947.
52 *Irish Independent*, 16 Sept. 1947.
53 *Anglo-Celt*, 11 Oct. 1947.
54 Gallogly, *Cavan's Football Story*, p. 113; Brady, *Cavan's Golden Years.*
55 This information was provided by Ms Mary Daly from Maudabawn, who attended the banquet.
56 Personal recollections of Mick Higgins. We are also grateful to Tom Sullivan, Cavan County Library, for this information.
57 O'Reilly, described by Mick Higgins as 'The greatest leader of men, on or off the field that I ever met', was a captain in the Irish Army, stationed at the Curragh camp in Kildare. Returning to play with his native Cornafean was not possible so he played his club football in Kildare. George Cartwright, *Up the Reds: The Cornafean Achievement GAA* (Cavan, 1985), p. 142.
58 Gallogly, *Cavan's Football Story*, p. 113.
59 *Anglo-Celt*, 11 Oct. 1947.
60 *Ibid*, p. 114. The surviving members were, Frank O'Grady, Michael Freehill, Michael McGerty, Peter Johnson, John McManus, Owen O'Reilly, Con McGerty and Peter Creighton.
61 See, for example, *Anglo–Celt*, 4 Oct. 1947, 11 Oct. 1947. This film, produced by the newly established National Film Institute of Ireland, was in fact the longest film shown up to then of any GAA game.
62 Gallogly, *Cavan's Football Story*, p. 125.
63 *Ibid*, p. 133.

The Emergence and Development of the GAA in Britain and Europe

1   Kevin O'Connor, *The Irish in Britain* (London, 1972), p. 7.
2   Roger Swift, 'The Historiography of the Irish in nineteenth-century Britain' in Patrick O'Sullivan (ed.) *The Irish in New Communities* (London, 1992), p. 63.
3   *Ibid*, p. 72.
4   Dónal McAnallen, Peter Mossey and Stephen Moore, 'The "Temporary Diaspora" at Play: The Development of Gaelic Games in British Universities', in *Sport in Society*, vol. 10, 3, pp 402–24.
5   'A Proud Record for London Hurlers' in *Gaelic World* (1985), p. 13.
6   *Trewman's Exeter Flying Post*, 13 Apr. 1845, reported a 'disgraceful occurrence' in Cornwall: 'when the annual game of hurling took place, about five hundred players' participated, causing thirty pounds worth of damage to the local plantation and general annoyance to the town's population. *Ibid*, 26 May 1869, also detailed how 'on Monday last a variety of amusements and athletics came off in the annual revel. The day's sports began by a game of hurling on the common, which was kept up for two hours with great spirit.'
7   *Morning Chronicle*, 31 May 1856.
8   *The Graphic*, 25 Mar. 1876.
9   Sean Meaney, *Our Name is on the Cup: The Stories of Liam MacCarthy and Sean Maguire* (London, 2008), p. 69.
10 *Irish Tribune*, 13 July 1895.
11 Seamus J. King, *The Clash of the Ash in Foreign Fields: Hurling Abroad* (Cashel, 1998), p. 42. See also *Reynolds Newspaper*, 29 Sept. 1895, which carried an advertisement for an Irish Athletic Association Gaelic sports club in south London that 'will be worked on strictly non-political lines, and Irishmen of all shades of opinion are eligible for membership.'
12 *Shan Van Vocht*, 2 Aug. 1897.
13 *SVV*, 1 Nov. 1897.
14 *Glasgow Examiner*, 11 Sept. 1897.
15 Joseph M. Bradley, *Sport, Culture, Politics and Scottish Society: Irish Immigrants and the Gaelic Athletic Association* (Edinburgh, 1998), p. 29.
16 *Irish News*, 05 July 1910.
17 Mike Cronin, 'Enshrined in blood: The naming of Gaelic Athletic Association grounds and clubs', in *Sports Historian*, vol. 18, 1 (May, 1998), p. 96.
18 Helena Duignan, *Keeping the Game Alive: One Hundred Years of Camogie in Britain* (Birmingham, 2004), pp 7–11, 14–16.

19   Minutes of the Ulster Council of the GAA, meeting of 3 July 1920, Cardinal Ó Fiaich Library and Archive, Armagh.

20   S. J. King, *Clash of the Ash*, p. 53.

21   Tony Beatty, *Brian Ború GAA Club (London) Centenary Story* (London, 2000), p. 167.

22   Report of the secretary of the Provincial Council of Britain for 1932; reprinted in Tommy Walsh, *The Gaelic Association in Britain: The History of the Provincial Council* (London, 2005), p. 26.

23   Walsh, *Provincial Council*, p. 27.

24   Report of the secretary of the Provincial Council of Britain for 1936, cited in Walsh, *Provincial Council*, p. 27.

25   *Ibid*, p. 27. For a proposal to form boys' hurling teams in Liverpool in 1926, see John Mitchel's Gaelic Football Club, *The Story of the GAA in Liverpool: Centenary Year 1884–1984* (Liverpool, 1984), p. 19.

26   Beatty, *Brian Ború*, p. 62.

27   Walsh, *Provincial Council*, pp 30, 148.

28   *GAA Digest*, Dec. 1948), p. 40. See also S. J. King, *Clash of the Ash*, p. 53.

29   Tracey Connolly, 'Emigration from Ireland to Britain during the Second World War' in Andy Bielenberg (ed.), *The Irish Diaspora* (London, 2000), p. 51.

30   Anon., *Clan na Gael London 1951–1998* (London, 1998), p. 63.

31   *Sunday Review*, 10 June 1962.

32   *Munster Express*, 3 June 1960, p. 12.

33   Roger Hutchinson, *Camanachd: The Story of Shinty* (Edinburgh, 1989), pp 59–60.

34   Interview with Tom Denning, former Chairman of Dulwich Harps GAA Club, 9 July 2008.

35   Bradley, *Sport, Culture, Politics and Scottish Society*, pp 74–5, 123–26.

36   Dónal McAnallen, Peter Mossey and Stephen Moore, 'The "Temporary Diaspora" at Play: The Development of Gaelic Games in British Universities', in Paul Darby and David Hassan (eds) *Emigrant Players: Sport and the Irish Diaspora* (Oxford, 2007), pp 70–92.

37   Interview with Gerry Kelly, official of the Irish Department of Foreign Affairs, 21 Aug. 2008.

38   R. J. Dickson, *Ulster Emigration to Colonial America, 1718–1775* (Belfast, 1988).

39   Enda Delaney, *Irish Emigration since 1921* (Dublin, 2002). p. 23.

40   Enda Delaney and Alan M. Barrett, 'Irish Migration: Characteristics, Causes, and Consequences', in Klaus F. Zimmermann (ed.), *European Migration* (Oxford, 2005), pp 43–65.

41   Delaney, p. 24

42   Damien Courtney, 'A Quantification of Irish Migration with Particular Emphasis on the 1980s and 1990s', in Bielenberg (ed.), *Irish Diaspora*, pp 287–316; Delaney, p. 24.

43   Ian Shuttleworth, 'Graduate emigration from Ireland: a symptom of Peripherality?' in Russell King (ed.), *Mass Migration in Europe: The Legacy and the Future* (Chichester, 1993), pp 83–95.

44   Jim MacLaughlin, *Ireland: The Immigrant Nursery and the World Economy* (Cork, 1997), p. 34.

45   Shuttleworth, 'Graduate emigration', pp 83–95.

46   Peter Clinch, Frank Convery and Brendan Walsh, *After the Celtic Tiger: challenges ahead* (Dublin, 2002), p. 20.

47   Mary J. Hickman, 'Migration and Diaspora' in Joseph Cleary and Claire Connolly, *Cambridge Companion to Modern Irish Culture* (Cambridge, 2005), pp 117–36.

48   Liam Ryan, 'Irish Emigration to Britain since World War 2'

in Richard. Kearney (ed.), *Migrations: The Irish at Home and Abroad* (Dublin, 1992), pp 45–69; Shuttleworth, 'Graduate emigration', p. 84.

49   Shuttleworth, 'Graduate emigration', p. 85.

50   Graeme Kirkham, 'The Origins of Mass Emigration from Ireland' in Kearney (ed) *Migrations*, pp 81–90.

51   See, for example, Eoghan Ó hAnnracháin and Cathal Davey, *More than a Sporting Experience: 30 Years of Gaelic Games in Luxembourg* (Luxembourg, 2008), pp 15–16.

52   David Hassan, 'The Role of Gaelic Games in the lives of the Irish Diaspora in Europe' in Darby and Hassan (eds), *Emigrant Players*, p. 61.

53   Grant Jarvie (ed.), *Sport in the Making of Celtic Cultures* (Leicester, 1999), p. 6.

54   *Ibid*, p. 6.

55   Terry Eagleton, 'The ideology of Irish studies' in *Bullán*, vol. 1, 1 (1997), p. 6.

The GAA in a Global Sporting Context

1   P. J. Cunningham, 'The Prod' in *A. N. Other* (Bray, 2001), p. 205.

2   A. E. S. Bairner, 'Sports and Nationalism' in Guntram H. Herb and David H. Kaplan (eds), *Nations and nationalism: A global historical overview*, vol. 3 1945–1989 (Santa Barbara, 2008), pp 991–1004.

3   Mike Cronin, *Sport and nationalism in Ireland: Gaelic games, soccer and Irish identity since 1884* (Dublin, 1999), p. 116.

4   David Daiches, *Robert Burns* (London, 1952), p. 9.

5   Garry Crawford, *Consuming Sport. Fans, Sport and Culture* (London, 2004), p. 6.

6   John Horne, *Sport in Consumer Culture* (Houndmills, Basingstoke, 2006), p. 27.

7   See Desmond Fahy, *How the GAA survived the troubles* (Dublin, 2001).

8   Adam Brown, Tim Crabbe and Gavin Mellor, 'Introduction: football and community – practical and theoretical considerations', in *Soccer and Society*, vol. 9 (3), 304 (2008), pp 303–12.

9   *Ibid*, p. 308.

10   *Ibid*.

11   Tom Humphries, *Green Fields: Gaelic sport in Ireland* (London, 1996), p. 5.

12   Richard English, *Irish Freedom: The history of nationalism in Ireland* (London, 2006).

13   A. E. S. Bairner, *Sport, nationalism, and globalization. European and North American perspectives* (Albany, New York, 2001).

14   Joseph Maguire, *Global Sport, Identities, Societies, Civilizations* (Cambridge, 1999).

15   Toby Miller, Geoffrey Lawrence, Jim McKay and David Rowe, *Globalization and sport: Playing the world* (London, 2001), p. 59.

16   Paul Darby and David Hassan, 'Introduction: locating sport in the study of the Irish diaspora' in Paul Darby and David Hassan (eds) *Emigrant Players: Sport and the Irish diaspora* (London, 2008), pp 2–3.

17   D. J. Taylor, *On the Corinthian spirit. The decline of amateurism in sport* (London, 2006), p. 31.

18   *Ibid*, pp 31–2.

19   *Ibid*, p. 32.

20   Ian Malin, *Mud, blood and money. English rugby union goes professional* (Edinburgh, 1997), p. 171.

21   http:///richmondfc.co.uk (Accessed, 15 April 2009).

22 John Kelly, *Flowers of Scotland? A sociological analysis of national identities, rugby union and association football in Scotland*. Unpublished PhD thesis, Loughborough University (2007).
23 Cited in Eamon Rafferty, *Talking Gaelic: Leading personalities on the GAA* (Dublin, 1997), p. 106.
24 Micheál Ó Muircheartaigh, *From Dún Síon to Croke Park: The autobiography* (Dublin, 2004), p. 236.
25 *Ibid*, pp 236–7.
26 *Ibid*, p. 237.
27 *Ibid*.
28 Bruce McKendry, *Champion – The players' story: The official story of the Ulster team in Europe* (Belfast, 1999).
29 Marcus de Búrca, 'The Gaelic Athletic Association and Organised Sport in Ireland', pp 100–111, in Grant Jarvie (ed.), *Sport in the Making of Celtic Cultures* (Leicester, 1999), p. 110.
30 Séamus J. King, *A history of hurling* (Dublin, 1998), p. 241.
31 Henri Lefebvre, *The urban revolution* (Minneapolis, 2003), p. 45.
32 Tom Inglis, Religion, identity, state and society, pp 59–77 in Joseph Cleary and Claire Connolly (eds), *The Cambridge companion of modern Irish culture* (Cambridge, 2005), p. 59.
33 *Ibid*, p. 74.
34 *Ibid*, p. 72.
35 J. J. Barrett, *In the name of the game* (Bray, 1997), p. 15.
36 Fahy, *How the GAA Survived*, p. 14.
37 T. Schirato and J. Webb, *Understanding globalization* (London, 2003), p. 88.

Cardinal Tomás Ó Fiaich and the GAA: an appreciation

1 *Irish Press*, 10 May 1990.
2 Con Short, Peter Murray and Jimmy Smyth, *Ard Mhacha 1884–1984: a century of GAA progress* (Armagh, 1984), p. 13.
3 Gene Larkin, 'The Last True Prince of Ulster' in *Creggan Journal*, no. 5 (1991), p. 43.
4 Kieran McConville (ed.), *Commemorative programme for the official opening of Páirc Phádraig, Cullyhanna* (1988), p. 3.
5 *Ibid*.
6 Joe McManus, 'Hall of Fame for Cardinal Tomas Ó Fiaich' in *Ulster Games Annual*, 1987–88, p. 12.
7 Seosamh Ó Dufaigh, 'Tomás Ó Fiaich, Scoláire' in *Seanchas Ard Mhacha*, ix, no. 1 (1978), p. 3.
8 Proinsias Ó hAodha, 'Memories of O'Neill's' in the programme for the official opening of Páirc Uí Néill An Phoirt Mhóir, 13 Aug. 1978, p. 7.
9 Tomás Ó Fiaich, 'Cuimhní Cinn an Ardeaspaig' in P. J. Toner, *The Armagh Camogie Story* (1978), p. 3.
10 Alan Rodgers, *Forever Young on the Fields of Moy* (Moy, 2008), p. 235.
11 Ó Fiaich, 'Cuimhní Cinn' in Toner, *Armagh Camogie Story*, p. 3.
12 Letter from Tomás Ó Fiaich to Alf Ó Muirí, 7 July 1959, contained in a collection of documents relating to Tomás Ó Fiaich, in the Cardinal Ó Fiaich Library.
13 Larkin, 'Last True Prince', p. 43.
14 Tomás Ó Fiaich, Foreword to Con Short, *History of the GAA in Crossmaglen, Co. Armagh 1887–1959: souvenir of opening of Blessed Oliver Plunkett Park, Crossmaglen*, 19 Apr. 1959.
15 Larkin, 'Last True Prince', p. 43.
16 Kevin McMahon, 'The Team' in *Creggan Journal*, no. 5 (1991), pp 75–80.
17 Deirdre Fee, 'Uncle Tom' in *Creggan Journal*, no. 5 (1991), p. 31.
18 Larkin, 'Last True Prince', p. 44.
19 Brian D'Arcy, 'I'll never forget "Fr. Tom"' in *Creggan Journal*, no. 5 (1991), p. 27.
20 Seamus McAteer, 'Gaelscrínte san Eoraip (Irish Shrines in Europe)' in *Creggan Journal*, no. 5 (1991), p. 72.
21 Tomás Ó Fiaich, 'History in your Club Names' in *Armagh Gaelic Athletic Association Year Book*, 1968, pp 3–6.
22 Tomás Ó Fiaich, 'Michael Cusack and the tradition of rural sport in Ireland', paper read at the Merriman Summer School, Ennis, Co. Clare, 22 Aug. 1969; contained in a collection of documents relating to Tomás Ó Fiaich, in the Cardinal Ó Fiaich Library.
23 Tomas Ó Fiaich, 'Ban the Ball' in Maynooth College Sigerson Cup programme 1974, pp 46–48.
24 Anon., 'Cardinal Tomás Ó Fiaich' on www.armagh-gaa.com, accessed on 5 Oct. 2009.
25 Tomás Ó Fiaich, Foreword to Con Short, *The Crossmaglen GAA Story 1887–1987* (Crossmaglen, 1987).
26 Anon., *St. Oliver Plunkett Park Crossmaglen: Saga of a sportsfield* (1977), p. 3.
27 Risteard Ó Glaisne, *Tomás Ó Fiaich* (Baile Átha Cliath, 1990), p. 135.
28 Tomás Ó Fiaich, Foreword to the Ulster Football Championship finals programme, 15 July 1984, p. 5.
29 *Ibid*.
30 Letter from Cardinal Tomás Ó Fiaich to Joe Lennon, Gormanston, 19 Jan. 1985, contained in a collection of documents relating to Tomás Ó Fiaich, in the Cardinal Ó Fiaich Library.
31 Anon., 'Cardinal Tomás Ó Fiaich' on www.armagh-gaa.com, accessed on 5 Oct. 2009.
32 Larkin, 'Last True Prince', p. 45.
33 *Ibid*, p. 46.
34 Pat O Neill, 'My Friend' in *Creggan Journal*, no. 5 (1991), p. 111.
35 *Irish News*, 16 May 1990.

The Search for John McKay:
The Ulsterman at the first meeting of the GAA

1 *United Ireland*, 8 Nov. 1884.
2 Marcus de Búrca, *Michael Cusack and the GAA*, p. 103.
3 Five of the other six men have been the subject of books or published articles. See, for example, Liam P. Ó Caithnia, *Micheál Cíosóg* (Baile Átha Cliath, 1982); Paul Rouse, 'Michael Cusack: Sportsman and Journalist' in Mike Cronin, William Murphy and Paul Rouse (eds), *The Gaelic Athletic Association 1884–2009* (Dublin, 2009), pp 47–59; Br. Seán McNamara, *The Man from Carron* [Ennis, 2006]; Séamus Ó Riain, *Maurice Davin (1842–1927): First President of the GAA* (Dublin, [1994]); Nancy Murphy, 'Joseph K. Bracken, GAA founder, Fenian and politician' in William Nolan and T. C. McGrath (eds), *Tipperary: History and Society* (Dublin, 1985), pp 379–393; Marcus de Búrca, 'The Curious Career of Sub-Inspector Thomas St George McCarthy' in *Tipperary Historical Society*, 1988, pp 201–204; Alf MacLochlainn, 'From Tipperary to Joseph's Prairie: the story of Joe Ryan, the seventh man in Hayes's Hotel' in *Tipperary Historical Journal*, 2002, pp 145–67
4 De Búrca, *Michael Cusack*, p. 104; Cumann Lúthchleas Gael, *A Century of Service 1884–1984* (Dublin, 1984), p. 46. Pádraig Puirséal, *The GAA in its Time* (Dublin, 1982), refers to 'Willie McKay, a Belfast man'. On the official GAA

website it is extrapolated from this information that McKay was from Co. Antrim (www.gaa.ie, accessed on 1 Oct. 2009).

5   See, for example, anon. 'Seven men of seven trades and the birth of the GAA' in *Irish Press GAA Golden Jubilee Supplement*, Apr. 1934, p. 4. Anon., 'A story of great endeavour' in programme for the official opening of the new Hogan Stand, Croke Park, 7 June 1959, p. 6, refers to McKay as 'a journalist of Cork'.

6   Thomas F. O'Sullivan, *Story of the GAA* (Dublin, 1916), p. xi.

7   Marcus de Búrca, *Michael Cusack and the GAA*, p. 104.

8   *Irish News*, 8 Dec. 1923.

9   *Ibid*, stated that 'his journalistic career began on the Belfast Morning News nearly half a century ago'.

10 Parnell Commission, minutes of evidence, 28 May 1889, pp 303–04, 306.

11 *Irish Independent*, 10 Dec. 1923.

12 *Cork Examiner*, 3 Nov. 1884.

13 O'Sullivan, *Story*, p. 9, states that McKay 'furnished his paper with reports of the meetings of the Association at which he attended.' De Búrca, *Michael Cusack*, p. 104, states that McKay also provided GAA reports for the *Cork Daily Herald*.

14 O'Sullivan, *Story*, p. 11.

15 Ó Riain, *Maurice Davin*, p. 60.

16 De Búrca, *Michael Cusack*, p. 122. See also O'Sullivan, *Story*, pp 21–2.

17 *Freeman's Journal*, 24 Feb. 1885; *United Ireland*, 28 Feb. 1885.

18 Ó Riain, *Maurice Davin*, p. 94. See also W. F. Mandle, *The Gaelic Athletic Association and Irish Nationalist Politics 1884–1924* (Dublin, 1987), p. 29.

19 *Cork Examiner*, 23 Apr. 1886.

20 *Freeman's Journal*, 21 Jan. 1899, 24 Jan. 1899; O'Sullivan, *Story*, pp 35, 140.

21 Registration of Marriage for John McKay and Ellen Browne, Registrar's District Cork no. 5, 19 Apr. 1883, General Register Office, Ireland (GROI).

22 O'Sullivan, *Story*, p. 34.

23 Registration of Birth for Patrick Joseph McKay, Registrar's District Cork no. 8, 28 Oct. 1887], GROI.

24 Parnell Commission, minutes of evidence, 28 May 1889, p. 303. See also Registration of Death of Maurice Henry McKey [sic], Registrar's District Cork no. 8, 19 Aug. 1889, GROI. The address of 36 Southern Road, Cork, may also have been a residence of McKay or his wife's family; John was present at that address when his son Maurice Henry died there in 1889.

25 Parnell Commission, minutes of evidence, 28 May 1889, pp 303–07.

26 *Irish News*, 8 Dec. 1923.

27 C.L.G., *Century of Service*, p. 46.

28 *Irish Independent*, 10 Dec. 1923.

29 *Cork Examiner*, 27 Nov. 1902.

30 *Cork Examiner*, 1 Dec. 1902.

31 Thomas Dooley, Cork GAA chairman, 1899–1905, had been involved with the association in the county since 1886 at least, and possibly as far back as 1884, and he was probably one of the few remaining officials in the country who knew McKay personally. Jim Cronin, *Making Connections: A Cork GAA Miscellany* [Cork, 2005], p. 40, relates that while the Cork County Board was lacking money Dooley would sometimes pay (out of his own pocket) the train-fares of his county's delegates to Thurles, and he would appoint *Cork Examiner* reporters as delegates in the knowledge that they would be attending anyway.

32 See, for example, *Cork Examiner*, 7 Jan. 1903, 24 Jan. 1903.

33 *Irish Independent*, 10 Dec. 1923.

34 *Cork Free Press*, 16 June 1910.

35 Peter Martin, *Censorship in the Two Irelands 1922–39* (Dublin, 2006), p. 9.

36 Patrick Maume, 'A Nursery of Editors: The Cork Free Press, 1910–16' in *History Ireland*, xv, no. 2 (Mar./Apr. 2007), p. 45.

37 *Irish News,* 8 Dec. 1923.

38 *Irish Independent*, 10 Dec. 1923.

39 Death certificate for John McKay, Lambeth, 2 Dec. 1923, General Register Office, England.

40 *Newry Reporter*, 11 Dec. 1923.

41 We have checked every edition of the *Cork Examiner* and *Cork Weekly Examiner* in December 1923.

42 *Irish News*, 8 Dec. 1923.

43 Irish News, 8 Dec 1923.

44 *Irish Independent*, 10 Dec. 1923.

45 *Irish Times*, 10 Dec. 1923.

46 *Irish News*, 8 Dec. 1923.

47 *Freeman's Journal*, 10 Dec. 1923.

48 See, for example, reports of Cork County Board meetings in *Cork Examiner*, 6 Dec. 1923, 13 Dec. 1923, 20 Dec. 1923.

49 Anon., 'Seven men of seven trades', *Irish Press GAA Golden Jubilee Supplement*, p. 4.

50 Death certificate for John McKay, Lambeth, 2 Dec. 1923,

51 Burial records of St Mary's Roman Catholic Cemetery, Kensal Green, London.

52 www.census.nationalarchives.ie/reels/nai001883145, accessed on 29 Aug. 2009.

53 Registration of Marriage for John McKay and Ellen Browne.

54 Registration of Death for Maurice Henry McKey [sic].

55 Register of baptisms, Catholic Diocese of Cork and Ross, St Finbarr's (South) Parish, Cork City.

56 Index of Birth for Patrick Joseph.

57 Registration of Death for Maurice Henry McKey [sic].

58 Among the other parish records checked were those of Dromara and Dromore parishes, Co. Down; those of Holy Rosary and St Matthew's parishes in Belfast; and those of the Cork City parishes of St Patrick, St Peter and St Paul, and St Mary and St Ann (North Cathedral). Considerable assistance was also provided by Kieran Wyse, Cork County Library; Armagh Ancestry; and Michael Anderson, Poyntzpass.

Where exactly in Co. Down did John McKay come from?

1   Letter from Jimmy McKay, Birmingham, to Philomena McKay, Belfast, *c.* 1978.

2   www.census.nationalarchives.ie/reels/nai001468081, accessed on 30 Oct. 2009.

3   Civil register of marriages, District of Down. We are grateful to Elizabeth Kennedy, Down District Council, for her assistance in obtaining this information. It appears that Catherine's family may have moved to Lisnamaul from Glassdrumman, near Annalong, as she was born there in 1857.

4   It is also worth noting that a John McKay, a 27-year-old farm labourer, was recorded in Cargagh in the 1911 census – as the only person there of that surname (www.census.nationalarchives.ie/reels/nai002224509, accessed on 2 Nov. 2009).

5   Jimmy McKay to Philomena McKay, *c.* 1878. This letter also mentioned how Anne Fitzpatrick, James' sister-in-law, married Hugh Tomelty, a farmer from Cargagh; how James'

daughter-in-law, Mary Nesbitt, married Hugh Keenan, a schoolmaster in the townland of Bonecastle; and how the Keenans' son and grandson (or James' grandson-in-law and great-grandson-in-law), Hughie and Paddy Keenan respectively, had continued to live in Cargagh.

6   *Ibid*, *c.* 1878. The father of John and James is referred to as James ('a farmer'), not Joseph, in Jimmy's letter. Perhaps his full name was Joseph James McKay, with the first and second names being used for official and familiar purposes respectively. It is perhaps relevant that John McKay's first son was named James Joseph; it was traditional back then in Ireland to name one's eldest son after one's father, and John may have done this.

7   R. S. J. Clarke, *Gravestone Inscriptions. Co. Down, vol. 21: Old Families of Downpatrick & District: from gravestone inscriptions, wills and biographical notes* (Belfast, 1993), p. 173. It appears likely that Doran was the maiden name of John McKay's mother Anne Jane. Jimmy McKay (her great-grandson), in his letter to Philomena McKay, claimed that his generation were 'second or third cousins of the Doran family' because 'Ann Doran married a James McKay'. Given that Jimmy referred to the father of John and James as James McKay, this last description may well be of their parents' marriage.

8   When Kieran McConville rang the Downpatrick Catholic parish office on 2 November 2009 to enquire about McKay baptisms, John Devaney, who had voluntarily gone to search through the same records to help us finish our search, was, unknown to Kieran, in the office at that exact time. Although initially finding no record of McKay baptisms, they established contact over the phone, and through collaboration were able to check through variant spellings and to verify that the children registered as McKees were in fact the McKays in question.

9   Register of baptism, Catholic Diocese of Down and Connor, parish of Downpatrick. We are grateful to Mary in the Downpatrick parish office for her assistance with this research.

10 Ambrose Macaulay, *William Crolly: Archbishop of Armagh, 1835-49* (Dublin, 1994), pp 1–2.

11 Aiken McClelland, *William Johnston of Ballykilbeg* (Lurgan, 1990).

12 Jimmy McKay to Philomena McKay, *c.* 1978.

13 *Irish Times*, 18 Oct. 1949.

14 Letter from Jimmy McKay, Birmingham, to Kevin McKay, Bray, *c.* 1980s.

15 *Daily Mirror*, 18 July 1922.

16 *Irish Times*, 18 Oct. 1949.

17 *Daily Express*, 18 Oct. 1949.

18 Census for England and Wales, 1911, 11 Great Russell Mansions, Great Russell Street, London.

19 Jimmy McKay to Philomena McKay, *c.* 1978.

20 *Irish Independent*, 25 June 1915. Around the same time he was reported to have a theatre company with P. T. Selbit, which ran revues such as *This is the Life* (*Irish Times*, 3 July 1915).

21 *Irish Times*, 7 Dec. 1922.

22 *Irish Independent*, 1 June 1930.

23 Sophie Tucker with Dorothy Giles, *Some of these Days: The Autobiography of Sophie Tucker* (New York, 1945), p. 185.

24 http://en.wikipedia.org/wiki/Elstree_Calling, accessed on 31 Oct. 2009.

25 *The Times*, 25 Mar. 1933.

26 *Irish Independent*, 1 Aug. 1931.

27 *The Times*, 25 Mar. 1933.

28 *The Times*, 23 Feb. 1937.

29 *The Times*, 21 Oct. 1949.

30 *Daily Express*, 18 Oct. 1949.

31 *Irish Times*, 18 Oct. 1949.

32 Jimmy McKay to Philomena McKay, *c.* 1978, stated that Joan and a relative were introduced to a rising theatrical star, Frankie Vaughan, at a show in London; Vaughan, who was born in 1928, did not move to London until the late 1940s.

INDEX